Authoritarian Liberalism and the Transformation of Modern Europe

OXFORD CONSTITUTIONAL THEORY

Series Editors

MARTIN LOUGHLIN
JOHN P MCCORMICK
NEIL WALKER

Oxford Constitutional Theory has rapidly established itself as the primary point of reference for theoretical reflections on the growing interest in constitutions and constitutional law in domestic, regional, and global contexts. The majority of the works published in the series are monographs that advance new understandings of their subject. But the series aims to provide a forum for further innovation in the field by also including well-conceived edited collections that bring a variety of perspectives and disciplinary approaches to bear on specific themes in constitutional thought and by publishing English translations of leading monographs in constitutional theory that have originally been written in languages other than English.

ALSO AVAILABLE IN THE SERIES:

Constitutionalism and the Paradox of Principles and Rules
Between the Hydra and Hercules
Marcelo Neves

Constituent Power in the European Union
Markus Patberg

Religion, Law, and Democracy
Selected Writings
Ernst-Wolfgang Böckenförde
Edited by Mirjam Künkler and Tine Stein

Constituent Power and the Law
Joel Colón-Ríos

Euroconstitutionalism and its Discontents
Oliver Gerstenberg

Beyond the People
Social Imaginary and Constituent Imagination
Zoran Oklopcic

The Metaethics of Constitutional Adjudication
Bosko Tripkovic

Carl Schmitt's State and Constitutional Theory
A Critical Analysis
Benjamin A Schupmann

Law and Revolution
Legitimacy and Constitutionalism after the Arab Spring
Nimer Sultany

Unconstitutional Constitutional Amendments
The Limits of Amendment Powers
Yaniv Roznai

Constitutional and Political Theory
Selected Writings
Ernst-Wolfgang Böckenförde
Edited by Mirjam Künkler and Tine Stein

Constitutionalism
Past, Present, and Future
Dieter Grimm

Europe's Functional Constitution
A Theory of Constitutional Beyond the State
Turkuler Isiksel

Post Sovereign Constitution Making
Learning and Legitimacy
Andrew Arato

Popular Sovereignty in Early Modern Constitutional Thought
Daniel Lee

The Cultural Defense of Nations
A Liberal Theory of Majority Rights
Liav Orgad

The Cosmopolitan Constitution
Alexander Somek

The Structure of Pluralism
Victor M Muniz-Fraticelli

Constitutional Courts and Deliberative Democracy
Conrado Hübner Mendes

Fault Lines of Globalization
Legal Order and the Politics of A-Legality
Hans Lindahl

The Cosmopolitan State
H Patrick Glenn

After Public Law
Edited by Cormac Mac Amhlaigh, Claudio Michelon, Neil Walker

The Three Branches
A Comparative Model of Separation of Powers
Christoph Moellers

The Global Model of Constitutional Rights
Kai Möller

Constituting Economic and Social Rights
Katharine G Young

Authoritarian Liberalism and the Transformation of Modern Europe

MICHAEL A WILKINSON

OXFORD
UNIVERSITY PRESS

OXFORD
UNIVERSITY PRESS

Great Clarendon Street, Oxford, OX2 6DP,
United Kingdom

Oxford University Press is a department of the University of Oxford.
It furthers the University's objective of excellence in research, scholarship,
and education by publishing worldwide. Oxford is a registered trade mark of
Oxford University Press in the UK and in certain other countries

First Edition published in 2021

Published in the United States of America by Oxford University Press
198 Madison Avenue, New York, NY 10016, United States of America

British Library Cataloguing in Publication Data
Data available

Library of Congress Control Number: 2020952643

ISBN 978–0–19–885475–3

DOI: 10.1093/oso/9780198854753.001.0001

Printed and bound in the UK by
TJ Books Limited

For Sigi and Tony

'A Klee painting named "Angelus Novus" shows an angel looking as though he is about to move away from something he is fixedly contemplating. His eyes are staring, his mouth is open, his wings are spread. This is how one pictures the angel of history. His face is turned toward the past. Where we perceive a chain of events, he sees one single catastrophe which keeps piling wreckage and hurls it in front of his feet. The angel would like to stay, awaken the dead, and make whole what has been smashed. But a storm is blowing in from Paradise; it has got caught in his wings with such a violence that the angel can no longer close them. The storm irresistibly propels him into the future to which his back is turned, while the pile of debris before him grows skyward. This storm is what we call progress.' (Walter Benjamin, 'Thesis IX', *On the Concept of History*).

Preface and Acknowledgements

The idea for this book can be traced back to 2012, when I was asked by Floris de Witte to contribute to 're:generation Europe', an initiative aimed at breathing life into what, at the height of the economic crisis, was looking like an asphyxiated entity. At the time, I was working on the idea of political constitutionalism as a way to understand the EU; transcending legal (and legalistic) analyses of its constitution by examining its political, institutional and power dynamics, but essentially bracketing material and economic issues. It was soon clear to me that this would not cut it as a means of dissecting the Europe that was emerging from the euro crisis. What was required was a direct confrontation with its material, as well as legal, and political elements.

I was struck that a project which always appeared voluntaristic and consensual (even if often detached and disconnected) was proceeding via increasingly authoritarian means; through coercion and cajoling, bypassing parliaments and public accountability, and yet all ostensibly in the furtherance of a project of economic liberalism (albeit, by then, often labelled 'neo-liberalism'). Market integration and conditionality programmes were not only insulated from democratic processes but, in the case of Greece, in direct defiance of them. I then became familiar with Hermann Heller's conjunction of 'authoritarian liberalism' to critique the ruling cabinets in late Weimar, and its later development, in quite different contexts, by authors such as Renato Cristi and Kanishka Jayasuriya. With this lens in mind, I wrote an article for the *German Law Journal*, published in 2013, titled 'The Spectre of Authoritarian Liberalism: Reflections on the Constitutional Crisis of the European Union'. This essentially presented the euro crisis as a conjunctural moment, with the exceptional situation of emergency or necessity used to justify departure from the norm of democratic and legal accountability, signalling the move from 'integration through law' to 'integration through fear', as Joseph Weiler remarked.

As my research progressed, this norm/exception framing appeared increasingly inadequate, for two reasons. First, it risked whitewashing the 'norm', when, in fact, as many scholars had identified, long before the euro crisis, and at least as far back as Maastricht, the EU already suffered from a series of legitimacy deficits—social, political and democratic. Second, the proper way to understand this conjuncture was not to see the EU as an externally imposed constraint, but as an integral feature of the process of state transformation. Chris Bickerton's work on European integration was invaluable in this regard.

I also began to think that Maastricht itself could not be the starting point for any enquiry. One of the dominant justificatory discourses for the post-war settlement—in which European integration played a key part—was that of 'constrained democracy', as outlined by Jan-Werner Müller. But this required deeper probing. A clue was in the stretching of language: on the one hand, 'militant democracy' (from the interwar writing of Karl Loewenstein), and, on the other, 'constrained democracy', as in Müller's own account. 'Militant democracy' was, in fact, a feature of the broader picture Hermann Heller had painted as 'authoritarian liberalism', despite the apparent contrast in terms.

The link with the interwar period was clear, but what I wanted to do now was to try and make sense of the full story, from Weimar to Athens, as it were. Was it possible that 'constrained democracy' was better understood as a long and entrenched version of authoritarian liberalism, signalling a slowly constructed passive transformation of Europe, depoliticizing the economy, and disarming any radical threats to the status quo? If so, how was it constructed? How was it maintained? And was it now entering a critical phase?

The book sets out to answer these questions by first offering a new interpretation of interwar breakdown, and then offering an account of each post-war stage of reconstruction, from Rome to Maastricht, Maastricht to Lisbon, and, finally, the euro crisis itself. It does so with a threefold analysis of inter-state, state-society and social relations, as a way of differentiating and describing the layers of a complex and interrelated totality which has changed over time, and shows signs of both continuity and discontinuity.

The book also aspires to open up debates on European integration and the post-war settlement where they appear so often to be closed down, polemicized around 'Brexit', and now the 'rule of law crisis', to be sure, but also frequently presumed in the academy to be sacred objects, however flawed, partly from fear that the alternatives could only be worse. A close analysis of the Weimar conjuncture prompted me to think that this might be an unwise strategy, just as the strategy of 'toleration' of 'authoritarian liberalism' (which Heller diagnosed too late), appeared to contribute to the collapse of liberal democracy in Weimar.

Even if one disagrees with the diagnosis, I hope that the book may be instructive nevertheless, and help to open the space to develop critical theories of European integration, not as some form of external constraint, or experiment gone awry, but as part of an ongoing structural transformation and, yet, one which need not be presumed as the inevitable horizon of any future political and constitutional arrangement.

Along its path this project has faced a good deal of opposition, but also some memorable and treasured support, and I owe a debt of gratitude to a great many people: more than I will be able to recall here. At the cost of inexcusably omitting some, I would like to mention a few.

First, I would like to thank Martin Loughlin, who read an entire first draft of this manuscript, and provided detailed commentary, both in the margins, and on the central thesis—which is not to suggest that he agrees with it! His help on this project was invaluable, and he has also provided deeper inspiration through his own work in constitutional theory. I would also like to thank Jacco Bomhoff and Peter Ramsay for their comments and suggestions on various parts of the manuscript, which proved tremendously beneficial, and improved the final product. Many other colleagues (past and present) have commented on aspects of this work over the years, particularly in the GOLEM seminar series (initiated by Damian Chalmers); and the LSE law department in general has provided a wonderful environment in which to pursue the project. As well as my colleagues, I would like to thank my students, who have provided a constant stream of inspiration over the last decade. Some of them I now have the pleasure of supervising as PhD students. Bob Roth, who is one of them, has worked tirelessly on helping me to compile the index, put together the bibliography, and organize the citations. I cannot thank him enough. And I have learnt, and continue to learn, a huge amount from my discussions with Signe Larsen (who has put me right on theories of the federation!) and Hjalte Lokdam.

Numerous conferences and seminars have helped to hone the arguments in the book, and I will only be able to mention a few of them here. At an early stage of the project, Marco Goldoni invited me to present a paper on authoritarian liberalism at the University of Glasgow, and I have benefitted from working with him on methodological issues in constitutional theory ever since. I had the pleasure of presenting the overall thesis of the book in Copenhagen, at the iCourts 'Centre of Excellence', thanks to the invitation of Jan Komarek, who has generously supported my work throughout. Massimo La Torre invited me to speak on the themes of authoritarian liberalism and populism at the University of Catanzaro, and, again, in Tallinn, Estonia, which provided valuable feedback as well as lively, critical and receptive audiences. I would also like to thank Agustin Menéndez and Matthias Goldman for 'Weimar Moments' in Madrid, and Graziello Romeo, for the opportunity to speak at Bocconi University in Milan. In February 2019, I was invited by Hajime Yamamoto to teach an intensive course on comparative constitutional law to a group of doctoral and postdoctoral scholars at Keio University, Tokyo, and this provided a wonderful opportunity to develop some of the themes of the book.

It has been a pleasure and a privilege, along the way, to contribute to a number of edited collections and special issues. This has provided the opportunity to get editorial feedback on aspects of the book at crucial stages. I would like to thank Günter Frankenberg and Helena Alviar for the chance to participate in their project in Paris, which culminated in the volume *Authoritarian Constitutionalism* (Elgar 2019), and Eva Nanopoulos and Fotis Vergis, who invited me to participate in their Cambridge conference, and contribute a chapter to their edited collection, *The Crisis Behind the Eurocrisis* (CUP 2019). I would also like to thank Vassilis Fouskas, who invited me to contribute to a symposium on neo-liberalism and ordoliberalism, which was published in a special issue of the journal *Critical Sociology* (2019). In 2019, I presented at two panels of the 'Historical Materialism' conference in Athens, and, along with my fellow panellists, I would like to extend a warm thanks to George Souvlis for his encouragement and hospitality, as well as to Jeremy Rayner, Susan Falls, and Taylor Nelms, his co-editors of the collection *Back to the '30s?* (Palgrave 2020).

In addition to those mentioned above, I would like to thank the following friends and colleagues for encouragement, discussion, comment, and criticism: Birsen Filip, Susan Marks, Conor Gearty, Christian Joerges, Mike Dowdle, Marco Dani, Johan van der Walt, Hauke Brunkhorst, Francisca Moya, Gareth Dale, Paul Blokker, Mikhail Xifaras, Denis Baranger, Olivier Beaud, Ulas Karadag, Pauline Trouillard, Werner Bonefeld, Zoran Oklopcic, Niklas Olsen, Michaela Hailbronner, Nikolas Vagdoutis, Saygun Gokariksel, Marleen Allemann, Giuliano Vosa, Jairo Lima, Andrew Woodhouse, Bowen Zhang, Jakub Bokes, Korina Pavlidou, Eirini Tsoumani, Magnus Wills, and Stefan Imhof.

At OUP, I would like to thank Jamie Berezin for sticking with me, despite numerous setbacks; Brianne Bello, for pushing me to completion within a reasonable time frame; and Mark Ajin for sterling work at the production stage. I would also like to thank the series editors, Martin Loughlin (again), and Neil Walker, who has supported my work since my formative years at the EUI, Florence.

Finally, I would like to thank Alexander Somek for providing some rather intangible, as well as very concrete, support for this project. His work has long been a source of inspiration, and when we were both invited, in 2015, to contribute to a special issue on Hermann Heller for the *European Law Journal*, at the invitation of Agustin Menéndez (again), I felt that I must be on the right track. Whether that is the case or not will be for others to judge, and I alone take responsibility for all and any faults in the final product.

In order to finish this project, Michelle, Gil, Cassia, and Stella—the people closest to me—have had to take some of the strain. My heart is with them always, and I look forward to being able to enjoy more time with them, now the book is complete. This book is dedicated to my mum and dad, both children of interwar Europe: one born in Leipzig, Germany, the other in Blackley, north Manchester; they formed a European Union long before the one discussed in this book.

Mike Wilkinson
London, Friday 5 March 2021

Table of Contents

List of Abbreviations

AfD	Alternative für Deutschland
AG	Advocate General
ASFJ	area of security, freedom and justice
BRIC states	Brazil, Russia, India, and China
CAP	Common Agricultural Policy
CDU	Christlich Demokratische Union Deutschlands (Christian Democratic Union)
CFP	Common Fisheries Policy
CFSP	Common Foreign and Security Policy
CSU	Christian Social Union
DGB	Deutscher Gewerkschaftsbund (National Federation of Trade Unions (Germany))
DiEM25	Democracy in Europe Movement 2025
DNVP	Deutschnationale Volkspartei (German National People's Party)
DPP	Deutsche Demokratische Partei (German Democratic Party)
EAW	European arrest warrant
EC	European Community
ECB	European Central Bank
ECI	European Citizens' Initiative
ECJ	European Court of Justice
ECSC	European Coal and Steel Community
EDP	excessive deficit procedure
EEC	European Economic Community
EFSF	European Financial Stability Facility
EFSM	European Financial Stability Mechanism
EFTA	European Free Trade Association
EIP	excessive imbalance procedure
EMS	European Monetary System
EMU	European Monetary Union
ENA	Ecole nationale d'administration
EPP	European People's Party
ESFS	European system of financial supervision
ESM	European Stability Mechanism
ETUC	European Trade Union Confederation
EU	European Union
FANGs	Finland, Austria, Netherlands, Germany
FPO	Freiheitliche Partei Österreichs (Freedom Party of Austria)
GDP	gross domestic product
IMF	International Monetary Fund
KKE	Communist Party of Greece
KPD	Kommunistische Partei Deutschlands (Communist Party of Germany)

LSE	London School of Economics
MPIfG	Max-Planck-Institut für Gesellschaftsforschung
NATO	North Atlantic Treaty Organization
NSDAP	Nationalsozialistische Deutsche Arbeiterpartei (Nazi Party)
OEEC	Organisation for European Economic Co-operation
OLP	ordinary legislative procedure
OMC	Open method of cooperation
OMT	Outright monetary transactions
PASOK	Panhellenic Socialist Movement
PCI	Partito Comunista Italiano (Italian Communist Party)
PIIGS	Portugal, Ireland, Italy, Greece, and Spain
QE	Quantitative Easing
SA	Sturmabteilung (Nazi Party's original paramilitary wing)
SEA	Single European Act
SGP	Stability and Growth Pact
SPD	Sozialdemokratische Partei Deutschlands (Social Democratic Party of Germany)
SS	Schutzstaffel (Nazi special police force)
TEU	Treaty on European Union
TFEU	Treaty on the Functioning of the European Union
TINA	'There is no alternative'
TSCG	Treaty on Stability, Coordination and Governance in the Economic and Monetary Union
UKIP	UK Independence Party
WTO	World Trade Organization

Introduction

Accounts of European integration typically begin with reconstruction following the devastation of the continent in the first half of the twentieth century. They begin by depicting a desire to start afresh, from a *Stunde Null*, in an attempt to ensure that the conflict of the preceding decades would never happen again. Blame for the preceding collapse is laid at the foot of a destructive nationalism, which was militarily aggressive and economically protectionist. The solution, directed primarily towards Germany, is to tame the impulse to rearm and to encourage the drive towards market integration. The simultaneous fulfilment of both aims, peace and prosperity, is symbolized by the Treaty of Paris of 1951 and its creation: the supranational institutions and structures that would be the hallmark of the European Union's development over the following sixty years.[1]

This book does not reject that story in its entirety, but it does offer an alternative explanation; one that highlights what that account misses and why, from a constitutional perspective, that omission is significant. In short, Europe is reconstituted, from the very beginning of the post-war period, in reaction to the fear of democracy that had threatened to unleash itself in the interwar period. This is significant because it suggests that the 'democratic deficit' identified since Maastricht, and which was described as a 'democratic default' in the euro crisis phase, is not merely a symptom of recent decades of the neo-liberal era, but characteristic of a far deeper condition.[2] It is also significant because it suggests that any remedy to that deficit would require a radical constitutional reimagining, or even a rupture from the post-war constitutional settlement.

It is hardly novel to argue that post-war Europe is conditioned by a fear of democracy, and hence by the perceived need for it to be 'constrained'. Jan-Werner Müller has presented this claim in detail, describing various formal and informal strategies designed to restructure existing institutions and create new ones, domestic as well as European, in order to build a constitutional architecture that depoliticizes the

[1] The two dominant narratives of integration are functionalist, focusing on economic interdependencies; and intergovernmentalist, focusing on inter-state bargaining. Weiler adds a structural, as well as ideological, messianic, component (see Joseph Weiler, 'The Political and Legal Culture of Integration: An Exploratory Essay' (2011) 9:3–4 International Journal of Constitutional Law 678); and van Mid delaar adds a normative vision, a 'Europe of Citizens' (based on an ideal of constitutionalism, in Luke van Middelaar, *The Passage to Europe: How a Continent Became a Union* (Yale University Press 2013).

[2] See Giandomenico Majone, 'From a Regulatory State to a Democratic Default' (2014) Journal of Common Market Studies 1. The seminal pre-crisis work on the democratic deficit is Simon Hix and Andreas Follesdal, 'Why there is a democratic deficit in the EU: A response to Majone and Moravscik' (2006) 44 Journal of Common Market Studies 533. But earlier still, see Jürgen Habermas, 'Remarks on Dieter Grimm's "Does Europe Need a Constitution"' (1995) 1 ELJ 303 and Joseph Weiler, Ulrich Haltern, and Franz Meyer, 'European Democracy and its Critique' (1995) 18 West European Politics 4.

Authoritarian Liberalism and the Transformation of Modern Europe. Michael A Wilkinson, Oxford University Press.
 DOI: 10.1093/oso/9780198854753.003.0001

activity of governing.[3] Müller's focus was on the cultural and political disciplining of mass democracy in post-war reconstruction in general, and the significance of the Christian democratic movement in achieving this goal in particular.[4] In his account, the post-war settlement was designed to discipline and stabilize liberal democracy, to prevent it from committing 'democratic suicide'. Much related work on the so-called 'counter-majoritarian' dilemma (including the inappositely named 'militant democracy') focuses on the supposed internal contradiction between the two poles of 'liberal democracy' and considers how to prevent democratic majorities from pursuing goals that would undermine liberalism.[5] Müller's insights have yet to be fully integrated into a constitutional history of the twentieth century, albeit that many of them were anticipated by the work of Carl Schmitt and have since been forgotten or discarded by liberal jurists.[6]

The focus here, however, is different: rather than the supposed internal contradiction in liberal democracy (and on the paradox of democratic self-destruction and the conceptual gymnastics involved in trying to resolve this), the critical issue is the material tension between democracy and capitalism. It is this heuristic that provides the explanatory framework for constitutional change.[7]

A critical, historical, and theoretical lens is used to analyse the object of this study: the material constitution of the state and the regional order in Europe and its reconstitution through the post-war period. The material constitution is a complex assemblage of ordering forces and structures: political unity, institutional power, social relations, and political-economic objectives.[8] Aspects of these, which are internally related to formal constitutional norms, will be developed throughout the chapters. At this stage, the object can be presented in simplified form as a representation of the relation between the political and economic realms.[9] Getting to grips with the way this

[3] See Jan-Werner Müller, *Contesting Democracy: Political Ideas in 20th Century Europe* (Yale University Press 2011). The claim is supported by much recent work in legal history on the origins of the integration project; see, eg Antonin Cohen, 'Constitutionalism without Constitution: Transnational Elites Between Mobilisation and Legal Expertise in the Making of a Constitution For Europe (1940s–1960s)' (2007) 32 L & Soc Inquiry 109; Antoine Vauchez, 'The Transnational Politics of Judicialisation: *Van Gend en Loos* and the Making of the EU Polity' (2010) 16 ELJ 1.

[4] Müller (n 3) ch 4.

[5] The term 'militant democracy' was coined in 1935 by Karl Loewenstein. For two recent critical readings, see Carlo Accetti and Ian Zuckerman, 'What's Wrong with Militant Democracy?' (2017) 65:1 Political Studies 182; and Anthoula Malkopoulou and Ludwig Norman, 'Three Models of Democratic Self-Defence: Militant Democracy and Its Alternatives' (2018) 66:2 Political Studies 442.

[6] See Benjamin Schupmann, *Carl Schmitt's State and Constitutional Theory* (OUP 2017).

[7] Although associated with the work of Wolfgang Streeck (see, eg *Buying Time: On the Delayed Crisis of Democratic Capitalism*), the dynamic tension has a deeper history in the Marxist tradition, see eg Ellen M Wood, *Democracy Against Capitalism: Renewing Historical Materialism* (CUP 1995).

[8] See Marco Goldoni and Michael A Wilkinson, 'The Material Constitution' (2018) 81:4 Modern Law Review 567. For a different kind of attempt to get beneath the 'visible architecture' of the EU and capture its 'political metaphysics' see Eva Nanopoulos and Fotis Vergis, 'The Inherently Undemocratic EU Democracy' in E Nanopoulos and F Vergis (eds), *The Crisis Behind the EuroCrisis: On the Multi-Systemic Failure of the EU* (Cambridge University Press 2019).

[9] It is significant that ordoliberalism is hardly given a mention in Müller's *Contesting Democracy*, even though Müller himself has elsewhere described its significance in post-war Germany as immense. Ordoliberalism will be discussed in Chapter 3, but it is immediately apparent that ordoliberalism does place centre stage the relation between the political and the economic, and also that it has largely been neglected until the euro crisis (for an exception see David Gerber, 'Constitutionalising the Economy: German

relation is reconstituted—through geopolitics and law, ideology, and class interests—is key to understanding the transformation of Europe in the twentieth and twenty-first centuries and its significance for constitutional theory. Or so it will be argued.

The argument presented in this book, in condensed form, is that the post-war European state system undergoes a structural transformation; a re-differentiation of the political and economic spheres. Specifically, this relation is transformed through a conditioning of democratic sovereignty over the economy, by taking economic matters out of the public domain of democratic power and accountability. The label 'authoritarian liberalism' is used to capture this phenomenon, a conjunction of political authoritarianism and economic liberalism.[10] To reduce it to its most basic formulation, it captures the phenomenon of a liberalism that is pursued by authoritarian means, in ways that avoid robust democratic accountability. It is liberal in the sense that it depoliticizes the economy, naturalizes inequalities, and values markets, competition, and private ownership.

Again, the claim that post-war Europe is conditioned by an attempt to reconstruct the tradition of classical liberalism initially through a mixed or 'embedded' version is not new.[11] The literature, however, rarely approaches this reconstruction in a critical manner or in a way that maps its trajectory. Authoritarian liberalism begins in the interwar period and then develops with a constitutional dynamic that takes place across various stages, beginning with the Treaties of Paris in 1951, and of Rome in 1957, gathering pace through the Single European Act 1986 and the Treaty of Maastricht in 1992, and accelerating in an extraordinary manner through the euro crisis phase (2008–). The book concludes that Europe has reached a critical juncture; entrapped in a fractious position, unable to move forward or backward.[12] Authoritarian liberalism is now fomenting the politics of an authoritarian populism that it was meant to prevent, but with which it appears to be mutually dependent.

Delimiting the claim

A few words of caution are required about the nature of the claim made here. The post-war reconstitution of the European state and state system has occurred gradually. It has not followed a strictly linear progression, nor has it affected the entire continent in

Neoliberalism, Competition Law and the "New Europe"' (1994) 42 American Journal of Comparative Law 25).

[10] I have developed this argument in a series of pieces; see Michael A Wilkinson, 'The Spectre of Authoritarian Liberalism: Reflections on the Constitutional Crisis of the European Union' (2013) 14 German Law Journal 527; 'Authoritarian Liberalism in the European Constitutional Imagination: Second Time as Farce?' (2015) 21 European Law Journal 313; 'The Reconstitution of Postwar Europe: Liberal Excesses, Democratic Deficiencies' in Michael Dowdle and Michael Wilkinson (eds), *Constitutionalism Beyond Liberalism* (Cambridge University Press, 2017); and 'Authoritarian Liberalism: The Conjuncture Behind the Crisis' in E Nanopoulos and F Vergis (eds), *The Crisis Behind the EuroCrisis: On the Multi-Systemic Failure of the EU* (CUP 2019).

[11] See, eg John Gillingham, *European Integration: 1950–2003 Superstate or New Market Economy?* (CUP 2003).

[12] See Claus Offe, *Europe Entrapped* (Polity Press 2014).

the same way. It is varied, uneven, and combined across European states. Although the EU plays a significant role, the reconstitution is not related exclusively to the project or institutions of the EU; it is as much a phenomenon of domestic constitutional change as it is an international and supranational one. Indeed, I argue, as have others, that these layers are connected: European integration is a process of state transformation, more than the building of an independent set of institutions and structures above, or separate from, the state.[13]

A different kind of study might attempt to trace several constitutional ideal types with related but distinct trajectories as they emerged in different constitutional cultures, and at different historical moments through the process of European integration, developing a kind of 'varieties of constitutionalism' literature for the European Union. At least four might be identified: the first, 'core Europe', would feature in those countries having direct experience of the collapse of liberalism through capitulation to fascism (the founding 'six'). For this first group, European integration is not a simple choice—an experiment which could as well be reversed, or a club which could be joined or left at will—it is in the DNA of their post-war constitutional identity, an escape from the burden of sovereignty. And Europe, in turn, bears the imprint of this identity, given the significance of the founding six on its form. The second, a southern fringe comprising Spain, Portugal, and Greece, would feature in those countries that applied to join the Union following post-war dictatorship. For these countries, entry to the EU signposted the promised land of political liberalism.[14] A third, comprising countries of the former Eastern bloc, would prevail in those countries for whom EU membership signalled readmission to 'the West'; an idea of Europe involving a rapid embrace of market capitalism, but also a reclaiming of sovereignty after decades of subjugation by an imperial power. For each of these three groups, the idea of 'Europe', in different ways, represents a form of emancipation from the past, perhaps with decreasing depths of attachment. A fourth and final category, more detached still, would consist of the sustained democracies of the UK and Nordic countries, for whom EU membership was always less than wholehearted as a constitutional choice, and signalled a more pragmatic stance; nothing fateful, still less emancipatory, was signified. In none of this fourth group had the decline of parliamentary democracy in the interwar—or post-war—periods been as severe; in none was the burden of the past as great. From that vantage point, particularly in the UK, Europe may be properly viewed as a voluntary project.[15]

[13] See especially Chris Bickerton, *European Integration: From Nation-State to Member State* (OUP 2013). From a constitutional perspective, see also Erik Fossum and Agustin Menendez, *The Constitution's Gift: A Constitutional Theory for a Democratic European Union* (Rowman & Littlefield 2011). For an overview of the literature, see Eva Nanopoulos and Fotis Vergis, 'The Inherently Undemocratic EU Democracy' in Nanopoulos and Vergis (eds), *The Crisis Behind the Eurocrisis* (CUP 2019).

[14] The Republic of Ireland might belong or relate to this group, in the sense that its successful independence from the UK is strongly associated with membership of the EU.

[15] Even for the UK, a strong voluntarism may be misleading. For the UK, membership of the EU has been presented as central to its constitutional modernization. See, eg Martin Loughlin, 'The British Constitution: Thoughts on the Causes of the Present Discontents' (2018) 16:1 New Zealand Journal of Public and International Law 1. But the modernization narrative does not capture the constitutional imagination in the same way as association of Europe with political emancipation.

A full evaluation of the significance for comparative constitutional law of these regional and culturally specific varieties, and the obvious objections and exceptions to which they would give rise, would require several book-length studies. The argument here will distil a complex and varied set of constitutional histories into one singular theory and constitutional trajectory: a path towards authoritarian liberalism. It is a trajectory that now comes under sustained pressure, not just from a single source, but from across the spectrum of political positions and across the geographical spread of the continent. The collapse of centrist parties (and rise of parties of the right and, to a lesser extent, the left), in particular, has affected countries belonging to all four 'varieties of constitutionalism'.[16] Authoritarian liberalism intertwines in different ways with each more particular constitutional trajectory. But the commonalities are enough to demand a more comprehensive thesis.

Authoritarian liberalism

The label 'authoritarian liberalism' may surprise, both in a conceptual and a historical sense.[17] Although it is not uncommon to consider neo-liberalism since the 1980s as an authoritarian phenomenon,[18] the immediate post-war period is often characterized as one in which democracy is consolidated. But that claim, when made, is then often qualified so much that democracy itself is barely distinguishable from liberalism.[19] It is a markedly constrained form of democracy that emerges: a 'passive authoritarianism'. Various shades of authoritarianism will be discussed throughout the chapters, beginning in late Weimar—when, as Hermann Heller noted, authoritarian government was invoked directly against democracy and, specifically, to defend the capitalist form of the economy—and ending in the euro crisis phase.[20]

Conceptually, 'authoritarian' is understood here in opposition and contrast to democratic government and particularly to democratic change, rather than, as is the case in some of the recent literature on the crisis of constitutional democracy, in opposition

[16] For analysis, see Chris Bickerton, 'The Collapse of Europe's Mainstream Centre Left' *New Statesman* (London, 1 May 2018).

[17] But see, eg Nicos Poulantzas, *State, Power, Socialism* (Verso 2000), first published in 1978 as *L'etat, le pouvoir, le socialism* (particularly Part 4: 'The Decline of Democracy: Authoritarian Statism'); Ishay Landa, *The Apprentice's Sorceror: Liberal Tradition and Fascism* (Brill 2010); Alexander Somek, 'Authoritarian Constitutionalism: Austrian Constitutional Doctrine 1933 to 1938 and its Legacy' in Joerges C and Ghaleigh NS (eds), *Darker Legacies of Law in Europe: The Shadow of National Socialism and Fascism over Europe and its Legal Traditions* (Hart Publishing 2003).

[18] See, eg Ian Bruff, 'The Rise of Authoritarian Neoliberalism' (2014) 26 Rethinking Marxism 113.

[19] See, eg Martin Conway, 'The Rise and Fall of Western Europe's Democratic Age, 1945–1973' (2004) 13:1 Contemporary European History 67, 71 (after suggesting that the best approximation of Western Europe between the late 1940s and early 1970s would be its 'democratic age', the author immediately notes that this 'risks emphasising the strengths rather than the limitations of the rather constrained form of democracy established after the Second World War').

[20] Hermann Heller, 'Autoritärer Liberalismus', Die Neue Rundschau 44 (1933) 289 (in English translation 'Authoritarian Liberalism?' European Law Journal 21 (2015) 295 (tr S Paulson)). Authoritarianism does not require a charismatic or autocratic leadership and the large-scale deployment of extralegal violence and coercion; it must be distinguished from fascism, dictatorship or totalitarianism, which is not to say that it cannot lead there (cf Juan Linz, *Totalitarian and Authoritarian Regimes* (Lynne Rienner Publishers 2000)).

or contrast to liberal government.[21] In political theory, notably the republican tradition and various writings in the radical democratic tradition, liberalism (particularly economic liberalism), is frequently described as being in tension with democracy and democratic politics.[22] Scepticism about the legitimacy of counter-majoritarian institutions is even prevalent amongst self-described liberals.[23]

With the aim of a general diagnosis in mind, the post-war reconstitution of Europe—including the project of integration—is, in a significant sense, *conservative*. Certainly, it has taken place 'in the shadow' of a federalist vision of European unification.[24] But this has never been more than a shadow; it has never materialized. In practice, the federalist project was almost immediately defeated. Instead, the constitutional architecture conserves a material order (and *telos*) of economic liberalism; one that was threatened in the interwar period, not only by a militaristic economic protectionism, but also by the prospect, however remote in practice, of democratic socialism: of public or collective control of the economy, and working-class autonomy. Safeguarding against this prospect was a concern of both ordoliberalism and neo-liberalism.[25] It was also a concern, and perhaps with more practical moment, of the Christian democratic parties that dominated the post-war political scene.

There is, in other words, an uneven but clearly marked de-politicization (qua de-democratization) of the economy written into the post-war reconstitution of

[21] For a recent overview of that literature, see Martin Loughlin, 'The Contemporary Crisis of Constitutional Democracy' (2019) 39:2 Oxford Journal of Legal Studies 435 . On varieties of authoritarianism, see Günter Frankenberg, 'Authoritarian Constitutionalism: Coming to Terms with Modernity's Nightmares' in Helena Alviar and Günter Frankenberg (eds), *Authoritarian Constitutionalism: Comparative Analysis and Critique* (Elgar 2019) 1.

[22] See, eg Sheldon Wolin, *Politics and Vision: Continuity and Innovation in Western Political Thought* (Princeton University Press 2004) chs 9 and 10; Chantal Mouffe, *The Democratic Paradox* (Verso 2000); and Cornelius Castoriadis, *Philosophy, Politics, Autonomy: Essays in Political Philosophy* (OUP 1991). See also Noberto Bobbio, *Liberalism and Democracy* (Verso 2005). Jürgen Habermas tries to resolve this tension, but his acknowledgement of it is central to his work (see *Between Facts and Norms: Contributions to a Discourse Theory of Law and Democracy* (MIT Press 1996)). In legal theory, see, egBrian Tamanaha, 'The Dark Side of the Relationship between the Rule of Law and Liberalism' (2008) 33 New York University Journal of Law and Liberty.

[23] See, eg Jeremy Waldron, *Law and Disagreement* (Clarendon Press 1999); Jeremy Waldron, 'Constitutionalism: A Skeptical View' in T Christiano and J Christman (eds), *Contemporary Debates in Political Philosophy* (Wiley Blackwell 2009) 267; Richard Bellamy, *Political Constitutionalism: A Republican Defence of the Constitutionality of Democracy* (CUP 2007). This work, however, tends to be normative in orientation, and abstracted from political economy and material constitutional development.

[24] The progressive federalist vision is often associated with Spinelli's 'Ventetone Manifesto' and the underground resistance movement during the Second World War, but opposed by the governments in exile, especially de Gaulle, who wanted to restore national sovereignty. See also Hannah Arendt, 'Parties, Movements and Classes' (1945) Partisan Review 12:4 and discussion in William Selinger, 'Arendt and European Federalism' (2016) Modern Intellectual History 13:2, 417, 419. Arendt argues that the collapse of parliamentary government in the interwar period, not only in Germany but across Europe, is a 'direct and logical consequence of the broader decline of the nation-state', maintaining that the only hope for Europe 'is to replace national sovereignty with federation'.

[25] This will be examined in Chapters 2 and 3. For an early assessment of ordoliberal thinking, see Carl Joachim Friedrich, 'The Political Thought of Neo-liberalism', American Political Science Review 49 (1955) 509. It is by now a commonplace that varieties of ordoliberalism and neo-liberalism, despite significant differences that will be examined in later chapters, both depend upon a strong state apparatus, partly to guard against politicization and democratisation of the economy. On their shared ideas and common roots see, eg P Mirowski and D Plehwe (eds), *The Road from Mont Pelerin: The Making of the Neoliberal Thought Collective* (Harvard University Press 2009).

Europe.[26] There was, undoubtedly, in the so-called *Les Trentes Glorieuses*, a significant taming of capitalism, which, in conjunction with the infrastructural rebuilding of war-devastated economies, contributed to a relative equalizing of conditions, as Piketty has documented.[27] This relative equalization was achieved through varieties of state interventionism, corporate bargaining, and social constitutionalism, in conditions of global economic growth. It was not a democratization of the economy, however, but a moderation of market forces that tamed capitalism; it was a coordinated capitalism or 'embedded liberalism' that emerged.[28] This emerged, not through democratic participation or an activated citizenry, but through a passive authoritarianism—led and managed by political elites, technocrats, and lawyers—domestically, as well as through informal transnational networks.[29] It was accompanied by ideological deradicalization, the erosion of parliamentarism, and a new political culture dominated by Christian democracy; replacing 'the politics of mass mobilisation that had defined the interwar period' with a political personalism, an 'individuated politics of interest representation'. Although electorally successful, it had 'little purchase on the hearts of many Europeans'.[30]

From this perspective, the 'neo-liberal' dynamic beginning in the later 1970s, continuing at Maastricht, and then accelerating in the euro crisis phase following the financial crisis of 2007, reflects a deepening of, rather than a departure from, the previous path of post-war development in general and European integration in particular.[31]

[26] Alan Milward's classic study, *The European Rescue of the Nation-State* (2nd edn, Routledge 2000), presents the Common Market as serving the material needs of the nation state, working to enhance and maintain its capacity to provide for the security and well-being of its people. European integration was thus ultimately about guaranteeing the renewed legitimacy and viability of the nation state form. However, by the second edition, at the turn of millennium, Milward acknowledges that in internationalizing policies, nation states were trying to 'restrict the force of postwar democratic pressures' at a serious cost to democratic legitimacy.

[27] Thomas Piketty, *Capital in the Twenty-First Century* (The Belknap Press of Harvard University Press 2014), 572. Piketty describes the period between the end of the Second World War and the beginning of the first oil crisis in 1973—variously called *les trente glorieuses*, *Wirtschaftswunder*, or the Golden Age of Capitalism—as an exceptional one where inequality was contained. But he suggests that the 'fundamental structural contradiction of capitalism' was ameliorated rather than overcome. Capitalism, in other words, continued to adhere to its immanent logic, independent of the politico-legal framework of society. Its effects were mediated by the countervailing forces of redistributive policies, and reconstruction in the aftermath of the levelling destruction caused by two world wars. This, however, only enabled 'the *illusion* that the fundamental structural contradiction of capitalism ($r > g$) had been overcome' ((italics added)).

[28] The term 'embedded liberalism', recalling Karl Polanyi, is associated with John Ruggie's 1982 article 'International Regimes, Transactions and Change: Embedded Liberalism in the Postwar Economic Order' (1982) 26:2 International Organization 379. Ruggie characterized embedded liberalism as a compromise, 'unlike the economic nationalism of the thirties, it would be multilateral in character; unlike the liberalism of the gold standard and free trade, its multilateralism would be predicated upon domestic interventionism' (ibid 393).

[29] The centrality of courts and constitutionalization in preserving elite hegemony and locking in liberal commitments against the vicissitudes of democratic politics gave rise to the term 'juristocracy', associated with the work of Ran Hirshl. See, eg *Towards Juristocracy: The Origins and Consequences of the New Constitutionalism* (Harvard University Press 2004).

[30] Bickerton (n 13) 84. This is discussed in Chapter 3.

[31] The claim is therefore similar, but also different, to Bickerton, who presents the neo-liberal turn beginning in the 1970s as a rupture. To be more precise, Bickerton's story is told in two acts, in some sense continuous and in others discontinuous. The first act is not the destruction wrought by the conflicts of the first half of the twentieth century but the initial stage of European integration itself, during *les trentes glorieuses*, a period of transition between the nation state and the member state, which became fully fledged only after the dismantling of the Keynesian welfare state in the 1970s and 1980s. The narrative is complex

The hollowing out of Western democracy, the rise of the juristic class, the transformation of the citizen into a consumer, and the escape from political freedom: all can be traced back to post-war reconstruction.[32] And in important respects, they are a reaction to interwar phenomena.[33]

The euro crisis response confirms this trajectory of 'authoritarian liberalism' and sharpens it. It represents a mutation in the EU's constitutional framework; a more pointed political authoritarianism, more coercive and executive in nature, as well as an increasingly asymmetric intergovernmentalism, and even the prospect of German hegemony. Yet, this reflects a 'conservative revolution' or 'revolution from above', aimed at shoring up the order of ideas and interests of economic liberalism (including a complex mix of class and national interests).[34] The label 'authoritarian liberalism' must now capture this mix, taking into consideration not only the curtailment and evasion of democracy pursued by domestic elites and transnational institutions, but—in light of the increasing spectre of a semi-hegemonic 'German Europe', with Germany as a 'reluctant leader'—in a less consensual configuration than in the founding decades of integration.[35]

Sovereignty and the autonomy of the political

To translate this claim into the language of constitutional theory requires some unpacking and reframing. The concept of sovereignty—as well as providing a longer background thread and fuller historical context—can help with this process. In the modern constitutional imagination, sovereignty is typically said to represent the autonomy of the political from the theological realm.[36] This reflects a process of secularization and modernization of the grounds of political authority. It expresses a new 'foundational constitutionalism' that emerged in the wake of the twin revolutionary traditions of the late eighteenth century in France and the US. This—by now traditional—model of constitutionalism attributes the authority of the constitution to the consent or authorization, however concretely or abstractly understood, of 'the

because Bickerton rejects Milward's [early] view that the initial phase was based on a democratic policy formation. It was already based on a growing depoliticization of society which combined class compromise, de-radicalization of organized labour, and the rise of corporatism. But, in that case, the continuities seem more significant than the discontinuities. This emphasis on the continuities also distinguishes my claim from that of Alexander Somek, who presents post-war 'Constitutionalism 2.0' as later giving way to a new form of 'Constitutionalism 3.0'; see Alexander Somek, *The Cosmopolitan Constitution* (OUP 2015).

[32] On the role of European integration in this dynamic, see R Daniel Kelemen, *Eurolegalism: The Transformation of Law and Regulation in the European Union* (HUP 2011)

[33] See Renato Cristi, *Carl Schmitt and Authoritarian Liberalism: Strong State, Sound Economy* (University of Wales Press 1997); on the links between Schmitt's interwar writing and neo-liberalism, see W Scheuerman, 'The Unholy Alliance of Carl Schmitt and Friedrich A Hayek' (1997) 4:2 Constellations 172.

[34] See Etienne Balibar, 'Europe's Revolution from Above', *The Guardian*, (London, 23 November 2011). This is tackled in detail in Chapter 5.

[35] See Ulrich Beck, *German Europe* (Polity Press 2013). The complexity of the term 'hegemony', as well as its application to German dominance within the EU, was recently discussed in Perry Anderson, *The H-Word* (Verso 2017). It will be addressed in Chapters 4 and 5.

[36] See Martin Loughlin, 'Why Sovereignty?' in Rawlings, Leyland, and Young (eds), *Sovereignty and Law: Domestic, Regional and Global Perspectives* (Hart Publishing 2013) 34.

people'.[37] In principle, it has been said that, 'all modern constitutions begin "We the people"'.[38]

If this claim is viewed in relation to a medieval mindset of divine right, once the word becomes deed, as the rupture of secularization is made flesh in Paris and Philadelphia, political autonomy all but follows as a matter of course. This course does not run entirely smoothly. But apart from the exceptional event of totalitarianism in the twentieth century, representing a return of religious absolutism in a different form, the modern constitutional path of liberal democracy is presented as the culmination of secular progress á la Hegel.[39] This triumph is fully complete as the Soviet exception is extinguished with the collapse of the USSR towards the end of the millennium, consecrated by a new 'end of history thesis' (since discarded by its author) and the triumph of liberal capitalism (and if the USSR is merely an anomaly, the completion of history can be dated much earlier).

The view of modern constitutionalism in the narrow light of a secularization thesis, based on the differentiation of the political from the religious, however, elides the action of constitutional development: the domain of political economy. If the autonomy of the political is presented as a *material struggle*, not merely—or not even primarily for—secularization, but for equality (or, as Etienne Balibar puts it, 'equaliberty'), set against the pre-modern fusion of political and economic power, the path of modern constitutionalism is immediately illuminated.[40] The continuous, if uneven, struggle for political equality, universal suffrage, and social rights, including women's movements, workers' movements, and—broadening the horizon—anti-colonial movements is highlighted.[41]

The 'march of the masses onto the stage of history' that began in the late eighteenth century and continued through the nineteenth century, reached a climax in the interwar era; a crucial turning point in constitutional history, a point at which political democracy was expanded, and there were calls for it to be extended to the economy, at the same time as capitalism experienced its most significant moments of crisis

[37] This foundational constitutionalism might be associated in Europe with the work of Dieter Grimm: see, eg 'Does Europe Need a Constitution?' (1995) 1 European Law Journal 282; 'The Constitution in the Process of Denationalisation' (2005) 12 Constellations 447; 'The Achievements of Constitutionalism and its Prospects in a Changed World' in Loughlin and Dobner (eds), *The Twilight of Constitutionalism* (OUP 2010).

[38] Simone Chambers, 'Democracy, Popular Sovereignty and Constitutional Legitimacy' (2003) 11 Constellations 153. As Neil Walker notes, modern constitutionalism 'helped create a new form of sovereignty rather than simply reign in an old form', in Walker, 'Sovereignty and Beyond: The Double Edge of External Constitutionalism' (2018) 57 Virginia Journal of International Law 799.

[39] The 'end of history' thesis has more recently been associated with Francis Fukuyama, and he has since abandoned it. But the basic secularization thesis is at the core of a French tradition of political thought that includes Marcel Gauchet, Claude Lefort, and Pierre Rosanvallon This makes up a so-called 'anti-totalitarian' position, which theorizes the autonomy of the political without sufficient regard to material forces. See, further: Michael A Wilkinson 'Public Law and the Autonomy of the Political: A Material Critique' in Wilkinson and Dowdle (eds), *Questioning the Foundations of Public Law* (Hart 2018).

[40] See Etienne Balibar, *Equaliberty: Political Essays* (Duke University Press 2014).

[41] The allure of the project of postnational constitutionalism and its political counterpart, the DiEM movement, is that they seem to represent a continuation of this modern project of democratization, taking the inclusionary dynamic a step further, beyond national borders. But for an alternative critical narrative of modernization, see, eg James Tully 'The Unfreedom of the Moderns in Comparison to Their Ideals of Constitutional Democracy' (2002) 65:2 Modern Law Review 204.

following the global depression of the early 1930s. In these critical moments, democratic capitalism—to adopt Wolfgang Streeck's terminology—appears unfeasible because of the heightened tension between its two poles; one demanding democratic solidarity and social protection, the other demanding market rationality and commodification. This polarity is represented by the extraordinary growth in inequality on the one hand, and an increasing class consciousness on the other; both with the organization of the working class, and with a high concentration of capital through monopolization and cartelization.[42] The state (through its governing institutions) has to act more coercively to maintain liberal economic order, in combination of its repression of domestic labour and expansion of imperial ambitions abroad. Because it so conspicuously enters the fray, extinguishing the myth of the 'neutral' or 'nightwatchman' state of classical liberal imagination, the material constitution comes more fully into view.[43] One or the other—democracy or capitalism—has to give.

As Hermann Heller diagnosed in 1932, just before the Nazis gained power, it was democracy that was set aside: liberalism became authoritarian through a series of presidential cabinets ruling late Weimar through decree, via emergency powers granted by the constitution.[44] This curtailment of parliament, and of democratic freedoms, was the prelude to democracy's full-scale collapse soon after, with the Nazi seizure of power in 1933 marking the end of the Weimar Republic; not, it should be noted, and contrary to a dominant constitutional myth, in conditions of democratic excess, but of democratic suppression.[45]

The material constitution

It is no surprise that the idea of the 'material constitution' surfaces in the interwar period, in the minds of both conservative and socialist scholars; the crisis of parliamentarism had exposed the instability of liberal constitutionalism in the face of competing political claims and the fragmentation and polarization of social forces.[46] And it is no surprise that material analysis has again begun to recapture the attention after the most recent crisis of democratic capitalism cast established institutions and the standard assumptions of their legitimacy into serious doubt.

But, by the present conjuncture, the 'foundational constitutionalism' of the French and American revolutionary tradition had already given way to a 'freestanding constitutionalism' driven by the motor of economism and the ideology (or utopianism)

[42] See Wolfgang Streeck, 'The Crises of Democratic Capitalism' (2011) 71 New Left Review 5; *Buying Time: The Delayed Crisis of Democratic Capitalism* (Verso 2013).

[43] For an earlier attempt to dispel the myth of the weak liberal state, see Franz Neumann, 'The Change in Function of Law in Modern Society' in *The Political and the Authoritarian State* (Free Press 1957) 22–68.

[44] Heller (n 20). This is examined in Chapter 2.

[45] This is examined in detail in Chapter 2. For a recent recycling of this myth see, eg JHH Weiler, 'The European Circumstance and the Politics of Meaning: Not on Bread Alone Doth Man Liveth (Deut. 8:3; Mat. 4:4)' (2020) 21 German Law Journal 96: ('Hitler and Mussolini were hugely popular at their time and came to power democratically').

[46] From Carl Schmitt, Eric Voegelin, and Constantino Mortati on the conservative authoritarian wing, to Antonio Gramsci on the radical wing via Hermann Heller in the social democratic centre (see Goldoni and Wilkinson (n 8), for discussion).

of individual human rights.[47] This constitutional discourse, driven by the material dynamic of global capital and the normative project of liberal individualism, had been the accompaniment to the gradual loss of any collective, democratic understanding of the constituent power.[48] That meant that when crises recently struck in Europe (and elsewhere) there was a political vacuum into which claims now frequently characterized—and often too casually dismissed—as politically populist would easily be channelled.[49]

The democratic ground had been vacated by decades of free-standing constitutionalism, the displacement of the idea of constituent power and a politics of 'extreme centrism' substituting even ordinary political contestation.[50] This was a period in which—in significant part due to the EU's own constitutional structure—there was a further 'hollowing out' of democracy, reflected in the emergence of a 'void' between rulers and ruled, as centre-left and centre-right merged in practice and ideology.[51] It also left the space open for new hybrids to emerge; inflections of authoritarian liberalism incorporating an uneasy but not unsuccessful mix of technocracy and populism.[52]

The discourse of 'reclaiming sovereignty' so prominent in the euro crisis, and in the Brexit debate, then seems to make much more sense (which is not to say that it will necessarily be realized). It is not that sovereignty had been lost by a return to the shackles of religious truth, however much one might like to think of Brussels bureaucrats as the high priests of Europe. It is that sovereignty has been perceived to have been lost through the erosion of democratic control over the economy.[53] 'Perceived' is an important word here. Constitutions do not exist only as norms; they exist in a universe where facts and norms are interrelated. They have a material existence, which is internally related to their formal prescriptions and proscriptions, and which depends in part upon the plausibility of their claims to political unity, the strength of their institutions and social supports, and the desirability of their political objectives. And care should be taken to highlight that democratic control does not necessarily equal effective control, at least in the short term.[54] This is borne out by the Greek crisis: the

[47] On 'freestanding constitutionalism' in the European Union, in contrast to the foundational constitutionalism of the modern revolutionary tradition, see Michael Wilkinson, 'Political Constitutionalism and the European Union' (2013) 76:2 Modern Law Review 191.

[48] See Samuel Moyn, *The Last Utopia: Human Rights in History* (Harvard University Press 2010).

[49] See, eg Jan-Werner Müller, *What is Populism?* (University of Pennsylvania Press 2016)

[50] The phrase was used by Tariq Ali to capture the neo-liberal consensus among political elites in the UK after 1989: (Tariq Ali, *The Extreme Centre: A Warning* (Verso 2015)). On 'extreme centrism' as a phenomenon of European integration, see Michael A Wilkinson, 'The Brexit Referendum and the Crisis of Extreme Centrism' (2016) German Law Journal 131.

[51] On the role of Europe in this process of depoliticization, see Peter Mair, *Ruling the Void* (Verso 2013) 115–19.

[52] See, eg Carlo Accetti and Chris Bickerton, 'Populism and Technocracy: Opposites or Complements?' (2017) 20:2 Critical Review of International Social and Political Philosophy 186.

[53] On the erosion of sovereignty in the euro crisis phase, see Martin Loughlin, 'The Erosion of Sovereignty' (2016) 45:2 Netherlands Journal of Legal Philosophy 57. The argument presented in this book traces this process of erosion back several decades earlier.

[54] The implication is not, it should be stressed, that leaving the EU or the eurozone would lift the material constraints on the democratic political process. Constraints would remain, not least the financial markets and geopolitical pressures that exist in a state system of radically unequal units. Neither would leaving the EU necessarily lead to the re-democratization of the economy: it may simply be controlled by a different set

economic cost of leaving the single currency, aside from the legal-technical obstacles, may have been considered practically prohibitive of any radical reclaiming of monetary and fiscal sovereignty that might follow an exit of the euro area.[55] But, in an era when virtually all constitutions pay at least lip service to the idea of democratic self-determination, withholding economic decisions from electoral contestation must overcome a high threshold of political justification, if it can be justified at all. The post-war justification, broadly understood as an attempt to regain liberal democratic and economic stability, can no longer hold even on its own terms; anti-systemic forces have returned and instability beckons.

The material conception of sovereignty advanced here is captured in a different discursive tradition of constituent power: one revived in the 1990s by Antonio Negri.[56] With the modern constitutional revolution, 'the people' do not suddenly become the source of authority; not in anything other than a purely symbolic sense. The real material struggles over constituent power unfold over time, in ebbs and flows, and across critical and even revolutionary moments (not only 1789, but also the revolutions of 1848, 1870, and 1918, the General Strike of 1926, the unrest of 1968, and the Occupy movements beginning in 2011). These involve class conflicts, identity conflicts, and (if we broaden the horizon) anti-imperial struggles: conflicts of material distribution as well as political recognition.[57] Struggles for constituent power may begin as informal social movements, becoming more formally channelled by political parties, as in the case of workers' rights, and more recently in the extraordinary rise (and decline) of Syriza. Their demands may become formalized, as with the inclusion of material social demands into a political programme, or even a constitutional text or international agreement. They may become juridified in the form of social rights, with all the accompanying difficulties of application, due to the institutional obstacles to courts giving effect to redistributive demands.[58] But they may also be obstructed or repressed, by formal constitutional means and informal, ideological, and coercive strategies; such as in the refrain that there is no alternative to neo-liberal structural reform ('TINA'), in the constitutionalization of austerity through judicial interpretation of the European Treaties in the euro crisis phase, or in the coercion and cajoling of debtor countries by formal and informal groupings in the same period.[59] To capture constitutional change is not only to take account of its formal channelling, but also of constitutionalism's

of elites. Whether to leave or remain in the EU is a complex political judgement, and no more will be said about it here.

[55] For an argument for Greece leaving the euro, see Costas Lapavitsas and Heiner Flassbeck, *Against the Troika: Crisis and Austerity in the Eurozone* (Verso Books 2015).

[56] See Antonio Negri, *Insurgencies: Constituent Power and the Modern State* (University of Minnesota Press 1999). Later, this material-historical approach appears to be have been abandoned by Negri in favour of a global 'multitude', as we will see in Chapter 4.

[57] On the variety of anti-capitalist boundary struggles, see Nancy Fraser, 'Behind Marx's Hidden Abode: For an Expanded Conception of Capitalism' (2014) 86 New Left Review 55.

[58] For discussion, see Emilios Christodoulidis, 'Social Rights Constitutionalism: An Antagonistic Endorsement' (2017) 44:1 Journal of Law and Society 123.

[59] cf Clemens Kaupa, *The Pluralist Character of the European Economic Constitution* (Hart Publishing 2016).

framing function: the way a constitution (understood broadly) establishes how political debate is to be organized and what its limits are.[60]

With this material understanding in mind, we can briefly present the post-war reconstitution of the European state and state system as not only conservative but also essentially *reactionary* in character; not only (and perhaps not even) to prevent society from turning toward fascism, but to prevent it from obtaining material control over the relations and forces of production.[61] This is expressed ideologically in the vesting of sovereignty in 'the constitution' rather than 'the people', and having the values of the constitution guarded by so-called 'independent institutions', independent of democratic will but not of liberal economic practices and ideas; indeed, often legally or even constitutionally bound to them. It may even be entrenched, as in the German case, by the notion of the 'eternity clause', attempting to make the sovereignty of the constitution unbreakable (ironically, given its prominence, the German Basic Law was not even a proper constitution and was meant to have been reconstituted with German reunification).[62] The idea of the sovereignty of the constitution or even the sovereignty of law, which epitomizes this transformation, has a reach far beyond Germany, often representing a broader moralization of constitutional theory and liberal judicial politics itself.[63] Underpinning this transformation is the belief that the people are no longer trusted to rule, not only by elites, but also by the people themselves: '*We* are afraid of the people', to adopt Möllers' apt expression.[64]

As the idea of the constitution as a basic and free-standing social contract gains ascendency, it is not only 'the people' but also 'the state' that fades into the background in the minds of constitutional scholars (liberal or otherwise), wholly disarming them for its return in the recent conjuncture, when the state is again called to act in order to maintain or regain order, in light of an inter-state system that—in the case of the EU—suffers legitimization crises of its own.[65]

[60] As Gavin Anderson puts it, 'constitutional discourse is always more than the rules it generates or legitimates ... setting the parameters not just for how politics is contested, but what is deemed politically contestable': see Gavin Anderson, 'Constitutionalism as Critical Project' in Stephen Gill, *New Constitutionalism and World Order* (CUP 2015) 283, quoting Emilios Christodoulidis.

[61] Note that the focus here is on the project of European integration as culminating in the European Union, officially born at Maastricht; but a similar story of conservative counter-revolution could be told about the European Convention on Human Rights (see, eg Marco Duranti, *The Conservative Human Rights Revolution: European Identity, Transnational Politics, and the Origin of the European Convention* (OUP 2017)). That story is compatible with what is told here, and partly intertwined, but the overall material significance of the EU is thought to far outweigh that of the ECHR.

[62] See Werner Heun, *The Constitution of Germany* (Hart 2010). The 'never again' narrative was only later read into this provisional and organizational document, as Michaela Hailbronner shows, see: Michaela Hailbronner, *Traditions and Transformation: The Rise of German Constitutionalism* (OUP 2015).

[63] This turn is often inspired by Ronald Dworkin's legal theory, eg in the work of Matthias Kumm, examined in Chapter 4.

[64] Christoph Möllers, '"We are (Afraid of) the People": Constituent Power in German Constitutionalism' in Martin Loughlin and Neil Walker (eds), *The Paradox of Constitutionalism: Constituent Power and Constitutional Form* (OUP 2007) 87–107. Already in 1950, Franz Neumann had written about the 'German's propensity to safeguard themselves against democracy through the means of jurisdiction and the provision of fixed basic rights' and described their 'constitutional fetishism' (see Clara Maier, 'The Weimar Origins of the West German *Rechtsstaat*, 1919–1969' (2019) 62:4 The Historical Journal 1081). More generally, see Michael Mandel, 'A Brief History of the New Constitutionalism, or "How we Changed Everything so that Everything Would Remain the Same"' (1998) 32:2 Israeli Law Review 250.

[65] For an overview of the waxing and waning of the concept of the state in constitutional theory, see H Patrick Glenn, *The Cosmopolitan State* (OUP 2013) ch 1. Note that there are important exceptions to

The constitutionalization of EU law

This material transformation is accompanied by a new constitutional imaginary, which emerges in domestic resettlements, as well as through the project of European integration.[66] The EU exaggerates and radicalizes these tendencies, not least with the gradual authorization of an unwritten European 'constitution' by 'we, the court'.[67] The disappearance of the democratic constituent power occurs not all at once, but in a gradual and incremental process of 'constitutionalization'.[68] This happens across various phases, beginning with the early years following the Treaty of Rome, when lawyer-activists were central to the project of forging a European constitution through instrumentalizing the judicial architecture created by the Treaty. This project would be reinforced with the Single European Act in 1986 and scaled up to the macroeconomic constitution of Economic and Monetary Union at Maastricht.[69] Constitutionalization reached an anticlimactic pinnacle with the Constitutional Treaty project in the new millennium, failing in referenda in France and the Netherlands in 2005. The constitutional idea was then formally abandoned, along with some of the symbolic accoutrements, but its content was repackaged in its essentials with the Treaty of Lisbon,[70] and the normative and explanatory appeal of constitutional discourse in the scholarship has barely diminished.[71]

The cumulative effect of constitutionalization in these phases, and especially in the post-Maastricht construction of Economic and Monetary Union (EMU), was transformative, as it delinked the sovereign powers of the state (especially the power to control money) from the constituent power of the people. This is a gradual but foundational shift, because central to the modern constitutional imagination had always been not only that the powers of the state must be limited (as liberalism recommends),

the recent decline in attention to the state in constitutional theory, eg Martin Loughlin, 'In Defense of *Staatslehre*' (2010) Der Staat 48 (1) 1 (and, more generally, Loughlin, *Foundations of Public Law* (OUP 2012). But a corollary of the fact that the state disappears in much legal and constitutional theory is perhaps that talk of a European federal state also dies in European studies (with Federico Mancini a rare exception in the mid 1990s), replaced by discourses of constitutional pluralism (as discussed in Part III).

[66] Of course, this has significant national variations. On the German context, see Ralf Ptak, 'Neoliberalism in Germany: Revisiting the Ordoliberal Foundations of the Social Market Economy' in Mirowski and Plehwe (eds) (n 25). On the European economic constitution, see Wolf Sauter, 'The Economic Constitution of the European Union' (1998) Columbia Journal of European Law 27

[67] See Miguel Maduro, *We The Court: The European Court of Justice and the European Economic Constitution* (Hart 1998).

[68] See Martin Loughlin, 'What is Constitutionalisation?' in M Loughlin and P Dobner (eds), *The Twilight of Constitutionalism* (OUP 2009).

[69] See Vauchez (n 3), Cohen (n 3).

[70] For analysis, see Christine Reh, 'The Lisbon Treaty: De-Constitutionalising the EU' (2009) 47:3 Journal of Common Market Studies 625.

[71] The literature on EU constitutionalism is too voluminous to cite here, and has not ceased in productivity. There are textbooks and even entire journals dedicated to exploring the EU in constitutional terms, eg The European Constitutional Law Review. For exceptions to those who embrace the constitutionalist discourse, see Peter Lindseth, *Power and Legitimacy: Reconciling Europe and the Nation-State* (OUP 2010); Bruno de Witte, 'The EU As International Legal Experiment' in Deburca and Weiler (eds), *The Worlds of European Constitutionalism* (CUP 2011). Weiler himself claimed to be a sceptic despite doing so much to spread the idea.

but that they be limited in the name of 'the people' or at least recognizable as a process of collective *self*-limitation (as popular sovereignty demands). In the post-war constitution, deepened and entrenched at Maastricht, the powers of the state are, by contrast, constrained; not by 'the people', but by 'the market' and the interstate system; by institutions that are technocratic rather than democratically responsive and geared to replicating or restoring, as far as possible, market rationality.[72]

The constitutionalization of economic liberalism is not a static settlement, establishing a clear demarcation of the political and the economic for the future. On the contrary, due to the dynamics underpinning neo-liberal and ordoliberal development, there is no neat separation of economic and political spheres because market logic tends to expand and extend, dominating the whole of political society, not only the economy narrowly conceived.[73] As Isiksel notes on the EU's own constitutional evolution, 'the expansion of the EU's operations has engendered the colonization of ever greater swathes of public policy by institutions designed primarily to create and govern a supranational market.'[74] This has occurred through political decisions and constitutional changes.

An obvious objection to characterizing these processes as authoritarian can be anticipated. In a trivial sense, membership in the EU remains a voluntary surrender of authority; states can, after all, (at least since Lisbon) formally leave the EU, now in accordance with Article 50 of the Treaty on European Union (TEU) and whatever domestic constitutional procedures are required. But this formalism misses precisely that the process of European integration is one of state and constitutional *transformation*, a change in domestic political institutions and elites (ruling arrangements) as well as the social constitutional imaginary (the ruling relationship).[75] It sets limits to what is politically possible, or at least what is politically feasible within current constitutional constraints, which of course may themselves change over time. The nature and extent of these limits, and their likelihood of change, does to some extent depend on which of the 'variety of constitutionalisms' adverted to above we are concerned with, and in particular on whether a member state of the EU is also a member of the euro area. The UK can leave the EU in a way that would not be open to a country in the eurozone. Within the eurozone, the 'variety of constitutionalisms', along with a variety of capitalisms, has been reduced to a singular logic through the euro crisis phase, if in fact this narrowing of political economic rationality can be traced back further.[76] The euro, according to the European Central Bank, is 'irreversible'.

Crisis, without doubt, has opened up the possibility of critique; this has led, in the case of Brexit, to the first significant possibility of rupture, and an undoing of the

[72] Bickerton, 'European Integration' (n 13) 67. See also Wolfgang Streeck, 'Markets and Peoples: Democratic Capitalism and European Integration' (2013) 73 New Left Review 63.

[73] In the critical literature on international relations, under the label of the 'new constitutionalism', this claim is relatively well established; see, eg Stephen Gill, *Power and Resistance in the New World Order* (Palgrave Macmillan 2003).

[74] Turkuler Isiksel, *Europe's Functional Constitutionalism* (OUP 2016) 19.

[75] This is one way of understanding the acknowledgement in the Miller case: see *R v Secretary of State for Exiting the European Union* [2017] UKSC 5.

[76] As we will discuss in Parts III and IV, the 'variety of capitalisms' literature is of limited explanatory purchase when confronted with the interconnections among various models of political economy.

post-war constitutional settlement in Europe.[77] It is an event of considerable moment and may yet brook momentum for a broader unravelling of the project. But because of the UK's particular material relation with the EU, it may be an outlier. Rupture remains a distant prospect in the core of Europe, as well as on the periphery.

The difficulties of Brexit show that, even outside of the single currency, the material constraints of membership and the costs of exiting (or the perception of such) are very real, as is the significance of membership of the EU in the constitutional imagination (discussed further in Chapters 3 to 5). For a core country such as Germany, France, or Italy, to leave the EU would signal a material change in their constitutions, perhaps a revolutionary one, even if formally permissible as a matter of legal logic.

Authoritarian populism?

From the present vantage point, the instability of the post-war resettlement—considered less than two decades ago as symbolizing a 'model for the nations of the world in the 21st century'[78]—now comes into full view. Europe finds itself, once again, in a critical condition following the global financial crisis.[79] Movements outside of the established centre have returned, and arguments for reclaiming sovereignty over borders, people, and capital have been resurrected. There has been much discussion about the phenomenon of right-wing nationalism in Hungary and, more recently, Poland, and of left-wing parties in Greece and Spain that have grown out of anti-austerity movements. But the reshaping of the political landscape has occurred not only in peripheral countries devastated by the economic crisis, but also in the core of Europe, and in creditor nations. In the 2017 federal elections, a far right party, the Alternative für Deutschland (AfD), entered the German parliament for the first time since the Second World War. The French presidential elections of the same year pitted Emmanuel Macron, leading a new formation En Marche, against Marine Le Pen of the Front Nationale. In Italy the following year, the refusal to appoint a Eurosceptic finance minister provoked a mini constitutional crisis after the election produced a coalition between the right-wing Lega and the centrist-populist Five Star Movement.

The passive authoritarian liberalism of the pre-euro crisis period, hardened through the crisis response, is now accompanied by an authoritarian populism that looks set to stay. The Polanyian double movement, in reaction to enforced, coerced, or elite-led marketization and commodification, takes the form of a conservative rather than progressive backlash, with politically illiberal features; in particular, with regard to freedom of the press and attitudes towards immigration.[80] This is all occurring from

[77] As explained above, the UK represents an atypical material position from the viewpoint of European integration as a whole, making it difficult to generalize the Brexit phenomenon. But the signs of discontent with the EU are widespread.

[78] See Mark Leonard, *Why Europe Will Run the 21st Century* (Fourth Estate 2005).

[79] Not long into the crisis, French philosopher Etienne Balibar described Europe as looking like a 'dead' political project; see 'Europe: Final Crisis? Some Theses' (2010) 13:2 Theory & Event .

[80] Karl Polanyi, *The Great Transformation: The Political and Economic Origins of Our Time* (Beacon Press 2001). Polanyi's theory is examined in Chapter 3.

within the European Union, and potentially poses a greater challenge to the project than the voluntary exit of the UK.

Significantly, the authoritarian populist reaction in Central and Eastern Europe to the brisk transition to market capitalism following accession to the EU, an inflection of—rather than rupture from—neo-liberal economics, has been permitted if not indulged, whereas the 'progressive' reaction—an attempt to break with neo-liberal austerity in Greece from the left—was harshly punished, if ultimately self-immolated in Syriza's capitulation.[81] The movement towards populism predated the euro crisis proper, growing in the core of Europe in the post-Maastricht phase, purporting to fill the void that had emerged in the decades of soft authoritarian liberalism.

With the blame for authoritarian populism now being laid by the ruling classes—as well as much of the academic commentary—on an excess of democracy rather than a deficit, political and constitutional elites double down on authoritarian projects of integration. Ordoliberalism is declared the only game in town;[82] those who contest it are caricatured as un-European, constituting the 'enemy within' the European project.[83] Increasingly there are also signs of a new 'enemy without' emerging, as Russia assumes a new geopolitical significance in the liberal imagination, but not yet one that could unite foreign policy across the continent.[84] If populism itself is simply derided; often dismissed in a careless and undifferentiated manner, its rhetoric is emulated by European elites in an attempt to co-opt its appeal.[85]

An incidental feature of this study is that, by illustrating the constitutional depths of the present conjuncture, it highlights the seriousness of the stakes, because it suggests that to break with European integration is not merely to mark a break with neo-liberal political economy, but with liberal constitutionalism. Where this conjuncture leads remains to be seen; the situation is fluid, the long period of crisis beginning in 2008 as yet unresolved. It could offer a return to a democratic path that had largely been

[81] The turn to 'authoritarian populism' in Eastern Europe has been described as continuing many of the policies of economic neo-liberalism. See Gareth Dale and Adam Fabry, 'Neoliberalism in Eastern Europe and the Former Soviet Union' in Damian Cahill, Melinda Cooper, Martijn Konings and David Primrose (eds), *The Sage Handbook of Neoliberalism* (Sage Publications 2018). On the link between financial crisis in Hungary, the imposition of austerity, and a populist turn, see Claire Kilpatrick, 'Constitutions, Social Rights and Sovereign Debt States in Europe: A Challenging New Area of Constitutional Inquiry' in Thomas Beukers, Bruno de Witte and Claire Kilpatrick (eds), *Constitutional Change Through Euro-Crisis Law* (CUP 2017) 279. Habermas described the approach towards Greece as punishment for Syriza daring to contest austerity from the left; see Philip Altermann, 'Jürgen Habermas' verdict on the EU/Greece Debt Deal—Full Transcript', *The Guardian* (London, 16 July 2015).

[82] See 'The Donald Tusk interview' ('Greece: Donald Tusk warns of extremist political contagion' *Financial* Times (London,16 July 2015) <https://www.ft.com/content/f6872342-2bd2-11e5-acfb-cbd2e1c81cca> accessed 21 November 2020; Mario Draghi has noted that the 'monetary constitution of the ECB is firmly grounded in the principles of ordoliberalism'; see 'Opening Remarks at the Session 'Rethinking the Limitations of Monetary Policy', speech by Mario Draghi, The Israel Museum, Jerusalem, 18 June 2013, available at <https://www.ecb.europa.eu/press/key/date/2013/html/sp130618.en.html>

[83] See, eg Udo di Fabio, 'Karlsruhe Makes a Referral' (2014) 15 German Law Journal 107.

[84] It is notable that in the Habermas–Derrida initiative launched in 2003, in response to the invasion of Iraq, it was the US that played the Schmittian foil to European humanism; see 'February 15th or What Binds Europeans Together?' (2003) 10 Constellations 291.

[85] As with Commission president von der Leyen's attempt at designating a portfolio to defending a 'European Way of Life', https://www.politico.eu/article/von-der-leyen-on-european-way-of-life-we-cant-let-others-take-away-our-language (accessed 21 November 2020).

abandoned over the last several decades, and all the opportunities and risks that come with it. But this is far from guaranteed.

The outline of the book

The narrative will unfold across five parts. *Part I* examines the interwar breakdown of liberal democracy, when ruling elites turned to an authoritarian liberalism in a failed attempt to shore up a system in crisis. The story begins in Weimar Germany (Chapter 1), not only because this sharpens the perspective, but because of Weimar's legacy for the post-war period. But authoritarian liberalism is also presented as a more general phenomenon, extending 'beyond Weimar' both in time and geographical space (Chapter 2).

Post-war Europe is then examined more fully in *Part II*, as its inter-state, state society, and social relations are reconstituted in such a way as to gradually restrain sovereignty, depoliticize the economy, and deradicalize politics. This occurs through various inter-state (Chapter 3), institutional (Chapter 4), and societal changes (Chapter 5). These are the result of domestic constitutional projects, supranational projects of European constitutionalization—particularly the process of 'integration through law'—and the ascendency of ordoliberalism and neo-liberalism in the constitutional imagination, buttressed by the political demobilization of the masses.

Part III charts the road from Maastricht to Lisbon, when increasing integration starts to be accompanied by various countermovements. The period after the fall of the Berlin Wall marks the return of the 'German question', but also a 'new intergovernmentalism' (Chapter 6). EU authority is extended to new areas but increasingly contested, notably by the German Constitutional Court, although contestation is evident in political arenas across Europe (Chapter 7). The differentiation of the political and the economic is scaled up through Economic and Monetary Union (EMU), imposing additional external constraints on sovereign power, and market rationality is deepened across a wider and more heterogeneous European space (Chapter 8).

In the euro crisis phase, examined in *Part IV*, the constitutional configuration is sustained only by further and harsher intervention and disciplining of member states. This occurs through an increasingly asymmetrical intergovernmental formation which raises the spectre of German semi-hegemony (Chapter 9). The significance of non-democratic transnational institutions, particularly the European Central Bank (ECB), becomes more conspicuous, but these institutions are only able to defer rather than resolve deep-seated structural problems (Chapter 10). Asymmetrical state interventions and institutional innovations are also accompanied by significant countermovements, offering, but ultimately failing, to reclaim popular sovereignty and democratic control over the economy (Chapter 11).

In conclusion, the 'new' phenomenon of authoritarian populism is considered, and judged to represent an inflection of authoritarian liberalism rather than a rupture.

PART I

INTERWAR: A PRE-HISTORY OF EUROPEAN INTEGRATION

Over the course of the 'long nineteenth century', from the French Revolution to the First World War, a myth of the liberal state emerges in Europe, in a threefold manner, as a sovereign, democratic and capitalist state.[1] The *sovereign state* is recognized as the only legitimate subject of international relations, with the right to determine its internal affairs and to decide on matters of war and peace, subject to conventions regarding civilized warfare. This *jus publicum europaeum* is based on a European 'balance of power' consolidated over a long period, from the early modern age of absolutism through to the 'golden age' of the interstate system and the Concert of Europe.[2] The *democratic state* is a state whose monopoly of legitimate force is based on secular foundations and the principle of political equality—in constitutional language, 'we, the people do solemnly ordain' our political and legal order— associated with the French and American revolutionary traditions of the late eighteenth century, but having roots in early modern Enlightenment thought.[3] Popular sovereignty ultimately serves as a foundation for political power, however ideological, mythical, or fictional this conception is considered to be. Finally, the *capitalist state* differentiates (and, on some accounts, effects a separation) between the state and the market, meaning that the political order and the economic order are relatively autonomous domains, and based on different logics or rationalities.[4] There is a political logic of collective security

[1] The 'long nineteenth century', a phrase associated with historian Eric Hobsbawm, also captures a period in the history of public law. Michael Stolleis, for example, presents 1914 as marking a break: a 'farewell to the nineteenth century': *A History of Public Law in Germany 1914–1945* (OUP 2004) 1–19.

[2] Carl Schmitt, *The Nomos of the Earth in the International Law of the Jus Publicum Europaeum* (GL Ulmen tr, Telos Press 2003 [first published 1950). cf Benno G Teschke, 'Fatal Attraction: A Critique of Carl Schmitt's International Legal and Political Theory' (2011) 3 International Theory 179; Marti Koskenniemi, 'International Law as Political Theology: How to Read *Nomos Der Erde*' (2004) 11:4 Constellations 492. According to Schmitt, the *jus publicum europaeum* implied a decisive rupture not only with divine right, but also with medieval just war theories, grounded in the moral universalism of the *respublica christiana*. A certain 're-moralisation' occurs in the aftermath of World War I, when Germany loses its right to wage war, as a result of Versailles and the League of Nations.

[3] See, eg Hannah Arendt, *On Revolution* (Penguin Books 2009 [first published 1963]); Martin Loughlin, *Foundations of Public Law* (OUP 2010) (Loughlin, 'Foundations') 37–46 . cf Martin Loughlin, *The Idea of Public Law* (OUP 2003).

[4] Max Weber, *Economy and Society: An Outline of Interpretive Sociology* (Guenther Roth and Claus Wittich eds, University of California Press 1978). The significance of Weber for early twentieth-century social sciences is general but also, for our purposes, particular, because of the philosophical and political influence he exerted in the Weimar debates, and over a significant number of protagonists, including Carl

or, in more republican-oriented conceptions, the public good, and an economic logic of capital accumulation and competition in a 'private sphere' of formal equality (presented in the Marxist tradition as a sphere of substantive inequality and exploitation).[5]

This sketch of a 'sovereign, democratic and capitalist' state simplifies a long and uneven historical process. It conceals the reality that each element is complexly interrelated with each other, and significant tensions, and even contradictions, emerge among them: between popular sovereignty and the limits imposed by an inter-state system, or between democracy and the constraints placed by private power in the economy. A different story can be told, depending on which element is taken to be dominant. Variations occur through distinct traditions; the state, as a unity, developing with a degree of relative autonomy. The myth is decidedly Eurocentric in its focus on the Western state tradition, and in bracketing the significance of imperialism.[6]

As a myth, it serves to crystallize a series of conceptual distinctions key to the constitutional *idea* of the modern European state: distinctions between international and domestic, state and society, the political and the economic realms.[7] It is in, and through, these distinctions that we can discern the basis for the complex set of practices and ideas that we might call liberalism. And it is in probing their interdependency, mutual irritations and even contradictions, that we can discern various strands of critical theory.[8] Therefore, internal to each domain is a dialectical narrative: the formal sovereign equality of states and the hierarchical structures of 'legalized hegemony',[9] the role of the theological mindset in shaping and reshaping the 'secularization' of state-society relationships,[10] and the differentiation and re-differentiation of the political and the economic realms, most evidently in periods of capitalist crisis.[11]

Schmitt. See, eg Duncan Kelly, *The State of the Political. Conceptions of Politics and the State in the Thought of Max Weber, Carl Schmitt, and Franz Neumann* (OUP 2003).

[5] See, eg Ellen M Wood, *Democracy Against Capitalism: Renewing Historical Materialism* (CUP 1995).

[6] cf Hannah Arendt, *The Origins of Totalitarianism* (Penguin Books 2017), identifying a direct link between the early modern political philosophy of Thomas Hobbes and the emergence of European imperialism and totalitarianism. On the influence of European colonialism on the early process of European integration, see Peo Hansen and Stefan Jonson, *Eurafrica: The Untold History of European Integration and Colonialism* (Bloomsbury 2014). Slobodian traces the imperialist mindset of the early European neoliberal globalists to that he calls the 'Geneva School': see Quinn Slobodian, *Globalists: The End of Empire and the Birth of Neoliberalism* (HUP 2018) ch 6.

[7] In Loughlin, 'Foundations' (n 3), the central foundational narrative is secularization, building on the work of the French philosopher Gauchet (ibid, 6–8).

[8] See, eg Edward Hallett Carr, *The Twenty Years Crisis 1919–1939* (Palgrave MacMillan 2016). 'Liberalism' in this broader sense thus includes forms of liberal internationalism, political liberalism *and* economic liberalism. Even within these forms, there is, of course, a large variety of *liberalisms*, but there is no space, nor need, to go into them here, nor to distinguish the new collectivist versions of liberalism that emerged towards the end of the nineteenth- and beginning of the twentieth century, and which started to replace the 'classical liberalism' of the Enlightenment. Critical theory, likewise broad in scope, almost invariably takes one or more of these distinctions and problematizes it.

[9] See Gerry Simpson, *Great Powers and Outlaw States: Unequal Sovereigns in the International Legal Order* (CUP 2004). cf Philip Bobbit, *The Shield of Achilles: War, Peace and the Course of History* (Anchor Books 2003).

[10] See, eg Marcel Gauchet, *The Disenchantment of the World: A Political History of Religion* (Oscar Burge tr, Princeton University Press 1997).

[11] See, eg Wood (n 5) .

Inter-state, state-society and social relations offer a structure with which to analyse the re-constitution of Europe through the development of a new *jus publicum europaeum* in the post-war era, as we will see in subsequent chapters. Much more could be said about these evolutionary narratives across the long nineteenth century. But this book is about their fate in the Europe of the twentieth century.

Our story begins after the First World War and the collapse of the regional inter-state system, with the breakdown of liberal constitutionalism, and severe social and economic crises culminating with the Great Depression of the early 1930s. If inter-state sovereignty had become inter-imperial rivalry long before that rivalry had degenerated into outright worldwide conflict in 1914, the period after the First World War had witnessed multiple failures to reconstruct a functioning framework for regulating international relations. This international and regional failure was underscored by the legacy of Versailles, the failure of the gold standard, and the weaknesses of the League of Nations.[12]

But it was the 'long march of the masses onto the stage of history' that resonated in the constitutional imagination. Initiated in the revolutionary periods of the late eighteenth century, and developing through the traditions of republicanism, socialism, and Marxism in the nineteenth century, by the interwar period the working class was armed with class consciousness, universal suffrage, and democratic representation. State-society relations, which remained shot through with the legacies of hierarchy, status and substantive socio-economic inequality, would now be based on real political equality. The growth of social democracy then threatened not only the material order of capitalism (and, in some cases, imperialism), but also, in the language of German *Staatslehre*, the bourgeois *Rechtsstaat* and its state form.[13] Severe socio-economic crisis tested the institutions and ideologies of the capitalist state and state system, and appeared to signal its breakdown, requiring the dramatic interpenetration of the state into society, and of the political into the economic realms, in an attempt to stabilize the bourgeois order.[14] In sum, there was a radical crisis in the modern liberal constitutional imagination.

The fallout from this multifaceted crisis of interwar authority is captured by Antonio Gramsci's notion of the interregnum, an 'in between' period, 'when the old is dying and the new cannot be born'.[15] In this period, the ruling class struggled to maintain hegemony, no longer 'leading', but only 'dominant', unable to rule on the basis of consent alone. 'Alienated from the mass of the population and torn with internal division', facing competing strategies for political hegemony and a detachment of the masses

[12] See Marti Koskenniemi, *The Gentle Civilizer of Nations: The Rise and Fall of International Law 1870–1960* (CUP 2001).

[13] The German tradition of *Staatslehre*, prominent at the turn of the twentieth century, was a distinct field of juristic thought where the constitution of the state was based on a trinity of territory, ruling authority, and people (See Loughlin, 'Foundations' (n 3) 190–196). On the anxiety of the bourgeoisie in the face of the threat of socialism, see Charles S Maier, *Recasting Bourgeois Europe: Stabilization in France, Germany, and Italy in the Decade after World War I* (Princeton University Press 2016) 23.

[14] Maier (n 13) 6–7 ('by the twentieth century most of the old elites had formed a conservative cartel with bourgeois political representatives.' Into the 1920s, bourgeois 'remained the code word for a matrix of relationships defined in opposition to what socialists suggested as alternatives'.)

[15] Antonio Gramsci, *Selections from the Prison Notebooks of Antonio Gramsci* (Quintin Hoare and Geoffrey Nowell-Smith trs, Lawrence and Wishart 2003) 276.

from traditional ideologies, the state turns to more coercive means of control.[16] The interregnum was characterized not only by a series of political and economic crises, but an *organic crisis*: 'a wider political and ideological crisis of legitimation' that revealed 'incurable structural contradictions of the political order' and threw up a variety of 'morbid symptoms'.[17] In the course of the struggle for hegemony that ensues, the myth of the liberal 'neutral state' of the long nineteenth century is discredited. The 'short twentieth century' begins.[18]

In the interwar period, in order to arrest the march of the masses and contain the dangers of parliamentary democracy, liberals turn to more authoritarian forms of governing, creating a series of constitutional conflicts. Although these are played out across the continent, the most intense battles would be fought in Weimar Germany, where, for historical reasons, liberalism was particularly fragile.

In late Weimar, the defection from parliamentarism, which would pave the way for the Nazi seizure of power, was launched by an 'anti-democratic and embittered ruling class'.[19] 'The fateful transition to authoritarianism', notes Eberhard Kolb, was coolly planned, 'and with the intention of drastically altering the constitutional system and the balance of social forces in favor of old elites of the army, bureaucracy and big business'.[20] Political and economic elites, refusing to countenance 'the inroads that democracy had made into their privileged position', were determined to destroy 'the political order and the social welfare provisions on which it rested'.[21] In this climate, it was a strange combination of forces—conservative and liberal—and their 'toleration' by social democracy, that emerged to defend the bourgeois order; it was the turn, as Hermann Heller explained, of an *authoritarian liberalism*.

Although tragically late, Heller's realization, in 1932, that it would be the ruling class that would resort to autocracy and dictatorship, fatally undermining the Republic in its last period before the Nazi takeover in early 1933, brings together into one arc his own critique of liberalism in the short conjuncture, and over the long durée. Liberalism's authoritarian tendency was not shallow and contingent or merely unleashed in the exceptional moment, it was profound: both cause and effect of the erosion and ultimate breakdown of democracy. Heller comes late to the realization that the liberal state is, in other words, a class state *and* a capitalist state, a state that would turn not only against socialism, but against democracy itself.

Chapter 1 sets out the interregnum of late Weimar, when Hermann Heller uses the term 'authoritarian liberalism' to capture the conjunction of political authoritarianism and economic liberalism in the presidential cabinets ruling Weimar by diktat and decree. The modus operandi of this regime was depoliticization, specifically of the conflicts in the economic sector that had been threatening the interests of capital. This was

[16] Rune Møller Stahl, 'Ruling the Interregnum: Politics and Ideology in Nonhegemonic Times' (2019) 43 Politics and Society 333.

[17] ibid.

[18] Kanishka Jayasuriya, 'The Strange Death of the Liberal International Order' (2010) 45 Economic and Political Weekly 75.

[19] See, eg Ian Kershaw, 'Introduction: Perspectives of Weimar's Failure' in Ian Kershaw (ed), *Weimar: Why did German Democracy Fail?* (Wiedenfeld and Nicholson 1990) 1–19

[20] Eberhard Kolb, *The Weimar Republic* (2nd edn, Routledge 2005) 116–135, 117–118

[21] Kershaw (n 19) 16.

'tolerated' by the social democrats, who, despite initial interest in radical democratization, had gradually abandoned it over the course of the 1920s, leaving behind not only options such as democratizing the economy, but also the parliamentary institutions of the Weimar Republic. The seizure of power by the Nazi party signals a continuation of the trajectory of depoliticization, and even the 'end of the political', although marking a break in heralding mass mobilization based on a cult of violence, redemption and racial identity.

In Chapter 2 we examine the broader constitutional tensions in interwar liberalism, specifically a result of its inability to respond to the social issue: the issue of socio-economic inequality. We will extend the lens beyond Weimar, turning to the political economy of various crises across Europe: in Italy, France, and Austria. As Karl Polanyi shows, in these contexts, the turn to authoritarian liberalism fatally weakened political democracy, and left it disarmed when faced with the fascist threat. And yet, proposals for neo-liberalism are already introduced before the onset of the Second World War, signalled by the organization of the Walter Lippman Colloquium in 1938, and the Mont Pelerin Society in 1947. The impact of these proposals, an attempt to create a new foundation for economic liberalism, is only fully realized in the post-war era (examined in Part II).

1
Authoritarian Liberalism in Late Weimar

1. Introduction

German Social Democrat and constitutional theorist Hermann Heller coined the term 'authoritarian liberalism' in the context of a crisis of the state, and its escalation in the late stages of the Weimar Republic. He used the term to capture the shift from a parliamentary democracy to an authoritarian presidentialism, which explicitly defended the market economy and the interests of the owners of capital and big businesses.[1] This 'authoritarian liberal' state, the last throw of the dice of the ruling order, was the precursor to the fully fledged collapse of the Weimar Republic in 1933 with the Nazi seizure of power. It was, therefore, largely overshadowed by the subsequent fascist dictatorship; but it was a crucial moment in Weimar's demise.[2]

The Nazis came to power, not, as the story so often goes, on the back of an excess of democracy, but of an excess of 'liberalism', in the sense of an economic liberalism pursued by political elites ruling in emergency mode. It was a regime which insisted on maintaining the illusion of a *distance* between state and society; the political and the economic realms. This was to be achieved through a strong state, the *qualitatively* total state, strong in effecting the differentiation of realms, as opposed to the *quantitively* total state proposed by the Social Democrats and those on the political left, which, according to its opponents—notably Carl Schmitt—would be a weak state, politicizing the economy and pluralizing the state. Authoritarian liberalism, it should be noted, although defending economic liberalism, was deeply *illiberal* in the meaning of 'political liberalism': intolerant of difference, impatient of parliamentary debate, and deeply fearful of democracy in mass society.[3]

It was, thus, a privation of parliamentary democracy that preceded its outright collapse in Weimar; formally through the exercise of emergency presidential powers and the bypassing of parliament, and informally through the exercise of paramilitary violence and political intimidation of opponents. The authoritarian liberals, backed by

[1] Hermann Heller, 'Autoritärer Liberalismus', Die Neue Rundschau 44 (1933) 289 (in English translation, 'Authoritarian Liberalism?' European Law Journal 21 (2015) 295 (tr S Paulson)). This was one of Heller's final publications before the Nazis took power in January 1933, and his premature death, in exile, in Madrid in November 1933.

[2] See, eg Peter C Caldwell, *Popular Sovereignty and the Crisis of German Constitutional Law: The Theory & Practice of Weimar Constitutionalism* (Duke University Press 1997)(Caldwell, 'Popular Sovereignty') 11–12. Caldwell notes that the conception of constitutional democracy associated with von Papen and Schmitt 'laid the groundwork for the Nazi takeover' and is 'obscured' by a conservative historiography that argues Weimar's republic was 'defenceless' and 'gave itself up'.

[3] Preuss describes 'mass democracy' as 'the political order of the Weimar Constitution': (Ulrich K Preuss, 'Carl Schmitt and the Weimar Constitution' in Jens Meierhenrich and Oliver Simons (eds), *The Oxford Handbook of Carl Schmitt* (OUP 2016) 472. In this chapter it is presented rather as an *irritant* to the political order.

Authoritarian Liberalism and the Transformation of Modern Europe. Michael A Wilkinson, Oxford University Press.
 DOI: 10.1093/oso/9780198854753.003.0002

capital as well as bureaucratic and military elites, were, above all, 'anti-Marxist' and 'anti-parliamentary'.[4] This is an important point to recall, and not only because it is so frequently forgotten, but because a very different, and largely misleading, story has such a powerful impact, resonating in a postwar emphasis in constitutional theory on 'over-democratisation', the misnamed 'militant democracy', 'democratic suicide', or the so-called 'tyranny of the majority'.[5]

This chapter begins by outlining the Weimar interregnum; a combination of political authoritarianism and economic liberalism, specifically the presidential cabinets ruling by diktat and decree, and the theorist that stood behind them: Carl Schmitt (section 2). This regime was supported by centrist and conservative parties and 'tolerated' by the Social Democrats. With much of the left, along with the trade unions, thereby abandoning any designs for radical democratization of society, let alone the overthrow of the capitalist system, a crisis of representation occurred (section 3). If, as many historians contend, authoritarian liberalism laid the grounds for the Nazi seizure of power, it was the suppression rather than excess of democracy that preceded Weimar's collapse. These various strategies of depoliticization are not reversed with the Nazi seizure of power; on the contrary, they are continued through the Nazi 'mass mobilization', ending the political (section 4) and replacing it with a cult of violence (section 5).

2. Authoritarian liberalism in late Weimar

The term 'authoritarian liberalism' was used by Hermann Heller specifically in reaction to the programme of centrist and conservative presidential cabinets ruling late Weimar Germany under President von Hindenburg. In this brief phase of presidential rule from 1930 to 1932, through Chancellors Brüning, von Papen, and then von Schleicher, government proceeded through emergency measures, bypassing parliamentary authority entirely. Supported by Germany's central bank, it proceeded to implement drastic cuts to state expenditure, pursue internal devaluation, and operate a deflationary policy, in part under pressure of servicing its war debts.[6]

After 1929, deeply affected by the Great Depression, as well as the liability for reparations payments, the economic situation, which had stabilized in the mid-period (1925–29), after the hyperinflations of the early 1920s, had again worsened. The German business community, increasingly frustrated with organized labour, hit by a dearth of foreign investment, and dependent on declining foreign exports, demanded 'greater expertise in the formulation and implementation of national economic policy', as well as 'authoritarian efforts to place the responsibility for economic decision

[4] Eberhard Kolb, *The Weimar Republic* (2nd edn, Routledge 2005) 116–35, at 117–18.

[5] For an analysis of the US use of, and influence on, the principle of 'militant democracy' in the context of the Cold War see Udi Greenberg, *The Weimar Century: German Emigres and the Ideological Foundations of the Cold War* (Princeton University Press 2014) ch 6.

[6] Heller, 'Autoritärer Liberalismus' (n 1) 295–301. According to Abraham, 'Brüning's strategy could be summarised as "deflation"; one he pursued in myriad ways' (David Abraham, *The Collapse of the Weimar Republic: Political Economy and Crisis* (Princeton University Press 1981) 276).

making in the hand of the Reich president'. This would enable economic policy to be implemented 'without going through parliament'.[7]

'Authoritarian liberalism' is offered pejoratively by Heller to capture the two dominant features of the regime: an avowed antipathy towards representative democracy in favour of autocracy and dictatorship, using emergency powers exercised under Article 48 of the constitution, and an ideological defence of free market liberalism and the protection of the interests of capital and major industrialists, a bloc which would soon support, with some reluctance, the transition to National Socialism.[8] In Heller's view, the presidential cabinets represented a new form of government; standing against the principles of democracy, parliamentarism, and majoritarianism, and appealing instead to a power that 'bears responsibility only before God', and to the 'miracles wrought by a dictatorship'.[9] Authoritarianism, Heller proclaims, is defined by its counterposition to *majority* rule.[10]

The concentration of state authority in an autocratic manner to deal ostensibly with emergency and exception, epitomized by the fascist dictatorship of Benito Mussolini, has a history, Heller notes, as old as the Roman Empire. But the true *experimentum crucis* of the new German version was to be found in a distinct place. It was to be found, not in the strength and extent of the political authority claimed by the state, but in the *limits* of that authority; it was to be found in its approach to the 'cardinal problem of the present', Heller declares, namely the question of the 'economic order'. Matching the sociological transformation of the bourgeoisie, as conservatism was drained of the last drop of 'social oil', and a major industrialist (Alfred Hugenberg, media magnate and former director of steel corporation Krupp) became Chairman of the former conservative party (DNVP), an authoritarianism emerged to defend *the free economy*; most appropriately this was to be addressed, Heller concluded, as 'authoritarian liberalism'.[11]

Exemplified in von Papen's ideas about the private economy, the authoritarian liberal insists, rhetorically, on the 'strict separation' of the state and the market.[12] In conceptual terms it thus represents the classical liberal belief in a society based on competition, exchange, and the price mechanism, but insists on a strong state in order to secure this market order. The authoritarian state has the positive task of maintaining the separation of politics and economics, more precisely to *depoliticize* the economy;

[7] Hans Mommsen, *The Rise and Fall of Weimar Democracy* (University of North Carolina Press 2007) 400–01.

[8] See Kolb (n 4) 116–35. According to Kolb these cabinets were supported not only by the Right but by a large part of the centre, as well as powerful economic interest groups and the army faction. Mommsen describes Hindenburg's plan as 'anti-parliamentary' and 'anti-Marxist' in terms of its basic organization (ibid 283). General von Schleicher had been pushing for such a government of the bourgeois right wing since as early as spring 1929 (ibid 282).

[9] Heller, 'Autoritärer Liberalismus' (n 1) 296.

[10] As Heller had made clear in Hermann Heller, *Sovereignty: A Contribution to the Theory of Public Law and International Law* (Belinda Cooper tr, OUP 2019) ('Sovereignty'), first published in 1927, the 'majority principle' is what links rulers and ruled.

[11] Heller, 'Autoritärer Liberalismus' (n 1) 299.

[12] Abraham (n 6) 277. As Abraham puts it, 'under Papen, the growing influence of the ministerial bureaucracy was joined to the central leadership of industrial and agrarian organizations so that the influence of the latter became wholly transparent. Wage and contract matters were to be shifted from the Labor to the Economics Ministry and *Sozialpolitik* reduced to a pure epiphenomenon of free-market considerations'.

so there is no resemblance to 'Manchester Liberalism', nor any residue of laissez-faire. On the contrary, the state must be active in pushing forward liberal modernization and loosening the bonds of solidarity, at least regarding socio-economic matters.[13] Above all, the objective of the authoritarian liberals—the 'feudalist clique that put Hitler into power'—was the elimination of socialism *and* democracy from politics by eliminating parliament, allowing the government to pursue its policies of austerity without political obstruction.[14]

The outward face of the regime—its claim to remain detached from the economy—was, in a significant part, ideological, because, in reality, Heller noted, it interfered ruthlessly in the economy in favour of certain class interests. It is therefore a formation that displayed a degree of slipperiness and hypocrisy; a difference between the rhetoric and the reality of its actions. The state that promised non-interference in the economy dismantled social policy with a 'heavy hand', feigned ideological neutrality while strongly inculcating a moral economy in the form of a duty to work necessary for the 'psychological happiness of the people', and supposedly retreated from interfering in cultural and educational policy whilst 'tripling' the costs of education.[15] The authoritarian liberal, Heller remarked contemptuously, fought against the welfare state with one hand, 'whilst subsidising large banks, large industry, and large agricultural enterprise' with the other.[16] It turned to other 'illiberal' forms of identity in order to maintain support, even acting with doses of 'authoritarian socialism' in a way that foreclosed the route of parliamentary or extra-parliamentary political contestation that might have democratically legitimated redistribution from the bottom up. What is 'decisive' for the political and social character of the authoritarian state, Heller concluded, is the '*capitalist form of the economy*'.[17]

A strong state, by then a 'thinly veiled dictatorship', asserted itself to remedy the weakness and disorder of the parliamentary system, which big business no longer trusted to deal with the economic issues of the day.[18] What was required, from the perspective of capital and heavy industry, was a government that could operate

[13] As Franz Neumann later noted, this picture of the liberal 'nightwatchman' state (a term used by socialist founder Ferdinand Lassalle to dismiss classical liberalism in the nineteenth century), was always an illusion (see Franz L Neumann, 'Economics and Politics in the Twentieth Century' in *The Democratic and the Authoritarian State* (The Free Press 1957) 258–59).

[14] Karl Polanyi, *The Great Transformation, The Political and Economic Origins of Our Time* (Beacon Press 2001) 246. The elimination of social democracy had been an aim of the German ruling class since Bismarck.

[15] Heller, 'Autoritärer Liberalismus' (n 1) 299. Adult education, in particular, was hit hard by austerity in the authoritarian liberal regime (see Mommsen (n 7)).

[16] ibid 300.

[17] ibid 298 (italics added). For the view that this policy of Brüning's was not without alternatives, see Carl-Ludwig Holtfrerich, 'Economic Policy Options and the End of the Weimar Republic' in Ian Kershaw (ed), *Weimar: Why did German Democracy Fail?* (Wiedenfeld and Nicholson 1990). Holtfrerich notes that although there were significant constraints on Brüning—including those posed internationally to Germany's foreign policy, and those placed by its domestic bank, excluded from devaluation in principle by the Young agreement of 1929/30, as well as fears of inflation from the early 1920s—, there remained political alternatives even after the summer of 1931. cf Harold James, 'Economic Reasons for the Collapse of Weimar' in Ian Kershaw (ed), *Weimar: Why did German Democracy Fail?* (Wiedenfeld and Nicholson 1990). Kolb (n 4) 122 also suggests that Brüning's chief priority was not to overcome the economic crisis but to get rid of the reparations burden.

[18] Mommsen (n 7) 292. German heavy industry, in particular, had fundamental doubts about the capacity of a parliamentary response to 'its demands that business be freed from excessive social costs and the fetters of collective bargaining' (Mommsen 267).

independently of party factions, pushing through dramatic cuts in public spending, and implementing various aspects of austerity; crucially, it reduced the system of unemployment insurance, which had been the occasion for Brüning's predecessor, the SPD chancellor Hermann Müller, to resign in March 1930.[19]

As historian Hans Mommsen puts it, 'The parliamentary constitution thus became an *empty shell* whose only function was to conceal the gradual transition to authoritarian government.'[20] Although presidential decrees had been used regularly since the early days of the Republic—first under Social Democrat president Ebert in response to violent insurrectionary uprisings—emergency politics would no longer be time-limited, nor restricted to non-budgetary matters. This manner of governing without the Reichstag, backed by coalitions of centrist, conservative, and nationalist forces, would take the violation of the principle of parliamentary democracy to the limits.[21] By 1931, state secretary Hans Schaffer would declare, 'from the budgetary point of view, we are already living in a military dictatorship'.[22]

The intellectual figure Heller had identified behind the new form of authoritarian liberalism was none other than Carl Schmitt, and in taking stock of the regime, even at this late moment, Heller was also targeting Schmitt's constitutional theory.[23] With its ability to bypass parliamentary accountability, the system of presidential cabinets was 'closer to Schmitt's heart than any other'.[24] Its techniques of government 'perfectly consummated the triumph of technocratic principles of bureaucratic-capitalist domination over political substance.'[25] In practice, its apparatus of political rule 'fell into line behind powerful economic lobbies'; the state bureaucracy, 'accountable only to the presidential cabinets and largely detached from its obligation to the parliamentary legislature', had become 'the primary location of decision-making power'.[26] Its aim of depoliticizing the economy reflected the concept of the political that Schmitt himself had theorized in his famous work of the same name, in the sense that the state had

[19] Abraham (n 6) 49–50: 'By 1930, virtually all sections of the dominant bloc agreed that post-crisis Germany must be spared the costliness and unreliability of an ineffective, democratic political structure and profit-devouring social-welfare system'.

[20] Mommsen (n 7) 317.

[21] Mommsen (n 7) 362.

[22] Mommsen (n 7) 396.

[23] 'When constitutional compromises such as those which characterized the Weimer Republic start to come apart, a conception of the state, "like Carl Schmitt's", which "declares rules and norms as insignificant and the exception as decisive" can, Heller ruefully added, achieve success' (Heller, 'Autoritärer Liberalismus' (n 1)).

[24] Chris J Thornhill, 'Carl Schmitt After the Deluge' (2000) 26 History of European Ideas 225, 237 (Thornhill, 'After the Deluge'); Chris J Thornhill, *Political Theory in Modern Germany: An Introduction* (Blackwell 2000) 88–89(Thornhill, 'Political Theory'): 'Between 1930 and 1933, Schmitt was intimately connected with the authoritarian, but non-Nazi, presidential cabinets which both temporarily checked and ultimately supported Hitler's rise to power'.

[25] Thornhill, 'After the Deluge' (n 24) 237. According to Ulrich Preuss, the regime (as late as 1932) 'was not an inescapable choice for an interim arrangement in an extraordinary time of emergency, but rather a blueprint for the kind of constitutional framework he had, right from the outset, regarded as appropriate constitutional setup to govern the political life of the German people even in ordinary times' (Preuss (n 3), 473). Schmitt was to join the NSDAP a year after this address and debate still rages as to whether Schmitt's philosophy was essentially and latently fascistic or whether his embrace of the Nazi party is better understood as merely opportunistic. For a recent evaluation, see, eg Benno Teschke, 'Decisions and Indecisions: Political and Intellectual Receptions of Carl Schmitt' (2011) 67 New Left Review 61.

[26] Thornhill 'After the Deluge' (n 24) 237.

finally grasped 'the enemy': the threat from the left to reconstitute the relation between the political and the economic realms, and erode the bourgeois *Rechsstaat.*[27]

In November 1932, Schmitt delivered an address to the German industrialists (the Langnamverein), entitled 'Strong State, Sound Economy', where he differentiated his position from the Social Democrats by explicitly distinguishing between the 'quantitatively' and 'qualitatively' total state.[28] The *quantitatively* total state, advocated by those on the left, was a weak state in Schmitt's view, interfering in the economy under the pressure of a plurality of interest groups. The *qualitatively* total state, on the other hand, drew 'a sharp line of separation vis-à-vis the economy', although, as Heller noted, ruled 'with the strongest military means and the means of mass manipulation' in culture and the media.[29] In other words, the authoritarian liberal state retreats from interfering in the sphere of distribution, and fights vehemently against the welfare state, but offers strong government to defend a militaristic and cultural conservatism.

3. Toleration by the Social Democrats: a crisis of representation

Heller, however, had made his diagnosis of authoritarian liberalism too late. With most important government business being conducted through Brüning's emergency decrees, the centrist parties in the Reichstag, including the Social Democrats (SPD), had done nothing except attempt to block 'no confidence votes' coming from the radical fringes. The SPD operated a policy of 'toleration' towards Brüning's authoritarian government; a *Tolerierungspolitik*, based, at least in part, on Heller's own prescriptions.[30] The formation of authoritarian liberalism, and the obstruction of representative democracy, in other words, were facilitated by the SPD's *own* position in the conjuncture, as well as over the long durée.[31]

Heller represented an orthodox left-Hegelian tradition in constitutional theory, placing his faith in the *soziale Rechtsstaat*, in the capacity of the Weimar state and its constitution, to deal with the social question and the issue of socio-economic

[27] Carl Schmitt, *The Concept of the Political* (George Schwab tr, expanded edn [1932], University of Chicago Press 2007). By November 1932, the KPD (Communist Party) had also made substantial inroads, increasing its vote, at the expense of the NSPAD, and obtaining 100 seats in the Reichstag.

[28] After previously rejecting the idea of the total state, Schmitt now found a way of defending it. This would be reprinted as an appendix in Renato Cristi, *Carl Schmitt and Authoritarian Liberalism: Strong State, Free Economy* (University of Wales Press 1998). Schmitt permitted the reprinting of this address twice in his lifetime, indicating it was a piece of some importance to him (see William E Scheuerman, *Carl Schmitt: The End of Law* (Rowman & Littlefield 1999) 288.

[29] Heller, 'Autoritärer Liberalismus' (n 1).

[30] Ellen Kennedy, 'The Politics of Toleration in Late Weimar: Hermann Heller's Analysis of Fascism and Political Culture' (1984) 5 History of Political Thought 109. According to Kennedy, this was justified by the SPD's parliamentary leader Breitscheid, on the basis of Heller's arguments made in *Europa und der Fascismus*, published in 1929.

[31] Although the dominant position in the SPD had become reformist, there were some, like Kirchheimer, who had maintained a more radical approach and rejected the 'toleration policy'. Thornhill describes Kirchheimer's position as a 'theoretical fusion of Marx and Schmitt' (Thornhill, Political Theory (n 24) 120).

inequality.[32] In continuing the legacy of the nineteenth-century state theory of Hegel, he followed and advanced a German idealism that presented the state as, in principle, *autonomous* from capitalist social relations, standing over and above civil society as a transcendental mediator of competing interests. Belief in the gradual reform (rather than revolution) of the state on the basis of the Weimar constitutional compromise and an 'equilibrium of class strengths' had become a dominant position in the SPD, following the founder of German socialism in the late nineteenth century, Ferdinand Lassalle, and represented by Eduard Bernstein's 'evolutionary path to socialism', as well as influenced by the work of Austro-Marxists Karl Renner and Otto Bauer.[33] It was this revisionist and reformist tradition, assuming socialism to be the 'legitimate heir' to the liberal order, that Heller represented in the German public law academy.[34]

In his book *Sovereignty*, published in 1927, Heller had been emphatic: only the self-identification of the people as sovereign could reflect a democratic relationship between rulers and ruled. Only then would the antithesis of monarchical sovereignty be achieved.[35] This could not be satisfied by the formal rule of law or a plebiscitary dictatorship. It required various devices of political representation ('such as elections, countersigning, parliamentarism, referendums, initiatives'), which should be understood as a means to guarantee juristically that 'power emanates from the people'. In practice, this must be understood on the basis of a 'majority principle', which, in order to function legitimately, requires the substantive 'homogeneity' of the people (a claim, as we will see in chapter 7, that reappeared in distorted form more than half a century later in the German Constitutional Court's Maastricht decision).[36] Heller was clear that homogeneity was, in large part, to be understood in terms of socio-economic equality, albeit buttressed and held together by a cultural community of values; a national culture.[37]

In 1927, Heller imagined the state as, potentially at least, a *neutral* state, equally open to different governmental regimes and capable of managing the problem of socio-economic inequality democratically. Even as late as 1931, during Brüning's reign as chancellor, Heller considered the authoritarian primacy of the state, and its dictatorship over society, necessary—albeit, from his perspective—to ensure the primacy of political authority *over* private economic power, and to *preserve* the institutions of the

[32] Caldwell, 'Popular Sovereignty' (n 2) 9, identifies Heller as a 'conservative social democrat'. See also Thornhill, Political Theory (n 24) 111–12 (Heller's thought 'reflects the very heart of SPD-orthodoxy in the 1920s').

[33] See, eg Otto Bauer, 'The Equilibrium of Class Strengths' in Mark E Blum and William Smaldone (eds), *Austro-Marxism: The Ideology of Unity: Austro-Marxist Theory and Strategy*, vol 1 (Brill 2015) 323–33.

[34] The SPD grew out of the Socialist Workers' Party of Germany, established when Lassalle, Bebel, Liebknecht, and others came together at Gotha in 1875, but soon banned under Bismarck's anti-socialist laws until 1890 (later splitting with the Independent Socialists in 1917). On Heller's relation with the tradition of Lassalle, see Hermann Heller, 'The Nature and Structure of the State' (1996) 18 Cardozo Law Review 1139 (tr David Dyzenhaus). On Bernstein's 'decisive' influence on the SPD, see Peter Gay, *The Dilemma of Democratic Socialism: Eduard Bernstein's Challenge to Marx* (2nd edn, Collier Books 1970) 252.

[35] Heller, 'Sovereignty' (n 10) 107

[36] ibid 108–09. In democratic states the relation between rulers and ruled, and hence the issue of representation, is a 'juristically significant factor' and, indeed, the 'crucial factor' in making sense of sovereignty.

[37] Kennedy (n 30) 125: 'Heller understood the ethical and normative task of socialism much as Fichte had understood culture—as cultivation, as the overcoming of subjectivity and isolation, as the attainment of harmony'. This was how Heller conceived integrating the working class into the unity of the national state.

Republic. He thus continued to advocate a strong state, standing above class conflict, asserting its autonomy from the capitalist economy and civil society, and using its governing institutions to maintain stability.

Heller's belief in the autonomy of the state persisted even as the material conditions became increasingly characterized by extreme inequality, and the political apparatus subject to the intense pressures of monopoly capitalism. This reflected a broader revisionist position in the SPD. Indeed, Social Democrats centred around Rudolph Hilferding, who had served as finance minister from 1928 to 1929, saw the concentration of capital and heavy industry in the late 1920s as potentially of instrumental value, more easily taken over and controlled by the 'class-neutral' state than a multitude of smaller enterprises.[38] The problem with the authoritarian liberal state, in other words, lay less in its authoritarianism than in its economic liberalism. Heller's 'faith in the state as the expression of community', as Chris Thornhill puts it, 'continued long after the German state had abandoned all interest in protecting the citizen from the economy'.[39]

To explain Heller's faith in the Weimar regime, even as its institutions were defecting from democracy, we have to consider the SPD's fear of the radical right on the horizon. The NSDAP (Nazi Party) was gaining electoral ground, and had dramatically increased its seats in the Reichstag in September 1930.[40] Rudolph Breitscheid, leader of the SPD, was, like Heller, concerned about further dividing the left; so long as there was a threat to Weimar from the NSDAP, 'nothing should be done to weaken Brüning and open the door to the fascists'.[41] On this interpretation, the SPD was 'forced to choose the lesser evil', in light of the Nazi Party's growing power.[42] Authoritarian liberalism was far from ideal, but it was better than the alternative, which, as far as the majority of Social Democrats could see, was only fascist dictatorship.

Far from protecting the Weimar Republic from the 'lesser evil', however, the government of the interregnum laid the path for the Nazi seizure of power. The toleration strategy fatally weakened the Social Democrats. It severed their link with the working class, as the harsh austerity which the governing regime pushed through, with the passive acceptance of the SPD, generated high levels of unemployment. Soaring unemployment, in turn, contributed to further weakening of the (already weakened) unions, which were further damaged by the direct undermining of the system of collective bargaining, as the authoritarian regime ordered reductions in wages and increases in working hours in the early 1930s.[43]

[38] Thornhill, 'Political Theory' (n 24) 110 ('Hilferding's brand of Marxism vacillates between an orthodox theory which asserts that modern government has been taken over by monopolies and general cartels, and a doctrine of organized capitalism, which argues that the modern state can itself resolve the contradictions between labour and capital').

[39] Thornhill, Political Theory (n 24) 112

[40] Becoming the second-largest party, with 107 seats.

[41] Kennedy (n 30) 111

[42] ibid 126–27. Kennedy notes that this was not only tactically wrong, but politically wrong, because it was not a policy *for* anything, and 'it was practised by a party that was not any longer in a position to tolerate anything. Its power, rights, and equality had already stripped away because the foundation for parliamentary democracy was gone'. The Communist Party was also increasing its parliamentary representation in the early 1930s.

[43] Ruth Dukes *The Labour Constitution: The Enduring Idea of Labour Law* (OUP 2014) 40

By the end of 1932, Heller appears to have realized the mistake. The idea of the 'neutral state' is now presented as a dangerous illusion, one which he tries desperately to dispel; this is the purpose of his polemic against authoritarian liberalism. By that stage, the state appears to him not only as a liberal formation, but as a class state and a *capitalist state*: one entrenched against socialism *and* democracy. The Social Democrats, however, had contributed to this predicament by abandoning their democratic convictions.

If the SPD's policy of tolerating the authoritarian liberals added an acute crisis of representation to the economic crises that preceded Weimar's collapse, this was the final chapter of a longer story in its own deradicalization. Despite the initial promise of extending political freedom into the economic realm, 'the economic constitution' advanced by the Weimar left after the birth of the Republic in 1918 had become little more than an adjunct. What had started as a project of socialization of the economy eventually performed merely a 'service function' for the democratic capitalist state, becoming 'co-extensive with the employer's aim of maximising production and profit'.[44] The Workers' Councils were gradually hollowed out, hampered by a lack of legislative action, subsumed by the unions, lacking in support from parties on the political left (including the communist KPD), and constitutionally weakened by the Reichsgericht's interpretation of Article 165 (providing for worker co-determination) as merely programmatic and not legally binding (as opposed to Article 153, which defended the right to private property).[45]

Labour lawyer Hugo Sinzheimer, associated with drafting the substantive part of the Weimar constitution, had advocated the economic constitution as a supplement to its organizational part, to reject the 'anarchy' of economic freedom in bourgeois society and to ensure the economy was run to achieve social ends.[46] This initially meant collective self-determination by Workers' Councils, which would integrate unions, becoming public law rather than private law bodies, and concerned with more than merely industrial conflict and maximizing economic gains.[47] But, as Ruth Dukes notes, Sinzheimer soon had a change of heart, suggesting instead that the unions should bear primary responsibility for the economic constitution, which was relegated to the negotiation of terms and conditions of employment, effectively abandoning the Workers' Councils.[48] Economic democracy, in other words, meant merely enhancement of workers' interests; it had little to do with collective control over the means of production, or political freedom. The unions and the SPD, in turn, became vast bureaucracies, alienated from the political struggle for democratic socialism and

[44] ibid 21–22.

[45] ibid 20 (examining the decision of the Reichsgericht of 11 February 1926). This left the 1920 Works Council Act as the main legislative frame.

[46] ibid 18. According to Sinzheimer, 'without economic democracy as a supplement to political democracy... the vast majority of the people remained unfree, subject to the control of a minority wielding economic power.' ('Only with economic democracy—the elimination of despotism at the workplace, of the control of the markets by capital, and of the state by the propertied classes—could true democracy be achieved').

[47] ibid 17–19.

[48] ibid 20. The revolutionary Workers' Councils had been violently repressed in 1920.

gradually reduced to economism, focussing narrowly on economic interests, collective bargaining, and corporatist arrangements.[49]

In Sinzheimer's reformist vision, the separation of the state and society could thus be maintained, with the state and its governing apparatus used to impose and maintain a better balance between labour and capital. Collective bargaining would take place 'in the shadow of the law' (such as factory legislation and law guaranteeing the freedom of association) in such a way as to temper substantive inequalities, but the law would be determined elsewhere. Economic democracy thus came to mean better regulation of the economy, rather than emancipation from capitalism. It followed that workers should be regulated by public labour laws, rather than dominated by private property (capital), but would be 'regulated' nonetheless, rather than autonomous. In this account, political democracy and economic democracy remained differentiated, albeit in a more socially inclined manner than according to classical liberalism. The functioning of private law rationality would be mediated but not transformed.[50]

The social policy pursued by the reformist wing of the SPD and the major unions, including protection of workers' rights, social welfare, rights of co-determination, and a system of public assistance and social insurance, had certainly promised a great deal to the working class and achieved some concessions from capital in the early years of the Republic. But it was not a break from the logic of the capitalist state. On the contrary, social policy presented a path to accommodate diverse social forces, and maintain a 'class equilibrium'; on many accounts, it depended on the success of the capitalist system in creating growth in order to facilitate redistribution of the social product.[51]

Socialization of the means of production did not materialize, partly due to opposition from the moderate left in the SPD, and trade unions. The unions were hampered by a narrow 'pressure group' mentality, a position which led them away from seeking radical *political* change.[52] By 1930 trade union membership had plummeted, strikes had declined, and organized labour was in close collaboration with the SPD.[53] Later, Franz Neumann (who had also supported the policy of 'toleration' to authoritarian liberalism) would suggest that social democracy and the unions failed because, in the mistaken belief that economic democracy was possible without political democracy, they had restricted the working class to economism and gradualism, and failed to create a 'democratic consciousness'.[54] Instead of extending political freedom into the

[49] Charles Maier describes the new institutional arrangement in the interwar era as 'corporatism', which, in his view, meant 'the growth of private power and the twilight of sovereignty' (Charles S Maier, *Recasting Bourgeois Europe: Stabilization in France, Germany, and Italy in the Decade after World War I* (Princeton University Press 2016) 9). He applies it as an ideal-type to Germany, France, and Italy.

[50] Dukes (n 43) 19 notes the likely influence of the Webbs, whose two volume *Industrial Democracy* was translated into German in 1898 .

[51] In a mirror image of Schmitt's position, Neumann had argued that the task for a socialist political theory of the state was 'to develop and concretely present the positive social content of the second part of the Weimar constitution'. Franz Neumann, 'The Social Significance of the Basic Laws in the Weimar Constitution' in K Tribe (ed), *Social Democracy and the Rule of Law: Otto Kirchheimer and Franz Neumann* (Allen and Unwin 1987) 43.

[52] Abraham (n 6) 252–80.

[53] Franz L Neumann, *Behemoth: The Structure and Practice of National Socialism, 1933–1944* (Ivan R Dee 2009) (Neumann, 'Behemoth') 17–20.

[54] Ibid 29. Neumann's position was complex and changing. There seemed to be a break in 1933, when he considered the Weimar compromise to have been doomed from the outset, given that capital remained the 'real owner of power': (Franz L Neumann, 'The Decay of German Democracy' in William E Scheuermann

economic domain, the left surrendered the political state to the bourgeoise and sought reconciliation and compromise within the system, even after it became increasingly apparent that the capitalist state would subsume any democratic elements once these were obstructing the commercial gains of large enterprises.[55]

In other words, just when the dominant political and economic classes were *politicizing* their struggle in the early 1930s, social democrats and the unions were reduced to reformist strategies, flatly refusing political strikes and underestimating the importance of political struggle.[56] The political weakness of the left, explicitly or tacitly accepting the organized and increasingly monopolized rule of capital, enabled reactionary parties to effectively destroy the 'constitutional platform for the emancipation of labour', namely Weimar's parliamentary democracy.[57]

The rise of authoritarian liberalism in late Weimar would repress the political-democratic management of the constitutional dialectic, tilting the balance in the conflict between democracy and capitalism decisively against democracy. This is eventually acknowledged by Heller to have been a failure of his own camp, an indictment of social democracy in Germany; in particular, of its longer-term failure to succeed in uniting its values with concrete political power.[58] The Social Democrats had made the cardinal error of thinking that the dialectic of fact and norm could be severed, detaching their normative values of social equality from the actual experience of political freedom.[59] Substituting formal agency for real autonomy, they had neglected the necessity of acting *politically*.[60]

'Nothing has corrupted the working class', in Walter Benjamin's words, 'so much as the notion that it was moving with the current'.[61] Social democracy since the Gotha

(ed), *The Rule of Law under Siege: Selected Essays of Franz L. Neumann and Otto Kirchheimer* (University of California Press 1996) 33) (Neumann, 'Decay'). For discussion, see Claus Offe, 'The Problem of Social Power in Franz L Neumann's Thought' (2003) 10 Constellations 211. According to Thornhill, Neumann's (and Heller's) support of the 'toleration policy' towards Brüning reflected the 'state-fidelity of the Weimar SPD in general' (Thornhill, *Political Theory* (n 24) 113).

[55] Thornhill, 'Political Theory' (n 24) 119–21. Kirchheimer again appears to have been an exception, insisting that capitalism and democracy are 'formally incompatible', and arguing for a 'mass participation' in political will-formation, with the state 'genuinely superseded by a worker's democracy'.

[56] Abraham (n 6) 259–60. Neumann, 'Behemoth' (n 53) 17.

[57] Neumann, Decay (n 54) 34–37. Any 'thought of cooperation on the left', which had been divided since the First World War, evaporated after the SPD-controlled police had violently put down unarmed communist demonstrators at a May Day celebration in 1929 in Berlin and, in any case, under direction from the Party in Moscow, the KPD repudiated any united front with the 'social fascists' and insisted on immediate insurrection, a strategy that had hopelessly failed in the early 1920s (Martin Jay, 'The Weimar Left' in PE Jordan and JP McCormick (eds), *Weimar Thought: A Contested Legacy* (Princeton University Press 2013). For further discussion of the broader divergence of left-wing political strategy, including in Weimar, and its relationship to the Russian Revolution in the interwar period, see Perry Anderson, *Antinomies of Antonio Gramsci* (Verso 2017).

[58] Heller traces this fundamental error back to Kant, in a way which strikingly mirrors the reflections of Dewey: John Dewey, *German Philosophy and Politics* (rev edn, GP Putnam's Sons 1942).

[59] Otto Kahn-Freund also suggested that the distance between the fine rhetoric of social democracy in constitutional texts such as the Weimar Constitution and the reality on the ground creates a severe problem of legitimacy; see Otto Kahn-Freund, 'The Weimar Constitution' (1944) 15 The Political Quarterly 229.

[60] Heller, 'Autoritärer Liberalismus' (n 1).

[61] Walter Benjamin, 'Theses on the Philosophy of History' in Hannah Arendt (ed), *Illuminations* (The Bodley Head 2015) 250. The theses were completed in spring 1940 and first published in *Neue Rundschau* in 1950.

Programme of 1875, confusing technological advances in work with political achievement, had adopted a conformist view of historical progress. As Benjamin noted, 'This vulgar Marxist conception of the nature of labour bypasses the question of how its products might benefit the workers while still not being at their disposal. It recognizes only the progress of the mastery of nature, not the retrogression of society; it already displays the technocratic features later encountered in Fascism'.[62]

4. Fascist dictatorship: the end of the political

Authoritarian liberalism, as well as being supported by liberals, conservatives, and Catholic centrists, and tolerated by social democrats, would be actively supported by a large section of the legal academy, many law professors having become critical of the Weimar republic—even 'actively anti-constitutional', in the sense of anti-parliamentary—by the early 1930s. As Michael Stolleis explains, the legal academy envisaged an 'outwardly and inwardly strong state' that could rise above the party factions and interests in civil society and reassert the stability of constitutional liberalism: an economic liberalism protected by the legal constitution and safe from the vicissitudes of democracy.[63] This could be understood as an attempt to restore de facto the pre-revolutionary monarchical regime, albeit without formally overturning the Weimar Constitution.

The political manoeuvres of authoritarian liberals would come to a head as a constitutional matter with von Papen's forceful deposition of the SPD government in Prussia, again using Article 48 of the Constitution. Carl Schmitt, as well as closely advising the presidential cabinets, would represent the Reich government of von Papen in the Staatsgerichtshof in this so-called 'Prussian coup', with Heller representing the Prussian side.[64] The coup was launched on the pretext of restoring public security, after von Papen's government had stoked violent clashes by lifting the ban on the SA, the original paramilitary wing of the Nazi Party. The real aim of von Papen's move was 'to wrest control' of Germany's largest state (Prussia) and its apparatus of executive power from the Social Democrats, as well as attract the support of the Nazis by helping them in their street battles with the Communists.[65] The court, in an ambiguous judgment, although finding the Prussian government not to have violated its duties to the federal Reich, held the federal government's actions to be justified. Occurring only months before the Nazi seizure of power in January 1933, the Preussenschlag was a key factor in ending the Republic, giving von Papen direct control of the Prussian government and police force, as well as helping to lay the grounds for the future Nazification of

[62] ibid 251.

[63] Michael Stolleis, 'Prologue' in Christian Joerges and Navraj Singh-Ghaleigh (eds), *Darker Legacies of Law in Europe: The Shadow of National Socialism and Fascism over Europe and its Legal Traditions* (Hart Publishing 2003) 8 ('Most of them were bourgeois and conservative and willing to cooperate with the new regime').

[64] For discussion, see Lars Vinx, *The Guardian of the Constitution: Hans Kelsen and Carl Schmitt on the Limits of Constitutional Law* (CUP 2015) 1–6.

[65] ibid 1.

Germany, with Hermann Göring's later installation as Prussian Minister of the Interior enabling the Nazis to use the secret police to brutally crush potential opposition.[66]

Authoritarian liberalism ultimately proved inadequate to deal with the political and economic situation. The cabinets failed either to unite the various fractions of capital, including heavy industry and agrarian interests, or to attract a mass of popular support.[67] By the end of 1932, 'crucial decisions were being made by a handful of men in leadership circles', cliques which bypassed not only parliament and parties but even the cabinets themselves.[68] Authoritarian liberalism was a counter-revolutionary formation that lacked a coherent political strategy and a political base, without which 'it was unable to effect any lasting transformation to an authoritarian state system'.[69] But it sufficiently undermined Weimar democracy so as to ease the transition to National Socialism, with the dominant classes eventually turning, however reluctantly, to the NSDAP, in order enlist popular backing.[70]

In late 1932, the Nazi vote would actually slump in federal elections.[71] But the diminished electoral support did not prevent Hitler's assumption of power in January 1933, which unfolded along lines that had already become customary with chancellors Brüning, von Papen, and von Schleicher. Hitler was appointed chancellor by President Hindenburg on 30 January 1933, in a short-lived coalition with Hugenberg's DNVP. New elections in March 1933, in a climate of violence and intimidation created by conditions of state-supported propaganda and state-sponsored terror, operationalized by the Gestapo and the SA, again failed to produce a clear Nazi majority. This was to be the last contested election in Germany in the interwar period.

The transformation from authoritarian liberal cabinets into a 'Führer State' would happen in a relatively short space of time.[72] The Reichstag Fire Decree of February 1933, issued by von Hindenburg on the advice of chancellor Adolf Hitler under the same Article 48 of the Constitution, just before the March election, nullified key civil liberties on the pretext of defending the state against the communist opposition. In reality, it was used as a legal basis for persecuting and imprisoning assorted opponents of the regime, and consolidating a one-party state. This decree, along with the Enabling

[66] James (n 17) 51. In 1934 oversight of the secret police (Gestapo) was handed to the head of the SS, Heinrich Himmler, with the Gestapo becoming a national agency. Hitler had ordered the Rohm Purge in 1934, after which the SA was significantly scaled down.

[67] On the difficulty for competing fractions of capital to form a coherent political response to the economic situation, see Abraham (n 6), 45–52. cf Nicos Poulantzas, *Political Power and Social Classes* (Verso 2018).

[68] ibid 51.

[69] Ian Kershaw, 'The Nazi State: An Exceptional State?' (1989) New Left Review 47–67.

[70] Dick Geary, 'Employers, Workers, and the Collapse of the Weimar Republic' in Ian Kershaw (ed), *Weimar: Why Did German Democracy Fail?* (Weidenfeld and Nicholson, 1990) 92, 104–5 ('a point had been reached whereby a bourgeois bloc including the Nazis could be envisaged as the road by which the hated welfare legislation and constraining labour law could be removed. Such a coalition may not have been the first preference of most industrialists. Many believed Hitler would prove malleable, especially after the Nazis lost two million votes in the second (November) Reichstag elections of 1932 and when an internal crisis began to grip the NSDAP. Yet the important point is that by 1933 industry wanted rid of the Weimar Republic'.)

[71] In the elections in November 1932, the Nazi vote fell by four per cent, and they lost thirty-four seats in the Reichstag.

[72] According to Stolleis, the transformation took 'about twenty-four months' (Michael Stolleis, *Public Law in Germany: A Historical Introduction from the 16th to the 21st Century* (OUP 2017) 101.

Act passed only weeks later, would provide the legal basis for Hitler's dictatorship, formally 'normalizing' the state of exception.[73]

To be sure, the ruling elites had completely underestimated the threat posed by Hitler. Complacency in the political class, convinced of its ability to control him, ranged from von Papen and Hugenberg to the SPD's own Rudolph Hilferding.[74] After the elections in November 1932, jubilant at the Nazis' decline, Hilferding had refused either to cooperate with von Schleicher or to join a united front with the Communist Party. The primary aim of the SPD, he had said, 'was the fight against Communism', prefiguring its Cold War position a decade later.[75]

But the reason the transition to Nazi dictatorship could occur so quickly was that the 'bourgeois elites' in the administration, the judicial system, and the military, were all willing to cooperate with the Nazi Party. They not only welcomed the end of Weimar parliamentarism, but cheered 'the end of the unions, the silencing of communists and social democrats, the expulsion of Jews, the job-creation measures and a foreign policy focused on ending the trauma of Versailles.'[76] Although there was some uneasiness in their relationship with the Nazi Party, the bourgeoisie were 'trapped' in a belief in the 'future usefulness' of the Nazis, seeing in their movement a 'department for mass mobilisation'. Mass mobilization and popular support did not mean mobilization in a political sense but, quite to the contrary, it meant mobilizing a 'culture of violence' and national redemption, and a determination to single out the 'Marxist enemy within as its prime target'.[77]

After the Nazi seizure of power in 1933, a debate had ensued among constitutional lawyers, particularly Schmitt and Nazi jurist Otto Koellreutter, over 'who could most radically purge from Nazi vocabulary the last remnants of traditional concepts of the German Constitution, now associated with liberalism'.[78] Although the rise of the Nazis was based on a 'national revolution', it was also designed, according to Koellreutter—initially in agreement with Schmitt—to *retain* the 'old German conservative heritage... in National Socialist countenance'.[79]

[73] Peter Caldwell, 'National Socialism and Constitutional Law: Carl Schmitt, Otto Koellreutter and the Debate over the Nature of the Nazi State, 1933–1937' (1994) 16 Cardozo Law Review 399, 407 (Caldwell, 'National Socialism'): 'The Enabling Law transferred the authority to issue laws, ordinances, and even constitutions to the executive power, eradicating the German tradition of limiting that power by a popular assembly. In effect, the law created a government able to exercise legislative power independent of either popularly elected body Reichstag or President'.

[74] James (n 17) 51–52.

[75] Neumann, 'Behemoth' (n 53) 32.

[76] Stolleis (n 72) 101.

[77] Bernd Weisbrod, 'Violence and Sacrifice: Imagining the Nation in Weimar Germany' in Hans Mommsen (ed), *The Third Reich Between Vision and Reality: New Perspectives on German History 1918–1945* (Berg 2001) 11.

[78] Caldwell, 'National Socialism' (n 73), 399–400.

[79] ibid 407. Although Koellreutter (who had been a Nazi member for some years) and Schmitt (who joined only in 1933) would soon explode in spectacular disagreement, Caldwell notes they both 'fully accepted the two tenets of Nazi rule: the *Fuhrer* principle; and the principle of the essential unity of *Artgleichheit* (unity of species, type, or race) of the German *Volk*' (408) the 'limit' to the *Führer*'s power would be found only 'in the *Volk*'s racial identity with the *Führer*'. He notes further that 'all the major Nazi theorists tended to reject positivism, with its distinction between law as a normative category, what "ought" to be, and factual reality'.

In legal terms, Koellreutter's interpretation gave National Socialism the form of what would later be theorized by Ernst Fraenkel as the 'dual state', 'a doubled pseudo-constitutional system: on the one side, "normal" judicial activity, on the other, "special" state action at the whim of the *Führer* or his deputies'.[80] This suggested other elements of apparent continuity with the old regime, beyond the conservative heritage of imperialism. In Fraenkel's view, the transition to Nazi dictatorship would be supported by large sections of capital and business for partly rational reasons: 'capitalism played handmaiden to dictatorship', wilfully embracing a violent, inhumane ideology because the Nazis promised to maintain not only the existing conditions of technical rationality, but 'an economic order which resembled the unfettered capitalism of old'.[81]

The theory of the 'dual state', the state based partly on prerogative power and partly on the remnants of a Rechtsstaat—part lawlessness, part law—would be superseded by a very different account of the Nazi regime, one offered by Franz Neumann in his monumental *Behemoth*.[82] Neumann focused on the political economy undergirding the transition to National Socialism; the Nazi governing apparatus supported by a broad hegemonic bloc combining four distinct groups: 'big industry, the party, the bureaucracy and the armed forces'.[83] The monopolization of industry and the cartelization of politics would combine; not in a state formation, but in a totalitarian form, together pursuing capitalism in an aggressive, imperialistic, and expansionary manner.

Neumann's account suggested that National Socialism (which he characterized as 'totalitarian monopoly capitalism' rather than 'state capitalism', as theorized by fellow Frankfurt Schooler Friedrich Pollock), was in some ways continuous with the Weimar era, but was fundamentally transformative in combining monopoly capital control with a command economy.[84] As a new regime of capital accumulation, with fewer fetters on capital than in liberal democratic form, it gave rise to a 'self-reinforcing dictatorship'.[85]

In terms of its constitutional-legal form, totalitarian monopoly capitalism marked a rupture, in Neumann's presentation, in the turn to an *irrational legal system*. For Neumann, this meant that the state, as Rechtsstaat, had ceased to exist in the Nazi dictatorship. In its place, there arose 'simply a decisionistic, situation-specific, deformalized law', a 'non-state system'.[86] Neumann suggested that the Nazi order should be understood as a 'form of society in which the ruling groups control the rest of the population *directly*, without the mediation of that rational though coercive

[80] ibid 413; Ernst Fraenkel, *The Dual State: A Contribution to the Theory of Dictatorship* (Edward Shils tr, OUP 2017).

[81] Jens Meierhenrich, *The Remnants of the Rechtsstaat: An Ethnography of Nazi Law* (OUP 2018) 199–200.

[82] Neumann, Behemoth (n 53).

[83] ibid 361.

[84] See, for discussion, Meierhenrich (n 81) ch 2. According to Meierhenrich, 'remnants of the Rechtsstaat' continued to have a 'structuring effect on social outcomes in the Third Reich, especially at the level of everyday law', notably in pre-war years, but even once war had begun, thus arguing in favour of Fraenkel's 'dual-state' thesis (p 3).

[85] ibid 30. Kirchheimer too, argued that National Socialism was 'the last, logical position in the accelerated concentration of capital and cartelization which characterised the Weimar period' (Thornhill, 'Political Theory' (n 24) 124).

[86] Kelly (n 4) 296.

apparatus' that was otherwise known as the state.[87] 'If general law is the basic form of right, if law is not only *voluntas* but also *ratio*', Neumann concludes, 'we must deny the existence of law' to National Socialism.[88]

In Neumann's characterization, totalitarian monopoly capitalism hardly qualified as a state; it was a regime in which the rule of general laws had been completely destroyed through 'decisionistic' legal thinking. 'Law', Neumann claimed, 'is now a technical means for the achievement of specific political aims. It is merely the command of the sovereign. To this extent, the juristic theory of the fascist state is decisionism. Law is merely an *arcanum dominationis*, a means for the stabilization of power.'[89]

Neumann's influence on post-war constitutional legalism is indisputable.[90] The liberal Rechtsstaat would be resuscitated in the post-war era in the thought that it would present a major bulwark to the decay of democratic capitalism into a fascist dictatorship. We will consider the influence of this reading of liberal democratic decay further in Part II.

But the accuracy of Neumann's characterization of National Socialism as a lawless regime based on a fully command economy is far from undisputed.[91] Fraenkel's account, which suggests that the law continued in the private sphere of the economy, well into the Second World War, seems in many ways superior.[92]

But Neumann's reference to the 'command of the sovereign' was misleading even on his *own* interpretation, since the Nazi 'sovereign' was not a unified state or really a 'sovereign' at all, but a cartel of powerful interest groups. Neumann's account in *Behemoth* is interesting less for its theory about the end of rational law, and more for what it suggests about the end of politics. Rather than bringing forth the truly political 'total' state, National Socialism in fact undermined the real source of legal and political power, namely the principle of 'sovereignty'.[93] The principle of sovereignty 'specific to the political sphere' made little sense in terms of sheer 'command'.[94] The Nazi system triumphed over the Weimar regime, in other words, not—or at least not primarily—through the destruction of legal rationality, but through the destruction of 'the political' sphere. The moment of 'genuine politics' was completely attenuated in National Socialism 'by technical and pluralist (private-legal) modes of coercion'.[95] It is quite possible that remnants of the Rechtsstaat in fact remained in Nazi Germany—'islands of legality in a sea of lawnessness'[96] —what disappeared was the political state.

[87] Neumann, 'Behemoth' (n 53), 470 (italics added).

[88] ibid 451: 'Law, as distinct from the political command of the sovereign, is conceivable only if it is manifest in general law, but true generality is not possible in a society that cannot dispense with power'.

[89] ibid 448.

[90] Meierhenrich (n 81).

[91] See ibid. See also R Ptak, 'Neoliberalism in Germany: Revisiting the Ordoliberal Foundations of the Social Market Economy' in Mirowski P and Plehwe D (eds), *The Road from Mont Pelerin: The Making of the Neoliberal Thought Collective* (HUP 2009), which describes it as a mixture of command economy and market capitalism.

[92] See William E Scheuerman, 'Social Democracy and the Rule of Law: The Legacy of Ernst Fraenkel' in Peter C. Caldwell and William E. Scheuerman, eds, *From Liberal Democracy to Fascism* (Humanities Press, 2000) 76–85.

[93] Kelly (n 4) 291.

[94] ibid.

[95] Thornhill, Political Theory (n 24) 127.

[96] Meierhenrich (n 81) 201.

5. A cult of violence

Although Neumann aimed his critique of decisionism partly at Carl Schmitt (of whom he was a student), Schmitt himself had quickly moved away from a decisionistic doctrine, distinguishing, in a work published in 1934, *three* types of juristic thought (based on 'norm', 'decision', and 'concrete order formation').[97] And as the Nazis consolidated their power, Schmitt would also distance himself from the concept of the state altogether.[98] Schmitt's earlier concept of the strong ('qualitatively total') state and his maintenance of a differentiation between the state and the Party, with the state retaining a hierarchy in this relation, had threatened to alienate him from the Nazi regime, which called for the rapid transcendence of the notion of the state. Even Schmitt's earlier concept of the political, based on the friend/enemy binary, was considered a bourgeois construct by the Nazis; unsuitable to a regime based on biological purity.

Schmitt soon pivoted, leaving behind his theory of the 'total state' with the publication of *State, Movement, Nation* (*Staat, Bewegung, Volk*).[99] If the 'state' remained present in Schmitt's scheme, it was now a kind of 'anachronism', narrowly defined as a bureaucratic apparatus; a static entity which carried out the political demands of the Führer, set into motion by the 'movement' of National Socialism. The movement, in turn, was the organized element of the ' "unpolitical" *Volk*'.[100]

In 1933, after Hitler's seizure of power, Schmitt proclaimed, 'On the 30 January, one can say accordingly, Hegel died'.[101] With the Nazi *movement* destroying the duality of state and society, the state would soon disappear from Nazi constitutional thought altogether, its 'liberal connotation' too embarrassing for jurists—including Schmitt—to countenance. Reinhard Hohn, a young Nazi jurist and SS member who succeeded both Schmitt and Koellreutter, then offered a 'total rethinking of legal scholarship on the basis of the *Führer* principle and racial equality', one which required that ' "science" once again become acquainted with "life." '[102] In that sense, the National Socialist regime clearly marked a departure, not only in the material economic rationality of its strategy of capital accumulation, but in its political form and ideology. An authoritarian leader would now directly represent the *Volk*, rather than any particular group, and the *Volk* would be identified on the basis of a *racial identity*. Its authority would be forged through cultivating and glorifying historical myths of violence and heroic self-sacrifice as a way to national redemption after the shame of defeat in the First World War and the punishment of Versailles.[103]

97 Carl Schmitt, *On the Three Types of Juristic Thought*, J Bendersky, tr (Praeger 2004).

98 The complexities of Schmitt's various moves cannot be dealt with here. For an attempt to systematize Schmitt's thought, see Martin Loughlin, 'Politonomy' in Jens Meierhenrich and Oliver Simons (eds), *The Oxford Handbook of Carl Schmitt* (OUP 2017).

99 See Jens Meierhenrich, 'Fearing the Disorder of Things: The Development of Carl Schmitt's Institutional Theory, 1919–1942' in Meierhenrich and Simons (n 3), . Meierhenrich gives the label 'racial institutionalism' to capture Schmitt's thought from 1933 to 1938.

100 Caldwell, 'National Socialism' (n 73) 416–17.

101 Carl Schmitt, *Staat, Bewegung, Volk* (Hanseatischer Verlaganstalt, 1933) 32.

102 Caldwell (n 73) 427.

103 Weisbrod (n 77) 12–13.

If the 'decisive role' in advancing the authoritarian liberal regime had fallen to the Catholic Centre Party (Zentrum),[104] the spectre of a more radical conservative nationalist movement in the background, drawing on myths of historical loss, biological superiority, and imperial expansionist ambitions, would be essential for the turn to National Socialism to succeed. The nationalist right-wing opposition to the Republic had, in 1930, still been seriously divided, with Hugenberg's 'pan-German' bourgeoise conservatism largely ineffective, and Hitler biding his time. But a neoconservative intelligentsia that was directed not only against Marxism and socialism, but also against democracy, liberal Enlightenment, and Western civilization more generally, would come to be supported by the various political constituencies of the capitalist economy.[105] A centrist constellation hostile to the 'cultural Bolshevism', and even aesthetic modernism, associated with urban life in Weimar would attract the support of the large agrarian section of society, in addition to the middle classes.

The bourgeois bloc would soon turn to the Nazi party once it had become clear that the defection from parliamentarism by the cabinets of authoritarian liberals would not hold any answers to the economic and political crises of the day.[106] As Hermann Heller had foreseen in 1929, a non-parliamentary Rechtsstaat (Heller comparing this to the model of the USA) would not be able to 'conform to the religion of violence'. Nor could it—and this, he emphasized, was the main thing—'remove the political economic difficulties of the ruling class'.[107] In a second move, he predicted, the bourgeoisie would thus likely 'throw itself into the arms of an irrational feudalism', partly inspired by Nietzsche, based on a resentment of its own laws, and a turn to a mythology of 'genius individualism without law' which values 'adventure and danger'.[108] The supreme article of faith of the bourgeoisie, 'unable to master the sociological situation either intellectually or morally and politically' would become 'force in itself, force as an end in itself';[109] thus, the appeal of an 'aestheticizing religion of violence, which is only bearable for the strong soul of the superior man'. In Heller's view, this was represented above all by Oswald Spengler's *Decline of the West*; a declaration of belief in the nobility as the 'genuine estate'. The bourgeoisie would be willing to turn to a strongman of 'Caesaristic dimensions'. From this new conservative perspective, the masses were 'a radical nothing'.[110]

Fraenkel's account of the 'dual state' suggests that Heller was only partly right. What had eluded Heller (and Neumann) was the possible juxtaposition of a legal *and* a prerogative state; the continuation of law in the sense of a private sphere of commercial predictability with its discontinuation as a matter of public political value.[111] Heller

[104] Mommsen (n 7) 288.

[105] Stolleis (n 72) 92: 'What Kurt Sontheimer called "anti-democratic thinking" was rapidly attracting a following, especially among young intellectuals'.

[106] Mommsen (n 7) 307.

[107] Hermann Heller, 'Rechtsstaat or Dictatorship?' (Ellen Kennedy tr, 1987) 16 Economy and Society 127, 137 (first published as Rechtsstaat oder Diktatur? *in Die Neue Rundschau* (S Fischer Verlag 1929) 721–35) ('Rechtsstaat or Dictatorship?').

[108] ibid.

[109] ibid 133.

[110] ibid 137, 139. Heller also compares this new conservatism to a corporate state, where 'professional estates' rule and the masses are reduced to political apathy.

[111] In a sense, Heller had captured this point without realizing it. He saw the turn to authoritarianism and dictatorship as primarily a turn away from law as democratic legislation; this is what he meant by a

thought that the bourgeoisie would be unable 'in one breath' to cry for the 'rationalisation of the economy' *and* for an 'arbitrary dictatorship'.[112] But, in fact, the normative state provided a continuation of technical rationality in the economy, and the prerogative state provided the irrational means to pursue the rational ends of violent military expansion, restructuring Germany as a military power. This would be a boon to the armaments industry, which was able to profit from the Nazis' aggressive creation of new markets and production needs. There remained, in other words, 'a rational core in an otherwise highly "irrational shell" '.[113]

The 'people', as an idea, in the totalitarian form of National Socialism were to be 'treated as essentially *unpolitical*, and located mainly with the private sphere'. This total *de-politicization* of the people would occur in tandem with their treatment as biological racial subjects; this was the Nazis' offering to overcome the class conflicts of the Weimar era. Although appealing primarily to the Mittelstand (petit bourgeois, peasant, and 'white collar'), the Nazi movement would be able to draw support from across the various strata of society, uniting diverse elements on the basis of an authoritarian populism, and calling into doubt the very concept of class consciousness.[114]

It was not only the narrative of national redemption after a humiliating military defeat that contributed to the collapse of liberal democracy in Germany. The 'cult' of violence and violent expansion (as distinct from political power) would also play a significant role.[115] In Hannah Arendt's view, violence is an anti-political concept and closely bound together with bureaucracy: 'rule by nobody'.[116] This suggests that it was not a *political* mass mobilization that ended Weimar. On the contrary, 'The unified constituent will of the people, which stood at the root of the democratic state' would, in the formulation of Nazi ideology, be forgotten. 'The people', in the Nazi regime, 'existed simply to be ruled'.[117] It was, in other words, an anti-political mobilization that ended the Weimar Republic.

turn away from a material understanding of the Rechtsstaat. The proletarian demand for social democracy, Heller suggested, had been merely the 'extension of a material Rechtsstaat to the order of work and commodities'. But what he had missed was the need for the working class to maintain and extend political democracy.

112 Heller, 'Rechtstaat or Dictatorship?' (n 107) 140.

113 Meierhenrich (n 81) (adopting Fraenkel's own language). On the Nazi economy in the late thirties and into the Second World War, see Adam Tooze, *Wages of Destruction: The Making and Breaking of the Nazi Economy* (Penguin 2008) (emphasizing Hitler's turn to the threat of US imperialism and anti-Semitism); cf Dylan Riley, 'The Third Reich as Rogue Regime: Adam Tooze's *Wages of Destruction*' (2014) 22:3–4 Historical Materialism 346.

114 On the various class make-ups of the electoral supports of the Weimar parties, see Abraham (n 6), 31 ('the key electoral contribution of the NSDAP consisted of uniting on the basis of an authoritarian populism the various Mittelstand groups').

115 On the significance of the cult of violence, and the 'trenchocracy', a remnant of the First World War, see Weisbrod (n 77). The conceptual distinction between power and violence is discussed in Hannah Arendt, *On Violence* (Harcourt 1970).

116 According to Arendt, 'the greater the bureaucratization of public life, the greater will be the attraction of violence. In a fully developed bureaucracy there is nobody left with whom one could argue, to whom one could present grievances, on whom the pressures of power could be exerted. Bureaucracy is the form of government in which everybody is deprived of political freedom, of the power to act; for the rule by Nobody is not no-rule, and where all are equally powerless we have a tyranny without a tyrant' (Arendt (n 115) 81).

117 Kelly (n 4) 293.

2

Beyond Weimar: The Long Crisis of Liberalism, the Political Economy of the Interwar Conjuncture and the Foundations of Neo-liberalism

1. Introduction

Authoritarian liberalism, although clarifying the immediate stakes in late Weimar as it was teetering on the brink of collapse, was far from unique to that particular interregnum.[1] On the contrary, it reflected a broader liberal quandary in the early twentieth century; how to contain mass democracy, specifically in light of the danger it posed to bourgeois society in a parliamentary system of government. A parliamentary democracy, with a growing representation of the working class and a constitution that could be read in a liberal or socialist direction, threatened the liberal *Rechtsstaat* by threatening to politicize the economy.

Heller had *already* offered a critique of liberalism long before it had turned to authoritarian rule in 1930, specifically criticizing its formalism and legalism.[2] In the period of relative economic stability (the mid-period of the Weimar Republic from 1924 to 1929). Heller noted that the liberal bourgeois bloc (*Bürgertum*) viewed the *Rechtsstaat* as a way of securing legal freedom in the commercial realm and the economic security that came with it; a goal it had maintained since the nineteenth century, evident from its response to the revolution of 1848.[3] In the Weimar Republic, this goal was threatened by a parliamentary democracy with a mass social democratic party: 'Through the roundabout way of politics', specifically legislation, a 'proletariat with equal civil and political rights' would become 'economically dangerous for the bourgeoisie'.[4]

One strategy of bourgeois and conservative jurists was to turn to the courts to frustrate the advent of social legislation, and prevent the creation of a social state. Heller describes the 1925 decision of the Reichsgerichtshof, when judges claimed a general

[1] See Renato Cristi, *Carl Schmitt and Authoritarian Liberalism: Strong State, Free Economy* (University of Wales Press 1998). Cristi traces Schmitt's own authoritarian liberalism back to at least 1923, when Schmitt published *A Crisis of Parliamentary Democracy*.

[2] Hermann Heller and David Dyzenhaus, *Sovereignty: A Contribution to the Theory of Public and International Law* (Belinda Cooper tr, OUP 2019), originally published in 1927 (Heller, 'Sovereignty').

[3] Hermann Heller, '*Rechtsstaat* or Dictatorship' (1987) 16 Economy and Society 127(Ellen Kennedy tr, originally published as '*Rechtsstaat oder Diktatur*' in 1929) ('Heller, Rechtsstaat').

[4] ibid 130. Heller notes the irony that, with the development of capitalism, democracy had come to threaten the very class which had created it.

Authoritarian Liberalism and the Transformation of Modern Europe. Michael A Wilkinson, Oxford University Press.
 DOI: 10.1093/oso/9780198854753.003.0003

power of constitutional review, as not only 'undoubtedly wrong' from a legal perspective, but a violation of the fundamental principle of the division of powers and an eccentric reading of equality based on private property. This 'degeneration' of the *Rechtsstaat* idea would be an 'effective security' for the bourgeoisie, against the possibility that the popular legislature might transform the liberal *Rechtsstaat* into a social *Rechtsstaat*, since the 'overwhelming majority of judges' were from the 'ruling class'.[5]

In fact, two distinct accounts of the liberal *Rechtsstaat* emerged in the interwar period: a formal-liberal account associated with Hans Kelsen, and a conservative-liberal account associated with Carl Schmitt. Although they offered distinct, and in some respects opposing, visions, both Kelsen's *nomocratic* and Schmitt's *autocratic* response to the conjuncture sought, in Heller's view, to disarm democracy and popular sovereignty, and to dematerialize the *Rechtsstaat*.

The liberal 'dematerialization' of the *Rechtsstaat* would achieve its purest form in Kelsen's Pure Theory of Law. This offered, in Heller's view, an empty, formal account of authority, insensitive to social inequality and the representation of a plausible political unity.[6] Conservative jurists, such as Carl Schmitt, offered a concrete account of sovereignty, but in an overly personalistic manner, presenting sovereignty as adhering in an 'organ' of the state or even in a dictator, similarly neglecting the construction of a democratic relationship between rulers and ruled.

Heller viewed both Kelsen's turn to legality and Schmitt's turn to dictatorship as reactions to the emergence of class consciousness and the disturbances caused by increasingly intense class conflict. Whereas Kelsen's position led to an unstable political relativism, Schmitt's led to an objectionable—and ultimately also unstable—political conservatism. Both theoretical frameworks were equally insensitive to the socio-economic conditions in which political unity could be successfully formed. Neither Kelsen nor Schmitt, in other words, had any answer to the social question.

Heller's own answer, however, was ambiguous (as we examined in Chapter 1). In 1927 Heller had clarified that the true meaning of state sovereignty had to be recovered, namely as popular sovereignty; meaning the concrete formation of the people as a unity through the process of political representation. But he later appears to have departed from his own counsel in advocating the 'toleration' of the presidential cabinets, until it was too late. In 1927 Heller had speculated that extreme inequality, a failure attributable to economic liberalism, could open the path to dictatorship, the working class finding its allure too strong in the presence of severe socio-economic disparities.[7] In *Authoritarian Liberalism*, however, he noted that it was the ruling class that would first defect from the liberal democratic regime, fearful not only of revolution but of any democratic (as well as revolutionary) road to socialism. Indeed, Heller's suggestion that the working class would resort to dictatorship was also in tension with his simultaneous diagnosis of substantive inequality, namely that in such conditions the ruling class *already* exerts a form of dictatorship within the liberal democratic

[5] ibid 131.

[6] ibid 132. This vision, in Heller's view, contributed 'in no small measure to the support of dictatorship among a youth that looks for moral justification and is hungry for reality'.

[7] Hermann Heller, 'Political Democracy and Social Homogeneity' in Bernhard Schlink and Arthur J Jacobson (eds), *Weimar: A Jurisprudence of Crisis* (University of California Press 2000)('Heller, 'Political Democracy').

system.[8] It was, in other words, possible that a dematerialized *Rechtsstaat* was already undemocratic: law would be made by and for the bourgeoisie, given their influence, which far surpassed their formal parliamentary representation, and included power wielded through the media, the judiciary, and the bureaucracy.

To introduce a more contemporary conceptual vocabulary, the tension between democracy and capitalism was not merely a conjunctural phenomenon; it was a generalizable conflict, which the liberal state of the early twentieth century had, somehow, to manage. With the advent of mass democracy and its social demands, it had severe difficulty in doing so. The repression of popular sovereignty and parliamentary democracy signalled not merely a crisis in the conjuncture, but the culmination of a crisis over the long durée.

As Karl Polanyi recounts, the pattern of authoritarian liberal response and reaction to interwar economic crises was far from unique to late Weimar. Right across the globe, the capitalist state tried to maintain the political-economic demands of the gold standard, fiercely resisting social democratic movements through exceptional measures, until, eventually but unevenly, states abandoned gold and market liberalism. This led, for example, to protectionism in Britain and the New Deal in the US.[9] According to Polanyi, the more fiercely countries resisted social democracy through authoritarian government in the name of economic liberalism and sound finances, the stronger and fiercer the eventual backlash (the protective 'countermovement').

A very different lesson from the crisis of interwar liberalism than the one offered by Polanyi, however, was being drawn by influential political and economic thinkers who rejected both laissez-faire and socialist planning. Laissez-faire had failed, but this only meant economic liberalism needed a new foundation. Democracy could no longer be trusted to secure it. But rather than offer a political programme that would renounce democracy, novel sources of authority would be proffered in the hope of establishing a new order based on scientific and technical expertise, managerialism, and class compromise: the foundations were thus laid for the neo-liberalism that would come to dominate in the post-war period.

The chapter begins by outlining how the crisis of the Weimar Republic in interwar Germany unfolded, in significant part, as a crisis over the meaning of the constitution and its modes of self-defence (section 2). Looking beyond Weimar, to the many crises of interwar liberalism as crises of democratic capitalism, with the help of Karl Polanyi, the generality of the phenomenon, as well as the particularities in various local state responses, will be examined (section 3). Finally, the legacy of authoritarian liberalism for post-war reconstruction is outlined: the ordoliberalism and neo-liberalism which began to germinate in the interwar period, and which shared a distrust of democracy and parliamentary sovereignty, but offered more structured responses for its containment than the harsh authoritarianism of the interwar conjuncture (section 4).

[8] ibid 262. 'Without social homogeneity', Heller warned, 'the most radical formal equality becomes the most radical inequality, and formal democracy becomes the dictatorship of the ruling class' (a factor which enables Heller to distinguish the European social problem from the 'Negro Question' in the US. He notes that 'nothing is more characteristic of the social disparity which threatens our democracy than the attempt to recast the economic disparity into an anthropological one' (ibid 264).

[9] Karl Polanyi, *The Great Transformation: The Political and Economic Origins of Our Time* (Beacon Press 2001), first published in 1944 ('Polanyi, The Great Transformation'), 250–65.

2. A liberal constitution in crisis: three models of constitutional self-defence

The Weimar Constitution, agreed in August 1919, established a parliamentary republic, and, although opposed both by many radicals and conservatives, would attract the allegiance of significant political parties of the centre, including the Social Democratic Party (SDP), the Catholic Centre Party (Zentrum), and the German Democratic Party (DPP). For the first time in German history, constitutional legitimacy was based on the principle of popular sovereignty.[10] Also for the first time in history, German democracy was subject to universal suffrage: the 1919 constitution granted votes to women, following a movement led by socialist organizations, feminists, and political radicals.[11] Parliamentary democracy, national integration, and industrial development had, however, come late to Germany. In conjunction with the humiliation of Versailles, economic costs of reparations, and ambivalence about the legacy of the monarchical principle, this gave the new republic a precarious cast.[12] In these conditions, popular sovereignty and constitutional legitimacy made for an uncomfortable pairing.

In reality, the Weimar Constitution reflected a series of compromises between interests and ideologies: between monarchism and republicanism, liberalism and socialism, presidentialism and parliamentary democracy, the internal unity of the Reich and the federal autonomy of its constituent states, and between the interests of capital and labour.[13] These compromises reflected tensions, in particular between the promises of a social state and a private capitalist economy, well understood by its liberal architect Hugo Preuss as well as the first president of the Republic, the Social Democrat Friedrich Ebert.[14] Throughout the course of the 1920s and early 1930s, the compromises would be severely tested, as Weimar faced a series of debilitating economic crises (first with hyperinflations, and later with deflation following the Great Depression). In addition, it was marked by serious political crises, growing social turbulence, parliamentary fragmentation, and extra-parliamentary unrest.

The constitutional settlement was viewed with suspicion by many conservatives and bourgeoise elites from the outset; considered a betrayal of the German Empire, and associated with the humiliation of defeat in the First World War and the punishment and 'war guilt' of Versailles. Many conservative scholars saw the proposed transition to a *Sozialstaat* as materially problematic, with social demands destabilizing the state through politicization of the economy, re-differentiating the relation between

[10] Peter C Caldwell, *Popular Sovereignty and the Crisis of German Constitutional Law: The Theory & Practice of Weimar Constitutionalism* (Duke University Press 1997) 1.

[11] Richard J Evans, 'German Social Democracy and Women's Suffrage 1891–1918' (1980) 15 Journal of Contemporary History 533.

[12] Michael Stolleis, *A History of Public Law in Germany 1914–1945* (OUP 2004) ('Stolleis, History of Public Law') 45–53.

[13] Michael Stolleis, *Public Law in Germany: A Historical Introduction from the 16th to the 21st Century* (OUP 2017) 73–74.

[14] See Hugo Preuss, 'The Significance of the Democratic Republic for the Idea of Social Justice' in Arthur J Jacobson and Bernhard Schlink (eds), *Weimar: A Jurisprudence of Crisis* (University of California Press 2000).

the political and economic realms.[15] Governing elites retained from the imperial era, still dominant in the civil service, army, and legal profession, had little attachment to Weimar's democratic regime, rendering it institutionally vulnerable.

The left was divided in numerous ways: SPD reformists (including legal thinkers like Hermann Heller) viewed the Republic as a vehicle for evolutionary social change; others (notably a group of Weimar labour lawyers, including Hugo Sinzheimer and Franz Neumann) insisted on the continuing process of democratization from the 'bottom up', by extending democracy to the workplace and the economy; and the radical left (including the Communist Party, the KPD) viewed the Republic as a capitalist state, which could only temper economic struggles but not properly resolve them. The radicals aimed at mobilizing the working class in the pursuit of political power, insisting on the revolutionary overthrow of the regime through class struggle. This created a clear schism. As Martin Jay puts it, 'whereas the SPD struggled to reconcile its defence of the democratic Republic with its advocacy of working-class interests', the KPD rejected the Republic as sham 'bourgeois democracy', but was tied to Moscow, and 'no less divided between its support for Soviet interests and those of the German working class as it understood them'.[16]

The political debates in Weimar were intense and polarized, and often accompanied by police and paramilitary violence on the streets. But they also frequently took the form of *constitutional argument*. The written document, in its second part, protected both economic liberalism (a qualified right to private property, Article 153) and social justice (Article 151). It even acknowledged the role of Workers' Councils as organs of economic democracy (Article 165), and the optional socialization of the means of production (Article 156).[17] Although the positive content of this part of the Weimar Constitution could, for many left-leaning Weimar lawyers, be brought to fruition as a 'labour constitution' through institutional means, as it 'contain[ed] the fundamentals necessary for the construction of a social *Rechtsstaat* whose objective is the realization of social freedom', jurisprudence would gradually turn this promise upside down.[18] In particular, Article 153 and the protection of private property would be

[15] John P McCormick, 'Weimar Legal Thought' in Peter E Gordon and John P McCormick (eds), *Weimar Thought: A Contested Legacy* (Princeton University Press 2013) 55: 'In general, most of the era's legal luminaries—Hans Kelsen, Richard Thoma, Hugo Preuss, Gerhard Anschütz, Heinrich Triepel, Erich Kaufmann, and others—analyzed the ensuing crisis of the Weimar Republic precisely in terms of a crisis of law accompanying a radical transition to the welfare state or *Sozialstaat*.').

[16] Martin Jay, 'The Weimar Left' in Peter E Gordon and John P McCormick (eds), *Weimar Thought: A Contested Legacy* (Princeton University Press 2013) 380. Jay notes that the various schisms of the Left were revealed with the outbreak of the First World War, and the decision of the SPD to support the war effort, ending the 'Second International' and the possibility of unity. He distinguishes Bernstein's revisionism, Kautsky's centrist orthodoxy, and a more radical revolutionary position represented by Rosa Luxemburg and Karl Liebknecht, without considering as a separate category the Labour Constitutionalists. These divisions continued after the 1918 revolution, with 'the SPD making a devil's pact with the army and the Freikorps, a volunteer para-military organization of veterans who relished in the brutal suppression of Bolshevik uprisings'.

[17] See Ruth Dukes, *The Labour Constitution: The Enduring Idea of Labour Law* (OUP 2014) 18.

[18] Franz Neumann, 'The Social Significance of the Basic Laws in the Weimar Constitution' in Keith Tribe (ed), *Social Democracy and the Rule of Law: Otto Kirchheimer and Franz Neumann* (Allen & Unwin 1987) 37. For Neumann, 'social freedom means that workers will determine their own working life; the alien power of the owners to command labour through their control of the means of production must give way to self-determination'.

utilized by liberals and conservatives in an attempt to frustrate the goals of socialism and the 'labour constitution'.[19] Through the juridical application of principles of economic freedom, Franz Neumann eventually lamented, the meaning of the Weimar Constitution was 'converted into its exact opposite'.[20]

The two most famous jurists associated with the Weimar era, Hans Kelsen and Carl Schmitt, represented opposing methodological and formal responses to the various criticisms of the constitution, which came from both left and right, conservatives and socialists.[21] The theme of constitutional defence on which these responses focused, and variations on this theme, would later be analysed under the label of 'militant democracy' through the influence of German émigré and constitutional lawyer, Karl Loewenstein (whose influence on post-war reconstruction is examined in Part II).[22] Heller offered a 'third alternative' but, as we will examine, it was hampered by ambiguity.

Kelsen's *Pure Theory of Law*

Hans Kelsen, better known now as one of the foremost exponents of legal positivism, rejected the idea of a 'militant democracy', associating democracy with proceduralism and political relativism and the constitution with its formal elements.[23] He famously theorized the state as having no independent juristic significance; the state was 'identical' with the positive legal order. In his *Pure Theory of Law*, Kelsen argued that there was nothing that stood 'behind the law', as it were; only a transcendental presupposition of its validity. This presupposition, necessary to make sense of any juristic knowledge—to understand law as *norm*—was also a way of ridding law and legal theory of foreign elements and ideological distortions. It was this presupposition, or *Grundnorm*, rather than a constellation of power or the expression of a metaphysical natural law, which authorized legal directives.[24]

The content of the legal order was entirely contingent, as Kelsen memorably argued using the example of revolution: if the revolution is successful, a new legal order and new Grundnorm comes into effect, and the revolutionaries will be regarded (retrospectively) as founders; if not, the old one remains in place and the revolutionaries will be treated as 'traitors' and punished accordingly.[25] The legal system as a whole

[19] Neumann saw that monopolization threatened even economic liberty: (Franz Neumann, 'On the Preconditions and Legal Concept of an Economic Constitution' in Keith Tribe (ed), *Social Democracy and the Rule of Law: Otto Kirchheimer and Franz Neumann* (Allen & Unwin 1987) (Neumann, 'On the Precognitions').

[20] ibid 56–57.

[21] Kelsen came to Germany only in 1930, but was central to Weimar juristic debates (see Caldwell (n 10)). Kelsen drafted the Austrian Constitution of 1920, at the request of Chancellor Renner, and had been inspired, in part, by the Weimar Constitution.

[22] This influence of the inappositely named 'militant democracy' is examined in Part II.

[23] Hans Kelsen, *The Essence and Value of Democracy* (Rowman & Littlefield 2013)(Kelsen, 'Essence and Value').

[24] Hans Kelsen, *Introduction to the Problems of Legal Theory: A Translation of the First Edition of the Reine Rechtslehre or Pure Theory of Law* (Bonnie L Paulson and Stanley L Paulson trs, Clarendon Press 1992)(Kelsen, 'Problems of Legal Theory').

[25] ibid.

was dependent on being, or in the course of revolution becoming, 'by and large effective', in the sense of reaching a general level of societal compliance, but there was no other social (or moral or political) relation that determined or even conditioned the constitutional order as such. In short, although Kelsen insisted that effectiveness is a condition of legal validity, he said nothing about the social or political conditions of effectiveness. The 'material constitution' was, thus, reduced to the formal norms that established and authorized law-making powers.[26]

Kelsen's view of democracy was that it expressed a political relativism; a denial of the possibility of accessing absolute truth or absolute values in the public realm. Relativism, he argued, 'is the Weltanschauung that the democratic idea presumes'. Democracy, he insisted, is based fundamentally on the principle of freedom and political equality, which yields a majoritarianism that nevertheless respects minorities, and the 'impossibility of claiming absolute validity ... for a political programme'.[27] Anything further than *formal* equality 'has nothing to do with democracy'.

In Heller's view, Kelsen's liberalism was the compliment to the bourgeois *Rechtsstaat*, not in the sense of protecting substantive private rights and freedoms, but in its formal account of the concept of *sovereignty*. As sovereignty is attributed to *norms* and no longer to the collective *will*, it becomes increasingly depersonalized and emptied of concrete political meaning, a process Kelsen took to its 'logical conclusion'. After the decline of the monarchical principle of the nineteenth century, rather than pushing for the more concrete understanding of sovereignty, Kelsen opted for a hollow formal version: a 'liberal rule of law rationalism'.[28] Kelsen's model was the culmination of a liberal theory that over the course of the nineteenth and early twentieth centuries had eroded the concept of the 'general will' and the principle of popular sovereignty entirely.

Kelsen's 'Vienna School' positivism, with its scientific orientation and strict separation of the 'is' and 'ought', the fact and the norm, was not sufficiently material and dynamic for Heller's social democratic orientation. But neither was it concrete enough for a conservative German public law academy that longed less for scientific clarification than 'for inner cohesion in a turbulent time'.[29] As conservative jurist Erich Kaufmann remarked, the neo-Kantian formalism that Kelsen represented was unsuited to 'paralysing the dangerous materialistic and utopian poison of Marxism', which was spreading on the left.[30] The traditional-authoritarian bourgeoisie had reluctantly, if at all, accepted the improvised parliamentarism thrust upon them, and longed for the 'competence, order and decency' that could only truly be protected by a monarchy.[31] Kelsen's political ideology was liberal democracy, and his orientation was realistic and pluralist; he did not advance an authoritarian liberalism.

[26] cf Lars Vinx, 'Hans Kelsen and the Material Constitution of Democracy' (2021 forthcoming Jurisprudence article).

[27] Kelsen, 'Essence and Value' (n 23).

[28] Heller, 'Sovereignty' (n 2) 67.

[29] Stolleis, 'Public Law in Germany' (n 13) 84.

[30] ibid 83.

[31] See Ellen Kennedy, 'Introduction' in Carl Schmitt, *The Crisis of Parliamentary Democracy* (Ellen Kennedy tr, MIT Press 1988) xxiv–xxix (Kennedy cites Thomas Mann, 'I want the monarchy, I want a passionately independent government ... I don't want politics. I want competence, order and decency.' (xxiv)). As Charles S Maier notes, 'bourgeois', after the First World War, 'served to describe the rallying

Schmitt's *Absolute Constitution*

In the early stages of the Republic, Schmitt and other conservative jurists had argued in favour of natural law-type solutions to the problems elicited by the social question, utilizing the courts to protect private property against legislative action, and specifically against the effects of the inflations of the early 1920s. These conservative jurists were involved in legal argumentation in the Reichsgericht against the expropriation of private property, and protested against the currency revaluation following the hyperinflation of 1923 to 1924, which hit middle-class savers in particular.[32] If, as Stefan Zweig had memorably suggested the annihilation of the value of money threatened to dissipate all other values, jurists had played their part in attempting to arrest this slide.[33] Constitutional provisions protecting formal equality and liberal constitutional principles would be raised against the arbitrariness of party democracy and the attempt, through legislation, to inflate away the national debt.[34] The judges of the Reichsgericht, unsurprisingly, sided with the creditors, defending their private rights against the 'despotism of the majority'.[35]

To the extent that conservatives, and even many in the political centre, supported Weimar parliamentary democracy, it was less out of any political conviction in the Republic than out of tactical considerations, to avoid the 'dictatorship of the proletariat' that they feared as the alternative.[36] Carl Schmitt shared this defensive posture and, in addition to judicial defence, would advance a dictatorial solution to the problem of constitutional self-protection, initially from within the Weimar regime.[37]

cry of anti-collectivist forces', describing the 'opposition to Social Democrats as well as to Marxists further left': Charles S Maier, *Recasting Bourgeois Europe* (Princeton University Press, 2016 [first published 1975]) x.

32 Another conservative jurist, Heinrich Triepel, had published a brief suggesting that the currency revaluation was unlawful (see Caldwell (n 10) 6, 148–53). Neumann described the judicial empowerment of the Reichsgericht as occurring through a 'revival of natural law' which was 'fulfilling counterrevolutionary functions'. He notes that the use of 'general principles of law' characteristic of the 'free law school', a 'kind of secret natural law', transformed the legal system by 'giving an immense amount of discretionary power to the judge' (Franz Neumann, 'The Change of the Function of Law in Modern Society' in *The Democratic and Authoritarian State: Essays in Political and Legal Theory* (Herbert Marcuse ed, Free Press of Glencoe 1957) (Neumann, 'Change of Function') 53–55.

33 Stefan Zweig, *The World of Yesterday: Memoirs of a European* (Anthea Bell tr, Pushkin Press 2011). For analysis of the impact of the myth that hyperinflation lead to the collapse of democracy, see Hjalte C Lokdam, 'Banking on Sovereignty: A Genealogy of the European Central Bank's Independence' (PhD Thesis, LSE 2019).

34 Caldwell (n 10) 148–53. See, further, Clara Maier, 'The Weimar Origins of the West German *Rechtsstaat*, 1919–1969' (2019) 62 The Historical Journal 1069, 1085–86.

35 Maier (n 34) 1086 (the implications of this are examined further in Chapter 3).

36 Stolleis, A History of Public Law (n 12) (citing Kaufmann: 'after the fall of the monarchy and in the maelstroms of the revolution, which left us with a choice only between a parliamentary majority rule and the "dictatorship of the proletariat", parliamentarism was the only tactical ground we could seek unless we wished to embrace, at least temporarily, the system of soviets after the Russian model. All political parties, from the German National to the majority social democrats, accepted the parliamentary system as such a tactical foundation, as a mere political "rule of the game" ').

37 Before his turn towards National Socialism in 1933 and1934, Schmitt was an 'implacable conservative opponent of the enemies of the Weimar state', especially those on the left. See Keith Tribe, *Strategies of Economic Order: German Economic Discourse 1750–1950* (CUP 1995) 175. As late as 1932, in *Legality and Legitimacy*, he was arguing that if the core of the second, substantial part of the Weimar Constitution could be stripped of its contradictions and developed in accordance with its inner logic, 'the idea of a German

On the basis of a 'commissarial' form of dictatorship, the president (using Article 48) should exercise emergency powers to defend the constitution, if necessary by setting some of its norms aside.[38] If the content of the constitution had been the result of a compromise, it was far from a sheer contingency for Schmitt; Weimar represented the prevailing bourgeois bloc (*Bürgertum*), which an authoritarian state apparatus should defend if necessary.[39]

Schmitt's constitutional theory was offered as an antidote to the relativism and fragmentation associated with democratization, statutory positivism, and political pluralization, which were weakening the ruling class and endangering the economically liberal aspects of the constitutional settlement long before 1930. His later turn to an authoritarian liberalism, examined in Chapter 1, thus represented a much deeper fear of the political awakening of the working class that could be traced back across the nineteenth century. This fear was laid bare in Schmitt's *Verfassungslehre*, published in 1928:

> Now the proletariat becomes the people, because it is the bearer of this negativity (that was Sieyes' 'third estate': which was nothing and shall become everything). It is the part of the population which does not own, which does not have a share in the produced surplus value, and finds no place in the existing order... Democracy turns into proletarian democracy, and replaces the liberalism of the propertied and educated bourgeoisie.[40]

As a matter of constitutional theory, Schmitt would attempt to obstruct any revolutionary move by distinguishing the constitutional text from the 'Constitution' as a political and existential phenomenon: the soul of the political community. The 'Constitution' stood above the temporary politics of competing social forces and the individual constitutional laws. It could be safeguarded and stabilized neither by judicial activism on its own, nor by the system of parliamentary democracy. Only an authoritarian government—more swiftly and sharply able to obstruct any exercise of parliamentary or revolutionary constituent power—could achieve this, by tempering and ultimately eroding the growing power of the working class.

The 'Constitution', for Schmitt, was, thus, not only the formal set of positive norms; it was also the expression of a unified substantial core: a 'constitutional identity'. Schmitt employed the term the 'Absolute Constitution' to connote this substantive identity, which must be protected from its opponents.[41] Constitutional identity could

constitution will be saved'. See Carl Schmitt, *Legality and Legitimacy* (Duke University Press 2004 [first published 1932]) 94. (Schmitt, 'Legality and Legitimacy').

[38] For an exploration of the difference between commissarial and sovereign dictatorship, in the move from Schmitt's *Die Diktatur* to *Political Theology*, and in the difference between crises in early and late Weimar, see John P McCormick, 'The Dilemmas of Dictatorship: Carl Schmitt and Constitutional Emergency Powers' (1997) Canadian Journal of Law and Jurisprudence 163.

[39] Schmitt's preference for a dictatorship allied with the Catholic Church was identified by Richard Thoma in 1925, in an early review of Schmitt's *Crisis of Parliamentary Democracy* (Kennedy (n 31) xiv).

[40] Carl Schmitt, *Constitutional Theory* (Seitzer tr, Duke University Press 2008) 271–72 (Schmitt, 'Constitutional Theory').

[41] Schmitt, 'Constitutional Theory' (n 40). For discussion, see Benjamin A Schupmann, *Carl Schmitt's State and Constitutional Theory: A Critical Analysis* (OUP 2017) 135–52.

be threatened not only by a Bolshevik-style revolution, but also by constitutional change through the ballot box, and through parliamentary legislation. What Schmitt 'feared most' in the Weimar era was the 'increased pace of the democratic revolution'; specifically, that in an age of universal suffrage and working-class consciousness, parliamentary democracy might overturn the liberal *Rechtsstaat*.[42]

The Weimar Constitution could, after all, be formally amended by a two-thirds majority, in respect to even its most fundamental provisions, leading Schmitt to fear that the 'entire system could be transformed through simple amendment procedure'.[43] The distinction between the formal part of the constitution (its organizational elements) and its second substantive part, which limited the political will of the community in the name of individual freedom, was meant to frustrate this,[44] with the latter providing the Weimar Constitution with its ultimate principles.[45] When it became apparent that the contradictions contained in the substantive provisions could not be reconciled, difficult as it was to protect both a bourgeois *Rechtsstaat* and social commitments (*soziale Rechtsstaat*) guaranteeing private property, as well as promising socialization of the means of production, Schmitt's answer was to pare the substantive provisions down to the bare liberal essentials: a minimal set of private rights based on an individualistic social order.[46] If, and when, decision was necessary, it would be made in favour of the liberal *Rechtsstaat* and against socialism, prioritizing negative liberties enforceable against the state above positive rights on the state.[47] The institution of private property was, thus, of central importance for Schmitt, both in ensuring the protection of the prevailing concrete order, and in precluding any instrumentalization of legislative change to achieve the aims of socialism or communism.[48]

Schmitt was anti-liberal to the extent that liberalism was politically weak in self-defence and philosophically hamstrung by its negation of the issue of sovereignty. Its unlimited tolerance of a plurality of competing interests and protection of civil rights of opponents pointed to an inability to secure its own principles against its political enemies. In practice, as Schmitt argued in the mid– to late Weimar period, the dictatorial powers conferred on the president by Article 48 could provide the means for the Weimar Constitution to defend itself; just as in a commissarial dictatorship, the exception should be used to protect the norm.

[42] See Cristi (n 1) 17 According to Cristi, making the distinction between liberalism and democracy enabled Schmitt's rapprochement with liberalism as early as 1923. Schupmann (n 41) 36 also cites Ingeborg Maus's analysis that 'Schmitt was motivated above all by a desire to protect bourgeoise property rights against the threat of socialism', although he himself suggests that protection of property rights was only a 'peripheral concern' for Schmitt.

[43] Jeffrey Seitzer, 'Carl Schmitt's Internal Critique of Liberal Constitutionalism: *Verfassungslehre* as Response to the Weimar State Crisis' (1997) 10 Canadian Journal of Law and Jurisprudence 203, 214; see further Olivier Beaud, *La puissance de l'État* (Presses Universitaires de France 1994). Beaud notes that Schmitt provided the first systematization of a substantive limitation on the power of amendment.

[44] Schmitt (n 40) 172.

[45] Schmitt, 'Legality and Legitimacy' (n 37) 90– 94; Schupmann (n 41) 180: 'Schmitt repeatedly argued that the Weimar Constitution contains a political decision to be a bourgeoise *Rechtsstaat*, which was above all oriented by its commitment to individual liberty.'

[46] Schupmann (n 41) 182–85. On the affinities between Schmitt's thought and Hayek see, further, William E Scheuerman, 'The Unholy Alliance of Carl Schmitt and Friedrich A Hayek' (1997) 4 Constellations 172.

[47] Schupmann (n 41) 187.

[48] Schmitt had argued, for example, against the expropriation without compensation of the princely houses, on which there was a referendum in 1926. See, further, Caldwell (n 10) 156–60.

Other conservative jurists sought, like Schmitt, to recreate the political balance of the nineteenth-century *Rechtsstaat* but looked more decisively to the courts for the answer. Heinrich Triepel, for instance, expressed a clear preference for 'enlightened or unenlightened despotism of a single person' rather than the 'despotism of the never enlightened rabble', and pleaded for the creation of a constitutional court with 'abundant powers' in order to restrict the legislative branch.[49] These jurists sought a return to the 'illusory stability of the system of constitutional monarchism, by allowing either the president or the value system of the basic rights to set a limit on party-political negotiations.'[50] Entrusting authority to the old elites, including much of the judiciary, who were rarely loyal to the democratic and social orientation of the Weimar Constitution, was a means of pursuing this aim. Their 'defence of the *Rechtsstaat*' might therefore also be read as '*counterrevolutionary*.'[51]

But if the exercise of judicial power might frustrate parliamentary democracy from becoming social, it would not prevent the bourgeoisie from turning to dictatorship. Only a conviction in parliamentary democracy could do that, and that conviction was conspicuously lacking.

Heller's *social democratic state*

Hermann Heller criticized both Kelsen's formal liberalism and Schmitt's conservative liberalism for repressing the concept of popular sovereignty. If Kelsen offered nothing more than the 'illusion' of 'rule without a ruler' (justified by the Grundnorm), Schmitt offered the spectre of a 'ruler without rules' (a theory of dictatorship). From Heller's perspective, both were essentially reactionary doctrines, inimical to a socialist vision based on an evolutionary democratic state.

Heller's dismissive view of Kelsen's liberalism was laid out clearly in 1927, when he took aim at Kelsen for 'degrading' the concept of sovereignty, breaking with the Rousseau–Hegel line of philosophical reflection on the state, and substituting the rationalism, legalism, and liberalism of the bourgeois *Rechtsstaat* for the idea of the 'general will'.[52] Kelsen's doctrine of 'legal sovereignty', one of 'the last remnants of the moral pathos of Enlightenment's universalist natural law', was not only a reflection of intellectual decline, or a harmless bourgeois illusion: it was a *reaction*, in the proper political sense of the word, based on concern of the middle class for its own personal security in an age of mass democracy.[53] Heller goes even further. Where class divisions have rendered the idea of a 'general will' improbable, even a formally democratic state,

[49] Ralf Poscher, 'Heinrich Triepel: Introduction' in Arthur J Jacobson and Bernhard Schlink (eds), *Weimar: A Jurisprudence of Crisis* (University of California Press 2000).

[50] Peter Caldwell, 'National Socialism and Constitutional Law: Carl Schmitt, Otto Koellreutter, and the Debate over the Nature of the Nazi State, 1933–1937' (1994) 16 Cardozo Law Review 399.

[51] ibid 403 (italics added).

[52] Heller, Sovereignty (n 2).

[53] ibid 67 (Heller warns against Kelsen's legal rationalism, and his 'logically incomprehensible answer' to the question of positive law's foundations, *presupposing* transcendentally the validity of a historically first constitution whose content is empirically determined (ibid 91)).

no longer materially representative, turns to the *ideology* of an objective rule of law to conceal class division and class dominance:

> A formal democracy that has lost the substantive idea of the *Rechtsstaat*– whose representative classes no longer believe in its right to represent them and whose class contradictions make a 'general will' unlikely – has an understandable interest in countering the idea of class dominance by propagating the ideology of a completely objective rule of law.[54]

A proper realization of popular sovereignty is 'logically impossible' in liberalism, since, Heller argues—in another echo of Rousseau— it either understands the people's will only as a sum of individual wills (the *volonté de tous* that Rousseau counterposed to the true *volonté générale*), or it proffers objective knowledge of the 'general will', culminating in the 'foolish' idea that we might live under the 'rule of law not of men'.[55] The liberal appeal to the written constitution does not help to resolve the problem: the text can be interpreted in very different ways, and be given very different meanings; there can be no objective knowledge of it.[56]

Kelsen's Pure Theory of Law, as the methodological conclusion of liberalism and its proclaimed freedom from the state, is 'the juristic mask' of liberal opposition to popular sovereignty.[57] It is, in other words, the methodological complement to a politics of anti-statism, a position which is not only 'theoretically false' but, Heller remarks, *politically misguided*: limitations on the exercise of sovereign powers lead neither to more democracy nor to greater individual freedom.[58]

Schmitt, on the other hand, although providing the 'sole' and 'highly significant' exception to the degradation of sovereignty in the academy, and a crucial corrective to Kelsen's abstract legal rationalism, errs in the opposite direction. Schmitt, who at that stage made only a cameo appearance in Heller's writing, was praised as offering a more robust conceptualization of sovereignty than Kelsen, but only by offering an overly personalistic account of dictatorship, which remained stuck in its own ambiguities: did Schmitt want to defend the Weimar Constitution or overthrow it?

Schmitt, in Heller's view, construed sovereignty in a dictatorial fashion, as inhering in an *organ* of the state.[59] This mirror image of the liberal rule of law ideology remains 'full of internal contradictions', Schmitt's conclusions on sovereignty in the debates on the meaning of the Weimar Constitution undermined by his own theoretical distinction between commissarial and sovereign dictatorship.[60] The president was not a

54 ibid 82 (almost replicating Soviet jurist Evgeny Pashukanis on this point: see his Evgeny Pashukanis, 'General Theory of Law and Marxism', in P Beirne and R Sharlet (eds), *Selected Writings on Marxism and Law* (Academic Press 1980)).

55 Heller, 'Sovereignty' (n 2) 108.

56 In Sovereignty, Heller (n 2) says relatively little about the concrete provisions of the Weimar Constitution.

57 ibid 183.

58 ibid 184.

59 In opposing the rationalist belief in law with a form of decisionism, Schmitt's turn to dictatorship is, in Heller's view, 'definitive' and 'a model for the study at hand' (ibid 101).

60 ibid (which Heller considers an otherwise 'excellent' distinction). Heller notes that Schmitt had avoided answering whether the president could perform 'acts of sovereignty' within the Weimar Republic. On the basis of Schmitt's distinction between commissarial and sovereign dictatorship, the president would appear

sovereign lawgiver, and was therefore unable to establish a new constitution or modify it in the exercise of constituent power, only to defend the existing one through the exercise of constituted powers.[61] This conclusion, however, would seem to contradict Schmitt's own earlier claim that 'sovereign is whoever decides on the exception', as he had famously declared in *Political Theology*, theorizing the state of exception to be jurisprudentially analogous to the miracle in theology.[62]

Schmitt's mistake was to confuse sovereignty for the personal attribute of an institution which was dedicated, in reality, only to conserving some aspects of the constitutional order; if necessary, by suspending other parts of it.[63] This, too, was not only a philosophical error. For Heller, it was politically misguided, a claim clarified by Heller's later critique of Schmitt's 'authoritarian liberalism': a regime that insists on conserving the liberal differentiation between state and society, and between the political and economic spheres, fatally weakens the bonds between rulers and ruled by exacerbating economic inequalities. More than passively tolerating authoritarian liberalism, as the Social Democrats had done, conservatives such as Schmitt had actively supported it, providing intellectual ballast for its defection from the parliamentary regime. But this was a defection buttressed by legal liberals such as Kelsen, who had turned their backs to the concept of popular sovereignty underpinning parliamentary authority.

Heller's own reformist position, which has recently been labelled a 'social model of democratic self-defence', avoiding the pitfalls of Kelsen's formalism and Schmitt's conservatism, faces a dilemma of its own.[64] For Heller, the big 'C' Constitution is political in nature, and must be understood in dynamic and relational terms.[65] Political unity is not a bare fact or existential antagonism, but is formed, constructed, and mediated through the political process, channelling competing claims over the common good. 'Democracy', says Heller, is a 'conscious process of the formation of political unity from bottom to top ... The people as a plurality is consciously to form itself into the people as unity'.[66] Political parties are essential to serve this function of unifying the multitude of wills of the citizenry into a coherent whole. In particular, through

merely a commissarial dictator, able to set aside the rules in order to preserve the whole (on the legal basis of Article 48 of the Weimar Constitution itself) but not 'sovereign' as such. (ibid, 102–03).

[61] On the ambiguities of Schmitt's position, concluding that ultimately Schmitt envisaged 'fusing elements of both commissarial and sovereign dictatorship', see William E Scheuerman, 'States of Emergency' in Jens Meierhenrich and Oliver Simons (eds), *The Oxford Handbook of Carl Schmitt* (OUP 2017) 553–57. cf Renato Cristi, 'Carl Schmitt on Sovereignty and Constituent Power' (1997) 10 The Canadian Journal of Law and Jurisprudence 189 (arguing that Schmitt's aim was to disarm the constituent power of the people).

[62] Carl Schmitt, *Political Theology: Four Chapters on the Concept of Sovereignty* (University of Chicago Press 2006).

[63] First and foremost, the sovereign decides whether the normal situation actually exists. For discussion, see Caldwell (n 10) 96–100; John P McCormick, *Carl Schmitt's Critique of Liberalism: Against Politics as Technology* (CUP 1998).

[64] Anthoula Malkopoulou and Ludvig Norman, 'Three Models of Democratic Self-Defence: Militant Democracy and its Alternatives' (2018) 66 Political Studies 442.

[65] Heller, 'Sovereignty' (n 2) 113 argues that 'homogeneity' is something that daily must be formed anew, approving Ernest Renan's formulation of nationalism with his metaphor of '*un plebiscite de toujours*'. For a relational conception of constituent power, building in part on Heller, see Martin Loughlin, 'The Concept of Constituent Power' in Michael W Dowdle and Michael A Wilkinson (eds), *Constitutionalism Beyond Liberalism* (CUP 2017).

[66] Heller, Political Democracy (n 7) 260.

its social policy, the Weimar Republic could still 'defuse' social conflicts; indeed, its ability to do so would 'decide its fate'.[67]

In order for the Constitution to accommodate a degree of conflict and channel man's 'unsocial sociability', there must be some prospect of *substantive* (socio-economic) equality 'between rulers and ruled', according to Heller. Although this can never be truly and finally achieved, because the social structure is 'necessarily antagonistic', Heller—rejecting the utopian Marxism of some of his opponents on the left—insists on the capacity of the political-social state to work through this tension, standing above the various competing interests and class conflicts.[68]

Substantive equality is both precondition and prospect of democracy; both cause and effect. This raises a profound dilemma for the liberal state. The merely formal equality (or 'civil homogeneity' as Heller puts it) of the liberal *Rechtsstaat* was not only entirely consistent with substantive *inequality*; it could also aggravate it.[69] This problem was so severe in Weimar that it was becoming increasingly difficult, if not impossible, to reconcile the formation of a 'general will' with its 'class state' (a state *divided* by class); precisely the difficulty that Rousseau and Hegel had pointed to (in an earlier age) in conditions of inequality and heterogeneity.[70] Equality appears to be a precondition for democracy, but, in the material reality of capitalist society, it can be—at most—an aspiration, and one that is thwarted by capitalism's own dynamic. Heller is caught in the Rousseau–Hegel bind, but now with a heightened tension between social demands made through parliamentary democracy, as well as extra-parliamentary means, on the one hand, and the autonomy of the privately regulated economy and capitalist interests on the other.

In such conditions, political power is unequally acquired and utilized by the ruling class to maintain its own position. This can occur through the normal political process because of the influence it can exert in its control of public opinion, media, and education. But in conditions of heightened socio-economic inequality, doubts might emerge as to whether liberal democracy is even capable of delivering the *minimal* conditions for a tolerable degree of social harmony. With strong populist reactions likely to ensue, Heller argues, electoral democracy itself might then be under threat, deemed inadequate for, or even an obstacle to, the necessary solidarity and social equality for society to politically constitute and reconstitute itself.

In other words, in the absence of political-democratic channels to respond to economic disparities, not only opposition within, but also, ultimately, *alternatives to* the liberal democratic process become alluring. Heller warned in 1928 that the relative

[67] Michael Stolleis, *History of Social Law in Germany* (Springer-Verlag 2014) 113.

[68] Heller, Political Democracy (n 7) 257. The dialectic of fact and norm is, in a democracy more than any other political form, dependent on and shaped by 'social equalisation' (ibid 261).

[69] ibid 264. According to Heller, social inequality 'transforms *summum jus* [supreme right] into *summa injuria* [supreme wrong]'.

[70] On Rousseau's struggle with political economy see, eg Marco Goldoni, 'Rousseau's Radical Constitutionalism and its Legacy' in Michael W Dowdle and Michael A Wilkinson (eds), *Constitutionalism Beyond Liberalism* (CUP 2017). On Hegel, see Frank Ruda, *Hegel's Rabble: An Investigation into Hegel's Philosophy of Right* (Bloomsbury 2011). Hegel uses the figure of the 'rabble' to capture the tendency of bourgeois society and industrial capitalism to lead to extremes of inequality and instability. From this perspective, it would appear to be no surprise that the rabble, having been dismissed, turns to 'non-liberal' alternatives.

tranquillity in the Federal Republic (the period from 1925 to 1928) would be short-lasting because social homogeneity was 'lacking to an extent unmatched in previous eras'.[71] His conclusion is implicit but clear: if the democratic route to social equality is perceived to be inadequate, the road to dictatorship is open. 'Once the proletariat believes that the democratic equality of its ever-powerful opponent condemns the democratic form of class struggle to hopelessness', Heller concludes, 'it resorts to dictatorship'.[72]

Heller's conclusion was both prescient and mistaken.[73] Dictatorship was on the cards, but not those held by the working class. It was the ruling elites that would resort to autocracy and then dictatorship, and big business allied to the middle class who increasingly 'warmed' to 'Germany's right-wing' and its anti-Marxist and anti-parliamentary agitation.[74] As the centre increasingly struggled to hold, it was not the dictatorship *of* the proletariat urged by those to Heller's left that would emerge, but a dictatorship *over* the proletariat. Authoritarianism beckoned, not as means of overturning the existing order, but as justification for maintaining, or attempting to maintain, *normality*: to preserve the status quo. Heller's dictum might well have been reversed: 'Once the *capitalist class* believes that the democratic equality of its ever-powerful opponent condemns the democratic form of *its* class struggle to hopelessness, it resorts to dictatorship'.[75]

3. Karl Polanyi and the political economy of the interwar conjuncture

With a longer historical arc in view, and a wider lens, the combination of political authoritarianism and economic liberalism as a reactionary force comes to appear less exceptional than normal in the development of the modern state and state system. Authoritarian government was the political means to defend the class interests of the bourgeoisie, but, without a mass political and social base, it then became dependent on various more extreme forces of conservativism and counter-revolution for support in the fight against socialism and communism.

The turn of the bourgeoisie and capitalist interests to authoritarian and then dictatorial government, eliciting support from conservative nationalist forces in the process, was a more generalizable phenomenon. Charles Maier notes that the 'new right' in the interwar period, which 'embraced a strident chauvinism, anti-Semitism, and

[71] Heller, Political Democracy (n 7) 262. This coincided with the forecast of the communist leaders, who had predicted an imminent collapse of the capitalist system.

[72] ibid 262.

[73] Another aspect in which Heller would have been entirely taken by surprise was the success of the racial aspect of National Socialist ideology and its biological conception of the *Volk* (see Heller (n 7)).

[74] See Hans Mommsen, *The Rise and Fall of Weimar Democracy* (University of North Carolina Press 2007) 301. In particular, pension and salary cuts in the public sector increasingly hit the middle class, who had already endured the losses of the hyperinflation. They often blamed this on the Social Democrats and refused to work together with organized labour due to considerations of 'status'. As we saw in Chapter 1, the Social Democrats, including Heller, tolerated the bypassing of parliament through the presidential cabinets.

[75] See, for a later analysis, Ian Kershaw, *'The Nazi State: An Exceptional State?'* (1989) 1:176 New Left Review 47.

anti-parliamentarism' would unite with the old conservative right in order to tackle 'Marxist socialism (and communism)'. This new right, even 'as it rhetorically lashed out against the parasites of finance or corrupt party politics', moved 'with violence against the major organized opposition to bourgeois institutions'.[76]

Despite its internal differences, a defensive bloc, including liberals and conservatives, would thus be formed against any move towards democratic or revolutionary socialism. 'Disillusioned liberals, traditional conservatives, nationalists, and new right-radicals' all 'converged in their hostility to socialism and the democracy that permitted it to thrive'.[77] Where the social democrats presented only moderate demands, and acquiesced in the economic ideas of the bourgeoisie, inclusive coalitions might form. But where the left presented radical demands, 'alarmed conservatives fought back': they resorted 'either to decentralized but simultaneous boycotts of government bonds and money (as in France), or to concerted political opposition to taxation (as in Germany), or to extralegal coercion (as in Italy)'.[78]

Karl Polanyi's account of the 'great transformation' of the state and market over the long nineteenth century opens up a broader point about the interwar conjuncture. The authoritarian state on which the defence of the interests and ideas of economic liberalism depended made its mark not only in the crisis *response* of the 1920s and 1930s, but in the initial *forging* of the market society across the nineteenth century. The market society was not spontaneous but often planned, and even coercively implemented, using a strong state apparatus, as the bourgeoisie deployed state power to overcome the fetters of the ancient regimes. Laissez-faire was *always* at least partly a myth, not only in its 'new version', with neo-liberalism now often shown to depend on a strong state, but in classical liberalism.[79] And to grasp the power of the state in stabilizing economic liberalism, we need to look not only at its exercise of authority domestically, but also in inter-state and imperial relations.[80]

In Polanyi's account, enforced commodification of labour, land, and money would lead to various spontaneous backlashes, as society tried to protect itself from the harsh consequences of marketization. Commodification was a general feature of economic liberalism, albeit often accelerated through periods of austerity. In reaction to the inequality sustained and exacerbated by the market society, there would be, in Polanyi's terminology, a re-embedding, in order for society to reconstitute itself as a political unity. How this re-embedding might occur is the crucial political-sociological question, following the inevitable crisis of market liberalism and the formal equality on which it is premised. Whereas a democratic society would pursue it through a bottom-up re-formation of political unity and the generation of social solidarity, authoritarian liberal government would attempt to maintain order in a top-down and paternalistic manner, setting aside democratic procedures if necessary. This repression of

76 Maier (n 31) 8.

77 ibid.

78 Maier (n 31) 581.

79 Polanyi, 'The Great Transformation' (n 9) 145–48. On neo-liberalism, see, eg Thomas Biebricher, *The Political Theory of Neo-Liberalism* (Stanford University Press 2018).

80 See, eg Hannah Arendt, The Origins of Totalitarianism (Harcourt 1966) ch 5. See, further, Domenico Losurdo, Liberalism: A Counter-History (Verso 2011); Giavanni Arrighi, Adam Smith in Beijing: Lineages of the Twenty-First Century (Verso 2007).

democracy, considered necessary for the stability and rationality of the system, places an enormous, and potentially overwhelming, stress on the constitutional framework of the sovereign, democratic, and capitalist state.

Polanyi devotes only slight attention to the brief and specific interregnum of authoritarian liberalism in late Weimar, instead sketching the route from market liberalism to outright fascism in diverse contexts and with broad brushstrokes. But he adds a geopolitical dimension to Weimar's decline, explaining the more general role of financialization in the global economy, and the different forms that social re-embedding subsequently took in the manner of the 'double movement'.[81] These movements were generally, albeit unevenly, repressed across different nations, and the manner and severity of their repression conditioned the political outcome.

Presented with the imperative of maintaining the gold standard, Polanyi depicts nation-states in the interwar period as facing a fundamental dilemma, either to maintain sound currency and sound budgets in order to bolster purchasing power, or to improve social conditions by depreciating the currency through higher wages, reduced exports, or deficit spending.[82] The UK and the US responded with protectionism and the New Deal respectively, both suspending the gold standard in time to avoid the perils of fascism, maintaining their status as 'masters not servants of the currency'.[83] With 'golden fetters' removed from monetary and fiscal policy, devaluations could play a positive role in fighting the effects of the Great Depression.[84] A strategy of reasserting sovereign political control over the economy appeared to succeed.[85]

But social democrat parties in Austria in 1923, Belgium and France in 1926, Germany in 1930, and the UK in 1931, were pushed to quit office to 'save the currency'. In these cases, sovereignty had been avoided and politics made submissive to the economy—specifically to the banking sector—able to obstruct any domestic move it happened to dislike. Governments, Polanyi recounts, felt they had to take the advice of bankers, who alone understood the effects of political measures on the capital markets and exchanges.[86] Where conservative governments subsequently reduced social services and tried to 'break the resistance of unions to wage adjustment',[87] the outcome

[81] Polanyi, 'The Great Transformation' (n 9) ch 20. On the complexities of the 'double movement thesis', see Gareth Dale, 'Karl Polanyi's The Great Transformation: Perverse Effects, Protectionism and *Gemeinschaft*' (2008) 37:4 Economy and Society 495–524.

[82] Polanyi, 'The Great Transformation' (n 9) 236

[83] ibid 242 (Roosevelt did so almost immediately on gaining power in 1933). According to Polanyi, the political dispossession of Wall Street by going off gold was the key to preventing the occurrence in the US of a 'social catastrophe of the continental type'. (ibid 238).

[84] See, further, Barry Eichengreen, *Golden Fetters: The Gold Standard and the Great Depression, 1919–1939* (OUP 1992).

[85] Polanyi, 'The Great Transformation' (n 9) appears to ignore his own counsel here, rejecting any local or historical explanations for the situation that gave birth to fascism, 'in reality' insisting that the part it played was determined by one factor: 'the condition of the market system' (ibid 250). In fact, he goes further, blaming not only liberalism's economic system but also its philosophy: 'freedom's utter frustration in fascism, is, indeed, the inevitable result of the liberal philosophy, which claims that power and compulsion are evil, that freedom demands their absence from a human community. No such thing is possible; in a complex society this becomes apparent' (ibid 266). Polanyi also argues that reforms were often rejected by Marxists as merely cosmetic, with orthodox Marxism and economic liberalism sharing the same dogmatic conception of freedom as 'indivisible' (echoing Heller's critique of Marxism in 'Sovereignty' (n 2)). He thus appears to miss the importance of political action (and inaction).

[86] ibid 237

[87] ibid 236.

was social disintegration. In practice, where questions of political organization were subordinated to the needs of currency stability and the maintenance of gold convertibility, states were unable to intervene to alleviate the social situation.

Polanyi summarizes the strength of interwar liberal economic opinion and its obsession with currency stability in a manner that would be strikingly resonant in the euro crisis phase (examined in Part IV):

> [In the 1920s] the stabilization of the currency became the focal point in the political thoughts of peoples and governments; the restoration of the gold standard became the supreme aim of all organized effort in the economic field. The repayment of foreign loans and the return to stable currencies were recognized as the touchstone of rationality in politics; and no private suffering, no restriction of sovereignty, was deemed too great a sacrifice for the recovery of monetary integrity. The privations of the unemployed made jobless by deflation; the destitution of public servants dismissed without a pittance; even the relinquishment of national rights and the loss of constitutional liberties were judged a fair price to pay for the fulfillment of the requirements of sound budgets and sound currencies, these *a priori* of economic liberalism.[88]

And yet, Polanyi notes, governments frequently *had* to intervene in the economy 'in order to reduce prices of monopoly articles, to reduce agreed wage schedules, and to cut rents.' The deflationist's ideal came to be a 'free economy under a strong government', but while the phrase meant what it suggested in terms of an authoritarian government: namely, the use of emergency powers and suspension of public liberties, 'free economy' meant, in practice, the opposite of what it said: namely, governmentally adjusted prices and wages. Economic adjustments were made, however, 'with the express purpose of restoring the freedom of the exchanges and free internal markets.'[89] There was, in other words, a version of militant market economics, where markets are suspended in the short run but only in order to save them in the medium to long run. The upshot of these strategies was that, although free markets had only been temporarily suspended, free government—meaning government that respected political democracy and principles of civil and political rights—had been sacrificed.

Where market liberal ideology was maintained and social democracy repressed in practice, with the market suspended but only in the interests of the ruling class and business elites, the conditions were created for a 'countermovement' of devastating proportions. Authoritarian liberalism had come at the enormous political cost of weakening social bonds, hollowing out the social core of democracy itself, and laying out the path for the fully-fledged fascist dictatorship. In this critical decade, 'the stubbornness with which economic liberals' had supported authoritarian interventionism 'merely resulted in a decisive weakening of the democratic forces which might otherwise have averted the fascist catastrophe'.[90]

[88] ibid 148.
[89] ibid 241.
[90] ibid 242

In the presence of the threat of extreme solutions, any movement towards a socialist response—although 'essentially the tendency inherent in an industrial civilization to transcend the self-regulating market by consciously subordinating it to a democratic society'—was suspected of being aimed towards the revolutionary overthrow of the political system.[91] Such suspicions, Polanyi notes, were liable to throw 'markets into confusion and start a universal panic'.[92] In these conditions, labour and capital, instead of achieving a social compromise, engaged in increasingly conflictual behaviour, eventually threatening the economic and political systems with complete paralysis.[93] And because of the rigid separation of the economic and the political, so central to the ideology of economic liberalism, such conflicts then became potentially grave and radical, immediately threatening social peace and harmony and destabilizing society's political forms. In such a climate of fear, 'the time was ripe for the fascist solution'.[94]

Although it had earlier antecedents in Italy, it was only in the third interwar period, after the crash of 1929, that the 'true significance of fascism became apparent', with the 'deadlock of the market system' which then precipitated the 'conjoint disintegration' of the political and economic system across the world.[95] The reaction to this economic deadlock, whether broken in the form of the New Deal in the US, Soviet collectivism in the 'second' Russian Revolution of the 1930s, British welfarism, or German National Socialism, all constituted the release of 'labour, land and money': the fictitious commodities around which the market society of capitalism was organized from subordination to the price system alone. Although reactions were similar only in discarding laissez-faire principles,[96] where liberals had obstructed social and economic reforms that might involve planning, regulation, or control, 'the victory of fascism was made practically unavoidable'.[97]

The policies of centralized fiscal orthodoxy pursued by the presidential cabinets in late Weimar, characterized by Heller as authoritarian liberal, were a prime example of democratic parliamentary obstruction, but far from the only case. For many 'liberals' of this period across Europe, socialism was perceived to be the greater danger than fascism—either on its own terms, or because of what it was suspected of leading to—justifying the suspension or bypassing of democracy altogether.[98]

[91] ibid 242–43

[92] ibid 243

[93] Ibid 244: 'The captains of industry were subverting the population from allegiance to their freely elected rulers, while democratic bodies carried on warfare against the industrial system on which everybody's livelihood depended. Eventually, the moment would come when both the economic and the political systems were threatened by complete paralysis'.

[94] ibid 244.

[95] Japan, Italy, and Germany 'sabotaging the crumbling institutions of peace, Germany leaving the League of Nations and the gold standard temporarily put out of action by its Anglo-Saxon creators' (ibid 252). Polanyi substantiates this argument by pointing out that, after the initial rise of fascism in the aftermath of the First World War , when, in the first period of fascism (1917 to 1923), government had sought its help to restore law and order, by 1924 to 1929—a period of relative political-economic calm—it had already faded out as a political force.

[96] Polanyi, 'The Great Transformation' (n 9) 252.

[97] ibid 265.

[98] See Karl Loewenstein, 'Autocracy versus Democracy in Contemporary Europe, I' (1935) 29 The American Political Science Review 571.

The erosion of parliamentary democracy and attempted depoliticization of the masses thus extended far beyond Weimar. Despite significant local variations, commonalities abounded, as did the desire to reconstruct economic liberalism on a new foundation. A few brief sketches are illustrative.

Austrian economic liberal Ludwig von Mises proclaimed that fascism, despite its dangers and makeshift nature, would be forever acclaimed for saving the continent from socialism and the attendant dangers to private property. He had approved Engelbert Dollfuss's crushing of labour and socialism in Austria in the 1930s, after its own experiments with democratic socialism, notably in 'Red Vienna'.[99] The Austrian version of 'authoritarian constitutionalism', in the period between 1933 and 1938, began, as Alexander Somek argues, with the 'myth' of the self-elimination of the Austrian parliament, and ended with the 'folk tale' that Austria was the first 'victim' of the Third Reich with the Anschluss in 1938.[100] Austrian interwar authoritarianism maintained structures of government and most of the features of constitutionalism 'with the noteworthy exception of (parliamentary) democracy itself'.[101]

The authoritarian regime of Christian Social chancellor Dollfuss governed on the basis of an emergency law that dated back to 1917, but had been incorporated into the Constitution of 1920, conferring wartime powers to enact economic regulations. His new constitution of 1934, ratified by a parliamentary rump after the banning of the Social Democrats, would combine authoritarian leadership with Christian corporatism. In terms of political ideology, it was explicitly animated by Catholic social philosophy, expressed by Pope Pius XI in his encyclical *Quadragesimo anno*, and the conservative corporatism of Othmar Spann. In Spann's vision, Heller had noted, a centralized power would not emerge through class struggle, from the bottom up, but only from the top down and, in reality, this could 'only mean dictatorship'.[102] It was aggressively anti-socialist in orientation, offering a model that 'subsumed the working class under a social function for the greater benefit of ruling elites'.[103]

In Italy, authoritarian liberals had facilitated the rise to power of Benito Mussolini in the early 1920s, in the hope that fascism would 'restore authority and correct a defective parliamentary system'. Support for fascism would take the form of a belief in 'resisting' the advance of democracy 'in the interests of liberalism'.[104] It fed off

[99] On the significance of von Mises in the relaunching of economic liberalism on the basis of consumer sovereignty, see Niklas Olsen, *The Sovereign Consumer: A New Intellectual History of Neoliberalism* (Palgrave 2019) ch 2. For the failure of Austro-Marxism in the interwar period, see Donald Sassoon, *One Hundred Years of Socialism: The West European Left in the Twentieth Century* (Bloomsbury 2014) 70–73.

[100] Alexander Somek, 'Authoritarian Constitutionalism: Austrian Constitutional Doctrine 1933 to 1938 and its Legacy' in Christian Joerges and Navraj Singh-Ghaleigh (eds), *Darker Legacies of Law in Europe: The Shadow of National Socialism and Fascism over Europe and its Legal Traditions* (Hart Publishing 2003).

[101] ibid 362. Somek adds that it is distinctive in pointing to a goal; in that case, social integration, 'that can only be achieved by authoritarian government'.

[102] Heller, Rechtsstaat (n 3) 139 ('through the means of corporations, workers should be made economically dependent on the dictator and become politically pliant').

[103] Somek (n 100) 375 (distinguishing it from post-war corporatism which seeks reconciliation through government-brokered deals). See, further Eric Voegelin, *The Authoritarian State: An Essay on the Problem of the Austrian State* (University of Missouri Press 1999).

[104] See Denis Mack Smith, 'Benedetto Croce: History and Politics' (1973) 8 Journal of Contemporary History 41 ('In private conversation Croce praised Mussolini as a brilliant politician and applauded 'fervently' the first speech of the fascist leader that he heard. There is nothing to suggest that he saw in fascism the negation of his own liberalism, at least not until it was far too late and the Liberals had helped Mussolini

bourgeois fear: less of a repeat of the Russian Revolution than of a class struggle that could take place through the factory councils and combine into a new hegemonic bloc with organic intellectuals and a revolutionary party, in the manner associated with Antonio Gramsci.[105] Fascism, in the view of Italian liberal thinker Benedetto Croce, was merely 'a bridge for the restoration of a more severe and a more authoritarian liberal regime'.[106] Variations on this position united what Robert Dahl would later label 'theorists of minority domination'—Robert Michels, Wilfredo Pareto, and Gaetano Mosca—who offered various justifications for elite rule.[107]

Corporatism was less advanced in France than in Germany and Italy. It had undergone a more gradual process of industrialization, and its bourgeoisie were less subject to pressures from radical factions.[108] But in 1935, under enabling laws that bypassed ordinary parliamentary debate, the French cabinet of Pierre Laval would also undertake authoritarian measures to avoid devaluation, fight speculation, and save the franc, under extreme constraints placed by the Bank of France to make budget cuts.[109] Laval's government would be replaced shortly after by Leon Blum's Popular Front, which took power along with a wave of strikes and unrest, and undertook its own (short-lived) experiment of 'social reform without revolution'.[110] Laval, who had earlier been a member of the Socialist Party, would collaborate under the Vichy regime, and succeed Philippe Pétain as Prime Minister in 1942, only to be executed by firing squad in 1945. Segments of the French intelligentsia with fascist leanings then looked to France's future as part of an 'authoritarian European order' under

into an invulnerable position. Fascism rather seemed to exemplify his own convictions that, in the interest of liberalism, the advance of democracy should be resisted.'). cf Richard Bellamy, 'Gramsci, Croce, and the Italian Liberal Tradition' (1990) 11:2 History of Political Thought 313.

105 Jan-Werner Müller, *Contesting Democracy: Political Ideas in Twentieth Century Europe* (YUP 2011) 61–63.

106 Bellamy (n 104) 323. As Maier (n 31) puts it: 'from 1920 through 1925, the liberals' attempt to make use of fascism as a force for order ... formed a major theme of Italian politics'. As a matter of constitutional theory, Mortati later presents a cultural 'material constitution', a product of Italian Fascist legal culture that bears some comparison with Gramsci's concept of hegemony, and is influenced by the theories of Schmitt and Heller, as well as the French institutionalists; see Massimo La Torre, 'The German Impact on Fascist Public Law Doctrine: Constantino Mortati's Material Constitution' in Christian Joerges and Navraj Singh-Ghaleigh (eds), *Darker Legacies of Law in Europe: The Shadow of National Socialism and Fascism over Europe and its Legal Traditions* (Hart Publishing 2003) 305–21. See, further, Marco Goldoni and Michael A Wilkinson, 'The Material Constitution' (2018) 81:4 MLR 567.

107 Robert Dahl, *Democracy and its Critics* (YUP 1989). See, for discussion, Hugo Drochon, 'Robert Michels, The Iron Law of Oligarchy, and Dynamic Democracy' (2020) 27 Constellations 185.

108 Sassoon (n 99) 52–53, noting the loss of the proletarian base of the French Socialist Party, and its increasingly reformist practice.

109 Otto Kirchheimer, 'Decree Powers and Constitutional Law in France under the Third Republic' (1940) 34:6 The American Political Science Review 1104. Citing Hauriou and Duguit, Kirchheimer notes that 'the practice of all-embracing delegation incorporated in the more recent French enabling acts was not compatible with the constitutional system in which a strict conception of separation of powers still prevail' (ibid 1117). Kirchheimer concludes that the 'degradation of Parliament to a mechanism recording votes of confidence and authorizing enabling bills only hastens the disintegrating process of parliamentary government as such' (ibid 1123). On the failure of proto-Keynesian policy in France, under pressure to maintain fiscal orthodoxy, see Bradford A Lee, 'The Miscarriage of Necessity and Invention: Proto-Keynesianism and Democratic States in the 1930s' in Peter A Hall (ed), *The Political Power of Economic Ideas: Keynesianism Across Nations* (Princeton University Press 1989).

110 Loewenstein (n 98) 571–93

German hegemony, with a younger generation 'swayed by a technocratic vision of the continent's future organisation'.[111]

4. The foundations of neo-liberalism

In his 1932 address to the German industrial association, the *Langnamverein*, Schmitt distanced himself from laissez-faire as well as from socialism, advocating a 'third form' of 'autonomous economic management'.[112] In this vision, a 'qualitatively total state' would maintain its distance from the 'free economy', upholding the separation of the political and the economic, while showing its strength in the domains of culture and the military.

The address clarified that the real enemy of authoritarian liberalism was less the 'statist' Social Democrats such as Heller than the more radical (if still non-revolutionary) left, which proposed the extension of political freedom into the economic domain and (at least in Kirchheimer's formulation) the politicization of the masses. It was politicization of the working class that might threaten the separation of the political and the economic spheres. If the goal was not (merely) to instrumentalize the social state (as Heller suggested) but to extend democracy to the sphere of *production* as well as distribution, it would radically upend the capitalist state. What Schmitt called for, on the contrary, was a process of *depoliticization*; specifically of the economy, returning to it a degree of relative autonomy, and protecting the sphere of 'the political'. This would be achieved by strong executive power, free from parliamentary interference: what Schmitt called for was the political decision to depoliticize the economy.[113]

To put the point bluntly, it was not only working-class revolution but the democratic road to socialism that liberals and conservatives needed to thwart. Liberal parliamentarism was not up to this task, nor was a liberal philosophy that underplayed the political antagonism of the moment; to that extent, it would be correct to describe Schmitt as anti-liberal. Schmitt's fear of the radical left in Weimar was so debilitating that it 'kept him looking in the wrong direction as the Nazis consolidated their power'.[114]

The authoritarian liberalism of late Weimar would not last long; and Schmitt, as we saw in Chapter 1, quickly adjusted his position accordingly when the Nazis seized

[111] Michael Sutton, *France and the Construction of Europe, 1944–2007* (Bergahn Books 2007) 21–22.

[112] Schmitt, 'Strong State, Sound Economy', reprinted as an appendix in Cristi (n 1). Schmitt does not, however, explain in any detail what this means. According to Cristi, it suggests affinities with a fascistic corporate order. Kelly, on the other hand, sees in it similarities with ordoliberal prescriptions (Duncan Kelly, *The State of the Political: Conceptions of Politics and the State in the Thought of Max Weber, Carl Schmitt and Franz Neumann* (OUP 2003) 253). cf (doubting ordoliberal connections) Christian Joerges, 'What is Left of the European Economic Constitution II? From Pyrrhic Victory to Cannae Defeat' in Poul F Kjær and Niklas Olsen (eds), *Critical Theories of Crisis in Europe: From Weimar to the Euro* (Rowman & Littlefield 2016) 146–47.

[113] To make conceptual sense of the distinction, it might help to consider the French *la politique* (politics) as opposed to *le politique* (the political). The process of depoliticization, in the sense of *politics*, is entirely compatible with a strong insistence on the foundations of the regime in terms of the category of *the political*.

[114] Schupmann (n 41) 36.

power. But the positions of political authoritarianism and economic liberalism that it combined would live on, and be reformulated in diverse contexts.

At the same time as Schmitt was giving his address to the *Langnamverein*, the Freiburg School of ordoliberalism—a group centred around German economist Walter Eucken—was laying its foundations.[115] The ordoliberals shared Schmitt's vehement anti-communism, obsession with order, distrust of economic democracy, and belief in a strong state. Schmitt's motto, 'strong state, sound economy', in fact neatly captures their own distance from the classical liberal idea of the minimal 'nightwatchman' state of the nineteenth century, even as that idea was itself highly misleading.[116] Unlike Schmitt, however, they believed that this could be constructed on an institutional and moral foundation; the economy protected by constitutional law, and a state apparatus guaranteeing rules established in advance, nurtured by a moral culture of scientific expertise, economic stability, and institutions dedicated to maintaining it.

In the 'Ordoliberal Manifesto', published in 1937, the founding fathers of ordoliberalism—Walter Eucken, Franz Böhm, and Hans Grossmann-Doerth—adapted Schmitt's language of the 'comprehensive decision' to their own intellectual programme.[117] The 'economic constitution' (*Wirtschaftsverfassung*) would be described as 'a general political decision [*Gesamtentscheidung*] as to how the economic life of the nation is to be structured'. This new form of economic liberalism would aim to suppress the democratic process, but in a softer manner than Brüning's autocratic version, bringing into effect 'scientific reasoning, as displayed in jurisprudence and political economy' for the 'purpose of constructing and reorganising the economic system'.[118]

Beyond Weimar, a related but distinct variety of economic liberalism, less dependent on, or threatened by, parliamentarism and mass democracy was emerging; one more successful at integrating labour and union leaders, and even attracting a significant part of the left, as well as conservatives and centrists. The political economy of corporatism, which began to evolve across Europe in the 1920s, offered a prospective path towards political stability, signalling not only the erosion of parliamentary democracy but, in Charles Maier's view, 'the growth of private power and the twilight of sovereignty'.[119]

Concurrently with the launch of the Ordoliberal Manifesto, a neo-liberal discourse would also begin to germinate in France. This would reconcile economic liberals, 'disillusioned socialists', and 'opponents of the 1936 experiment' of Leon Blum's

[115] Eucken was professor of economics at the University of Freiburg from 1927 until his death in 1950. On the link between Schmitt and the ordoliberals, see Werner Bonefeld, 'Authoritarian Liberalism: From Schmitt via Ordoliberalism to the Euro' (2017) 43 Critical Sociology 747.

[116] See Neumann, 'Change of Function' (n 32) 22–23.

[117] Franz Böhm, Walter Eucken, and Hans Grossmann-Doerth, 'The Ordo Manifesto of 1936' in Alan T Peacock and Hans Willgerodt (eds), *Germany's Social Market Economy: Origins and Evolution* (Macmillan 1989) 24. Originally published in 1937 as 'Unsere Aufgabe' in Franz Böhm (ed), *Die Ordnung der Wirtschaft* (Kohlhammer 1937). Franz Böhm, *Wettbewerb and Monopolkampf* (Nomosverlag 2010) 120 directly cites Schmitt's idea of the comprehensive decision over the type and form of the political unity. On the depth of Eucken's affinity with Schmitt, see Tribe (n 37) 212.

[118] Böhm, Eucken, and Hans Grossmann-Doerth (n 117) 23.

[119] Maier (n 31) 9.

Popular Front.[120] Pre-eminent among them would be Louis Rougier; professor, political activist, and active promoter of an 'intellectual renewal of economic liberalism'.[121] Rougier, after organizing a French translation of Walter Lippman's *The Good Society*, convened the Lippmann Colloquium in Paris in 1938, bringing together economists, lawyers, senior civil servants, and intellectuals. This hand-picked group included Austrian School economist Ludwig von Mises; two of the architects of the German 'social market economy', Wilhelm Röpke and Alexander Rüstow; Cold War liberals such as Raymond Aron (who would later leave the group in 1960), and Friedrich von Hayek. Hayek, often presented as a more extreme or dogmatic theorist than the ordoliberals, would, in a 1939 publication, sketch the liberal economic consequences of inter-state federalism in a way remarkably prescient for future developments in the EU.[122]

The Walter Lippman Colloquium itself has been described as marking the 'birth' of neo-liberalism, with a 'second birth' occurring a decade later in Switzerland, with the formation of the Mont Pelerin Society in 1947 (with Hayek as a founding member).[123] The colloquium included diverse figures who would come to play a significant political role in post-war resettlement. Jacques Rueff, a French conservative free market economist, strong opponent of Keynesianism, and leading member of the Mont Pelerin Society, who was 'close in spirit to the Ordo theorists', would be called upon in 1958 by De Gaulle to advise on French economic policy, pushing through radical currency reform as well as structuring tariff dismantlement under the EEC.[124] He would later become a judge on the European Court of Justice.[125] Another prominent member was Robert Marjolin, a French economist and politician whose instincts were not economically liberal, but whose initially functionalist views on European integration would extend into the 'new neo-liberalism' of the 1970s and 80s.[126]

[120] François Denord, 'French Neoliberalism and Its Divisions: From the Colloque Walter Lippmann to the Fifth Republic' in Philip Mirowski and Dieter Plehwe (eds), *The Road From Mont Pelerin: The Making of the Neoliberal Thought Collective* (HUP 2015) 46.

[121] ibid.

[122] Friedrich Hayek, 'The Economic Conditions of Inter-state Federalism' in *Individualism and Economic Order* (The University of Chicago Press 1948) 255–72. For similar neo-liberal accounts of federalism, see Wilhelm Röpke, *International Order and Economic Integration* (D Reidel Publishing Company 1959) and Lionel Robbins, *Economic Planning and International Order* (Macmillan and Co Limited 1937). As we will see in Parts II and III, there are clear structural and consequential similarities between Hayek's vision and the EU and EMU.

[123] Thomas Biebricher, *The Political Theory of Neo-Liberalism* (Stanford University Press 2018) 13. On the significance of the Walter Lipmann Colloquium for laying the foundations of neo-liberalism, and emphasizing the 'scalar organization of neoliberal governmentality' see Arnaud Brennetot, 'The Geographical and Ethical Origins of Neoliberalism: The Walter Lippmann Colloquium and the Foundations of a New Geopolitical Order' (2015) 49 Political Geography 30.

[124] Sutton (n 111) 142.

[125] Antoine Vauchez describes Rueff's later vision as one of an 'institutional market', as opposed to laissez-faire: Antoine Vauchez, *Brokering Europe: Euro-lawyers and the Making of a Transnational Polity* (CUP 2015) 56. Arnaud Lechevalier recounts how Rueff has recently been described, accurately, as an 'ordoliberal' (see Arnaud Lechevalier, 'Why and How has German Ordoliberalism Become a French Issue? Some Aspects about Ordoliberal Thoughts we can Learn from the French Reception' in Josef Hien and Christian Joerges (eds), *Ordoliberalism, Law and the Rule of Economics* (Hart Publishing 2017) 24.

[126] Marjolin, a young PhD student at the time (and identified as a Keynesian or even socialist), would be involved in the Marshall Plan, lead the French delegation in the negotiations for the Rome Treaty, and would later be the co-author of the OECD's MacCracken Report of 1977, which while 'mostly modest and warning in its language, first opened the door to the contemporary neoliberalism of the 1980s by arguing for

Rougier initially described the objective of the Lippmann Colloquium as 'an international crusade in favour of *constructive liberalism*'. Although there was significant disagreement among the participants, even on naming their doctrine, some favouring 'individualism', others 'positive liberalism', eventually 'neo-liberalism' became prevalent for 'strategic reasons'.[127] It was meant to connote that 'laissez-faire' was redundant, albeit there remained differences between those who accepted state and regulatory intervention (the German ordoliberals), corporatists, and the more classical liberal or libertarian strands. As Francois Denord puts it, 'At the end of the 1930s, neoliberalism appeared to offer a possible compromise between different factions of the ruling elite trying to safeguard the autonomy of the economic field'.[128]

What also emerged in conjunction with the foundations of neo-liberalism were new ideas of political organization based on scientific management and industrial efficiency, imported into Europe from the United States and perceived as the 'motor of American prosperity'. 'If the 1920s began with the left pressing for democratization of the factory', Maier notes, 'it ended with the right calling for rationalization, Americanism, Fordism, the Bedeaux plan'.[129] Based on the authority of the professional engineer, the progressive businessman, the entrepreneur, and the technician, rather than on class conflict and the authority of political representatives, these schemes were received enthusiastically by parties across the political spectrum. Organized labour would also be integrated into some of these schemes, particularly the neo-corporatist frameworks, even though labour would itself then be seen as 'another form of capital'. US concepts of stable financial international order had buttressed these visions, with material deflationary pressures placed through the international economic system, reinforcing corporatist and bourgeois social settlements.[130]

Although the Second World War put an abrupt end to the neo-liberal ideas germinating in the late 1930s, they would soon be resurrected after the war. In post-war Europe they would represent not only a faith in the price mechanism and the logic of the market, but, ideologically, 'the strength of anticommunism' in the new Cold War.[131] What also appeared to be shared among the various strands of this new liberal 'thought collective', to adopt the term used by Mirowski and Plehwe, was the strong sense that the development of mass society was centrally responsible for the collapse of interwar liberalism. A new order of economic liberalism needed to be constructed that

greater flexibility of capital and labour' (see Hagen Schulz-Forberg, 'Crisis and Continuity: Robert Marjolin, Transnational Policy-making and Neoliberalism, 1930s–70s' (2019) 26 European Review of History 679); cf Katje Seidel, 'Robert Marjolin: Securing the Common Market Through EMU' in Kenneth Dyson and Ivo Maes (eds), *Architects of the Euro: Intellectual in the Making of the European Monetary Union* (OUP 2016) 51 (suggesting that Marjolin's proposals for economic cooperation in the 1960s reflect an 'essentially neo-functionalist outlook on European integration').

[127] Denord (n 120).
[128] ibid 50–51.
[129] Maier (n 31) 583.
[130] Maier (n 31) 590.
[131] Denord (n 120) 52. As Tribe (n 37) 206–07 notes, the 'Social Market Economy' would be 'both geographically and intellectually in the frontline of the struggle against socialism'. But he also notes that the model against which it was originally built was less the Soviet Union than the economic management of Nazi Germany.

could be kept safe from the vicissitudes of democratic politics and parliamentarism, but without raising the spectre of authoritarianism and dictatorship.[132]

The insistence on an economic constitution in order to prevent the cartelization and monopolization of industry that was blamed for the collapse of Weimar is sometimes considered to be an originality of ordoliberalism, distinguishing it from its neo-liberal cousin. A version of this claim could, in essence, have been found in the writings of Franz Neumann.[133] But in complete contrast to Neumann—particularly to his post-war writings—the ordoliberals would identify the domain of freedom not in the political realm, but in the purely private realm of the economy: the freedom to participate in society as an individual agent or consumer.[134] This, crucially, also meant the abolition of class consciousness and class conflict from the political domain. There were, in other words, other routes to depoliticization than through the cult of violence and national redemption offered by the Nazis; there was space for a new liberalism to be constructed on a firmer foundation. Whereas socialism 'had appealed to man as worker from its origins', new European conservative movements of the interwar period 'sought to make social roles outside the sphere of production the major determinants of political allegiance'.[135] The 'New Right' sought to change the terms of debate, appealing to man 'insofar as he was concerned as consumer or as saver about the value of money, as a newspaper reader about the prestige of his nation-state, or even as a commuter about his rights to uninterrupted tram service'.[136] It appealed to the individual not as *Homo faber*, still less a political citizen, but as 'audience man' (a term which would reappear in the form of 'audience democracy' in the 1990s, as we will see in Part III).[137] And, Maier notes, much of the left, sooner or later, followed suit in this economistic turn.[138]

As we will explore in Part II, corporatism, ordoliberalism, and the related tradition of 'social market economy' (coined later by Müller-Armack, early adviser to the Nazi regime, and another Mont Pelerin member), had a powerful political ally in the post-war period, in the form of Christian democracy. This added a further twist in the path of depoliticization: the intertwining of political with religious identities in the formation of confessional parties that opposed the materialism of both 'bourgeois

[132] (Oddný Helgadóttir, 'The Bocconi Boys go to Brussels: Italian Economic Ideas, Professional Networks and European Austerity' (2016) 23 Journal of European Public Policy 392.Italy's post-war liberalism also 'emphasized skepticism of mass politics and the state and preferred markets instead'. Ludwig Einaudi, a renowned European federalist, 'was an active member of the transnational liberal networks that established Colloque Lippman (1938) and the Mont Pelerin Society (1947), both of which played a crucial role in the formation of modern neoliberalism' (ibid 397).

[133] Neumann, 'On the Preconditions' (n 19). In conditions of monopoly capitalism (which was a natural progression from competitive capitalism), the case for the generality of law was an absurdity for Neumann. To deal with the emergence of monopolies in the economy, a strong, interventionist state was required, in order to pursue a positive principle of equality. Neumann, in this way, has been interpreted as apparently offering a 'very particular development and modification of Schmitt's position' on the qualitatively total state. Both seemed to concur that democracy and liberalism had to be 'disentangled' (Kelly (n 112) 272).

[134] Franz Neumann, 'The Concept of Political Freedom' (1953) 53:7 Columbia Law Review 901. Ordoliberalism is discussed further in Chapter 3.

[135] Maier (n 31) 584.

[136] ibid 585.

[137] See, especially, Chapter 8.

[138] Maier (n 31) 586.

liberalism' and 'atheistic Marxism'.[139] Varieties of neo-liberalism and Christian democracy were able to coalesce ideologically in their opposition to socialism, and even to form a transnational hegemonic bloc that would prove far more stable than any liberal political movement in the interwar era.

In the German context, the success attributed to Ludwig Erhard and Leonard Miksh for the currency reform and abolition of price controls (the *Leitsätzegesetz*) in 1948 (after a decade of rationing) gave the ordoliberal ideology and social market economy the credibility to establish a myth through which economic planning and a socially guided economy could be denounced.[140] The formidable force of Christian democracy, corporatism, ordoliberalism, and social market economy would later also be able to combine with a moderated social democracy to pursue various constitutional and political compromises. The German SPD's own post-1959 modernization programme, complete renunciation of Marxist class struggle, and acceptance of free market principles and the project of European integration (after initial opposition), reflected a more general revisionism of social democracy across Europe.

In retrospect, Social Democrats such as Heller had appeared to be directly and deeply conflicted about the possibility of change towards a socialist system within the liberal constitutional order.[141] Heller was clear that liberals such as Kelsen and conservatives like Schmitt aimed to repress (in their very different ways) the concept of popular sovereignty as a revolutionary constituent power; as a power which might emerge to overturn the inter-state, state-society, and social relations of the liberal constitutional imagination. Heller's own position, however, was ambivalent: insisting on popular sovereignty, but within the confines of the existing constitutional settlement, and without a belief in the working class as an agent of revolutionary (or even reformist) change, in line with a broader culture in the SPD that 'was wary of . . . the "spontaneity" of the working class'.[142] The upshot of interwar collapse for many socialists was the abandonment not only of revolutionary socialism, but of democratic socialist ideals altogether. This widespread reformism, as we will see in Part II, would be bolstered in the post-war period by a deradicalization of Western communist parties, particularly in the later turn to 'Eurocommunism'.

[139] Carlo Invernizzi Accetti, *What is Christian Democracy? Politics, Religion and Ideology* (CUP 2019) ch 1. cf Stathis N Kalyvas, *The Rise of Christian Democracy in Europe* (Cornell University Press 1996).

[140] Rudolph Ptak, 'Neoliberalism in Germany: Revisiting the Ordoliberal Foundations of the Social Market Economy' in Philip Mirowski and Dieter Plehwe (eds), *The Road from Mont Pelerin: The Making of the Neoliberal Thought Collective* (HUP 2009); Tribe (n 37) 209 (comparing them to 'prophets for the new Germany').

[141] In retrospect, Neumann also rejected the possibility that the Weimar Constitution offered a path towards democratic socialism, describing the 'so-called revolution of November 1918' as 'no real revolution but only the collapse of the monarchy' (Franz L Neumann, 'The Decay of German Democracy' in William E Scheuermann (ed), *The Rule of Law under Siege: Selected Essays of Franz L Neumann and Otto Kirchheimer* (University of California Press 1996) 30). And, in an intriguing later 'contrast and compare' of Heller and Harold Laski, Neumann insisted that Heller (to his detriment) rejected the Marxist theory of the state. Neumann added, dismissively, that 'in Heller's book one can read on every page the German idealistic philosophy which constitutes its origins' (see Franz L Neumann, 'On the Marxist Theory of the State' in Keith Tribe (ed), *Social Democracy and the Rule of Law: Otto Kirchheimer and Franz L Neumann* (Allen & Unwin 1987) 83).

[142] Jay (n 16).

Throughout the postwar period, the authority of parliamentarism would steadily decline, with political power shifting structurally towards the executive, judicial, and administrative branches of government. This process would culminate in a so-called 'state-party cartel', theorized by Neumann's Frankfurt School compatriot, Otto Kirchheimer, an aspect of a phenomenon later described as 'constrained democracy' or, in more critical vein, the 'hollowing out' of democracy (examined in Part III). With a growing consensus around a moderate capitalism, 'political problems' would be 'transformed into ostensibly non-political, technical, administrative issues, so that the essentially political questions of power and inequality are expunged effectively from political discourse'.[143] After 1945, bourgeois Europe did not cease to exist, but it 'faded from concern'.[144] 'Stratification, inequality, and corporatist power remained', but, unlike in the interwar era, few sought to abolish them.[145]

Economic liberalism would be stabilized in the post-war era in a depoliticized form, in less coercive fashion than in late Weimar, and without the need to turn to conservative nationalist forces for support. It would be able to draw from the benefits of Cold War superpower rivalry, global economic growth, various corporate and class compromises, and the scaling up of political-technical authority in the process of European integration. It would be based, in part, as we will now examine, on a more subtle, passive authoritarianism, deriving its sustenance from a fear of collective self-government, of sovereignty, and of democratic freedom; a fear that grew in part from a dominant, but misleading, narrative of interwar decline.

143 Peter Cocks, 'Towards a Marxist Theory of European Integration' (1980) 34 International Organization 9, 26.

144 Maier (n 31) 14.

145 ibid 15.

PART II

POST-WAR EUROPE

The Reconstitution of Inter-State, State-Society and Social Relations

If the linchpin of the European constitutional state of the 'long nineteenth century' was the idea of sovereignty in domestic and international affairs, political authority based on the constituent power of 'the people', and a liberal market economy, this framework—and each of its pillars—was placed under interminable pressure in the interwar period (as outlined in Part I). The *jus publicum europeaum* had ended, constituent power had imploded, and economic liberalism had failed. The sovereign democratic and capitalist state and state system in Europe would need to be reconstituted on a new foundation, in material conditions quite different from those which had given rise to it.

The reconstitution of post-war Europe would be a formidable task, as well as a complex and uneven one. Three guiding threads are distinguished here and elaborated in turn. First, the framework of *interstate relations* as well as the myth of the state would be reconstructed on a new basis of *restrained sovereignty*, most evidently in the defeated nations, and in those whose descent into fascism had been most marked and most destructive: Germany and Italy. In France and the Benelux countries too, the need for a new type of regional internationalism was apparent, specifically to tie Germany to a European future and a peaceful post-war recovery. With the failure of the federalist project of European unification, what emerges instead is a patchwork system of external constraints on the exercise of sovereign powers, pursued through the Council of Europe, with the creation of regional human rights instruments, such as the European Convention on Human Rights, and the Community institutions and trade agreements of the Treaty of Paris in 1951, consolidated and extended by the Treaty of Rome in 1957.[1] This occurs in the shadow of the Cold War, the heat of US involvement in post-war reconstruction through the Marshall Plan, and a new imperialism heralded by the growing hegemony of its project of global capitalism.[2] In the regional resettlement of Europe, inter-state relations between 'the founding six'

[1] The 'Treaty of Rome' refers to the EEC and Euratom Treaties, making three distinct entities along with the European Coal and Steel Community established in Paris.

[2] See Leo Panitch and Sam Gindin, *The Making of Global Capitalism* (Verso 2012); on 'Americanization from above', see Philipp Gassert, 'The Spectre of Americanization: Western Europe in the American Century' in Dan Stone (ed), *The Oxford Handbook of Postwar European History* (OUP 2012).

gradually come to resemble domestic more than external affairs. External state sovereignty is restrained, but without being scaled up to the supranational level.

Second, *state-society relations* would be reconstituted through a process of internal depoliticization. European elites attributed the collapse of interwar liberal democracy to over-politicization, to a crisis of democracy rather than of capitalism.[3] The message that resonated was a modified version of Karl Loewenstein's plea for a 'militant democracy'.[4] What this meant was that liberal constitutionalism must fight harder for its own survival, and protect itself *from* democracy if necessary. 'Militant liberalism' would, therefore. be a more accurate characterization, expressing concern for the supposedly anti-liberal and even tyrannical tendencies of an unrestrained majoritarianism. Constitutional scholarship turns away from concern for the social-economic *causes* of the interwar collapse, and focuses its attention on the *consequences* of the constitutional breakdown, particularly in the German case. The conclusions it draws are curiously Schmittian: the Weimar constitution was not defended militantly enough; its substantive provisions were too ambitious; legal positivism is sometimes blamed; what was needed was stronger constitutionalism, with more rigid checks and balances.

Legal scholarship would not look to presidentialism or plebiscitary dictatorship as a means of constitutional defence, but to judicial guarantees of fundamental rights and human dignity, and a more robust ideological anti-positivism.[5] The anti-positivist shift is just as pronounced in constitutional as in legal theory, and of more practical moment for the institutional analysis and concrete institution-building that accompanies it. To put it crudely, the masses were not trusted to maintain liberal democratic institutions without the strong moral guidance of constitutional and political elites.[6] Whilst there was also an element of collective self-distrust, and the desire for collective self-commitment to liberal values, exemplified in the German case, the key constitutionalist programmes were elite-led and elite-managed. This was nowhere more evident than in the project of European integration, culminating in a 'constitutionalism without a constitution', a legal constitutional doctrine but without political constitutional support, but it was, as we will examine, a process that integrated national and supranational orders.[7] Through this process, a soft authoritarianism emerges,

[3] See, eg Jan-Werner Müller, *Contesting Democracy* (YUP 2011). This is particularly the case with the ordoliberals. As we will also discuss below, this perception of crisis persists even in the response of 'critical theorists' such as Jürgen Habermas to the legitimation crisis of the 1960s and 1970s.

[4] See Karl Loewenstein, 'Militant Democracy and Fundamental Rights, I' (1937) *31* American Political Science Review 417; 'Autocracy versus Democracy in Contemporary Europe, I' (1935) *29* American Political Science Review 571 (which was, itself, a modified version of Carl Schmitt's constitutional theory, as we examined in Chapter 2).

[5] This post-war turn is closely associated with both US and West German post-war constitutional discourse. The focus here is on Europe, but for some comparisons, see Michaela Hailbronner, *Tradition and Transformations: The Rise of German Constitutionalism* (OUP 2015); and, on the synergies between them, Jacco Bomhoff, *Balancing Constitutional Rights* (CUP 2013). On the US influence on the German Basic Law, see Rande Kostal, *Laying Down the Law: American Legal Revolutions in Occupied Germany and Japan* (HUP 2020).

[6] See, eg Christoph Möllers, 'We are (Afraid of) the People: Constituent Power in German Constitutional Discourse' in Martin Loughlin and Neil Walker (eds), *The Paradox of Constitutionalism: Constituent Power and Constitutional Form* (OUP 2007).

[7] See Joseph HH Weiler, *The Constitution of Europe: 'Do the New Clothes have an Emperor?' and other Essays on European Integration* (CUP 1999). On the synthesis between national and supranational orders, see John Erik Fossum and Agustin José Menéndez, *The Constitution's Gift* (Rowman & Littlefield 2011).

repressing popular sovereignty, parliamentarism, and the democratic ethos itself, in favour of a hierarchical system of authority with deference to technical expertise.

Third, democracy is reconfigured through a new constitutional imaginary, a vision of *social relations* based on individual economic freedom. The restoration of economic stability would require the repair and restructuring of economies laid to waste as a result of the Second World War, and the imperatives of capital accumulation and advancing corporate interests would require suppression of the claims of radical socialist forces, emboldened throughout the war by their involvement in the resistance movements.[8] The fear was not only a repeat of the uncoordinated protectionism that characterized national response to the depression of the 1930s and proved so regionally (as well as globally) catastrophic, but also, from a liberal perspective, how to forestall the prospect of democratic (as well as revolutionary) socialism that had briefly surfaced in the interwar period.[9] The presence of the Soviet Union and strong communist parties within Europe may well have had a tempering effect on economic inequality, moderating the excesses of capitalist democracy during the Cold War period. But from a constitutional perspective, the mixed political economy based loosely on a coupling of ordoliberalism and social market economy (and other variants of Christian democracy) would come to signify a broader ideological shift: a new economic constitution based not on laissez-faire, but on strong rules and institutions. European integration played a key part in contributing to this new arrangement of law and political economy, providing the institutional architecture and aspirational ideology to support it. Although this would take several decades to fully mature, its foundations were laid in the 1950s (and based on ideas that had been germinating from the early 1930s).

In the quest for the reconstitution of Europe after the Second World War, three key interconnected questions therefore emerge, relating respectively to state sovereignty, political authority, and socio-economic relations. These involved more specific material goals: how to resolve the 'German question' (to stabilize power relations in central Europe and prevent a return of German hegemony); how to prevent domestic descent into political extremism, and how to stabilize the European (and world) economic system.

In each case the motive is to restore and maintain a liberal political and economic order after its interwar breakdown. The task was to reconstruct the constitutional state in such a way that it would be able to suppress popular sovereignty and democratic

[8] Communist parties were particularly strong in Italy and France (in 1951 the Italian Communist Party had attained 37 per cent and the French Communist Party 29 per cent of the vote) as well as Czechoslovakia (with 38 per cent of the vote in 1946). Even the German SPD initially viewed socialism as Europe's future, its first program in 1946 supporting a 'democratic and socialist federation of European states', although it soon changed course, by the late 1950s accepting the German version of capitalist compromise advocated by ordoliberals and Christian democrats: a 'social market economy'. See Thomas Risse and Daniela Engelmann-Martin, 'Identity Politics and European Integration: The Case of Germany' in Anthony Pagden (ed), *The Idea of Europe: From Antiquity to the European Union* (CUP 2002) 298–300. Udi Greenberg notes that this marked an 'ideological reversal' for the SPD, and notes the additional significance of the SPD's embrace of NATO by 1960 (Udi Greenberg, *The Weimar Century: German Emigres and the Ideological Foundations of the Cold War* (Princeton University Press 2014) 76–77)).

[9] It is notable that Britain's own membership occurs in the period of so-called 'ungovernability', when Tony Benn—who, as Secretary of State for Industry, had offered a programme of democratic socialism—led the campaign for a Leave vote in the 1975 referendum, on the basis that membership would frustrate its achievement.

excesses (associated with aggressive nationalism and economic protectionism), which were credited with the interwar collapse.[10] If the influence of 'militant democracy' was apparent, for reasons already hinted at, but developed further below, militant democracy is a seriously misleading expression for this new constitutional settlement because it is, in a significant sense, *reactionary*: it is constructed in reaction, and opposition, to the forces of mass democratization and class consciousness that were unleashed in the interwar period.[11]

This reactionary aspect of post-war reconstitution is overlooked in much of the literature because so often the story of European integration begins from ground zero—a *Stunde Null* of post-war devastation—as if the scene were to be restaged from scratch after the catastrophe of the Second World War and the experience of Nazism and fascism. As a result, vague platitudes are offered in the literature, suggesting, for example, that European integration and the post-war settlement were based on ideals of 'peace and prosperity', as if these were capable of providing a distinctive constitutional *telos*.[12] All but the immediate past is largely erased as an explanatory background, suppressed by a 'rhetoric of peace, reconciliation and anti-communism', as a new threat from the East quickly emerges in the post-war liberal imagination.[13]

The point to be emphasized is that there is no *Stunde Null*, no *creatio ex nihilo*.[14] As Hannah Arendt reported, there was no new beginning or revolutionary rupture, even in post-war Germany, which had experienced the most dramatic descent into the horrors of Nazism.[15] The constitutional technologies and ideas that are developed; designed to discipline and domesticate democracy, to avoid the perceived danger of it turning towards extremism of the left or right, derive in part from a reactionary imagination, not only to the historical experience of fascism but—something that is underplayed in the literature—the perceived threat of democratic socialism. This conforms

[10] See, eg Wilhelm Röpke, *International Economic Disintegration* (William Hodge & Co 1942).

[11] On the general significance of the concept, see Jan-Werner Müller, 'Militant Democracy' in Michel Rosenfeld and András Sajó (eds), *The Oxford Handbook of Comparative Constitutional Law* (OUP 2012). As we noted at the end of Chapter 2, this radical scepticism of mass democracy united members of the 'neoliberal thought collective'.

[12] cf Weiler (n 7), who, as mentioned in Chapter 1, notes that democracy was not uppermost in the minds of the 'founding fathers' of Europe, but never explores *why* that was the case, or with what consequences (and later laments the undemocratic nature of the project as decisive in its legitimacy problem).

[13] See Hauke Brunkhorst, 'Collective Bonapartism—Democracy in the European Crisis' (2014) 15 German Law Journal 1177.

[14] On the difficulties faced in attempting to begin with a blank slate, through a process of legal de-Nazification, see RW Kostal, 'The Alchemy of Occupation: Karl Loewenstein and the Legal Reconstruction of Nazi Germany 1945–1946' (2011) 29 Law and History Review 1. This only scratches the surface of the more general difficulties of de-Nazification in the social and economic-industrial spheres. Also significant in regard to the project of integration is the rehabilitation of Hans Peter Ipsen; see Christian Joerges, 'Europe: A Grossraum: Shifting Legal Conceptualisations of the Integration Project' in Christian Joerges and Navraj Singh-Ghaleigh, *Darker Legacies of Law In Europe* (Hart Publishing 2003). On the perceived continuities between the Third Reich and the Federal Republic, see Hans Kundnani, *Utopia or Auschwitz: Germany's 1968 Generation and the Holocaust* (OUP 2009).

[15] Hannah Arendt, 'The Aftermath of Nazi Rule: Report from Germany' in *Essays in Understanding 1930–1954* (Schocken Books 1994) 249 ('The reintroduction of truly free enterprise meant handing over the factories and the control of economic life' to a German business class, 'who … had been staunch supporters of the regime for all practical purposes' and, thus, regained 'their old power over the working class—that is, the only class in Germany which … had never been wholeheartedly Nazi'.)

with a myth of interwar breakdown,[16] which, occluding the authoritarian liberalism of late Weimar, presents the Nazi seizure of power as a fully democratic transition, and identifies moral relativism and legal positivism, in combination with political tolerance and legislative supremacy, as responsible for democratic decay.[17]

In the conceptual schema outlined in Part I, the post-war constitution re-differentiates the relationship between the political and the economic, through reorganization of the international and domestic, state and society, and public and private spheres. Inter-state, intra-state and interpersonal relations are increasingly, albeit unevenly, *depoliticized* (more precisely in the sense of being *de-democratized*). The role of European integration, as pursued through the Treaties of Paris and Rome, is to separate the political domain from the economic by establishing technocratic and juridical mechanisms of market integration, problem-solving, regulation and conflict resolution. This is pursued by laying down the foundations for a common European market, motivated by classical economic imperatives of attaining efficiency through competition, now guarded by new non-democratic institutions. It begins with the removal of tariffs and quotas in the aim of establishing a common market, and progresses to include the elimination of non-tariff barriers and harmonization of technical standards, with the aim of creating an internal market in which undistorted competition would flourish, including through the application of rules against state subsidies.[18] Overall, democracy is restrained not for the purpose of maintaining a strong democratic ethos, which appears a contradictory notion, but for the purpose of promoting economic liberalism. It is, properly understood, authoritarian in character. But it is an authoritarianism based on an eclipse of political freedom that has a class character as well as a socio-psychological dimension; it is not only that elites fear and distrust the people, but also that the people fear and distrust themselves.[19] This eclipse of political freedom is, as we will examine, captured by the substitution of constitutional rights for constituent power, the decline of parliamentarism and the rise of administration, the transition from mass democracy to the professionalization of politics, and the displacement of the citizen for the icon of the consumer.[20]

This Part unfolds as follows: Chapter 3 details the new regional geopolitics of inter-state relations, the interdependence of internal and external domains of state action, and the change in the abstract meaning of sovereignty it entails.[21] Materially, inter-state

[16] Clara Maier, 'The Weimar Origins of the West German *Rechtsstaat*, 1919–1969' (2019) 62 The Historical Journal 1069.

[17] For an earlier busting of this myth, see Michael Mandel, 'A Brief History of the New Constitutionalism, or "How we Changed Everything so that Everything Would Remain the Same"' (1998) 32 Israeli Law Review 250.

[18] Stefano Bartolini, *Restructuring Europe: Centre Formation, System Building and Political Structuring between the Nation State and the EU* (OUP 2005) 180–181.

[19] The notion that a 'fear of freedom' underpins the turn to interwar authoritarianism is explored as a social psychological phenomenon in the work of Erich Fromm; see *The Fear of Freedom* (2nd edn, Routledge 2001 [originally published 1941]). As a transition in the fortunes of the concept of constituent power, see Christoph Möllers, '"We are (Afraid of) the People": Constituent Power in German Constitutionalism' in Martin Loughlin and Neil Walker (eds), *The Paradox of Constitutionalism: Constituent Power and Constitutional Form* (OUP 2007) 87–107.

[20] Herbert Marcuse, *One-Dimensional Man: Studies in the Ideology of Advanced Industrial Society* (Taylor and Francis 2013).

[21] As Cowen and Smith argue, geopolitics was never only about a state's external relations, but involved a more encompassing 'geopolitical social' that both crosses and crafts the distinction between inside

relations in Europe are reconstituted through extraneous factors of Cold War superpower rivalry, as well as through the project of European integration. This is supported by domestic developments, with constitutional commitments to internationalism and Europeanism detaching state sovereignty from popular sovereignty. Through its functionalist ideology (Schumann's 'de facto solidarity'), institutional set-up (voting weights, independent institutions, Luxembourg veto), and de-politicization by juridical avenues (eg, by formalizing non-retaliation between states), European integration makes a significant contribution to the idea of sovereign restraint. The seeds of a European 'federation' are sown by the suspension of sovereignty over the economy, but warfare and welfare, along with the power of taxation, remain formally with states, and outside any federal arrangement. This produces an inconclusive picture of its political form, from the perspective of constitutional theory.[22]

Chapter 4 tracks the development of a new political constitutionalism through the substitution of constitutional rights for constituent power. This substitution, and the transformation in state-society relations it signals, has international and European, as well as domestic, dimensions, which are themselves interrelated. It contributes significantly to the narrative of domestic depoliticization, in combination with a demobilization of the masses, and a deradicalization of parties of the left. The turn to law, and to lawyers as constitution-builders, is captured by a number of movements and metaphors: 'sovereignty of law', 'integration through law', 'constitutional supremacy', 'juridification', 'legal constitutionalisation', 'juristocracy', and so on.[23] These movements begin before the sharper turn to neo-liberal de-democratization starting in the 1980s, which will be considered in the Part III. The transformation of political problems into technical or legal issues, along with the decline of parliamentarism as a touchstone of political legitimacy, and the constitutionalisation of the Treaties by the ECJ, was facilitated (and opposition to it disarmed) due to the relatively high levels of economic growth during the *Trente Glorieuses*. This permitted a welfare corporatism to complement the constitution of a soft authoritarian liberalism.

In Chapter 5, the political economy of this constitutional turn is traced, by examining the re-foundation of economic liberalism after its demise in the interwar period, especially through the influence of ordoliberalism and neo-liberalism in the constitutional imagination. This is practically tempered because of the impact of social and Christian democratic ideas, the realpolitik of a programme of social market economy, and the process of European economic integration itself (a mixed assemblage of economic liberalism, 'planning for competition', and agricultural subsidies). But the economic constitution is entrenched along with the 'end of ideology' in Europe, as even notionally communist parties turn towards the political mainstream and rescind any

and outside national state borders; see Deborah Cowen and Neil Smith, 'After Geopolitics? From the Geopolitical Social to Geo-Economics' (2009) 41 Antipode 22. On the representation of this phenomenon as 'late sovereignty' in the European Union, see Neil Walker, 'Introduction' in Neil Walker (ed), *Questioning Sovereignty* (Hart Publishing 2004).

[22] cf Signe Larsen, *The Constitutional Theory of the Federation and the European Union* (OUP 2021) (making a compelling case for understanding the EU as a federation from the outset of the Rome Treaty).

[23] I refer to this type as 'freestanding constitutionalism'; see Michael A Wilkinson, 'Political Constitutionalism and the European Union' (2013) 76 Modern Law Review 191.

revolutionary ambitions, long before the end of history is proclaimed in the aftermath of the fall of the Soviet Union.[24] The economic constitution does not signify the triumph of liberal democracy, but of technocratic managerialism, establishing a path that would be deepened at Maastricht, and then pursued more aggressively still in the euro crisis phase, when it also comes up against semi-serious opposition (dealt with in Parts III and IV, respectively).

[24] The alleged 'end of ideology too' is a much earlier phenomenon, predating the era commonly referred to as neo-liberal. See Daniel Bell, *The End of Ideology: On the Exhaustion of Political Ideas in the Fifties* (HUP 2000 [originally published 1960]). Robert Dahl calls this the new democratic 'Leviathan'; see Robert Dahl, 'Epilogue' in Robert Dahl (ed), *Political Oppositions in Western Democracies* (YUP 1966). On the connection between the end of ideology and the project of European integration, see, eg Peter Cocks, 'Towards a Marxist Theory of European Integration' (1980) 34 International Organization 9, 26.

3

Restraining State Sovereignty: Imagining a 'European Germany'

1. Introduction

A key geopolitical question in post-war Europe was how to constrain Germany to prevent its re-emergence as a militarily or politically hegemonic central European power. This concern was based on distrust—felt particularly keenly in France, for obvious historical reasons—of German state sovereignty.[1] But fear of German hegemony was a domestic issue on the part of the ruling elites in Germany too, captured by Michael Mann's plea to avoid the nightmare of a 'German Europe', and to realize the dream of a 'European Germany'.[2]

On the international canvas, the significance of European powers was, however, fading. The 'German question' was thus to some extent displaced during the period from the Treaty of Paris (1951) until the Treaty of Maastricht (1992) due to factors beyond the European sphere of influence: the division of Germany in the context of the Cold War, the wider impact of the US-led reconstruction through the Marshall Plan, and the collapse (and reinvention) of European colonial ambitions.[3] Germany in this period has been described as 'semi-sovereign', a status more broadly and materially shared by other former European powers, but a special feature of Germany's post-war constitutional identity.[4]

We will first examine this status of semi-sovereignty in more detail, along with the Franco-German relationship so central to its development, in order to situate European integration in a regional geopolitical perspective (section 2), before turning to the 'supranational compromise' itself, where sovereignty is more generally

[1] See, eg Mette Eilstrup-Sangiovanni and Daniel Verdier, 'European Integration as a Solution to War' (2005) 11 European Journal of International Relations 99.

[2] For discussion, see Thomas Risse and Daniela Engelmann-Martin, 'Identity Politics and European Integration: The Case of Germany' in Anthony Pagden (ed), *The Idea of Europe: From Antiquity to the European Union* (CUP 2002).

[3] See Peo Hansen and Stefan Jonsson, 'Building Eurafrica: Reviving Colonialism through European Integration', 1920–1960' in Kalypso Nicolaidis, Berny Seby, and Gabrielle Maas (eds), *Echoes of Empire: Memory, Identity, and Colonial Legacies* (IB Tauris 2015).

[4] Peter Katzenstein, *Policy and Politics in West Germany: The Growth of a Semisovereign State* (Temple University Press 1987), focussing on the domestic aspects of semi-sovereignty, which are explored in Chapter 4. Although the term 'semi-sovereign' was developed by Katzenstein, he notes that its provenance is older (adapted 'from one of the classics of American political science', Elmer E Schattschneider, *The Semisovereign People: A Realist's View of Democracy in America* (Holt, Rinehart and Winston 1965)), the term referring to an analysis of American political institutions and organizations as a mobilization of specific class bias; a 'heavenly chorus' that 'sings with a strong upper-class accent'. In fact, the term was already used by Heller in 1927, in Hermann Heller and David Dyzenhaus, *Sovereignty: A Contribution to the Theory of Public and International Law* (OUP 2019) 161, in discussion in international law of dependent polities, vassal states, or member states of a federation.

Authoritarian Liberalism and the Transformation of Modern Europe. Michael A Wilkinson, Oxford University Press.
 DOI: 10.1093/oso/9780198854753.003.0004

restrained in the 'founding six' members of the EEC, without being reconstructed at a supra-state level (section 3).

2. A semi-sovereign state at the heart of Europe

In the immediate post-war period Germany was not a fully sovereign nation, but divided into East and West under the auspices of the Cold War superpower rivalry, and controlled from without by foreign occupation.[5] The Cold War dynamic gradually changed the emphasis of the German question: from the US perspective it became less a question of preventing German domination of Europe, and more a question of ensuring Germany's ability to act as a bulwark to Soviet expansion. A weak Germany rather than a strong one might be more problematic from this newly emerging Cold War perspective.[6]

After NATO was formed in 1949 through the signature of the North Atlantic Treaty (with France and Italy among its founding members), the United States became the driving force of Western European rearmament; a process which accelerated with the Korean War, placing increasing pressure on European states both in terms of remilitarization and economic reconstruction. Obligations imposed by NATO extended deep into the economic life of its members. For those requiring economic assistance, significant conditions were attached to aid. This was combined with the broader effects of the Marshall Plan, coordinated by the Office of European Economic Co-operation (OEEC). The OEEC was established by treaty in 1948, serving economic reconstruction and trade liberalization as well as the geopolitical ends of stabilizing European liberal democracy against any movement towards socialism.[7] This coordination involved an extraordinary amount of political-economic planning from above, 'an event without precedent in history—the first effort of European states to engage in economic planning on a European scale'.[8] Such planning required detailed examination of existing assets and logistical assessment for regaining economic stability for each of the sixteen nations involved, and across Europe as a whole.[9] Without this aid, bankruptcy in Europe could well have followed—and quite possibly communism too—with all the implications for trade with the US and geopolitical reversals that would have entailed.[10] Marshall had publicly declared that if the Italian Communist Party

[5] In Simon Bulmer and William E Paterson, *Germany and the European Union: Europe's Reluctant Hegemon?* (Red Globe Press 2018) 22–25, the authors describe the period from 1949, when the Federal Republic was created, until 1955, when the Occupation Statute ended, as the 'pre-sovereign' period. On the US influence on post-war legal reconstruction in Germany (and Japan), see Rande Kostal, *Laying Down the Law* (HUP 2019).

[6] As van Middelaar puts it, 'Washington made it clear that the German question took second place to the struggle against the Soviet Union' (Luuk van Middelaar, *Passage to Europe: How the Continent Became a Union* (Yale University Press 2013) 139–40).

[7] See Paul Sweezy, 'Is the Marshall Plan an Instrument of Peace?' (1949) 1 Monthly Review 80.

[8] Karl Loewenstein, 'The Union of Western Europe: Illusion and Reality I. An Appraisal of the Methods' (1952) 52 Columbia Law Review 55, 82.

[9] The sixteen nations were Britain, France, Italy, Belgium, Luxembourg, the Netherlands, Denmark, Norway, Sweden, Switzerland, Greece, Turkey, Ireland, Iceland, Austria, and Portugal.

[10] See Tony Judt, *Postwar: A History of Europe Since 1945* (Pimlico 2007) 93–99.

were elected to power, Italy would be excluded.[11] Even the creation of a Common Market itself was considered an important feature of the transatlantic bulwark against the spread of communism—not only from outside Europe but from the internal threat of communist parties—as well as a vehicle for restraining German ambitions by tying Germany into a European future.[12]

Whatever its precise material significance for economic reconstruction, the Marshall Plan clearly signalled the complete suspension of sovereignty over trade, as participating states were subjected to controls over their economic life by both the OEEC and the US government, to an extent 'incompatible with the nature of the sovereign state'.[13] Under the subsequent Mutual Security Act, interference in domestic affairs was even greater; the receiving state frequently having to subscribe 'to the American principles of decartelization, free trade and the promotion of free enterprise,'[14] as well as a prohibition on those selling strategic material to the Eastern bloc. This was a high-intensity example of 'planning for laissez-faire', as Polanyi had detailed in an earlier age of enforced market liberalization from above, and would prefigure the type of change that would eventually be institutionalized through the creation of the European Coal and Steel Community (ECSC), and then extended through the Common Market by the founding six.

The broader perception was that the classical European nation state was no longer fully in control of its own destiny: 'dwarfed by the United States and the Soviet Union', the European state system was, 'for the first time since the seventeenth century, firmly embedded in an international order dominated by others'.[15] If the European state, 'born of international threat and internal mobilisation', had finally become a civilian state, confirming 'Schumpeter's pacific image of the bourgeois political order', the sterilization of high politics and its bureaucratic insulation was reinforced because the entire field of international relations was dominated by the US.[16] This reflected a large-scale material and ideological reconfiguration of international power.

The abdication of sovereignty by European states was made clear not only through their acceptance of the economic and political planning demanded by the US; it was clearly borne out in concrete terms by US geopolitical power, exemplified by the pressure that drove the resolution of the Suez crisis, humbling the pretensions of the United Kingdom and France to foreign policy autonomy and signposting a postcolonial future for regions previously under European control.[17] The decline of European

[11] Alan Milward, *The European Rescue of the Nation-State* (Routledge 2000) 332. De Gasperi, founder of the Christian Democratic Party and first Prime Minister of the Italian Republic, also saw a Western European bloc as the 'spiritual rampart against the ideological assault of Communism' (ibid 333).

[12] See Wolfram Kaiser, *Christian Democracy and the Origins of the European Union* (CUP 2007) 199.

[13] Karl Loewenstein, 'Sovereignty and International Cooperation' (1954) 48 The American Journal of International Law 222, 230. Loewenstein adds, 'Internal and external self-determination of nominally sovereign states has thus become the frequent objective of counsel, criticism, and censure by the Government and Congress of the United States and, of course, American public opinion at large, which offers generous if unsolicited advice concerning, for example, the tax structure in France, management techniques of British business, industrial policies of Italy, or budgetary practices of Greece'.

[14] ibid 231.

[15] Miles Kahler, 'The Survival of the State in European International Relations' in Charles S Maier (ed), *Changing Boundaries of the Political: Essays on the Evolving Balance between the State and Society, Public and Private in Europe* (CUP 1987) 288.

[16] ibid 289.

[17] See, eg Perry Anderson, *The New Old World* (Verso 2009) 10.

imperial ambitions was evident more generally in the new configuration of global power: countries would either be clients, satellites, or allies of one or the other global superpower, with the world bipolarized in a way that would significantly alter the meaning of material self-determination.

That the notion of self-determination in Europe had been transformed after the Second World War was a conclusion uniting otherwise divergent thinkers such as Carl Schmitt and Alexander Kojève.[18] In Carl Schmitt's narrative, US control over the new and decisive geopolitical element after the sea and land of earlier epochs (the Leviathan and Behemoth), in its dominance of air power, underwrote no less than a new *nomos of the earth*.[19] But as new regional constellations of political community developed above the nation state, political conflict would be reproduced at a supranational level among continental blocs. For Kojève, the end of the classic European state, along with advances in technology, material progress, and the growing global economy, all signalled the 'neutralisation' of the political, and even the end of 'domestic politics' itself.[20] Kojève's thesis of the 'withering away' of politics through administration was a forerunner of the 'end of history' thesis more famously echoed a half-century later by Francis Fukuyama albeit subsequently abandoned.[21]

Despite their disagreements, the broadly shared diagnosis of Schmitt and Kojève was that the 'German question', the geopolitical issue that had preoccupied the European region over the previous half-century, had faded into the background.[22] Domestically, Adenauer's West Germany—abdicating any regionally or globally hegemonic ambitions, which in any case would have been blunted by its position sandwiched between the rival superpowers—made the decisive political choice at the beginning of the Cold War to align itself with the US and with Western liberalism more generally; even at the expense of forgoing the possibility of early reunification with the East as a 'neutral power' offered by Moscow.[23] This choice, and the division within Germany it entailed, was cemented in 1955 with West German membership of NATO, shortly followed by the Soviet Union establishing the Warsaw Pact of Eastern bloc countries. German reunification would anyway have been difficult to accept for the rest of Western Europe at this historical juncture, given Germany's ability and propensity to dominate the continent over the preceding half-century. Few in Europe in the early 1950s believed that Germany's official rejection of Nazism was 'more than

[18] See, eg Walter Rech and Janis Grzybowski, 'Between Regional Community and Global Society: Europe in the Shadow of Schmitt and Kojève' (2017) 13 Journal of International Political Theory 143.

[19] Carl Schmitt, *The Nomos of the Earth in the International Law of the Jus Publicum Europaeum* (GL Ulmen tr, Telos Press 2003) 352–53.

[20] Rech and Grzybowski (n 18) (citing Kojeve's letter to Carl Schmitt's dated 2 May 1955).

[21] ibid 147 (citing Kojeve's letter to Carl Schmitt dated 16 May 1955). The post-Cold War iteration of the 'end of history' is examined in Part III.

[22] Schmitt (n 19) 352–53.

[23] See Risse and Engelmann-Martin (n 2) 296. cf Otto Kirchheimer who, writing in 1953, presents this as hardly a choice at all, but as entirely inevitable. See 'Notes on the Political Scene in Western Germany' in Frederic Burin and Kurt Shells (eds), *Politics, Law and Social Change: Selected Essays of Otto Kirchheimer* (Columbia University Press 1969).

superficial and temporary'.[24] The Germans, Karl Loewenstein lamented in 1952, 'are still feared, and again mistrusted'.[25]

The West German turn inward to focus on resurrecting its economic fortunes coincided with the fabled *Wirtschaftswunder* under economics minister Ludwig Erhard, a staunch economic liberal and Atlanticist.[26] This was facilitated by the cancelling and restructuring of large portions of its national debt in the so-called 'London Agreement' of 1953, as well as the avoidance of any reparations payments to the USSR or other countries that had suffered German aggression.[27] In a different vernacular, the fresh start given to Germany with debt cancellation signalled nothing less than a new *nomos* of the European area: in commenting on its use in classical Greece, Schmitt noted that *nomoi* and the Aristotelian notion of *politeia* could be created not only by land division but also by the liquidation of debt.[28]

The Bonn Republic transitioned from a 'non-sovereign' to a 'semi-sovereign' state after the first decade of its existence. Due to the military and diplomatic context of the Cold War, continuing dependence on the US for its security, and domestic constraints on its exercise of sovereign powers (discussed in Chapter 4), it did not regain full sovereignty with the termination of the Occupation Statute in 1955. Although an absence of full sovereignty was a characteristic shared by other European states at that time, for the Federal Republic it was its 'defining mark', due to its defeated, divided, and dependent status and need to 'forg[e] a new identity around a European vocation'.[29] Institutional memberships of organizations such as the EEC were not merely instruments *of* policy, they were normative frameworks *for* policy, and this was understood domestically, and by Germany's neighbours.[30]

With the new alignment of core Europe, and a German 'culture of restraint', it would be a Franco-German partnership that would become the new 'motor' of regional geopolitics, symbolized with the Elsyée Treaty signed by President de Gaulle and Chancellor Adenauer in 1963.[31] The Elsyée Treaty would christen a new Franco-German relationship, sealing reconciliation after a period of devastating antagonism,

[24] Karl Loewenstein, 'The Union of Western Europe: Illusion and Reality II. An Appraisal of the Motives' (1952) 52 Columbia Law Review 209, 236.

[25] ibid.

[26] Erhard, who would succeed Adenauer as Chancellor, and has been described as father of the 'Social Market Economy', as well as being a member of the Mont Pelerin Society, had close ties to the ordoliberals, examined below (see Ralf Ptak, 'Neoliberalism in Germany: Revisiting the Ordoliberal Foundations of the Social Market Economy' in Philip Mirowski and Dieter Plehwe (eds), *The Road from Mont Pelerin: The Making of the Neoliberal Thought Collective* (HUP 2009)).

[27] According to Kenneth Dyson, The London Agreement on German External Debts, agreed in 1953, 'was a central pillar of the German "economic miracle"', see Kenneth Dyson, *States, Debt and Power: Saints and Sinners in European History and Integration* (OUP 2014) 594. The fact that this was connected to recovery rather than conditionality would be brought up, to no avail, during the Greek debt crisis some sixty years later.

[28] Schmitt (n 19), 68.

[29] William E Paterson, 'Beyond Semi-Sovereignty: The New Germany in the New Europe' (1996) 5 German Politics 167, 167.

[30] ibid 170: 'Over the longer term, the Federal Republic's commitment to making policy "In Europe's Name" contributed significantly to the unanimous acceptance by Germany's neighbours of German unity.'.

[31] ibid: 'when German governments sought to change or advance the Community agenda, their first reflex was to look for French support and to present it as a Franco-German initiative'.

and begin an era of regularized and constructive intergovernmentalism. Although, to De Gaulle's displeasure, Elysée would not displace NATO; it would cement, expand and intensify a key bilateral partnership, providing a framework to achieve a 'permanent concertation' between France and Germany, providing organizational coherence and procedures for interaction, as well as requiring mutual consultation 'before every important decision in all important questions of foreign policy'.[32]

In the decades that followed the Elysée Treaty, the Franco-German directorate would evolve institutionally to the extent that it became second nature among public officials of both states to consider their relations closer to domestic than foreign affairs. A regional form of 'cooperative hegemony' had emerged, where France's political leadership, particularly in European matters, could legitimize the rise of Germany as an economic power.[33] The hope was that, overall, any overt fear of German hegemony would be neutralized by French political dominance on the process of integration. This delicate compromise would transition through a number of stages before being seriously transformed in the wake of German reunification in 1990: this subject will be examined more fully in Chapter 6.

Although central to regional geopolitical development, the Franco-German relationship was conditioned by a fundamentally divergent view on the nature and *telos* of the European project. From a French perspective, represented by De Gaulle, the project was about European *cooperation*, offering a balance to US global imperialism by reinforcing the sovereignty and autonomy of the Western European states under French leadership.[34] For many in Germany, it was about European *integration*, overcoming ambitions of national sovereignty, maintaining dependence on the US and NATO and, in utopian moments, presenting a path to a federal state in the making. These differences would continue into the 1970s, even if diluted, in the less ideological and more pragmatic politics of Giscard and Schmidt, leading to further compromises such as the institutional regularization of European Council summits, as insisted on by the French in 1974; and then the direct election of the European Parliament, as requested by the Germans and supported by the smaller member states, in 1979.[35]

Although there were a number of significant developments in terms of strengthening bilateral cultural networks and exchanges, and cultivating 'parapublic ties', the Franco-German interaction did not bring about a true cross-border public sphere.[36] The basic disagreements, different constitutional imaginaries and institutional designs they reflected, and the lack of any common political language would be

[32] Ulrich Krotz and Joachim Schild, *Shaping Europe: France, Germany and Embedded Bilateralism from the Elysée Treaty to Twenty-First Century Politics* (OUP 2013) 55.

[33] Bulmer and Paterson (n 5) 74 (citing Thomas Pedersen, *Germany, France and the Integration of Europe: A Realist Interpretation* (Pinter 1998)).

[34] Michael Sutton, *France and the Construction of Europe, 1944–2007* (Bergahn Books 2007) 1–14.

[35] It would also be under President Valery Giscard d'Estaing (President from 1974 to 1981) that ordoliberal and neo-liberal thought (discussed in Chapter 5) came to dominate in France, introduced by Raymond Barre (Prime Minister from 1976 to1981, economics professor and former European Commission vice president) and linked to France's integration into the European market. See Arnaud Lechevalier, 'Why and How has German Ordoliberalism Become a French Issue? Some Aspects about Ordoliberal Thoughts we can Learn from the French Reception' in Christian Joerges and Josef Hien (eds), *Ordoliberalism, Law and the Rule of Economics* (Hart Publishing 2017) 23–48. Sutton (n 34) describes Barre as a 'pivotal figure' in the turn away from dirigisme, 145.

[36] Krotz and Schild (n 32) 111–12.

compounded in time by diverging growth patterns and political-economic strategies. Even in its earlier parity and its original, relatively balanced institutional form, it was partially fear, distrust, and difference that conditioned this core European inter-state relationship. Later, as a more overt disequilibrium emerged with the ascendance of the Deutschmark in the 1970s and 1980s,[37] and then when the spectre of hegemony returned with German reunification and the end of the Cold War in the 1990s, the Franco-German relationship would be defined by a series of asymmetries (which will be examined in Chapter 6).[38]

Regional geopolitics was constructed in and through the wider project of European integration, and must be understood in this broader, and partially autonomous, context; closer in some respects to the German than the French view, but with the gradual fading of any federal horizon. The notion of restrained sovereignty, in other words, would be part of the constitutive politics of European integration; semi-sovereignty would come to characterize both the member states *and* their union, in what has been termed a 'supranational compromise'.

3. The supranational compromise

Within the framework of integration, and under the auspices of the Franco-German axis, the creation of the ECSC at Paris, and then the EEC at Rome, signified that West German sovereignty was a collective question involving Europe as a whole. Structurally, the framework of integration would gradually change the nature of inter-state relations, restraining expressions of state sovereignty; in the first instance, by pooling sovereign powers and establishing common, competitive markets in coal and steel production, following the Schuman Declaration. As well as stimulating economic growth, this would safeguard against German rearmament, suppressing control over the factors of war-making, and against the temptation for Germany to look eastwards, towards reunification under the aegis of Moscow.[39]

The Schuman plan would also assuage fears of working-class militancy; initially it was strongly opposed by German Social Democrats, who saw its designs as 'conservative, clerical and capitalist'.[40] But it was not a return to a mythical nineteenth-century laissez-faire. In the words of Robert Marjolin, French economist and member of the inaugural European Commission, the Treaty of Paris represented 'an original combination of liberalism and planning', providing 'a controlled system of free competition'.[41] Thanks, in large part, to Dutch diplomacy,[42] as well as initiatives of 'the two

[37] Pierre Grémion, 'State, Europe, and Republic' in Anand Menon and Vincent Wright (eds), *From the Nation State to Europe? Essays in Honour of Jack Hayward* (OUP 2003) 53: 'the Franco-German partnership, though no less a reference after 1978, indeed more so, came to represent a group of decision-makers increasingly preoccupied with exchange rates, whilst other social and intellectual spheres of Franco-German co-operation showed signs of decline'.

[38] See Krotz and Schild (n 32) 54–59.

[39] Gerhard Bebr, 'The European Coal and Steel Community: A Political and Legal Innovation' (1953) 63 The Yale Law Journal 1

[40] Hans Kundnani, *The Paradox of German Power* (C Hurst & Co 2014) 30.

[41] Cited by Bebr (n 39) 37.

[42] Milward (n 11) 196, describes Dutch foreign minister Beyen's proposals for a customs union as 'the bridge which led from the ECSC to the EEC'.

great federalists' Paul-Henri Spaak and Jean Monnet, the process would then be expanded significantly by the Treaty of Rome in 1957 to encompass the aim of securing free movement of all the factors of economic production, using the same supranational operating system introduced at Paris, with the European Commission broadly replicating the structure of the ECSC's executive branch (the High Authority).[43]

Post-war European institution-building would prolong the durability of the constitutional nation state within Europe's evolving regional setting by curtailing its scope for external interference. This occurred most dramatically in the constitutional imaginary by bracketing the question of war,[44] and redefining the concept of security, to emphasize economic rather than military matters.[45] In this view, not just the bilateral Franco-German relationship but European integration among 'the six' was about reimagining inter-state politics as a form of domestic rather than foreign politics. In other words, it was based on the idea that 'traditional "international relations" between states' could develop in 'new "constitutional" ways'.[46] As well as the aim of preventing war, this came with a more immediate material rationale: contributing to domestic socio-economic prosperity and internal security was perceived to be the best way to avoid political extremes, which would have external as much as domestic costs in a tightly integrated and interconnected region.

The project for creating a 'United States of Europe' was sidelined early on, despite its support in Germany, and from sources as diverse as Winston Churchill and Altiero Spinnelli.[47] Efforts to establish a European Political Community and a European Defence Community failed; rejected in the French parliament, contested by the German Social Democrats in the Federal Constitutional Court, and more generally lacking in popular support.[48] The French elites were, at that moment, preoccupied with transforming their overseas empire into a French Union rather than constructing a new European one, and among the masses, particularly in France, there was little support for a federalist project.[49] Instead of trying to rally the people in support of some clearly defined goals, Jean Monnet and his followers preferred, in Pascal Lamy's words, 'to get on without telling [the people] too much about what was happening'.[50]

Plans for political union would thus be superseded by a supranational technocratic and juristic project which would be constructed in tandem with a symbolic

[43] ibid 119 (Bebr (n 39) described the supranational powers of the ECSC as 'mark[ing] a basic departure from the conception of all previous international organizations' (at 1)).

[44] Eilstrup-Sangiovanni and Verdier (n 1).

[45] See Milward (n 11).

[46] Neil Walker, 'The Idea of Constitutional Pluralism' (2002) 65 Modern Law Review 355. In that specific sense, to the extent generalizable, European integration presented as a true 'federation'. See Christoph Schönberger, 'Die Europäische Union als Bund' (2004) 129 Archiv des öffentlichen Rechts 81, 104. According to Schmitt, internally, the federation necessarily signifies pacification, a 'civil peace' between its partners (Carl Schmitt, *Constitutional Theory* (Duke University Press 2008) 386).

[47] See Risse and Engelmann-Martin (n 2) 298.

[48] For analysis of this conflict, politicizing the Court for the first time, see Karl Loewenstein, 'The Bonn Constitution and the European Defense Community Treaties' (1955) 64 The Yale Law Journal 805. The SPD's concerns about the Defence Community related to the prospect of German rearmament.

[49] Pierre Grémion, 'State, Europe, and Republic' in Anand Menon and Vincent Wright (eds), *From the Nation State to Europe: Essays in Honour of Jack Hayward* (OUP 2003) 48.

[50] Cited in Giandomenico Majone, 'The Limits of Collective Action and Collective Leadership' in Damian Chalmers, Markus Jachtenfuchs, and Christian Joerges (eds), *The End of the Eurocrats Dream: Adjusting to Diversity* (CUP 2016) 226.

re-foundation of the domestic constitutional state (examined in Chapter 4). Integration would be pushed forward by complementary and occasionally competing dynamics—along technocratic-economic, teleological-juridical, and symbolic-constitutional lines—as well as pushed forward pragmatically by intergovernmental interests.[51] The exercise of inter-state political power and authority, and the self-understanding of the role of the state (largely through the self-understanding of its elites) in the regional state system would be modified significantly, as a result of the process of European integration.

The 'supranational compromise', as theorized by US commentators, was a delicate bargain between competing objectives, 'serving not only to satisfy but also to quiet major political forces'.[52] Those who had advocated a more integrated, federal Europe retreated from grand ideas of political accountability into a bureaucratic template of 'technocratic administration'.[53] Monnet's strategy of 'elite-led gradualism' attempted to lock in interested organizations, including 'business, labour, and national administrative agencies', rather than to politically activate the public or to rouse political passions.[54] Democratic legitimacy, to the extent that it mattered, was left in the hands of nation states; the security of the entity as a whole would be managed by the US (initially, 'the monetary and military integration of the Western European states was guaranteed by their Atlantic integration').[55]

If the technocratic project to create a Common Market based on a functional logic of interdependence was associated with Monnet—and steps of 'de facto solidarity', in the words of the Schuman Declaration—the juristic plan to create a federal-legal form of union was associated with the early jurisprudence of the European Court of Justice (ECJ)—particularly *Van Gend en Loos* and *Costa v ENEL*—and a wider community of lawyers.[56]

Walter Hallstein, first president of the Commission, lawyer, federalist, and German Christian Democrat, framed integration as a phenomenon in which the 'majesty of law' was to replace the high passions of politics as the means to manage and regulate inter-state relations on the European continent, and ultimately to unite Europe.[57] If Hallstein's vision foundered politically on the intergovernmental intransigence of

[51] The classic neofunctionalist account was given by Ernst Haas, *The Uniting of Europe* (Stanford University Press 1958). A competing account, based on the obstinacy of the nation state, was offered at an early stage by Stanley Hoffman, 'Obstinate or Obsolete? The Fate of the Nation-State and the Case of Western Europe' (1966) 95 Daedalus 862.

[52] Leon Lindberg and Stuart Scheingold, *Europe's Would-Be Polity* (Prentice Hall 1970) 16.

[53] See William Wallace and Julie Smith, 'Democracy or Technocracy? European Integration and the Problem of Popular Consent' in Jack Hayward (ed), *The Crisis of Representation in Europe* (Routledge 1996) 139.

[54] ibid 140.

[55] Stefan Bartolini, *Restructuring Europe. Centre Formation, System Building and Political Structuring between the Nation State and the EU* (OUP 2005) 367.

[56] *Van Gend en Loos v Nederlandse Administratie de Belastingen* [1963] ECR 1 (26/62), *Costa v ENEL* [1964] ECR 585 (6/64); see Antoine Vauchez, 'The Transnational Politics of Judicialization: *Van Gend en Loos* and the Making of the EU Polity' (2010) 16 European Law Journal 1; Antonin Cohen, 'Constitutionalism without Constitution: Transnational Elites Between Mobilization and Legal Expertise in the Making of a Constitution For Europe (1940s–1960s)' (2007) 32 Law & Social Enquiry 109; Morten Rasmussen, 'The Origins of a Legal Revolution: The Early History of the European Court of Justice' (2008) 14 Journal of European Integration History 77.

[57] Walter Hallstein, *Die Europäische Gemeinschaft* (ECON 1979) 33.

De Gaulle, it would be retained as a juristic project, and even a constitutional one, through the European courts. The quasi-federalist project could only materialize with the help of these significant interventions, combining European and domestic juristic practice. Through international organizations—Paul Reuter, legal advisor to the French government, noted in 1958—'jurists could occupy a place they had lost in the national order'.[58]

At least on this limited point, analogies with US federalism are instructive.[59] Through the process of judicial activism, it has been noted in relation to *Marbury v Madison* and its progeny, that 'the provisions of the US constitution became positivised, de-politicized, individualized, and legalized'.[60] Although borne from quite different circumstances, the Treaty of Rome would be subjected to a similar fate, with similar consequences for the EU legal order and—because of the judicial architecture of the Union and the legal doctrines developed by the Court of Justice—for the national legal orders it depended on to function.

Legal integration would thus occur through national as much as supranational developments; domestic courts, in particular, proving essential allies to the European Court of Justice, if also occasionally inconvenient ones, in the project of constitutionalizing the Treaties, an issue examined in Chapter 4.[61] The combination of political functionalism and legal constitutionalism would dominate juristic opinion in the core, uniting French functionalists and German jurists, and together leaving political sovereignty to one side.

The EU, accordingly, would operate, at most, as a 'quasi-federal' polity, with an idiosyncratic split between normative-technocratic authority on the one hand—strongly supranationalized through the jurisprudence of the ECJ and the bureaucratic expertise of the European Commission (and later the monetary authority of the European Central Bank (ECB))—and political power on the other, which remained formally with the component national units of the member states.[62] This last point would be practically highlighted by the so-called 'empty chair crisis', which was resolved only by De Gaulle's Luxembourg compromise, maintaining the national veto when issues

[58] Paul Reuter, 'Techniciens et Politiques dans l'organisation Internationale' in *Politique et technique* (Presses Universitaires de France 1958) 195; cited in Antoine Vauchez, *Brokering Europe: Euro-Lawyers and the Making of a Transnational Polity* (CUP 2015) 13.

[59] See, eg Ernst Mestmäcker ('According to a widespread opinion in the United States and represented also by an influential lobby in Brussels, there is only one direction in which European law should develop: in the direction of American law.'): Ernst Mestmäcker, 'European Touchstones of Dominion and Law' (2007) The Ordo Yearbook of Economic and Social Order 3. According to Cohen (n 56) 113, the development of a constitutional comparativism in which the US Constitution was 'the central point of reference' was the result of the investments of a number of 'European and American transnational entrepreneurs in the definition of a new international order and of the legal investments of different law professionals (both American and European) in the formalization of a model of federalism based on the comparison of different forms of federations'.

[60] Martin Loughlin, *Foundations of Public Law* (CUP 2010) 293.

[61] As early as 1967, the German Constitutional Court argued that, as a result of the Treaty of Rome, 'a new public authority has thereby been created, which is autonomous and independent vis-à-vis the public authorities of each Member State'. (Case No 1 BvR 248/63 and 216/67). See Andrew Oppenheimer (ed), *The Relationship between European Community Law and National Law: The Cases* (CUP 1994) 413.

[62] See Joseph HH Weiler, 'The Transformation of Europe' (1991) 100 The Yale Law Journal 2403.

of importance were at stake and relegating the European Commission to the political margins.[63]

Commitment to substantive member state equality was an important feature of the institutional framework in the foundational period, pushing beyond the merely formal—and in practice illusory—sovereign equality of international law. So, for example, as integration proceeded, a balance would be sought between large and small member states through allocation of voting in the European Council, digressive proportionality of seats in the European Parliament, and strict unanimity in the rules for treaty amendment. Informally, the Luxembourg compromise demanded unanimity even for ordinary law-making, ensuring a degree of sovereign control over the political process, albeit one that was powerless to prevent the simultaneous constitutionalization of the treaty commitments occurring through judicial avenues.[64]

This relatively successful construction of European integration can only be understood in tandem with a domestic re-foundation, which launched a new constitutional ethos based on individual human dignity, fundamental rights, and international commitments. These principles were often codified in basic constitutional texts, most notably in West Germany; the Basic Law of the Federal Republic promised an 'openness' to international law, and committed West Germany to the establishment of a 'united Europe'.[65] The constitutions of France in 1946 (paragraph 15 of its preamble) and Italy in 1948 (Article 11) also declared consent to *limitations of sovereignty* necessary 'for the realisation and the defence of peace', and 'to establish an order ensuring peace and justice among nations', respectively.[66] Despite initial ambiguity in the Belgian constitution regarding the constitutionality of international commitments, and the transfer of powers to international organizations such as imposed by the Treaty of Rome, it soon integrated the demands of supranationalism. The Benelux countries as a whole were generally open to binding international commitments, not least since the principle of sovereignty was downplayed—even absent entirely—from the Dutch constitution, easing the path of supranational compromise.[67]

Such domestic constitutional refoundation had, as its twin aims, regional integration, and international alliance with the US. The 'limitation of sovereignty' clauses that facilitated this would become constitutionally significant in permitting the approval and entry into force of treaties that would otherwise have required constitutional revision.[68] All of the 'big three' countries of the founding six (Germany, France, and Italy) could thus approve the Treaties of Paris and Rome without making constitutional

[63] Piers Ludlow, 'De-Commissioning the Empty Chair Crisis: The Community Institutions and the Crisis of 1965–66' in Jean-Marie Palayret, Helen Wallace, and Pascaline Winand (eds) , *Visions, Votes and Vetoes* (Peter Lang 2006) 90–91.

[64] On the claim that political intergovernmentalism was the flip side to legal supranationalism, see Weiler (n 62).

[65] Preamble and Article 23(1) of the Basic Law.

[66] See further, Bruno de Witte, 'The European Union as an International Legal Experiment' in Gráinne de Búrca and Joseph HH Weiler (eds), *The Worlds of European Constitutionalism* (CUP 2012) 19 (de Witte, 'EU as Legal Experiment').

[67] See Bruno de Witte, 'Do Not Mention the Word: Sovereignty in Two Europhile Countries: Belgium and the Netherlands' in Neil Walker (ed), *Sovereignty in Transition* (Hart Publishing 2003) 364 , suggesting the Benelux as a 'laboratory of post-sovereignty'.

[68] de Witte, 'EU as Legal Experiment' (n 66) 27.

amendments, bypassing the need to reignite the principle and practice of constituent power.

Even if not immediately incorporated into post-war constitutional resettlements, European integration would, over time, become a central feature of the new domestic constitutional imagination, playing both a real and symbolic role in framing the exercise of political authority. Beyond the various constitutional texts, commitments to belong to the European Union and be part of the project of European integration would be strongly enshrined informally, as part of a new constitutional culture, and across a 'variety of constitutionalisms', or different 'paths to constitutionalism', in Bruce Ackerman's words.[69]

The reshaping of the geopolitical constitution of Europe through restrained sovereignty—initially of the founding 'six'—would thus grow after the 1970s into an ever-enlarging project in which the construction of an overarching sovereign political entity became less likely as Europe expanded demographically, geographically, and culturally. This would be entirely in line with leading ordoliberal ideas. As Wilhelm Röpke had put it, 'to diminish national sovereignty' was 'most emphatically one of the urgent needs' of the time. 'But', he went on, 'the excess of sovereignty should be abolished instead of being transferred to a higher political and geographical unit'.[70] In this way, German ordoliberal preferences conveniently matched the interests of the ruling classes in powerful states such as France and the United Kingdom who wanted to avoid full political union for their own domestic reasons. Integration would thus occur without the construction of a sovereign superstate, even if the faint shadow of such remained—maintained by sceptics and proponents alike for diametrically opposed reasons—the first to harness Eurosceptic opinion, the second to keep the promise of genuine political union alive among the faithful.[71]

The obligations of EEC (and later EU) membership, although guaranteed by institutions partly external to the member states, should be understood as long-term collective self-commitments, not comparable to the obligations one enters on joining (and exits on leaving) a club on a whim. Even the goal of restraining (German) state sovereignty based on distrust of German power has been reinterpreted as a collective *self-limiting* device; European integration was the external dimension of a strategy of domestic self-prevention (described as the 'German interest paradox': that it is in the German interest that German interests are not perceived as German interests).[72]

[69] Bruce Ackerman, *Revolutionary Constitutions: Charismatic Leadership and the Rule of Law* (Belknap Press 2019); Bruce Ackerman, 'Three Paths to Constitutionalism—and the Crisis of the European Union' (2015) 45 British Journal of Political Science 705.

[70] Wilhelm Röpke, *Economic Order and International Law* (Academie de Droit International de la Haye, Recueil de Cours, Volume 86/II: Kluwer International Law 1954) 250 . On the broader significance of Röpke's ideas for the international investment regime, see Ntina Tzouvala, 'The Ordoliberal Origins of Modern International Investment Law: Constructing Competition on a Global Scale' in John Haskell and Akbar Rasulov (eds), *New Voices and New Perspectives in International Economic Law* (Springer 2019) 37–54.

[71] It would be revived in the academy, briefly, by Federico Mancini after Maastricht, and then, as we will examine in Chapter 5, in mutated legalized form, by the 'new constitutionalists' that emerged in the euro crisis period.

[72] See Franz Mayer, 'Rebels without a Cause? A Critical Analysis of the German Constitutional Court's OMT Reference' (2014) 15 German Law Journal 111.

In sum, what is created as a matter of political form can be described as akin to a federation but not to a federal state.[73] State sovereignty over economic matters is suspended, eventually exercised neither at national nor at supranational level.[74] Neither of the classic material attributes of modern state formation—the capacity to provide warfare and welfare—are determined at the European level, with total European expenditure at only around 1 per cent of GDP. However, the member states are not fully self-determining, presented as they are with supranational limits on governmental activity in ever-expanding areas of common concern.

As a matter of constitutional theory, there is a delinking of the connection between state sovereignty and popular sovereignty. Monnet's dictum (*nous ne coalissons pas les états, nous unissons les hommes*) is transformed.[75] States are united, but only through their ruling elites: this is how the exercise of state power is restrained. Democracy rests—in a reclined manner—at the national level, its upscaling to Europe a non-starter due to the lack of popular support or political channels. The so-called 'no *demos* thesis', so prominent in the literature after Maastricht (examined in Part III) is integral to understanding this trajectory, right from the outset of the project.[76]

European integration would thus modify conceptions of legitimate government through its institutional structures and especially its legal system, notably with the doctrines of direct effect and supremacy of Community law. Alongside the principle of *effet utile* and non-retaliation, this would distinguish European from classical international law.[77] It would gradually distance Community law from the normal politics of international agreements, lending it the symbolic appearance of a constitutional project and, as domestic courts were co-opted into its practice and discourse, the practical effects of one too.[78] As we shall see, these developments required, and depended on, internal political and constitutional arrangements as much as supranational juristic initiatives.

European integration can be seen as a soft authoritarian project from its origin, restraining inter-state relations not on the basis of, or in a manner accountable to, a democratically active citizenry but on the basis of US influence and involvement, geopolitical power imbalances and historical fears of German domination. Even more significant than this geopolitical frame, however, were the institutional structures

[73] See Olivier Beaud, *Théorie de la Fédération* (PUF 2007); Signe Larsen, *The Constitutional Theory of the Federation and the European Union* (OUP 2021).

[74] In this sense, there is a similarity with Hayek's inter-state federation, discussed further in Chapters 5 and 8 (Friedrich August von Hayek, 'The Economic Conditions of Interstate Federalism' in *Individualism and Economic Order* (University of Chicago Press 1942)).

[75] Jean Monnet, *Mémoires. Nous ne Coalisons pas des Etats, Nous Unissons des Hommes* (Fayard 1976).

[76] See John Gillingham, *European Integration 1950–2003: Superstate or New Market Economy?* (CUP 2003). As Krotz and Schild (n 32) 111 note, despite the various attempts at building parapublic institutions, there isn't even a public sphere between France and Germany, let alone a 'European-wide public sphere'.

[77] See William Phelan, *In Place of Inter-State Retaliation: The European Union's Rejection of WTO-Style Trade Sanctions and Trade Remedies* (OUP 2015).

[78] Ulrich Haltern and Joseph HH Weiler, 'Constitutional or International? The Foundation of the Community Legal Order and the Question of Judicial Kompetenz-Kompetenz' in Anne Marie Slaughter, Alec Stone Sweet, and JHH Weiler (eds), *The European Courts and National Courts—Doctrine and Jurisprudence* (Hart Publishing 1998); Joseph HH Weiler, 'In Defense of the Status Quo, Europe's Constitutional Sonderweg' in JHH Weiler and Marlene Wind (eds), *European Constitutionalism Beyond the State* (CUP 2003). On domestic courts' reception, see Karen Alter, *Establishing the Supremacy of European Law: The Making of an International Rule of Law in Europe* (OUP 2003).

manned and expanded by bureaucratic elites, a demobilization of the masses, and a series of domestic class compromises. The restraint of state sovereignty would be a project pursued through institutional frameworks at both national and European levels, where these are often intertwined (both in terms of the procedures and the institutional personnel involved), most obviously with Europe's quasi-federal legal structure. To make sense of the political and constitutional nature of this 'soft authoritarianism', we have to examine how the processual union of states reflects a reconfiguration of the ruling relationship *within* the state. This reconfiguration transforms the understanding of constituent power undergirding modern political authority, and it is to this that we turn in the next chapter.

4

De-democratization of the Political Constitution

1. Introduction

In the aftermath of the Second World War, many European (as well as US) political elites attributed the interwar collapse of European liberalism to over-politicization: to a crisis of democracy rather than a crisis of capitalism. This was particularly the case for the German ordoliberals, who saw the development of 'mass society' as 'the central reason for the demise of the Weimar Republic'.[1] From their perspective, a 'new liberalism' needed to be reconstructed, which contained the dangers of mass democracy; the version proposed by ordoliberals would be 'economic liberalism without any element of political liberalism', revealing, according to Philip Manow, a 'profound authoritarian disposition'.[2]

The post-war version of authoritarian liberalism did not function through the hard diktats and emergency decrees of presidential cabinets, as it had in late Weimar, but in a softer way, through a decentralized constitutional system, constraining democracy through various veto points and institutional channels. It represented the domestic side of the 'semi-sovereign' state.[3] This would be combined, in practice, with a moderated capitalism; the hard edges of the capitalist economy softened through a welfare state corporatism (that had originated with Bismarck) and varieties of coordinated capitalism, which coexisted, sometimes uncomfortably, with ordoliberal precepts.

[1] Ralf Ptak, 'Neoliberalism in Germany: Revisiting the Ordoliberal Foundations of the Social Market Economy' in P Mirowski and D Plehwe (eds), *The Road from Mont Pelerin: The Making of the Neoliberal Thought Collective* (HUP 2009) 104. See also, eg Philip Manow, 'The Uneasy Compromise of Liberalism and Corporatism in Postwar Germany' (1999) University of California, Berkeley, Centre for German and European Studies Working Paper 5/88 < https://pure.mpg.de/rest/items/item_1235351/component/file_1235350/content > accessed 22 November 2020: ('Ordoliberalism revealed a very strong authoritarian, anti-parliamentary leaning' and 'the central message in the contributions of Eucken, Rüstow, and others was that the present crisis of the German economy and society resulted from a political crisis, from a crisis of the political and constitutional order of Weimar. In their view it was not a sign of a (secular) crisis of capitalism' (ibid).

[2] Manow (n 2). In the early 1950s, ordoliberalism was described as 'German neoliberalism' (see, eg Otto Kirchheimer, 'Notes on the Political Scene in Western Germany' in FS Burin and KL Shells (eds), *Politics, Law and Social Change: Selected Essays of Otto Kirchheimer* (Columbia University Press 1969) 219).

[3] See Manfred G Schmidt, 'The Parties-do-matter Hypothesis and the Case of the Federal Republic of Germany' (1995) 4 German Politics 1 ('What we find in the Federal Republic of Germany is thus a type of democracy which resembles the classical prescription of "political mixing" and moderation; its democracy is a "moderate democracy", in which a large array of powerful constraints on the will of the majority exists. Within this context, the scope of democracy and the leeway for political choices on the part of the central government in general and the incumbent parties in particular is considerably smaller than the leeway for action in a more "sovereign" state, such as in a pure majoritarian democracy').

Authoritarian Liberalism and the Transformation of Modern Europe. Michael A Wilkinson, Oxford University Press.
 DOI: 10.1093/oso/9780198854753.003.0005

In attempting to bypass traditional ideologies of socialism and nationalism, political elites adopted strategies of pragmatism, and looked towards transnational solutions and consensus underpinned by a principle of economic liberalism.[4] The domestic refoundation of political authority and the project of European integration were thus initially conceived as twin components of a depoliticization of state-society relations, restraining democracy so as to deter any renewed threat to the liberal order.[5] If the interwar period had problematized a vision of liberal constitutionalism underscored by popular sovereignty, the post-war response was to remodel sovereignty, making the constitution and constitutional politics safe for economic liberalism.

More specifically, democracy would be contained through a variety of mechanisms, including federal divisions of power, as well the outsourcing of political authority to 'counter-majoritarian' institutions—independent regulatory agencies, independent central banks, and strong constitutional courts—whose legitimacy depended not on popularity but on expertise.[6] Oversight of these institutions would also be removed from the political-democratic process, vested increasingly in other administrative and judicial bodies that would themselves be insulated from democracy and—to the extent that parts of the constitution are considered unamendable—even from the constituent power that undergirded the modern political-constitutional order.[7] These various constitutional devices and institutions would domesticate democracy, to avoid the perceived danger of politics turning towards extremism of the left or right, or making illiberal or otherwise 'irrational' decisions. In other words, the idea was to lock in the constituent and constituted powers through commitments that would be placed outside direct political control, sundering the constitution from the authority of the people.[8] This *militant economic liberalism* would be achieved through the construction of limits to the ordinary political-democratic process, and limits to more fundamental methods of constitutional change.

Theoretically, of course, the extralegal or extraconstitutional (revolutionary) channels of political change remained, at least in versions of constitutional theory that maintained the idea of an original or 'underived' constituent power: the power to make or remake the constitution. But to understand the post-war transformation in full, it is necessary to capture the informal, as well as formal, transformation of the constitutional dynamic; to capture, in other words, the dynamic of changing state-society relations, which disarmed even the original constituent power.

[4] See Daniel Lerner and Morton Gorden, *Euratlantica: Changing Perspectives of the European Elites* (MIT Press 1969) 241–61 (describing 'the new pragmatism' of European elites and their attachment to the US and NATO).

[5] See Jan-Werner Müller, *Contesting Democracy: Political Ideas in Twentieth-Century Europe* (YUP 2011); and Christopher J Bickerton, *European Integration: From Nation-States to Member States* (OUP 2012).

[6] See Pierre Rosanvallon, *Counter-Democracy: Politics in an Age of Distrust* (Arthur Goldhammer tr, CUP 2006).

[7] See, eg Peter Lindseth, *Power and Legitimacy: Reconciling Europe and the Nation-State* (OUP 2010).

[8] See Christoph Möllers, '"We Are (Afraid Of) the People": Constituent Power in German Constitutionalism' in Martin Loughlin and Neil Walker (eds), *The Paradox of Constitutionalism: Constituent Power and Constitutional Form* (OUP 2007). This is scaled up to a more general understanding of a 'post-constituent constitutionalism'; see Neil Walker, 'Post-Constituent Constitutionalism? The Case of the European Union' in Martin Loughlin and Neil Walker (eds), *The Paradox of Constitutionalism: Constituent Power and Constitutional Form* (OUP 2008).

This section begins by looking specifically at the demobilization of the masses, at the depoliticization of institutions that mediated conflicts of interest between state and society—such as political parties and organized labour—and at the decline of parliamentarism as a forum of democratic legitimization (section 2); it continues by examining the transformation of authority away from the constituent (or even constituted) power of the people to the authority, or even 'sovereignty', of the *law* (section 3); and, finally, it looks at how this process was complemented, and scaled up to the supranational level, in the project of European integration, through the so-called 'constitutionalization' of the European Treaties (section 4).

2. Demobilization of the masses and the decline of parliamentarism

The post-war remodelling of popular sovereignty, through the displacement of constituent power and the depoliticization of state-society relations, came with significant practical moment. Over time, it profoundly reshaped the constitutional imagination and restructured national constitutional politics, fundamentally de-democratizing, and hence disarming, the notion of popular sovereignty. It is not only that the power to remake a constitution (or remould one through interpretation) became juristic, technocratic, removed from the ordinary; even, in some cases, an *extraordinary* political process.[9] There was also a growing, informal deradicalization of state-society relations through the changing role of political parties, and transformation of constitutional cultures in a way that demobilized the masses.[10]

In the post-war period, political parties began to operate in a manner removed from traditional sources of democratic authority and class consciousness. Post-war reconstitution thus coincided, in Continental Europe, with the 'Christian Democratic moment', a reaction to the turmoil of the interwar period, as well as the perceived threat of socialism and communism (both from outside and inside). This domestic-constitutional resettlement sought, above all, political and economic *stability*, safeguarding against the vicissitudes of democratic politics.[11] In this objective, 'Western Europeans fashioned a highly *constrained* form of democracy, deeply imprinted with a distrust of popular sovereignty—in fact, even a distrust of parliamentary sovereignty', as Jan-Werner Müller has recounted in some detail.[12]

[9] cf Chris Thornhill, *A Sociology of Transnational Constitutions: Social Foundations of the Postnational Legal Structure* (CUP 2016). Thornhill argues that constituent power is then exercised through the enforcement of individual rights. But this individualized notion changes the meaning of constituent power, as argued below.

[10] cf Elite theories of democracy from the early twentieth century: Schumpeter's 'minimalist democracy', and Mosca and Pareto's 'minority domination', as well as lesser-known figures such as Robert Michels (see, eg Hugo Drochon, 'Robert Michels, The Iron Law of Oligarchy and Dynamic Democracy' (2020) 27 Constellations 185 (following Pareto's lead, 'Michels viewed the mass as generally immobile and passive, in need of a leader to guide them and towards whom they felt gratitude' (ibid 187).

[11] See Müller (n 5) 132–50.

[12] ibid 128. Alan Milward notes that, for the European 'saints'(De Gasperi, Schuman, and Adenauer), 'democratic theory was summoned to the defence of religious liberty', and, for Schuman, 'Christianity and democracy were indistinguishable' (Alan Milward, *The European Rescue of the Nation-State* (Routledge 2000) 328).

Stability was to be achieved through a commitment to political centrism, Christian social thought (especially Catholic, but incorporating Protestant variants), and a political economy of high productivity and growth. In this way, the impact of capitalism was moderated, as well as democracy constrained.[13] The settlement would be based partly on national policy formation, but also pushed by transnational networks, particularly on the centre-right, with 'transnational Christian democracy' characterized as 'hegemonic' in Western Europe in first two decades of the post-war era, dominating the formation of the EEC, and having 'fundamental long-term repercussions' even into the present-day EU (explored in Parts III and IV).[14]

After a period of mass mobilization during the Second World War, political elites in the 'founding six' were substantially concerned with 'the problem of demobilizing popular movements, and winding down popular ambitions' rather than activating them.[15] The 'retreat to privatism' this entailed had the backing of many public intellectuals in the post-war period, particularly those associated with Cold War liberalism such as Raymond Aron and Isaiah Berlin.[16] It was not a path forced coercively onto the masses. On the contrary, 'once the rush of liberation had passed, Europeans seemed all too eager to disengage from wider political and ideological agendas, in order to "return" to the private sphere',[17] tending to ask 'not what they could do for their rulers, but what their rulers could do for them'.[18] Rather than a democracy based on an active, mobilized citizenry, a passive, soft authoritarianism emerged, based on a fear of political freedom, as well as the desire to escape from politics altogether into individualism and lifestyle choice.

The vitality of the working class, in Hannah Arendt's view, had been exhausted by the 'tragic history of the German socialist parties' in the interwar years. Never before had it 'been in a less revolutionary mood'. Although 'there is a certain embittered resignation to a system that is "sold" to them under the trade name of democracy', this is 'almost a guarantee that any regime, however good or bad, will be acceptable, as a matter of indifference'.[19] Arendt's early assessment of the post-war Republic was later

[13] On the significance of Christian democracy and Catholic thought, more generally, on the foundations of the European Union, see Wolfram Kaiser, *Christian Democracy and the Origins of European Union* (CUP 2007).

[14] ibid 9. The dominance of Christian democracy was achieved through informal transnational networks, as well as national party structures. Kaiser also notes that 'apocalyptic fears of socialist-bolshevist revolution' in the interwar period had led the Vatican 'to support any right-wing anti-communist authoritarian regime from Miklós Horthy in Hungary to Francisco Franco in Spain' (ibid 54). The Catholic 'centre party' had supported Brüning's regime of authoritarian liberalism in the interwar period. Even after the war, 'large sections of the Christian democratic electorate were initially not fully reconciled to parliamentary democracy' (ibid 169).

[15] James Heartfield, 'European Union: A Process Without a Subject' in Christopher J Bickerton, Philip Cunliffe, and Alexander Gourevitch (eds), *Politics Without Sovereignty: A Critique of Contemporary International Relations* (Routledge 2007) 137.

[16] Müller (n 5) 126. Martin Conway, 'Democracy in Postwar Europe: The Triumph of a Political Model' (2002) 32 European History Quarterly 5, 67 (Conway, 'Democracy in Postwar Europe')(a 'characteristic of postwar democracy ... was its reliance on the individualist and essentially negative definitions of freedom developed by anti-Communist liberals such as Isaiah Berlin and Raymond Aron, and propagated by Cold War propagandizing organizations such as the Congress for Cultural Freedom').

[17] Martin Conway, 'The Rise and Fall of Western Europe's Democratic Age, 1945–1973' (2004) 13 Contemporary European History 67, 76; see also Müller (n 5) 130.

[18] Conway (n 17).

[19] Hannah Arendt, 'The Aftermath of Nazi Rule: Report from Germany' in *Essays in Understanding 1930–1954: Formation, Exile, and Totalitarianism* (Schocken Books 1994).

shared by Carl Jaspers, looking back in 1967 after nearly two decades of the Bonn Republic: the result had been a 'parliamentary democracy of passive subjects who did not know the proper point of voting in elections'.[20]

More generally, across Western Europe, it was a 'governed democracy' that had emerged after the war, in which 'legitimacy was derived *from* the will of the people but not exercised *by* the people'. Once they had exercised their right to vote, 'the people were expected to retreat from the political stage and allow their representatives to act in their name'.[21] Democracy was legitimized by 'fridges and motor cars' for the masses, in combination with new bureaucratic and administrative roles for privileged and established elites and the professional middle classes, who would often move seamlessly between national and supranational, private and public vocations.[22] The working class of Europe, who were the 'incontrovertible social victims of the war' were 'strangely invisible' in much of the political life of post-war Europe.[23] The language of class struggle was disappearing, subdued by the security of the bureaucratic and transnational 'iron cage' and a paternalistic elite-led politics.

The founding period of European integration was thus characterized by a growing depoliticization of state-society relations: a combination of class compromise, the deradicalization of the trade union movement, and the rise of the national corporatist state.[24] If the new post-war social contract was based on a Keynesian consensus, this was on the stabilization of the capitalist system, rather than any emancipatory goal; an aim apparently accepted by organized labour, which dropped political militancy in exchange for a share in the benefits of sustained economic growth.[25] The stress on technocracy (technically correct solutions to social and economic problems) meant that 'conflict could be reduced significantly', and 'ideals of industrial democracy and worker self-administration', so prevalent in the interwar period, would be discarded.[26]

Technocracy was by no means always smoothly implemented. The contradictions between elite-led political and economic rationalization and active republican democracy, which had existed in different ways since the Revolutionary period of the late eighteenth century, were apparent in post-war France, for example, and these generated friction. And, if the goal of economic rationalization and modernization was

[20] Karl Jaspers, Antwort—Zur Kritic meiner Schrift—Wohin treibt die Bundesrepublik? (R Piper & Co 1967) 67, cited and translated in Kari Polonen, 'The Search for a New Beginning' in Marco Goldoni and Christopher McCorkindale (eds), *Hannah Arendt and the Law* (Hart Publishing 2012) 162. The lack of a 'new beginning', and fundamental failure of renewal in the post-war era, is also remarked on by Jürgen Habermas (see Müller (n 5)143).

[21] Conway, 'Democracy in Postwar Europe' (n 16)66.

[22] ibid 75 (Conway views this as, in significant ways, continuous with movements from the 1920s onwards).

[23] ibid 76.

[24] See, generally, Philippe C Schmitter and Gerhard Lehmbruch (eds), *Trends toward Corporatist Intermediation* (Sage Publications 1979); Bickerton (n 5) 78–80.

[25] John H Goldthorpe, 'Problems of Political Economy After the Postwar Period' in Charles S Maier (ed), *Changing Boundaries of the Political: Essays on the Evolving Balance between the State and Society, Public and Private in Europe* (CUP 1987) 365 (Goldthorpe notes that 'the triumph of Keynesianism' was not the defeat of free-market capitalism: 'It was characterized by its strictly limited extent; and second, by its considerable reliance on the market itself as an instrument of control' (ibid 364–65)). This should be no surprise, given that Keynes himself was a technocrat more than a democrat, and spoke of the 'euthanasia of politics' in economic policymaking (Müller (n 5) 144).

[26] Müller (n 5) 143.

deemed essential after defeat in the Second World War, so a goal of re-democratization also appeared pressing after the authoritarian rule of the Vichy era. The first goal, however, was far more successfully achieved than the second. A huge nationalization programme and a strong dirigiste philosophy pushed through plans of economic modernization. Although the Fourth Republic rebuilt parliamentary democracy to some degree, 'the state-led modernization drive' primarily empowered experts: 'the knowledgeable top civil servants and politicians who used centralized planning, the ministerial bureaucracy, nationalized enterprise, and the financial circuitry of the Treasury to channel resources'.[27] The creation of the ENA (Ecole nationale d'administration) provided a new generation of civil servants with an 'elite identity' and the expertise to help guide the modernization process, which 'was not effected by major institutions but by small activist minority networks working in a conspiratorial way'.[28] In France, as elsewhere, it was the state apparatus, not the socialist party, that brought about the Keynesianization of society in the first two post-war decades.[29]

Major post-war economic initiatives—including the development of electricity and transport infrastructure, nuclear power, urban planning and rebuilding, expanding the new social security system, and modernizing agriculture—thus 'concentrated power in the state administration and its 'technocrats'.[30] With de Gaulle's centralization of power in the executive (signalled in his referendum on direct election of the president, transforming the constitution of the Fifth Republic), the drive towards technocracy continued. Parliamentary democracy was increasingly sidelined, the French state of the Fifth Republic described as 'a ravaged parliament with an executive power in the hands of a technocratic leadership'.[31] If the state elite would prove more adept at working with business lobbies and the Brussels bureaucracy than integrating the concerns of its own public, this lent a dynamic edge to its post-war economic recovery, but did not produce a constitutionally stable mix, and the intertwinement of state and society would, not infrequently, be disrupted by political crises. In widening the gap between the state and the public, and 'consigning a large measure of democracy to the streets', the state of the Fifth Republic eventually 'served as much to sow as to quell disorder',[32] culminating with the turbulence of the late 1960s (examined in Chapter 5).

The process of institutional depoliticization should be understood as part of a broader phenomenon of the transformation of the party system, and the genesis of what Otto Kirchheimer called the 'catch-all party': rational, pragmatic, and based on ideological demobilization of the masses.[33] It would emerge in tandem with the new

[27] Herrick Chapman, 'The State' in Edward Berenson et al (eds), *The French Republic: History, Values, Debate* (Cornell University Press 2011) 170(Chapman, 'The State').

[28] Pierre Grémion 'State, Europe, and Republic' in A Menon and V Wright (eds), *From the Nation State to Europe? Essays in Honour of Jack Hayward* (OUP 2003) 47.

[29] cf Pierre Rosanvallon, 'The Development of Keynesianism in France' in Peter A Hall (ed), *The Political Power of Economic Ideas* (Princeton University Press 1989).

[30] Chapman, 'The State' (n 27) 170. See, further, Herrick Chapman, *France's Long Reconstruction: In Search of the Modern Republic* (Harvard University Press 2018).

[31] Otto Kirchheimer, 'France From the Fourth to the Fifth Republic' in Frederic S Burin and Kurt L Shells (eds), *Politics, Law and Social Change: Selected Essays of Otto Kirchheimer* (Columbia University Press 1969) 241.

[32] Chapman, 'The State' (n 27) 172

[33] Frederic S Burin and Kurt L Shells (eds), *Politics, Law and Social Change. Selected Essays of Otto Kirchheimer* (Columbia University Press 1969). For discussion, see André Krouwel, 'Otto Kirchheimer and

philosophy of political personalism and belief in human rights that was embraced by many Christian democrats (often under the influence of French Catholic philosopher Jacques Maritain), and a realignment of class forces within the left parties towards the professional middle class.[34] The emergence of the 'catch-all party' signalled a 'separation between organisations representing societal interests ... and the political parties concerned with winning votes and office'.[35] It later incorporated a deradicalization of the communist Left, with its turn to a reformist 'Eurocommunism', most notably in Italy (examined in more detail in Chapter 5).

At the same time as a Keynesian consensus was emerging at home, a very different type of political economy was in the process of being constructed 'abroad'. France, again, is illustrative. After the failure of the European Defence Community in the French parliament, the second attempt at integration, at Rome, was 'quietly' establishing itself without public opinion really even noticing. The Rome Treaty signalled an attempt at integration 'more economic, more pragmatic, more liberal'.[36]

Juxtaposed with an 'endogenous model of state-driven modernization' would thus be the 'modernization process set in motion by the policy of liberalization in Europe'. This reflected 'one of the major thrusts of American policy', but was also supported by the French socialist party (SFIO).[37] Thus, paradoxically, if it was a Gaullist state apparatus that developed a domestic project of Keynesian reconstruction, it would be a socialist government (under Guy Mollet, French Prime Minister from 1956 to 1957) that brought about trade liberalization and laid the ground for the construction of a free market in Europe. This would coincide with the German SPD's own modernization programme, renunciation of Marxist class struggle, embrace of Christian ethics, and acceptance of free market principles—and of the EEC itself— at Bad Godesberg in 1959.[38] It reflected a more general revisionism of social democratic parties across

the Catch-All Party' (2003) 26 West European Politics 23 (The 'catch-all party' theorized by Kirchheimer captures the erosion of parliamentary democracy as a result of 'vanishing political antagonism and principled opposition', the formation of a 'state-party cartel', where parties are disconnected from their social foundations, the professionalization of party organization, and appeal to personal politics and 'extensive depoliticisation, political apathy of the mass population and the waning of the classic separation of legislative, executive and judicial powers' (ibid 31)).

[34] On the significance of Maritain, whose views were underpinned by a 'strong Thomist notion of natural law', see Müller (n 5) 135–38. European integration contributed to French de-industrialization by increasing the accessibility of German coal and steel.

[35] Claus Offe, 'New Social Movements' in Charles S Maier (ed), *Changing Boundaries of the Political: Essays on the Evolving Balance between the State and Society, Public and Private in Europe* (CUP 1987) 67 ('The prevalent concern with growth and real income led working-class spokesmen to renounce more extensive projects of societal change, in exchange for a firmly established status in the process of income distribution (ibid 66–67)).

[36] Grémion (n 28) 48

[37] ibid 50. Mollet later led the SFIO into oblivion (via the Algerian War and support for de Gaulle).

[38] Sassoon notes that, in supporting the EEC, the SPD, previously critical of the Schuman Plan, was, for the first time, approving a major foreign policy initiative of the Christian Democratic Union (CDU), and, in so doing, also distancing itself from German reunification (Donald Sassoon, *One Hundred Years of Socialism: The West European Left in the Twentieth Century* (Bloomsbury Publishing 1996) 237). Sassoon also notes, more generally, that the socialist parties of Western Europe in the 1950s showed a lack of conviction and originality with 'their adoption of a non-socialist and fundamentally bipartisan concept of international political and economic relations', renouncing the ambition of developing non-capitalist relations and beginning the long 'revision' of the socialist tradition that continued into the 1980s and 1990s (ibid 239–40).

Europe, with their abandonment of Marxism, discarding of working-class identities, and dilution of any commitment to anti-capitalism.[39]

Throughout this foundational period, parliamentary authority was in decline, with political power shifting structurally towards the executive and administrative branches of government. Together, this would reflect a process culminating in a so-called 'state-party cartel',[40] later described as a significant feature in the 'hollowing out' of democracy after Maastricht (as we will examine in Chapter 8). With a growing consensus around a capitalism moderated by varying degrees of social corporatism, 'political problems [were] transformed into ostensibly non-political, technical, administrative issues, so that the essentially political questions of power and inequality [were] expunged effectively from political discourse'.[41] In sum, the supranational compromise represented by the Treaty of Rome, which characterized the first three post-war decades in Europe, amounted to 'enlightened administration on behalf of uninformed publics, in cooperation with affected interests'.[42]

3. Sovereignty of the law

The apparent success of the post-war liberal constitutional reimagining, displacing constituent power and sidelining political democracy, was such that, by 1966, Loewenstein concluded, 'the task of checking the bureaucracy which [Max] Weber had assigned to parliament was now effectively fulfilled by courts'. Parliamentarism, which in nineteenth century liberalism 'seemed to be the ultimate in political wisdom', had, in the space of two post-war decades, suffered from 'widespread devaluation'.[43]

The displacement of constituent power, and even of the constituted powers of the legislative branch, left a gap that would be partly filled by the idea of the rule of law and the institutional authority of a constitutional court (in Germany and Italy), or constitutional council (in France). In part, this too was a reaction to the interwar breakdown of liberalism, based on a specific diagnosis of legal positivism's weakness in protecting the values of legality, and its complacency in separating law and morality. In legal theory, this reaction was associated with Gustav Radbruch's conversion to natural law, and in the Anglo-American academy with Lon Fuller's procedural natural law and, later, the moral interpretivism of Ronald Dworkin.[44] Whereas, in the

[39] ibid 241–73. Udi Greenberg, *The Weimar Century: German Émigrés and the Ideological Foundations of the Cold War* (Princeton University Press 2014) 77 argues that the SPD's shift had deeper roots in its anti-communism of the interwar era.

[40] See Krouwel (n 33).

[41] Peter Cocks, 'Towards a Marxist Theory of European Integration' (1980) 34 International Organization 126.

[42] William Wallace and Julie Smith, 'Democracy or Technocracy? European Integration and the Problem of Popular Consent' in J Hayward (ed), *The Crisis of Representation in Europe* (Routledge 1996) 143.

[43] Müller (n 5) 148 (quoting Karl Loewenstein, *Max Weber's Political Ideas in the Perspective of our Time* (University of Massachusetts Press 1966) 48). See also Otto Kirchheimer, 'The Waning of Opposition in Parliamentary Regimes' in Mattei Dogan and Richard Rose (eds), *European Politics: A Reader* (Little, Brown & Co 1971).

[44] See Lon Fuller, *The Law in Quest of Itself* (The Law Exchange 2012)(originally published in 1940), and, later, famously, in his debate with Herbert Hart, seeLon Fuller, 'Positivism and Fidelity to Law–A Reply to Professor Hart' (1958) 71 Harvard Law Review 630. cf Franz Neumann, *Behemoth: The Structure and Practice of National Socialism, 1933–1944* (, Ivan R Dee 2009) 153 (originally published in 1944), rejecting

US, constitutional theory would consist in a distinct but related long-running battle over the so-called 'counter-majoritarian dilemma', this did not explicitly materialize in European constitutional thought.[45] On the contrary, there was a large degree of convergence around the claim that the '*Rechtsstaat* had become the ultimate aim of politics; democracy itself served merely as a means to its realization'.[46] In Germany, antipositivism would not only be a philosophical position, it would come to constitute 'the legitimatory core of the Basic Law'.[47]

German lawyers, in conjunction with their American tutors, and returned émigrés such as Loewenstein, followed a rather simplistic reading of Nazism as an extension of German state worship, blaming Hegelian philosophy, legal positivism's weakness in constitutional defence, or the inevitable irrationality of mass democracy.[48] The 'standard argument', as Michaela Hailbronner calls it, runs like this: 'because the Nazis came to power with the support of the German people ... the people (and their representatives) could after 1945 no longer be trusted to protect fundamental human rights'. On the strength of this 'myth' (ignoring that the Nazis seized power in a context of political violence and the complete suspension of parliamentary democracy), it would be 'inevitable' that a 'strong counter-majoritarian institution' would emerge to the fore. The process reflected not only an institutional change, but a 'revolutionary shift' in legal discipline; a transformation from '"state theory" (*Staatsrechtslehre*) to constitutional theory', and a turn to constitutionalism in a negative, limiting sense.[49]

There was far from an immediate ascendance of the notions of the sovereignty of the law and legal constitutionalism. In the early post-war period, on the contrary, the distrust of lawyers initially prevailed, not least since they had played such a significant role in the Nazi administration of justice, including the organization of the Holocaust.[50] Given the complicity of ordinary lawyers and judges in the Nazi takeover, a new independent body would be required to protect the liberal order: a constitutional court, sitting in Karlsruhe. This was a specialized 'Kelsenian court', exercising

the conflation of morality and law as being inimical to the fight against National Socialism, and specifically objecting to Fuller's thesis, as well as Carl Schmitt's. As Müller puts it, natural law thinking 'underwent a major renaissance after the war' (Müller (n 5) 128).

[45] On the broader spread of *constitutional review* in Europe, as opposed to—but, ultimately, in convergence with—American *judicial review*, see Alec Stone Sweet, 'Why Europe Rejected American Judicial Review and Why It May Not Matter' (2003) Yale Faculty Scholarship Series 81(Stone Sweet, 'American Judicial Review').

[46] Clara Maier, 'The Weimar Origins of the West German *Rechtsstaat*, 1919–1969' (2019) 62:4 The Historical Journal 1069, 1070 ('severing the connection between the political production of laws and the law itself appears as the fundamental purpose of Radbruch's conception of the law'(ibid 1073)).

[47] ibid 1076. Not everyone agreed: Forsthoff, for example, lamented the 'far-reaching de-politicization of the era' (see Jacco Bomhoff, *Balancing Constitutional Rights* (CUP 2013)117)(Bomhoff 'Constitutional Rights').

[48] On the significance of the US influence on German (and Japanese) post-war reconstruction, see Rande Kostal, *Laying Down the Law: The American Legal Revolutions in Germany and Japan* (Harvard University Press 2019).

[49] Michaela Hailbronner, *Transitions and Transformations: The Rise of German Constitutionalism* (OUP 2015) 41–42. Hailbronner herself is sceptical of the overriding practical significance of the dignified response to Nazism in explaining the West German constitutional development. See also Jo EK Murkens, *From Empire to Union: Conceptions of German Constitutional Law Since 1871* (OUP 2013).

[50] Maier (n 46).

constitutional review rather than ordinary US-style judicial review. The Basic Law, although including a catalogue of rights, did not, at first, even provide for an individual complaint mechanism (although one had been granted by statute). But, in 1969, it was amended for this purpose on the insistence of the Social Democrats.

The Basic Law itself was meant only to be a provisional 'constitution', rather than a real 'Constitution'; a temporary affair until reunification with the East, hence its less than majestic title.[51] The structure of the Basic Law prioritized the protection of fundamental rights (beginning with the protection of human dignity), and relegated the organizational aspect of the state to the second part, flipping Weimar's ordering, and—just as Carl Schmitt had suggested—placing value emphasis (with regard to spheres of personal liberty) above value neutrality.[52] Ernst Forsthoff, a close associate of Schmitt, would also restate Schmitt's Weimar-era distinction between, and prioritization of, justiciable liberal rights and non-justiciable social principles, in this manner seeking to 'preserve traditional state prerogatives from judicial intervention' and 'leave room for a strong state'.[53]

Over time, and particularly after its Lüth decision, the court 'frequently engaged highly political questions while grounding its authority on a traditional judicial and distinctly hierarchical basis of legitimacy'.[54] If the creation of a dedicated constitutional court was a clear break from Weimar, it would not take long before Weimar controversies were emulated; the court soon declaring itself the 'guardian of the constitution', as it engaged in increasingly politicized decisions. 'Constitutional populism', as Möllers remarks, had not disappeared; it had simply migrated from one institution, the president, to another—the constitutional court— signalling, at the same time, the complete 'legalisation' of the constituent power.[55] Although many legal scholars had initially been sceptical of the Karlsruhe Court, their eventual support and construction of constitutional doctrine strengthened the idea that 'constitutional law could only be reliably trusted to legal experts'.[56]

The new liberal conception of the *Rechtsstaat* advanced not merely a philosophical conception of law and its relationship to morality; it implied a complete view (even if implicit) of the legitimacy of the state, and of the relationship between state and society. It had clear institutional implications for the constitutional structure and the relationship among the branches of government, contributing to the relegation of the legislature from its previously privileged position.[57] As Alexander Somek notes, classifying a

[51] See Werner Heun, *The Constitution of Germany: A Contextual Analysis* (Hart Publishing 2010).

[52] See Benjamin Schupmann, *Carl Schmitt's State and Constitutional Theory: A Critical Analysis* (OUP 2017) 180, 204. Schmitt later reversed this position, complaining against the 'tyranny of values' instigated by the Lüth decision.

[53] Hailbronner (n 49) 80.

[54] ibid 79. The effect of the Lüth decision, that the constitution had created an objective order of values, 'fully established basic rights as the primary political and legal principle of the West German state' (Maier (n 46) 1080). Alec Stone Sweet describes Lüth as a 'juridical coup d'etat', and notes that its impact would be contested by civil courts (Alec Stone Sweet, 'The Juridical Coup d'etat and the Problem of Authority' (2007) 8 German Law Journal 915(Stone Sweet, 'The Juridical Coup d'etat')).

[55] Möllers (n 8).)

[56] Hailbronner (n 49) 86.

[57] See Alexander Somek, *The Cosmopolitan Constitution* (OUP 2014)(Somek, 'The Cosmopolitan Constitution'). As Somek notes, 'The judiciary becomes a censorial body that watches over the implementation of the constitution, understood as the ultimate final programme of politics. This is the core idea of the "value order": The system of values, which centres on the dignity of the freely developing person within

new 'Constitutionalism 2.0', contrasting with the foundational Constitutionalism 1.0 of the modern revolutionary period:

Within a human rights-based constitution, the legislature can no longer claim to be the intra-constitutional representation of the pre-constitutional sovereign since the sovereign does not exist as a collective body ... but only as an act of recognition that transforms the constitution into a carrier of morally compelling demands'. In this new constitutional configuration, 'the constituent power is passive, not active.[58] The rise of a liberal conception of constitutionalism also suggests a certain historical forgetting. Basic rights of a liberal variety had been invoked by conservative scholars in early Weimar as means to prevent the move to a democratic socialist society, as Franz Neumann had contemporaneously recalled.[59] His (and his Weimar associates') critical perspective on the liberal *Rechtsstaat* would be essentially lost in the post-war constitutional culture, along with Hermann Heller's statist-social critique (outlined in Chapter 2). The 'renaissance of natural law in the post-war period' operated under other 'false assumptions', since it was quite apparent that the Nazi state had by no means functioned on a positivist understanding of the law.[60] On the contrary, 'the Nazi regime had itself deployed strongly anti-positivist polemics precisely against the positivism of the Weimar Constitution'.[61] As Clara Maier puts it:

> Both the interpretation of basic rights and the idea of an abstract order of values were key components of these criticisms [of Weimar's legislative positivism]. In unearthing and re-evaluating these concepts, post-Second World War constitutional theorists established a continuity between the conservative thought of the Weimar period and the legitimation of the Bonn Republic.[62]

The myth that legal positivism and legislative supremacy led to the collapse of the Weimar Republic was curious in another respect (in addition to the reality that legislative supremacy was disabled by the presidential cabinets that bypassed parliament). There had, in fact, as we saw in Chapter 2, been an *increase* in assumption of judicial powers of review in early Weimar (by the Reichsgericht), in particular to protect private property and the interests of creditors in the context of the hyperinflation of 1923 to 1924, a move supported by conservative jurists such as Schmitt. The judges' defence of the 'liberty claims' of the creditors, against the legislator, was presented as a necessary defence again the 'absolutism of the majority',[63] an early instantiation of the fear

society, must be seen as fundamental to all areas of law. This value system, which centres upon dignity of the human personality developing freely within the social community, must be looked upon as a fundamental constitutional yardstick for measuring and assessing all actions in the areas of legislation, public administration, and adjudication. The legislature no longer has a privileged position in such a constitutional system' (ibid 16).

58 ibid 15.
59 See, eg Franz Neumann, 'The Decay of German Democracy' (1933) 4 Political Quarterly 525.
60 Maier (n 46) 1082.
61 ibid 1082.
62 ibid 1083.
63 ibid 1086.

of the 'tyranny of the majority' so characteristic of liberal constitutionalist thought in the post-war era.[64]

Both Heller and Neumann had cautioned *against* judicial review of parliamentary legislation, as they believed that it presented an 'immense danger to democracy' when coexistent with the 'predominant bourgeois interpretation of basic laws'.[65] Judicialization would be seized by the middle classes, who dominated the judiciary, in an effort to prevent the democratic-legislative transformation of the liberal *Rechtsstaat* into a social *Rechtsstaat*.[66] Constitutional thought in post-war Germany, despite seeking to distance itself both from the Weimar period and from Nazism, thus in fact 'showed strong *continuities* with precisely those legal arguments from the Weimar period, which had been effectively used to undermine the state's legitimacy and its ability to expand the provision of welfare'.[67]

If the constitution of the Federal Republic of Germany had made a 'basic decision' in favour of a 'substantive understanding of democracy, a set of values that had to be defended against its declared enemies', these were, in other words, the values of the bourgeois *Rechtsstaat*.[68] Although the threat of a military-style fascist movement had largely disappeared, the liberal order declared its new enemies to be the extreme left (the communist threat 'remains a danger to which the Federal Government is ever alive', in the words of the first West German chancellor, Konrad Adenauer), and nationalism itself (which, for Adenauer, violated not only the political but the 'divine order', in line with other Catholic leaders sceptical of traditional notions of sovereignty).[69] In the process of forging a new constitutional identity, 'Germany's own past as well as Communism constituted "the others" against which a 'Christian occidentalism' could

[64] The term 'tyranny of the majority' is often associated with early US constitutionalism. See Alexander Hamilton, James Madison, and John Jay, *The Federalist* (Cass R Sunstein ed, HUP 2009) No 51, 343; Alexis de Tocqueville, *Democracy in America* (Harvey C Mansfield and Delba Winthrop trs, University of Chicago Press 2000) 239–42. It appeared to make a revival in the post-war era, on both sides of the Atlantic: see, eg Stephen Holmes, *Passions and Constraints: on the Theory of Liberal Democracy* (University of Chicago Press 1995) and, in modified version, through the work of Rosanvallon: see, eg Rosanvallon (n 6).

[65] Duncan Kelly, *The State of the Political: Conceptions of Politics and the State in the Thought of Max Weber, Carl Schmitt and Franz Neumann* (British Academy 2003) 273.

[66] See Hermann Heller, '*Rechtsstaat* or Dictatorship?' (1987) 16 Economy and Society 127 (originally published in 1929, tr Ellen Kennedy). For Heller's deeper critique of liberalism (discussed in Chapter 2), on the basis of its reduction of the popular sovereignty of the general will into a legalistic individualism, see Hermann Heller, *Sovereignty: A Contribution to the Theory of Public and International Law* (David Dyzenhaus ed, OUP 2019) (originally published in 1927).

[67] Maier(n 46) 1090.

[68] Jan-Werner Müller, 'A "Practical Dilemma Which Philosophy Alone Cannot Resolve": Rethinking Militant Democracy: An Introduction' (2012) 19 Constellations 536. For a survey of militant democratic practices in Europe, see Angela Borne and Fernando Bertoa, 'Mapping Militant Democracy: Variation in Party Ban Practices in European Democracies (1945–2015)' (2017) 13 European Constitutional Law Review 221.

[69] Konrad Adenauer, *World Indivisible—With Liberty and Justice For All* (George Allen & Unwin 1956) 9, 25; Thomas Risse and Daniela Engelmann-Martin, 'Identity Politics and European Integration: The Case of Germany' in A Pagden (ed), *The Idea of Europe: From Antiquity to the European Union* (CUP 2002) 315: 'Almost single-handedly, Chancellor Adenauer constructed the Federal Republic's European identity in order to justify and legitimize a foreign policy oriented towards the West'. Adenauer had been active in the pro-European wing of Zentrum, a Catholic party that was the predecessor of the CDU, during the Weimar Republic. After the Second World War, there was a tendency to conflate fascism and communism under the label of 'totalitarianism', which continues, even in the official discourse of the European Union.

be constructed. And, in the context of the Cold War, this 'left no other choice' than to commit to the 'Free World' under US tutelage.[70]

In the construction of this new liberal constitutional identity, the backing of powerful legal institutions such as the constitutional court was central. Political deradicalization in the Federal Republic would famously be juridified and given a formal constitutional stamp of approval, with the Karlsruhe court banning the Communist Party of Germany (KPD) in 1956, in accordance with Article 21 of the German Basic Law, forbidding parties that 'seek to undermine or abolish the free democratic basic order'.[71] The aim of the KPD, it was alleged, was 'to establish a socialist-communist system by means of a proletarian revolution and the dictatorship of the proletariat'. The KPD did not deny this, instead arguing that Article 21 was itself in violation of the free democratic order, an argument rejected by the Court.

The conception of democracy constructed was, thus, more in line with Carl Schmitt and Rudolf Smend,[72] than it was with Hans Kelsen, who had strongly rejected the concept of militant democracy, favouring a procedural over a substantive version of democracy (as we saw in Chapter 2).[73] As Zuckerman and Accetti note, in rejecting the KPD's argument, the Court was forced to rely on the idea of a supposedly manifest 'political will' of the constitution's framers, 'which clearly reflects the lingering influence of the Schmittian idea of a constitutional core'.[74] The decision, described as setting the benchmark for its new 'militant democracy',[75] contains an 'inherent arbitrariness' over who is to be treated as an "enemy" of democracy, and even 'implies a "decisionist" and authoritarian exercise of power': one which 'contradicts the very logic of the system it is supposed to protect'.[76]

Even though appearing fundamentally *anti-democratic* in the abstract, this authoritarian framework would be legitimized by the idea of 'constitutional patriotism', a cultural appendage to militant democracy associated with Jürgen Habermas, which operated as a substitute for 'the traumatized national self-esteem of West Germans'.[77] This new loyalty to the liberal constitution would be cemented by counter-majoritarian institutions: not only the Federal Constitutional Court, but also the Bundesbank would benefit from a cultural deference to expertise. Like the constitutional court, the Bundesbank was bolstered by its own set of myths constructed out of interwar

[70] Risse and Engelmann-Martin (n 68) 296. Milward ascribes Adenauer's view of Russia as a 'barbaric non-European country' to a racial prejudice prevalent in mainstream German conservatism (Milward (n 12) 329).

[71] *KPD Case*, BVerfGE 5, 156.

[72] On the influence of Smend, see Jud Mathews, *Extending Rights' Reach: Constitutions, Private Law and Judicial Power* (OUP 2018) 54–56.

[73] Hans Kelsen, *The Essence and Value of Democracy* (Nadia Urbinati and Carlo I Accetti eds, Brian Graf tr, Rowman & Littlefield 2013).

[74] Carlo I Accetti and Ian Zuckerman, 'What's Wrong with Militant Democracy?' (2016) 65 Political Studies 182, 191.

[75] See Donald P Kommers and Russell A Miller, *The Constitutional Jurisprudence of the Federal Republic of Germany* (Duke University Press 2012) 291.

[76] Accetti and Zuckerman (n 74) 190. Schupmann (n 52) 212, although attempting to defend a version of militant democracy, appears to acknowledge its contradictions, and suggests 'constrained democracy' as a more appropriate label, noting that 'another name for this phenomenon could be "authoritarian liberalism"'.

[77] Ulrich Preuss, 'Political Order and Democracy: Carl Schmitt and his Influence' in Chantal Mouffe (ed), *The Challenge of Carl Schmitt* (Verso 1999).

prehistory, such as the links between political interference with central bank independence, hyperinflation, and democratic collapse.[78]

The German post-war model was not merely one among several developing in parallel. What Franz Neumann, in 1950, had critiqued as constitutional fetishism became feted far beyond the Federal Republic. The 'constitutional culture ... anchored by the post-World War II German constitution' became 'the most influential in the world', according to one recent commentator.[79] The ideas of militant democracy, and then constitutional patriotism, would transfer particularly smoothly to jurisdictions, such as Italy, which had experienced a similar national trauma of a descent into fascism. The Italian version was formulated through the idea of a 'protected democracy' (*democrazia protetta*), advanced by powerful Christian democratic forces. As a matter of constitutional theory, as Marta Cartabia puts it, fundamental constitutional rights would form a constitutional core in this world view. Rights would constitute 'an acceptable basis for the collective identity of a *demos* founded on a community of values', able to replace 'the old-fashioned *demos* based on nationality, race, blood, or other factors'.[80]

Within Western Europe more generally—particularly, but not exclusively, in countries tainted by the rise of fascism—political democracy came to be limited through the juridification of the constitution. The judicial protection of individual rights, and legalization of other constitutional rules, emerges through an expansion of judicial review and an increase in the power and authority of the juristic class (including specialized jurisdictions separate from the judiciary).[81] This process expanded and accelerated throughout the post-war period, even in jurisdictions, such as France, normally and historically resistant to the notion of 'government by judges'.[82] The ending of this resistance, which had been maintained since the French Revolution, was, as Stone Sweet shows, prefigured in the interwar attacks on the 'Jacobin despotism' of legislative supremacy associated with Rousseau's general will.[83] In 1971 it would, effectively, be finalized when the French Conseil Constitutionnel began to incorporate a Bill of Rights, based on the preamble, into

[78] Even though, as we saw in Part I, deflation was the proximate cause for democratic collapse. For discussion on the early years of the German central bank, see Jörg Bibow, 'On the Origin and Rise of Central Bank independence in West Germany' (2009) 16 The European Journal of the History of Economic Thought 155. See, further: Hjalte C Lokdam, 'Banking on Sovereignty: A Genealogy of the European Central Bank's Independence' (LSE, PhD Thesis 2019).

[79] Kim Lane Scheppele, 'Jack Balkin is an American' (2013) 25 Yale Journal of Law & the Humanities 23.

[80] Marta Cartabia, 'The Legacy of Sovereignty in the Italian Constitutional Debate' in Neil Walker (ed), *Sovereignty in Transition* (Hart Publishing 2003) 305, 317–18 (Cartabia speaks of the 'sovereignty of values' at 317–18). See, further: Marco Dani, 'The Subjectification of the Citizen in European Public Law' in Loïc Azoulai, Ségolène Barbou des Places, and Etienne Patuat (eds), *Constructing the Person in EU Law* (Hart Publishing 2016) (in Dani's view, the post-war constitution began as democratic and social, and only lost these qualities at a later stage, in line with the Single European Act).

[81] See Alec Stone Sweet, *Governing with Judges: Constitutional Politics in Europe* (OUP 2000). This is a phenomenon with global dimensions. See, eg Bruce Ackerman, 'The Rise of World Constitutionalism' (1997) 83 Virginia Law Review 771. On the 'juristocracy', see Ran Hirshl, *Towards Juristocracy: The Origins and Rise of the New Constitutionalism* (HUP 2004).

[82] See Mitchel Lasser, *Judicial Transformations: The Rights Revolution in the Courts of Europe* (OUP 2009).

[83] Stone Sweet, 'American Judicial Review' (n 45) (noting the significance of Hauriou and Duguit).

1958 Constitution of the Fifth Republic, despite the firm rejection of such a move at its inception.

The most profound symbol of democratic limitation would be the use of the 'eternity clause' to prohibit constitutional amendment, in an attempt to avoid constitutional politics, taming the so-called 'derived', and perhaps even the original, constituent power.[84] Together with other provisions, this clause, it has been said, 'provides the legal backbone of German militant democracy'.[85] It is transformed into an even broader and vaguer limit through the later development of the doctrine of 'constitutional identity', where an explicit or implicit (and therefore easily expandable) core of constitutional values is protected by constitutional courts against modification. The notion of constitutional identity (or 'basic structure') suggests that there are substantive constitutional limits, not only on ordinary law, but on constitutional amendments. We thus arrive at the paradoxical idea of an 'unconstitutional constitutional amendment'.[86]

The silencing of the popular constituent power through the juridical operationalization of constitutional identity represents the legalization of Carl Schmitt's distinction between the big 'C' Constitution and constitutional laws, now guarded by a court rather than a presidential institution.[87] Instead of dealing with underlying constitutional conflicts, this process of legalization, however, would merely conceal them,[88] depoliticizing constitutional conflict in a way that would end up politicizing the court.[89]

In this process of legal constitutionalization, and of the judicialization of the principle of constitutional identity, international and supranational courts play a prominent role, not least since their own doctrines (particularly those of the European Court of Justice) effectively turn *ordinary courts* into *constitutional courts*. But, as we will see, this is also an ambiguous development, since domestic constitutional identity would eventually come into open judicial conflict with aspects of European integration.[90]

[84] This is generally associated with the German Basic Law, but has travelled beyond: see, eg Jacques Ziller, 'Sovereignty in France: Getting Rid of the Mal de Bodin' in Neil Walker (ed), *Sovereignty in Transition* (Hart Publishing 2003) 270–72; Cartabia (n 79). Taming the original constituent power may appear impossible, as a matter of legal form, but, as we will examine in Chapter 7, this is one reading that emerges from the Maastricht and Lisbon decisions of the German Constitutional Court.

[85] Hailbronner (n 49) 51.

[86] Yaniv Roznai, *Unconstitutional Constitutional Amendments: The Limits of Amendment Powers* (OUP 2017).

[87] cf David Dyzenhaus, 'Constitutionalism in an Old Key: Legality and Constituent Power' (2012) 1 Global Constitutionalism 229, 257 ('constituent power is at best a distraction for constitutional theory'); David Dyzenhaus, 'The Politics of the Question of Constituent Power' in Loughlin and Walker (eds), *The Paradox of Constitutionalism* (OUP 2007) ('the question of constituent power simply does not arise for a liberal account of the rule of law').

[88] See Bomhoff, 'Constitutional Rights' (n 47) 236, citing Norbert Elias, *The Germans: Power Struggles and the Development of Habitus in the Nineteenth and Twentieth Centuries* (Polity Press 1996).

[89] See JAG Griffith, 'The Political Constitution' (1979) 42 Modern Law Review 1, for an early diagnosis of this dilemma in a different context (the UK), but in way which is generalizable.

[90] This is explored in more detail in Chapter 7, as its significance becomes clearer after the Maastricht decision of the German Constitutional Court.

4. Constitutionalization of the European Treaties

Just like the restrained inter-state sovereignty discussed above, restrained popular sovereignty (restraining not only ordinary politics but also the constituent power) would be achieved through external as well as domestic institutions, in a combination of international and national commitments. The inter-state developments already mentioned, including the creation of a regional human rights agreement—the European Convention on Human Rights—and especially the trade agreements and supranational Community institutions created by the Treaty of Paris in 1951, and consolidated and extended by the Treaty of Rome in 1957, would thus have an impact not just on the state's external action but on its domestic political authority.[91] The way in which this emerged as a constitutional constraint requires a more detailed excursion into the role played by courts and other legal actors.

It is often reiterated in the literature that the European Court of Justice (ECJ) 'constitutionalized' the European Treaties, beginning from the early 1960s in the cases of *Van Gend en Loos* and *Costa v ENEL*, with its doctrines of direct effect and primacy.[92] The Court presented the legal order as independent, distinct from ordinary international law; and later as 'autonomous', and based on Treaties that established a 'constitutional charter'. Faced with some resistance from the German Constitutional Court, the ECJ would soon extend European legal primacy over even constitutional norms at the national level, based, essentially, on functional principles of 'effectiveness' (*effet utile*),[93] in the process claiming to protect individual 'fundamental' rights and freedoms in its own way.[94]

The effect of the 'constitutional juggernaut' of *Van Gend en Loos* was, according to one commentator—comparing it to the decision of the Supreme Court in *Marbury v. Madison*—both to 'radically disaggregate the State' by employing national courts

[91] On the origins of the ECHR and its role in constraining democratic socialism, see Marco Duranti, *The Conservative Human Rights Revolution: European Identity, Transnational Politics and the Origins of the European Convention* (OUP 2017).

[92] Case 6/44 *Costa v ENEL* [1964] ECR 585. In *Costa v ENEL*, the ECJ claimed that EEC law, 'an independent source of law, could not, because of its special and original nature, be overridden by domestic legal provisions, however framed, without being deprived of its character as Community law and without the legal basis of the Community itself being called into question'. A year after *Costa v ENEL*, the following article was published by the influential US scholar Stein: Eric Stein, 'Towards the Supremacy of Treaty-Constitution by Judicial Fiat: On the Margin of the Costa Case' (1965) 63 Michigan Law Review 491.

[93] See Case 11/70 *Internationale Handelsgesellschaft v Einfuhr -und Vorratstelle fur Getreide und Futtermittel (Solange I)* [1970] ECR 1125. On the early reception of the ECJ's doctrines in Germany, see Bill Davies, *Resisting the European Court of Justice: 1949–1979: West Germany's Confrontation with European Law* (CUP 2012).

[94] Although Advocate General Lagrange had already described EU law as a 'constitution' in his opinion in *Costa* (the Treaty of Rome, he said, had 'the nature of a real constitution'), and had used the term 'autonomy' as early as 1956 in his opinion in *Mirrosevich v High Authority* (Case 10/55 *Miranda Mirossevich v High Authority* [1956] OJ 18, 399), the term 'constitutional' would not be used by the ECJ until Case 294/83 *Parti Ecologiste 'Les Verts' v European Parliament* [1986] ECR 1339. The autonomy of the Community legal order would be reiterated by the Court of Justice in Opinion 2/13 on the accession of the EU to the European Convention of Human Rights [2014] OJ C65/2, and in *Kadi*, discussed in Chapter 10. The principle has not been undisputed. See, eg Theodor Schilling, JHH Weiler, and Ulrich Haltern, 'Who in Law is the Ultimate Judicial Umpire of European Community Competences? – The Schilling–Weiler/Haltern debate' (1996) Jean Monnet Papers 96/10.

in the service of EU law, and to 'recalibrate the Community system' in the normative turn to the individual.[95] In the construction of a new supranational legal order, the individual becomes the bearer of directly effective legal rights, and even, in one account, becomes the 'jurisgenerative' unit par excellence in Community law.[96]

Although this narrative would occasionally be advanced with warnings attached—Weiler, for example, belatedly noted that a system with individuals at its centre is liable to degrade into self-centred individualism[97]—it would generally be celebrated in the scholarship.[98] Despite notable instances of resistance, European constitutionalism would also largely be embraced by domestic courts. The elevation of the constitutional rights (the material aspects of which are discussed further in the next chapter) as parameters of legitimation thus occurred across two tracks, which were intertwined. They were formally intertwined through the preliminary reference procedure established by the Treaty of Rome (now Article 256 of the Treaty on European Union (TEU)), which meant that the ECJ was largely dependent on cooperation with national courts. And they were informally intertwined through the limited cadre of judicial appointments and narrow legal culture, in terms of the class and educational background of judges.[99] The idea of the 'sovereignty of law' could only be given historical sense if understood 'as a shorthand for the power of the juristic class'.[100]

The substitution of constituent power with constitutional rights as the framing idea for the whole constitutional order thus occurred in the light of national, as much as transnational, and supra-national processes of constitutionalization.[101] Both regionally and domestically, these processes 'came as a masterly and opportune substitute for a real constitution, and law as a convenient expedient for politics', effectively neutralizing political disputes by turning them into mere 'technical matters'.[102] Although occurring on the basis of specialized and often obscure cases on tariff and non-tariff barriers to goods, these technical matters would come to be dressed in the garb of grand-sounding constitutional doctrine such as direct effect and supremacy (which would be extended to more politically salient domains in the later jurisprudence discussed in Part III).

In other words—despite the early failures to establish a European political community based on a constitution authorized by the 'peoples of Europe'—the European

[95] Daniel Halberstam, 'Pluralism in *Marbury* and *Van Gend*' in Miguel P Maduro and Loic Azoulai (eds), *The Past and Future of EU Law* (Hart Publishing 2010).

[96] ibid. As we discuss below, this was not the empowerment of 'the individual' but, rather, predominantly 'the firm'.

[97] Joseph HH Weiler, 'Van Gend en Loos: Individual as Subject and Object and the Dilemma of European Legitimacy' (2014) 12:1 International Journal of Constitutional Law 94.

[98] See, eg Francis Jacobs, *Sovereignty of Law: The European Way* (CUP 2007).

[99] On the background of judges and *referendaires* of the ECJ, see Angela Zhang, 'The Faceless Court' (2016) 38 University of Pennsylvania Journal of International Law 71.

[100] See Marti Koskenniemi, 'Conclusion: Vocabularies of Sovereignty – Powers of a Paradox' in Hent Kalmo and Quentin Skinner (eds), *Sovereignty in Fragments: The Past, Present and Future of a Contested Concept* (CUP 2009) 229.

[101] See Martin Loughlin, 'What is Constitutionalisation?' in Martin Loughlin and Petra Dobner (eds), *The Twilight of Constitutionalism* (OUP 2010).

[102] Antonin Cohen, 'Constitutionalism without Constitution: Transnational Elites Between Mobilisation and Legal Expertise in the Making of a Constitution For Europe (1940s–1960s)', *Law and Social Enquiry* 32 (2007) 109.

Court of Justice, and the European legal community more generally, pursued, at times aggressively, the *legal fiction* of a constitution.[103] It was this fiction that authorized the shift from political constitution-making to judicial constitutionalization, substituting the older idea of constituent power for a new idea of constitutional rights. As Shapiro famously noted:

> The Community [is presented] as a juristic idea; the written constitution as a sacred text; the professional commentary as a legal truth; the case law as the inevitable working out of the correct implications of the constitutional text; and the constitutional court as the disembodied voice of right reason and constitutional teleology.[104]

Despite the undoubted significance of German constitutionalism, and of the German Constitutional Court itself, the elevation of the juristic class was not merely a German affair, nor one lacking a longer genealogy. *Van Gen en Loos* and *Costa v ENEL* were themselves decided under the presidency of Judge Robert Lecourt, a French Christian democrat. They had followed in the wake of the Constitution of the Fifth Republic of 1958, which had, in its own way, signalled the erosion of domestic parliamentary supremacy in France.[105] The ideological origins have been said to be found 'in the ambition of eighteenth–and nineteenth-century rationalists, from Francois Quesnay to Saint-Simon'. This was 'for a "despotism" of the law, for a rational and efficient administration that would ultimately dispense with the messiness, brutality, and particularism of politics'.[106] The notion of 'law without state' could be traced even further back in history, to the medieval jurists attempting to unify European legal culture based on Roman and canon law, and to a pre-modern constitutional imaginary that accorded with a fragmentation of authority and a legal pluralism based on universal values.[107]

Whatever its precise scholastic origins, the overall trajectory of the process of domestic and transnational juridification was not only to depoliticize and de-democratize state-society relations, but also to replace political and democratic deliberation with juridical and technocratic forms of decision-making and norm-setting. This trajectory would often be combined with a deep cultural conservatism; an attempt to restore an older wisdom and guidance of those in authority, and the stability and security that was perceived to come with it.[108]

Although direct comparisons between *Van Gend en Loos* and *Marbury v Madison* must be offered with caution,[109] there are illuminating parallels, particularly in terms

[103] ibid.

[104] Martin Shapiro, 'Comparative Law and Comparative Politics' (1980) 53 Southern California Law Review 537, 538.

[105] Ziller (n 83) 261–77.

[106] See Tony Judt, *A Grand Illusion? An Essay on Europe* (Hill and Wang 1996).

[107] See further, eg Ralf Michaels and Nils Jansen, 'Private Law Beyond the State? Europeanization, Globalization, Privatization' (2016) 54 The American Journal of Comparative Law 843. This is developed further in Part IV, when, after Maastricht, theories of constitutional pluralism become dominant in the academy.

[108] On post-war Germany's 'technocratic conservatism', based on a longing for stability and security, see Dirk van Laak, 'From the Conservative Revolution to Technocratic Conservatism' in Jan-Werner Müller (ed), *German Ideologies Since 1945: Studies in the Political Thought and Culture of the Bonn Republic* (Palgrave MacMillan 2003) 147.

[109] cf Halberstam (n 95).

of the process of conflating fundamental law and ordinary law, set in motion and sustained by the judicial branches in the US, as in the European Union. Through the process of judicial constitutionalization, it has been argued, specifically in relation to *Marbury v Madison* and its progeny, that, 'the provisions of the US constitution became positivised, de-politicized, individualized, and legalized'.[110] The provisions of the Treaty of Rome have been subjected to a similar fate, with similar consequences for the EU legal order, as well as for national constitutional orders, through the judicial architecture of the Union, and—proactively—by the legal doctrines developed by the Court of Justice.[111] Integration through law, which became a scholarly movement in the 1980s, signified that law would be both the object and the agent of integration. This movement did nothing less than to 'shap[e] the contours of EU law as an academic discipline'.[112] As the editors of the *Integration Through Law* volumes identified, the challenge was one of 'seduc[ing] the individuals' loyalty—at least in part—away from the state'.[113]

The differences between European and US federalist discourses, however, are significant. In the US, constitutionalization takes place alongside a myth of political emancipation, based in the idea of 'We the People' as the grounds of authority. The difference, thus, has less to do with the commonly supposed presence or absence of a '*demos*', of cultural or linguistic homogeneity, and more to do with the narrative that develops in distinct historical-political contexts. To put the point starkly, where the American project is accompanied by a revolutionary narrative, the post-war European project appears to be counter-revolutionary, an effort to arrest the progress of the democratic constituent power; 'to stem the tide of revolution', as Arendt put it.[114]

The evolutionary constitutionalization pursued in the judicial framework of European integration is, in certain key respects, closer to the emergence of a 'common law constitutionalism',[115] which happens piecemeal, spontaneously, is judge-led and elitist. In that limited sense, it is closer to Hayek's vision of a liberal *cosmos* than a legislatively designed *taxis*.[116] But there is little in the narrative that appears as natural or spontaneous. On the contrary, the argument that the Court proceeded by stealth, and

[110] Loughlin (n 101) 293.

[111] In the words of Mestmäcker, 'According to a widespread opinion in the United States and represented also by an influential lobby in Brussels, there is only one direction in which European law should develop: in the direction of American law'; see Ernst-Joachim Mestmäcker, 'European Touchstones of Dominion and Law' (2007) 58 The Ordo Yearbook of Economic and Social Order 2. According to Cohen (n 102), the development of a constitutional comparativism in which the US constitution was 'the central point of reference' was the result of the investments of a number of 'European and American transnational entrepreneurs in the definition of a new international order and of the legal investments of different law professionals (both American and European) in the formalization of a model of federalism based on the comparison of different forms of federations' (ibid 113).

[112] Daniel Augenstein and Mark Dawson, 'Introduction: What Law for What Polity? "Integration through Law" in the European Union Revisited' in Daniel Augenstein (ed), *'Integration through Law' Revisited: The Making of the European Polity* (Ashgate Publishing 2012) 1.

[113] ibid 26.

[114] Hannah Arendt, *On Revolution* (Penguin Books 1990), 135.

[115] See, eg Somek, 'The Cosmopolitan Constitution' (n 57).

[116] See Friedrich Hayek, *Law, Legislation and Liberty* (Taylor & Hudson 1982). It is no coincidence that Hayek favoured what he thought was the spontaneity of the common law in preference to legislation. See discussion in Raymond Plant, *The Neo-Liberal State* (OUP 2009).

against the wishes of the member states, is captured in the often-repeated claim that it committed a 'judicial coup'.[117]

Although this process would occasionally encounter resistance from domestic courts, resistance rarely amounted to a significant blockage or pushback. The interlinking of the supranational narrative with domestic constitutional developments was articulated in the celebrated 'dialogue' between European courts and national courts through the so-called *Solange* jurisprudence, which prompted the construction of a set of unwritten principles of human rights law by the ECJ, as well as through the Europeanization of domestic projects of constitutional reform.[118]

To be sure, this early constitutionalization was, in many ways, an ersatz and unbalanced process, not only in the sense of bypassing political and constituent power, but even in respect of the value of legality itself. The ECJ was weak on Fundamental Rights protection and notoriously bad at developing a doctrine of judicial review of EU law. The latter was nowhere more evident than in its own excessively strict standing requirements, and its reluctance to annul any EU legislation.[119] This reluctance was justified, in part, for reasons of Treaty construction, although textual limits did not prevent the ECJ from expansive rulings elsewhere.[120] What is clear is that its constitutionalization of Treaty law was a means of self-authorization and enforcement, rather than a means of constructing a robust rule of law in the republican sense of horizontal checks and balances against the excessive concentration of supranational power.

The two aspects of authority are of course intertwined: the more that EU law could present itself as legitimate, the more its authority would be acceptable, and accepted by domestic institutions. But there was always the suspicion that the ECJ's increasing juridification of superior Fundamental Rights norms was aimed primarily at elevating its own juridical authority over that of national courts, especially domestic constitutional courts. If the 'surface language' of the Court's jurisprudence was the language of human rights, Joseph Weiler famously argued, the 'deep structure' was all about supremacy.[121]

The early *Solange*-style conflict would not capture the political attention in the way later clashes would, such as *Viking* and *Laval* (see Chapter 8) or *OMT* and *Weiss* (see

[117] Alec Stone Sweet, *The Judicial Construction of Europe* (OUP 2004); Stone Sweet, 'The Juridical Coup d'etat' (n 54) (also describing the Lüth decision of the German Constitutional Court, and the 1971 incorporation of the rights in the preamble into the 1958 Constitution by the French constitutional council, as 'juridical coup d'états').

[118] cf Brun-Otto Bryde, 'The ECJ's Fundamental Rights Jurisprudence – A Milestone in Transnational Constitutionalism' in Loïc Azoulai and Miguel P Maduro (eds), *The Past and Future of EU Law* (Hart Publishing 2010).

[119] For a critique of overly narrow standing requirements, see Opinion of Advocate General Jacobs delivered on 21 March 2002, Case C-50/00P *Unión de Pequeños Agricultores v Council of the European Union* [2002] ECR I-6677. As Bartolini put it, 'when we examine the process from the point of view of the formation and consolidation of the new European central hierarchy, its peculiarity is not "constitutionalization", but, on the contrary, a very clear lack of this. There is a noticeable lack of clear provisions for limited government, there is no vertical or horizontal separation of powers, and finally, only a weak net of protections for citizens exist in areas other than those of their capacities as economic agents' (Stefano Bartolini, *Restructuring Europe: Centre Formation, System Building, and Political Structuring Between the Nation State and the European Union* (OUP 2005) 165).

[120] Most famously, perhaps, *Les Verts v European Parliament* (n 93), where it also spoke of the Treaties as the 'Constitutional Charter' of the EEC.

[121] Joseph HH Weiler, 'The Transformation of Europe' (1991) 100 Yale Law Journal 2403.

Chapter 10), when the political-economic implications of constitutionalizing free movement provisions, or of empowering the ECB, became far clearer and more controversial in terms of disrupting sensitive domestic choices. Provided there was no outright conflict between domestic and supranational courts, the system could remain functional, and the contests presented as productive, or at least not destructive.

Functionalism and a normative attachment to judicial power would eventually give rise to various theories of constitutional pluralism, pluralist constitutionalism, contrapuntal law, and so on.[122] Ironically, but tellingly, these justificatory discourses only gained significant ground when European constitutionalism came to be increasingly *contested* after the Treaty of Maastricht; once, in other words, constitutionalization of EU law started to become more obviously *dysfunctional*, and its legitimacy was called into question with the return of political sovereignty and issues of constituent power (examined in Part III).

More generally, the upshot of these competing claims of constitutional rights was their eventual *devaluation*—from initially being cast as liberal 'trumps', defeating governmental policy prescriptions, in Dworkin's influential narrative[123]—they would come to be considered merely as ubiquitous interests to be 'balanced'. With the inflation of rights undermining their rhetorical power, the doctrine of proportionality increasingly came to dominate discussion of constitutional and administrative review in both domestic and transnational settings.[124] But proportionality was merely a way of further judicializing political and social conflict, now with a fictional Hercules as sovereign, capable of identifying the correct answer.[125]

Law, lawyers, and legal ideology thus played a central role in the constitutional imaginary of Europe, and the building of the European polity.[126] This hardly made Europe unique in the historiography of modern state- or polity-building. The insight that 'lawyers' law' played a fundamental role in the project of European integration, as well as constitutionalism beyond the state more generally, provides a sense of continuity with a phenomenon that has been pronounced domestically: the rise of the jurist as 'guardian' and, even, as 'state-builder'.[127] It reflects the more

[122] See, generally, Jan Komarek and Matej Avbelj (eds), *Constitutional Pluralism in the European Union and Beyond* (Hart Publishing 2012). These ideas are examined further in Chapter 7.

[123] Ronald Dworkin, *Taking Rights Seriously* (HUP 1978).

[124] See Jacco Bomhoff, *Balancing Constitutional Rights* (CUP 2013); cf David Beatty, *The Ultimate Rule of Law* (OUP 2005).

[125] As Paul Kahn puts it, if we ask what the figure of Hercules—whose decisions always represent the 'true' meaning of the law—represents, we have no better answer than 'the sovereign' (Paul Kahn, *Political Theology: Four New Chapters on the Concept of Sovereignty* (Columbia University Press 2011) 81); he continues, 'the court's decisional authority is inseparable from its claim to speak in the voice of the sovereign people ... not the moral authority of Hercules but the political authority of We the People'.

[126] Cohen (n 102) noted that, 'of all the various social groups that Eric Stein once identified as major players in the 'making of a transnational constitution - judges and Advocate Generals of the ECJ, members of the legal services of the European Commission and the Council of Ministers, legal consultants of the national ministries, legal scholars, and law professors, to which one should add the "middlemen" of European integration, ie private lawyers and attorneys—most remain to be studied as social groups' (citing Eric Stein, 'Lawyers, Judges, and the Making of a Transnational Constitution' (1981) 75 The American Journal of International Law 1 and Stuart Scheingold, *The Law in Political Integration: The Evolution and Integrative Implications of Regional Legal Processes in the European Community* (Harvard University Press, 1971).

[127] See Martin Loughlin, *Foundations of Public Law* (OUP 2010) 307, drawing on Tocqueville. The Basic Law is described as 'lawyers' law' rather than 'layman's law' by Möllers (n 8).

general ascendency of contemporary liberal constitutionalism, whose project is of 'abolishing politics, or of so constraining it by legal and constitutional formulae that it no longer matters what are the outcomes of political deliberation'.[128] Law, in an age of rights and an emerging 'juristocracy', increasingly becomes a 'straightjacket' for politics.[129] If the EU is at the vanguard of this movement, it was largely created by states' in their own image'.[130]

If legal agents 'followed the same path taken by their ancestors; they produced "some State"';[131] less remarked upon in the academy was the kind of state they were producing. Constitutionalization tended to reinforce a liberal (or neo-liberal) political-economic rationality, due both to the nature of the Treaty law the Court was interpreting, and to the kind of litigation (and litigants) that came before it. It was not the 'abstract individual', but mobile economic operators, transnational enterprises, and commercial organizations that were privileged by the law of the European Economic Community.[132]

The type of state that judicial constitutionalization was 'producing' largely followed an ordoliberal vision, of a strong state and strong institutional guarantees for the flourishing of economic liberalism and a competitive free market economy. The substantive implications for the political economy of the member states, and the more general principle of democratic control over the economy, would emerge once it became clear that the substitution of constitutional rights and proportionality for constituent power and democratic politics was not merely a formal exchange of ideas. Once European integration was placed fully into focus, juridification of its rules would substantively to impact on domestic constitutional ordering by elevating economic freedoms (in the form of fundamental freedoms to trade) and undistorted competition above political autonomy, social and welfare provisions, and other non-economic concerns.[133]

To understand this transformation in full, we have to turn directly to a third dynamic of constitutional change in the project of post-war reconstitution and European integration: economic constitutionalism. Although this came into academic consciousness at a relatively late stage,[134] its potential should have been evident right from the start, symbolized by the case of *Costa v ENEL*, a case famously establishing the principle of the primacy of European law, based, as is rarely remembered, on an

[128] Martin Loughlin, *Sword and Scales: An Examination of the Relationship Between Law and Politics* (Hart Publishing 2000) 4–5, quoting John Gray, *Enlightenment's Wake: Politics and Culture at the Close of the Modern Age* (Routledge 1995). See also Adam Tomkins, 'In Defence of the Political Constitution' (2002) 22 Oxford Journal of Legal Studies 157.

[129] See Loughlin (n 128).

[130] Anthony Pagden, 'Introduction' in Pagden (n 69) 31.

[131] Cohen (n 102) 131.

[132] See Damian Chalmers and Luis Barroso, 'What van Gend en Loos Stands for' (2014) 12 International Journal of Constitutional Law 105.

[133] See Fritz W Scharpf, 'The Asymmetry of European Integration: or Why Europe Can't Have a Social Market Economy' (2010) 8 Socio-Economic Review 211. See, further, Alexander Somek, 'Constituent Power in National and Transnational Contexts' (2012) 3 Transnational Legal Theory 31.

[134] But see, already, Ernst Joachim Mestmäcker, "Power, Law and Economic Constitution' (1973)11:3 German Economic Review 182. Mestmäcker is described by Slobodian as 'the most important figure in combining Hayek with Böhm and scaling up the economic constitution to the suprastate level' (Quinn Slobodian, The Globalists: The End of Empire and the Birth of Neoliberalism (Harvard University Press 2018) 208).

(unsuccessful) challenge to the nationalization of the Italian electricity industry.[135] Economic constitutionalism is a phenomenon combining domestic and transnational dimensions, and support in legal, as well as political, domains. Understanding its material development also requires a consideration of how informal opposition to the post-war status quo was disarmed and deradicalized.

[135] On the historical background to the case, see Cohen (n 102).

5

The Material Constitution: Ordoliberalism, Neoliberalism, and the Deradicalization of Political Opposition

1. Introduction

The transformation of the post-war European state through depoliticization, legalization, and the making of a supranational constitution (outlined in Chapter 4) was not a value-neutral development. In practice, the demobilization of the masses, decline of parliamentarism, and construction of a transnational rule of law meant that politics would be reduced to a narrow centre ground, decision-making would be increasingly technical and remote from democratic debates, and, over time, socio-economic regulation would be subject to constitutional constraints entrenching economic freedoms, market logic and undistorted competition.

Even more fundamentally, the transformation signified a shift in the constitutional imagination, away from a political and towards an economic conception of freedom. 'Economic constitutionalism' would come to signify more than the conditioning of political authority by particular economic interests and ideas; it would signify *the economic* as the principal ground of authority for the 'constitution' of the polity as a whole.[1] With 'the economic' becoming foundational, market logic would colonize the totality of social and political relations.[2] This presaged the later TINA ('There Is No Alternative') narrative, positing that there was no alternative to structural reform, which came to fruition in the Maastricht era, and was hardened through the euro crisis phase (examined in Parts III and IV, respectively). But, in reality, the foundations were laid much earlier, from the era of the Treaty of Rome.[3] As the young Habermas put it, writing on the cusp of the new neo-liberalism emerging out of the economic crises of

[1] Foucault captured this reversal between state and market in ordoliberal thought in his lectures in the late 1970s; see Michel Foucault, *The Birth of Biopolitics—Lectures at the College de France 1978–1979* (Graham Burchell tr, Palgrave MacMillan 2008). See, further, Owen Parker, *Cosmopolitan Government in Europe: Citizens and Entrepreneurs in Postnational Politics* (Routledge 2013) 27–50.

[2] See Emilios Christodoulidis, 'The European Court of Justice and "Total Market" Thinking' (2013) 14 German Law Journal 2005. Even systems theorists came to recognize this threat; see, eg Gunter Teubner, *Constitutional Fragments: Societal Constitutionalism and Globalization* (OUP 2013).

[3] In the view of Brian Bercusson, although the Treaty of Paris 1951 had suggested an active labour policy, the period following Paris, in complete contrast, 'was characterised by a strategy of neo-liberal laissez-faire, reflected in the almost total absence of social policy and labour law provisions in the Treaty of Rome of 1957' (Brian Bercusson, *European Labour Law* (2nd edn, CUP 2012) 102. See also Wolfgang Streeck, 'The Internationalisation of Industrial Relations in Europe: Prospects and Problems' (1998) 26 Politics and Society 429 430 (Streeck, 'Industrial Relations in Europe'): 'by the time of the Treaty of Rome, the preferred approach for the integration of the European economy, and presumably European society, had become the integration of markets, and no longer of planning authorities on the older model of the ECSC'.

Authoritarian Liberalism and the Transformation of Modern Europe. Michael A Wilkinson, Oxford University Press.
 DOI: 10.1093/oso/9780198854753.003.0006

the early 1970s, the civil privatism of late capitalism had meant 'high-output orientation versus low-input orientation'. This corresponded to the constitutional structures of a 'depoliticised public'.[4]

In this chapter, we will first examine the establishment of a new economic constitutionalism based on ordoliberal ideas in practical combination with a social market economy (section 2). We then turn to consider the scaling up of the economic constitution through European integration, and its deepening in the period commonly referred to as 'neo-liberal', beginning in the mid- 1970s (section 3), before finally outlining how opposition to this post-war constitutional dynamic was disarmed and deradicalized by its own turn away from class politics and popular sovereignty (section 4).

2. The economic constitution and ordoliberalism

As we saw in Chapter 1, the idea of an 'economic constitution' was prefigured in the interwar period by Frankfurt School theorists Franz Neumann and Hugo Sinzheimer.[5] For those left-leaning labour lawyers in early Weimar, it signalled political-democratic control over the economy, the logical progression of the constitutional idea originating in the modern revolutions of the late eighteenth century: the autonomy of the political realm. It represented the move from a bourgeois constitution to a labour constitution; a move, in Marxist terminology, from political emancipation towards full human emancipation, with collective autonomy over the means of production.[6]

In the course of post-war reconstruction, however, the economic constitution became associated with the Freiburg ordoliberals, and its meaning inverted: the economic constitution became a political decision for the autonomy of the economic realm, a realm characterized by inequality and exploitation. The point was no longer to move forward to a labour constitution, or to economic democracy, but to restore and prolong classical liberal ideals into a new era, protecting the basic rules underlying free market competition. This would be restored, not through any outmoded return to laissez-faire, but through renewing a constitutional and institutional culture prioritizing political and economic stability, and a rule-based culture that was deemed essential for the free market to function efficiently.[7] Economic constitutionalism

[4] Jürgen Habermas, 'What does a Legitimation Crisis Mean Today? Legitimation Problems in Late Capitalism' (1973) 40 Social Research 643.

[5] See Franz Neumann, 'On the Preconditions and the Legal Concept of an Economic Constitution' in Otto Kirchheimer and Franz Neumann (eds), *Social Democracy and the Rule of Law* (Leera Tanner and Keith Tribe trs, Allen and Unwin 1987)(Neumann, 'On the Preconditions'). See also Ruth Dukes, *The Labour Constitution: The Enduring Idea of Labour Law* (OUP 2012).

[6] See Karl Marx, *Economic and Philosophical Manuscripts of 1844* (Dover Publications 2007). This would, thus, have resolved the 'comprehensive contradiction' that Marx noted, in commenting on the French Constitution of 1850, 'The classes whose social slavery the constitution is to perpetuate, proletariat, peasantry, petty bourgeoisie, it puts in possession of *political power* through *universal suffrage*. And from the class whose old *social power* it sanctions, the bourgeoisie, it withdraws the *political guarantees* of this power ... (f) rom the ones it demands that they should not go forward *from political to social emancipation*; from the others that they should not go back *from social to political restoration*': (Karl Marx, 'The Class Struggles in France, 1848 to 1850' in K Marx, F Engels (eds), *Marx and Engels 1849–51* (Lawrence & Wishart 1978) 79.

[7] See David Gerber, 'Constitutionalising the Economy: German Neoliberalism, Competition Law and the "New Europe"' (1994) 42 American Journal of Comparative Law 25.

then came to be seen as analogous, in the economic domain, to the efforts of 'militant democrats' in the political domain, namely to depoliticize (qua de-democratize) the basic rules of political economy. Accordingly, whereas its initial formulation in early Weimar pointed at democratization of the economy, in the post-war era it came to mean the opposite: keeping democracy at bay, closed off from the economic sphere as far as possible.[8]

The ordoliberal economic constitution would, in fact, need to perform a twofold function, insulating the economy from both public and private power; from corruption by democratic interference as well as from excessive concentrations of capital. If this would, at times, require intervention, it could only be a liberal interventionism (a 'Marktkonforme Intervention'), working 'in the same direction as the rules of the market, not against them'.[9] At both the macro and micro levels of the economy, constitutional, technocratic, and legal solutions would need to be found in order to maintain the conditions of a free market. Ordoliberalism thus called for the constitutionalization of the economic sphere in the double sense of protecting it from the irrationality of monopoly control, and from political-democratic planning.

The ordoliberals' founding meeting in Freiburg in 1933 had coincided with Carl Schmitt's address to the *Langnamverein*, discussed in Part I: 'strong state, sound economy'.[10] Sharing Schmitt's vehement anti-communism, obsession with order, distrust of economic democracy, and belief in a strong state, the motto captured their own distance from the classical liberal idea of the minimal 'nightwatchman' state of the nineteenth century.[11] Ordoliberals and defenders of the (politically related) tradition of 'social market economy' considered the laissez-faire of classical liberalism to be socially and politically bankrupt. As against Friedrich von Hayek's outmoded brand of 'palaeoliberalism', they presented the free economic order as constructed and maintained by a strong state apparatus and strong constitutional rules, and not by a spontaneous evolution of the free market and market relations.[12] The conditions for competition would not simply take care of themselves; unbridled capitalism would be as destructive as unfettered democracy. That was the lesson the ordoliberals had drawn from the collapse of the Weimar Republic. In contrast to the Austrian (and later Chicago-style) neo-liberals, ordoliberals thus presented capitalism, as well

[8] See, eg Hauke Brunkhorst, 'Collective Bonapartism' (2005) 15:6 German Law Journal 1188: 'The *first stage* of the constitutional evolution was triggered by the invention of the *economic constitution* of Europe that consisted in the *structural coupling of law and economics*. In 1957 treaty negotiations, German Ordoliberals—then strongly backed by the conservative American government—took the chance to realize their old dream of a mere *technical constitution without government and legislator*'.

[9] Friedrich A Lutz, 'The Functioning of the Gold Standard' in Alan T Peacock and Hans Willgerodt (eds), *Germany's Social Market Economy: Origins and Evolution* (Palgrave MacMillan 1989). Published originally as 'Goldwährung und Wirtschaftsordnung' (1935) 41 Weltwirtschaftliches Archiv 224.

[10] On the link between Schmitt and the ordoliberals, and the significant of both for the euro, see Werner Bonefeld, 'Authoritarian Liberalism: From Schmitt via Ordoliberalism to the Euro' (2017) 43 Critical Sociology 747.

[11] The term, coined pejoratively by Ferdinand Lassalle, was already misleading in the nineteenth century, as Neumann notes (Franz Neumann, 'The Change in Function of Law in Modern Society' in *The Political and the Authoritarian State* (Free Press 1957) 22–68).

[12] As we noted in Chapter 3, Hayek's position was more nuanced, particularly in his theory of inter-state federalism.

as democracy, as potentially inimical to the competition-based market society.[13] Capitalist innovation and spontaneity, in and of itself, could not be trusted to overcome the problem of monopoly power and anticompetitive practices.

The analogy with Schmitt is instructive. For the ordoliberals, the economic constitution had to be grounded in a political decision; a comprehensive political decision on the nature and form of a liberal economy. The institutions to guarantee it must not be undermined, either by democratic efforts to control the economy, or by monopolistic attempts to control the market. The ordoliberal's faith in the economic constitution thus required the accompaniment of a strong technocratic-juridical governance apparatus to maintain efficient market conditions, as well as an ideological and cultural commitment to the market values it was tasked with protecting.[14] The free economy, in other words, required a concrete order (an *ordo*): a complex cultural, as well as institutional and legal, achievement. But once this order was constituted, political intervention could, and should, be limited.

If to put the law above man, as Rousseau quipped, '*il faudrait des dieux*' (one would need gods), the ordoliberals answered the call for a new set of elites, who, confounding Rousseau, could, like gods, finally 'give laws to men'.[15] The ordoliberal programme was the culmination of a German brand of political rationalism; a way to tame the passions of an erratic 'people', and avoid democracy turning away from liberalism. If, in other words, both democracy and capitalism needed to be tamed to prevent their self-destruction, economic constitutionalism was the means to achieve this aim; to establish the conditions of the free market through constitutional rights, technical intervention, and legal regulation. With the right institutions in place, personal freedom could be maintained through the market mechanism.

The relationship between ordoliberalism and European economic integration is not a straightforward one, with some ordoliberals (and neo-liberals) viewing the EEC as too interventionist, and (particularly in its 'Eurafrican' extension) a potential impediment to a more global free trade regime.[16] Ordoliberalism had a clear, if latent, influence on what has been called the 'microeconomic' constitution of the EEC, through the establishment and enforcement of competition rules, and cultivation

[13] Although it was already Franz Neumann who had identified the threat of organized capitalism to the rule of law in the 1920s (Neumann, 'On the Preconditions' (n 5)). See, further, William E Scheuermann (ed), *The Rule of Law Under Siege* (University of California Press 1996).

[14] See Bonefeld (n 10). See, further, Quinn Slobodian, *Globalists: The End of Empire and the Birth of Neoliberalism* (HUP 2018) 210–14.

[15] Hannah Arendt, *On Revolution* (Penguin 1958) 184. According to Hannah Arendt, the vicious circle at play in new foundations can be overcome by recalling the principle inherent in the new beginning itself. This new beginning, as we have seen, was largely absent in the post-war imagination.

[16] See Slobodian (n 14) 214, distinguishing between the 'universalists' (such as Röpke), initially opposed to the EEC and in favour of global economic integration in a world market, and the constitutionalists, for whom the EEC offered a 'realization of the double government dreamed of by Hayek since the 1930s', a 'model of supranational governance that had not only liberal principles at its core but a mechanism of enforcement capable of evading contamination by democratic claims-making'. According to Lechevalier, 'the ordoliberal approach played a key, yet not exclusive, role in the architecture of the Treaty of Rome'. Alfred Müller-Armack, a pivotal figure in the negotiations, eliminated most of the dirigiste elements, along with Hans von der Gröben, Director General for competition at the European Commission (Arnaud Lechevalier 'Why and How has German Ordoliberalism Become a French Issue? Some Aspects about Ordoliberal Thoughts We Can Learn from the French Reception' in Joerges and Hien (eds), *Ordoliberalism, Law and the Rule of Economics* (Hart Publishing, 2017) 40.

of market logic and economic freedoms.[17] This was not born immediately with the Treaty of Rome, but, as examined above, was delivered largely through its subsequent judicial constitutionalization. In time, the more contentious notion of constitutionalizing macroeconomic policy choices by making monetary stability and open financial markets as constitutionally enshrined as private property and contractual freedom would become vital both to German economic development, and to the later shape of European integration. In the ordoliberal imagination, stability of monetary policy came to be considered as constitutionally significant as the protection of property.

Although, initially, ordoliberals were sceptical that price stability would be best achieved by central bank independence, favouring the more objective constraints of a gold standard, over the course of an almost decade-long political battle with chancellor Adenauer, they came to support political independence of the central bank (along with the independence of the judiciary).[18] This coincided with the entrenchment of the myth, through significant leverage of public opinion linking interwar collapse (especially the memory of the hyperinflation of the early 1920s) to political control of the German central bank.[19] The deflation and crisis of capitalism that was the proximate cause of Weimar's demise could, thus, be conveniently forgotten. What emerged was the monetary equivalent of the popular distrust in the people themselves to protect democracy, based on the parallel myth of legal, and especially statutory, positivism's responsibility for its collapse in the interwar period (examined in Part I).

Although the ordoliberal monetary framework was only supranationalized and entrenched with the rule-based structure of Economic and Monetary Union at Maastricht (discussed in Part III),[20] the motivating ideas can be identified much earlier.[21] Not only was the post-war 'European liberal' persuaded that 'the next stage of economic unification' could only be achieved 'by relying on the common denominator of national economic policies: namely, the monetary policy'; more than that, 'concerning fiscal policies', the liberal believed that 'a day will necessarily arrive at which it will be requested from the Federated States what today they demand from their regional and local authorities: a balanced budget'.[22]

By the mid 1970s, West Germany would be fully converted to a policy of monetary stability, in an 'unholy alliance with US conservatism'. A monetary counter-revolution had taken place through 'the back door', with a permanent reinterpretation of the 'Growth and Stability Law'—initiated by Erhard (as Chancellor), and passed by SPD finance Minister Schiller—which, 'little by little', replaced an equality of aims,

[17] See, eg Kaarlo Tuori and Klaus Tuori, *The Eurocrisis: A Constitutional Analysis* (CUP 2014). See also Philip Manow, Armin Schäfer, and Hendrik Zorn, 'European Social Policy and Europe's Party-political Center of Gravity, 1957–2003' (2008) 15 Journal of European Public Policy 20; Christian Joerges, 'What is Left of the European Economic Constitution? A Melancholic Eulogy' (2005) 30 European Law Review 461.

[18] See Peter Bernholz, 'Ordo-Liberals and the Control of the Money Supply' in Alan T Peacock and Hans Willgerodt (eds), *German Neoliberals and the Social Market Economy* (Palgrave MacMillan 1989) 208 (citing Otto Veit)..

[19] See Hjalte C Lokdam, 'Banking on Sovereignty: A Genealogy of the European Central Bank's Independence' (LSE PhD Thesis, 2019).

[20] See, generally, Tuori and Tuori (n 17).

[21] See Foucault (n 1) 139 ('what is to be saved, first of all and above all, is the stability of prices').

[22] François Bilger, *La Pensée Economique Libérale dans l'Allemagne Contemporaine* (Librairie Générale de Droit et de Jurisprudence1964), cited in Lechevalier (n 16) 39 fn 74.

alongside full employment and equitable distribution of incomes, with 'a hierarchy of aims in which monetary stability comes first'.[23]

There was no pristine application of ordoliberalism, either domestically or in the context of European integration. The reinvention of economic liberalism for the post-war European age was based, initially, on the reconciliation and compromise between capitalist and socialist demands, liberalism and intervention, rather than any pure vision. In practice, during the 'golden age' of growth from 1945 to 1975, a post-war consensus tempered ordoliberalism: specifically, through the national (neo-)corporatist state that tamed capital as well as democracy, and was founded on a social contract between social classes.[24] Capitalism, in other words, was tempered not only by maintaining the conditions for competitive markets, but by forging relatively harmonious labour relations (presaging the severe wage restraint of German labour in the neo-liberal period).[25] Social and labour policy, in the initial stages, was not significantly affected by the Treaty of Rome, and a 'twin-track' process could emerge that would protect an 'embedded liberalism'.[26]

The European post-war state was responsible, in other words, not only for ensuring the conditions of fair competition and price stability, but also for moderating excesses of inequality in a capitalist society. Rather than any pretension of the state to reclaiming internal or external sovereignty, it was its success in negotiating these 'diplomatic' missions that came to be seen as its *raison d'etre* (a vision that continues through to the neo-liberal era). In Germany, the new style of macroeconomic policy was based on a 'magic triangle', consisting of aspects of Keynesianism, the Freiburg School of ordoliberalism, and the neoclassical synthesis.[27] Belief in the ability of this complex economic rationality to create and sustain the affluent society extended to Social Democratic politicians, as well as liberals and Christian Democrats.[28]

It is important to stress, however, that the relative equality of conditions was a product of compromise within capitalism, rather than any emancipation from it. Consensus around economic growth, distribution, and security (including social security) in the two post-war decades was supported 'by a "civic culture" that emphasized the values of social mobility, private life, consumption, instrumental rationality, authority and order'. If nominally democratic, this consensus, in fact, 'de-emphasized political participation'.[29] The proponents of economic democracy, so prevalent in early Weimar, were, in the words of Claus Offe, 'reduced to virtual insignificance'.[30]

[23] See Wilhelm Hankel, 'Monetary Stability and the Welfare State' The German Tribune, June 6 1976, 6–7 (reprinted in Peter Katzenstein, *Policy and Politics in West Germany: The Growth of a Semisovereign State* (Temple University Press 1987) 115–17, at 116).

[24] See Chris Bickerton, *European Integration: From Nation-States to Member States* (OUP 2012) 74–113.

[25] This is examined more closely in Part III.

[26] See John G Ruggie, 'International Regimes, Transactions and Change: Embedded Liberalism in the Postwar Economic Order' (1982) 36 International Organization 379 (examined further below, in the context of European integration).

[27] Karl Schiller, *Konjuncturpolitik auf dem Wege zi einer Affluent Society*, vol 54 (Kieler Vortrage, Institut für Weltwirtschaft 1968) in Katzenstein (n 23) 112–14 (Schiller was West German economics minister for the SPD from 1967 to 1972).

[28] Katzenstein notes that Schiller, who became minister of economics in 1967, 'did not press for a sharp break with Erhard's neoliberalism', but complemented it with 'global guidance' (ibid 90).

[29] Claus Offe, 'Challenging the Boundaries of Institutional Politics: Social Movements Since the 1960s' in CS Maier (ed), *Changing Boundaries of the Political: Essays on the Evolving Balance between the State and Society, Public and Private in Europe* (CUP 1987) 67–68.

[30] ibid 68.

Although social democratic policies contributed to the 'saving of capitalism from above' by contributing to the construction of variants of the European welfare state, in the main it was Christian democracy that had undertaken responsibility for this task.[31] As Conway puts it, 'Welfare reform, as it developed after the war, was piecemeal and ... its expansion often took place within established insurance structures ... [i]n this respect, it proved to be Christian Democracy, with its principles of subsidiarity and concern for the interests of families, that had a considerably greater influence on postwar welfarism than did Social Democracy.'[32]

The post-war compromise was not a triumph of social democracy (at least outside of Scandinavia), or even of Christian socialism, but essentially of Christian democracy.[33] Within Christian democracy, 'Christian socialist rhetoric soon gave way to more traditional market-oriented economic policy-making with limited state interventionism and moderate social reforms.' This shift was especially marked in the case of the German Christian Democratic Union (CDU), which, as early as 1949, with the launch of its Düsseldorfer Principles, under the strong influence of the ordoliberal Ludwig Erhard, 'developed the idea of the "social market economy" with strong liberal connotations and limited state interventionism.'[34]

Although other Christian democratic parties in core Europe adopted compromised packages of economic programmes, and despite the various differences across states, and distinct internal fault lines, 'all Christian democratic parties', according to Kaiser, 'were united', not only 'in their support for a mixed economy', but in 'their opposition to socialist centralisation.'[35] Social Catholicism was explicitly anti-socialist, in accordance with Pope Leo XIII's encyclical on the 'inviolability of private property', and was based on a rejection of social conflict; nature ordaining that capital and labour must dwell in harmony. Despite the rhetoric of personalism and Christian solidarity, left-leaning visions of Christian democracy 'were soon sidelined in favour of more market-friendly versions'.[36]

The class character of the post-war settlement can also be clearly discerned, emboldening the bourgeoisie and quietening the working class. 'Middle-class liberal-conservative elites', Kaiser notes, dominated the post-war networks of Christian

[31] See Tony Judt, *Ill Fares the Land* (Penguin Books 2010) 47.

[32] Martin Conway, 'Democracy in Postwar Europe: The Triumph of a Political Model' (2002) 32 European History Quarterly 59, 67–68 (Conway, 'Democracy').

[33] cf Sheri Berman, 'Institutions and the Consolidation of Democracy in Western Europe' in Orfeo Fioretos, Tulia Falleti, and Adam Scheingate (eds), *The Oxford Handbook of Historical Institutionalism* (OUP 2016) 413. Although Berman describes the institutions that consolidated post-war European democracy as unequivocally social democratic at the domestic level, she also notes that this 'ended up being partially contradicted by developments at the regional level in Europe', namely the mismatch between intense regional economic integration and the political deficit which appeared 'during the earliest stages of the integration process'. Many other commentators regard it, with some justification, as Christian democratic rather than social democratic. See, eg Jan-Werner Müller, *Contesting Democracy: Political Ideas in Twentieth-Century Europe* (YUP 2011) 130 (describing Christian democracy as 'the most important ideological innovation of the post-war period). He notes that, even in the UK, an outlier in some sense, many of the architects of the welfare state, such as Beveridge, were 'liberals' rather than 'socialists'.

[34] Wolfram Kaiser, *Christian Democracy and the Origins of the European Union* (CUP 2007) 177. Erhard himself had also fiercely opposed harmonization of social welfare legislation at the Treaty of Rome (Alan Milward, *The European Rescue of the Nation-State* (Routledge 2000) 213–14).

[35] Kaiser (n 34) 177.

[36] Müller (n 33) 138.

democracy, 'with a common project for creating an integrated Europe based on a curious mélange of traditional confessional notions of occidental culture and anti-communism and broadly liberal economic ideas'. Consensus was obtained through consociational patterns of governance, geared towards interest mediation, and 'combined with a deliberately conservative, dull form of political representation and decision-making by indistinguishable "men in suits"'.[37]

The dominant combination of ordoliberal idealism and Christian democratic political authority coincided with the loss of power and visibility of the industrial working class. Trade unions were an inadequate political mechanism for working-class autonomy, 'fiercely divided', as they were, 'between communist, socialist and Catholic organisations', and with the non-communist unions 'embroiled in a prolonged and ultimately somewhat fruitless pursuit of influence through state-encouraged structures of corporatist negotiation'.[38] This must be understood in the broader cultural context of the post-war period, when even left-wing vanguard parties that had previously been officially committed to revolution, including the French and Italian communists, came to support emerging liberal democratic orders in Western Europe.[39]

Although they did not initially make up a majority within national parties, let alone domestic politics and parliaments, Christian democrats soon largely succeeded, through methods of transnational cooperation and networking, in 'implanting their core ideas in supranational European integration'.[40] The strategy of Christian democratic leaders such as Adenauer, Schuman, and De Gasperi to 'bore core Europe into supranational integration' thus appeared largely successful; and, to a significant extent, even more so than at the domestic level.[41]

3. An economic constitution writ large and the transition to neo-liberalism

The reconstruction of a durable and functional set of liberal economic rules would require a transnational framework, as economic interdependencies among European nations grew. It would require a regional, as well as national, settlement to depoliticize the economy, otherwise economic 'irrationalities' would simply be displaced from the domestic to the regional or global inter-state system. The inter-state aspect of this project has been outlined above (in Chapter 3), with the binding of Germany to a

[37] Kaiser (n 34) 172 (citing Conway). See, further, Carlo Invernizzi Accetti, *What is Christian Democracy? Politics, Religion and Ideology* (CUP 2019) ch 8.

[38] Martin Conway, 'The Rise and Fall of Western Europe's Democratic Age, 1945–1973' (2004) 13 Contemporary European History 67, 74 (Conway, 'The Rise and Fall'): 'The success of notable elites in regaining control of the political process ... becomes more comprehensible if one recognises how the war years had simultaneously strengthened the power and profile of such notables while demobilising and weakening the working class.'

[39] See Müller (n 33) 128.

[40] Kaiser (n 34) 10. Although the methods of elite interaction were transnational, conservativism continued to mobilize nationalism, as well as religion, and belief in technical expertise, in order to stall the advance of socialism (see Michael Mann, 'Sources of Variation in Working Class Movements in Twentieth-Century Europe' (1995) New Left Review 14).

[41] ibid 172.

European future, as a geopolitical equal to France, in the early stages of the Paris and Rome Treaties. But the project of integration also contributed to a political-economic differentiation in the domestic constitutional state, which recalibrated a complex set of social relations and political ideologies. In short, the constitutional imagination would increasingly become dominated by the idea of individual economic freedom, substituting the political freedom that was so central to mass movements of the early part of the twentieth century.

The task of differentiating the economic from the political was one in which European integration would play a key part. As Giandomineco Majone puts it:

> The possibility of separating economics and politics was a key, if implicit, assumption of the founders of the EEC. It was not a new idea but rather a return to a classical liberal tenet which in the nineteenth century and up to World War I had made it possible for the world economy to develop in such a fashion that 'between national and international economic integration there was only a difference in degree but not in kind'.[42]

The broader belief that economic benefits would be gained from free trade through the comparative advantage of different regimes had, of course, been part of the vernacular of classical liberalism since David Ricardo, although there was also growing recognition that unregulated free trade in the world market would increase inequality where levels of regional development were asymmetrical.[43] Classical liberalism, in any case, had few defenders at this historical juncture, as there was sufficient historical memory of its failures.

European integration would square the circle of economic modernization and social protection; market competition would emerge together with widespread material prosperity and the building of the domestic welfare state. Although Hayek had already foreseen the economically liberal consequences of an inter-state federation in the interwar period,[44] the project of European integration did not initially resemble this vision; it was a much messier and mixed affair, encompassing a twin-track process, analogous to what would later be characterized as 'embedded liberalism'.[45]

Embedded liberalism in the post-war period of regional integration captured the idea that liberal economics is pursued internationally, and aspects of social democracy are maintained domestically; in other words, 'Smith abroad and Keynes at home'. Government intervention in the economy was widely accepted as legitimate

[42] Giandomenico Majone, *Rethinking the Union of Europe Post-crisis* (CUP 2014) 149 (citing Wilhelm Röpke, 'Economic Order and International Law' (1954) Recueil des Cours 86, 218–50).

[43] See Gunnar Myrdal, *Economic Theory and Underdeveloped Regions* (Gerald Duckworth & Co 1957). Myrdal was executive secretary of the UN Economic Commission for Europe. The critique that free trade may increase inequality returned to mainstream political economy in the work of Dani Rodrik (see Chapter 8).

[44] Friedrich August von Hayek, 'The Economic Conditions of Interstate Federalism' in *Individualism and Economic Order* (University of Chicago Press 1942) 269. Hayek saw the 'abrogation of national sovereignties and the creation of an effective international order of law' as the 'necessary complement and logical consummation of the liberal programme'. See John Gillingham, *European Integration 1950–2003: Superstate or New Market Economy?* (CUP 2003) on Hayek's significance for the early EU.

[45] See Ruggie (n 26).

and necessary, albeit less under the direct influence of Keynesian social democracy, and more influenced by Christian democracy and the Social Market Economy of the ordoliberals, as we have seen. Free trade was pursued, internationally and regionally, through institutional developments that respected, or at least permitted, this sphere of domestic social protection. European integration was initially considered to fit this paradigm, developing its four freedoms (of goods, services, workers, and capital), while respecting, or at least not overly interfering with, domestic welfare regimes.[46]

The precise contribution of European integration to economic growth and relative equalizing of conditions during the 'golden age' period is disputed.[47] Social welfare regimes themselves had nothing specifically to do with European integration, but neither were they contradicted or thwarted by it.[48] If anything, social spending (including health care, education, pensions, and social security), which would remain resolutely national, could benefit from any 'fiscal dividend' from the growth facilitated by the single market. But, although it is relatively undisputed that European integration, in European versions of embedded liberalism, was at least compatible with the pursuit of a 'social market' at the national level, it is also apparent that this delicate bargain would gradually be unravelled.[49]

European integration itself encompassed a curious mix of freedom of movement of the factors of production, rules against anticompetitive practices, and common policies on the state-managed subsidies of agriculture (CAP) and fisheries (CFP). The dominance of a Christian democratic 'farmer-bourgeois alliance' contributed to this mix of restrained capitalism, bureaucratic planning, and transnational market integration.[50] Catholic politicians played 'by the rules of democracy, not because they believed in them, but because it was more advantageous to be inside the game than outside'.[51] Although not democratically inclined, the power of agricultural lobby groups, in conjunction with Christian democratic politics, was credited with a significant contribution 'to the stability of the postwar order by forestalling any resurgence in rural support for the extreme right'.[52]

With specific regard to the single market, advances were initially limited largely to the removal of tariff barriers and the free circulation of goods. This gradual and incremental market integration was accompanied by relatively low levels of capital mobility in the foundational period. The whole enterprise proceeded slowly, in light of the political obstacles to supranational integration (especially the French veto); but

[46] See, eg Wolf Sauter and Harm Schepel, *State and Market in European Union Law: The Public and Private Spheres of the Internal Market Before the EU Courts* (CUP 2009). Note that there was, in time, some social support through structural and investment funds, although European expenditure would remain minimal as a percentage of GDP.

[47] See Barry Eichengreen, *The European Economy Since 1945: Co-Ordinated Capitalism and Beyond* (Princeton University Press 2007), noting the significance of 'catching up' with the US, reconstruction of war-damaged economies, and global factors, as well as coordinated capitalism and the integration of Western Europe (ch 6); cf Perry Anderson, *New Old World* (Verso 2009) 95–98.

[48] Stefan Giubboni, *Social Rights and Market Freedom in the European Constitution: A Labour Law Perspective* (CUP 2006) 15–17.

[49] See Diamond Ashiagbor, 'Unravelling the Embedded Liberal Bargain: Labour and Social Welfare Law in the Context of EU Market Integration' (2013) 19 European Law Journal 303.

[50] Kaiser (n 34) 188.

[51] Müller (n 33) 134.

[52] Conway, 'Democracy' (n 32) 77.

it was given structural impetus by the European Court of Justice, in conjunction with domestic courts and transnational lawyers, in the strategy of 'constitutionalisation by stealth' (outlined in Chapter 4).[53] What this 'quiet revolution' constitutionalized would exclusively be the principle of market freedom, by virtue of the almost total absence of social provisions in the original Treaty framework; a 'genetic anomaly' from a social democratic perspective, and one whose defects would be drawn out over time, as regulatory competition replaced upward harmonization.[54]

If lessons had been learnt about the complicity of classical liberal economics—enforced marketization, rigid adherence to monetary stability—in exacerbating high levels of socio-economic inequality and the collapse of democracy in the interwar period, they were soon to be forgotten.[55] From the 1970s, domestic politics and European integration alike were gradually redirected, signalled by the renaissance of Hayek, and by ideas that only thirty years previously had been considered defunct.[56] This period presaged the acceleration of economic constitutionalism in the period of neo-liberalism.[57]

The constitutional implications of neo-liberalism would be wide-ranging; political identity was fragmented, social relations were increasingly commodified, society itself even denied. Citizenship was quantified, recalibrated as a particular collection of individualist tastes and preferences, effectively replacing the political citizen with a simple consumer of economic benefits, or totem of public opinion. In significant ways, this too was a deepening and radicalization of pre-existing trends; prefigured, for example, by Kirchheimer's analysis of post-war politics (discussed in Chapter 4), which noted that, with the transformation of political parties, the citizen became a consumer of political products, sold by a professional cadre of detached elites.[58]

In the neo-liberal era, what changes, in terms of the responsiveness of the state and its institutions, is that, with the increasing financialization of the economy and the emergence of the 'debt state', the constituency that matters in terms of placing pressure

[53] As Giubboni puts it, the dynamic of judicial integration and spillover of the economic freedoms was one of the most decisive aspects of the transformation of the European economic constitution, although that, too, has to be understood in a context of acquiescence, at the very least, by the 'Masters of the Treaty' (Giubboni (n 48) 23).

[54] ibid 27 (citing Massimo D'Antona, 'Armonizzazione del diritto del lavoro e federalismo nell'Unione europea', *Rivista Trimestrale di Diritto e Procedura Civile* 1994, 695ff, 704). Giubboni himself identified a 'symbolic turning point' in the Single European Act, but acknowledged the founding asymmetry between economic integration and social rights, a result of the 'road not taken' at Rome (see, further, Stefano Giubboni, 'Social Rights and Market Freedom in the European Constitution: A Reappraisal' (2010) 1:2 European Labour Law Journal 161). Christian Joerges argues that the balance between domestic social policy and European market remained stable for 'a decade' or so (n 17) 461.

[55] See Karl Polanyi, *The Great Transformation: The Political and Economic Origins of Our Time* (Beacon Press 2001) (originally published in 1944). Polanyi also, in a sense, predicted the neo-liberal revival, noting that liberals would always claim that the problems were that markets were not free enough.

[56] See Dieter Plehwe, 'Introduction' in Philip Mirowski and Dieter Plehwe (eds), *The Road from Mont Pèlerin: The Making of the Neoliberal Thought Collective* (HUP 2009). Specifically for Hayek's influence on European integration, see Gillingham (n 44).

[57] cf Foucault (n 1).

[58] André Krouwel, 'Otto Kirchheimer and the Catch-All Party' (2003) 26 West European Politics 23. Observing the birth of the French Fifth Republic, Kirchheimer noted the 'conversion of the participant citizens into bewildered, bemused, or embittered spectators', in Otto Kirchheimer, 'France From the Fourth to the Fifth Republic' in FS Burin and KL Shells (eds), *Politics, Law and Social Change: Selected Essays of Otto Kirchheimer* (Columbia University Press 1969) 215.

on the political process is less the *Staatsvolk* than the *Marktsvolk*, in Wolfgang Streeck's memorable expression. As the dominant means for the state to collect resources shifts from reliance on its citizens through direct taxation to reliance on financial investors in the global marketplace, a 'new stage in the relationship between democracy and capitalism' is inaugurated.[59] This occurs in a manner that disarms the Frankfurt School critical theorists, who identified a legitimation crisis but were viewing society with the wrong lens, with communication theory having substituted political economy.

As a matter of constitutional form, the 1970s signalled the transition of the neo-corporatist nation state into what Chris Bickerton has termed the European 'member state', bound increasingly by external constraints that bear little resemblance to a process of collective self-commitment. Political checks and balances were increasingly outsourced to a transnational managerial class and a set of institutions far removed from the democratic process. Substantively, this transition involved the dismantling of the social contract between labour and capital, the unravelling of post-war class compromise, and the freeing of capitalism from political constraints, including those deriving from concern for conceptions of the 'public good'.[60] In the era of the member state, economic privatization was combined with the rise of administration and regulation, and the (constitutional) role of the state and its institutional apparatus became predominantly one of correcting for market failures.[61] Under neo-liberal ideology, market liberalization, economic efficiency, productivity, competitiveness, and corporate empowerment become constitutional 'ends in themselves'. Economic liberalism moves into an increasingly authoritarian mindset, as captured by the response to the report of the Trilateral Commission in 1975 on 'ungovernability', which blamed instability and the 'crisis of democracy' on excessive demands of the working class, a reiteration in some respects of the myth-building about hyperinflation in the interwar period.[62]

In attempting to rewrite the terms of the post-war social contract, and to recover and enforce the more laissez-faire approach to political economy that had been dismissed in the interim, two distinct avenues were pursued.[63] The first was to introduce a strict determinacy to political discourse; that of 'There is no Alternative' (TINA) to economic liberalization. Although particularly associated with Margaret Thatcher, and her powerful legacy on neo-liberal and third way successors, the pressure faced by socialist President Francois Mitterand, who abandoned his socialist programme in 1983 for fear of currency devaluation under the weight of the Deutschmark, is perhaps more indicative of the shift in Continental Europe.[64] The second avenue along which

[59] See, eg Wolfgang Streeck, *Buying Time: The Delayed Crisis of Democratic Capitalism* (Verso 2014) 10–20, 79–88(Streeck, 'Buying Time').

[60] See Bickerton (n 24) ch 3.

[61] Bickerton (n 24) 107.

[62] Bickerton (n 24) 93–94. See Michael J Crozier, Samuel P Huntington, and Joji Watanuki, *The Crisis of Democracy: Report on the Governability of Democracies to the Trilateral Commission* (New York University Press 1975); see, further,Michael C Behrent, 'The Origins of the Anti-Liberal Left: The 1979 Vincennes Conference on Neoliberalism' (2017) 35 French Politics, Culture & Society 44.

[63] See Bickerton (n 24) 95, citing the 'Goldthorpe Report': (John H Goldthorpe, 'Problems of Political Economy after the Postwar Period' in C S Maier (ed), *Changing Boundaries of the Political: Essays on the Evolving Balance Between State and Society, Public and Private in Europe* (CUP 1987).

[64] See Leo Panitch and Sam Gindin, *The Making of Global Capitalism: The Political Economy of American Empire* (Verso 2012) 196–99. According to Ulrich Krotz and Joachim Schild, *Shaping Europe: France,*

neo-liberal movement accelerated involved the turn to transnational rules and obligations to regain domestic and global political and economic stability, which had been shaken by the crises of the 1970s. This turn to formalize external constraints would become key to the construction of European Monetary Union (EMU), the basis for which was established at Maastricht (examined in Part III).

The neo-liberal transformation was materially underpinned by the collapse of the Bretton Woods system, 'stagflation', and two oil crises, in the 1970s, and then the dramatic increase in regional and global capital flows in the subsequent decade, highlighted by the changing role of the US, as it moved from a productive economy to one based on consumption. With the election of Nixon in 1972, a welfare-oriented 'fiscalism' would be replaced by a 'conservative monetarism': a 'victory' replicated in the Federal Republic of Germany.[65] To the geopolitical context must be added the emergence of 'national champions' of industry that were becoming pan-European corporations, 'operating regional value chains across the expanded European market', deepening productive links and financial integration, and presaging the transformation of the domestic bourgeoisie, if not the formation of a transnational capitalist class.[66]

To be sure, as Stefano Bartolini explains, the pure logic of the 'Internal Market' of 1987 differed in certain respects from that of the 'Common Market' of 1957. The European market was no longer conceived as a means to connect consumers and producers beyond national borders within established productive structures. Instead, it became a tool to *modify the productive structures themselves*, in order to improve their competitiveness 'to better face the world market'.[67] This openness and boundary removal would be extended to the free circulation of capital in 1990, liberalizing commercial credits, direct investments, personal capital movements, European stock market flows, and short term currency exchange.[68] The removal of obstacles to trade

Germany, and Embedded Bilateralism from the Elysée Treaty to Twenty-First Century Politics (OUP 2013) 190, Mitterand's decision to keep the franc inside the EMS in March 1983, accepting its constraints, marked a 'historic break in French economic policy'. After this policy U-turn, 'France had to forego any autonomy in monetary policy-making'. But, in fact, in 1976 'Giscard d'Estaing's new prime minister, the economist Raymond Barre, [had] adopted an anti-inflationary plan based on the liberal principles favored by West German Social Democrats', after which 'absolute priority went to restoring France's balance of payments equilibrium; salary increases were abruptly curbed, and unemployment was used to pressure workers to moderate their demands' (Behrent (n 62) 49). See, further, Andrew Glynn, 'Social Democracy and Full Employment' (1995) New Left Review 33, arguing that, despite the genuine constraints of economic globalisation, particularly international financial flows, international integration was not a fundamental block to full employment policies.

[65] Hankel (n 23). On the weakness of Keynesianism in post-war Germany, see Christopher Allen, 'The Underdevelopment of Keynesianism in the Federal Republic of Germany' in Peter Hall (ed), *The Political Power of Economic Ideas: Keynesianism Across Nations* (Princeton University Press 1989) 263.

[66] See Christakis Georgious, 'Unification from Above and Its Contradictions' in Eva Nanopoulos and Fotis Vergis (eds), *The Crisis Behind the Eurocrisis: On the Multi-systemic Failure of the EU* (CUP 2019) 295–314; cf Nicos Poulantzas, 'Internationalisation of Capitalist Relations and the Nation-State' (1974) 3 Economy and Society 145. Paradoxically, an industrial policy of European mercantilism would come up against Commission competition policy that protected small and medium-sized enterprises.

[67] Stefano Bartolini, *Restructuring Europe: Centre Formation, System Building, and Political Structuring between the Nation-State and the European Union* (OUP 2005) 181 (italics added).

[68] This was foreseen in the Treaty of Rome (Article 67), but was relaunched by directives in 1986 and 1987, to be established on 1 January 1990.

and 'fair and undistorted competition', pursued through the Court and the highly discretionary activities of the European Commission, would, over time, by tackling national subsidies and anticompetitive practices, 'modify the balance between internal boundary removal and external boundary setting'. The overall effect of the policies adopted into the 1980s was, thus, to open European economies 'towards the international market as much as (if not more than) it opened them with respect to each other'.[69]

And, yet, the essential idea and impetus behind the neo-liberal trends of market liberalization had *already* been constitutionalized in theory and substantially effected, if not yet perfected, in practice. If, initially, the potential of certain Treaty provisions had lain 'dormant', they could quickly be brought to life, given the foundational logic (including with respect to the free movement of capital) that had already been laid, and then entrenched by the Court, in conjunction with domestic legal and political authorities. In the words of Colin Crouch:

> [I]n the absence of parliamentary government responsible to mass suffrage, the first quarter-century of the European Communities reproduced an almost ideal-typical capitalist polity: neither democracy nor organized labour interfered with the business of managing the affairs of capitalism. If there was a European citizenship it was enjoyed by the business interests which lobbied the Commission and national governments.[70]

To grasp the disequilibrium of the political-economic relation that was set in train, and appreciate its constitutional roots and structural constraints, we can turn to the work of Fritz Scharpf. In Scharpf's powerful narrative, a neo-liberal bias is written into the EU's overall structural asymmetry, by prioritizing liberal over republican readings of the constitution, and economically liberal over social welfare models of the relationship between state and society.[71] As Scharpf argues, the ECJ played a significant role in this constitutional transformation by elevating European market rules into directly effective and supreme 'constitutional' law. The end would be to gradually homogenize an otherwise heterogeneous set of domestic economies.[72] Judicial authority, as the judgment of *Cassis de Dijon* clarified, would be far more easily utilized in the service of deregulation of the economy than politics would be in its re-regulation.[73] This led to a deep and structural 'deregulatory bias', as Damian Chalmers notes:

[69] Bartolini (n 67) 185 (Bartolini contrasts this, at the other extreme, with the Common Agricultural Policy (CAP), which is designed to eliminate internal obstacles but set a 'strong external boundary-building policy' (ibid 186)).

[70] Colin Crouch, 'Breaking Open Black Boxes: The Implications for Sociological Theory of European Integration' in Anand Menon and Vincent Wright (eds), *From the Nation State to Europe: Essays in Honour of Jack Hayward* (OUP 2003) 207.

[71] See Fritz Scharpf, 'Legitimacy in the Multi-Level European Polity' in Martin Loughlin and Petra Dobner (eds), *Twilight of Constitutionalism* (OUP 2010).

[72] ibid.

[73] Case 120/78 *Rewe-Zentral AG v Bundesmonopolverwaltung für Branntwein (Cassis de Dijon)* [1979] ECR 649.

> In the 1960s and 1970s, the vesting of one vision, the Gaullist one, in the political institutions through the Luxembourg Accords, and the other, that of a pan-European political community, in the Court of Justice, led to a peculiar dynamic ... [t]he Court gave a series of integrationist judgments, elaborating rights which could be invoked by individuals against national governments ... [j]uxtaposed with the inertia of the legislature, this led to the development of a deregulatory bias whereby national policies were ... tightly restricted by the Court, without there being any substitute EU legislation to take their place.[74]

The constitutional grounds for what is commonly referred to as neo-liberalism had, thus, been laid far earlier than suggested by its association with the Thatcher–Reagan revolution, or Mitterand's capitulation to the bond markets in 1983. Embedded liberalism, pursuing the dual goals of 'Keynes at home, Smith abroad', was already 'by its very nature "an unstable chemical compound" '.[75] Once the market had been constitutionalized by the European Court, the direction of travel in political economy would be largely one way, if far from strictly linear.

As a structural and ideological matter, the foundations of the asymmetry were laid not only with the decoupling of market and social policy, but with the post-war substitution of 'integration through politics' by 'integration through law'. This placed a set of supranational laws with the potential for an inbuilt economically liberal basis in the hands of a juristic class and a limited constituency of litigators.[76] Even though it was not until *Cassis de Dijon* that the potential was fully realized, at least in the domain of free movement of goods, the groundwork was set by the constitutionalization of a set of market-liberal rules. This was not merely a feature of the 1980s, associated with the Single European Act or Maastricht Treaty, significant though these would be in sharpening the asymmetries (as we will explore in Part III). The groundwork was laid in the 1950s and early 1960s and, in fact, reflected an ethos that had its roots in the interwar philosophy of the ordoliberals, complemented by Christian democracy and elements of political pragmatism. This early foundation is often overlooked, perhaps overshadowed by the more brutal forms of disciplinary neo-liberalism pursued in the euro crisis phase, or perhaps masked by the relatively high growth and low inequality of the thirty years following the end of the Second World War,[77] defined by more mixed forms of political economy. But, in order to understand how the groundwork for a new economic liberalism could be laid and maintained, it must now be recounted how radical opposition to the post-war settlement was disarmed.

[74] Damian Chalmers, Giorgio Monti, and Gareth Davies, *European Union Law* (4th edn, CUP 2019) 18.)

[75] Giubboni (n 48) 18 (citing Salvatore Veca, *Cittadinanza. Riflessioni filosofiche sull' idea di emancipazione* (Feltrinelli 1990) 42).

[76] See Fritz Scharpf, 'The European Social Model: Coping with the Challenges of Diversity' (2002) Journal of Common Market Studies 645.

[77] See Thomas Piketty, *Capital in the Twenty-First Century* (HUP 2014). According to Piketty, the countervailing forces of redistributive policies and reconstruction in the aftermath of the levelling destruction caused by two world wars only enabled 'the *illusion* that the fundamental structural contradiction of capitalism ($r > g$) had been overcome' (ibid 572 (italics added)).

4. Political deradicalization

Whereas, in Germany, political deradicalization had become a formal constitutional cause taken up by constitutional institutions armed with a doctrine of militant democracy, in France and Italy it would be less 'decisionistic' and authoritarian, and occur in a more gradual and informal way. It would be undertaken, in part, by the radical left parties themselves, as they abdicated revolutionary constituent ambitions. The so-called 'Eurocommunist' parties gradually adopted strategies of constitutionalism and broad political alliance, most notably in Italy, eventually buying into a 'historic compromise' with the political centre and establishment. If there were strategic reasons for this turn—partly fearing a 'strategy of tension' from the right, wary of the dangers of counter-revolution, and partly through fears of sabotage of the type inflicted on leftist regimes abroad, such as Allende's in Chile—there were deeper ideological factors involved too.[78]

Compromise with forces of social democracy and Christian democracy was considered the second stage of a progressive sequence that began with a first stage of broad anti-fascist resistance during the Second World War (the unity of which was only broken because of the Cold War). 'Eurocommunism', it has been said, 'was inseparable from the legacies of fascism', specifically the left's defeats in Italy and Spain in the interwar period. This historical memory now inspired a new strategy of allegiances; the Italian Communist Party for example, becoming the 'bulwark of democratic legality, the shield of the constitution', turning decisively away from any notions of class struggle and the dictatorship of the proletariat.[79]

If the theoretical and practical tensions raised by the prospect of an ostensibly revolutionary political movement turning towards constitutionalism and reformism were apparent,[80] those raised by its turn to an embrace of the European project would be palpable. The Italian Communist Party (PCI), initially hostile to the EEC (seeing it as part of a Euro-Atlantic capitalist bloc), would revise its position through the 1960s, as it adopted a more favourable stance towards economic expansion, and modernization more generally. This revision was fairly swift and sharp, the PCI soon starting to present anything other than Europeanism and the unity of the European Left as a doomed attempt to return to autarky or defunct 'monolithism'.[81] To hold out instead for a mass movement at the European level would become an article of faith for much of the radical Left across the continent: the road to socialism would be through Europe, or not at all.[82]

[78] See, eg Geoff Eley, *Forging Democracy: The History of the Left in Europe 1850–2000* (OUP 2002) 408–17.

[79] ibid 411.

[80] See Ralph Miliband, 'Constitutionalism and Revolution: Notes on Eurocommunism' (1978) 15 Socialist Register 158.

[81] Donald Sassoon, 'The Italian Communist Party's European Strategy' (1976) 47 The Political Quarterly 253.

[82] See, in particular, the writings of Ernest Mandel, Belgian Marxist and Trotskyist activist: Ernest Mandel, *Europe versus America? Contradictions of Imperialism* (New Left Books 1970); cf Nicos Poulantzas, 'Internationalisation of Capitalist Relations and the Nation-state' (1974) 3 Economy and Society 145, reprinted in Nicos Poulantzas, *The Poulantzas Reader: Marxism, Law and the State* (James Martin ed, Verso 2008) 220 (accusing Mandel of going along with 'bourgeoise propaganda about the 'united Europe' (ibid 247)).

Although Italian Communists recognized the increasingly 'authoritarian process' of constructing the European community, and recognized the need for a popular sovereignty to counter Europe's bureaucratic apparatus, this, as a matter of principle as well as strategy, was not to be achieved at the level of the nation state. Only the autonomy of a unified European polity could fully unleash the productive forces, compete with American capital, and liberate Europe from the two opposing superpower blocs.[83] By the 1970s, under Enrico Berlinguer, the PCI had not only embraced European integration but abandoned official opposition to NATO, and, by the late 1970s, it had even come to accept a political economy of wage restraint and austerity.[84]

In the words of Herbert Marcuse, evaluating it in discussion with Jürgen Habermas in 1979, Eurocommunism had become 'the true reflex of existing power relations on the one hand', and 'of the inner and outer embourgeoisement of the working class on the other'.[85] This shift had a decisive electoral impact: in June 1979 the Italian Communist Party lost 1.5 million votes, and by 1991 it had dissolved, having declared the era of Eurocommunism over with the collapse of the Soviet Union. The French and Spanish Communist Parties pursued similar paths in the 1970s and suffered a similar fate, albeit with distinct local variations.[86]

Political demobilization and deradicalization, far from challenged by the series of events represented in the date 'May 1968', would effectively be reinforced by them. Although there would be no single interpretation of these 'events' (*les événements*, as they would be characterized in France), they did represent, at least in part, a revolt against the hierarchy and authoritarianism of the post-war constitutional settlement[87] There would also, concurrently, be a return of a working-class militancy in some areas, with industrial unrest and strike waves occurring, not just in France, but also in Germany and Italy throughout the 1960s. But there was an apparent political and social discrepancy at play: while 'more workers than ever before were expressing their discontent, fewer and fewer socialist activists belonged to the working class'.[88] The pattern of social and political conflict that grew out of the events of 1968 would be 'the polar opposite of the class conflict model', with the new areas of struggle for recognition 'occupied by middle-class radicals' and other 'post-socialist' demands mobilized under various banners of group identity.[89]

The legacy of 1968 would remain politically contested. But as a constitutional moment, its effects were marginal or non-existent. The events generated interest in the

[83] Sassoon (n 81) ('If the development of the productive forces is part of an advance to socialism and if this development depends on the creation of an autonomous Europe, that is of a new relationship between Europe and the USA, then it follows that it is no longer possible to conceive (in Europe) of an advance to socialism on the basis of the nation'). This was a position held, more generally, by communist parties and Marxist theorists across Europe (see Poulantzas (n 82)).

[84] Eley (n 78) 412.

[85] Herbert Marcuse, Jürgen Habermas, and Friends, 'A Discussion on Democracy and Critical Theory' (1979) 1 New Political Science 19.

[86] Eley (n 78) 413.

[87] For an overview, see Martin Klimke, '1968: Europe in Technicolour' in Dan Stone (ed), *The Oxford Handbook of Postwar European History* (OUP 2012). Sassoon ((n 80) 369) describes the event as being like a semiotician's 'open text'.

[88] Sassoon (n 81) 381.

[89] Offe (n 29) 79. See, later, Nancy Fraser, 'From Redistribution to Recognition? Dilemmas of Justice in a "Postsocialist Age"' (1995) New Left Review 68.

student movements; a new politics of personal identity and subjectivity, a turn towards cultural politics and against professional authority, as well as a new wave of feminism, and the 'unparalleled expansion of the university system throughout Western Europe'.[90] But they had little lasting structural impact on the political system, the constitutional order, or the dynamic of its political economy.[91] To the extent that 1968 represented a remobilization of society, it was not a political remobilization, still less a reawakening of the constituent power. In the words of Claus Offe, its unconventional character signalled a 'mobilisation for non-institutional political action'.[92]

As has been noted elsewhere, from one perspective, the spirit of cultural libertarianism left over from 1968 was entirely compatible with the new economic liberalism reasserting itself in the wake of the 1973 economic crisis. With the political importance of the 'self' acquiring a mass following, Freud would replace Marx 'as an unlikely ideological sponsor of the politics of the younger generation'.[93] Or, as more colourfully expressed in 1978 by Régis Debray, *l'esprit de mai* had given way to 'neo-liberalism', and the 'children of Marx and Coca-Cola' (as Jean-Luc Godard famously dubbed the sixties generation) had become 'the legitimate offspring of hashish and Raymond Aron'.[94]

The French intellectual turn away from Marxism and materialism in the 1970s—under the influence of the *nouveaux philosophes*, an anti-totalitarian political front, and a 'second left' associated with socialist politician Michel Rocard—would reinforce this new liberalism, albeit often in the guise of a postmodernist reaction.[95] It would also, somewhat paradoxically, be reinforced by Michel Foucault's own ambivalent position towards neo-liberalism, even as he brilliantly diagnosed both neo-liberal and ordoliberal postwar trends and the emergence of new forms of liberal governmentality in his lectures at the end of the 1970s.[96]

In an important sense, then, the reaction to the crises affecting Western democracy towards the tail end of the 'golden age' of managed capitalism merely buttressed the political and constitutional status quo. The official Left's response to landmark events had often been 'the mirror image of that of its opponents'. Francois Mitterand, for example, in demanding in 1968 that parliament support an '"exceptional government" ... imitated the strategy adopted by de Gaulle a decade previously', supported by the French Communist Party 'stubbornly maintaining a strategy of Left unity and

[90] Sassoon (n 81) 394.

[91] Hailbronner does suggests a link between the rebellion against professional authority and the introduction of dissents in 1971 (Michaela Hailbronner, *Tradition and Transformations: The Rise of German Constitutionalism* (OUP 2015) 87).

[92] Offe (n 29) 77–80

[93] Sassoon (n 81) 397.

[94] Behrent (n 62) 53 (citing Régis Debray, *Modest Contribution aux Discourses et Cérémonies Officielles du Dixieme Anniversaire* (Francois Maspero 1978)).

[95] For a broad survey of the antecedents to this turn, as well as its legacy, see Göran Therborn, 'After Dialectics: Radical Social Theory in a Post-Communist World' (2007) 43 New Left Review 63.

[96] See Serge Audier, 'Neoliberalism Through Foucault's Eyes' (2015) 54 History and Theory 404. On Foucault's problematic conflation of power and domination, see Jan Rehmann, 'The Unfullfilled Promise of the Late Foucault and Foucauldian "Governmentality Studies"' in Daniel Zamora and Michael C Behrent (ed), *Foucault and Neoliberalism* (Polity Press 2016) 134. On Foucault's significance for public law, see Martin Loughlin, *Foundations of Public Law* (OUP 2010), 167–70, noting, however, that Foucault's argument 'avoids altogether the normativity of political engagement' (ibid 168–69).

abandoning any hopes of an insurrectionary politics'.[97] The elections of 1968 resulted in losses for the Left, with the Gaullists obtaining more working-class votes than the Communists. Left-wing opinion would soon be further tarnished by the USSR's invasion of Czechoslovakia months after the election in France. In drawing up the balance sheet, Donald Sassoon concludes that May 1968, 'far from being the proof that a violent revolution in the West was possible, confirmed what had become evident since 1945, namely that it was inconceivable'.[98]

The cumulative effect of a turn away from the state, from popular sovereignty and constituent power, and towards a transnational or even global discourse of human rights has been documented elsewhere.[99] The role of European integration played a central part too; not only, as we saw above, in dampening the revolutionary spirits of radical parties by offering the prospect of a future utopia, but in reinforcing the same consumer society that the events of May 1968 had called into question. If 'May 1968 represented ... a repudiation of the élites who had carried through *endogenous* modernization', the *exogenous* modernization that the very same elites were pursuing through membership of the Common Market would be left to achieve its full effect.[100]

Throughout the 1970s and early 1980s, and particularly after the major structural decision of the European Monetary System (EMS) in 1979, following West Germany's elevation of an anti-inflationist strategy, the notion of *Europe* 'became an authority that could exercise coercion in a social climate that was uncooperative'. The Common Market had become a project that would offer 'a substitute for an inadequate reforming ethos'.[101] This would accelerate with the combination of Delors and Mitterand in the 1980s, after which 'a linear relationship' would emerge 'between the decline of socialist ideas and the increasing centrality given to Europe'.[102]

The impact of neo-liberalism and economic globalization on the conditioning and curtailing of democracy would be acknowledged by certain contemporary commentators and critics. The organizers of a major conference at the University of Vincennes in 1979, featuring prominent intellectuals such as Noam Chomsky, Michel Foucault, Henri Lefebvre, and Nicos Poulantzas, had proposed a 'remarkably coherent concept', and coined a term for a 'new internal order' based on this, '[the] soft way'. This term 'sought to account for how a complete restructuring of the capitalist system' could have gone 'hand-in-hand with cultural liberalization and democratic rollback'.[103] There was, thus, not only a 'recognition of how neo-liberal economic policies systematically dismantled the post-war economy and the welfare state', but also an appreciation of the new capitalist order's 'global scope', and an 'analysis of the distinctive form of ideological hegemony that accompanied it'.[104]

[97] Sassoon (n 81) 398.
[98] ibid 399.
[99] See Samuel Moyn, *The Last Utopia: Human Rights in History* (HUP 2012).
[100] Pierre Grémion, 'State, Europe, and Republic' in A Menon and V Wright (eds), *From the Nation State to Europe? Essays in Honour of Jack Hayward* (OUP 2003) 48–49.
[101] ibid 53.
[102] ibid 54.
[103] Behrent (n 62).
[104] ibid.

If neo-liberal economic restructuring would be achieved, in part, by co-opting 'the libertarian spirit of the sixties', it was, in practice, politically authoritarian in its erosion of the spirit of collective autonomy and democratic power. An anarchic social liberalism would be a wholly inadequate, if perhaps reflexive, response to the authoritarian economic liberalism that was emerging in this period through formal, as well as informal, mechanisms. The more common response, even among self-described critical theorists, would be to accept the TINA narrative and present the logic of economic globalization, and with it a disembedded liberalism, as inexorable.[105] But authoritarian liberalism was about to rapidly accelerate, and then be extended and entrenched after Maastricht, in response to, and in conjunction with, the deeper economic globalization of the 1980s and 1990s. This will be the subject of Part III.

[105] See, eg Giubboni (n 48) 21: 'In an age of overwhelming globalization of financial markets and increasing internationalization of production processes, in which nation-states saw themselves as *inexorably* losing control over their own economies, the embedded liberalism metaphor therefore seemed destined to have to give way to its opposite: to disembedded or, even, subversive liberalism' (italics added).

PART III
THE ROAD FROM MAASTRICHT TO LISBON
Constitutional Movements and Counter-Movements

The reconstitution of post-war Europe was passively rather than actively authoritarian. Democracy was constrained in a way that reflected a sense of collective self-restraint as much as a process of the suppression of mass democracy. In combination with relatively benign economic circumstances, conditions were conducive for the emergence of a 'permissive consensus' on the elite-driven project of European integration.[1] As outlined in Part II, building a strong vibrant democracy was not part of post-war reconstruction, either domestically or supranationally, but neither was there significant opposition to the post-war settlement in general, and the project of European integration in particular, even outside the political mainstream.[2] In sum, there was a degree of congruence between domestic and supranational constitutional projects of constraining democracy through formal and informal means.

As a matter of political economy, the limited integration that followed the Treaty of Rome left space for national divergences and mixed economies, encompassing France's state-led capitalism and Germany's social market economy.[3] Although narrowing in range, the different social contracts would remain intact, each supported by overall economic growth, compromises between labour and capital, and elements of corporate bargaining. Enlargement of the European Economic Community was relatively slow-paced in comparison to the post-Maastricht era, the 'Europe of

[1] The term 'permissive consensus' was coined by Lindberg and Scheingold in 1970: Leon N Lindberg and Stuart A Scheingold (eds), *Regional Integration: Theory and Research* (HUP 1970) 62.

[2] The significance of the Christian democratic parties is well documented, but, as we examined in Chapter 5, it was not only centrist parties of the Left and Right, but also supposedly radical parties such as 'Eurocommunists' that came to support the project.

[3] The diversity of post-war welfare capitalism was famously captured by Gøsta Esping-Anderson, *The Three Worlds of Welfare Capitalism* (Polity Press 1990), and the varieties of capitalism in Peter A Hall and David Soskice, 'An Introduction to Varieties of Capitalism' in Peter A Hall and David Soskice (eds), *Varieties of Capitalism: The Institutional Foundations of Comparative Advantage* (OUP 2001) 1–68. By the mid 1990s there was concern that this (limited) diversity was being eroded. According to Fritz Scharpf, the different versions of the capitalist welfare state 'depended on the capacity of the territorial state to control its economic boundaries', a capacity that would be lost 'through the globalization of capital markets and the transnational integration of markets for goods and services', bringing to an end the 'golden age' of the welfare state. Instead, countries are then forced into regulatory competition (Fritz W Scharpf, 'Negative and Positive Integration in the Political Economy of European Welfare States' in Gary Marks et al (eds), *Governance in the European Union* (Sage Publications 1996) 16–17).

six' doubling in number between Rome and Maastricht, but over the course of several decades. The novelty of supranational institutions was genuine, and the jurisprudence of the Court of Justice genuinely innovative. But the overall scheme was juristically rather than politically ambitious, with the EEC's competences formally limited to the aim of completing the common market, progress towards which would, anyway, be initially slow and gradual.

According to one influential account, a duality and even equilibrium between law and politics prevailed, captured in the theory of 'dual supranationalism': if normative and technocratic authority was supranationalized in the Court and Commission, this was balanced by the firm retention of real political power at the national level.[4] In reality, however, as we saw in Part II, this produced a constitutional asymmetry that tilted strongly in favour of market logic.[5] To the extent that political power remained with the nation states, it was concentrated in executive, governmental, and administrative branches. There was an erosion of parliamentarism and a 'hollowing out' of democracy, and little sign of either re-emerging beyond the state.

Although the post-war settlement appeared relatively stable, the sharpening of its trajectory after the economic crises of the 1970s would highlight serious disequilibria. Soft authoritarianism would, then, be no substitute for robust popular support. Integration through law was a fragile foundation for a polity, particularly one which was to embark on a more ambitious and contested project of 'deepening and widening' as the end of the millennium approached. The plan to integrate in fields such as common foreign and security policy, judicial and police matters and, most conspicuously of all, to embark on Economic and Monetary Union, were bound to provoke more active forms of contestation. These were areas which went to the heart of the sovereign powers of the modern state, highly salient to partisan politics. Theories of equilibrium and consensus, already cracking, were about to be shattered.[6] Maastricht would mark a turning point.

To be sure, many changes inaugurated at Maastricht were foreshadowed by events during the 1970s and 1980s and, particularly, by the Single European Act of 1986. These included the new legislative procedure of cooperation, providing for Qualified Majority Voting and increased powers of the European Parliament; increased lobbying by transnational pressure groups for completion of the Common Market; the appointment of Jacques Delors as Commissioner (in 1984); President Mitterrand's U-turn on his socialist programme in the early 1980s (signifying the collapse of national Keynesianism); and the liberation of capital, with the relaxation of currency controls portending a new era of financialization of the economy (as we saw in Chapter 5). Institutionally, aspects of political intergovernmentalism and differentiated integration in foreign policy and EMU were also foreshadowed by European

[4] Joseph HH Weiler, 'The Transformation of Europe' (1992) 100 The Yale Law Journal 2403 (Weiler, 'The Transformation') (outlined earlier in Joseph HH Weiler, 'The Community System: The Character of Supranationalism' (1981) 1 Yearbook of European Law 267). National courts were also essential, as a significant conduit of supranational legality.

[5] Theorized in some detail, at an early stage, by Fritz W Scharpf, 'The Joint Decision Trap: Lessons from German Federalism and European Integration' (1988) 66 Public Administration 239.

[6] As Weiler himself acknowledged, in 'The Transformation' (n 4).

Political Cooperation and the Werner report (in the 1970s), the Schengen regime (signed in 1985), and the European Monetary System (initiated in 1979).

But unlike these earlier developments and the Single European Act itself, which passed through ratification smoothly, Maastricht presented significant political obstacles, and in a number of different member states.[7] As William Wallace and Julie Smith tersely put it, reflecting on events shortly after ratification, 'only after the signature of the Maastricht Treaty were the democratic credentials of European integration directly challenged'.[8] The sense of 'indirect legitimacy' for the project, which had characterized the earlier experience of integration, 'no longer existed'. And despite the introduction of European Parliament elections (in 1979), European integration had actually become 'subjectively more remote from "the people"—the mass public—over the years'.[9] More bluntly, as Jacques Delors put it in an unguarded moment, the phase of 'benign despotism' was over.[10]

The sharp turn of Europe in the short period from the Single European Act to the Maastricht Treaty is dramatized by the change in the British attitude towards it. From enthusiastic supporter and, arguably, key player, in the mid 1980s,[11] the British government had become the most fervent opponent. This shift was signalled by Thatcher's Bruges speech of 1988, announcing a disquiet that would reverberate well into the new century.[12] British intransigence would have practical repercussions for the EU itself. Thatcher's domestic neo-liberal revolution not only imposed its stamp on the single market project, it opposed integration of social and welfare rights in particular, cementing obstacles to further political union.

[7] In Majone's view, the success of the Single European Act was due precisely to the fact it 'avoided any grandiose institutional reform': Giandomenico Majone, *Dilemmas of European Integration: The Ambiguities and Pitfalls of Integration by Stealth* (OUP 2005) 11. Majone concludes that book by declaring that the EU, despite 'underhand efforts to steer it in the direction of full political union', is the 'leading model of the post-modern confederation designed to prepare the economies of its component polities to the challenges of globalisation' (ibid 221).

[8] William Wallace and Julie Smith, 'Democracy or Technocracy? European Integration and the Problem of Popular Consent' in Jack Hayward (ed), *The Crisis of Representation in Europe* (Routledge 1995) 150. In the same volume, Weiler, Haltern, and Mayer offered a standard account of the 'democratic deficit'(in 'European Democracy and its Critique' (ibid 4)).

[9] Wallace and Smith (n 8) 153. They continue by stating that, if 'technocratic policy-making was acceptable among six countries, with a limited agenda and within the wider context of American leadership and the external Soviet threat', the situation looked very different in an enlarged EU, 'without constructive American guidance or the solidarity engendered by any clear and present external danger'. In the new post-Maastricht conditions, there could be 'little hope of generating any comparable permissive consensus' (ibid 154).

[10] Vernon Bogdanor, 'Futility of a House with no Windows', *The Independent* (London, 26 July 1993) <https://www.independent.co.uk/voices/futility-of-a-house-with-no-windows-1487252.html>

[11] See, eg John Gillingham, *European Integration 1950–2003: Superstate or New Market Economy?* (CUP 2003) 164.

[12] 'The very success of the single market project that the Iron Lady had supported', notes Ludlow, 'stimulated the appearance of multiple other European ambitions to which she was opposed' (N Piers Ludlow, 'Problematic Partners: De Gaulle, Thatcher and their Impace' in Erik Jones, Anand Menon, and Stephen Weatherill (eds), *Oxford Handbook of the European Union* (OUP 2012) 212). Thatcher's own fall from power was then 'tightly bound up with the European issue' (ibid 212), revealing her own impotence, unable to prevent collective decision on the starting of EMU despite strident opposition to it, and showing, as with de Gaulle, that 'isolated Euroskeptic leaders can only have a comparatively limited impact on the integration process', such is their reduced capacity to control it (ibid 216).

British exceptionalism, however, appeared a relatively minor inconvenience in light of the broader regional and international context, reflecting the geopolitical, political and economic changes of the Maastricht period. These generated tremendous optimism, with the collapse of the Soviet bloc opening Europe to the East, and the proclaimed triumph of liberal capitalism cementing the end of ideology; even, some famously predicted, the end of history.[13] With the Cold War coming to an end, Europe appeared in need of a new geopolitical vocation, since it was no longer required as a Western bulwark to US imperialism against the threat of Soviet Communism.[14] The collapse of the Soviet Union offered an obvious path forward, the enlargement programme opening up the EU to the countries of Central and Eastern Europe, on condition they satisfied the 'Copenhagen' pre-accession criteria, respecting broad principles of liberal democracy and market economy. The 'widening and deepening' of integration coincided with this normative re-foundation; a new constitutional identity for the EU, based, on paper at least, on democracy, human rights, and the rule of law.[15] The new optimism among political elites would soon lay the ground for the Constitutional project, which began in earnest with the Laeken declaration, following the Treaty of Nice in 2001.[16]

But the Maastricht era also generated certain new anxieties and rekindled old ones. The reunification of Germany altered internal regional power dynamics, and even reopened the question of German hegemony, which had been closed down by the Cold War superpower rivalry of the post-war era, and eased by relative parity in the Franco-German partnership. The discourse of constitutional 'finality' (signalled by Joschka Fischer's 'Humboldt speech')[17] proved ill-fated, the Constitutional project rejected by referenda in two core founding states, France and the Netherlands, in 2005. In France, especially, fears of the project's neo-liberal political economy, and a sense that it reneged on Delors' social promise, were major factors in its rejection.[18] The notion of

[13] Francis Fukuyama, *The End of History and the Last Man* (The Free Press 1992).

[14] Robert Kagan noted the irony of Europe's 'Venus' having depended on 'America's Mars'. It was the United States that had provided the solution to the age-old 'German problem', permitting Europeans to relinquish force (quoted in Étienne Balibar, *We, the People of Europe? Reflections on Transnational Citizenship* (Princeton University Press 2004) 216 (Balibar, 'We, the People of Europe?'). Balibar went on to argue that Europe's political capacity was entirely illusory).

[15] Article 2 Treaty on European Union. After accession, these criteria would bear little weight until rhetorically resuscitated in the so-called 'rule of law crisis'.

[16] For a constitutional analysis of the constitution-making period, see John Erik Fossum and Agustin Menendez, *The Constitution's Gift: A Constitutional Theory for a Democratic European Union* (Rowman and Littlefield 2011).

[17] See Joschka Fischer, 'From Confederacy to Federation: Thoughts on the Finality of European Integration' in Christian Joerges, Yves Meny, and JHH Weiler (eds), *What Kind of Constitution for what Kind of Polity: Responses to Joschka Fischer* (Jean Monnet Program Online Papers 2001) <http://hdl.handle.net/1814/4110>.

[18] See Gilles Ivaldi, 'Beyond France's 2005 Referendum on the European Constitutional Treaty: Second-Order Model, Anti-Establishment Attitudes and the end of the alternative European Utopia' (2006) 29 West European Politics 47 ('In many respects, the rejection of the ECT in 2005 was first and foremost a retrospective vote on the process of European integration itself, and the unilateral termination by a majority of voters of the "social welfare and economic growth" confidence pact that they had made with their national political elites on the occasion of the Maastricht Treaty referendum in 1992 . . . [T]he novelty of the 2005 contest was the critical view of the EU model of social and economic governance in a wide segment of those, and more particularly left-wing voters of the middle class, who had subscribed to the alternative utopian European project defended by President François Mitterrand 13 years earlier' (ibid 49).

finality also foreshadowed the still unresolved geopolitics of Europe's borders, raising issues of exclusion of outsiders from 'Fortress Europe', concerns about febrile EU–Russia relations, and questioning of cultural and religious identity, with the prospect of Turkish accession.[19]

Although the failure of the European Constitutional project signposted a clear unsettling of the trajectory of integration, this could, in fact, be identified in the variations established at Maastricht itself. The member states would agree to launch a single currency, but one which did not unite them all. The attempts to go beyond market Europe, by integrating Common Foreign and Security Policy and Justice and Home Affairs, were pursued intergovernmentally, excluding the law-making process and the ECJ's jurisdiction; citizenship was added to the Treaty, but as a pale imitation of the real thing—an adjunct—merely complementary to national citizenship, and in line with the logic of market freedoms, in terms of its emphasis on non-discrimination and transnational mobility.[20]

Domestically, the fractious nature of the European constitutional arrangement was increasingly evident in the decade following Maastricht. With the end of the permissive consensus, doubts over the legitimacy of the EU's authority began to resonate more loudly, with dissent gradually moving from the margins to the mainstream. If, in the post-war period, European integration was considered compatible with relatively autonomous and diverse domestic political and constitutional arrangements, the Maastricht era would signal an uneasiness with national autonomy, not through its supersession by the construction of a United States of Europe, but through a much messier set of formulas that would signal multiple points of conflict. What Maastricht finally made clear (at least to some) was that 'the integrated Europe of the European Union will never be a supranational state on the model of European nation-states'. Instead, something quite different was developing: 'a polity of a new kind: an international order, controlled by intergovernmental relations between sovereign nation-states, that serves as a domestic order for a transnational economy'.[21]

The post-Maastricht phase thus presents a paradox. On the one hand, there was increasing enthusiasm about the project in elite and academic circles; a sense generated by a 'culture of total optimism'.[22] Around the turn of the millennium, Europe continued to be presented as 'a paragon of international virtues'; a 'model to the

[19] On the uncertainties of Europe's constitutional identity in this period, see Étienne Balibar, 'Europe's Vanishing Mediator' in 'We, the People of Europe?' (n 14) 203.

[20] See Fossum and Menendez (n 16). See, further, Niamh Nic Shuibhne, 'The Resilience of EU Market Citizenship' (2010) 47 Common Market Law Review 1597.

[21] Wolfgang Streeck, 'Neo-Voluntarism: A New European Social Policy Regime?' in Gary Marks et al (eds), *Governance in the European Union* (Sage Publications 1996) 64. Streeck presciently continues, 'This combination of executive intergovernmentalism and economic transnationalism would give rise to a "historical coalition" between political nationalism and neoliberalism' (ibid 65), a conclusion which forces a radical dissociation from the received wisdom of 'teleological federalism' and its accompanying utopia of a gradually emerging social Europe (ibid 68).

[22] Giandomenico Majone, *Rethinking the Union of Europe Post-Crisis: Has Integration Gone too Far?* (CUP 2014) 58. This was, apparently, the same Majone who had fully justified the EU as non-majoritarian: a regulatory regime on the structure of a confederation based on principles of economic liberalism. As Perry Anderson notes, the 'magisterially evasive term "non-majoritarian"' was, in fact, in deep contradiction with democracy (Perry Anderson, *The New Old World* (Verso 2009) 112).

nations of the world'; a 'beacon of light' in troubled times.[23] We would be entering 'the new European century', an era in which sovereignty itself would be transcended. In fact, according to one influential legal scholar, we had already moved 'beyond the sovereign state'.[24] In domestic politics, there was a convergence on a new 'third way' neo-liberalism, embodied in the triumvirate of Blair, Schröder and Jospin, as domestic political-economic strategies gradually fell into line with a new, neo-liberal 'Maastricht orthodoxy'.[25]

On the other hand, as European integration accelerated, albeit in discrete and compartmentalized domains, it would be accompanied by a growing set of *countermovements*, signalled by the return of the discourse of state sovereignty, as domestic constitutional challenges to the project of integration increased in number and intensity. These challenges occurred through formal institutions such as constitutional courts, and in popular referenda, buttressed by the growth of nationalist political parties. Countermovements tended to be based on nationalism and identity politics rather than a reinvigoration of local or partisan forms of democratic representation, let alone a democratic constituent power, not least since so many left-wing intellectuals had effectively abandoned meaningful Euroscepticism.[26] These movements, however, would often merely reinforce the executive intergovernmentalism that was leading the project of integration.

The disconnect between rulers and ruled that emerged post-Maastricht is strongly pronounced in constitutional theorizing on the European Union. The normative turn in constitutional theory took leave of the material elements of constitutional change, discarding questions of political economy and institutional legitimacy, and overlooking democratic and social deficits.[27] Much of this disconnect was simply concealed in the dominant political and constitutionalist rhetoric of the time: constitutional pluralism,[28] democratic experimentalism, and[29] cosmopolitanism.[30] The EU was perceived as a 'stepping stone to a world society', as Europe's leading political philosopher put it.[31] The project of constitutionalization appeared increasingly 'free-standing', divorced from geopolitical changes, shifts in party political programmes and fortunes, and changes in state-civil society relations and political economy.[32] If a

[23] Anderson (n 22) 47–49 (respectively quoting Tony Judt, Marcel Gauchet, Jeremy Rifkin, and Mark Leonard).

[24] Neil MacCormick, 'Beyond the Sovereign State' (1993) 56 Modern Law Review 1, 18.

[25] See Christopher J Bickerton, Dermot Hodson, and Uwe Puetter, 'The New Intergovernmentalism: European Integration in the Post-Maastricht Era' (2015) 53 Journal of Common Market Studies 703.

[26] Some of the leading radical philosophers of the era had abandoned domestic politics entirely for the abstract agency of the global 'multitude' (see Michael Hardt and Antonio Negri, *Empire* (HUP 2000).

[27] See, eg Neil MacCormick, *Questioning Sovereignty: Law, State and Nation in the European Commonwealth* (OUP 1999). In *Questioning Sovereignty*, there is little discussion of the impact of market integration on democracy or social values.

[28] cf Neil Walker, 'The Idea of Constitutional Pluralism' (2002) 65 Modern Law Review 317.

[29] See Oliver Gerstenberg, 'Law's Polyarchy: A Comment on Cohen and Sabel' (1997) 4 European Law Journal 343.

[30] See, eg Ulrich Beck, *The Cosmopolitan Vision* (Polity Press 2006). This coincided with the turn to governance in European studies and the diagnosed death of the modern nation state, see, eg Markus Jachtenfuchs, 'Theoretical Perspectives on European Governance' (1995) 1 European Law Journal 123.

[31] Jürgen Habermas, *The Postnational Constellation: Political Essays* (MIT Press 2001).

[32] See Michael A Wilkinson, 'Political Constitutionalism and the European Union' (2013) 76 Modern Law Review 191.

new constitutionalism was being forged without democratic support or popular constituent backing, this could not be sustained other than by authoritarian means.[33]

This Part analyses the *continuities* and *discontinuities* in the trajectory of the post-war reconstitution outlined in Part II. The continuities, and even accelerated dynamics, of a passive authoritarian liberalism are evident: inter-state relations are further depoliticized, but without the creation of a supranational political-democratic centre; the realignment of state-society relations continues with further depoliticization (and de-democratization) of decision-making, and concomitant growth of technocracy and juristocracy; and, finally, the neo-liberalization of political economy continues apace, now with the differentiation of the political and economic scaled up to a macro level through EMU's separation of the state from its money supply, and the restriction of its fiscal autonomy. The constitutional dynamic that launched post-war reconstruction is reinforced, and deepened in significant respects, supplementing the soft authoritarianism of the founding era with a harsher neo-imperial aspect, due to the dramatic inequalities among a diverse set of new member states, as well as between existing ones. Inter-state, state-society, and social relations are increasingly disconnected from democratic political contestation, precariously sustaining a 'void' between rulers and ruled, of ever-growing proportions.[34]

And, yet, in each of these dimensions, irritants emerge, reflecting various discontinuities and even countermovements, both systemic and anti-systemic: a regional configuration that would reveal stark asymmetries among the members, and even a re-emergence of German hegemony; re-politicization through national and constitutional identity politics; the fomentation of social discontent with an 'extreme centrism', and 'third way' neo-liberalism that left little choice to voters, other than disenchantment with establishment politics. Movements and countermovements, thus, appeared largely intertwined, and even symbiotic. If the impact of these countermovements remained—by and large—latent, subdued, and incapable of breaking through the constitutional surface to have any significant impact, they revealed a series of tensions in the post-war project—contradictions, even—laying the groundwork for the more spectacular conflicts that would erupt through the euro crisis phase that begun shortly after the ratification, in 2009, of the Treaty of Lisbon (examined in Part IV).

Chapter 6 presents the geopolitical constitution of Europe as it develops in the period from 'Maastricht to Lisbon'. This period is characterized by further constraints on the exercise of sovereign powers among states. But this is structured through a 'new intergovernmentalism' rather than traditional forms of supranationalism. This feature, along with the move towards differentiated integration, signals the end of the 'federal dream'. It also marks the return of the German question, as the reunification of Germany, and its increasing influence through the Eastern enlargement of the Union, raises the spectre of German hegemony.

Chapter 7 examines political constitutionalism after Maastricht, a paradoxical configuration in which EU authority is augmented, but subject to increasing domestic contestation. This generates heightened constitutional conflicts in formal arenas, and social and political contestation and opposition in informal ones. Sovereignty and

[33] As was noted by Martin Loughlin, 'In Defence of *Staatslehre*' (2009) 48 Der Staat 1.
[34] See Peter Mair, *Ruling the Void: The Hollowing of Western Democracy* (Verso 2013).

constituent power resurface after their post-war sublimation, but without obvious practical moment, and the judicial practice and academic discourse of European constitutionalization continues apace, disconnected from democratic support.

Chapter 8 turns to the constitution of economic liberalism, especially through the construction of Economic and Monetary Union (EMU), and the ideological shifts that it reflects and entrenches. This is the domain in which the deepening and widening of post-war trends is most evident, the logic of the market being brought to bear on macro-economic policy with a nearly complete political abdication to ordoliberal and neo-liberal demands. And, yet, in the socio-economic domain, too, certain discontinuities can be identified, with growing social fractures developing, and opposition to the Maastricht settlement and its political orthodoxy bubbling below the surface, without being channelled into a significant political movement.

6

Restraining State Sovereignty or the Return of the German Question?

1. Introduction

As a matter of regional geopolitics, the 1992 Treaty of Maastricht, on its face, looked like a continuation of the European project along the route constructed from its outset. The process of restraining state sovereignty and depoliticizing inter-state relations would be extended from a single market for the productive economy to the areas of monetary policy, foreign policy, political and judicial cooperation, and citizenship itself. The project was opened to a much-enlarged set of members; the motto of a 'return to Europe' for countries of Central and Eastern Europe, after having escaped the yoke of Soviet domination, signalling a reunion with a continuous, and even fateful, historical path.[1] On the surface, and in official discourse, the project that began at Rome was 'widened and deepened' at Maastricht. The 'European Union' itself was officially born, symbolizing the move beyond its original economic remit.

And, yet, this would be a superficial and misleading analysis if left without supplement. Due to the particular and dramatic geopolitical changes, with the fall of the Berlin Wall presaging the reunification of Germany, the original question of state sovereignty—of how to prevent German domination of the European continent—returned to the discourse of European constitutional politics, having lain dormant for four and a half decades.[2] The end of Cold War superpower rivalry, disequilibrium in the Franco-German axis, political-economic imbalance between a northern core and outer peripheries, and what has been called, retrospectively, the 'new intergovernmentalism', strengthened the power of European executives and new European institutions at the expense of traditional supranationalization of the Union, as well as of domestic representation.[3] The material constitution of the Union, thus, became characterized by increasing divisions, due, notably, to constitutional differentiation (section 2); growing imbalances between core nations, and even the spectre

[1] See Marise Cremona, 'Introduction' in Marise Cremona (ed), *The Enlargements of the European Union* (OUP 2003).

[2] According to Krotz and Schild, the issue of German power in Europe '[re]appeared in scholarly discourse in the 1990s when observers pointed to Germany's "dominant and growing ... tremendous influence" and characterised Germany's position in Eastern Europe as "hegemonic"' (Ulrich Krotz and Joachim Schild, *Shaping Europe: France, Germany, and Embedded Bilateralism from the Elysee Treaty to Twenty-First Century Politics* (OUP 2013) 15). According to Bulmer and Paterson, 'unification and the associated move to the Berlin Republic prompted a gradual reappraisal of how to analyse Germany's role' (Simon Bulmer and William Paterson, *Germany and the European Union* (Red Globe Press 2019) 8.

[3] Christopher J Bickerton, Dermot Hodson, and Uwe Puetter, 'Something New: A Rejoinder to Frank Schimmelfennig on the New Intergovernmentalism' (2015) 53 Journal of Common Market Studies 731.

Authoritarian Liberalism and the Transformation of Modern Europe. Michael A Wilkinson, Oxford University Press.
 DOI: 10.1093/oso/9780198854753.003.0007

of inter-state domination (section 3); and stark *asymmetries* with the unfolding of the project of Eastern enlargement of the Union (section 4).

2. Differentiated integration and the 'new intergovernmentalism'

If the French bet had always been that further and deeper integration would bind Germany to the European project in a manner that would mitigate the risk of its renewed domination, the post-Maastricht era proved to be a huge gamble. The 'Europe of twelve' agreed, at Maastricht, to confer the new entity with dramatic new competences. This signalled, symbolically, the path from single market to political union, with the domestication of inter-state relations in the new areas of monetary union (EMU), Common Foreign and Security Policy, and justice and home affairs, as well as the inclusion of citizenship of the Union. But these areas of further integration would be pursued in the absence of a single constitutional structure, the Community method of law-making restricted to the first, market-based pillar.[4] EMU would be governed through the Community's institutional powers, including new ones such as the European Central Bank (ECB), but would be subject to the opt-outs of the UK, Denmark and, de facto, of Sweden, and would be rolled out over a transitional period that would depend upon convergence criteria.

The Maastricht Treaty itself had been negotiated along twin tracks; one—Intergovernmental Conference—was rather haphazard, and dealt with political union, and the other—more thoroughly prepared—dealt with EMU itself. The result, in addition to the infamous pillar structure, was a series of opt-outs and opt-ins. This multi-speed, variegated structure would prove to be an enduring feature of the new settlement, and would be extended at the Treaties of Amsterdam (1997), and Nice (2001). Maastricht, according to one influential voice, marked the 'end of the post-1985 *rélance* of European integration, rather than the big leap forward that Delors had wanted'.[5] The variation and differentiation of EMU was to be a new 'metaphor' for integration, in the words of another commentator.[6]

The move from economic to political Union was largely illusory. Its most prominent symbol was the creation of Union citizenship, an apparently dormant creature that the Court of Justice nevertheless breathed some life into during the first decade of its existence, in a series of bold and controversial judgments promoting cross-border mobility and prohibiting discrimination on grounds of nationality.[7] But outside the

[4] See Deirdre Curtin, 'The Constitutional Structure of the Union: A Europe of Bits and Pieces' (1993) 30 Common Market Law Review 17. See also Paul Demaret, 'The Treaty Framework' in David O'Keefe and Patrick M Twomey (eds), *Legal Issues of the Maastricht Treaty* (Wiley Chancery 2003).

[5] See Giandomenico Majone, 'The Limits of Collective Action and Collective Leadership' in Damian Chalmers, Markus Jachtenfuchts, Christian Joerges (eds), *The End of Eurocrats' Dream: Adjusting to Diversity* (CUP 2016) 230. In fact, Majone notes, the Commission had very little influence over the negotiations on political union.

[6] Francis Snyder, 'EMU—Integration and Differentiation: Metaphor for the European Union' in Paul Craig and Gráinne de Búrca (eds), *The Evolution of EU Law* (OUP 2011) 687–716.

[7] Agustín José Menéndez, 'European Citizenship after *Martinez Sala* and *Baumbast*: Has European Law Become More Human but Less Social?' in Miguel Poiares Maduro and Loïc Azoulai (eds), *The Past*

context of interstitial and ad hoc claims made by the transnationally mobile, political union was nominal at most, with little attempt to construct any supranational political government, or to integrate the European citizen into the domestic political life of the host state. Notably, non-nationals' voting rights were restricted to local and European Parliament elections, thus excluding them from the most significant political life of the nation.[8] Indeed, far from representing a rupture with the dominant neo-liberal economic trajectory, member states would, by incorporating the views of mobile non-national taxpayers into policymaking, favour 'mobile capital and the richer EU citizens over immobile labour and poorer citizens'.[9]

Disunity and fragmentation were the more pervasive features of the era; and, it would seem, far from temporary ones.[10] Accordingly, although Maastricht formally gave birth to the new entity called the European Union, it did not supplant the economic pillar of the European Community, but merely supplemented it, and in an institutionally uneven manner. This was described at the time, and quite appositely, as creating a Europe of 'bits and pieces'.[11] The goal of federalism was dropped, at the insistence of the British, and substituted for the nebulous principle of 'subsidiarity', a principle whose impact on scholarly interest was inversely proportional to its effect on constitutional law.[12] In foreign affairs, Europe would continue to express less than the sum of its parts, the failure of political capacity to materialize on the world stage confirming Henry Kissinger's famous adage that spoke to Europe's overall geopolitical irrelevance.[13] To the extent that influence was exerted, it would continue to be in Paris, Berlin, and London, rather than Brussels.[14] Significant divisions remained among the major European powers, most notably over the Iraq war; this split old and

and Future of EU Law; The Classics of EU Law Revisited on the 50th Anniversary of the Rome Treaty (Hart Publishing 2010) 363–93.

[8] On the 'political riddle' of European citizenship, see Joseph HH Weiler, 'To be a European Citizen: Eros and Civilisation' in *The Constitution of Europe: 'Do the New Clothes have an Emperor?' and other Essays on European Integration* (CUP 1999) 324–57. See, further, Richard Bellamy, 'The Liberty of the Moderns: Market Freedom and Democracy in the EU' (2012) 1:1 Global Constitutionalism 141–72. The extension of citizenship and welfare claims, to some extent, re-politicizes the issue of free movement, but not in the sense of a pan-European partisan politics; rather, as a further domestic node of contestation.

[9] Floris de Witte, *Justice in the EU: The Emergence of Transnational Solidarity* (OUP 2015) 65–69

[10] Some would prove to be, such as the UK opt-out from the Social Chapter. The Republic of Ireland and Denmark would also obtain protocols on abortion and second-home ownership, respectively.

[11] See Curtin (n 4). Weiler (n 8) 233 describes Maastricht as a 'rebellion' against a 'federal-type constitutionalism'.

[12] Article A of the draft Treaty text had read, 'This Treaty marks a new stage in the process leading gradually to a Union with a federal goal'. In earlier Christian democratic and Catholic thought, subsidiarity was framed to 'limit the scope of state intervention in the economy and society' (see Wolfram Kaiser, *Christian Democracy and the Origins of the European Union* (CUP 2007) 307–08). In the EU, it was intended to safeguard the exercise of competence at the national level, but would have very limited legal impact; see Paul Craig, 'Subsidiarity, A Legal and Political Analysis' (2012) 50 Journal of Common Market Studies 72; cf Carlo Invernizzi Accetti, *What is Christian Democracy? Politics, Religion and Ideology* (CUP 2019), claiming its central political significance.

[13] Kissinger famously had 'no one to call' to ask for Europe's position on an important geopolitical matter.

[14] cf Chris Bickerton, *From Nation-States to Member States* (OUP 2012) 27–33, which argues against the claim that the Common Foreign and Security Policy (CFSP) was built around the primacy of national sovereignty, but also the claim that it was moving in a neo-functionalist manner towards a pan-European solution. It was, rather, being constructed as a 'consensus-generating machine' through committees.

new Europe, in the early years of the new millennium, on the most decisive foreign policy issue for a generation.

In reality, therefore, Maastricht also signalled a departure—if initially thought to be temporary—from the path of European unification, with the launching of what was variously referred to as 'multi-speed Europe', 'variable geometry', or 'differentiated integration': the ability to pursue different levels of integration through opt-ins and opt-outs. This would be given more precise formalization at the Treaty of Amsterdam in 1997, be modified again at the Treaty of Nice in 2001, and would survive in the period after the Treaty of Lisbon was signed, in 2007.[15]

The most ambitious plan to extend integration, aside from EMU (examined in Chapter 8), was the creation of an area of freedom, security and justice (AFSJ). Building on earlier cooperation in non-economic fields, stretching back to the 1970s and 1980s, such as the Pompidou Group on drugs, the Trevi Group on antiterrorism, the Schengen Agreement on common borders, and the Dublin Convention on asylum application, the AFSJ, officially established at Amsterdam, developed the pillar on justice and home affairs introduced at Maastricht (TEU Article K). This proceeded in an intergovernmental fashion, using a special set of legal instruments to the almost total exclusion of the Community apparatus, leaving out the core institutions of European Parliament, Court of Justice, and Commission, and functioning on the basis of unanimity of decision-making among the member states. Although partially 'communitarized' at Amsterdam, with visas, asylum, immigration, and other policies related to the free movement of persons integrated into the Community pillar, the title on police and judicial cooperation in criminal matters remained intergovernmental, proceeding through the adoption of common positions, framework decisions, and conventions. But it also laid the ground for a number of semi-autonomous bodies to develop, notably Europol (and later Eurojust), and formally excluded the constitutional quality of its rules, bolstering the power and authority of executive branches of the member states, and sidelining constitutional guarantees.[16]

In an imitation of its earlier foundational rulings on direct effect and supremacy within the single market, the Court of Justice again proved to be an active force, de facto constitutionalizing framework decisions despite the Treaty having explicitly ruled out their direct effect,[17] extending EU competence into criminal matters where there was a functional spillover from the internal market,[18] eroding the principle of national autonomy in criminal law,[19] and offering preliminary rulings even where

[15] This was the era of 'semi-permanent' Treaty revision, described as a 'constitutional conversion', albeit one almost totally bypassing the people (Bruno de Witte, 'The Closest Thing to a Constitutional Conversation in Europe: The Semi-Permanent Treaty Revision Process' in Paul Beaumont, Carole Lyons and Neil Walker (eds), *Convergence and Divergence in European Public Law* (Hart Publishing 2002).

[16] On the constitutional aspects of the AFSJ, see Neil Walker, 'In Search of the Area of Freedom, Security and Justice: A Constitutional Odyssey' in Neil Walker (ed), *Europe's Area of Freedom, Security and Justice* (OUP 2004) 3–40. Even with the subsequent collapse of the pillar structure at Lisbon, this area stubbornly resisted supranationalization.

[17] Case C-105/03 *Maria Pupino* [2005] ECR I-5285.

[18] Case C-176/03 *European Commission v Council of the European Union* [2005] ECR I-7879 (environmental crimes), and Case C-440/05 Commission v Council [2007] ECR I-9097 (ship-source pollution).

[19] Joined Cases C-187 and 385/01 *Gözütok and Brügge* [2003] ECR I-1345.

jurisdiction was formally excluded.[20] If the member states continued to claim the monopoly of the legitimate use of physical force within their territory, with national security, in particular, being emphasized as remaining the 'sole responsibility of each Member' (Article 4), this did not prevent a number of incursions into autonomous rights of defence protected at the national level, 'the extremity' of which were constitutionally significant.[21]

The logic of mutual recognition of judgments and requests, in comparison to its originating domain of free movement, would be reversed under the European arrest warrant (EAW), in the sense that it empowered rather than disarmed the governing apparatus of the state.[22] It facilitated extradition of suspected criminals even in the absence of shared standards of criminal justice or definitions of offences.[23] But in one respect, it followed a continuous logic, highlighting a new aspect of authoritarian liberalism: the erasure of borders in a way that would undermine civil rights of the accused, extending police powers to such a degree that it would eventually be subject to a series of constitutional challenges in domestic courts. Application of the EAW was a particular area of concern for domestic constitutional courts, tasked with upholding rights of defence that were often protected in written constitutional documents.[24] Initially held up by liberal constitutionalists as a good illustration of an area in which the EU ought to have increased powers, execution of the arrest warrant became increasingly contested as a means through which rights of defence, and of a fair trial, might become progressively weakened and even eroded. The effective operation of these increased police powers was predicated on the assumption that a high degree of mutual trust and respect existed among the member states, a condition that would be severely tested in the critical decade following Lisbon, with the emergence of authoritarian populism, and the so-called 'rule of law crisis'.

More generally, the process of integration outside the core economic constitution was increasingly occurring *without* constitutionalization, in the interstices of accountability, through 'grey areas' of law and politics. Maastricht had called an end to the singleness of the Community method of law-making, inaugurating an era dominated by visions of 'new governance', 'experimentalism', and the 'open method of coordination (OMC)'; an era in which integration would no longer necessarily proceed in

20 Case C-354/04 *Gestoras Pro Amnistía, Juan Mari Olano Loan and Julen Zelarain Errasti v Council* [2007] ECR I-1579.

21 In a stock-taking exercise in relation to the Third Pillar, published in 2009, a 'striking imbalance' was identified, 'between the Union's enthusiasm for investing in crime control and its reticence about ensuring appropriate protections for defence rights'; see Estella Baker and Christopher Harding, 'From Past Imperfect to Future Perfect? A Longitudinal Study of the Third Pillar' (2009) 34 European Law Review 25.

22 ibid: 'In the single market context, the role of mutual recognition is rights-enhancing for individuals in promoting freedom of movement and economic opportunity. In the context of JHA, however, it operates differently, promoting the movement ... of official decisions against individuals, thus rights-restricting in outcome'. See also Sandra Lavenax, 'Mutual Recognition and the Monopoly of Force: Limits of the Single Market Analogy' (2007) 14 Journal of European Public Policy 762.

23 The EAW (Council Framework Decision (EU) 2002/584/JHA of 13 June 2002 on the European arrest warrant and the surrender procedures between Member States ([2002] OJ L 290/1)) abolished the requirement of double criminality (eroding the principle *nullum crimen, nulla poena sine lege*) with respect to thirty-two crimes, if punishable by a maximum sentence of at least three years.

24 This was exemplified already in the case of *Melloni*: see Case C-399/11 *Stefano Melloni v Ministerio Fiscal* [2013] OJ C114/12.

a legal-constitutional fashion, but through 'soft law' and other informal avenues of 'governance'.[25] This also signalled a departure from the neofunctional logic that economic integration would prompt political integration, and that politicization would then force elites to engage mass publics in European matters, eventually precipitating a process of Euro-democratization.[26] On the contrary, integration proceeded apace, but with a new intergovernmental inflection, fragmentary, under the radar of constitutional legitimacy, and further removed from democratic and legal accountability.[27]

An 'integration paradox' thus emerged after Maastricht: member states 'pursue[d] more integration but stubbornly resist[ed] further supranationalism', representing a turn to what was appositely characterized as the 'new intergovernmentalism'.[28] The federalizing dynamic created by the extended use of qualified majority voting in Council, following the Single European Act, which facilitated a move from negative integration to positive harmonization of rules, appeared to be checked after Maastricht.[29] While there was a formal increase in the power of the European Parliament in the legislative process, with the introduction of 'co-decision' (later renamed the 'ordinary legislative procedure'), there was no concomitant increase in popular legitimacy.[30] There was deliberation among political and economic elites, often behind closed doors, but no deliberative democracy worthy of the label. The combination of consensus-seeking among member states (often through the committee structure of 'comitology'), driven primarily by national governments and their perception of the 'national interest' (subject to lobbying by powerful economic interest groups), was better captured by the term 'deliberative intergovernmentalism', as opposed to the 'deliberative supranationalism' in vogue at the time.[31]

[25] See, eg Joanne Scott and David M Trubek, 'Mind the Gap: Law and New Approaches to Governance in the European Union' (2002) 8 European Law Journal 1. In 2001 the European Commission proclaimed the turn to 'governance' in its White Paper, Commission, 'European Governance: A White Paper' (White Paper) COM (2001) 428 final. For critical reflection, see Christian Joerges, 'Guest Editorial: The Commission's White Paper on Governance in the EU: A Symptom of Crisis?' (2002) 39 Common Market Law Review 441, and the symposium in Christian Joerges, Yves Meny, and Joseph HH Weiler (eds), 'Mountain or Molehill? A Critical Appraisal of the Commission White Paper on Governance' (Jean Monnet Working Paper No 6/01, 2001).

[26] See Lisbet Hooghe and Gary Marks, 'A Postfunctionalist Theory of European Integration: From Permissive Consensus to Constraining Dissensus' (2009) 39 British Journal of Political Science 1, 5.

[27] The dangers inherent in the post-Maastricht approach were well understood at the time (see, eg David Marquand, 'Reinventing Federalism: Europe and the Left' in David Miliband (ed), *Reinventing the Left* (Polity Press 1994)).

[28] Bickerton, Hodson, and Puetter (n 3) 731. As they note, 'The extension of the ordinary legislative procedure in successive treaty revisions does not *eo ipso* signal more supranationalism. Pushes to expand qualified majority voting and legislative decision-making competences to the domain of social policy-making, for instance, have failed to generate a new wave of legislation, a centralization of power or the harmonization of social standards.'

[29] The turn to governance was foreshadowed by the new approach to harmonization; see Francis G Snyder (ed), *The Europeanisation of Law: The Legal Effects of European Integration* (Hart Publishing 2000).

[30] The introduction of the co-decision process, at Maastricht, was meant to help remedy the democratic deficit. In reality, the turn to trialogues reflected a new legislative culture, which, although not mentioned in the Treaty, became semi-formalized, rendering EU law-making increasingly secretive and bureaucratic (see, eg Anne E Stie, *Democratic Decision-Making in the EU: Technocracy in Disguise?* (Routledge 2012)).

[31] cf Christian Joerges and Christian Neyer, 'From Intergovernmental Bargaining to Deliberative Political Processes: The Constitutionalisation of Comitology' (1997) 3 European Law Journal 273. In this period, there was tremendous optimism about the democratic possibilities of integration, often building on the work of US scholars; see, eg Joshua Cohen and Charles Sabel, 'Directly-Deliberative Polyarchy' (1997) 3 European Law Journal 313. But there were also isolated critical voices, eg William Scheuermann, arguing

From the very beginning of the postwar period, the prospect of a European federalism had cast its shadow over the process of integration; or, for those more inclined towards it, cast its light over a path to the 'promised land'.[32] After Maastricht, this more ambitious, constructivist, vision of European integration—which had always existed alongside, sometimes in conflict with, ideas of reinventing, preserving, or transcending the sovereign nation state— was fading. To the extent that the federal project remained alive at all, it was thanks to the efforts of EU scholars.[33] Notwithstanding this, the notion of a common European identity as central to the development of a constitutional programme of closer union was never entirely sidelined. It was briefly revitalized by Jürgen Habermas and Jacques Derrida, representing the two most prominent and distinct voices of Franco-German public intellectual discourse in the late twentieth century, as a counterweight—in their view—to the belligerent, imperialist, market fundamentalist values of the United States. This was outlined in their February 15 'manifesto' for Europe, launched in reaction to the US-led invasion of Iraq.[34] In reality, it did little more than to highlight increasing governmental divisions: as a matter of foreign affairs, it revealed the continuing cleavages *within* Europe, pitting the so-called states of 'new Europe'—more in tune with Washington—against 'old Europe', a last-ditch attempt to preserve an element of autonomy in foreign affairs before Sarkozy's later capitulation.[35]

If the chances of political elites pushing forward with a supranational federal state, legitimized through a pan-European representative democracy, had always appeared slim, it would not only be politically marginalized, but would inhabit a constitutional 'no man's land', in the post-Maastricht period. With the German Constitutional Court's infamous 'Maastricht decision', the warnings against further integration were clearly marked.[36] But although that decision was widely and often harshly criticized in the literature, what was less frequently noted was that it was the Lisbon decision of the same court that more decisively dashed any dreams of a European federal state.

that their models were simply synchronizing with high-speed capitalism, and were suspect in their legitimacy; see William E Scheuermann, 'Democratic Experimentalism or Capitalist Synchronization? Critical Reflections on Directly-Deliberative Polyarchy' (2004) 17 Canadian Journal of Law and Jurisprudence 101.

[32] cf Joseph HH Weiler, 'Federalism and Constitutionalism: Europe's Constitutional Sonderweg' in Kalypso Nicolaidis and Robert Howse (eds), *The Federal Vision: Legitimacy and Levels of Governance in the US and the EU* (OUP 2001).

[33] See Andrew Glencross and Alexander H Trechsel (eds), *EU Federalism and Constitutionalism: The Legacy of Altiero Spinelli* (Lexington Books 2010). On the federal statist paradigm, cf Federico Mancini, 'The Case for Statehood' (1995) 4 European Law Journal 29; Joseph HH Weiler, 'The Case Against the Case for Statehood' (1998) 4 European Law Journal 43.

[34] Jürgen Habermas and Jacques Derrida, 'February 15, or What Binds Europeans Together: A Plea for a Common Foreign Policy, Beginning in the Core of Europe' (2003) 10 Constellations 291. This followed on from Habermas's urging of a European Constitution, which, in his view, could act as a bulwark against globalization, see ' Jürgen Habermas, 'Why Europe Needs a Constitution' (2001) 11 New Left Review 5. For a critique of the selective and highly idealistic nature of this manifesto, in its attempt to outline a 'exclusivist moral geography' see Owen Parker, *Cosmopolitan Government in Europe: Citizens and Entrepreneurs in Postnational Politics* (Routledge 2013) 105.

[35] Sarkozy, in 2009, symbolically returning France to NATO's military command, forty years after de Gaulle's refusal.

[36] *Brunner v The European Union Treaty* [1994] 1 Common Market Law Review 57 (*Maastricht* decision) (BVerfG).

The ambiguous 'not yet' in its Maastricht decision morphed into a decisive 'never' with Lisbon, at least outside a revolutionary constitution on the basis of a new act of German constituent power; a rather unlikely prospect, to say the least. The most powerful domestic court in the region raised the protection of Germany's core domestic constitutional identity above the demands of European political union, at once criticizing the EU's democratic legitimacy *and* proscribing further democratization.[37] The legitimacy question thus ended in a 'catch-22': the EU suffered from a democratic deficit which it was prohibited from remedying lest it transcend, and thereby abandon, the domestic democratic sphere, which, in practice, would be to violate the constitutional protection of democracy itself. The constitutional constraints imposed by the German court were significant, not only on the shape of the Union, but on domestic inter-institutional and state-society relations, and we will return to these in Chapter 7.

3. The return of the German question

The EU was not only becoming more intergovernmental in new ways, it was also becoming more asymmetric in terms of economic and political power among states, and yet more consensual in terms of a narrowing of political-economic ideology within them. These two patterns combined to reinforce the authority of an elite consensus around a framework of market liberalism, which would be further solidified through the enlargement of the Union.

In the decades following the Second World War (as outlined in Chapter 3), the Franco-German directorate had become institutionalized to the extent that it was second nature amongst public officials of both states to consider their relations closer to domestic than foreign affairs.[38] In this process, a 'cooperative hegemony' had emerged, where France's political leadership legitimized the rise of German power.[39] But with the end of the Cold War, and German reunification, along with successive waves of enlargement, Germany's economic and security interests would change, and the bilateral relationship at the core of Europe would become unbalanced.[40] With the power of Germany enhanced, and the role of France diminished, the parity on which their relationship had been built following the Elysée Treaty was upset. France's self-perception transformed from being Europe's 'firstborn son' in the post-war period

[37] Judgment of 30 June 2009, 2 BvE 2/08 (*Lisbon* decision) (BVerfG).

[38] In that sense, the European integration presented as a true 'federation' (see Christoph Schönberger, 'Die Europäische Union als Bund: Zugleich ein Beitrag zur Verabschiedung des Staatenbund-Bundesstaat-Schemas' (2004) 129 Archiv des öffentlichen Rechts 81. According to Schmitt, , the federation, in an internal sense, necessarily signifies a 'civil peace' between its partners (Carl Schmitt, *Constitutional Theory* (Duke University Press 2008) 386 (emphasis in original)). See, further, Signe Larsen, *The Constitutional Theory of the Federation and the European Union* (OUP 2021).

[39] Thomas Pedersen, *Germany, France and the Integration of Europe: A Realist Interpretation* (Continuum 1998).

[40] According to Krotz and Schild (n 2) 148, due to 'Germany's export-portfolio and its geographical proximity, export and investment opportunities in dynamic markets in countries with high capital formation needs promised to profit Germany's economy more than others', albeit, in their view, that security interests proved to be even more important than economic ones.

to its 'neglected middle child' in the Maastricht era.[41] With this disequilibrium in the Franco-German core, and a German sphere of influence in Central and Eastern Europe on the horizon, a prospect returned that had haunted Europe from the first half of the twentieth century: a German-dominated Mitteleuropa.

This prospect had been advanced positively at the beginning of the First World War by liberal politicians as a way to stabilize the region, before Carl Schmitt adapted the idea as an existential and cultural unity to oppose the new enemy in the interwar era: Soviet Russia.[42] In Schmitt's various schemas, a German Mitteleuropa or Middle European *Grossraum* would be based successively on a distinct theological-romantic idea of Catholicism as the atheistic opposite to communism, on political institutionalism and a concrete order, and on the appropriation of the territorial land itself.[43] As we saw in Chapter 3, these projects receded from view after the Second World War, and there was a consensus among otherwise divergent thinkers around the decline, if not quite the 'death of the state'.[44] As a global geopolitical matter, Cold War superpower rivalry had entirely superseded the German question.

The prospect that returned with German reunification in the 1990s was of a qualitatively and quantitatively different kind. Germany would re-emerge as an economically (rather than militarily) dominant state, and one powerful enough to upset the balance of power, but not powerful enough to exercise full leadership. This prospect had a significant impact on the geopolitical, political, and economic reconstitution of the European Union in the post-Maastricht era.[45]

The disparate, differentiated, constitutional structure of Europe, described above, was itself a sign of growing German influence. In 1994, two prominent German Christian Democrats, Wolfgang Schäuble and Karl Lamers, had prepared a document innocuously entitled, 'Reflections on European Policy', which suggested that a group of core states should be able to move forward with political union, and to utilize flexible tools from within the EU toolkit to pursue the project of further integration.[46] The term 'multi-speed Europe' was intended to signify that the role played by an advanced core would be short-lived, reuniting once the laggards had caught up. But it unquestionably provided additional opportunities for a core group of states to 'exert forms of leadership' over others.[47]

[41] See Mark Vail, 'Europe's Middle Child: France's Statist Liberalism and the Conflicted Politics of the Euro' in Matthias Matthijs and Mark Blyth (eds), *The Future of the Euro* (OUP 2015).

[42] See John P McCormick, 'Carl Schmitt's Europe: Cultural, Imperial and Spatial Proposals for European Integration, 1923–1955' in Christian Joerges and Navraj Singh-Ghaleigh (eds), *Darker Legacies of Law in Europe: The Shadow of National Socialism and Fascism over Europe and its Legal Traditions* (Hart Publishing 2003).

[43] ibid. See, further, Stuart Elden, 'Reading Schmitt Geopolitically: Nomos, Territory and Grossraum' (2010) Radical Philosophy 18.

[44] See Walter Rech and Janis Grzybowski, 'Between Regional Community and Global Society: Europe in the Shadow of Schmitt and Kojève' (2017) 13 Journal of International Political Theory 143.

[45] See Anne-Marie Le Gloannec, 'Germany's Power and the Weakening of States in a Globalized World: Deconstructing a Paradox' (2001) Les Cahiers Européens de Sciences Po 3.

[46] Karl Lamers and Wolfgang Schauble, *Reflections on European Policy* (European Policy Documents No 189/96, 7 September 1994) ('Lamers & Schauble Report').

[47] Vincent Della Sala, 'Leaders and Followers: Leadership Amongst Member States in a Differentiated Europe' in Erik Jones, Anand Menon, and Stephen Weatherill (eds), *Oxford Handbook of the European Union* (OUP 2012) 312.

The growing imbalance in power relations among national governments, in line with the geoeconomic developments of the period, and domestic shifts in the balance of class forces, would be reflected in the increasing pressures of liberalization. This would have a pronounced deregulatory effect on continental 'coordinated market economies', as well as 'liberal market economies', terms made famous in the 'varieties of capitalism' literature.[48] The flattening of the varieties of capitalism would also coincide with divergence in distinct growth patterns and demand-side dynamics. In terms of economic and trade performance, there would be marked differences between countries pursing an export-led growth model (such as Germany, the Netherlands, Belgium, and Austria), on the one hand, and those pursuing mixed regimes with substantial demand-led growth (such as Italy, Spain, Greece, and Portugal), on the other.[49] Divergence would accelerate dramatically after the entry into force of the single currency, and into the first decade of the twenty-first century. Its effects would be felt acutely in the euro crisis phase, which we will examine in Part IV. But the conditions were laid in the Maastricht era, and the foundations even earlier, with the 'undervaluation regime' of Germany being traceable back to the 1950s.[50] The growth strategies depended on wage restraint in 'northern' Europe, and asset bubbles in the south, which 'reinforced and exacerbated forms of unevenness' that could be traced back to the origins of the single market, with free trade policies more generally tending to 'reproduce long-standing developmental asymmetries and polarizing conditions between countries'.[51]

The return of the German question, as one of geo-economic domination, also depended on a relative weakening in the situation of France. As Vivien Schmidt noted, at the cusp of the global financial crisis, the political-economic consequences of the decline of France's leadership role in the 1990s were deep and varied.[52] French leaders were forced to abandon plans for an EU-level industrial policy and, after a long period of resistance, to concede to deregulation of *services publics* (public utilities) in telecommunications and electricity. State aid rules and competition policy would further impinge on the state's capacity to intervene in its own domestic political economy. With regard to EMU, the reforms would be huge, covering structural, institutional, and

[48] Peter A Hall and David Soskice, 'An Introduction to Varieties of Capitalism' in Peter A Hall and David Soskice (eds), *Varieties of Capitalism: The Institutional Foundations of Comparative Advantage* (OUP 2001); cf Wolfgang Streeck, *E Pluribus Unum? Varieties and Commonalities of Capitalism* (2010) MPIfG Discussion Paper 10/12; Lucio Baccaro and Chris Howell, *Trajectories of Neoliberal Transformation: European Industrial Relations Since the 1970s* (CUP 2017).

[49] Peter A Hall, 'Varieties of Capitalism and the Eurocrisis' (2014) 37:6 West European Politics 1223. For recent analysis of the growth model as an alternative view (from varieties of capitalism) on comparative political economy, see Lucio Baccaro and Jonas Pontusson, 'Rethinking Comparative Political Economy: The Growth Model Perspective' (2016) 44 Politics & Society 175.

[50] See Martin Höpner, *The German Undervaluation Regime under Bretton Woods: How Germany Became the Nightmare of the World Economy* (2019) MPIfG Discussion Paper 19/1. Höpner defines this as a regime (meaning 'institutions, organizations, and ideologies') 'with features that steer behavior towards the deterioration of the real exchange rate and thereby towards the accumulation of export surpluses', and argued that German policymakers 'discovered Germany's distinct ability to generate export surpluses after the payments account crisis in 1950/51'.

[51] Andreas Bieler, Jamie Jordan, and Adam D Morton, 'EU Aggregate Demand as a Way out of Crisis? Engaging the Post-Keynesian Critique' (2019) 57 Journal of Common Market Studies 805, 809.

[52] Vivien A Schmidt, 'Trapped by their Ideas: French Elites' Discourses of European Integration and Globalization' (2007) 14 Journal of European Public Policy 992.

substantive aspects of the economy, including concessions on austerity budgets and pensions cuts. Through EMU, Schmidt notes, 'France fully transformed its monetary system from a state-directed credit allocation system informed by neo-Keynesianism to an EU-driven interest-rate based system informed by monetarism.'[53]

We will return to the neo-liberalization of integration in general, and EMU in particular, in Chapter 8, as it reflected deeper changes in political economy, affecting the various layers of the material constitution, including state-society and social relations, as well as geopolitical imbalances. But as a geopolitical matter, the disparity between France and Germany would be extended, particularly through the process of enlargement of the Union, and in a way that would fundamentally alter the nature of the project.

With the newly reunified Germany playing a more dominant role in leading the project in its Eastern expansion, the successive enlargements of the Union after Maastricht would change the constitutional dynamic of integration. First, the 'Europe of twelve' that signed the Maastricht Treaty would soon become the 'Europe of fifteen' with the accession of Austria, Finland, and Sweden in 1995. This so-called 'EFTA enlargement', unlike the previous Mediterranean enlargements of the 1980s (in which Greece, Spain, and Portugal joined), raised the prospect of an emerging 'Germanic bloc' at the heart of the EU, a fear felt particularly keenly in a 'French political elite imbued by geopolitical thinking'.[54] The French concern was both that enlargement would undermine the project for a *Europe puissance* (Europe as a world power) due to the neutral inclinations of the new EFTA members, and would increase the likelihood of a *Europe espace* (Europe as a free trade area) due to the prospective dilution of any plan towards a 'social Europe'.[55] Both concerns would prove prescient.

After initial French resistance to enlargement—an obstructionist policy that risked international isolation, as well as the souring of relations with candidate countries—proved futile, France's shift in attitude occurred under the cover of the formal adoption of a European Ostpolitik. This would be strongly supported by the UK, if ostensibly for different reasons than Germany, as the UK believed that any widening would necessarily imply a shallowing; that 'expansion must mean defederalizing'.[56] This may have been true, but expansion also invoked a different spectre. Although the global geopolitics of the end of the twentieth century would look very different from earlier epochs, with the US emerging as sole global superpower following the collapse of the Soviet Union, European nations themselves had rediscovered 'traditional imperialist postures', and even began to 'carve out clienteles' in Central and Eastern Europe.[57] The Europe of the post-Maastricht era would come to resemble a system of concentric circles, with an inner core of leading nations, a second zone of 'inner colonization', and a third zone of 'predatory capitalism'.[58] Even liberal commentators would warn of this

[53] ibid 996.

[54] Krotz and Schild (n 2) 145.

[55] ibid.

[56] See Perry Anderson, *The New Old World* (Verso 2009) 45.

[57] See Étienne Balibar, *We, the People of Europe? Reflections on Transnational Citizenship* (Princeton University Press 2004) 167. This will become more evident as the euro crisis unfolds, as explored in Part IV.

[58] ibid 169, 171 (Balibar even comparing Europe to apartheid-era South Africa because of the sense of second-class citizenship).

as a dangerous harbinger for future developments, concerned that the 'neo-colonialist attitude of West Germans' towards their compatriots in the East throughout the process of reunification might be generalized across the new European constitutional space.[59]

4. Enlargement of the Union: stark utopia, stark asymmetries

It was not only German economic and security interests that drove the process and form of European enlargement in the post-Maastricht era. Ideology also played a significant role, particularly in the constitutional politics of the new members. Accession to the European Union was presented as a 'return to Europe', or as the 'reunification of Europe' following the 'rectifying revolution' heralded by the fall of the Soviet Union.[60] This promised the restoration of cultural unity with the West,[61] the new members' rejection of the Soviet Union slotting neatly into the Christian democratic myth of post-war European reconstruction, to the extent that aspects of the fascist experience (shared with Germany in the interwar years) 'could even be commemorated in the name of anti-Communism'.[62] At the same time, it reinforced the exclusive territorial boundaries of 'Fortress Europe' and the particular identity of a 'Christian Europe', and even a 'European civilization'; one 'separating Europe from alien times ("communism", "Islam") as well as from alien places ("Islam", "Russia")'.[63]

There would be no material relaunching of the European Union after Maastricht to signify the historical achievement of enlargement. There was little sense (at least internally) that Central and Eastern accession countries would be reconstituted in the manner of the post-fascist countries, on the basis of restrained democracy, or a new ideology of post-sovereignty or supranationalism. Their own post-Soviet constitutions made no reference to this attitude, and for obvious reason: this was not a re-foundation in reaction to a breakdown that had been caused by the perception of an excess of democracy, or an internal backsliding. On the contrary, the return to the West represented an emancipation from an external authority: the old hegemony of the Soviet Union. The new members had no desire, as the joke went, to substitute

[59] ibid 169, citing Timothy Garton-Ash. Leading the reunification negotiations for the FRG was Wolfgang Schäuble. On the context of privatization of East German assets under the auspices of the 'Treuhand' agency, see Charles S Maier, *Dissolution: The Crisis of Communism and the End of East Germany* (Princeton University Press 1997) 290–303. See, further, Ben Gook, 'Backdating German Neoliberalism: Ordoliberalism, the German Model and Economic Experiments in Eastern Germany after 1989' (2018) 54:1 Journal of Sociology 33.

[60] Jürgen Habermas, 'What does Socialism Mean Today? The Rectifying Revolution and the Need for New Thinking on the Left' (1990) 1 New Left Review 183.

[61] For discussion, see Jiri Přibáň, *Legal Symbolism: On Law, Time and European Identity* (Ashgate 2007).

[62] James Mark, *The Unfinished Revolution: Making Sense of the Communist Past in Central-Eastern Europe* (YUP 2010) 94. This would be mirrored from the East ('From post-Communist Russia, by contrast, came a revival of Soviet-era anti-Fascist memory. Under the Putin presidency, the heroic role of the Soviet Red Army in saving Europe from the horrors of Fascism was positioned at the heart of a newly assertive national identity whose paradigms it sought to export to the rest of the continent') (ibid 95).

[63] See Talal Assad, 'Muslims and European Identity: Can Europe Represent Islam?' in Anthony Pagden (ed), *The Idea of Europe: From Antiquity to the European Union* (CUP 2002) 219.

authoritarian rule from Brussels for diktat from Moscow, regaining sovereignty only to immediately lose it. As a result, national sovereignty, far from being downplayed in Central and Eastern Europe, would be rhetorically embraced, and the idea of supranationalism explicitly rejected, foreshadowing later developments in regard to the so-called 'rule of law crisis' under Orban and Kaczynski, in Hungary and Poland.[64]

In contrast to previous accessions, particularly the Mediterranean enlargements which followed the removal of dictatorships in Greece, Spain, and Portugal in the 1970s, the Europe of the new millennium was not about opening the path to liberal democracy, despite the rhetorical gestures.[65] On the contrary, European integration would be perceived by the new members primarily as a source of the promotion of market liberalism, and 'as a *threat* to democracy'.[66] The attitude of many of the new member states towards Europe was based on a distinct cultural myth, focused on shared Christian roots and historical alignment, rather than political values. In the absence of the transformative effect of a political revolution, it was the forces of nationalism that would be awakened; 'forces which had been suppressed during the communist period'.[67] In the absence of a political constituent power, the 'apolitical constituent power of the ethnos', even though essentially a contradiction in terms, was left to fill the vacuum.[68]

Without the experience of liberal democracy as a political way of life, it was expected to be imposed from above, 'without democrats'.[69] What appeared was another TINA narrative, something 'disturbingly familiar' to countries of the former Soviet bloc; they were, again, as one commentator puts it, 'simple marionettes in a historical process that takes place independently of their will and drags them with it to a better future'.[70] There would be 'revolutionary changes in the political and constitutional system', but without a 'revolution as such'. If the totem of the French-style revolution of the late eighteenth century was the guillotine, in 1989 it was 'the round table'.[71] Thus,

[64] See, eg Wojciech Sadurski, *Constitutionalism and the Eastern Enlargement of Europe* (OUP 2012). This is examined further in Part IV and the concluding chapter.

[65] According to Iglesias, although it transformed the Francoist regime into a liberal democracy (a 'constitutional monarchy'), the new '78 regime in Spain left the economic elites from the Franco era untouched, and tied the unions to wage restraint, while building a consensus (excluding Basque and Catalan nationalist parties) around a neo-liberal order. This included the pragmatic 'Eurocommunist' Spanish Communist Party (Pablo Iglesias, 'Understanding Podemos' (2015) 93 New Left Review 7.

[66] ibid 103.

[67] Ulrich Preuss, 'The Exercise of Constituent Power in Central and Eastern Europe' in Martin Loughlin and Neil Walker (eds), *The Paradox of Constitutionalism: Constituent Power and Constitutional Form* (OUP 2007) 224(Preuss, 'Constituent Power'). Preuss had anticipated the possibility of Central and Eastern European countries 'falling prey' to an ethnic conception of democracy; see Ulrich Preuss, 'Constitutional Powermaking for the New Polity: Some Deliberations on the Relations between Constituent Power and the Constitution' (1993) 14 Cardozo Law Review 639, 649 (Preuss, 'Constitutional Power').

[68] Preuss, 'Constituent Power' (n 67) 227. With the almost complete absence of labour or Left political counterpositions to the EU, nationalist Euroscepticism was the only galvanizing force offering opposition to this new status quo.

[69] See Jan Komárek, 'Waiting for the Existential Revolution in Europe' (2014) 12 International Journal of Constitutional Law 195.

[70] ibid.

[71] Gábor Attila Tóth, 'Hungary's Constitutional Transformation from a Central-European Comparative Perspective' in Henning Glasser (ed), *Norms, Interests and Values: Conflict and Consent in the Constitutional Basic Order* (Nomos Verlagsgesellschaft 2015) 132 (noting that, in Hungary, the Roundtable Talks of 1989 had neither a mandate for constitution-making, nor popular authorization to make law for the new regime).

'in Poland, Hungary, Bulgaria, and the German Democratic Republic', it was 'legal' and 'constitutional' revolutions that were sought, with the notion of 'civil society' acting as a stand-in for the revolutionary constituent power.[72]

In significant respects, the countries of Central and Eastern Europe were returning to a Europe already markedly different from its founding form; a West that had significantly changed, in material ways, from its earlier phase of post-war class compromise, neo-Keynesianism, corporatism, and the welfare state. A neo-liberal consensus had become cemented by the time accession unfolded, even if—in a new 'third way' inflection—it was a version that retained certain compensatory aspects of embedded liberalism. In this context, accession itself, framed as 'catching up' with the West, meant adopting an even stricter and starker form of the market liberal utopianism that had come to dominate the imagination in Western Europe. It was one that resonated with the global political economy of neo-liberalism that was becoming more generally ascendant, now in the radical form of a 'forced decollectivisation' or 'shock therapy'.[73] Although some scholars, thus, still identified the EU as an 'embedded neo-liberalism', which incorporated certain demands of labour movements and social democracy, this could be distinguished from the 'market radical' variant imposed on the new members, where the EU 'export[ed] the core of its deregulatory programme' into a context in which labour was in an even weaker bargaining position than in the West.[74] Through a mixture of economic power and conditionality, and the euphoria around the idea of membership, as Dorothée Bohle explains, 'the EU managed, during the 90s, to push the Central and Eastern European countries towards adopting a specific, neo-liberal reform model'.[75]

The focus on economic integration, regulatory alignment, and the creation of a robust state-market apparatus of enforcement not only concealed domestic inequalities in the new members, but also inequalities between East and West, underwriting a dynamic of difference reminiscent of old colonial relations, and the 'informal empire' of US-led global capitalism.[76] The European Commission's expectation of economic

Hungary was unique in failing to adopt an entirely new constitution after the fall of communism; the 1989 constitution codified the previous constitution of 1949.

[72] Andrew Arato, 'Dilemmas Arising from the Power to Create Constitutions in Eastern Europe' (1992) 14 Cardozo Law Review 661.

[73] Peter Gowan, 'Neo-Liberal Theory and Practice for Eastern Europe' (1995) New Left Review 3 ('shock therapy' was the name given by Jeffrey Sachs to his own model); cf Adam Fabry, 'The Origins of Neoliberalism in Late "Socialist" Hungary: The Case of the Financial Research Institute and "Turnabout and Reform"' (2018) 42:1 Capital and Class 77 (arguing that the origins of Hungary's neo-liberal transformation *preceded* the formal transition to a market economy). On the 'blind neoliberal belief in self-regulating markets and the withdrawal of state regulations', which had 'helped prosperity in the short-run, and gave a huge spurt to globalization', see Ivan T Berend, 'From Oil Crisis to Financial Crisis 1973–2009' in Dan Stone (ed), *The Oxford Handbook of Postwar European History* (OUP 2012) 417.

[74] Dorothée Bohle, 'Neoliberal Hegemony, Transnational Capital and the Terms of the EU's Eastward Expansion' (2006) 88 Capital & Class 57 (using the concept of 'embedded neo-liberalism' developed in Bastiaan van Apeldoorn, *Transnational Capitalism, and the Struggle over European Integration* (Routledge 2002)).

[75] Bohle (n 74) 70.

[76] See Antony Anghie, *Imperialism, Sovereignty and the Making of International Law* (CUP 2005). See also John D Haskell and Boris N Mamlyuk, 'Capitalism, Communism and Colonialism? Revisiting "Transitology" as the Ideology of Informal Empire' (2009) 9 Global Jurist 7 ('democracy in Central and

growth and reform through market integration, macroeconomic stabilization, regional free trade and commerce was accompanied by an incongruent emphasis on local responsibility for the emerging conditions, as well as selective protectionism by Western states, in certain sectors. The point of 'catching up' was not to gain comparative advantage over the West but to normalize institutional frameworks for neo-liberal economic development, in particular those which presented opportunities for the direct investment of Western capital. The upshot in the acceding states was the normalization of structural inequalities, high levels of unemployment, and radical welfare divergence from existing European social models (which were themselves in the process of severe erosion).[77] Another related consequence, particularly of the large-scale direct foreign investment, was the emergence of a new set of 'reform elites' in accession states, a feature of the more general process of transnational class formation, which compensated for the lack of a traditional domestic bourgeoisie.[78]

The new relationship of putatively formal political equality qua member state of the European Union (a status itself deferred under transition arrangements that gave new members second-class status) would not only conceal the deep substantive and structural inequalities between the regions, it would also—in conjunction with the constitutional right to free movement established under EU law, and the absence in the East of strong industrial relations—put downward pressure on any commitment to social Europe, whether in East or West.[79] The accession deals would be sealed with structural and cohesion funds, emphasizing money transfers instead of a politics of redistribution in a way that would mould unequal relations into dependent ones, resembling core-periphery models analysed elsewhere in the developing world.[80]

What was emerging, in broader terms, was a new inter-state dimension to the post-war authoritarian liberalism of self-restraint, discipline, and compromise. Constraints on the democratic process would now, increasingly, be presented as necessary features of integration with—and be demanded by—*other states*. Asymmetries would be highlighted and reinforced, serving the interests of transnational capital and even, on some neo-Gramscian accounts, a new hegemonic historical bloc.[81] This did not, however, signal the transformation of the European Union from a federation of political equals into a hegemonic federation straightforwardly dominated by one, or one-half, of a Franco-German axis. If Germany was 'semi-sovereign' in the post-war era,

Eastern Europe, then, is not about self-representation or real determination; rather, it is a function of capitalism—a tool by which American informal empire expands and legitimizes itself').

[77] On the diversity of political economy and variety of 'market societies' among the new members, see Dorothée Bohle and Bela Greskovits, *Capitalist Diversity on Europe's Periphery* (Cornell University Press 2012) 3. They identified three capitalisms: a neo-liberal type in the Baltic states, an embedded neo-liberalism in the Visegrad countries, and a neo-corporatist type in Slovenia.

[78] Bohle (n 74) (describing the passive revolution as a 'bourgeoise revolution without a bourgeoisie').

[79] See, eg Alain Supiot, 'Under Eastern Eyes' (2012) 73 New Left Review 28.

[80] On dependency practices more generally in the context of the imperialism of modern liberal constitutionalism, see, eg James Tully, 'Modern Constitutional Democracy and Imperialism' (2008) 46 Osgoode Hall Law Journal 461.

[81] Bohle (n 74) (describing a new a transnational neo-liberal constellation, based on post-Fordist production, the pressure exerted by the European Round Table of Industrialists, export-oriented capital, and the subordination of labour).

it graduated to becoming, at most, 'semi-hegemonic' in the post-Maastricht phase.[82] This would lead to an unstable situation—a disequilibrium—that remained unresolved in the decade leading up to Lisbon, and was exacerbated through the euro crisis (examined in Part IV).

To understand why, we need to consider not only external factors, but look to the domestic constitutional dimension, through which inter-state relations are conditioned, constrained, and restructured over time.[83] Domestic political and constitutional constraints prevented the development of a European federal state or a straightforward exercise of leadership by Germany, particularly as consent around the project of integration was starting to fray, and the permissive consensus in the core countries itself was beginning to collapse. This did not, however, prevent a different kind of constitutional-ideological hegemony emerging, which proclaimed, despite the facts, that Europe had moved 'beyond the sovereign state'. It was, on the contrary, just at this moment that sovereignty would begin to mark its comeback.[84]

[82] Peter J Katzenstein, *Policy and Politics in West Germany: The Growth of a Semisovereign State* (Temple University Press 1987). The term semi-sovereign was examined in Chapter 3.

[83] See Bulmer and Paterson (n 2).

[84] See, further, Michael A Wilkinson, 'Beyond the Post-Sovereign State? On the Past, Present and Future of Constitutional Pluralism' (2019) 12 Cambridge Yearbook of European Legal Studies 6.

7

The Post-sovereign Constitution or the Return of Sovereignty?

1. Introduction

Although the official narrative was that Maastricht would launch the 'widening and deepening' of the Union, the material reality was that it initiated a 'decade of self-doubt'; a growing of the Union's powers but a weakening of its legitimacy. This culminated in the failure and then abandonment of the 'European Constitution' project in 2005, followed by the symbolic 'deconstitutionalization' of the Treaty of Lisbon, which was ratified just as the global financial crisis was beginning to place the whole construction under severe pressure (examined further in Part IV).[1]

This chapter examines the reconstitution of state-society relations in the period from Lisbon to Maastricht. An ambiguity is evident, and reveals a deep disconnect. On one hand, there was a continuation and acceleration of the trajectory of 'judicial constitutionalization', pushed particularly vigorously in the academy as well as the courts, with the proliferation of theories celebrating a new liberal normative order: 'global constitutionalism', 'world constitutionalism', 'societal constitutionalism', and 'constitutional pluralism'.[2] In different ways, these would posit the transcendence of the state, or of sovereignty, and even of the political constitution of society itself. This stance was not restricted to mainstream opinion, but adopted even by critical theorists and, in variation, by some in the Marxist tradition (such as Hardt and Negri's celebration of the 'multitude').[3] I have, elsewhere, used the term 'freestanding constitutionalism' to convey this theoretical orientation, to capture the claims that the authority of a constitutional order depends upon its congruence with 'higher' cosmopolitan ideals of political morality; ideals that, in one influential understanding, emerged out of a juridical practice of constitutional interpretation of basic principles and fundamental rights.[4]

[1] See Christine Reh, 'The Lisbon Treaty: De-Constitutionalizing the European Union?' (2009) 47 Journal of Common Market Studies 625.

[2] For a collection of essays on these themes, see Matej Avbelj and Jan Komárek (eds), *Constitutional Pluralism in the European Union and Beyond* (Hart Publishing 2012). Weiler would later describe constitutional pluralism 'as the only party membership card which will guarantee a seat at the high table of the public law professoriate' (see Joseph HH Weiler, 'Prologue: Global and Pluralist Constitutionalism—Some Doubts' in Gráinne de Búrca and Joseph HH Weiler (eds), *The Worlds of European Constitutionalism* (CUP 2011) 8).

[3] See Michael Hardt and Antonio Negri, *Empire* (Harvard University Press 2000). For some early sceptical reactions to Hardt and Negri in the Marxist and radical traditions, see Gopal Balakrishnan (ed), *Debating Empire* (Verso 2003).

[4] Michael A Wilkinson, 'Political Constitutionalism and the European Union' (2013) 76 Modern Law Review 191. For some contemporary scepticism, even at the 'high point' of Euro-constitutionalism, see, eg

Authoritarian Liberalism and the Transformation of Modern Europe. Michael A Wilkinson, Oxford University Press.
 DOI: 10.1093/oso/9780198854753.003.0008

On the other hand, this trajectory appeared increasingly *disconnected* from concrete constitutional, political, and social developments, which reflected various reactions against the supranational, postnational, and cosmopolitan leanings of constitutional elites and scholars. These reactions took place through formal channels, such as domestic constitutional courts and national referenda, and, informally, through the rise of Eurosceptic parties and social movements. Ironically, the very turn towards legal constitutionalization and judicial power supranationally would come up against its own version at the domestic level, with constitutional courts harnessing constitutional identity and counter-limits against the European Court.[5] Political sovereignty, having been folded into legal constitutionalism and other forms of technocratic rule in the post-war period (as we saw in Part II), also begins to spring back into action, just at the moment it was being declared obsolete by the legal academy. To use Habermas's own terminology, there appeared to be a growing mismatch between 'system' and 'lifeworld'; ironically, one which his own theoretical and political moves only aggravated, his 'post-national constellation' offering up the EU as a stepping stone to the constitution of a world society increasingly removed from any *demos*, just as the actual *demoi* appeared to be shaken from their post-war passivity.[6]

To capture this complex and ambivalent set of developments, we will first examine the discourse of post-sovereign constitutionalism (section 2); then outline the return of sovereignty claims (section 3), and argue that this combination, understood dialectically, shows a disconnect between juristic and popular constituent power, and reveals a hollow authoritarian liberal constitutionalism (section 4).

Carol Harlow, 'Voices of Difference in a Plural Community' (2002) 50 American Journal of Comparative Law 339: 'To some theorists of Europe, participatory proceduralism can be used strongly to promote pluralist democracy; in practice, however, it contains a powerful bias towards elitism or forms of corporate governance in which interest groups obtain a stranglehold on policy.' Other significant dissenting voices included, eg Martin Loughlin, *The Idea of Public Law* (OUP 2003); Peter Lindseth, *Power and Legitimacy: Reconciling Europe and the Nation-State* (OUP 2010). The last-mentioned argued for an 'administrative not constitutional' reading of the EU.

[5] Although the return of sovereignty is most closely associated with the German Constitutional Court, supranationalism was rejected bluntly in the Polish Constitutional Court's ruling on the validity of the accession Treaty (Judgment concerning the constitutionality of Poland's accession to the European Union [2005] K18/04, 11 May 2005). For a survey on the use of identity provisions, see, eg Barbara Guastaferro, 'Beyond the Exceptionalism of Constitutional Conflicts: The Ordinary Functions of the Identity Clause' (2012) 31 Yearbook of European Law 263.

[6] Jürgen Habermas, *The Postnational Constellation: Political Essays* (MIT Press 2001) (Habermas, 'Postnational Constellation'). For an astute critique, see Perry Anderson, 'Arms and Rights' (2005) New Left Review 5, 18 (noting that once democracy 'is redefined as principally a matter of "communication" and "consciousness", political participation and popular will become residuals that can be bypassed in the design of a cosmopolitan legal order'). Elsewhere, Habermas would note that a postnational constitution was in danger of being merely a hegemonic facade if it failed to bridge the liberal and republic conceptions of democracy, and later suggested that the EU was moving into a 'post-democratic' future (*The Guardian* (London, 10 November 2011)), exposing a level of dissonance in his writings that was becoming increasingly hard to reconcile.

2. Post-sovereign constitutionalism

By the time of the Maastricht era, it had become commonplace to regard European Union law as 'constitutional' in type. In 1996, Joseph Weiler and Ulrich Haltern had declared the alleged 'rupture' or 'mutation' of the European Union legal order from public international law and its 'transformation into a constitutional legal order' as one of the 'great perceived truisms, or myths' of European integration.[7] This referred to the process by which the EC Treaties had 'evolved from a set of legal arrangements binding upon sovereign states into a vertically integrated regime conferring judicially enforceable rights and obligations on all legal persons and entities, public and private, within EC territory'.[8] The logic of constitutionalization had, in effect, long been asserted by the European Court of Justice, as it turned itself into a supranational and de facto 'constitutional court' through the post-war era, in its seminal case law beginning in the early 1960s (as outlined in Part II above).

But although the groundwork had long been laid by the Court, as well as earlier scholars such as Eric Stein, and then Weiler himself, there was an inflation in constitutionalist discourse between Maastricht and Lisbon that is hard to exaggerate. It was not only that commentators would routinely describe EU law and the Court of Justice as 'constitutional' in their academic texts on the 'constitutional law' or 'constitutional principles' of the European Union.[9] It was also that this discourse was invested with a deep theoretical and normative significance, transcending national scholarly boundaries, encompassing Kantian constructivists, as well as Hegelian idealists.

According to Armin von Bogdandy, adopting a methodology of 'doctrinal constructivism', European law (and international law) inhabited an autonomous area, a 'middle level' between natural law and positive law, and should be interpreted in terms of basic constitutional principles. From this perspective, influenced by Ronald Dworkin's legal theory, the 'primary law' of the EU would not only justify the exercise of public power, it would 'legitimize acts of the EU, create a citizenship, grant fundamental rights, and regulate the relationship between legal orders, between public power and the economy and between law and politics'.[10] These principles would be discerned not only from the written texts themselves but from their juristic reconstruction. They would then be presented as forming a coherent whole, through the

[7] Ulrich Haltern and Joseph HH Weiler, 'Constitutional or International? The Foundation of the Community Legal Order and the Question of Judicial Kompetenz-Kompetenz' in Anne-Marie Slaughter, Alec Stone Sweet, and Joseph HH Weiler (eds), *The European Courts and National Courts—Doctrine and Jurisprudence* (Hart Publishing 1998) It was, of course, a myth that Weiler himself had helped create.

[8] ibid. According to Paul Craig, arguing in favour of the constitutional thesis, this captured the transformation of the Community legal order from a 'relationship binding upon states qua states, to an integrated legal order that confers rights and obligations on private parties'; see Paul Craig, 'Constitutions, Constitutionalism and the European Union' (2001) 7 European Law Journal 125, 128.

[9] There are far too many to cite. For a representative example and set of surveys, see Armin von Bogdandy and Jürgen Bast (eds), *Principles of European Constitutional Law* (Hart Publishing 2006).

[10] Armin von Bogdandy, 'Founding Principles of EU Law: A Theoretical and Doctrinal Sketch' (2010) 2 European Law Journal 95. Bogdandy acknowledged the debt to Ronald Dworkin, and *Law's Empire*.

elaboration of principles conceived as specifically juristic, autonomous from society or the political process that uneasily accompanied them.[11]

Even supposedly critical social theorists would take this route, mapping out a projection of their constitutional vision 'beyond the state', based on deliberative democracy or the right to justification.[12] The translation into English of Jürgen Habermas's *Between Facts and Norms* in 1995 (and then *The Postnational Constellation* in 2001) had a profound impact on normative theory, and gave a veneer of intellectual credibility to European, postnational, and cosmopolitan constitutionalisms.[13] By incorporating principles of deliberative democracy into constitutional design, and into the discourse of political justification, *Between Facts and Norms* legitimized the transcendence of notions of constituent power, popular sovereignty, and concrete forms of mass democracy.[14] According to Habermas, popular sovereignty no longer 'circulated in a collectivity, or in the physically tangible presence of the united citizens or their assembled representatives'. It would, henceforth, take effect only 'in the circulation of reasonably structured deliberations or decisions', leading to the 'harmless' conclusion that there could no longer be a sovereign in the constitutional state itself.[15]

Habermasian projects would be pursued in various registers—an ethics of constitutional tolerance, legal-moral principles of adjudication, post-sovereign constitutionalism, dialogical consensus, institutional harmony, and contrapuntal law—often collected under the label of 'constitutional pluralism'.[16] In each case, the assumption was that some *normative order* above the conflicting systems could, and would, resolve (or at least defer) any deep-seated political or social conflicts. Order depended on the ability to identify, and, in so doing, generate a universal *ratio*: these projects were, in other words, essentially monist, despite their appellation.[17] This monism would be

[11] ibid. By the early 2000s, it was claimed that, of all the initial mysteries accompanying European legal integration, 'none of them are very mysterious anymore' (Ulrich Haltern, 'Pathos and Patina: The Failure and Promise of Constitutionalism in the European Union' (2002) 9 European Law Journal 14, 19–38).

[12] See Jürgen Neyer, *The Justification of Europe: A Political Theory of Supranational Integration* (OUP 2012), building on Rainer Forst, *The Right to Justification. Elements of a Constructivist Theory of Justice* (Columbia University Press 2012). cf Danny Nicol, 'Can Justice Dethrone Democracy in the European Union? A Reply to Jürgen Neyer' (2012) 50 Journal of Common Market Studies 508; Alexander Somek, 'The Darling Dogma of Bourgeois Europeanists' (2014) 20 European Law Journal 688.

[13] See Jürgen Habermas, *Between Facts and Norms: Contributions to a Discourse Theory of Law and Democracy* (Polity Press 1996)(Habermas, 'Between Facts and Norms'); Habermas, 'Postnational Constellation' (n 6).

[14] The explicitly cosmopolitan outlook in constitutional theory included work inspired by Rawls, as well as Habermas. After his *Theory of Justice*, Rawls later built his political liberalism on the constructed ground of 'reasonable' conceptions of shared 'constitutional essentials'; on the assumption that political power should only be used in ways that citizens 'may reasonably be expected to endorse in the light of principles and ideals acceptable to their common human reason' (John Rawls, *Political Liberalism* (Columbia University Press 1993) 137). On an explicit attempt to apply Rawls's overlapping consensus to the EU, see Charles F Sabel and Oliver Gerstenberg, 'Constitutionalising and Overlapping Consensus: The EJC and the Emergence of a Coordinate Constitutional Order' (2010) 16 European Law Journal 511.

[15] See Habermas, 'Between Facts and Norms' (n 13) 136.

[16] Avbelj and Komárek (n 2) identify six versions in their Introduction. Much of this work was inspired by Neil MacCormick; see Neil MacCormick, *Questioning Sovereignty: Law, State, and Nation in the European Commonwealth* (OUP 1999)(McCormick, 'Questioning Sovereignty').

[17] See Hans Lindahl, 'Democracy, Political Reflexivity and Bounded Dialogues: Reconsidering the Monism-Pluralism Debate' in Emilios Christodoulidis and Stephen Tierney (eds), *Public Law and Politics: The Scope and Limits of Constitutionalism* (Ashgate 2008) 103–16; Alexander Somek, 'Monism: A Tale of the Undead' in Jan Komárek and Matej Avbelj (eds), *Constitutional Pluralism in the European Union and Beyond* (Hart Publishing 2012).

represented by principles of legality or subsidiarity, or economic rights themselves, although much of the constitutional scholarship of this era was completely detached from the ordoliberal moorings of the actual EU constitution, as well as its neo-liberal drift.[18] Constitutionalism, once freed from its Westphalian straitjacket, and its false dichotomies of domestic and international, internal and external, could 'give way to a graduated approach' that extended constitutional authority 'to fora and layers of governance other than nations', and which treated those 'layers of governance ... as on[e] overall complex'.[19] This was a period of tremendous constitutional optimism, at least in the academy, with constitutionalism set to 'rule the world', as one collection suggested, based on the authority of its universalist values.[20]

Neil MacCormick, by no means the most exuberant of the constitutional optimists, had already declared, in the emphatic conclusion of his Chorley Lecture in 1993, that we were 'beyond the sovereign state'.[21] Many others followed suit, without any of MacCormick's later nuances and qualifications.[22] So confident was the legal academy of its liberal constitutionalist project that sovereignty was declared dead, redundant, or simply passé.[23] Neither the French *petit oui* in 1992 (the French approving the Treaty of Maastricht by 51 to 49 per cent) nor even the rejection of the Constitutional Treaty (following the Laeken Convention on the Future of Europe launched after Nice) in referenda in France and the Netherlands in 2005 did much to dent this constitutional enthusiasm.[24] Nor did the increasingly neo-liberal cast of Europe's political economy sound the alarm, even for scholars who self-described as social democratic.[25] Constitutional theory was so detached from its political moorings that it had not perceived them shifting in the sand.

[18] For an exception, see Ernst-Ulrich Petersmann, 'State Sovereignty, Popular Sovereignty and Individual Sovereignty: From Constitutional Nationalism to Multilevel Constitutionalism in International Economic Law?' in Wenhua Shan, Penelope Simons, and Dalvinder Singh (eds), *Redefining Sovereignty in International Economic Law* (OUP 2008). Petersmann applied his models to European, as well as international, economic law.

[19] Martin Loughlin, paraphrasing Cottier and Hertig; see Martin Loughlin, 'In Defence of *Staatslehre*' (2009) 48 Der Staat 1, 21.

[20] Jeffrey Dunoff and Joel Trachtman (eds), *Ruling the World: Constitutionalism, International Law and Global Governance* (CUP 2012); see also MacCormick, 'Questioning Sovereignty' (n 16) 95.

[21] Neil MacCormick, 'Beyond the Sovereign State' (1993) 56 Modern Law Review 1, 18.

[22] For MacCormick's later, more qualified position, see, eg Neil MacCormick, 'Sovereignty and After' in Hent Kalmo and Quentin Skinner (eds), *Sovereignty in Fragments: The Past Present and Future of a Contested Concept* (CUP 2010).

[23] Post-sovereignty became a project to be pursued at all costs. 'The real lawyerly task is to neutralise' the question of sovereignty, according to one commentator. See András Jakab, *European Constitutional Language* (CUP 2016) 116: 'Our task is to avoid or prevent the question, and if someone still poses it, then we should give a "solution" that does not say anything practical for conflicts'. He goes on to suggest that the language of *Staatslehre* is 'redundant'.

[24] On the contrary, see, eg Herman van Gunsteren, 'The Birth of the European Citizen Out of the Dutch No Vote' (2005) 1 European Constitutional Law Review 406. For a more cautious assessment, see Neil Walker, 'Post-Constituent Constitutionalism? The Case of the European Union' in M Loughlin and N Walker (eds), *The Paradox of Constitutionalism: Constituent Power and Constitutional Form* (OUP 2008).

[25] MacCormick's declared political goal was to pursue a soft version of social democracy, firmly rejecting any 'purely market-economical view of the good society' (MacCormick, Questioning Sovereignty (n 16) 174–75)). As a matter of political philosophy, he explicitly attacked voluntaristic liberalism of the social contract variety in favour of contextual individualism associated with the communitarian tradition (eg ibid 162–63). Yet, in *Questioning Sovereignty*, despite its focus on the European Union, one looks in vain for any discussion of the impact of market integration on social values, or the likely impact of the single currency

3. The return of sovereignty claims

Ironically, given the thousand ships of post-sovereignty launched in its wake, Maastricht was precisely the moment that sovereignty would begin to mark its return, after a hiatus of half a century. It would return not only in a geopolitical sense, with heightened asymmetries in inter-state relations, as recounted in Chapter 6, but as a political-constitutional concept. The project of denationalizing the constitution was coming unstuck, just at the moment that it was proclaimed rhetorically triumphant by its adherents.

In the juridical arena itself, the judicialization of European rights had led not to the perfection or triumph of liberal constitutionalism, but to increasing conflicts over its terms.[26] In the absence of supranational political channels, these would be played out predominantly as *domestic* concerns and constitutional conflicts.[27] From Maastricht itself through to the Lisbon Treaty, there would be various complaints made against further integration. The most significant was the resistance from the German Constitutional Court, which will be our focus in this part, but it reflected disquiet elsewhere.

Although traceable to the 1970s (and the *Solange* jurisprudence outlined in Part II), Karlsruhe's judgments grew more constitutionally challenging with the Maastricht Treaty decision.[28] The Maastricht decision generated enormous academic controversy over its so-called 'no *demos* thesis'. It also brought back into the spotlight the jurisprudence of Weimar, and of Schmitt and Heller in particular, and themes which had largely been overlooked in the intervening years. This would be an early sign of the later conflicts taking place through the euro crisis phase over the guardian of the constitution, which we will come to examine in Part IV.[29]

The Maastricht debates occurred in the context of recent German reunification, which had altered the geopolitical dynamics of regional integration, and potentially put questions of domestic constituent power and sovereignty back on the table after half a century. But they remained largely repressed.[30] In fact, the speed with which the German treaties of reunification were conceived, 'the secrecy with which they were

on macroeconomic policy choices. It is not as if these were unknown, as the work of Scharpf, Streeck, and others was already prominent.

[26] But see Matthias Kumm, 'How Does European Union Law Fit into the World of Public Law? *Costa*, *Kadi*, and Three Conceptions of Public Law' in Jürgen Neyer and Antje Wiener (eds), *Political Theory of the European Union* (OUP 2010) 125.

[27] This is an often complex domestic constitutional phenomenon; the *judicial empowerment* thesis, developed by Karen Alter, shows how constitutional doctrines of EU law strengthened lower domestic courts vis-à-vis higher national courts and other domestic institutions (see Karen J Alter, *Establishing the Supremacy of European Law: The Making of an International Rule of Law in Europe* (OUP 2003)).

[28] *Brunner v European Union Treaty* [1994] 1 CMLR 57.

[29] Weiler's extraordinary reaction to the Maastricht decision set much of the tone, accusing it of an ethnic reading of national sovereignty despite the actual text of the decision; see Joseph HH Weiler, 'Does Europe Need a Constitution? Demos, Telos, and Ethos in the German Maastricht Decision' (1995) 1 European Law Journal 219, 248(Weiler, 'Does Europe Need a Constitution?').

[30] For an assessment of the impact of the suspicion of popular sovereignty and democratic constituent power in the context of German reunification, contrasting Germany with the South African case in a similar period, see Simone Chambers, 'Democracy, Popular Sovereignty, and Constitutional Legitimacy' (2004) 11 Constellations 153. See, again, Christoph Möllers, 'We are (afraid of) the People: Constituent

negotiated, and their extraordinary bulk and complexity', foreclosed the opportunity for democratic scrutiny.[31] The process of reunification 'was consciously organized as a technical-bureaucratic matter for experts—in which neither the *Länder* and their parliaments, nor indeed even the population of both German states, had a share that was worthy of mention'.[32] Article 146 of the German Basic Law had attempted to codify the constituent power, holding it open for the future but immunizing it for the present. Although it was not triggered, for fear of awakening a discourse of popular sovereignty from its slumber, the European question would soon raise profound domestic constitutional issues of democracy and sovereignty.[33]

Despite the German court ultimately giving the Maastricht Treaty the seal of approval, it refused to give up guardianship of the constitution, and of the limits of EU powers (the so-called question of *Kompetenz-Kompetenz*), maintaining the possibility of an ultra vires review if the EU (including the ECJ) violated the principle of conferral. It also warned that the member states needed to be left 'sufficiently important spheres of activity of their own in which the people of each can develop and articulate itself in a process of political will-formation'. Only if they retain this political capacity, it proposed, could they 'give legal expression to what binds the[ir] people together (to a greater or lesser degree of homogeneity) spiritually, socially and politically'.[34] Although this could have been interpreted as a signal to contest the increasing depoliticization and re-differentiation of powers entrenched by the European economic constitution, particularly given the significance of the single currency to the complaint, the focus of the academic response was, instead, preponderantly on the court's allegedly ethno-nationalistic overtones.[35]

It *was* curious that the German court cited Hermann Heller for the proposition on relative homogeneity. This, without any reference to Heller's insistence on the centrality of socio-economic equality (discussed in Chapter 2), was disingenuous. But these reactions to the judgment were still more curious, given the absence of any actual reference to ethnicity. A more apposite criticism was made shortly after by Jürgen Habermas: given the court's concern with the democratic legitimacy of the European construct, it was perverse to have given the green light to the Maastricht Treaty at all, in light of the increasing deficits of the Union.[36] Instead of drawing the obvious conclusion, however, that the court (and others) should have been bolder in halting

Power in German Constitutional Discourse' in Martin Loughlin and Neil Walker (eds), *The Paradox of Constitutionalism: Constituent Power and Constitutional Form* (OUP 2007).

[31] Peter E Quint, 'Constitution-Making by Treaty in German Unification: A Comment on Arato, Elster, Preuss, and Richards' (1992) 14 Cardozo Law Review 691, 695 ('the details of unification were basically determined by a small group of (primarily western) party leaders – principally the leadership of the dominant Christian Democratic Union ("CDU"), including the main technician and theorist of unification, West German Interior Minister Wolfgang Schauble').

[32] ibid 695, fn 18.

[33] Möllers (n 30) 96–97.

[34] *Brunner* (n 28) [44].

[35] Weiler, Does Europe Need a Constitution? (n 29); cf Loughlin (n 4) 95.

[36] The democratic deficit, Habermas noted, was 'expanding day by day because the economic and social dynamics even within the existing institutional framework perpetuate the erosion of national powers through European law' (Jürgen Habermas, 'Remarks on Dieter Grimm's "Does Europe Need a Constitution?"' (1995) 1 European Law Journal 303).

or critiquing the integration dynamic, Habermas (and his followers) refused his own counsel, only seeing supranational (and ultimately cosmopolitan) progression in their vision.[37] This neo-Kantian orientation stood in for a philosophy of history; a 'linear postulation of a future constituted ultimately by more of the present'.[38] Critical theory was left behind.

Despite paving the way for ratification, the constitutional symbolism of the Maastricht ruling remained profound. As a matter of constitutional theory, the 'no *demos* thesis' would be further developed by Dieter Grimm, one of the justices on the court. In brief, the thesis stated that, in the absence of a European *demos*, there could be no real European constitution. The irony of this claim, given that the German Basic Law itself had introduced 'precisely the opposite approach', was not lost on all of the justices.[39] But Grimm's thesis was not predicated on the historical context of the German Basic Law, but on a deeper philosophy of constitutionalism, which stretched back to the modern Revolutionary period of the late eighteenth century.

In noting that 'responsibility for the basic order of the EU' could not be 'ascribed to the constituent power of the people', Grimm maintained that the EU order lacked 'an element of any somewhat meaningful notion of a constitution'.[40] Any sense that constitutionalism beyond the state might *compensate* for the existing, genuine limitations on—and transfers of public power from—the sovereign nation state, would only be an 'illusion'.[41] Grimm acknowledged the material reality of supranational and international governance, conceding that there was no longer congruence between public power and the state, and that the state constitution had ceased to regulate public power 'coherently and comprehensively'. But he concluded that the growing 'gap' in-between could only be mitigated by domestic controls.[42] In contrast to Habermas, Grimm denied that the subjection of power to the combination of the rule of law and the authority of 'the people' could, in any sense, be replicated 'beyond the state'.

With the domestic constitution controlling 'what passes for political authority in the state',[43] the prospects, suggested Grimm, looked bleak. The pathological tendencies of modernity—the globalization of capital, fragmentation of traditional communities and cultural ways of life, and the depoliticization resulting from internal and external pluralism—had come to wreak havoc on the bonds of citizenship and the powers of the state. The possibilities for supranational citizenship and statehood to

[37] The position of left-liberal intellectuals such as Habermas reflected a more profound shift: the turn away from radical positions amongst European Left parties in general, and even a view of the EU as a positive ground for a socialist alternative, whether on pragmatic and reluctant, or idealist grounds, covering positions from strong reformism to weak reformism and even 'uncritical pro-integrationism', taking withdrawal completely off the table. See Richard Dunphy, *Contesting Capitalism? Left Parties and European Integration* (Manchester University Press 2004) 3–6.

[38] John P McCormick, *Weber, Habermas, and Transformations of the European State: Constitutional, Social, and Supranational Democracy* (CUP 2007) 291.

[39] See Udo Di Fabio, 'A European Charter: Towards a Constitution for the Union' (2001) 7 Columbia Journal of European Law 159, 162.

[40] Dieter Grimm, 'The Constitution in the Process of Denationalisation' (2005) 12 Constellations 447, 459.

[41] Dieter Grimm, 'The Achievements of Constitutionalism and its Prospects in a Changed World' in Martin Loughlin and Petra Dobner (eds), *The Twilight of Constitutionalism?* (OUP 2010) 22.

[42] ibid 16. 'To the extent that statehood is eroding', Grimm laments, 'the constitution is in decline'.

[43] ibid 16.

mitigate these risks were severely limited, however. Although the EU came close to comparison with the 'central unit of a federal state', regulated by a 'closely meshed net of legal norms',[44] it was not 'an expression of the self-determination of a people or a society about the form and substance of their political union'.[45]

Never, or not yet? In the later *Lisbon* decision, the German Constitutional Court would develop and refine its jurisprudence, but also change course.[46] It moved away from its emphasis, in the *Maastricht* decision, on the social and cultural preconditions for constitutional democracy—the 'no *demos* (yet) thesis'—and towards a more legalistic reading of the constitutional restraints placed on further integration by the German Basic Law (ie, the right to vote for members of the German parliament guaranteed by Article 38).[47] If the concern of the *Maastricht* decision was for the necessity of a degree of social and political homogeneity, combined with a principle of *openness* towards the process of further European integration, the emphasis of the *Lisbon* decision was on sovereignty, constitutional identity, and the *closure* of the process of integration by virtue of the constitutional guarantees protected by the eternity clause (Article 79(3)).

In affirming that the EU is an association of states based on conferred powers, that the member states are the 'Masters of the Treaty', and that 'EU citizenship does not constitute a European people with the right to self-determination',[48] the *Lisbon* judgment of the German court merely restated its own constitutional orthodoxy. And, yet, it had the effect of making necessary what it had previously suggested was only contingent; namely, the national configuration of the democratic constitutional form.[49]

The judgment, therefore, signalled an inflection in the constitutional imagination. The foundation of constitutional authority was fully transformed from a collective people towards an individual 'right' to vote. An insistence on the 'right to vote', in terms of strict 'democratic equality', was considered incompatible with the 'degressive proportionality' of seats in the European Parliament (the system of allocating seats in a way which disproportionately protects smaller states), raising the so-called 'Maltese question' (why should a Malteser weigh more than a German?). This strict insistence on the principle of 'one person, one vote' appeared disingenuous given the federal structure of the German court's own constitutional system.[50] In fact, it served

[44] ibid 17.

[45] ibid 17.

[46] *Lisbon Case*, BverfG, 2 BVE 2/08, 30 June 2009. The decision spawned voluminous academic commentary, largely critical, but not in the same way as the Maastricht ruling. According to Christoph Schonberger, 'There is probably no other judgment in the history of the Karlsruhe Court in which the argument is so much at odds with the actual result.' See Christoph Schonberger, '*Lisbon* in Karslruhe: *Maastricht*'s Epigones at Sea' (2009) 10 German Law Journal 1201, 1201.

[47] It is only because the German court read Article 38 in a broad and substantive way, demanding that the body elected by the German people should maintain substantial policy choices in important areas, that it is able to draw a chain of inference to Article 20 and then Article 79(3) GG.

[48] Dieter Grimm, 'Defending Sovereign Statehood Against Transforming the Union into a State' (2009) 5 European Constitutional Law Review 353, 363 (Grimm, 'Defending Sovereign Statehood').

[49] According to Schönberger (n 46) 1208, this represents 'an unprecedented arrogation of power by the Court'.

[50] The court seems unable to think about democracy in anything but nation-statist terms, which Grimm describes as 'irritating' (Grimm, 'Defending Sovereign Statehood' (n 48) 367). For discussion on the difficulty of reconciling the democratic principle with any kind of federal structure, taking into account quality of states as well as persons, see Christopher Lord and Johannes Pollack, 'Unequal but Democratic? Equality According to Karlsruhe' (2013) 20 European Journal of Public Policy 190.

to underline the key rationale, which was not the democratic process, but a new principle of individual *sovereignty*. This was a peculiar kind of sovereignty: not popular sovereignty of the German people, but sovereignty of the German constitution and its unamendable core.[51] In practice, this took sovereignty further from the people and vested it in the court's own hands.[52] Indeed, as a more general theoretical matter, it would be noted that the principle of 'constitutional identity' (which was raised to salience in constitutional courts across the EU) conveyed the 'opposite values' to sovereignty as traditionally understood. Whereas sovereignty was associated with 'absolute power, the primacy of politics over law, [and] of the collective over the individual', constitutional identity 'signified the limitation of power, the reign of law, the primacy of the individual over the group, and of identity politics over power politics'.[53]

Although less criticized by European constitutionalists than the Maastricht ruling, the *Lisbon* ruling, in reality, presented a far greater obstacle to further European integration. The door left open by Maastricht—the possibility that the Basic Law might permit the gradual development of a European state that would include the Federal Republic of Germany—was firmly closed.[54] Permission to transform the EU into a federal state, the court suggested, 'can only be given by the people through a new constitution'.[55]

No amount of gradualism, but only something akin to a constitutional revolution—an exercise of original constituent power—could mark a break with the European state, and state system, of the post-war era. But precisely this possibility was meant to have been displaced by the post-war constitutional settlement. Although using the language of sovereignty, the court was not protecting popular sovereignty, or even parliamentary sovereignty, but a semi-sovereign constitutional identity that had functioned to constrain those very democratic dynamics, in an attempt to insulate the constitution from political change.

The German constitutional *Finalität* announced post-Lisbon was very different from the *finalité* imagined by European federalists of previous eras, who viewed democracy in the European Union as eventually accompanying a European sovereign state, or at least something in the vicinity. Such a development, however, was ruled out by the court; not even constitutional amendment could authorize the German authorities

[51] Even though the notion of 'sovereignty' is not explicitly mentioned in the Basic Law, Thym notes that the term 'sovereign(ty)' is mentioned no less than forty times in the judgment. See Daniel Thym, 'In the Name of Sovereign Statehood: A Critical Introduction to the Lisbon Judgment of the German Constitutional Court' (2009) 46 Common Market Law Review 1795, 1797.

[52] JHH Weiler famously noted that, '[t]o protect national sovereignty is passé; to protect national identity ... is à la mode': Joseph HH Weiler, 'On the Power of the Word: Europe's Constitutional Iconography' (2005) 3 International Journal of Constitutional Law 173, 184.

[53] François-Xavier Millet, 'The Respect for National Constitutional Identity in the European Legal Space: An Approach to Federalism as Constitutionalism' in Loïc Azoulai (ed), *The Question of Competence in the European Union* (OUP 2014), 271.

[54] Even if, as Grimm notes, the eternity clause is not restricted to preventing a return to National Socialist dictatorship, but protects against 'every enemy of the free democratic order', this does not mean, as he concedes, that it prevents the re-establishment of democracy at a higher, supranational, level. This conclusion would follow only if democracy could be realized only within the nation state. According to Grimm, an amendment to the Basic Law to provide for a referendum on a European state would suffice: 'a new constitution, as the Court thinks, would not be indispensable'. See Grimm, 'Defending Sovereign Statehood' (n 48) 368.

[55] Grimm, 'Defending Sovereign Statehood' (n 48) 359.

to surrender national constitutional sovereignty.[56] Stated simply, 'the EU is not permitted to constitute itself'.[57] But neither may the EU be explicitly transferred 'essential state tasks' from the member states; or, at least, not from Germany.[58] Meanwhile, since the EU institutions have the 'tendency to political self-empowerment',[59] it was essential that the German court retained control over the 'creeping competences' of the European Union.

The *Lisbon* ruling, in other words, would signal both a heightened surveillance over the exercise of EU powers (ultra vires review) *and* establish a 'red line' against the transfer of further powers, crossing which would violate the constitutional identity of the Basic Law (identity review).[60] These signals were often considered merely as threats, reflecting a court that might 'bark' but would never 'bite'.[61] Nevertheless, the judgments would lay the groundwork for the more aggressive stance adopted in the *OMT* and *Weiss* rulings (considered in Part IV), when, through the euro crisis, the exercise of powers of the European Central Bank would further blur the (already blurred) lines between monetary and economic policy in a manner that would become materially relevant to German 'constitutional identity'.

The German court, thus, resurrected a version of militant democracy, but now asserted its own authority to protect a domestic constitution not just from surrender to a dictator within, but to a supranational Union without. The question of who was the 'guardian of the constitution', so central to the debates in Weimar, had marked its return to the European stage. Although it was the domestic court rather than the president of the Republic that was asserting itself in this role, the task of defending a constitutional identity unamenable to majoritarian amendment recalled Schmitt's authoritarian position in late Weimar.

The German Constitutional Court was now clearly offering itself as the guardian of the post-war constitutional settlement. But it was not merely a formal constitutional identity it was guarding, or one without implications for the substantive constitution of the EU. It was guarding a constitutional settlement that, in its Maastricht reading, insisted on 'economic integration as an apolitical phenomenon'. In reality, this meant

[56] Grimm, 'Defending Sovereign Statehood' (n 48) 367. The paradox is apparent: only because there is no 'founding will' and the EU 'is exactly not laid out in analogy to a state' does it comply with the principle of democratic sovereignty, but only if it were laid out in analogy to a state could it become truly democratic in any meaningful sense: the sense implied by the guarantee of equality of voting essential to human dignity.

[57] Grimm, 'Defending Sovereign Statehood' (n 48), 360.

[58] ibid 357ff. As Grimm notes, drawing a clear line on permissible transfer of powers to the EU is difficult, if not impossible (Dieter Grimm, 'Sovereignty in the European Union' in Jeffrey Ellsworth and Johan WG van der Walt (eds), *Constitutional Sovereignty and Social Solidarity in Europe* (Nomos/Bloomsbury 2015) 52; Grimm, 'Sovereignty in the European Union'.

[59] *Lisbon case* (n 46) para 237.

[60] In the *Honeywell* case, it would set out the conditions for ultra vires review (Judgment of 6 July 2010, BVerfGE 126, 286 *(Honeywell* decision) (BVerfG)).

[61] See Joseph HH Weiler, 'The "Lisbon Urteil" and Fast-Food Culture' (2009) 20 European Journal of International Law 505. Later, Dieter Grimm—noting that the role of the ECJ itself is perceived as 'a promoter of integration rather than that of a neutral umpire', very rarely finding EU acts ultra vires—would then suggest, commenting on the *Honeywell* case (BVerfGE 126, 298), that, although the role of guardian of member states' rights must lie with national constitutional courts, it is 'rather unlikely it will ever find a violation' (Grimm, 'Sovereignty in the European Union' (n 58) 53).

the supranationalization of ordoliberal principles of sound finances and balanced budgets, buttressed by the 'politically neutral' notion of price stability.[62]

The same constitution towards which liberal democratic commentators such as Habermas had urged patriotism in the post-war era now thwarted their very European federalist ambitions.[63]

4. Excavating the dialectic: an authoritarian constitutionalism

The constitutional discrepancy in the post-Maastricht period is glaring. The discourse of European, postnational, and global constitutionalism grew apace in the academy, supposedly completing the transcendence of the state, and moving beyond sovereignty itself. The material reality, however, was of a growing systemic differentiation and formal constitutional contestation of this discourse, channelled through domestic constitutional courts, political parties, and popular referenda in the member states.

For some, this disjunction signified only that the practice and discourse of EU constitutionalization was incomplete. It had established 'constituted' power—the subjection of political authority (both at the national and the supranational level) to the normative order of the law—but not yet established a European constituent power. It had achieved only 'one half' of a proper constitutional discourse. It was, thus, suggested that, owing to the efforts of the European Commission and the Court of Justice (in conjunction with domestic courts), Europe had developed 'constitutional practices without any underlying legitimizing constitutionalism';[64] or, more poetically, that European integration had resulted in 'a constitutional body without a soul'.[65] All the paraphernalia associated with strong 'normative' supranationalism—direct effect, supremacy, effectiveness of the law—was in place but the 'political' culture of constitutionalism was merely a hollow shell. If the political constitution remained stubbornly national, the assumption was that it simply needed to 'catch up' with the legal academy, pushed along 'from the top down' through projects of European constitution-building and symbolic myth-making, as with the failed Constitutional Treaty of 2005.

In reality the process of constitutionalization beyond the state, as a 'freestanding process of rationalist constitutional design', operating without the fiction of authorization by 'the people', suggested something quite distinct. It suggested an 'authoritarian

[62] Christian Joerges and Florian Rödl, '"Social Market Economy" as Europe's Social Model?' (2004) EUI Working Paper Law No 2004/8, 7 <https://cadmus.eui.eu/bitstream/handle/1814/2823/law04-8.pdf?sequence=1&isAllowed=y> accessed 22 November 2020.

[63] Other constitutional courts would adopt, and adapt, the rhetoric of the German Constitutional Court in the service of enhancing their own constitutional authority, but with relatively minimal impact, directed more at the domestic balance of institutional powers than at the material constitution of the European Union. See, eg Jan Komárek, 'Playing with Matches: The Czech Court's Ultra Vires Revolution' in Maximilian Steinbeis, Alexandra Kemmerrer, and Christoph Möllers (eds), *Krise and Konstitutionalisiering in Europa* (Verfassungsblog I, Recht im Context, Nomos 2015) 101–07.

[64] Joseph HH Weiler, *The Constitution of Europe* (CUP 1999) 298.

[65] Miguel Poiares Maduro, 'Europe and the Constitution: What if this is as Good as it Gets?' in Joseph HH Weiler and Marlene Wind (eds), *European Constitutionalism Beyond the State* (CUP 2003) 77. It might be more apt to describe it as a constitutional body without a soul: informed more by reason than by passion.

constitutionalism', through which a new 'imperial network' would 'seek to secure the legitimacy of its global rule'.[66] Within the EU, this 'imperial network' transcended the democratic spheres of the sovereign states, but did not inhabit a free-floating domain. It did not even bypass the governments of the member states, but partly empowered them, and, at the same time, immunized them from mechanisms of domestic accountability.[67]

Constitutionalism was increasingly resulting in 'an overall depoliticized and essentialist view of democratic politics', one which denied 'any role of the larger *demos* and civil society'.[68] This legal-liberalization of the constitution was particularly marked in its exportation to the 'new democracies' of Central and Eastern Europe. Not only were there no grand refounding moments to mark the momentous changes announced by the enlargement of the Union, as noted in Chapter 6: even the idea of the *demos* was almost entirely missing in the democratic transitions that took place in accession countries.

In a sense, the absence of constituent assemblies in the post-communist transitions, which coincided with 'the explosion of constitutional courts', mimicked precisely the soft authoritarian liberalism of the post-war European core, particularly in adopting the German model of centralized constitutional review.[69] 'In nearly all post-communist European states', Sadurski noted, 'constitutional courts established themselves as powerful, activist players, dictating the rules of the political game for other political actors'.[70] Given that the term 'civil society' had first been reintroduced by Central and Eastern European scholars, it was, ironically, Western social theorists in the 1990s that 'passionately embraced the concept'; and, just at the same time, Eastern European intellectuals were 'becoming wary of it', unsure 'that a concept elaborated essentially as a tool of opposition to the totalitarian communist state' could serve the same useful purpose in the rebuilding of their societies.[71]

The process of generating an authoritarian constitutionalism in a manner removed from popular constituent power and democratic politics was not new in its essentials, as we have seen in Part II. It was a continuation of a process that began at Paris and Rome in the 1950s. What was new, over the long decade after Maastricht, was that the 'permissive consensus' was starting to fray. What was new, in other words, was the degree to which 'consensus' was politically and socially contested, at the same time as it was abruptly transplanted in the East. The German court's rulings reflected the growing turbulence and discontent beneath the formal constitutional surface. But they, too, functioned to deflect from domestic pressures; Karlsruhe served 'as [a]

66 Loughlin (n 19).

67 Simon Hix and Andreas Follesdal, 'Why There is a Democratic Deficit in the EU: A Response to Majone and Moravcsik' (2006) 44 Journal of Common Market Studies 533.

68 Paul Blokker, *New Democracies in Crisis? A Comparative Constitutional Study of the Czech Republic, Hungary, Poland, Romania and Slovakia* (Routledge 2014) 5.

69 See Ruti Teitel, 'Post-Communist Constitutionalism: A Transitional Perspective' (1994) 26 Columbia Human Rights Law Review 167, 172.

70 Wojciech Sadurski, *Constitutionalism and the Enlargement of Europe* (OUP 2012) 101.

71 Krishan Kumar, 'On Civil Society: A Further Note on Civil Society' (2000) 41 European Journal of Sociology 167, 167.

missing channel for Germans to voice their Euroscepticism'.[72] Elsewhere in the EU (and eventually in Germany too), Euroscepticism would have its more direct channels of political expression.

Despite the considerable attention given to the judicial shadow-boxing between Luxembourg and Karlsruhe, the underlying material dynamic of the constitutional order escaped serious interrogation. The Maastricht orthodoxy was not neutral with respect to political economy; in conjunction with the impact of the single currency and the process of enlargement, as the single market freedoms were extended to accession countries at very different stages of political-economic development, growth models were diverging within the EU. Imbued in discourse analysis and a 'culture of total optimism', the concrete implications of Economic and Monetary Union (EMU) and neo-liberalization were largely overlooked.[73]

To the extent that the constitutional discourse did attend to material changes, scaling-up to a level above the nation state was often *assumed* to be the only antidote to neo-liberal globalization. Habermas again led the charge of critical theorists by offering the EU as a bulwark against global capitalism: only 'more Europe' could redeem the promise of the postnational constellation.[74] The 'scalarist' eschatology so dominant in liberal constitutional theorizing was reinforced by a sentiment that anything short of European constitutional patriotism betrayed a recidivist ethnonationalism.[75] On the other hand, the state-based but legalistic reaction of the German Constitutional Court did nothing to counter the material transformation of EMU, but merely legitimized it, while sounding some rhetorical warning shots. It did not, and could not, resolve the political and democratic deficits.

To make sense of the growing disconnect between the optimism of the constitutional discourse and the material reality of integration, we have to move away from normativist, positivist, or ideal constitutional theory. Concealed by the panegyrics to constitutionalism, whether proto-cosmopolitan or state-based, was a dynamic of further depoliticization of state-society relations, and countermovements that attempted to resist this. The challenges to the EU were substantive as well as formal, relating to the economic impact of the single currency, the financial impact of free movement, the lack of procedural safeguards in the European arrest warrant framework, and the erosion of social rights and industrial relations. Challenges were occurring inside and outside the corridors of constitutional courts, in between state and society. These were expressed through a rising tide of nationalism, the return of sovereignty claims, and of constituent power, and social discontent manifested through popular referenda on the EU (from the France *petit oui* and Danish 'no' on the Maastricht Treaty in 1992, and the Irish rejection of the Nice Treaty in 2002, to the French and Dutch 'no' to the

[72] Klaus Garditz, 'Beyond Symbolism: Towards a Constitutional Actio Popularis in EU Affairs? A Commentary on the OMT Decision of the Federal Constitutional Court' (2014) 15 German Law Journal 189.

[73] cf Bernard H Moss (ed), *Monetary Union in Crisis: The European Union as a Neoliberal Construction* (Palgrave 2005). EMU is examined in detail in Part IV.

[74] Jürgen Habermas, 'Why Europe Needs a Constitution' (2001) 11 New Left Review 5.

[75] For a more nuanced assessment of the 'no *demos* thesis', identifying a variety of positions on a spectrum, see Lars Cederman, 'Nationalism and Bounded Integration: What it Would Take to Construct a European Demos' (2001) 7 European Journal of International Relations 139.

Constitutional Treaty in 2005). Disconnect was also expressed through the decline of established political parties and the rise of Eurosceptic parties and social movements in the UK, France, Austria, and Italy, and these would be complemented by others through the euro-crisis phase.[76]

What was emerging, in other words, was not merely a democratic 'deficit' but an increasing material and ideological 'disconnect'.[77] European constitutional discourse had become divorced from the concrete political and social reality characterizing the domestic life of the member states, and from the material impact of growing asymmetries in inter-state relations. As well as being divorced from domestic politics, the language of post-state law and postnational constitutionalism was tracking the global flows of capital and international trade and their universal economic rationality. It is difficult to improve on Stefano Bartolini's formulation of the problem: that, 'in connection with economic activities', the 'new legal universalism' assumed that the role of supranational orders was 'to limit regulatory and legislative intervention by the domestic political systems, and bring to an end the historical phase characterised by the close grip of politics on the economy through law'.[78]

This loss of grip of politics on the economy through law was now complemented by an underworld of legal pluralism, as semi-autonomous transnational fields of corporate governance developed, exacerbated by the financialization of the economy and the securitization of assets. It contributed to the de facto erosion of state sovereignty across the European Union, just as EMU would contribute to its *de jure* erosion.[79] To pursue this further, we have to turn directly to the evolving material constitution of the Union in the period after Maastricht. This will be the subject of Chapter 8.

[76] See Peter Mair, *Ruling the Void: The Hollowing of Western Democracy* (Verso 2013). UKIP was founded in 1993 by LSE professor Alan Sked, who was ousted by Nigel Farage in 1997; the Front Nationale was an established party, founded in 1972, but its support began to grow in the 1990s (Jean-Marie Le Pen won 15 per cent of the presidential vote in 1995, and achieved a shock second place in the first round in 2002); the Freedom Party of Austria made a decisive electoral breakthrough in 1991; and, after the collapse of the post-war Italian political system, Forza Italia was formed in 1994, later becoming an electoral force. For analysis, see Mabel Berezin, *Illiberal Politics in Neoliberal Times: Culture, Security and Populism in the New Europe* (CUP 2009).

[77] cf Peter Lindseth, *Power and Legitimacy: Reconciling Europe and the Nation-State* (Oxford University Press 2010) 28.

[78] Stefano Bartolini, *Restructuring Europe: Centre Formation, System Building, Political Structuring between the Nation State and the European Union* (OUP 2005) 372.

[79] See, further, Gralf-Peter Calliess and Peer Zumbansen, *Rough Consensus and Running Code: A Theory of Transnational Private Law* (Hart Publishing 2010); Peer Zumbansen, 'Transnational Private Regulatory Governance: Ambiguities of Public Authority and Private Power' (2013) 76 Law and Contemporary Problems 117.

8
The Material Constitution: There is no Alternative . . . or is There?

1. Introduction

To examine the material layers of the constitutional landscape after Maastricht, we need to look at the underlying shifts in political economy and ideology, specifically in regard to the relation between the political and the economic spheres. This relation would be reconstituted through the processes of integration and domestic constitutional reform, a deepening of the economic liberalism of the Union, in general, and through economic and monetary union (EMU), in particular. In other words, it was not merely an 'authoritarian constitutionalism', but, materially, an 'authoritarian liberalism' that was resurfacing in Europe, not (yet) in an emergency mode, but in a steady development of post-war trends outlined in Part II.[1]

The geopolitical and political constitutions of the post-Maastricht era that we examined in Chapters 6 and 7 did not evolve autonomously; they were interrelated. As a totality, the period between Maastricht and Lisbon presents a puzzle. When viewed over the long durée, there was a deepening of the post-war disjuncture between domestic democratic politics and European policymaking, with passive authoritarianism increasing in line with the delegations of tasks to counter-majoritarian institutions. Yet, there were growing geopolitical imbalances and bubbling currents of domestic resentment; challenges to the way the European Union and its member states were constituted.[2]

To get a firmer grasp on this tension, we need to examine the material layers underneath the constitutional surface. In particular, we need to examine the significance of Economic and Monetary Union (section 2); the deepening of market liberal ideology (particularly the TINA narrative: 'There Is No Alternative') in the core, and its

[1] This was a much broader phenomenon, extending beyond the European scene. See, eg Philip Bobbitt, *The Shield of Achilles: War, Peace, and the Course of History* (Anchor Books 2003) (on the substitution of the twenty-first-century 'market state' for the twentieth-century 'nation-state'); Kanishka Jayasuriya, 'Globalisation, Sovereignty and the Rule of Law: From Political to Economic Constitutionalism' (2001) 8 Constellations 442; Stephen Gill, *Power and Resistance in the New World Order* (2nd edn, Palgrave MacMillan 2008); Ran Hirshl, *Towards Juristocracy: The Origins and Consequences of the New Constitutionalism* (HUP 2007). For the impact of US-led global capitalism on the project of integration, see Alan W Cafruny and Magnus Ryner, *Europe at Bay: In the Shadow of US Hegemony* (Lynne Rienner 2007).

[2] Weiler, otherwise a frequently sage observer of the EU, characterized Maastricht as being 'greeted by the *typical* indifference with which the elite-driven European construct was habitually met'; and '[t]hat, indeed, *has always been the Achilles Heel of the European construct*—the question whether the undoubtedly noble project enjoys popular legitimacy' (Joseph HH Weiler, 'In the Face of Crisis: Input Legitimacy, Output Legitimacy and the Political Messianism of European Integration' (2012) 34 Journal of European Integration 825, 826 (emphasis added)).

Authoritarian Liberalism and the Transformation of Modern Europe. Michael A Wilkinson, Oxford University Press.
 DOI: 10.1093/oso/9780198854753.003.0009

widening through the accession of new member states (section 3); and, as various counter-movements, the growing political and social resentment towards the elite-driven projects of integration (section 4).

2. Economic and Monetary Union

Economic and Monetary Union (EMU) was a central factor in the deepening of economic liberalism effected by the Treaty of Maastricht. The reasons for the eventual adoption of EMU included the geopolitical calculations discussed in Chapter 6, and the particular timing and objectives of the European project, conditioned by the increasing strength of German capital.[3] The French saw EMU as a strategy to contain the hegemony of the Deutschmark, which was anticipated to grow, in light of German reunification and re-emergence as a central European power.[4] If the French got the single currency they wanted, it was under the conditions the Germans demanded, with the rules of EMU structured in accordance with ordoliberal precepts, and the European Central Bank (ECB) closely modelled on the structure of the Bundesbank, in some ways radicalizing its independence from political control.[5]

But inter-state bargaining and fears of geopolitical asymmetries only tell part of the story. The blueprint for EMU had been drawn up by Jacques Delors, with a group of monetary experts and central bank governors, after a meeting of the European Council in Hanover in 1988, and *prior* to the prospect of German reunification.[6] The European states were operating within a system that was *already* led by Germany; the Deutschmark had de facto dominated the exchange rate mechanism since the European Monetary System (EMS) was set up in 1979, and a power shift in favour of Germany in monetary affairs had, in fact, been visible since 1968.[7] EMU developed as a monetarist project from within this regional power imbalance, but, just as significantly, within a context of widespread consensus among domestic elites on monetary policy objectives (price stability and currency stability), and the institutional independence from democratic politics needed to achieve it.[8] In this changing belief system,

[3] See, eg Ulrich Krotz and Joachim Schild, *Shaping Europe: France, Germany, and Embedded Bilateralism from the Elysée Treaty to Twenty-First Century Politics* (OUP 2013) 183–211.

[4] See, eg Giandomenico Majone, *Rethinking the Union Post-Crisis: Has Integration Gone Too Far?* (CUP 2014) 29.

[5] See Elie Cohen, 'The Euro, Economic Federalism, and National Sovereignty' in Anthony Pagden (ed), *The Idea of Europe: From Antiquity to the European Union* (CUP 2002) 269: 'The European Central Bank had to be an exact replica of the Bundesbank, or at least as independent and dedicated to the fight against inflation. The barter was concluded along the following lines: the sharing of monetary power was granted to "the Twelve" in exchange for allowing Germany to set the rules of the game'.

[6] See, further, Harold James, *Making the European Monetary Union: The Role of the Committee of Central Bank Governors and the Origins of the European Central Bank* (Belknap 2012) 211–16. In addition to a power struggle between states, he emphasizes the pull of a European identity, the entrepreneurship of the Commission under Delors, and the product of a global debate on economic financialization and international tensions following the Volker shock. He also notes that although 'the *Bundesbank* appeared to be the institution most opposed to institutionalized European and global monetary cooperation', the 'solution devised was to imitate or adopt as much of the *Bundesbank* model as possible' (ibid 211).

[7] Krotz and Schild (n 3) 211.

[8] See Amy Verdun, 'The Institutional Design of EMU: A Democratic Deficit?' (1998) 18 Journal of Public Policy 107.

divorced from the neo-Keynesianism that had persisted until the early 1970s, anti-inflationary doctrine had become hegemonic. EMU, thus, presented an opportunity to allow for central bankers to bypass national parliaments and the awkwardness of domestic party politics.

The effect of the single currency would be to alter the shape of inter-state relations by removing a key lever of domestic power: the power to control a currency vis-à-vis other states in the regional and global economy. EMU also changed the relationship between state and society by constituting an *external* constraint on domestic politics and policy (a *vincolo esterno*, as the Italians put it).[9] It conditioned domestic political and economic structures through the empowerment of technocratic bodies, the dominance of neo-liberal ideas, and the entrenchment of ordoliberal rules, together representing a material reconfiguration of social relations. This rapidly accelerated the de-democratization of the economy that began in the foundational period of integration in the post-war era.

In other words, if the Treaty of Rome (and its subsequent judicialization) had effected an initial and limited 'geo-separation' of the political and the economic spheres by creating a European 'microeconomic' constitution that guaranteed the free movement of the factors of production, the Treaty of Maastricht would extend this logic to the 'macroeconomic' sphere.[10] The idea, broadly following ordoliberal principle, would be to directly constrain (and depoliticize) the domain of monetary policy and, indirectly, the domain of economic policy, by tying the hands of domestic governments.[11] As Lechevalier puts it, 'the resulting institutional balance' led EMU to reflect core principles of ordoliberalism, and, in fact, to 'move closer towards the ordoliberal model than Germany itself ha[d] ever done'.[12]

EMU, contrary to its name, was a form of monetary union *without* economic union. Departing from the earlier recommendations of the Werner Report, as well as other analyses of monetary union, in the 1970s, Delors offered no new institution of supranational economic government to flank the monetary authority.[13] Maastricht,

[9] See Kenneth Dyson and Kevin Featherstone, 'Italy and EMU as a *vincolo esterno*: Empowering the Technocrats, Transforming the State' (1996) 1 South European Society & Politics 272 ('The *vincolo esterno* involved a particular version of a two-level game: here the domestic "reverberation effects" were of prime importance. EC-level developments and commitments were used by Italian elites to restructure the domestic policy process, thereby revising the balance of power between key actors and opening up new opportunities for policy reform at home'. However, 'the attraction of EMU as a "*vincolo esterno*", empowering Italian technocrats to overcome domestic constraints, was not matched by substantial Italian leverage in the two-level game' (ibid 291–92). See, further, Kenneth Dyson and Kevin Featherstone, *The Road to Maastricht: Negotiating Economic and Monetary Union* (OUP 1999).

[10] This way of conceptualizing it comes from Klaus Tuori and Karlo Tuori, *Eurozone Crisis: A Constitutional Analysis* (CUP 2013).

[11] ibid.

[12] Arnaud Lechevalier, 'Why and How Has German Ordoliberalism Become a French Issue? Some Aspects about Ordoliberal Thoughts We Can Learn from the French Reception' in Josef Hien and Christian Joerges (eds), *Ordoliberalism, Law and The Rule of Economics* (Hart Publishing 2017) 42 (he continues that, 'by shifting power towards "enlightened despots" (such as the ECB or Commission) . . . the ordoliberal rule-based approach has led to a deprivation of democratic sovereignty in the Eurozone' (ibid 43)).

[13] The MacDougall Report in 1977 had suggested a minimum federal budget of 5 to 7 per cent of EU GDP to complement monetary union (Commission, 'Report of the Study Group on the Role of Public Finance in European Integration—Volume 1' ('MacDougall Report', COM Doc II/10/77, April 1977) <http://ec.europa.eu/economy_finance/emu_history/documentation/chapter8/19770401en73macdougallrepvol1.pdf> accessed 6 September 2020)

therefore, signalled an arrest of the functional logic that economic integration would prompt political integration, and that politicization would push elites to engage mass publics in European matters, eventually precipitating a process leading to full political union with a pan-European democracy.[14] On the contrary, EMU entrenched the further *depoliticization* of a key aspect of macroeconomic policy, removing an important lever of power from the political pillars of the member states, but without reconstructing it at the supranational level, or establishing a future plan to do so.

The new monetary institution, the European System of Central Banks, would take independence in a radically new direction. The ECB itself would be independent from the state; not just from the individual member states of the EU, but from any state or state apparatus at the supranational level. It would be based on a treaty-constitution close to unamendable (in contrast, the Bundesbank's independence was guaranteed only via statute) and, unlike the Bundesbank, it would be disembedded from the public. The new 'currency without a state' was not only democratically unaccountable; it also lacked the social and political bonds of a supranational community. The introduction of the euro had, in effect, achieved the denationalization of money advocated by Friedrich von Hayek,[15] as 'increased capital mobility, and independence of competition authorities and central banks now exerted direct market discipline on political society'.[16]

While radically independent in a formal sense, the ECB would be radically *dependent* on a particular material economic ideology written into its founding document, the Maastricht Treaty. The Bank was given extremely limited discretion in setting policy, being mandated exclusively to the goal of avoiding inflation. This marked a clear break from even the muted Keynesianism of the post-war years, and clearly differentiated it from its counterparts in the US and the UK (the Federal Reserve and Bank of England were charged not only with safeguarding against inflation, but also against unemployment).[17]

The ECB's independence from government was, thus, an illusory form of independence: the ECB was *dependent* on, and constrained by, a single logic: the aim of 'price stability'. And this aim was effectively constitutionalized, based on Treaty provisions close to unamendable, since amendment would require unanimous consent

[14] See Gary Marks and Lisbet Hooghe, 'A Postfunctionalist Theory of European Integration: From Permissive Consensus to Constraining Dissensus' (2009) 39 British Journal of Political Science 1, 5.

[15] On the 'subtle' influence of Hayek, see the speech by Professor Otmar Issing, 'Hayek, Currency Competition and European Monetary Union' (Annual Hayek Memorial Lecture hosted by the Institute of Economics Affairs, London, 27 May 1999) available at <https://www.ecb.europa.eu/press/key/date/1999/html/sp990527.en.html> accessed 7 September 2020.

[16] Magnus Ryner, 'The Authoritarian Neoliberalism of the EU: Legal Form and International Politico-economic Sources' in Eva Nanopoulos and Fortis Vergis (eds), *The Crisis Behind the Eurocrisis: On the Multi-Systemic Failure of the EU* (CUP 2019) 91. In Dyson's view, the monetarism of the Chicago School had by then come to exert more influence on the Bundesbank than ordoliberalism, noting that 'Milton Friedman trumped Eucken': Kenneth Dyson, 'Ordoliberalism as Tradition and Ideology' in Josef Hien and Christian Joerges (eds), *Ordoliberalism: Law and the Rule of Economics* (Bloomsbury Publishing 2017) 95. On the influence of the ordoliberals on Hayek, see Sean Irving, 'Limiting Democracy and Framing the Economy: Hayek, Schmitt and Ordoliberalism' (2018) 44 History of European Ideas 113.

[17] According to economic orthodoxy, a bank's independence was considered 'perfect' if it had price stability as 'the only or major goal, and in case of conflict with government [the central bank] has final authority to pursue policies aimed at achieving this goal' (Alex Cukierman, *Central Bank Strategy, Credibility, and Independence: Theory and Evidence* (MIT Press 1992)).

from all of the member states. This made its mandate more resistant to change than many entrenched domestic constitutional provisions, and a hostage to future intergovernmental bargaining. Price stability, in other words, became the '*Grundnorm* of the Eurozone's economic constitution'.[18]

EMU required surrender of monetary sovereignty by the individual member states, but without corresponding gains in the Union's economic authority. This diminution of national sovereignty, without its transfer to a higher political level, replicated Röpke's ordoliberal principle, enunciated in the 1950s.[19] Also in accordance with ordoliberal thinking was the primacy of price stability in the conduct of monetary policy (and in the conduct of economic policy, more broadly), established in Articles 119 (2) and 127 (1) of the Treaty on the Functioning of the European Union (TFEU), proscribing exchange rate arrangements and general economic policies that might threaten it. The de facto constitutionalization and depoliticization of monetary policy objectives was the final piece of a jigsaw puzzle that had been in the making for several decades.[20]

The spectre that had so haunted early Weimar in the eyes of fiscal conservatives would be finally banished from Europe, as a whole, in a continent-wide field experiment. From the perspective of fiscal conservatives, inflation had been as dangerous as war in 'erod[ing] the social fabric of society' and, ultimately, putting 'the very foundations of democracy and freedom at risk'.[21] This was, according to Otmar Issing, 'one of the lessons of the bitter history of the 20th century, which was a century of hyperinflation in the wake of wars and wars in the wake of hyperinflation'.[22] The deflation and unemployment of the early 1930s that was the proximate cause of Weimar's collapse is all but airbrushed from history, buried with the fact that the hyperinflation had occurred under an independent central bank.[23]

The attachment to the myth of hyperinflation as the cause of social and political ills was not only the preserve of fiscal conservatives and ordoliberals. It was, according to German economic elites, so widely accepted by the German public that to question it would seem 'taboo'.[24] But it also resonated beyond Germany, with French neo-liberals associated with the interwar Walter Lippman Colloquium (introduced in Chapter 2) having lauded the German economic post-war success. Jacques Rueff, influential in the French section of the Mont Pelerin Society, and leading architect of the liberalizing reforms under de Gaulle, 'went even further than Eucken in sketching a rules-based market order and in anticipating the design features of the successive EMU'.[25] The

[18] Chiara Zilioli and Martin Selmayr, 'The European Central Bank: An Independent Specialized Organization of Community Law' (2000) 37 Common Market Law Review 591, 628.

[19] See Chapter 3.

[20] See, further, Chiara Zilioli and Martin Selmayr, *The Law of the European Central Bank* (Hart Publishing 2001): in parallel to its denationalization, the EMU constitutional framework has led 'to a complete depoliticization of monetary policy' (ibid 34, emphasis in original).

[21] Otmar Issing, *Should We Have Faith in Central Banks?* (The Institute of Economic Affairs 2002) 23–24.

[22] ibid.

[23] See, further, Hjalte C Lokdam, 'Banking on Sovereignty: A Genealogy of the European Central Bank's Independence' (PhD Thesis, LSE 2019).

[24] Hans Tietmeyer, 'The Role of an Independent Central Bank in Europe', in Patrick Downes and Reza Vaez-Zadeh (eds), *The Evolving Role of Central Banks: Papers Presented at the Fifth Seminar on Central Banking* (Central Banking Department, IMF 1991) 182–83.

[25] See Dyson (n 16) 93. See, further, François Denord, 'French Neoliberalism and its Divisions: From the Colloque Walter Lippmann to the Fifth Republic' in Philip Mirowski and Dieter Plehwe (eds), *The Road*

reaction to the stagflation of the 1970s cemented the end of Keynesianism and the turn to monetarism (as we saw in Chapter 5), symbolized by the award of the Nobel Prize, in 1976, to Milton Friedman, and led a second generation of neo-liberals influenced by the Chicago school to offer a new narrative of economic crises as products of the democratic political process rather than of capitalism.[26] Just as, in response to the interwar period, a new myth emerges in response to the ungovernability of the 1970s, linking democratic excess, hyperinflation (now in the form of 'stagflation'), and liberal constitutional breakdown.[27]

The consequences of extrapolating the myth of hyperinflation to a European level would be revealed spectacularly when the structure came under pressure in the euro-crisis phase, but politics needed to deal with *deflation* (discussed in Part IV). For now, it might be noted that this myth helped legitimize an extraordinary rigidity in constitutional structure, as well as an ideological convergence that would prove a serious obstacle when conditions changed.

Since there was no clear legal avenue of exit from the single currency, EMU was effectively an 'alienation' rather than an 'agency' contract (to adopt Jean Hampton's terminology).[28] In other words, there was no formal option of reclaiming sovereignty over money (until Lisbon, there wasn't even a clear legal avenue of exit from the EU). The dedication of Mitterrand and Kohl to 'make EMU and with it European integration "irreversible" moved the EMU project steadily forward'.[29] Unlike Ulysses's voyage, there would be no end destination at which the ties could be unbound once the Sirens' calls had been safely circumnavigated.

To complement the separation of monetary policy from fiscal authority, and the guarantee of price stability, EMU would be underpinned by a predominant, if unwritten, logic of market discipline and the avoidance of moral hazard. In this configuration, the retention of fiscal authority by the member state—its capacity to spend, and repay its existing debts—would be based on the state's own ability to raise resources from the financial markets. In the new era of the 'debt state', revenue would increasingly be generated that way, rather than from the taxpayer, not least due to the potential for tax arbitrage in a regional setting where capital was guaranteed to move freely.[30]

from Mont Pelerin: The Making of the Neoliberal Thought Collective (HUP 2009) 45–67. On the similarities and differences between French neo-liberalism and German ordoliberalism, see, further, Bruno Amable, 'Dirigism and Modernism vs Ordoliberalism' in Josef Hien and Christian Joerges (eds), *Ordoliberalism: Law and the Rule of Economics* (Bloomsbury Publishing 2017) 13–21.

[26] The McCracken report for the OECS, co-authored by Robert Marjolin in 1977, which contributed to the global discrediting of Keynesianism, blamed a rise in aspirations, union demands, and public concerns over income distribution for the economic crises of inflation, without the 'benefit of either information or research' (Robert Keohane, 'Economics, Inflation, and the Role of the State: Political Implications of the McCracken Report' (1978) 31:1 World Politics 108, 113).

[27] For a powerful counter-narrative, see Wolfgang Streeck, *Buying Time: The Delayed Crisis of Democratic Capitalism*, (Verso 2014).

[28] See Jean E Hampton, *Hobbes and the Social Contract Tradition* (CUP 1986), especially ch 9.

[29] Krotz and Schild (n 3) 211.

[30] See Agustin Menéndez, 'The Existential Crisis of the European Union' (2013) 14 German Law Journal 453; Streeck (n 27).

The disciplining of member states' fiscal policies would be taken care of, in theory, by bond yields set at a level appropriate to the soundness of a state's finances, with the aid of credit rating agencies and other information available to financial investors on the creditworthiness of the investment.[31] This would not entirely dispense with the need for fiscal rules, as acknowledged by the agreement to set maximum deficit and debt levels. The inadequacy of market discipline, on its own, to exert sufficient pressure on the member states, especially in a heterogeneous union such as the eurozone, was thus vaguely understood; hence, the creation of a loose structure of *public discipline*, the Stability and Growth Pact (SGP). This was violated in the early period of EMU by France and Germany, and the 'rules' were under-enforced by the European Council and the European Court of Justice, reflecting a more general move away from traditional supranationalism, hard law, and the *acquis communautaire* in the period between Maastricht and Lisbon.[32] The open method of coordination (OMC), a turn to 'soft law' and 'new governance', was *celebrated* by many as a sensible departure from a Community method of law-making that was too centralized and 'one-size-fits-all', unable to accommodate the constitutional diversity within the Union.[33] The fact that the 'rules' of the Stability Pact—if that is even an appropriate label for its requirements—were leniently interpreted, and under-enforced, was given relatively little attention at the time.

The material impact of EMU on its members was significant: a radical convergence of yields on government bonds. By the time of the introduction of the hard currency in 2002, interest rates on ten-year government bonds were virtually identical across the eurozone. This was accompanied by huge movements of capital from northern banks towards the periphery, which inflated their domestic demand and helped to create asset bubbles in the private sector.[34] In retrospect, this also raised the spectre of another aspect of EMU's incompleteness: the absence of any proper banking union or supervision of financial markets.[35]

Competitiveness in countries whose growth model was export-driven was increased through wage suppression and neo-liberal labour market reform, often pursued by ostensibly centre-left parties, as with the Hartz IV reforms in Germany under the auspices of Schröder's 'Agenda 2010'.[36] This symbolized both a 'retrenchment of the

[31] Market discipline was central to the logic of EMU. According to a 2007 ECB working paper, 'Accurate asset pricing implies that governments pursuing unsound fiscal policies will be forced to offer higher yields to attract risk-averse investors, in order to compensate them for the higher default risk. Via this channel, progress in financial integration will ultimately reinforce any market-driven disciplinary effect.' (Simone Manganelli and Guido Wolswijk, 'Market Discipline, Financial Integration and Fiscal Rules: What Drives Spreads in the Euro Area Government Bond Market?' (2007) ECB Working Paper Series No 745. <https://www.ecb.europa.eu/pub/pdf/scpwps/ecbwp745.pdf>).

[32] Case C-27/04 *Commission v Council* [2004] ECR I-6649.

[33] For contemporary discussion, see, eg Oliver Gerstenberg, 'The New Europe: Part of the Problem — or Part of the Solution to the Problem?' (2002) Oxford Journal of Legal Studies 563; cf Christian Joerges, 'What is Left of the European Economic Constitution? A Melancholic Eulogy' (2005) 30 European Law Review 461, 478ff.

[34] See Menendez (n 30).

[35] See Erik Jones, 'The Forgotten Financial Union: How You Can Have a Euro Crisis without a Euro' in Matthias Matthijs and Mark Blyth (eds), *The Future of the Euro* (OUP 2015).

[36] The reforms came with significant political cost; sparking protest, effectively ending Schröder's career, and splitting the Left by giving rise to Die Linke (see, further, Abraham Newman, 'The Reluctant Leader: Germany's Euro Experience and the Long Shadow of Reunification' in Matthias Matthijs and Mark Blyth (eds), *Future of the Euro* (OUP 2015) 127–28).

German Welfare State' *and* the 'spread of neoliberal policies on the continent'.[37] The significance was not only the specific downward effect on wages and working conditions, but 'the undisguised expulsion of labour from its traditional place in the corporatist structure of the German economy'. This further 'demot[ed] the German working class as a political player',[38] and coincided with the German SPD losing 300,000 members between 1990 and 2005.

The full significance of the huge financial flows that took place in the long decade after Maastricht would only be discovered when they dried up after the collapse of Lehman Brothers in 2008, and the market reaction to the realization of higher Greek deficit levels in 2009 (examined in Part IV). The constraints on the political economies of the members of the eurozone, in general, and on the possibility of producing a social Europe, in particular, were, again, an exaggeration of earlier trends, rather than a departure from them. The 'profoundly conservative system' of the EU, and the structural and ideological attachment to European integration, meant that, even when twelve out of fifteen members were led by centre-left governments, there was no prospect of escape from the straitjacket of economic liberalism.[39] Social democracy, or what was left of it, had to face 'institutions against politics' as well as markets against politics, in addition to its own ideological attachment to integration.[40]

In another respect, convergence of interest rates, and ideological convergence in political economy, were reinforcing and reproducing material *divergence*. Even before the negotiation of the Maastricht Treaty, the national economies of the eurozone had been on different economic growth paths. The future debtor states 'were mainly pursuing policies of financially-driven growth that were dependent on an expansion of private credit and on increasing asset prices in the markets for commercial and residential property'.[41] Germany and the Netherlands, on the other hand, were pursuing an export-driven policy based on the suppression of wages. The problems in the political economy of Europe, in other words, were structural and combined. If consensus around EMU appeared to conceal them at first, in fact it exacerbated them, setting a trap for countries that would later be unable to tackle loss of competitiveness through currency devaluation.

There were warnings against the construction of monetary union without fiscal union. Even mainstream economic analysis on optimal currency theory from the 1960s suggested that the eurozone may not have been an optimal currency area, given the relatively low degree of labour movement and flexibility.[42] And, as early at 1971,

[37] ibid 128. It was only after 2005 that Germany began to benefit from faster growth and lower unemployment (and then, in contrast to France).

[38] Costas Lapavitsas, *The Left Case Against the EU* (Polity Press 2019) 47.

[39] See Gerassimos Moschonas, 'Reformism in a "Conservative" System: the European Union and Social Democratic Identity' in John Callaghan and others (eds), *In Search of Social Democracy: Responses to Crisis and Modernisation* (Manchester University Press 2009) 183 ('With the second project of integration, social democrats have found themselves in a *non-conjunctural* position of ideological inferiority in European political space. They have lost ground as well as a great part of their programmatic freedom of manoeuvre. Social democracy exhibited strong signs of programmatic destabilisation and exhaustion.')

[40] ibid 183.

[41] Simon Deakin, 'Social Policy, Economic Governance and EMU: Alternatives to Austerity', in Niklas Bruun, Klaus Lörcher, and Isabelle Schömann (eds), *The Economic and Financial Crisis and Collective Labour Law in Europe* (Hart Publishing 2014) 90.

[42] See Robert A Mundell, 'A Theory of Optimal Currency Areas' (1961) 51 The American Economic Review 657.

following the early forerunner of EMU, the 'Werner Plan', Nicholas Kaldor had predicted that monetary union without political union, far from facilitating political integration, would actually make such integration *less* likely, quite possibly even precipitating the break-up of the Union.[43] After Maastricht, it was said that the problem with the set-up of EMU was less the fact of central bank independence per se, than the difficulty that would arise if the anti-inflationary objectives EMU entailed were no longer generally supported, but yet unable to be readily modified. This could (and later would) raise substantial democratic concerns.[44] These would largely be overlooked, however, due to the broader ideological ascendency of neo-liberalism, and the decline of social democratic opposition to the status quo.

3. Deepening and widening of market liberal ideology

The Maastricht formula for sound finances emerged in the middle of a new phase of economic integration in Europe, which complemented the neo-liberal revolution of the 1980s, and the political dominance of monetarism unleashed in the Anglo-American world by Thatcher and Reagan (following Pinochet's experiment in Chile). The turn to financialization of the economy had been facilitated by the dismantling of fetters on capital accumulation and a loosening of capital controls, with the free movement of capital eventually becoming a fundamental legal and even constitutional right in the EU.[45] As a result of capital mobility and the threat of capital flight, the capacity of the state to raise revenue through taxation was diminished;[46] and, in conjunction with the right of free establishment in the EU, extended in the ECJ's *Centros* decision, domestic powers to tackle tax evasion would be further curtailed and corporate tax competition fuelled.[47]

The structural deepening of the EU's economic liberalism within EMU, and in the Internal Market more generally, can only be understood in conjunction with the broader ideology ascendant in the period. This had already been grasped in the Maastricht moment, with contemporary commentators observing (and occasionally lamenting) 'the dominant trend' in the 1980s and 1990s 'for the retreat of state powers, and 'the privatisation of public space'.[48] In fact, as was later noted, from the

[43] Nicholas Kaldor, 'The Dynamic Effects of the Common Market' *New Statesman* (London, 12 March 1971). This repeated arguments he had made in 1963 (see Nicholas Kaldor, 'Escape from Socialism' *New Statesman* (London, 26 July 1963)).

[44] See Verdun (n 8) 127 ('even though at first sight the democratic deficit of EMU appears to be not much worse than that in the "pre-EMU status quo", democratic accountability and legitimacy could become highly problematic if the majority of European citizens failed to support the chosen policies. The Maastricht Treaty leaves insufficient possibilities for changes in the conduct of monetary policies.')

[45] See, eg Menendez (n 30) 453–526.

[46] ibid.

[47] Case C212/97 *Centros* [1999] ECR I-1459. See, further, Philipp Genschel, 'One Trap, Many Exits, but No Free Lunch: How the Joint-Decision Trap Shapes EU Tax Policy' in G Falkner (ed), *The EU's Decision Traps: Comparing Policies* (OUP 2011) 54–72.

[48] Andrew Gamble, 'Economic Recession and Disenchantment with Europe' in Jack Hayward (ed), *The Crisis of Representation in Europe* (Routledge 1996) 171 (citing Helen Wallace). Gamble argues that 'moves to implement the neoliberal agenda for European integration will end by deepening the crisis of legitimacy' (ibid 173).

1980s onwards, in old members such as France and Italy, as well as new members such as Spain, privatization was fast and furious, Europe having eliminated, in a relatively short span of time, 'one of the main characteristics of its postwar economic model: the mixed economy'.[49]

After several decades of gradual construction, the beginning of the 1990s culminated in 'a certain ideational uniformity' prevailing among 'European political elites regarding the primacy of price stability, the limits of government intervention and the superiority of markets over planning as the pillars of societal organization'.[50] The EU itself (most obviously through EMU) served as a means to cement this ideology, and establish a differentiation of the political and the economic that would 'free European elites from the growing constraints of their internal national, democratic and welfare states'.[51] European integration, specifically the 'setting of a core economic constitution as an external constraint', was a way for domestic elites 'to externalise the pressure for domestic change and reform and, at the same time, to externalise the political costs of economic rationalisation'.[52] The creation of the European single market in 1986 was not 'a collective burst of idealism' but, rather, a 'convergence of national interests around the new patterns of policy-making: not the Keynesian synthesis of the 1950s and 1960s but the neoliberal regulatory programme of the 1980s'.[53]

The rhetoric of 'TINA', outlined in Chapter 5, and closely associated with Margaret Thatcher's domestic project of neo-liberal reform, was far more widely adopted in the aftermath of the collapse of the Soviet Union. As well as announcing the emergence of the United States as sole global superpower, and liberal capitalism as 'the only game in town', it signalled the decline of critical theory as a serious oppositional force. 'Since 1989', Habermas—the standard-bearer of the Frankfurt School—suggested, it had 'become impossible to break out of the universe of capitalism; the only remaining option', he concluded, was 'to civilize and tame the capitalist dynamic from within'.[54] This was, apparently, the same Habermas who, in response to the German court's Maastricht decision, lamented the democratic deficit of the EU as growing ever greater by the day, eroding the capacity of the democratic state to perform its job of taming capitalist excesses.[55]

[49] Ivan T Berend, 'From Oil Crisis to Financial Crisis 1973–2009' in Stone (ed), *The Oxford Handbook of Postwar European History* (OUP 2012) 414.

[50] Chris Bickerton, Dermot Hodson, and Uwe Puetter, 'The New Intergovernmentalism: European Integration in the Post-Maastricht Era' (2015) 53 Journal of Common Market Studies 703, 708 ('this was the moment when the planning and big government instincts of the postwar era were finally jettisoned. Nation-states in Europe had become Member States.' (ibid 709)). Colin Crouch notes that the US was at the forefront of this trend, which he calls 'post-democracy', setting an example for elites around the world (Colin Crouch, *Post-Democracy* (Polity Press 2004) 11).

[51] Stefano Bartolini, *Restructuring Europe: Centre Formation, System Building, and Political Structuring between the Nation-State and the European Union* (OUP 2005) 246.

[52] ibid 247.

[53] Robert O Keohane and Stanley Hoffmann, 'Institutional Change in Europe in the 1980s' in Robert O Keohane and Stanley Hoffmann (eds), *The New European Community: Decision-Making and Institutional Change* (Routledge 1991) 23.

[54] Jürgen Habermas, *The Crisis of the European Union: A Response* (Polity Press 2012) 106, 113.

[55] Jürgen Habermas, 'Remarks on Dieter Grimm's "Does Europe Need a Constitution?"' (1995) 1 European Law Journal 303. This suggests that the cognitive dissonance identified in Chapter 7 had deep roots in Habermas's thinking.

Despite the promise of Jacques Delors for a social Europe, the capture of the integration process by neo-liberal forces and their harnessing of the 'big market' project soon closed any openings that may have existed for the development of a different kind of Community, 'redefining the European Community in purely market terms as a huge field for the free play of private interests, increasingly open to global trade and investment flows and only minimally supervised by the tiny apparatus of the EC Commission'.[56] Through the increasing internationalization of trade, and the integration of global markets, the European 'common market' would lose much of its earlier meaning, which had been 'related to a degree of closure of the European economic system'. Instead, the *single market* would simply become a 'section of the global market', in the process 'eroding the idea of a European juridical space'.[57]

With political consensus on the need for labour market flexibility, deregulation, and trade union reform, the single market was viewed as potentially levelling the various technical barriers to full scale competition across the continent. At the same time, it would 'accelerate the dissolution of national economies as distinct objects of control, thus excluding any repetition of the French experiment' of the early 80s, when Mitterrand's U-turn marked a decisive end to continental Keynesianism.[58] In the context of the dominance of supply-side economics, the discourse of labour market flexibility had come to assume centrality in the political economy of the European state and, by the end of the twentieth century, it had come to replace the aim of full employment.[59]

If it was less liberal democracy than neo-liberal capitalism that became seen as invulnerable — at 'the end of history'— since there seemed, literally, to be no alternative to the free market ideology, what was the function of democracy any longer? In much theorizing, it had disappeared as a meaningful process, let alone any radical movement. 'Democratization' was often simply conflated with 'liberalism', 'constitutionalism', or 'modernization'.[60]

Underwriting the hegemony of 'third way' neo-liberalism, however, were not merely theoretical conflations, but the deepening and acceleration of a social dynamic, captured in the movement from 'citizen' to 'consumer',[61] and 'civic' to 'market'

[56] According to Stefan Giubboni, the 'metamorphosis' of the SEA and Maastricht periods was clear; the new laws of the transnational economy had become 'direct and explicit constraints that—aided by the supremacy of Community law—prevail[ed] over (formerly protected) national sovereignty in social policy', signifying a substantial reduction in member states' de facto autonomy, 'overturning the original constitutional balance' (Stefano Giubboni, *Social Rights and Market Freedom in the European Constitution: A Labour Law Perspective* (CUP 2006) 25).

[57] Bartolini (n 51) 370. This coincided with the then-Director-General of Competition for the European Commission boasting that the EC Treaty was 'the most strongly free market oriented constitution in the world': see Claus-Dieter Ehlermann, 'The Contribution of EC Competition Policy to the Single Market' (1992) 23 CMLR 257, 273.

[58] John Grahl and Paul Teague, 'The Cost of Neoliberal Europe' (1989) 174 New Left Review 33, 34. See, further, Ben Clift, 'The Political Economy of French Social Democratic Economic Policy Autonomy, 1997–2002: Credibility, *Dirigisme* and Globalisation' in John Callaghan and others (eds), *In Search of Social Democracy: Responses to Crisis and Modernisation* (Manchester Press University 2009).

[59] Bo Strath (ed), *After Full Employment: European Discourses on Work and Flexibility* (Peter Lang 2000).

[60] See, eg Bartolini (n 51) 89.

[61] See Wolfgang Streeck, 'From Citizens to Consumers: Considerations on the New Politics of Consumption' (2012) 76 New Left Review 27.

freedom.[62] This vision of citizenship, and of freedom, based on the exercise and enjoyment of individual liberty, was underpinned in the constitutional imagination much earlier than commonly supposed. It was not merely a result of neo-liberal changes from the 1980s, which is not to deny the significant material changes to the economy and society that occurred in that period. As laid out in Chapter 5, the focus on individual rights, economic freedoms, and market competition—engineered with the deliberate aim to remove class struggle from the political domain—was a goal shared by Christian democrats, ordoliberals, and other post-war 'planners for laissez-faire', including social democrats and even some radicals.[63] Although there were various class compromises forged at the coalface of industrial relations in the varieties of post-war coordinated capitalism, the dominant vision in the constitutional imaginary was of the individual as consumer, free from interference by others (often termed 'negative liberty').[64]

Although the move from industrial to finance-led capitalism, and various defeats of the industrial working class in the 1980s, did not, therefore, bring about a fundamental change in the constitutional imagination, they did signify a major realignment of class power within the various post-war compromises. This was spectacularly effected in the UK, as represented by Thatcher's multiple electoral and ideological victories, particularly with the miners' strike of 1984 and 1985, and her confident declaration that 'there is no such thing as society'.[65] Thatcher would later be tormented by the issue of Europe, a legacy handed down to future generations of Tory leaders; but, ironically, given its later Eurosceptic turn, British conservatism had stamped its influence on the course of European integration. Its own strategy of labour market deregulation had spelled the end of the Social Action Programme of the mid 1970s, leading to the abandonment of a European legislative strategy in labour policy, and precipitating the turn to 'social dialogue'.[66] The Conservative party had, more generally, moulded the Single European Act; most notably, through the influence of Lord Cockfield, 'Father of the Single Market', and his radical approach to economic integration. This approach had favoured mutual recognition of regulation, bypassing the need for common standards wherever possible, in an echo of—and aided by—the Court's earlier *Cassis de Dijon*

[62] See Richard Bellamy, 'The Liberty of the Moderns: Market Freedom and Democracy in the EU' (2012) 1:1 Global Constitutionalism 141 (on how the EU serves to expand modern market liberty, and erode the union of modern market liberty and the political liberty of the ancients achieved by the nation state, drawing on Benjamin Constant's famous distinction).

[63] We also saw that there was some critique of these trends, particularly in light of the authoritarian approach apparent in the report of the Trilateral Commission (see Michael C Behrent, 'The Origins of the Anti-Liberal Left: the 1979 Vincennes Conference on Neoliberalism' (2017) 35 French Politics, Culture & Society 44).

[64] Isaiah Berlin, 'Two Concepts of Liberty' in Henry Hardy (ed), *Liberty: Incorporating Four Essays on Liberty* (2nd edn, OUP 2002). The notion of 'consumer sovereignty' has roots even earlier, in the interwar philosophy of Austrian neo-liberal Ludwig von Mises (see Niklas Olsen, *The Sovereign Consumer: A New Intellectual History of Neoliberalism* (Palgrave MacMillan 2019)).

[65] Thatcher's 'authoritarian populism' (as it was characterized by contemporary commentators such as Stuart Hall and Andrew Gamble), which developed from a position of influence within the EU in the 1980s, may, in hindsight, have been a precursor to the wave of authoritarian populism emerging in the late euro crisis phase. This is explored further in Conclusion of this book (Stuart Hall, 'Gramsci and Us' in Stuart Hall (ed), *The Hard Road to Renewal: Thatcherism and the Crisis of the Left* (Verso 1988) 161–73).

[66] Brian Bercusson notes that this, inadvertently, led to some successes at the European level, as British trade unions turned to Brussels: Brian Bercusson, *European Labour Law* (2nd edn, CUP 2009) 17.

ruling.[67] The pressures of 'planning for laissez-faire' had wide-ranging impacts, particularly in conjunction with the financialization of the economy (and of the corporation), and deindustrialization of major economies: so much so that, by the end of the 1990s, 'French and German financial and corporate governance systems had more in common with those found in Britain than they had with their own post-war systems.'[68] Continental capitalism, in other words, had become increasingly Atlanticized, and this had occurred in conjunction with the decline of European trade unions and the expansion of employer discretionary power, and, on some accounts, 'an emergent European transnational capitalist class'.[69]

Financial integration and the opening up of the market for public procurement would substantially liberalize the single market in new areas, on the assumption that efficiencies, flexibility, and reductions in transactions costs would restore Europe's "lost dynamism". If this reflected a neo-liberal developmental agenda based on rhetorical optimism around economic modernization and rationalization, in reality it also meant that integration would occur less through market competition among small and medium-sized firms than through large multinational corporations, including American and Japanese concerns, paving the way, not for the Europeanization promised by Delors but for further globalization of Europe's economic life.[70] By 2004, it had been estimated that, 'Europe had become the most globalised region, and Belgium the most globalised country, of the world'.[71] In conjunction with the loss of monetary autonomy instantiated by the EMS, and later EMU, there were already concerns that this would have an asymmetrical impact; that 'the weaker economies of Europe, especially low-income Mediterranean countries, could pay a high price' for 'enforced alignment with the restrictive policies of West Germany'.[72] This narrative would be played out in the post-Lisbon era in a more dramatic fashion, in the wake of the global financial crisis (examined in Part IV).

In the area of free movement, the European Court of Justice, which had been so active in liberalizing trade for goods, exemplified in *Cassis de Dijon*, appeared to scale

[67] According to Lord Cockfield, '[t]he gradual limitation of national sovereignty is part of a slow and painful forward march of humanity', in *The Guardian* (London, 11 November 1988), cited by Alan Milward, *The European Rescue of the Nation State* (Verso 1992) 2. Cockfield, European Commissioner for the Internal Market from 1985 to 1988, was the author of the White Paper on 'The Completion of the Internal Market'.

[68] Orfeo Fioretos, 'Coordinated Versus Liberal Market Economies' in Erik Jones, Anand Menon, and Stephen Weatherill (eds), *Oxford Handbook of the European Union* (OUP 2012) 300. See, further, Richard Deeg, 'Change from Within: German and Italian Finance in the 1990s' in Wolfgang Streeck and Kathleen Thelen (eds), *Beyond Continuity: Institutional Change in Advanced Political Economies* (OUP 2005) (Streeck and Thelen, 'Beyond Continuity').

[69] On institutional convergence and shifting class power across a variety of capitalisms in the post-Fordist era, see Lucio Baccaro and Chris Howell, *Trajectories of Neoliberal Transformation: European Industrial Relations Since the 1970s* (CUP 2017). On the emergence of a transnational capitalist bloc, see Bastiaan van Apeldoorn, 'Transnational Class Agency and European Governance: The Case of the European Round Table of Industrialists' (2000) 5 New Political Economy 157, 157. See, further, Bastiaan van Apeldoorn, *Transnational Capitalism and the Struggle Over European Integration* (Routledge 2002).

[70] Grahl and Teague (n 58) 42. On Europeanization and globalization as complementary as well as competing processes, see Francis Snyder, 'Globalisation and Europeanisation as Friends and Rivals: European Union Law in Global Economic Networks' (1999) EUI Working Paper Law No 99/8 <http://hdl.handle.net/1814/153> accessed 22 November 2020.

[71] Berend (n 49) 417.

[72] Grahl and Teague (n 58) 45.

back its ambitions in its *Keck* case, excluding non-discriminatory domestic selling arrangements from the Treaty prohibitions.[73] But this proved to be brief respite from its insistence on the logic of market integration, the Court soon limiting the consequences of *Keck* in subsequent case law.[74]

In the *Viking* and *Laval* line of cases, the European Court of Justice then put its own considerable juridical weight behind the increasingly neo-liberal market drift, and, in more sensitive areas of domestic political economy, extending the application of free movement of services and establishment against trade union laws and trade union actions.[75] In *Viking*, appositely described as Europe's '*Lochner* moment', the European Court would rule that industrial action, although a basic legal right common to the constitutional traditions of the member states (and protected in the Charter of Fundamental Rights), must not disproportionately infringe on a firm's fundamental economic freedom; its right to freedom of establishment, as protected by the Treaty (Article 49 TFEU).[76] With the imposition of a duty of justification on the exercise of the right to strike, and the extension of free movement provisions in their horizontal dimension (against non-state parties), the prioritization of economic liberty would be significantly advanced.[77] This would mean not only that the economic freedoms would trample on sensitive national arrangements and structures of autonomous bargaining, but that they would do so in areas where the EU itself had no legislative competence, and therefore no means to close any regulatory gap.[78] Commentators may have been waiting for Polanyi, but it was Hayek who would greet them.[79]

The Court's 'fundamentalist' approach to economic freedom would, in effect, overturn the original 'de-coupling' of national social spheres and supranational market law, since any distortion of competition or obstacle to market access was now presumed

[73] Case C-267/91 *Keck and Mithouard* [1993] ECR I-6097.

[74] For a nuanced assessment, see Wolf Sauter and Harm Schepel, *State and Market in European Union Law: The Public and Private Spheres of the Internal Market Before the Courts* (CUP 2009). They note that, although in some ways *Keck* marked a more restrained ECJ, in free movement of services and capital the ECJ continued its activist course of liberalization; and, in social security cases, proceeded to add 'another nail to the coffin of embedded liberalism' (ibid 9).

[75] Case C-341/05 *Laval v Svenska Byggnadsarbetareförbundet* [2007] ECR I-11767; Case C-438/05 *International Transport Workers' Federation and Finnish Seamen's Union v Viking Line* [2007] ECR I-10779. See Christian Joerges and Florian Rodl, 'Informal Politics, Formalised Law and the Social Deficit of European Integration: Reflections after the Judgments of the ECJ in *Viking* and *Laval*' (2009) 15 European Law Journal 1.

[76] Danny Nicol, 'Europe's Lochner Moment' (2011) Public Law 308.

[77] Fritz Scharpf, 'The Double Asymmetry of European Integration: or Why the EU Cannot be a Social Market Economy' (2010) 8 Socio-Economic Review 211–50 (since the early 1980s, 'economic integration has accelerated and intensified, and the liberal transformation, which Hayek had expected, has, indeed, been taking place in the multilevel European polity' (ibid 212). Scharpf emphasized the structural asymmetry favouring 'non-political actors' over political actors, and negative integration over positive integration, and identified integration through law as a significant factor. Harm Schepel, 'Constitutionalising the Market, Marketising the Constitution, and to Tell the Difference: On the Horizontal Applications of the Free Movement Provisions in EU Law' (2012) 18 European Law Journal 177.

[78] Scharpf (n 77). Or, as in the case of the Monti II Regulation, fails to gain adequate political support for regulation.

[79] Martin Höpner and Armin Schäfer, 'Polanyi in Brussels? Embeddedness and the Three Dimensions of European Economic Integration' (2010) MPIfG Discussion Paper 10/8<https://EconPapers.repec.org/RePEc:zbw:mpifgd:p0088> accessed 22 November 2020.

to be caught by the Treaty prohibitions, and subject to proportionality testing.[80] Although building on earlier trends (direct effect and supremacy, as well as mutual recognition), its case law would become increasingly salient as a matter of political economy, making the Court a more conspicuous institution. This was exacerbated by its privileging of free movement of capital and rights of investors over state intervention in the economy, consolidating the wave of privatizations which had occurred in the 1980s and 199's in its *Golden Shares* rulings, which demanded justification for the state's special rights in privatized companies, in light of their potentially dissuasive impact on investment.[81] The depth of liberalization was reflected in the Court's abandonment of a discrimination-based approach to free movement, captured by Advocate General Tizzano's invocation of the dystopian prospect of a 'market without rules'.[82] This broader, and more common, interpretation of liberalization would come to include all efforts at reform, referring to a shift away from regulation and public ownership of enterprises, 'to a greater reliance on market mechanisms and incentives to pursue consumer welfare, industrial, regional and/or employment objectives'. It included mechanisms such as structural reorganization, privatization, and antitrust enforcement.[83]

Liberalization had cut deep into models of domestic political economy, highlighted clearly by its impact on the French system. Even, and especially, in those areas where the French model had been so distinctive—in public services and industrial policy—the single market would contribute to neo-liberal restructuring.[84] Similar stories would be repeated in other domains: the single market, in network sectors such as electricity, gas, telecommunications, railway, air transport, and postal services, demonstrated a practical and transformative power, particularly where the lines between public authority and private power had become increasingly blurred. Integration through stealth would accelerate in this period, with the Commission breaking up natural monopolies, opening service provision to competition, and expanding market regulation to the supranational level, where the difficulties of obtaining political agreement were acute.[85]

The *deepening* of market liberal ideology would be reinforced through its *widening*, as the Union extended eastwards. Accession had prompted a swift and brutal transition to market economies for many of the former Soviet bloc countries (as we examined in Chapter 6). Despite the formal refounding of the Union on the principles of democracy and the rule of law, these principles were not on the central horizon of

[80] See Mitchel Lasser, 'Fundamentally Flawed: The CJEU's Jurisprudence on Fundamental Rights and Fundamental Freedoms' (2014) 15 Theoretical Inquiries in Law 229.

[81] Case C-367/98 *Commission v Portugal (Golden Shares)* [2002] ECR I-4731.

[82] Case C-442/02 *CaixaBank France v Ministère de l'Économie, des Finances et de l'Industrie* [2004] ECR I-8961, para 63 (AG Tizzano).

[83] Niamh Dunne, 'Liberalisation and the Pursuit of the Internal Market' (2018) 43 European Law Review 803 (citing Rauf Gönenç, Maria Maher, and Giuseppe Nicoletti, 'The Implementation and the Effects of Regulatory Reform: Past Experience and Current Issues' (2001) OECD Economic Studies No 32, 2001/I, 12.)

[84] Krotz and Schild (n 3) 176 (citing Peter Becker, *Die Deutsche Europapolitik und die Osterweiterung der Europäischen Union* (Nomos 2011) 156–57). See also Vivien Schmidt, 'Trapped by their Ideas: French Elites' Discourses of European Integration and Globalization' (2007) 14 Journal of European Public Policy 992 (Schmidt, 'Trapped by their Ideas').

[85] Scharpf (n 77).

integration. The economic transformation that was demanded was, on the other hand, conspicuous, and its effects extreme: compared by commentators to natural or man-made disasters such as 'floods, earthquakes, famines or wars', in terms of the enormity of the social dislocation.[86]

The predominance of market-making over democracy-building, in the 'return to Europe', was exacerbated by the absence of solid social foundations for democracy; the absence of civil society after years of Soviet rule.[87] And, as we saw in Part II of this book, constructing a vibrant civil society was never part of the package of membership of the European Union; on the contrary, membership of the Union was part of a package of a constrained democracy and depoliticization. In a significant sense, the neglect in attending to the construction of active democratization was not, therefore, a departure from, but entirely in keeping with, the post-war European trajectory of passive authoritarian liberalism.

What was new was that authoritarian liberalism now traversed a geopolitical space and operated, in part, through the asymmetries of regional integration. As one commentator put it, enlargement was a means to 'assert political and economic control over the unstable and impoverished eastern part of the continent ... [i]t was about conquering, reforming, and regulating new emerging markets. In essence it was about securing peace and prosperity in the future Europe through the skilful use of EU membership conditionality'.[88]

The term 'conditionality' would, of course, acquire a specific significance in the context of the euro crisis, when it came to mean the austerity attached to financial assistance (as we will examine in Part IV). For the new members, the manner of reform required was clear from accession itself, which demanded radical state transformation in the domain of the economy.[89] Vaclav Klaus took a prominent position in this transformation, and 'together with other free market liberals in post-communist Europe', and 'an army of Western advisers', would prescribe a version of neo-liberal 'shock therapy'.[90] As Jan Komarek puts it, after many dissidents left politics soon after 1989, 'their place was assumed by 'grey zone' technocrats and the former members of nomenklatura, who quickly learned the new language of democracy, human rights, the rule of law and, of course, market economy'.[91]

[86] Shafiqul Islam and Michael Mandelbaum (eds), *Making Markets: Economic Transformations in Eastern Europe and the Post-Soviet States* (Council on Foreign Relations Press 1993).

[87] Dorothée Bohle and Béla Greskovits note that East Central European democracies had a 'hollow core' at their inception (see Dorothee Bohle and Béla Greskovits, *Capitalist Diversity on Europe's Periphery* (Cornell University Press 2012). See also Jan Zielonka, *Europe as Empire: The Nature of the Enlarged European Union* (OUP 2006) ch 1.

[88] Zielonka (n 87) 44–45. The EU Accession Partnerships conditioned reception of Union pre-accession aid to the fulfilment of economic criteria.

[89] According to the Copenhagen criteria, '[m]embership requires that candidate country has achieved stability of institutions guaranteeing democracy, the rule of law, human rights, respect for and protection of minorities, the existence of a functioning market economy as well as the capacity to cope with competitive pressure and market forces within the Union. Membership presupposes the candidate's ability to take on the obligations of membership including adherence to the aims of political, economic and monetary union'.

[90] Jan Komarek, 'Waiting for the Existential Revolution' (2014) 12 International Journal of Constitutional Law 190–212.

[91] ibid.

The dominance of market integration in the process of enlargement was reinforced by the fact that the EU had, by Maastricht, already become deeply intertwined with the neo-liberalization of the European economy as a whole. Market liberalization, particularly of financialized capitalism, was the new meaning of modernization. This occurred in a context of trade union decline, with membership of unions, and industrial rights, already having been weakened in the Western nations. There would be no compensation for this through EU-level measures.[92] On the contrary, 'the years after 1992 marked a progressive move away from policies of harmonisation in the social and labour fields', and a move from hard law to soft governance methods of regulation in the social policy field.[93] The European Trade Union Confederation (ETUC) could not compensate for the lack of social legislation; on the contrary, even if it had been competent to organize industrial action at the supranational level, the possibilities for transnational strike action were 'limited by the profound difficulties involved in forging and re-forging transnational solidarities between "European" citizen-workers'.[94]

The context of social-democratic decline is significant in understanding the developments after Maastricht, but must not disguise the fact that 'disorganized capitalism', as it was sometimes referred to, was the result of clear political, legal, and constitutional *organization*: the single market project was 'a highly politicized choice of ethos, ideology, and political culture: the culture of "the market" itself'.[95] If the EU increasingly functioned as a liberalization machine, this was not a machine that operated itself: the ECJ was driving its 'engine'.[96] By the new millennium, 'laissez-faire' had also become the Commission's position on social dialogue, operating without intervention 'under the guise of respect for freedom of association'.[97]

Enlargement exacerbated the difficulties in developing forms of social organization that might counter or resist these developments, not least because, in some of the new member states, trade union membership levels were already drastically low or close to non-existent. The effect of the mismatch this represented between the reality of market-making and economic integration, on the one hand, and the rhetoric of democracy and constitution-building, on the other, is well illustrated in the case of Hungary, and is worth examining in some more detail.

Hungary was initially the 'poster boy' of neo-liberal transformation in the region, with successive governments in the 1990s promoting market liberal policies,

[92] Jelle Visser, 'More Holes in the Bucket: Twenty Years of European Integration and Organized Labor' (2006) 26 Comparative Labor Law & Policy Journal 477. On the broader dynamics of institutional change in this period, see Wolfgang Streeck and Kathleen Thelen, 'Introduction: Institutional Change in Advanced Political Economies' in Streeck and Thelen, 'Beyond Continuity' (n 68).

[93] Ruth Dukes, *Labour Constitution: The Enduring Idea of Labour Law* (OUP 2014) 143. Wolfgang Streeck characterized this new regime as one of 'neo-voluntarism', somewhere between coercion and anarchy (Wolfgang Streeck, 'Neo-Voluntarism: A New European Social Policy Regime?' in Gary Marks and others (eds), *Governance in the European Union* (Sage Publications 1996)). There was, in the 1990s, an optimism about the role of the Commission, with its threat to propose legislation as a substitute for 'classic weapons of class struggle' (see Dukes, above, 146, citing Bercusson).

[94] Dukes (n 93) 150.

[95] SeeJoseph HH Weiler, 'The Transformation of Europe' (1991) 100 Yale Law Journal 2403, 2478.

[96] Dunne (n 83) 809.

[97] Bercusson (n 66) 554 (Bercusson describes this phase as, at best, demonstrating the Commission's 'benign neglect' towards social policy. He concludes that, in the period after 2004, 'with respect to all Member States, new and old, laissez-faire is the Commission's position on social dialogue' (ibid 632).

including low corporate tax rates, investor-friendly policies of privatization, and laws ensuring transnational corporations the right to expatriate profits and the benefits of state subsidies. Hungary's 'variety of neoliberalism', 'based on extreme openness to foreign capital and high dependency on exports', as well as privatization of state assets, was received well by mainstream economists and international institutions such as the WTO, NATO, and the EU, despite leading to chronic underemployment and high levels of poverty and inequality.[98] As an indicator of the degree of rapid interdependence generated in the period, by the end of 2005, German companies accounted for 28 per cent of all direct foreign investment in Hungary.[99] The integration of supply and value chains, and, in particular, relocation of German firms into the Visegrad states, was greatly facilitated by accession into the single market.

At the same time as this transition to a market economy was implemented, a new 'reform' class of domestic bourgeoisie was created in the accession countries; not one interested in ideas of political emancipation, but embedded in new technocratic government and positions of expert authority. In combination with the formation of a substantial underclass (the result of drastic cuts in welfare spending, weakened trade unions, and the legitimization of austerity measures), this exacerbated inequalities without a significant process of democratization or emergence of a public sphere.[100] As we will explore in Part IV, the later turn, exemplified by Viktor Orban (initially a strong advocate of neo-liberal reforms and European integration), to an authoritarian populism (with illiberal elements), after the election of the Fidesz party in 2010, could be seen as a 'Polanyian counter-movement in one person', although it retained many aspects of economic neo-liberalization. The stage for this had been set in the long decade after Maastricht.

Although, as we have noted, the period from Maastricht to Lisbon—and, particularly, in the run up to the adoption of the euro as a hard currency in 2002—was characterized by tremendous Euro-enthusiasm among political elites, and the growing hegemony of a neo-liberal ideology in both East and West, below the surface rhetoric and the soothing message of converging bond yields, there were signs of cracks in the 'permissive consensus': and right in the core of Europe, as we will now examine.

4. Decline of traditional mass parties and the emergence of social resentment

As a domestic matter, the project of European integration had become increasingly intertwined with the 'third way' politics of Schröder, Blair, and Jospin. In conjunction with the narrowing of political positions, and a neo-liberal drift, in economic matters, on the part of social democratic parties, this could appositely be labelled a

[98] On the limitations and contradictions in Hungary's neo-liberal accumulation regime between 1990 and 2006, see Adam Fabry, *From State Capitalism to Authoritarian Neoliberalism* (Palgrave 2019) ch 4.

[99] See Eva Kiss, 'Foreign Direct Investment in Hungary: Industry and Its Spatial Effects' (2007) 45 Eastern European Economics 6. On the significance of foreign direct investment for the political economy of the Visegrad countries more generally, see Bohle and Greskovits (n 87) ch 4.

[100] See Bohle and Greskovits (n 87).

constellation of 'extreme centrism'.[101] The relationship between Europeanism and political centrism was not contingent: on the contrary, it was structural and ideological. As Simon Hix and Andreas Follesdal demonstrated in their classic article on the democratic deficit, despite the growing law-making powers of the European Parliament, the process of integration would entrench a centre-right bias in the law because of the constitutional primacy of market-making, multiplication of veto points, and the character of European Parliamentary elections.[102] European integration, as Chris Bickerton persuasively argued, functioned increasingly as a means to bypass domestic representative politics; part cause and part effect of the hollowing out of democracy.[103]

The EU's own institutions, largely insulated from public view, would become more conspicuous after Maastricht. Subject to the same kind of corruption scandals that had affected the EU member states, the Jacques Santer era culminated in the dramatic mass resignation of the entire Commission in March 1999, after the publication of the report of a committee of independent experts, on charges of fraud, mismanagement, and nepotism, after which it was seriously weakened.[104] Even the modest attempts to remedy the democratic deficit by increasing the formal law-making powers of the European Parliament were stymied by the legislative culture of secrecy and expert management, with negotiations taking place through so-called 'trialogues' between Parliament, Council, and Commission, which empowered bureaucratic decision-making behind closed doors.[105] Despite giving the European Parliament increased law-making powers, turnout for its elections continued to drop, falling below 50 per cent in June 1999 (and reflecting low levels of support for the EU, as recorded in the Eurobarometer surveys in 2000 and 2001).[106]

The 'democratic deficit' was, in fact, far deeper than any analysis of the EU's changing law-making processes (formal or informal), or of its popularity index, would reveal. To the extent that all European economies had become 'semi-sovereign', generalizing the post-war West German case described in Chapter 3, with the *demos* subject 'to a set of constraints and persuasions that lie outside [its] own direct control', the scope of partisan politics itself had been severely limited, affecting the capacity of parties to act as representative agents of popular or class interests.[107] The accelerated

[101] The term was later used by Tariq Ali to capture neo-liberal hegemony (see Tariq Ali, *The Extreme Centre: A Warning* (Verso 2015)).

[102] Simon Hix and Andreas Follesdal, 'Why There is a Democratic Deficit in the EU: A Response to Majone and Moravcsik' (2006) 44:3 JCMS 533–62.

[103] Chris Bickerton, *European Integration: From Nation-States to Member States* (OUP 2012).

[104] Giandomenico Majone, 'The Limits of Collective Action and Collective Leadership' in Damian Chalmers, Markus Jachtenfuchts, and Christian Joerges (eds), *The End of Eurocrats' Dream: Adjusting to Diversity* (CUP 2016) 230–31.

[105] Anne Elizabeth Stie, *Democratic Decision-making in the EU: Technocracy in Disguise* (Routledge 2013); Christine Reh and others, 'The Informal Politics of Legislation: Explaining Secluded Decision Making in the European Union' (2013) 46 Comparative Political Studies 1112; Christopher Lord, 'The Democratic Legitimacy of Codecision' (2013) 20 Journal of European Public Policy 1056; Katrin Huber and Michael Shackleton, 'Codecision: A Practitioner's View from Inside the Parliament' (2013) 20 Journal of European Public Policy 1040.

[106] Archived Eurobarometer reports are available at <https://ec.europa.eu/commfrontoffice/publicopinion/index.cfm/Survey/index#p=1&instruments=STANDARD> accessed 7 September 2020.

[107] Peter Mair, 'Political Parties, Popular Legitimacy and Public Privilege' in Jack Hayward (ed), *The Crisis of Representation in Europe* (Routledge 1996) 46. See also Fritz Scharpf, 'Democratic Legitimacy Under Conditions of Regulatory Competition: Why Europe Differs from the United States' in Kalypso Nicolaidis

decline of traditional partisan politics, and the transformation in the role of political parties, away from representative agencies and towards 'public office holders', was intimately connected with a process of integration that was emptying politics of content outside a narrow centre ground. If parties could no longer make a difference, it 'would then hardly be surprising to find that ordinary voters might also have despaired of a partisan intent'.[108] Nor was it surprising that the post-Maastricht period would coincide with a decline in party membership (relative to the electorate), 'reinforcing the sense of erosion in the position of the party on the ground'.[109] This sense of political limits would be heightened in the sheer range of coalition alternatives, where virtually all possible permutations and combinations of governing parties were tried and found wanting, none capable of offering a credible alternative to the status quo.

To be sure, a significant part of this narrowing of political possibilities was down to the more general decline or blurring of traditional identities within civil society, leading to the 'erosion of traditional boundaries based on class and religion, the changing patterns of social stratification, and the emergence of a greater emphasis on individualistic or particularistic identities'.[110] The individual as consumer rather than citizen had little need for political representation, existential meaning being conveyed by lifestyle choices that required only an enhanced personal freedom. This type of freedom would be increasingly regulated through provisions of non-discrimination, where EU law and policy would play a prominent role. Unlike traditional social policy, anti-discrimination law and policy was not about creating solidarity among the members of a collective, but about eliminating arbitrary factors that might affect individual choice.[111]

The erosion of traditional class identities and their political representation would be reinforced by a turn of the Liberal Left towards a politics of multiculturalism, cultural identity, and a moralizing discourse of inclusion, largely abandoning class struggle and emancipatory movements of solidarity.[112] This, too, was a continuation of earlier trends: the legacy of 1968, the new social movements of the 1970s, and the deradicalization of major communist parties in continental Europe, followed by their collapse with the end of the Cold War, and the rise of the 'New Right' thereafter.

Party decline, in itself, was only part of the story of changing social and political dynamics. Although divorced from class or popular bases, parties were, in another sense, becoming more powerful, more autonomous, and able to access far greater resources, not least due to the frequency with which they were able to access public office through coalition formation. The decline in membership did not mean a decline in funds; European parties, in fact, had more money at their disposal than ever before.

and Robert Howse (eds), *The Federal Vision: Legitimacy and Levels of Governance in the United States and European Union* (OUP 2001).

108 Mair (n 107) 47.

109 ibid 46.

110 ibid 50. See also Crouch (n 50).

111 See Alexander Somek, *Engineering Equality: An Essay on European Anti-Discrimination Law* (OUP 2011).

112 Alexander Somek, 'From Workers to Migrants, from Distributive Justice to Inclusion: Exploring the Changing Social Democratic Imagination' (2012) 18 European Law Journal 711. See also Moschonas (n 39).

What it signalled was a qualitative transformation; not only a disembedding from class, but also a re-embedding in the state; moving away from civil society towards integration into the state apparatus and a new establishment culture. From that position, parties could derive income, office, and access to state-regulated broadcasting, a combined strategy to increase their public profile and privileges.[113] A mutual dependency between state and party would then develop, connected to organizational and technological changes, with the growth of national media as the preferred form of communication with the electorate.[114] This even gave rise to a new ideal type; a form of representative government where the electorate appears 'above all, as an *audience* which responds to the terms that have been presented on the political stage', heralding rule by media expert.[115]

Although Peter Mair traces this trajectory back to the 1970s, and changes to the global economy associated with the era commonly described as neo-liberal, we saw in Part II that its roots were deeper, lying in the pacification of the *demos* from the 1950s. But Mair, correctly, noted that participation in the project of European integration could only act as an accelerant of this decline, with the opacity of European law-making and the Europeanization of policy-making further narrowing the scope for politics or, in Mair's own words, blurring differences within the mainstream to 'almost non-existence'.[116] What was new after Maastricht was the recognition that this transformation could no longer produce an equilibrium. On the contrary, a disequilibrium or contradiction appeared, between the decline of the representative role of parties and their increased set of public powers. Like Tocqueville's nobles, the status of political parties had increased while their popular relevance had 'eroded'.[117] This process was reinforced by the enhanced power and legitimacy of the state's bureaucratic apparatus (courts, regulatory agencies, independent commissions),[118] reaffirming 'people's belief in the existence of an undifferentiated political *casta* that rules in unrepresentative ways'.[119]

The most 'essential elements in the formation of social democracy's historical identity' were undermined by the EU: the orientation of social democratic appeals to the state, welfare politics, the link with the working class, and the belief in the primacy of

[113] Mair (n 107) 53–54 ('this movement from civil society to the state can be seen as part of a strategy by which the parties consciously attempt to ensure their own survival. The state, in this sense, is not some 'neutral' or 'external' agency which comes to the aid of the parties; rather, that state is the parties, or the parties are the state, in that it is the parties that are drawing up and then implementing the laws and proposals from which they benefit').

[114] These phenomena were picked up by theorists of radical democracy such as Chantal Mouffe and Ernesto Laclau, who advocated a Left populism as a means to fill in the void, thereby accelerating the distance of this new Left to Marx and class struggle (Chantal Mouffe and Ernesto Laclau, *Hegemony and Socialist Strategy: Towards a Radical Democratic Politics* (Verso 1985)). This came to prominence only in the euro crisis phase (examined in Part IV), with the advance of Syriza, Podemos, and Corbyn's Labour Party, all of which remained 'trapped in Europe'.

[115] Bernard Manin, *The Principles of Representative Government* (CUP 1997) 220 (one of three ideal types alongside parliamentarism and party democracy). Manin, extraordinarily, considers the channels of public communication in an audience democracy to be 'politically neutral, that is, non-partisan' (ibid 228).

[116] Mair (n 107) 47.

[117] ibid 55.

[118] Richard S Katz and Peter Mair, 'Changing Models of Party Organization and Party Democracy: the Emergence of the Cartel Party' (1995) 1 Party Politics 5.

[119] Bickerton, Hodson, and Puetter (n 50) 710.

politics.[120] Moreover, just as it contributed to severing its link to the working class, the EU would also be a mechanism for social democracy, which had become more firmly pro-European, 'to connect better with the salaried and educated middle strata of the population', reinforcing the tendency of the left to turn away from material politics, and towards cultural liberalism.[121]

Yet, the transformation in parliamentarism and party politics, significantly facilitated through the project of European integration and its 'external constraints', was unlikely to occur without a reaction, just as any relational theory of the constituent power would suggest.[122] As early as 1995, the stirrings of Euroscepticism across the continent, and across all parts of the political spectrum, but particularly on the Right, were identified as significant phenomena, the European project being a 'most appealing target for those seeking to highlight the gap between the people and the political elite'.[123] Although this would cause limited turmoil at the time, at least outside Italy, since Eurosceptic parties generally remained unable to break through in terms of electoral success and, therefore, remained outside governmental power, it exposed political and constitutional fault lines.

Although the formal constitutional challenges came from the German court, it was the French scene that exposed the material cracks. The French Left had suffered a traumatic ideological and political defeat in the early 1980s with Mitterrand's U-turn on Keynesian policies, and an embrace of austerity policies in anticipation of the reaction of the financial markets. It was not only that this marked the end of a *dirigiste* approach 'in favour of an "ordo-liberal", anti-inflationary and market-conforming solution', but that once the 'appropriate' development was conceived in these terms, it would set the path for future development, and all this 'despite the absence in France of the wider framework of (corporatist) institutions' upon which German ordoliberalism was itself predicated.[124]

In a significant respect, this failure anticipated the turn of the French liberal Left, and the larger part of the whole European Left, to a politics of Europeanism, under the promise, represented by Delors, of building a European social policy over the top of the single market.[125] That this would fail to materialize, even when social democratic

[120] Moschonas (n 39) 183.

[121] ibid 184.

[122] See Martin Loughlin, 'The Concept of Constituent Power' (2014) 13 European Journal of Political Theory 218.

[123] Andrew Gamble, 'Economic Recession and Disenchantment with Europe' in Jack Hayward (ed), *The Crisis of Representation in Europe* (Routledge 1996): 'Many new fringe parties outside the political centre have sought to take advantage of the new political climate. They include Fascist and Racist parties, as well as Green, nationalist and regionalist parties ... A characteristic which they all shared was populism' (ibid 159).

[124] Clift (n 58) 78–79.

[125] The legacy of Delors on the British Left was extraordinary. His speech to the TUC in 1988 signalled the practical end of a tradition of left-wing Euroscepticism, which lived on only on the fringes of the Labour party and broader movement. As Helen Thompson puts it, 'At a time when the Labour party still did not have a clear electoral strategy for returning to power, Delors effectively told the left that inside the EC it could protect what remained of its post-1945 political victories by insulating them in a "social European" sphere away from the reach of a Conservative government. Within a few years of Delors' speech, virtually all meaningful debate within the Labour party over the EC ended, even though very few in the party had any interest in pursuing Delors' general vision of a European political union built around monetary union': Helen Thompson, 'Returning to Democracy: The British Left and the Constitutional Temptation of the European Union' in Richard Ekins and Graham Gee (eds), *Judicial Power and the Left: Notes on a Sceptical Tradition* (Policy Exchange 2018). This is all the more extraordinary given that Delors' prescriptions were, in the

parties occupied the seats of power in a majority of member states in the late 1990s, demonstrated the structural difficulties, if not impossibility, of the task. The struggles of French statism were compounded by a German chancellor Schröder inclined towards the 'third way' discourse of Tony Blair, signalling the decline of the Rhineland model and embrace of a more Anglo-Saxon-style neo-liberal economy.[126]

The absence of any significant concrete achievements for social-democracy in the supranational constellation was not for lack of rhetorical critique aimed at Europe's neo-liberal market drift. Even centrist politicians were concerned about the dangers of European liberalization, exemplified by French prime minister Lionel Jospin's stark warning, in 2001, that a broader perspective on integration was required 'if Europe is not to decay into a mere market, sodden by globalization'.[127] Although it would become more celebrated through the euro crisis phase, Dani Rodrik's theorization of the 'trilemma' of economic integration, national sovereignty, and democratic mass politics had already led to wide acceptance of the 'diminished democracy' thesis.[128]

The French *petit oui* in the Maastricht referendum signalled the depth of the social cleavage. But this would profit mainly the far Right, the Left having largely surrendered the terrain of meaningful Euroscepticism.[129] As early as 1990, French political philosopher Marcel Gauchet had captured this phenomenon with the metaphor of a 'wall' emerging between the elites and the people, 'between an official, respectable France, which prides itself on its noble feelings, and a country of the marginalised', the 'ignoble', bitter from the denial even of its existence.[130] It was out of this 'social fracture', reinforced by the collapse of the Communist Party, that the Front Nationale's popularity grew, and would only increase as the state retreated further away from the discourse of sovereignty, and materially transferred more sovereign powers to the EU. Whereas the Left (and much of the intellectual class) would put its faith in a future EU as a complement for this process, the Right would present it as a scapegoat for the loss.[131]

words of Ralf Dahrendorf, 'an astonishing mixture of Keynes and Friedman, and conservative and traditional in inspiration' (cited in John Gillingham, *European Integration 1950–2003: Superstate or New Market Economy?* (CUP 2003) 160).

[126] On the unravelling of the German model of coordinated market economy in the process of neoliberalization, see Baccaro and Howell (n 69) 97–121.

[127] Quoted by Habermas 9 (n 54) ('In his magnificent speech of May 28, the French Prime Minister [Lionel Jospin] spoke of this "European way of life" as the content of a political project.').

[128] Dani Rodrik, 'How Far Will International Economic Integration Go?' (2000) 14 The Journal of Economic Perspectives 177. cf Giandomenico Majone, *Dilemmas of European Integration: The Ambiguities and Pitfalls of Integration by Stealth* (OUP 2005) 181–220 (in the same book, Majone suggested that a 'transnational constitutionalism' could supplant the need for European democracy, and downplayed the democratic deficit (23–24)).

[129] See Richard Dunphy, *Contesting Capitalism? Left Parties and European Integration* (Manchester University Press 2004).

[130] Marcel Gauchet, 'Les Mauvaises Surprises D'une Oublieé: La Lutte Des Classes' (1990) 60 Le Débat 257 (my translation).

[131] On the revival of nationalisms and connection with integration, see James Heartfield, 'European Union: A Process Without a Subject' in Christopher J Bickerton, Philip Cunliffe, and Alexander Gourevitch (eds), *Politics without Sovereignty: A Critique of Contemporary International Relations* (Routledge 2006).

The 'quiet revolution' that had been occurring through the project of integration would not go politically and socially unchallenged.[132] The Bolkestein Directive on the liberalization of trade in services had provoked intense debate and even mass protests in various EU countries, including France, Belgium, Denmark, and Sweden. On 21 March 2005, it was estimated that nearly 100,000 people marched in Brussels to protest against the Directive. Critics argued that it would erode many of the member states' regulations governing industry and the environment, and would lead to competition between workers in different parts of Europe, resulting in a general decline in income levels. The trope of the 'Polish plumber' became famous during the French debate, with social critics depicting the EU as a neo-liberal Trojan Horse, enforcing rules and policies that would lead to social dumping, as companies and jobs were relocated to Central and Eastern Europe to benefit from lower costs, less regulated economies, and weaker labour sectors.

Parts of the French Left, no longer subdued by Delors' promise, would then begin to openly revolt, protesting against the Constitutional Treaty on the grounds that it represented a further neo-liberalization of the economy. The French rejection of the Constitutional Treaty in 2005 (along with the Dutch) would highlight a more general rupture from the Delors consensus, as 'the temptation grew to switch from attempts to upload French (socialist) preferences to the European level towards a defensive stance, protecting the national French model from European-level intrusions'.[133] As Vivien Schmidt noted, with the Constitutional Treaty referendum, the EU's 'direct effects' on French politics were evidenced by 'cross-cutting cleavages for parties on the right as much as the left'. Indirectly, the EU, by 'removing more and more policy areas from the national political arena', was further 'narrowing the policy repertoire and space for political deliberation' and leading to an increase in domestic 'politics without policy'. In this context, national electorates would become 'frustrated by the inability of elected leaders to deal directly with the questions which are of greatest concern to them, such as globalization and immigration'.[134]

All of this contributed to the ongoing political disconnect: 'voter demobilization, on the one hand—evident in the increasing levels of abstentionism in French elections—and voter extremism—evident not only in the referendum on the Constitutional Treaty but also in the 2002 presidential election'.[135] The increasing disconnect of the project of integration from the popular masses would simultaneously reinforce the power of elites *and* make the whole edifice more fragile. As we examined in Chapter 6, domestic political elites transformed their constituency: accountability shifted away from electoral and representative devices towards peer review, new forms of delegation, and public management. Even 'ideational convergence' among the member states did not lead directly or straightforwardly to further supranationalization, but, rather, to intergovernmentalism and the creation of *de novo* bodies to manage the

[132] Krotz and Schild (n 3) 175 (citing Nikolas Jabko, *Playing the Market: A Political Strategy for Uniting Europe: 1985–2005* (Cornell University Press 2006)).

[133] Krotz and Schild (n 3) 173. See, further, Owen Parker, *Cosmopolitan Government in Europe: Citizens and Entrepreneurs in Postnational Politics* (Routledge 2013) 91–92 ('it was the *non* campaign mobilized by the left . . . that was arguably decisive in securing the rejection of the constitution').

[134] Vivien A Schmidt, *Democracy in Europe: The EU and National Polities* (OUP 2006) ch 4.

[135] Schmidt, 'Trapped by their Ideas' (n 84) 996–97.

integration process.[136] Institutional diversity remained, and there was only relatively weak public support for the new neo-liberal European social contract. The advances made, reflecting intergovernmental deliberation and elite-led consensus (often under the auspices of the new governance agenda or comitology), were not based on any popular programme, or on mass political mobilization. In fact, as exemplified in the French case, they occurred in spite of increasing popular discontent.

Elite concessions would be largely symbolic, as with the removal of 'free competition' from the preamble, and the 'repacking' of the Constitutional Treaty at Lisbon by jettisoning the symbols of European statehood (the flag and anthem), but without any substantial repatriation of sovereign powers. The warning signs, however, should have been obvious. The declared goal of the Laeken Declaration (drafted by a group of 'wise men') had been to bring the EU's institutions 'closer to its citizens'.[137] But it turned out that many of its citizens didn't much like what they saw. This resentment, and the social fractures underlying it, which were essentially domestic constructs, would remain relatively dormant and inconsequential until the euro crisis phase, to which we can now turn.

[136] Bickerton, Hodson, and Puetter (n 50). Ambivalence towards further supranationalization can even be seen in the ECJ itself, as in the Court's ruling on the Stability and Growth Pact (n 32) in July 2004, 'which underlined Member States' sovereignty in economic policy'.

[137] The group of 'wise men' comprised Belgian prime minister Dehaene, Italy's prime minister Giuliano Amato, former Commission president Jacques Delors, former Polish foreign minister Geremek, and future UK foreign secretary David Miliband. It would be chaired by 75-year-old former French president, Valery Giscard d'Estaing. See, further, Paul Berman, 'From Laeken to Lisbon: The Origins and Negotiation of the Lisbon Treaty' in Andrea Biondi, Piet Eekhout, and Stefanie Ripley (eds), *EU Law After Lisbon* (OUP 2012).

PART IV
EURO CRISIS: THE UNFINISHED CONJUNCTURE

The ink was barely dry on the Treaty of Lisbon when the global financial crisis demonstrated that the EU was not fit for the purpose of tackling it. Signed in December 2007, Lisbon had adopted most of the substantive aspects of the failed Constitutional Treaty but abandoned its symbolic adornments. It took two years to come into force, ratification being held up by (another) Irish referendum rejection, resistance by Czech president Vaclav Klaus, and constitutional challenge in Germany.[1] When it was finally ratified in December 2009, it closed a decade-long set of intergovernmental negotiations that had begun in Nice, with the Laeken declaration. It was thought to have brought an element of finality to the reform process; the last Treaty change for a generation, after a protracted and troubled road.[2] It was soon evident that the trouble had only just begun.

At the dawn of the new millennium, Europe had been hailed as a 'model for the nations of the world'.[3] The euro was set to become a global reserve currency, rivalling or even displacing the dollar for world economic importance. The European Union had attained a 'stable constitutional equilibrium'; its democratic deficit and market liberal trajectory entirely justifiable, according to leading commentators.[4] Authoritarian liberalism was flourishing, not least in those parts of the academy intent on dismissing the 'ignorant, irrelevant and ideological' populace from participation in the process,

[1] The *Lisbon* decision of the German Constitutional Court, examined in Chapter 4.

[2] See Paul Berman, 'From Laeken to Lisbon: The Origin and Negotiation of the Lisbon Treaty' in Andrea Biondi, Piet Eekhout, and Stefanie Ripley (eds), *EU Law After Lisbon* (OUP 2012): 'It spanned a Convention, two Intergovernmental Conferences (IGCs), the agreement and abandonment of a Constitutional Treaty, six referendums in Member States including three critical 'no' votes, a 'period of reflection', successive fraught negotiations and last-minute deals at European summits, long debates in national Parliaments, and, even after the text had been agreed and signed, the negotiation of two further Protocols and other texts to get the Treaty over the finishing line' (ibid 3).

[3] See Perry Anderson, *The New Old World* (Verso 2009) 47–48.

[4] Andrew Moravcsik, 'In Defence of the Democratic Deficit: Reassessing Legitimacy in the European Union' (2002) 4 Journal of Common Market Studies 618; Andrew Moravcsik, 'The European Constitutional Compromise and the Neo-Functionalist Legacy' (2005) 2 Journal of European Public Policy 349. European issues, Moravcsik argued, were not that important to voters, being, in their nature, of minimal political and economic salience. Writing in 2008, Moravcsik opined that the integration process had reached an 'institutional plateau', which he labelled the 'European constitutional settlement' (Andrew Moravcsik, 'The European Constitutional Settlement' (2008) 31 World Economy 157).

after they had dared to reject the Constitutional Treaty.[5] Even some less supine voices remained eager to defend the status quo, and celebrate the EU's unique achievements as a *sui generic* or post-state polity, pursuing its chosen *Sonderweg* in the face of recalcitrant populations.[6]

'Constitution-making has hitherto been a response to situations of crisis', it was noted by Jürgen Habermas, in a celebrated essay from 2001 that signalled the prelude to the ill-fated constitutional experiment. But, 'where', he asked, 'is such a challenge . . . in today's rather wealthy and peaceful societies of Western Europe?' Less than a decade later, this would seem both ironic, and distant in tone, as the euro crisis response tore up the already-weakened social contracts in the debtor states.[7]

Despite the Panglossian veneer, it could not be said that the troubles the EU came to face in the decade after Lisbon were entirely unforeseen. Dissenting voices had existed, and not only in the margins of the academy or the fringes of Eurosceptic political parties. In the 'decade of self-doubt' that followed the Maastricht Treaty, there had been a growing concern over Europe's social, political, and democratic deficits, and a growing sense of its impending legitimacy crisis.[8] These were clearly signposted at the national level by the German Constitutional Court, and the ensuing debate on the legitimacy of the European construct and its compatibility with domestic constitutions. Outside of the academy, the warnings were sounded even by centrist pro-European politicians.[9] Others, too, had concerns about its liberal economic logic, and articulated problems of a similar type, lamenting the market-driven ethos of the EU, and its lack of political market-correcting capacity.[10] But, as we saw in Part III, the social cleavages exposed by the *petit oui* at Maastricht, amid other signs of apathy and alienation—such as declining voter turnout, particularly for European Parliament elections—were largely exploited by the right, the liberal left cleaving hard to its European vocation.

[5] Andrew Moravcsik, 'What can we Learn from the Collapse of the European Constitutional Project?' (2006) 47 Politische Vierteljahresschrift 219 (Moravcsik considered the collapse of the constitutional project to demonstrate the EU's stability and success).

[6] Joseph HH Weiler, 'In Defence of the Status Quo: Europe's Constitutional Sonderweg' in JHH Weiler and Marlene Wind (eds), *European Constitutionalism Beyond the State* (CUP 2003) 7–27; cf Joseph HH Weiler, *The Constitution of Europe: 'Do the New Clothes have an Emperor?' and other Essays on European Integration* (CUP 1999) ch 7 (Weiler, 'The Constitution of Europe').

[7] Jürgen Habermas, 'Why Europe Needs a Constitution' (2001) 11 New Left Review 5(Habermas, 'Why Europe Needs a Constitution').

[8] On the general issue of the EU's legitimacy post-Maastricht see, eg Gráinne de Búrca, 'The Quest for Legitimacy in the European Union' (1994) 59 Modern Law Review 349. Joseph Weiler talked of a 'crisis of ideals' that the Europe of Maastricht suffered from, in 'The Constitution of Europe (n 6) 238–40. See, further, Carol Harlow, 'Citizen Access to Political Power in the European Union' (1999) EUI-RSCAS Working Papers 99/02. Specifically on its social deficit, see Christian Joerges, 'What is Left of the European Economic Constitution? A Melancholic Eulogy' (2005) 30 European Law Review 461. On the general democratic deficit of the Union, see Simon Hix and Andreas Follesdal, 'Why There is a Democratic Deficit in the EU: A Response to Majone and Moravcsik' (2006) 44 Journal of Common Market Studies 533.

[9] In his speech in 2001, Lionel Jospin, for example, warned that Europe might 'decay into a mere market, sodden by globalization' (quoted approvingly by Habermas, 'Why Europe Needs a Constitution' (n 7) 9: 'In his magnificent speech of May 28, the French Prime Minister [Lionel Jospin] spoke of this "European way of life" as the content of a political project.').

[10] This refrain grew after Maastricht, and found powerful and concise articulation in the work of Fritz Scharpf and then, particularly through the crisis phase, Wolfgang Streeck. See Fritz W Scharpf, *Governing in Europe: Effective and Democratic?* (OUP 1999); Wolfgang Streeck, *Buying Time: On the Delayed Crisis of Democratic Capitalism* (Verso 2014).

If the political (and academic) discontent, although real, remained largely inconsequential in the post-Maastricht era, this would change with the global financial crisis. This ostensibly began in the US in 2008 with the collapse of Lehman Brothers, but soon centred on Europe, and the eurozone in particular. Initially, the 'fin de millennium' European triumphalism was replaced with a shrug. This was, in essence, an 'American problem'; or, when it became apparent that it would not be contained there, one rooted in the interconnectedness of transnational capitalism and its inflated financial sector.[11] Once attention shifted to the eurozone, in 2010 and 2011, evaluations of the European Union, and especially the eurozone, were quickly and dramatically downgraded.[12] Complacency soon gave way to grim pessimism, the euro crisis conjuncture heralding no less than the 'end of the West', according to David Marquand.[13] Unless it finds the capacity to start again 'on radically new bases', Etienne Balibar lamented, 'Europe is a dead political project'.[14] Even on a more sober assessment, such as that made by Weiler in 2011, there was 'grave crisis' in Europe, the EU reaching a 'nadir which one cannot remember for many decades'.[15]

As outlined in Parts II and III, the reconstitution of Europe in the post-war and Maastricht eras had laid the ground for this conjuncture, as well as establishing the conditions for its *irresolution*. Maastricht, signed in 1992, and soon complemented by the 1997 Treaty of Amsterdam, had established the (incomplete) constitutional structure of EMU, absorbed the Schengen regime, opened the door to differentiated integration, and anticipated the enlargement of Europe to the East. It had also marked a change in the material and ideological balance of power: reunification reinstated the 'German question', and the end of any really existing alternative to liberal capitalism unleashed an ideologically hegemonic neo-liberalism, with not only centrists but erstwhile critical theorists calling an end to any emancipatory projects.[16] The long process of depoliticization had reached its apogee in domestic contexts of a 'third way politics' that offered little alternative to the neo-liberal paradigm, and in many cases deepened it. European integration reinforced the edifice of authoritarian liberalism through its

[11] Magnus Ryner, 'Europe's Ordoliberal Iron Cage: Critical Political Economy, the Euro Area Crisis, and its Management' (2015) 22 Journal of European Public Policy 275.

[12] cf Armin von Bogdandy, who began an article, published well after the troubles in the eurozone, with the remarkably understated, 'Europe is not a democratic showcase', but went on to argue that democracy beyond the state does not substitute but 'complements domestic forms': see Armin von Bogdandy, 'The European Lesson for International Democracy: The Significance of Articles 9 to 12 EU Treaty for International Organizations' (2012) 23 European Journal of International Law 315, 322. Any other conclusion would be 'useless' for legal doctrine, since, unable to give meaning to a term of positive law, the 'democracy' of Article 2 TEU (ibid 323). European Union can provide a model for the democratization of the international arena, we were informed, without a trace of irony.

[13] David Marquand, *The End of the West: The Once and Future Europe* (Princeton University Press 2012).

[14] Étienne Balibar, 'Europe: Final Crisis? Some Theses' (2010) 13 Theory & Event.

[15] Joseph HH Weiler, '60 Years Since the First European Community—Reflections on Political Messianism' (2011) 22 European Journal of International Law 303.

[16] Most notably Jürgen Habermas, declaring that, since 1989, 'it has become impossible to break out of the universe of capitalism; the only remaining option is to civilize and tame the capitalist dynamic from within', in Jürgen Habermas, *The Crisis of the European Union: A Response* (Polity Press 2012) 106 (the same Habermas who would later declare Brexit the defeat of capitalism by populism; see Thomas Assheuer, 'The Players Resign—Core Europe to the Rescue: a Conversation with Jürgen Habermas about Brexit and the EU Crisis' *Die Zeit* (Hamburg, 12 July 2016) <http://www.zeit.de/kultur/2016-07/juergen-habermas-brexit-eu-crises-english> accessed 24 September 2020).

institutional procedures of consensual law-making, constitutionalization of the Treaty provisions, and entrenched commitments to market liberalism and technocratic authority. In the absence of any robust supranational democratization, it left member states with 'politics but no policies', and the EU with 'policies but no politics'.[17]

In the absence of channels to contest the direction of European politics, the only option was to politically contest Europe itself. And, yet, due to the profound grip of European integration on post-war cultural imagination, as well as on dominant material interests and identities, there was limited appetite to channel this dissent.[18] The permissive consensus of the founding period, which had given way to a 'constraining dissensus' after Maastricht, was fuelling 'a destructive dissensus', as the divide grew 'between integrationist leaders and a sceptical public'.[19] Developments through the euro crisis phase would, then, cast doubt on the very sustainability of the EU: it became an existential crisis.

The concentration of power in executive branches of government continued and accelerated a trend that was launched in earnest at Maastricht. Through the euro crisis, intergovernmental authority and informal power would be exercised in an increasingly coercive fashion, and elected heads of governments would be dispatched and replaced with technocratic leaders, notably in Italy and Greece. Developments lacked even the semblance of conventional supranational institution-building or law-making, often under the guise of 'necessity' and 'emergency'.[20] Experimentation, new governance, and deliberative supranationalism were forgotten, replaced with 'post-democratic executive federalism'.[21] In this period, a formal institution—the European Central Bank—and a 'formally informal' and intergovernmental 'Eurogroup' (finance ministers of the euro area member states) would take the lead, along with Germany's chancellor, Angela Merkel, and her finance minister, Wolfgang Schäuble.[22] Previously tempered by global geopolitics and institutional constraints (as outlined in Parts II and III), asymmetries of sovereign power hardened; among blocs of states, as much as bilaterally. Germany took on a more dominant role, but one which fell short of the clear

[17] See Vivien Ann Schmidt, *Democracy in Europe: The EU and National Polities* (OUP 2006) ch 4.

[18] One of the extraordinary effects of the Brexit vote was that a 'Remainist' class was politically re-awakened when it felt that its interests and identity were threatened (see Daniel Cohen, 'Loud, Obsessive, Tribal: The Radicalisation of Remain' *The Guardian* (London, 13 August 2019) <https://www.theguardian.com/politics/2019/aug/13/brexit-remain-radicalisation-fbpe-peoples-vote> accessed 24 September 2020.

[19] Dermot Hodson and Uwe Puetter, 'The European Union in Disequilibrium: New Intergovernmentalism, Postfunctionalism and Integration Theory in the Post-Maastricht Period' (2019) 26 Journal of European Public Policy 1153, 1154.

[20] Jonathan White, 'Emergency Europe' (2016) 63 Political Studies 300.

[21] See Christopher J Bickerton, Dermot Hodson, and Uwe Puetter, 'The New Intergovernmentalism: European Integration in the Post-Maastricht Era' (2015) 53 Journal of Common Market Studies 703.

[22] As Stefano Bartolini put it, the monetary subsystem is a 'federal subsystem in a non-federal system': Stefano Bartolini, *Restructuring Europe: Centre Formation, System Building, and Political Structuring between the Nation-State and the European Union* (OUP 2005) 374. On the Eurogroup's origins in the late 1990s, see Uwe Puetter, 'The Informal Eurogroup: A New Working Method and Institutional Compromise' (2001) ConWEB No 02/2001. <https://www.wiso.uni-hamburg.de/fachbereich-sowi/professuren/wiener/dokumente/conwebpaperspdfs/2001/conweb-2-2001.pdf>. As Bickerton explains, the Eurogroup is neither supranational nor merely intergovernmental ('its working methods resemble more those of an epistemic community than they do of an intergovernmental forum' (Chris Bickerton, *European Integration: From Nation-States to Member States* (OUP 2012) 36)).

hegemonic leadership required to 'stabilize' the region, suggesting a 'semi-hegemonic' formation in which Germany was powerful enough to prevent collapse, but not powerful enough to resolve structural tensions. This 'in-between' status was due to supranational, as well as domestic, political and constitutional constraints. It meant that crisis could be deferred, but not resolved: Europe would stumble rather than fall.

What has been described here as a passive form of authoritarian liberalism became more active in the repression of democracy; particularly once opposition to the 'Troika' (the ECB, Commission, and IMF) and associated conditionality turned from disorganized resentment into more focussed political struggle against 'austerity', and the prospect of a rupture of the post-war settlement from the Left emerged in Athens.

What was new, in response, was the more explicit closing down of any alternatives, and the identification of an ideological enemy to the European economic project. Some commentators explicitly identified 'bad Europeans' as those who disregarded the economic stability criteria.[23] According to Donald Tusk, then European Council president, the notion that there could be any alternative to austerity was an 'ideological illusion'. Tusk, approving the ordoliberal world view, even associated resistance to austerity as somehow 'anti-German':

> If I look for something inspiring when it comes to the economy, I am ready to look towards something wise and responsible ... For me, maybe the best school of thinking is the so-called 'ordoliberals' in Germany, in this critical time after the Second World War. Very pragmatic, no ideology, no illusions. Books and also practical politics from [Ludwig] Erhard, [Walter] Eucken, [Wilhelm] Röpke. This, for me, is the source of thoughts that can be very useful for today. Wilhelm Röpke thought—and I think it's very relevant here today—we have too much Rousseau and Voltaire and not enough Montesquieu.[24]

It was always possible that a domestic electorate might acquiesce in the narrative that 'there is no alternative' to neo-liberal structural reforms, or even embrace this narrative as a political ideology. But through the euro crisis phase, structural reform was not offered as one path among many; it was a constitutional constraint of membership, structurally and ideologically hegemonic despite its *partisan* nature. Austerity would be partisan in both political-economic and geopolitical terms, favouring the class interests of those with assets, and countries with export-led growth models,[25] even as its apparent irrationality as a curb on overall economic growth was entering the mainstream of debate.[26]

[23] Identifying the 'enemy within' the neo-liberal constitutionalism as those 'bad Europeans' who disregarded the stability criteria, see Udo Di Fabio, 'Karlsruhe Makes a Referral' (2014) 15 German Law Journal 107. For Di Fabio, the crisis was caused not by financial problems accumulated over years of neo-liberal excesses (as even many of its architects conceded), but by 'massive violations of the law', without explaining the chain of causation. He also appeared to query the independence of the ECJ because it had a Greek president.

[24] See Peter Spiegel, 'The Donald Tusk Interview: Annotated Transcript' *Financial Times* (London, 16 July 2015) <https://www.ft.com/content/ff50e5a9-7b15-3998-a9f1-c11359dc01b8> accessed 24 September 2020.

[25] As Mark Blyth argued: see Mark Blyth, *Austerity: The History of a Dangerous Idea* (OUP 2013).

[26] See, eg Paul Krugman, 'Europe's Austerity Madness' *New York Times* (New York, 27 September 2012) <https://www.nytimes.com/2012/09/28/opinion/krugman-europes-austerity-madness.html> accessed 24 September 2020.

The heightened authoritarianism that was used to push through structural reform was, thus, both transformative yet also conservative of the post-war constitutional constellation. To be sure, it could be argued that the euro regime mutated from a nominally rule-based structure, accompanied by market discipline, to a discretionary order reinforced by bureaucratic power.[27] This would not be a temporary suspension of normality, in response to a situation with a clearly demarcated end point, or with the limits of a sunset clause. It was open-ended and future-oriented. And it had *a conservative aim*.[28]

This is not to say that there was nothing new in the material constitution of neo-liberalism as a specific regime of capital accumulation, so dependent, as it had become, on financialization of the economy, privatization, and the opening up of new markets, as we saw in Chapter 8.[29] The 'consolidation state' of the euro crisis decade differed from the 'debt state' of the neo-liberal period beginning in the late 1970s, and the 'tax state' of the 'golden age' that preceded it. This was most obvious in the management of resource accumulation and distribution, and the changing capital-labour relations that emerged with the economic and political weakening of the working class.[30] But the aim of the institutional mutations, substantively, was not to change, but *to maintain*, the existing material constitution of Europe, including its geopolitical configuration, and its fundamental market-driven objectives.

What was ultimately striking was the lack of any alternative to the post-war project of integration in the European constitutional imagination, just when it appeared to be most needed. The contestation that was generated did not lead to any definitive resolution, but only to a series of fudges, often played out in judicial disputes.[31] Authoritarian liberalism was sustained, in the final analysis, not as a result of *supranational* constraints, but as a symptom of the loss of political freedom, and of the disappearance of the practice and discourse of constituent power—the power to establish a new constitutional order—marking a decline that had begun with the post-war settlement. What were decisive were the *supraconstitutional* constraints; those which limited the constitutional imagination to legal constitutionalism and deliberative democracy, and suppressed notions of popular sovereignty.[32]

[27] This was argued by Michael Ioannidis, 'Europe's New Transformations: How the EU Economic Constitution Changed During the Eurozone Crisis' (2016) 53 Common Market Law Review 1237, drawing on Ackerman's notion of a constitutional moment. It is notable, however, that Ioannidis, as many others, focussed on moral hazard in a completely one-sided manner, focussing on the risk in dis-incentivizing prudent economic management on the part of the public debtor, and neglecting the recklessness of the private creditor.

[28] On the internal link between a policy regime governed by rules and far-reaching discretion, see Jonathan White, 'Policy Between Rules and Discretion' in Josef Hien and Christian Joerges (eds), *Ordoliberalism, Law and the Rule of Economics* (Hart Publishing 2017) 289.

[29] For a useful account, see Ben Fine and Alfredo Saad-Filho, 'Thirteen Things You Need to Know about Neoliberalism' (2017) 43 Critical Sociology 685.

[30] Streeck (n 10).

[31] This would continue after the OMT saga in the *Weiss* case: see Michael A Wilkinson, 'Flight, Fight or Fudge: First Reflections on the PSPP Judgment of the German Constitutional Court' (*Verfassungsblog*, 6 May 2020) <https://verfassungsblog.de/fight-flight-or-fudge/> accessed 24 September 2020.

[32] See, further, Alexander Somek and Michael A Wilkinson, 'Unpopular Sovereignty?' (2020) 83 Modern Law Review 955.

The extent of these informal constraints became clear through the pivotal event of the decade, and the focal point of this chapter: the election, in January 2015, of an anti-austerity, but pro-European, party in Greece; this appeared, momentarily, to have pushed matters to a head, its flamboyant finance minister Yanis Varoufakis leading rhetorical confrontation with the Eurogroup. Syriza eventually came armed with the extraordinary democratic mandate of the '*oxi*' referendum of July 2015, when the Greek electorate, against all expectations, voted 'no!' (*oxi*) to the conditionality programme. But Syriza had no credible exit plan.[33] With its eventual capitulation shortly after, the tension between Syriza's social democratic programme and European economic integration was resolved decisively in favour of remaining in the EU. As Greece signed up to a memorandum imposing even harsher conditionality than the one rejected in the referendum, the lights appeared to go out on any alternative to the status quo.

This Part examines the latest act in the drama: the decade since the global financial crisis, strangely inconclusive yet clearly indicative of future prospects. The series of tensions identified after Maastricht, and examined in part III (constitutional differentiation and the return of the 'German question', post-sovereign constitutionalism and the return of political sovereignty, the dominance of neo-liberalism and the emergence of anti-systemic alternatives) become contradictions, and if resolved at all, only in a tentative, provisional manner, giving rise to new problems, not least the rise of authoritarian populism from within the EU (to be addressed in the Conclusion).

Part IV proceeds as follows: Chapter 9 examines inter-state sovereignty after Lisbon, and through the eurozone crisis. On its surface, Lisbon represented a fudge: maintaining much of the substance of the constitutional project, but without the constitutional symbolism, and lacking popular support in key states. Through the euro crisis, this fudge became unsustainable: the issue of sovereignty could no longer be held in suspension, but would increasingly be exercised outside the EU legal framework. New informal formations took centre stage—notably the 'Troika' and the Eurogroup— exercising both de facto power and *de jure* authority, to avoid the formal constraints of the Maastricht Treaty, while maintaining its ordoliberal spirit and substance. Sovereignty was increasingly drained of any content, at least for some states, its loss appearing as the quid pro quo for accepting financial assistance. All of this puts the issue of German hegemony back on the agenda, suggesting a regional authoritarian liberalism writ large, more coercive and less consensual than in the foundational period.

Chapter 10 examines the political constitution of Europe in the post-Lisbon era. The disconnect identified in Chapter 7 grows apace: postnational discourse incongruent with the fetters on further integration placed by a rigid Treaty and (one of) the member states' domestic constitutions. This is exemplified by the OMT saga, in

[33] In the end it was Wolfgang Schäuble who would table 'Grexit', which should really have been little surprise since the same Schäuble, never convinced that countries like Greece (or even Italy) belonged in the eurozone at all, had argued for an exclusive core Europe already, in the 1990s (as we saw in Chapter 6). On the possibility and desirability of exit from EMU, see Costas Lapavitsas, 'Planning an Exit from the EMU' in Eva Nanopoulos and Fotis Vergis (eds), *The Crisis Behind the Eurocrisis: The Eurocrisis as a Multidimensional Systemic Crisis of the EU* (CUP 2019) 403–19; Heiner Flassbeck and Costas Lapavitsas, *Against the Troika: Crisis and Austerity in the Eurozone* (Verso 2015).

which the German Constitutional Court threatened, after decades of barking, to finally 'bite'; and against an ECB programme that had existential implications for the eurozone. The ECJ's assertive ruling in response did not, however, signal the perfection of the European constitutionalist project (as the 'new constitutionalists' claimed) but revealed its precarity, in effect rubber-stamping a programme that was of a dubious legitimacy.[34] If this would 'buy time' for the Union, and assuage fears that strict enforcement of the Maastricht rules might lead to its unravelling, it would do so in a way that merely concealed its dysfunctionality. Authoritarian liberalism was left intact and juridically fortified, but left open to further institutional contestation.

Chapter 11 turns to the material constitution of the decade-long crisis, specifically the dominance of ordo- and neo-liberalism, and the erosion of democracy. The imposition of austerity was a function of ideological commitments that stretched back to the Maastricht era and earlier, deepening the economic liberal market rationality of integration, but now dismantling domestic social contracts in a harsher manner, in a more disciplinary mode; if, ultimately, still under the guidance of domestic elites. This did not go uncontested by popular movements. Extraordinary countermovements emerged to try to break out of the straitjacket of economic liberalism, notably through the election to government in Greece, in January 2015, of a left-wing anti-austerity party, Syriza, which reflected broader anti-systemic currents across Europe. Syriza's subsequent capitulation symbolized not merely the increasingly powerful (but also dysfunctional) external constraints of EU membership, but the home-grown roots of the dominant constitutional imaginary: a fear of popular sovereignty, and of radical democracy, under the veil of an ideological Europeanism.

[34] See Claire Kilpatrick, 'On the Rule of Law and Economic Emergency: The Degradation of Basic Legal Values in Europe's Bailouts' (2015) 35 Oxford Journal of Legal Studies 325; Jonathan Tomkin, 'Contradiction, Circumvention, and Conceptual Gymnastics: The Impact of the Adoption of the ESM Treaty on the State of European Democracy' (2013) 14 German Law Journal 169.

9
Authoritarian Liberalism Writ Large: the Spectre of a 'German Europe'

1. Introduction

A tension in the geopolitical constitution of Europe had emerged in the post-Maastricht era. This tension arose between further enlargement of the political space and deeper integration (in discrete but significant policy areas) on the one hand, and increasing intergovernmental differentiation, asymmetry, and even the spectre of German semi-hegemony on the other. If the official EU discourse was of a 'widening and deepening' of the Union, the reality was a fragmentation of authority and a loosening of its foundational support. The single currency was the symbol—at once—of unity, a new area of transfer of sovereign powers; of one of the key 'markers of sovereignty'; *and* of an incomplete Union with differentiation among its members, subject to opt-outs and transitional arrangements. This tension was captured by the 'new intergovernmentalism' and the prospect, if not (yet) the reality, of German ascendency (as detailed in Chapter 6).

After Lisbon, this tension between expansion and extension of the EU's powers, and a weakening in its authority and support, would heighten. Enlargement continued, with the accession of Croatia in 2013, and continuation of negotiations with the states of the Western Balkans, and the Treaty of Lisbon would, again, prescribe further and deeper integration in discrete policy areas. But the pace of enlargement was reduced in comparison with the Maastricht era, and Europe's external borders became more geopolitically consequential with the emergence of friction with Russia. Regionally, the spectre of German hegemony appeared closer on the horizon.

Integration proceeded, but without the unitary symbolism of a single constitutional document or constitutional moment. The member states remained firmly the 'Masters of the Treaty', and, for the first time, Lisbon granted them the formal authority to leave the Union. To the extent that democracy had not already been 'hollowed out', it was restricted to the domestic arena. This was only highlighted by innovations such as the European Citizens' Initiative (ECI), and the attempts to empower national parliaments through dialogue and warning systems based on the principle of subsidiarity.[1] These proved to be ineffective at generating democratic engagement with the Union, either at domestic or supranational level.

Lisbon itself was a masterpiece of ambivalence, signalling 'both the beginning and the end of a European constitution depending on whether one is an optimist or a

[1] Christine Reh, 'The Lisbon Treaty: De-Constitutionalizing the European Union?' (2009) 47 Journal of Common Market Studies 625, 641. On the 'early warning system' and Barroso Initiative, see Davor Jančić, 'The Barroso Initiative: Window Dressing or Democracy Boost?' (2012) 8 Utrecht Law Review 78.

Authoritarian Liberalism and the Transformation of Modern Europe. Michael A Wilkinson, Oxford University Press.
 DOI: 10.1093/oso/9780198854753.003.0010

pessimist'. It was a geo-constitutional fudge (section 2).[2] This ambivalence would be resolved through the euro crisis phase, as major changes occurred outside the Treaty altogether, bypassing its mechanisms of legal and political accountability, and ending the democratic federal dream (section 3). In the process, the EU would come to resemble a semi-hegemonic 'German Europe', the kind of political form which integration was originally intended to prevent (section 4).

2. The Lisbon Treaty: a geo-constitutional fudge

The prospect of accession to the EU would no longer represent merely an invitation to join (or rejoin) European liberal market democracy, but to participate in a 'geopolitical game' involving Washington and the Kremlin as well as Berlin, Paris, and London. Although the ideological battles of the Cold War were long over, the geopolitical tensions were not, with the question of the positioning of Ukraine, Moldova, and Georgia reigniting the issue of the boundary between Euro-Atlantic and Russian zones of influence on the continent.[3] The question of Turkish EU membership would also remain unresolved. External boundary issues, and the precise contours of Europe's geographical space, would be studiously avoided by the Treaty of Lisbon, despite the assertion of its constitutional finality.

The introduction of a secession clause (Article 50 TEU), a development cautioned against by representatives of the 'founding six', and also intended as a merely symbolic gesture, primarily for public consumption as means to highlight the voluntarism of the endeavour, nevertheless formally changed the basic rules of the game, and possibly the nature of the entity.[4] Although its significance was little appreciated at the time, the formalization of exit would not only be central to the 'Brexit' event that would take place in 2016, but would also be used by a new brand of European constitutionalists to justify increasingly centralized *juridical* authority exerted by the ECJ (examined more fully in Chapter 10).

Article 50 would underline member state *sovereignty*. It was considered to cement the authority of the 'Masters of the Treaties', and to strengthen the hand of large member states, in particular, who could threaten its use to gain advantage in inter-state bargaining. The possibility of exit introduced a 'territorial flexibility unimaginable in any thick constitution',[5] adding a sense of 'deconstitutionalization' that was reinforced by dropping the 'primacy of EU law' from the foundational text and relegating it to a declaration attached to the Treaty. To the extent that the Union was brought 'closer to the citizen', it was largely through the attempt to empower national parliaments, giving

[2] Chris Bickerton, *European Integration: From Nation-States to Member States* (OUP 2012) 43.

[3] Luuk van Middelaar, *The Passage to Europe: How a Continent Became a Union* (YUP 2013).

[4] Voluntary exit contradicts the political form of the federation, which, in so many other respects, the EU resembles (see Signe Larsen, *The Constitutional Theory of the Federation and the European Union* (OUP 2021)). It also contradicts the foundational jurisprudence: in *Costa v ENEL*, the ECJ had declared that membership entailed '*permanent* limitation of sovereign rights' (see Chapter 3). A common view, prior to Lisbon, was that there was no unilateral right to withdraw from the EU.

[5] Reh (n 1) 637.

them the opportunity through the 'early warning system' to issue a 'yellow card' and 'orange card' against legislative proposals from the Commission.[6]

The Lisbon Treaty formally achieved the replacement of Maastricht's pillar structure with a single framework, albeit comprising two texts of equal value: the Treaty on the Functioning of the European Union (TFEU), and the Treaty on European Union (TEU). Although it declared a new foundation—Article 2 TEU proclaimed the Union to be based on the values of respect for human dignity, freedom, democracy, equality, the rule of law, and respect for human rights—these potentially conflicting and deeply contestable provisions were given little political direction or substantive attention. Furthermore, their sincerity would be somewhat undermined by the failure of the EU (in violation of Article 6(2) TEU) to accede to the European Convention on Human Rights.[7] This failure, based on the ECJ's negative opinion on the matter, cast doubts on its own commitment to human rights, and cemented the ECJ's position as the guardian of an 'economic constitution without qualifiers'. Its own 'European exceptionalism' would only underline the hypocritical instrumentalization of human rights as the legal source for contesting later developments in Hungary and Poland.[8]

In the reformulation of the EU's foundational commitments, extending rhetorically far beyond the narrow economic remit of Rome, *democracy* would paradoxically be *reduced* to a mere value alongside others, with which it might compete, rather than privileged as the process through which to realize, achieve, or negotiate competing visions of the public good.[9] According to Article 10 TEU, the Union was to be founded on the principle of representative democracy. But, if the European Parliament had gained increased powers, there was little reconnection with voters (turnout fell in every election until 2019, reaching a low of 42.5 per cent in 2014), and mobile Union citizens were politically disenfranchised from the most significant domestic elections and referenda.[10]

The 'democracy deficit' also pervaded the process of enlargement.[11] It would be for the Commission to decide whether the Copenhagen criteria had been satisfied, an 'exercise in liberal imperialism' designed 'to give the Union control over developments in the post-Communist space'.[12] Although enlargement was not the first attempt to remake European societies from above, it may have been the first not to be attempted through force. But if this 'revolution from above' was not coercive, it was, nevertheless,

[6] See Marco Goldoni, 'Reconstructing the Early Warning System on Subsidiarity: The Case for Political Judgment' (2014) 39 European Law Review 647.

[7] It did promulgate its own 'Charter of Fundamental Rights of the European Union', but this was considered by many as merely declaratory (which also meant that the UK and Poland obtaining a protocol distancing themselves from it was of limited juridical significance).

[8] Turkuler Isiksel, 'European Exceptionalism and the EU's Accession to the ECHR' (2016) 27 European Journal of International Law 565; cf Daniel Halberstam, 'It's the Autonomy Stupid: A Modest Defence of Opinion 2/13 on EU Accession to the ECHR, and the Way Forward' (2016) 16 German Law Journal 105.

[9] The preamble to the TEU at Maastricht had given precedence to liberty and democracy over human rights and fundamental freedoms, and the rule of law. Instead, dignity (mimicking the German Basic Law), would now take pride of place.

[10] This became a major topic of discussion after the Brexit referendum.

[11] David Marquand, *The End of the West: The Once and Future Europe* (Princeton University Press 2011) ch 5.

[12] ibid 149 (quoting Jan Zielonka, *Europe as Empire: The Nature of the Enlarged European Union* (OUP 2007) 54).

achieved in a 'scandalously undemocratic way', far removed from electorates in both East and West.[13]

As a matter of constitutional structure, supranational discipline was extended, after Lisbon, to police and judicial cooperation. This was far from fully fledged 'communitization' of policy: the UK and Ireland were exempt (with the possibility of opting-in), and Denmark obtained less flexible opt-outs. But the emphasis laid by British and Danish officials was still on compromise and cooperation with their peers; Adler-Nissen concluded that 'the management of opt-outs' reflected 'a *retreat* from national sovereignty rather than an expression of it'.[14] Emergency brake procedures were added, more generally, in matters deemed to touch on fundamental aspects of criminal justice or social security, strengthening the role of the European Council; and Article 4(2) TEU declared that essential state functions would be respected, placing particular emphasis on national security remaining with the member states. Although it was no longer a Europe of 'bits and pieces', but, instead, simplified and streamlined with respect to legislative procedures and removal of the three-pillar structure, it was far from a unified entity. Lisbon strengthened the executive branches of the member states, and also left untouched the informal, less traditional modes of law-making that had emerged in the post-Maastricht era including the open method of coordination—and the regulatory activities of networks and agencies. It, ultimately, left unresolved the legitimacy issues raised by a type of 'governing without government', or 'governing without law'.[15]

The Lisbon Treaty signalled the abandonment of the more federal-sounding 'constitutional concept', and, after the partially opened-up and more inclusive 'Convention process' following Laeken, it announced the return to the normal path of closed intergovernmental bargaining. This would be launched under the presidency of German chancellor Angela Merkel in 2007. The nature of the Lisbon 'Reform Treaty' was 'more closed and accelerated than any other to date', with its lack of transparency, exclusion of national parliaments, and the dismissal of national referendum results in France and the Netherlands.[16] And, in the only country that held a referendum on Lisbon, the Treaty was rejected; the Irish made to vote again after concessions were offered in a legally binding declaration.[17]

In terms of the development of external and inter-state sovereignty, Lisbon was, again, a mixed affair. It created a new post of High Representative in Foreign and Security Affairs, assisted by an External Action Service, and it established a

[13] Marquand (n 11) 152.

[14] Italics added. Adler-Nissen warned against seeing opt-outs as expressions of national sovereignty in light of the day-to-day practice; see Rebecca Adler-Nissen, 'Opting-out of an Ever Closer Union: The Integration Doxa and the Management of Sovereignty' (2011) 35 West European Politics 1092.

[15] See Colin Scott, 'Governing Without Law or Governing Without Government? New-ish Governance and the Legitimacy of the EU' (2009) 15 European Law Journal 160; Kenneth Armstrong and Claire Kilpatrick, 'Law, Governance, or New Governance? The Changing Open Method of Coordination' (2007) 13 The Columbia Journal of European Law 649.

[16] See Damian Chalmers, Giorgio Monti, and Gareth Davies, *European Union Law: Cases and Materials* (3rd edn, CUP 2014) 39.

[17] On 12 June 2008, 53.4 per cent of voters rejected the Treaty in the Republic of Ireland. The declaration stated that nothing in the Treaty would affect the Articles of the Irish constitution on right to life, education and the family, tax, the EU's competence on tax, and Irish neutrality. The result was a 'yes' vote of 67 per cent on 2 October 2009.

semi-permanent president of the European Council, with considerable agenda-setting powers. But the role of High Representative was a watered-down version of the post in the Constitutional Treaty, a member not only of the Council but also the Commission, acting as a 'bridge' to assuage fears of imbalance in favour of large member states. It hardly answered Kissinger's infamous question ('who you gonna call?') with any certainty. Article 48 established the possibility of a simplified procedure for Treaty revision, a 'passerelle clause', meaning that the EU, through the Council, and with the consent of Parliament, could make small Treaty modifications (including to its own decision-making rules) without having to go to an Intergovernmental Conference.[18] But this bypassing of the normal route of Treaty change, which would later be realized with the Council decision amending Article 136 TFEU to allow the establishment of a stability mechanism for the eurozone, would, along with bypassing the surrounding publicity, reinforce the executive branches of the state.[19]

The various antinomies reflected in the Lisbon fudge would be captured neatly by Chris Bickerton's integration paradox, based on his analysis of the form and content of the shift from 'nation state' to 'member state'. Lisbon revealed 'the *continued centrality of national executives* in an integration process that *appears as external to and separate from* national governments'; governments which are, themselves, distanced from their domestic publics, and oriented instead to their peers through abstract rules and norms of a 'technical rather than a political nature'.[20] Inter-state asymmetries were deeply embedded in this paradox, and also more conspicuous now that the supposedly technical matters were, clearly, highly political in nature.

The Franco-German 'partnership' was evolving into a more clearly one-sided affair. As we saw in Chapter 6, this relationship, so central to the early dynamic of integration, was already threatened in the Maastricht era by German reunification, differentiated integration, and growing power imbalances. But it was only through the eurozone crisis and the political and constitutional reactions to it, along with the abrupt collapse in the 'Community method' of law-making, that the inter-state nature of the polity, and the contours of a new 'German question', would be revealed.

3. Euro crisis: the end of the democratic federal dream

In the EU, unlike the US, the global financial crisis became a sovereign debt crisis, and then a full-blown existential crisis, heralding a series of economic, political, and constitutional crises, and even a 'comprehensive geopolitical crisis of the post-cold war era'.[21] The stock explanation for the difference is that, in the aftermath of the

[18] Fearing that this may undermine state sovereignty, the German court, in its *Lisbon* decision, insisted on close involvement of the Bundestag if the 'passerelle clause' is triggered (Judgment of 30 June 2009, 2 BvE 2/08, recitals 316–21).

[19] For discussion of Article 48, concluding, contrary to Jürgen Habermas, that it retained the member states as 'Masters of the Treaty', see Dieter Grimm, 'Sovereignty in the European Union' in Jeffrey Ellsworth and Johan WG van der Walt (eds), *Constitutional Sovereignty and Social Solidarity in Europe* (Nomos/Bloomsbury 2015) 48–50. The amendment to Article 136 would be challenged in *Pringle*, discussed below.

[20] Bickerton (n 2) 47–48.

[21] Adam Tooze, *Crashed: How a Decade of Financial Crises Changed the World* (Allen Lane 2018) 20.

collapse of Lehman Brothers in 2008, there was an initial hesitation on the part of the leading European powers—in contrast to the relatively quick and decisive action in the US— even when the crisis, initially considered an Anglo-American affair, became centred in Europe in 2010. The European crisis was notable in being 'self-inflicted', with millions suffering 'for no good reason'. If individual actors—Germany, France, the International Monetary Fund (IMF)—acted logically, the collective result 'was a disaster', inflicting political harm 'from which the EU may never recover'.[22]

But it is precisely in the competition between these individual logics, the structural constraints they reflected, and the ideological dominance of the 'Maastricht orthodoxy', that an explanation is to be found. The constitutional differentiation, emerging inter-state domination, and stark asymmetries (outlined in Chapter 6) combined to extinguish the prospect, already dim from the outset, of a democratic, federal Europe. In turn, they would expose a harsher aspect to the authoritarian liberalism of the previous decades, through an emergency-driven and ad hoc set of responses.

The problems began outside the eurozone, when, in 2007 and 2008, new members experienced severe economic shocks, particularly affecting those who had swiftly transitioned from the former Eastern bloc to market economies. As global markets collapsed, 'eager disciples of market liberalisation and financial globalisation' were especially vulnerable,[23] being hugely dependent on foreign credit and investment.[24] An assistance package agreed between Hungary, the IMF, and the EU, conditional upon austerity, sparked a bitter political backlash. Its 'neocolonialism' recalled, for some, Hungary's treatment by the Allied powers at the Treaty of Trianon, after World War I,[25] and set the stage for the advance of *Fidesz*, who won a conclusive electoral victory in 2010. *Fidesz* would remain in government and consolidate its power, over the next decade, under the leadership of Viktor Orban, raising a different concern for the EU, often captured under the label of authoritarian populism and the 'rule of law crisis'.[26]

A collective EU solution to the problems on Europe's eastern fringe was out of the question for Berlin, since the German ruling class opposed any proposals that would entail mutualization of debt or shared financial commitments. If this was motivated by electoral calculations, it was also consistent with, and—in part—demanded by, the Maastricht settlement. The European Central Bank (ECB) was also uninterested in any sort of intervention on behalf of the candidate countries, its mandate being based on narrow ordoliberal principles and the avoidance of moral hazard. Abandonment to the IMF revealed the first signs of the absence of any meaningful solidarity to come, as well as signalling the general pattern of development through the euro crisis: the preference of northern European states to impose austerity on others and to avoid, above all, having to bail out their own banks. In fact, as one paper put it at the time, examining the harsh conditionality attached to loans in the cases of Hungary, Latvia,

[22] ibid 15.
[23] ibid 228–30.
[24] The build up of which, we examined in Part III.
[25] Tooze (n 21) 231.
[26] On the link between the constitutional mutation in Hungary, and the debt crisis, see Claire Kilpatrick, 'Constitutions, Social Rights and Sovereign Debt States in Europe: A Challenging New Area of Constitutional Inquiry' in Thomas Beukers, Bruno de Witte, and Claire Kilpatrick (eds), *Constitutional Change Through Euro-Crisis Law* (CUP 2017) 279–326.

and Romania, it was the 'European rescue of the Washington consensus' that was in motion, the EU insisting on harsher neo-liberalism than even the guardians of the global capitalist order.[27]

In the aftermath of Lehman Brothers' collapse, it was decreed that the guarantee that no systemically important financial institution would be allowed to fail should be given by each country acting on its own, not by the European Union acting jointly. Although it was Merkel who initially insisted on this,[28] it was not only the preserve of the Christian democratic centre-right in Germany, but included prominent social democrats.[29] In reaction to dramatic action taken by the US to tackle the economic crisis, Peer Steinbruck, German finance minister and SPD member, had immediately rejected the idea of a similar European fund, arguing against fiscal stimulus, and insisting that the only solution was to double down on austerity.[30] In an hour of great urgency, perhaps the greatest since the Second World War, the de facto solidarity that had been promised by Schuman more than a half-century previously had swiftly evaporated.

When attention shifted to Greece in October 2009, as its prime minister, George Papandreou, revealed a budget deficit much higher than previously thought, and Greece's credit rating was subsequently downgraded (just a few months after the IMF had praised its economic performance), Merkel moved swiftly, again, to stress national responsibility, deriding the 'problem children' in the eurozone.[31] This would not be the last of such household metaphors, with the famous Swabian housewife offered up as the paradigm of the cautious saver, in contrast to the spendthrift Mediterranean. It echoed the idea that the eurozone constitution must protect a 'community of stability', one that had been entrenched in the German post-war political imagination, and given approval by its constitutional court in the Maastricht ruling. This constitutional vision, appealing to moderation and frugality—a 'European stability *ideology*', as Ashoka Mody puts it— would be cultivated with great political success by Angela Merkel.[32]

Earning the nickname 'Mutti', the German chancellor offered a maternal inflection of authoritarian liberalism, geared towards a domestic audience, as well as a bloc of countries that had endured their own austerity programmes (later nicknamed the 'FANGs'—Finland, Austria, the Netherlands, and Germany—after their reluctance to agree to any mutual efforts to combat the impact of the COVID-19 pandemic in 2020). With Greece trying to be the good student, the fiscal austerity measures it announced in 2009, applauded both by Germany and France (notably by then French finance minister, Christine Lagarde, later to become head of the ECB), were, in reality, trapping it in a vicious debt spiral, with higher interest rates on new bonds not only raising the debt burden but constricting economic growth. By the beginning of 2010,

[27] Susanne Lütz and Matthias Kranke, 'The European Rescue of the Washington Consensus? EU and IMF Lending to Central and Eastern European Countries' (2013) 21 Review of International Political Economy 310.This article discusses the harshness of EU conditions compared to the IMF's.

[28] See George Soros, *The Tragedy of the European Union: Disintegration or Revival* (Public Affairs 2014) 18.

[29] Ashoka Mody, *EuroTragedy: A Drama in Nine Acts* (OUP 2018) 217.

[30] ibid.

[31] ibid 237.

[32] ibid 47.

it looked like some kind of default or debt restructuring was necessary. But neither was palatable.[33]

The Maastricht Treaty, as outlined in Chapter 8, was a serious obstacle to intervention, with the so-called 'no bailout clause' of Article 125 TFEU prohibiting the assumption of mutual debt, and Article 123 TFEU prohibiting direct central bank financing of the government. Treaty change, as well as being highly demanding, politically, with its unanimity requirements, was not on the agenda after the Constitutional Treaty debacle, and Lisbon's air of finality. Although the 'no bailout clause' was directed, in the first instance, at preventing the moral hazard associated with irresponsible lending, ensuring that private creditors would bear the burden of default, and disincentivizing reckless behaviour, that ship had already sailed. Lending had accelerated with the post-Maastricht turn to financialization and securitization of the economy, combined with a lenient approach to rules, in an era of legal pluralism, 'soft law', and 'decentred regulation'.[34] The political economies and growth strategies of member states, in the previous decades, had depended on extraordinary levels of lending to the periphery, in large part by northern European banks.[35] Greece, in other words, was too small to worry about in isolation, but by 2010 was 'too big to fail', given the possible spillover effects. The rhetorical trick was to present austerity as the solution to Greece's troubles, not only in an attempt to avoid debt restructuring, but to help spin the morality tale that the issue was of public-sector profligacy rather than private-sector excesses. This began what would later, appositely, be called 'the greatest bait and switch in history', as taxpayers would end up shouldering the economic burden instead of the banks.[36]

The ordoliberal and neo-liberal narratives of financial rescue combined to attribute the crisis to a series of unconnected domestic problems caused by undisciplined member states and their irresponsible electorates.[37] It was not financialization of the economy, irrational financial markets, or the economic liberalism of Economic and Monetary Union (EMU), but the *demoi* that were responsible. This narrative would be reinforced with the crisis prevention mechanisms: the so called six-pack of regulations, and the Fiscal Compact. It was also emphasized by the ECB,[38] which, radically committed to low inflation and hamstrung by its own constitution as well as domestic (German) constraints, added a tightening of monetary policy to the fiscal austerity, exacerbating the problems by *raising* interest rates in 2011, at the height of the crisis.[39]

[33] Wolfgang Schäuble eventually mooted the possibility of 'Grexit', as we will examine in Chapter 11. Debt restructuring was anathema to northern European leaders. The French were particularly adamant in their opposition to it (see ibid 245, 252–53).

[34] Julia Black, 'Decentring Regulation: Understanding the Role of Regulation and Self-Regulation in a "Post-regulatory" World' (2001) 54 Current Legal Problems 103. cf Günter Teubner, 'A Constitutional Moment? The Logic of "Hitting the Bottom"' in Poul F Kjaer, Gunther Teubner, and Alberto Febbrajo (eds), *The Financial Crisis in Constitutional Perspective: The Dark Side of Functional Differentiation* (Hart 2011).

[35] For a detailed account, see Agustin Menendez, 'The Existential Crisis of the European Union' (2013) 14 German Law Journal 453.

[36] See Mark Blyth, *Austerity: The History of a Dangerous Idea* (OUP 2015).

[37] In fact, by 2012, the Commission estimated that 4.5 trillion euros had been spent rescuing banks in the EU. See Commission, 'A Roadmap towards a Banking Union' (Communication) COM (2012) 510 final, 3.

[38] Mody (n 29) 281.

[39] Initial hesitation on the part of the member state governments was, thus, matched by an extremely sluggish response by the ECB, albeit curtailed by an extremely narrow mandate, and one that would be kept under constant review by the most powerful domestic court in the region, the Bundesverfassungsgericht,

Greece's economic situation, predictably, deteriorated, in accordance with the emerging consensus—at least outside the European establishment—that Greece could not, realistically, repay its debts in full, and that austerity would likely make things worse due to the 'fiscal multiplier' effect.[40]

But it was important that Greek bankruptcy be avoided, for fear that it would panic the financial markets, in the absence of sufficient firewalls to protect other indebted member states, and, potentially, lead to an uncoordinated unravelling of the monetary system. The eventual prompt to collective action was, thus, not solidarity but *fear*; less the concern for the impact of austerity on Greece's suffering population than the possibility of contagion, which was particularly threatening for other heavily indebted countries, including much larger and more significant economies such as Italy. The first Greek bailout of 110 billion euros, agreed in May 2010 by the eurozone members and the IMF; and the second, of 130 billion euros, agreed in March 2012, through the European Financial Stability Facility (EFSF), were both presented as essential to ensure the stability of the eurozone, and were subject to harsh conditionality, including privatizations, social cuts, reduced wages for public sector workers, and labour market reforms. Conditionality had been negotiated through memoranda of understanding (MOU) with the by-now infamous 'Troika' of institutions, imposing a strict micro-management of budgetary powers, and mandating specific reforms in areas where the EU would normally have limited competence, such as health, education, and industrial relations.[41] The Greek bailouts faced fierce political resistance in Germany, but the public reaction in Greece (and elsewhere) was visceral, thousands rebelling on the streets against the structural reforms, beginning a process that would end in July 2015 with the '*oxi*' referendum. Even as it quickly transpired that the problems in the eurozone went far deeper and wider, and bore little relation to the relatively minor issue of Greece's budget deficit, it was the Greek crisis, politically and constitutionally, that took centre stage in the conjuncture, and we shall return to it in Chapter 11.[42]

The patchwork of rescue programmes would eventually be consolidated into the European Stability Mechanism (ESM), established in September 2012 by eurozone governments. Like the EFSF, it was created as a private company in Luxembourg, but would use the EU's own institutions, in addition to the IMF.[43] It would continue the

raising constitutional issues that it had developed in its *Maastricht* and *Lisbon* rulings. As we will explore in the next section, Merkel's domestic audience was not only the electorate, but the Karlsruhe court.

[40] Mody (n 29) 287–89.

[41] See Mark Dawson and Floris de Witte, 'The Constitutional Balance of the EU after the Euro-Crisis' (2013) 76 Modern Law Review 817.

[42] Bailouts were soon required for the Republic of Ireland and Portugal, and bank recapitalization through the ECB would be offered to Spain and Italy. In each case, the conditions and ailments were different, but the proposed remedy similar, if highly legally complex, involving the European Financial Stability Mechanism (EFSM), a relatively small fund based on Article 122(2) TFEU, and the European Financial Stability Facility (EFSF), a larger but temporary fund, characterized by Varoufakis as 'even more toxic than Wall Street's noxious derivatives: Yanis Varoufakis, *And the Weak Suffer what they Must? Europe, Austerity and the Threat to Global Stability* (Penguin Books 2016) 167.

[43] This had already raised concerns in Germany, and was challenged by the German Constitutional Court, which insisted on important concessions regarding the protection of the prerogatives of the Bundestag in its ESM (temporary injunction) decision. See Judgment of 18 March 2014, 2 BvR 1390/12 (*temporary injunction*) (BVerfG).

requirement of negotiating strict conditionality with the Troika in return for assistance, which would be formalized by way of amendment to Article 136 TFEU, using the simplified revision procedure (agreed at Lisbon, it thereby avoided the need for an Intergovernmental Conference).[44] In the ESM itself—a substantial rescue fund of 500 billion euros—voting rights would be weighted according to capital contributions, with political influence formally and directly reflecting the financial strength of the member states: 'who pays, says'. Rather than trying to at least respect a principle of member state equality, if not attempting to give it a substantive element (which had existed in some degree from the outset of the project at Rome) that might protect smaller states, the innovations would be driven by de facto member state *inequality*.

To avoid political and constitutional constraints, the response to the crisis took place outside the constitutional architecture of the Union, in an ambiguous grey area, a twilight zone between the 'Community method' and the pure intergovernmentalism of international agreement.[45] The reforms were undertaken through 'executive emergency constitutionalism', and 'authoritarian managerialism', with the manner of negotiating the memoranda eroding any vestige of parliamentary democracy for the debtor states (even if, formally, a matter of sovereign governmental decision).[46] The increase in executive power effected through the euro crisis management would obtain its legitimacy not from any democratic mandate, but primarily from its economic 'credibility', and the capacity of the Troika and Eurogroup to act outside the normal rules. It would be a functional, 'market-conform' logic, rather than a democratic or constitutional logic, that would drive the process of integration, albeit incrementally and often subject to strong domestic contestation. It would be a logic that, if necessary, and with apparent impunity, would disregard the principles associated with 'integration through law' and the principle of the equality of member states, not to mention the various guarantees of representative democracy, solidarity, and social rights (in Treaty Articles, as well as domestic constitutional law). The overall effect, according to many commentators, was to shred the credibility of the EU's commitments to constitutionalism.[47]

If these developments appeared to mark a turning point, appearances were, in one sense, deceptive. Certainly, after the earlier years of hyperlegal constitutionalization, the EU appeared to be an increasingly *unconstitutional* Union, managed through ad hoc emergency politics and exceptional technocratic powers of control and

[44] According to Article 136(3), '[t]he member states whose currency is the euro may establish a stability mechanism to be activated if indispensable to safeguard the stability of the euro area as a whole. The granting of any required financial assistance under the mechanism will be made subject to strict conditionality.'

[45] This led to a new method of governance: the 'Union method'. See Edoardo Chiti, Agustín José Menéndez, and Pedro Gustavo Teixeira (eds), 'The European Rescue of the European Union: The Existential Crisis of the European Political Project', Report 3/12 (ARENA 2012) 395.

[46] ibid 417 (accordingly, 'the in and out' from the constitutional framework operates as a precondition for the rise of executive emergency constitutionalism, as it tends to minimize public debate and to avoid the ordinary filters of the democratic constitutional state'; Christian Joerges, 'Europe's Economic Constitution in Crisis and the Emergence of a New Constitutional Constellation' (2014) 15 German Law Journal 985.

[47] Nicole Scicluna, 'Integration through the Disintegration of Law? The ECB and EU Constitutionalism in the Crisis' (2017) 25 Journal of European Public Policy 1874; Nicole Scicluna, 'Can the EU's Constitutional Framework Accommodate Democratic Politics?' (2017) 9 Perspectives on Federalism 98; Nicole Scicluna, 'Politicization without Democratization: How the Eurozone Crisis is Transforming EU Law and Politics' (2014) 12 International Journal of Constitutional Law 545.

surveillance, and functioning outside the usual procedural guarantees and safeguards of the democratic constitutional state.[48] But this bypassing of the Treaty rules, although more notable in the euro crisis phase, was, in fact, prefigured in the lax response to earlier violations of the Stability and Growth Pact by France and Germany.[49] And since Maastricht, and particularly after Lisbon, the political authority of the EU had *already* been fragmenting, with the fragility of integration through law becoming more evident over time.

Deconstitutionalization, over the long trajectory, can be best understood as the flip side of the over-constitutionalization of the foundational period: as a different way of maintaining the same logic of avoiding the politicization of underlying conflicts.[50] Although the soft, permissive authoritarianism was mutating into a harder, more coercive, variety, the dynamic was clearly recognizable. Albeit now in a distinct mode of emergency, the more active forms of authoritarian liberalism were following a similar 'scientific-technocratic' logic as before.[51]

The European Court of Justice (ECJ), adopting an accelerated procedure, quickly rubber-stamped the ESM, holding that agreeing to it outside the Treaty was legally permissible.[52] The ECJ's reasoning was derided for its formality, and even 'dishonesty'.[53] But its options were limited, given the significance of the ESM for the survival of the single currency. The constitutional implications, however, were significant: by giving its stamp of approval to the ESM, the Court not only mandated the conditionality (in effect, 'austerity' as a condition) of assistance, it also made explicit the de facto '*constitutional* status of the curtailment of sovereignty which beneficiary states must accept' as a price for financial aid.[54] It did this by insisting that the ESM satisfied the objectives of EMU; in particular, the logic behind the 'no bailout clause' (Article 125 TFEU), the maintenance of fiscal discipline. Ingeniously, the Court found there to exist a 'higher objective' of 'financial stability of the euro area as a whole' (para 164) behind the narrower goal of fiscal discipline. But, and this was a key point, the ESM could, therefore, only satisfy the Maastricht rules if strict conditionality were included as a quid pro quo

[48] See, eg Christian Kreuder-Sonnen, 'Beyond Integration Theory: The (Anti-)Constitutional Dimension of European Crisis Governance' (2016) 54 Journal of Common Market Studies 1350, 1358.

[49] These violations were sidestepped by the Court of Justice in Case C-27/04 *Commission v Council* [2004] ECR I-6649.

[50] On over-constitutionalization, and deconstitutionalization as a solution, see Fritz W Scharpf, 'De-constitutionalisation and Majority Rule: A Democratic Vision for Europe' (2017) 23 European Law Journal 315.

[51] Independence of the central bank itself is a good example. In the words of the German court, although such independence undoubtedly restricts democracy, 'it is compatible with democratic principle because it takes the tested and *scientifically* documented special character of monetary policy into account' (para 59 of the OMT judgment, Order of 14 January 2014, 2 BvR 2728/13 ('*Gauweiler*' order)).

[52] Case C-370/12 *Thomas Pringle v Government of Ireland and Others* [2012] OJ C26/15. On the ECJ as a rubber stamper, see Marijus Bernatavičius, 'Independence of the ECB and the ECJ During the Sovereign Debt Crisis: From Active Leadership to Rubber-Stamping?' (2020) 35 Journal of Common Market Studies 1. Accordingly, the ECJ acted as 'the implicit agent of the principal'.

[53] See Paul Craig, '*Pringle*: Legal Reasoning, Text, Purpose and Teleology' (2013) 20 Maastricht Journal of European and Comparative Law 1; cf Michelle Everson, 'An Exercise in Legal Honesty: Rewriting the Court of Justice and the Bundesverfassungsgericht' (2015) 21 European Law Journal 474. According to Everson, it was 'legal trickery in the politicised service of a brute functionalist rescue of the Euro' (ibid 480).

[54] Karlo Tuori and Klaus Tuori, *The Eurocrisis: A Constitutional Analysis* (CUP 2012) 18 (Tuori and Tuori mount a qualified defence of *Pringle*).

for assistance. Moreover, because the ESM was determined outside EU law, guarantees that the Court had rhetorically constructed in its fundamental rights jurisprudence would not apply; the conditionality negotiated between the Troika and a recipient state could not, for example, be challenged on the grounds of violating social rights or labour protection.[55]

The asymmetrical power balance between debtor and creditor states would, thus, be replicated and reinforced by a substantive asymmetry between the harshly enforced market liberal principles and the (further) neglected social policy dimension of the Treaties. This would subsequently be buttressed by the formalization of budgetary controls over national parliaments, as contained in the Fiscal Compact, and the control and surveillance model in the European Semester, reinforcing the so-called 'six-pack of regulations'.[56] This package 'generalise[d] the austerity requirements that were initially imposed on debtor states' and 'invest[ed] the Commission with practically unlimited authority to investigate economic conditions in Member States'.[57]

The governance of the euro regime threatened to become increasingly 'hard', including sanctions against members for macroeconomic imbalances, even if they appeared a 'total departure from any claims to rule-bound legitimacy'. In the words of Fritz Scharpf, the excessive imbalance procedure established an 'entirely discretionary regime whose scope of delegated authority far exceeds the limits of generally allowable delegation in constitutional democracies'.[58]

The promise of a 'constitution to come', always central to the discourse of European integration, would come to appear increasingly threadbare. The headline attempt to re-politicize integration—pushed by the European Parliament for the process of selecting Commission president, the so-called '*Spitzenkandidaten* process'—had an ambiguous legal basis (Article 17(7) TEU merely required the European Council to 'take into account' the results of the European Parliament election in proposing a candidate, with the European Parliament only able to accept or reject the Council's nomination). But the process would not only prove a failure (underlined by the appointment, in 2019, of Ursula von der Leyen, despite her not being a *Spitzenkandidaten*); it also demonstrated the increasing de facto authority of the German chancellor.[59]

[55] cf Claire Kilpatrick, 'Are the EU Bail-Outs Immune to Social Challenge Because they are not EU Law?' (2014) 10 European Constitutional Law Review 393. See, further, Dawson and de Witte (n 41).

[56] See Alicia Hinarejos, *The Euro Area Crisis in Constitutional Perspective* (OUP 2015) 29–32.

[57] Fritz Scharpf, 'After the Crash: A Perspective on Multilevel European Democracy' (2015) 21 European Law Journal 384, 390.

[58] ibid 393. Although formally outside the EU legal framework, the Fiscal Compact is substantially within it. On this legal ambiguity, see Chiti, Menéndez, and Teixeira (n 45). The 'six-pack' enhanced the role of the Commission in policing national budgets and sanctioning member states, particularly through the macroeconomic imbalance procedure (MIP), which strengthened the preventive arm of the Stability and Growth Pact. If a member state does not make any adjustments, the Commission can trigger an excessive imbalance procedure (EIP) equal to 0.1 per cent of national GDP. The Commission can also enforce discipline through the excessive deficit procedure (EDP), which is part of the corrective arm of the Stability and Growth Pact, and deals with situations in which the government deficit or debt is above the reference values set out in the Treaty (an annual deficit above 3 per cent of GDP). If the country under the EDP does not take effective action to reduce its deficit, the EU can issue fines, as a last resort.

[59] See Marco Goldoni, 'Politicising EU Lawmaking? The *Spitzenkandidaten* Experiment as a Cautionary Tale' (2016) 22 European Law Journal 279.

If the dream of a democratic, federal constitutional project had ended, the euro crisis developments suggested another spectre was on the horizon; of a quite different sort to that imagined by the founding fathers of post-war integration, and one diametrically opposed to the original remit of preventing a 'German Europe'. Hegemony was back on the agenda.

4. The emergence of semi-hegemony in a 'German Europe'

In terms of the balance of inter-state relations, the numerous mechanisms and institutions aimed specifically at preventing the marginalization of smaller member states, and avoiding their domination by larger and more powerful states, would be seriously eroded through the euro crisis.[60] The return of stark material asymmetries, in combination with the power exercised by 'informal' intergovernmental organs such as the Eurogroup, and supranational technocratic institutions such as the ECB, made the state sovereignty of (some) member states appear entirely illusory. This affected even the core Franco-German bilateral relationship, albeit that increasing divergence in economic performance pointed more to 'structural weakness in the French economy' than any particular German strengths.[61]

For the debtor states, the euro crisis would have a more extreme impact on their exercise of sovereign powers than anything experienced in the previous decades. Even the notion of 'receivership' was too mild a term for the status that countries in the periphery were reduced to, following suspension of the normal democratic process. 'Occupation' by the Troika was more appropriate, suggesting as it did, 'the consequences of military defeat'. These were not the words of a Greek radical, but a mainstream Italian political scientist, Giandomenico Majone.[62] Of the March 2012 bailout, when the terms negotiated through the European Financial Stability Facility (EFSF) were being debated in the Bundestag, amidst rioting in Athens, German sociologist Ulrich Beck would note, with alarm, his realization that 'today the Bundestag will decide the fate of Greece'.[63]

Germany, in Beck's view, needed to assume its historic responsibility for Europe; it had 'become too powerful to be able to afford the luxury of indecision'.[64] The difficulty

[60] See Dawson and de Witte (n 41): '[w]ithin the EU, the instruments for the protection of spatial balance are those of the overrepresentation of smaller Member States in voting arrangements, an independent mediator for the initiation of policy proposals, the system of competences that protects against majoritarianism in sensitive areas, and the rigid treaty revision system, that requires consent of all Member States to 'change the rules of the game'. They note, in detail, how this spatial balance has altered as a result of reforms since the financial crisis.

[61] Ulrich Krotz and Joachim Schild, *Shaping Europe: France, Germany, and Embedded Bilateralism from the Elysée Treaty to Twenty-First Century Politics* (OUP 2013) 209 (they find 'empirical evidence for a new type of Franco-German asymmetry and a powerful position of Germany', particularly when it comes to setting the benchmark for fiscal discipline, replicating its monetary power of the 1970s and 1980s (ibid 208–09)). On Germany's own social decline, see, eg Oliver Nachtwey, *Germany's Hidden Crisis: Social Decline in the Heart of Europe* (Verso 2018).

[62] Giandomenico Majone, *Rethinking the Union of Europe Post-Crisis* (CUP 2014) 200 (extending it to the treatment of the Republic of Ireland in 2011).

[63] Ulrich Beck, *German Europe* (Polity Press 2012).

[64] ibid 3.

was that ordoliberal prescriptions, so dominant in its own post-war constitutional imaginary, put a sizeable obstacle in the way. These were buttressed, not only by domestic political constraints, but by its own constitutional court, and the Maastricht rules that the court entrenched and attempted to protect (as we will examine in Chapter 10). Instead, a political bloc led by Berlin could only prescribe severe doses of austerity, and a tightening up of the rules in line with ordoliberal ideas of 'sound money'. This found strong support in countries with export-led growth strategies such as the Netherlands and Finland, as well as among ruling elites and professional networks in countries such as Italy, which had formalized ideas of 'expansionary austerity' and solidified them in mainstream economics.[65]

'Of decisive importance', in the new balance of powers, was the disequilibrium in the Franco-German relationship, so central to integration since the founding period.[66] In this core bilateral partnership, the power shift in favour of Germany was 'nowhere more visible than in monetary affairs', reflecting long-term trends: as far back as 1968, monetary integration was seen as a way to tie down the 'German Gulliver'. In return, France (and eventually the rest of Europe) had to pay the price of becoming 'more German', emulating its stability-oriented model.[67] The imbalance had been attributed to a variety of factors, including the process of deindustrialization in France, its loss of world market share, and comparative lack of economic dynamism, culminating in 2012 with a downgraded credit rating.[68]

Since sovereign debt was now issued in a currency the member states had no control over, (some) states would be highly vulnerable to attacks from the financial markets, and there would, effectively, be only one way for them to regain 'competitiveness': 'internal devaluations'. In the absence of currency devaluation as a tool with which to restore competitiveness, internal devaluation—meaning neo-liberal structural reform (spending cuts and reductions in labour costs)—was pressed as the only way of restoring economic health. Through the euro crisis, the euro would turn out to be a foreign currency with foreign masters for some of its member states. As Michel Aglietta puts it, there is a sense in which the euro is a foreign currency for every country; but, he continues, there is 'one country for which the euro is less external than it is for the others: Germany'.[69]

Germany, *as a member state*, had become more powerful in European affairs since Maastricht, despite initial economic difficulties in dealing with reunification. After Lisbon, and through the euro crisis, its influence would increase further, due to its stronger economic fundamentals, as well as the fact that it was playing a game based on its own preferred rules. The diminution of France's status had been complemented not only by the growth of Germany, with its economic power and sizeable contribution

[65] See Oddný Helgadóttir, 'The Bocconi Boys go to Brussels: Italian Economic Ideas, Professional Networks and European Austerity' (2016) 23 Journal of European Public Policy 392 (identifying the role of Bocconi University, and the legacy of Ludwig Einaudi).

[66] Simon Bulmer and William E Paterson, *Germany and the European Union: Europe's Reluctant Hegemon?* (Red Globe Press 2018) 13.

[67] Krotz and Schild (n 61) 211.

[68] France lost its triple-A rating in November 2012, no longer 'able to sustain even the appearance of equal partner' (Bulmer and Paterson (n 66) 210).

[69] Michel Aglietta, 'The European Vortex' (2012) 75 New Left Review 15.

to the EU budget, but also by Germany's geostrategic turn to the East, with the prospect of a 'Weimar Triangle' (Paris, Berlin, and Warsaw) replacing the bilateral core. Economically, Germany was also looking increasingly outside of the EU altogether, with its strong and growing export performance towards the 'BRIC states' loosening its dependence on the single market.[70] By 2018, Germany had announced the world's largest current account surplus, 'bigger even than China's'.[71] The effects of German economic strategy and ordoliberal ideology, thus, extended far beyond its relationship with France, or even with the European periphery.

In the process of becoming 'more German', Europe was also becoming 'more coercive', with Germany using its 'unprecedented power to impose its economic preferences' on the eurozone as a whole.[72] As a result of euro crisis management, Merkel was 'shaping the entire policy framework of eurozone member states'.[73] After the imposition of the Fiscal Compact, the whole of Europe was 'speaking German', with Merkel assuming the role of Europe's 'de facto chancellor'.[74]

Yet, there was a limit to Germany's geopolitical power in the region. Germany was reluctant to use its full leverage, or incapable of doing so; unwilling to play the role of hegemon, or to take on responsibility as 'hegemonic stabilizer' in an increasingly turbulent regional space. The category of a 'hegemonic stabilizer' could be traced to the work of Charles Kindleberger, who had argued that stabilization of the world economy depended upon leadership exercised by one dominant power. It was this type of hegemony that was missing in the 1930s: a feature which contributed to the interwar breakdown, in his view.[75] Hegemony of this sort was not at issue in Europe, not least since Germany entirely lacked the military might of previous global powers such as the US and Britain, and was militarily weaker than many European powers, including France.[76] The global geopolitical and economic significance of the US (both its political leadership and dollar influence) in any case had continued, and remained evident throughout the euro crisis.[77]

With its exercise of political-economic power, Germany, in tandem with the Troika, pursued an 'aid-in-driblets strategy',[78] providing enough to keep debtor states

[70] Krotz and Schild (n 61) 161.

[71] See Bulmer and Paterson (n 66).

[72] Hans Kundnani, *The Paradox of German Power* (C Hurst & Co 2016) 98–99.

[73] Mody (n 29) 323.

[74] See Leonard FM Besselink and Jan-Herman Reestman, 'The Fiscal Compact and the European Constitutions: "Europe Speaking German"' (2012) 1 European Constitutional Law Review 1.

[75] Charles Kindleberger, one of the architects of the Marshall Plan, argued that, for the world economy to be stabilized, 'there has to be a stabilizer, one stabilizer', regretting the US's reluctance in the interwar period to take this role over from the UK: Charles Poor Kindleberger, *The World in Depression, 1929–39* (University of California Press 1973) 305.

[76] In an important sense, this did not matter so long as the US pursued its global security role. If the US reneged on this role, Germany's dependence on France might grow, rebalancing the bilateral relationship. This factor would be exacerbated with the election of President Trump, potentially removing the international linchpin of European security, and quite possibly making Germany more geopolitically dependent on France.

[77] See Magnus Ryner, 'Europe's Ordoliberal Iron Cage: Critical Political Economy, the Euro Area Crisis and its Management' (2015) 22 Journal of European Public Policy 275. For broader discussion of the importance of US imperialism for European integration, see Alex Callinicos, 'Brexit and the Imperial Constitution of Europe' in Eva Nanopoulos and Fotis Vergis (eds), *The Crisis Behind the Eurocrisis: The Eurocrisis as a Multidimensional Systemic Crisis of the EU* (CUP 2019).

[78] Mody (n 29) 326.

propped up, but never enough to relieve them of their servitude; pursuing 'brutal neo-liberalism to the outside world, consensus with a social-democratic tinge at home'.[79] Even in economic terms, however, the imbalance in the eurozone was less the result of Germany's success than others' failures. The German economy was marked by 'mediocre growth, high unemployment and low inflation', with poor levels of domestic investment; its export success was due, largely, to wage suppression and the benefits of the single currency.[80] Domestically, German society was suffering from downward mobility, precariousness, and attenuated social equality: symptoms of a 'regressive modernization' often overlooked in a context of post-Cold War neo-liberal triumphalism.[81] It was, therefore, more appropriate to describe Germany as, in Christoph Schönberger's words, *Hegemon wider Willen*, the 'reluctant hegemon'.[82]

Constitutional scholars from previous generations had argued that the idea of hegemony properly made sense only within a federal-type structure, where one state would become a regional 'determining influence'.[83] Although this came closer to the mark in capturing Germany's position in the EU, there remained complicating factors. Despite its increasingly prominent role thorough the euro crisis, Germany's 'extreme reluctance' to play the 'role of a true leader' extended beyond comparative power credentials.[84] There were obvious historical factors in play: restrained sovereignty was a significant part of the post-war constitutional settlement, as we examined in Part II, and its legacy had not disappeared. In view of the historical record, and the mutual mistrust that remained latent but ready to resurface, it was 'almost unimaginable that the members of the EU, large or small, would be willing to accept a German hegemony'. The only occasions on which the 'peoples of Europe seem to display solidarity', Majone cautiously noted, 'is when they *oppose* the hegemonic aspirations of one of the states of the continent'.[85] European integration was designed, in the post-war period, precisely to avoid the return of such a scenario.

The notion of *semi-hegemony*, developed in an earlier era by German historian Ludwig Dehio, appeared more apposite: not powerful enough to simply impose its

[79] Beck (n 63) 51–52 (a mutant version of Smith abroad, Keynes at home: so familiar from the earlier foundational period).

[80] Costas Lapavitsas and others, *Crisis in the Eurozone* (Verso 2012) 22–29.

[81] See Nachtwey (n 61).

[82] Christoph Schönberger, 'Hegemonie Wider Willen: Zur Stellung Deutschlands in der Europaischen Union' (2012) 66 Merkur 1.

[83] Such as German scholar Heinrich Triepel (see Perry Anderson, *The H-Word: The Peripeteia of Hegemony* (Verso 2017)).

[84] The notion of the 'reluctant hegemon' (used by Schönberger, as well as Ulrich Beck, and Bulmer and Paterson) is a flawed analysis, according to Majone, with its 'implicit assumption that, barring a total collapse of the EU, European integration will remain stable at the present level, or even resume its march towards 'more Europe' once the crisis is over'. In fact, Majone argues that 'integration is becoming more differentiated, and there are also clear indications of a retrograde movement in several respects. Thus, the goal of a truly integrated European market appears to be less and less feasible; and it can even be argued that the European market is actually less integrated today than twenty or thirty years ago. This is because of the growing importance of services, which, as was noted above, are still largely regulated domestically; but also because growing socio-economic heterogeneity within the Union makes policy harmonization increasingly problematic' (Giandomenico Majone, 'The Limits of Collective Action and Collective Leadership' in Damian Chalmers, Markus Jachtenfuchs, and Christian Joerges (eds), *The End of the Eurocrats Dream: Adjusting to Diversity* (CUP 2016) 235).

[85] ibid 232 (citing Ludwig Dehio, *Deutschland und die Weltpolitik im 20 Jahrhundert* (Fischer Bücherei 1961)) (italics added).

will, but strong enough to be perceived as a threat to the balance of power.[86] According to one recent commentator, the age-old 'German question' that semi-hegemony invoked had now re-emerged in a distinct 'geo-economic form'.[87]

Although Germany already materially conditioned 'the economies of the other member states in important respects', hegemony, even in the more limited sense of determining influence within a federation, required two things absent from the inter-state relations of Europe: first, Germany lacked *de jure* or de facto authority within the 'federal government' of the eurozone; and, second, there was not the full consent of other states to its leadership role.[88] On the first, the array of intergovernmental and technocratic powers was too unwieldy to be determined from a single source; it was not charismatic authority but a 'bureaucratic Caesarism' that emerged in the euro crisis.[89] On the second, in order to become more fully hegemonic, Germany would have had to act in a more *flexible* manner, willing to relax its strict insistence on austerity, making short-term concessions in order to serve long-term interests; offering a kind of Marshall Plan-style programme for the debtor countries, emulating the role of the US after the Second World War. It would have had to abandon the economic liberalism that was so central to its own constitutional imagination, and which, as we have seen, had become a crucial plank in the constitutionalization of the European Union. Abandoning its commitment to sound money, at least temporarily, would, in turn, have made it more acceptable as a hegemon from the perspective of the debtor countries, simultaneously increasing both its capacity to lead and the consent of those led.

Germany's insistence on economic stability—the 'stability culture' entrenched at Maastricht—not only prevented it from taking on a leadership role; it was, ironically, creating great political *instability* (in addition to cementing its own lack of economic dynamism). The formal and material constitution of authoritarian liberalism had come to be a fetter on the exercise of its inter-state power and a source of increasing discontent, both at home—because of strong domestic sentiment that the euro crisis management was not ordoliberal *enough*—and abroad, due to the disastrous economic and social consequences of austerity. As we will see in Chapter 11, there was a rationale to Germany's authoritarian liberalism as a strategy of capital accumulation *and* a limit to the political instability it would foment elsewhere, due to the acceptance by domestic elites of the lack of any alternative to EU membership.

If the country with the largest economy had made a trade surplus a '*de facto* reason of state',[90] this economic strategy had a long lineage, based on Germany's entry into

[86] See Kundnani (n 72) 8 (as Kundnani puts it, from 1871 to 1945, Germany's size and central location made it 'too powerful for a balance of power but not powerful enough to exercise hegemony' (ibid 107)). On German semi-hegemony in the monetary area in the run-up to the ESM, see Anne-Marie Le Gloannec, 'Germany's Power and the Weakening of States in a Globalized World: Deconstructing a Paradox' (2001) 10 German Politics 117.

[87] Kundnani (n 72).

[88] ibid.

[89] See Cédric Durand and Razmig Keucheyan, 'Bureaucratic Caesarism: A Gramscian Outlook on the Crisis of Europe' (2015) 23 Historical Materialism 23.

[90] Helen Thompson, 'Austerity as Ideology: The Bait and Switch of the Banking Crisis' (2013) 1 Comparative European Politics 729, 730 (according to Thompson, '[t]he euro-zone simply cannot endure in a way that is compatible with democratic politics if the state with the largest economy and most fiscal credibility makes a trade surplus a de facto reason of state').

international political economy in the nineteenth century as a late industrializer, and its dependence on foreign trade 'that survived two depressions and world wars'. This position goes 'beyond geo-economics', since it is attributable to domestic as well as inter-state relations, and transcends the historical context in which it developed, 'reverberat[ing] powerfully in the present'.[91] The 'long-run specialisation in the export of capital and durable consumer goods', and 'the accumulation of a consistent trade surplus as a source of domestic stabilisation', would, according to Julian Germann, present 'an almost insurmountable hurdle for German crisis managers to pursue anything other than an export-led recovery in the wake of the global financial crisis'.[92]

To make sense out of this situation requires a nuanced analysis; not, as Ulrich Beck suggested, a bifurcation. In Beck's view, Europeanization of the continent could assume one of two very different forms, '*either* participation on terms of equality (reciprocity) *or* hierarchical dependence (hegemony)'.[93] Equality and dependency are more complex notions, resistant to such binaries. Admittedly, a key element of the 'ideology' of European integration was, as Majone argued, the 'basic equality and equal dignity' of the member states; a historical legacy of the very 'German question' that had now returned. But Majone's choice of words was revealing. Member state equality was not merely formal: it was *ideological*. Formal equality, as anyone even cursorily acquainted with critical and Marxist traditions would immediately recognize, is entirely compatible with hierarchical dependence. As Michel Aglietta puts it:

> There can be no cooperative policy-making in Europe if the currency is external to all member-states. There is, however, one country for which the euro is less external than it is for the others: Germany. If Berlin were to agree to play the role of benevolent leader—that is, taking onboard the interests of the monetary union as a whole, while pursuing its own policies—it might have been possible to arrive at a second-best scenario; but it has done nothing of the sort.[94]

Viewed from the perspective of the EU as a whole, there appeared to be a certain incoherence in an ordoliberal response to the euro crisis. Germany could not 'coherently' insist that all other states have a macroeconomic policy 'that looks like its own', this argument continued, 'because such a result is definitionally impossible'.[95] The

[91] Julian Germann, 'Beyond "Geo-Economics": Advanced Unevenness and the Anatomy of German Austerity' (2018) 24 European Journal of International Relations 590, 597–98 ('the excessive export orientation that some observers see as trumping Germany's "civilian power" today . . . has roots that reach far back into the history of German capitalism. It emerged not only from the particular world market pressures and opportunities that German industrialisation encountered, but also from the strictures and incentives imposed by Germany's social composition.').

[92] ibid 601 ('The consistent and growing trade surplus that Germany has posted since 1951 . . . and the staggering increase in its export ratio since the introduction of the euro (from 26.5% of GDP in 1998 to 46% in 2016)' are part of a 'long-run trajectory').

[93] Beck (n 63) 64 (italics added).

[94] Aglietta (n 69) 23–24 (he continues: 'Historically, monetary unions have gone in one of two directions: either they have been dissolved—the Latin and Scandinavian unions—or they have moved towards constituting political sovereignty, as when the Zollverein customs union formed the basis for the German Reich.').

[95] Thompson (n 90). See also Wolfgang Munchau, 'The Wacky Economics of Germany's Parallel Universe' *Financial Times* (London, 16 November 2014) <https://www.ft.com/content/

German-led response, as Mark Blyth argued, was based on the 'fallacy of composition';[96] put simply, 'it is not possible for all euro area member states to run surpluses, unless there is a massive increase in the current account surplus to the rest of the world'.[97]

Viewed in the whole, ordoliberalism was not only economically suspect; it was constitutionally problematic. Scaled up to the European level and entrenched at Maastricht, ordoliberal emphasis on price stability, competitiveness, and fiscal discipline not only constrained the EU response (particularly the ECB), it also became increasingly incompatible with democracy in *other* parts of the eurozone. But a neo-Keynesian style rescue programme involving transnational cost-sharing and steps towards political union would have been incompatible with the German constitution, as interpreted by the Karlsruhe court (as we saw in Chapter 7).

This suggests that it is misleading to treat the eurozone (let alone the EU) as a coherent whole, and more instructive to view it as a complex ensemble of inter-state, state-society, and social relations. Through an unfolding intergovernmentalism, the crisis response revealed a distinct tension: German capital's relative power, on the one hand, and the lack of Germany's political state capacity to become a fully hegemonic leader, on the other; due, in part, to the very nature of the European Union as a quasi-federal project, and not (yet) a coercive state apparatus.

It was not through military power or traditional geopolitics, but geoeconomic power *and* ideological constraints, that domination occurred in the EU; and it was not countries in their totality that were dominated, but classes within countries, often with the compliance of the domestic ruling class and political and economic elites. To pursue this further, we need to look beyond doubts about whether Germany was powerful enough to assume leadership in the way the US and UK had in previous epochs, or whether it was held back by the historical legacy of the age-old 'German question'. We need to consider the constitutional architecture and ideology of the integration project, as well as the material constitution undergirding it. These are the subjects of Chapters 10 and 11, respectively.

e257ed96-6b2c-11e4-be68-00144feabdc0> accessed 24 September 2020: 'the ordo-liberal word view is asymmetric. Current account surpluses are considered more acceptable than deficits. Since the rules are based on national law, ordo-liberals do not care about their impact on the rest of the world. When they adopted the Euro, the rest of the world suddenly did start to matter.'

[96] Blyth (n 36) 140–42.
[97] Ryner (n 77) 280.

10
The New Constitutionalism and its Discontents

1. Introduction

In order to explain the structure of Germany's governmental power—relative to the power of other member states—we need to consider the institutional dimension, in addition to the inter-state asymmetries examined in Chapter 9. First, institutions, and the relations among them, mattered, both 'horizontally' (among supranational institutions, and among domestic institutions) and 'vertically' (between domestic and supranational institutions). The European Union was the main vehicle through which Germany exercised its power, and integration both enhanced *and* constrained that power. Although, as we have seen, member states would not hesitate to move forward with certain aspects of integration outside the constraints of Treaty, if necessary, this remained an exceptional route, and had to be justified and approved by the European Court of Justice. Other EU institutions, which also enjoyed a relative autonomy from the member states, would play an even more crucial role through the crisis, precisely because of their constitutional independence; the most notable of these was the European Central Bank.[1]

Second, domestic institutions also obstructed the activation of German hegemony; a result of the post-war constitutional settlement itself. The German Constitutional Court would prevent Germany from becoming an overt hegemon, even if its political class had the desire to occupy such a position. The most serious institutional challenges to the 'rescue regimes' thus came, not from debtor states deprived of their fiscal sovereignty, but from the region's most powerful constitutional court, sitting in Karlsruhe. Ironically, a German constitution deliberately constructed to safeguard liberal democracy, and to prevent a return to dictatorship, would be utilized to resist the democratization of supranational institutions in Europe. Domestic constitutional patriotism, in other words, was obstructing a European constitutional patriotism 'writ large'. There was, however, a deeper irony. A domestic constitution deliberately constructed to protect liberal democracy in Germany, and a supranational economic constitution modelled on its ordoliberal ideas, would rigidify a structure that was contributing to the decline of democracy *elsewhere* in Europe.

In practice, the Maastricht formula for Economic and Monetary Union (EMU) had an increasingly substantial impact on domestic state-society and social relations throughout the euro crisis. Democracy was collateral damage; the price that had to be paid for economic interdependence : '[the] gutting of Greek and Italian democracy'

[1] The ECB might be described as the only 'truly federal institution'; more so than the ECJ, which relied to a greater extent on its domestic counterparts.

Authoritarian Liberalism and the Transformation of Modern Europe. Michael A Wilkinson, Oxford University Press. © Michael A Wilkinson 2021. DOI: 10.1093/oso/9780198854753.003.0011 was the result of a 'toxic combination of massive financial integration with Berlin's dogged insistence on intergovernmentalism'.[2] The flip side of the European Union being a voluntaristic association of formal equals was that there was always the option of leaving. But how real was this option?

The institutional constraints depended not just on constitutional texts; they operated within a political and constitutional context. This can be captured by the term 'constitutional imagination'.[3] The constitutional imagination, and its limits, mattered, in Germany and across all the member states. The European Union was not only a vehicle of German power; it was a vehicle through which the ruling elites in *other* member states exercised and maintained their own power, supported by the absence of any popular alternative to EU membership in the constitutional imagination.

This chapter begins by examining the orientation towards a free-standing European constitutional discourse, which continued regardless of the asymmetric intergovernmentalism and emergency executive politics of the euro crisis. It even assumed a global, cosmopolitan aspect, particularly under the influence of Jürgen Habermas (section 2). The concrete constitutional developments, however, contradicted this posture, with challenges from domestic courts reaching a crescendo in the OMT (outright monetary transactions) saga. This was the first time there was direct contact between Karlsruhe and Luxembourg, and on an issue of profound significance: the Weimar question of the 'guardian of the constitution' had returned (section 3). This prompted a generation of 'new constitutionalists' to assert a *finalité* of integration through the juristic supremacy of the European Court of Justice (section 4), but in a manner which resembled Schmitt's decisionistic federation rather than Habermas's normative federalism, insisting on the very real prospect of constitutional exit (and even expulsion), from the EU, despite the erosion of sovereignty that rendered this prospect illusory (section 5).

2. The globalization of European constitutional discourse

Even if, from a legal point of view, the 2005 Constitutional Treaty was formally just another international treaty, as a political matter, it was said to have a constitutional aspect.[4] Invocations of Philadelphia were far-fetched, but the Constitutional Treaty would have symbolized at least a partial claim on the constituent power of the peoples of Europe, drafted, as it was, in the name of 'the will of the citizens and States of Europe'.[5] Following its failure, the Lisbon Treaty that replaced it was, on the contrary,

[2] Adam Tooze, *Crashed: How a Decade of Financial Crises Changed the World* (Penguin 2018) 412 ('What defined the parameters of an acceptable solution to the eurozone crisis was the constitution of the Federal Republic, the autonomy of its central bank and the political interests of the German centre-right' (ibid 413–14)).

[3] See Martin Loughlin, 'The Constitutional Imagination' (2015) 78 Modern Law Review 1.

[4] See Chris Bickerton, *European Integration: From Nation-States to Member States* (OUP 2012). cf Joseph HH Weiler, 'On the Power of the Word: Europe's Constitutional Iconography' (2005) 3 International Journal of Constitutional Law 173 (calling it a Treaty 'masquerading as a Constitution'). For an exploration of what was missing from the Constitutional Treaty and absent from the subsequent Treaty of Lisbon, see Alexander Somek, 'Postconstitutional Treaty' (2007) 8 German Law Journal 1121.

[5] See Luuk van Middelaar, *The Passage to Europe: How a Continent Became a Union* (YUP 2013) 289 ('European citizens were ascribed constituent power', a 'huge step').

politically international, signposting the continuation of the post-Maastricht trend towards the concentration of executive power; not only did it retain the member states as the sole authors of the Treaty, but it also formalized the European Council as the main driving force of the project.[6]

Despite the obvious warning signs in various referenda, buttressed by the German Constitutional Court's erection of a solid blockade against further integration in its Lisbon case, in a move far more materially significant than its previous rulings, the failure of the Constitutional Treaty had dented little of the constitutional Euro-enthusiasm in the academy. Constitutional discourse was increasingly juristic and 'free-standing', detached from any notions of popular constituent power.[7] It was barely even irritated by popular rejection of the constitutional project in two core founding states (France and the Netherlands), ignoring the deeper democratic discontent this signalled.

As we saw in Chapter 7, Jürgen Habermas was a key intellectual figure in the discourse of postnational constitutionalism, with his work in democratic theory—presented as a dialectical resolution of republicanism and liberalism, popular sovereignty and human rights—being well suited to a transcendence of the state tradition.[8] His co-originality thesis of public and private autonomy, and the claim that democracy and the rule of law were 'internally related', were widely influential as abstract claims, building upon his earlier theory of communicative action.[9] They could still offer a critical, if increasingly blunted, riposte to the market-liberal and passive authoritarian vision of democracy that dominated the post-war constitutional imagination. But when it came to European integration, it was not a renewal of republicanism that drove his narrative forward, but a Kantian liberal universalism, combined with a Weberian functionalism and a moralistic reaction to nationalism, based on historical (and perhaps also personal) experiences of the Federal Republic of Germany.

In reflecting on the EU after the onset of the euro crisis, Habermas presented both the sociological and political-moral dynamics of globalization in highly naturalistic terms; as unstoppable social evolutionary forces bound up with a capitalist dynamic of 'functionally-driven opening', followed by 'socially integrative closure'. Even with the initial failures of the EU in the euro crisis laid bare, European integration, specifically in terms of the process of constitutionalization, still represented 'an important stage', not towards European unification, but along the route to a 'politically constituted world society'.[10] The political fragmentation precipitated by the crisis was merely

[6] Although de facto the European Council had been meeting since 1974, as part of the solution to the 'blockades resulting from the Luxembourg Veto', it found its way into the formal text (see Luuk van Middelaar, 'Spanning the River: The Constitutional Crisis of 1965–1966 as the Genesis of Europe's Political Order' (2008) 4 European Constitutional Law Review 98).

[7] See Michael A Wilkinson, 'Political Constitutionalism and the European Union' (2013) 76 Modern Law Review 191.

[8] Jürgen Habermas, 'Three Normative Models of Democracy' in Seyla Benhabib (ed), *Democracy and Difference: Contesting the Boundaries of the Political* (Princeton University Press 1996).

[9] Jürgen Habermas, 'On the Internal Relation between the Rule of Law and Democracy' (1995) 3 European Journal of Philosophy 12.

[10] Jürgen Habermas, *The Crisis of the European Union: A Response* (Polity Press 2012) 2(Habermas, 'Crisis').

a stumbling block on the path of the 'civilising force' of constitutional law and transnational integration.[11]

The failure of the Constitutional Treaty had not made the slightest dent in Habermas's constitutional enthusiasm, nor on that of many of his followers. In fact, the failure of the Constitutional Treaty, and its symbolic difference with the Lisbon Treaty, often barely registered, Habermas opening his *Crisis* book with the observation that Europe 'is now *more than ever* a constitutional project'.[12] After noting the similarity between the EU's self-consciously supranational form and previous federations, empires, and alliances of the pre-democratic era, Habermas would distinguish the Union on the basis that, unlike these, it *declares itself to be democratic*. He would add that, in its declamatory terms (Articles 9 to 12), the Lisbon Treaty 'leaves nothing to be desired', as if democracy could now be satisfied by its sheer pronouncement.[13] The democratic deficit of the Union would, elsewhere, be emphasized by Habermas, intensifying the aura of cognitive dissonance. Deficits must be overcome by postmetaphysical force of right reason, Habermas having persuaded himself (and many of his readers) to overlook them, and focus instead on a future horizon of pan-European democracy, identity, and solidarity, albeit based on a constituent power now curiously split at its root.

The EU constitution, 'in spite of the fact that one of the two supporting pillars is composed directly of collectivities [member states]', has, like all modern legal systems, 'a strictly individualistic character', Habermas argued. It rested ultimately 'on the subjective rights of citizens'.[14] The dual constituent power is therefore not a combination of states *and* European citizens, but a combination of citizens of states and citizens of the Union (although since the Union, for some unspecified reason, is not a 'collectivity', according to Habermas, it is unclear what it really means to be a citizen of it). The EU, in the language of constitutional theory, has the character of a *pouvoir constituant mixte*.[15] Rather than seeing citizens of the states—or 'future EU citizens'—as the constitution-founding subject, 'it is theoretically more convincing to conceive of the individuals, who are (simultaneously) citizens of the states and of the Union, as the only subjects of legitimation'.[16]

[11] ibid 1–12.

[12] ibid 1 (Habermas talks about the Constitutional Treaty without mentioning its failure as a result of significant public opposition in two founding member states, and fails to note that it was not even put to the public vote in Germany (ibid 30). Later, he suggests that the Lisbon Treaty made no difference, at least regarding its format, in terms of dual constituent power (ibid 34–35), and then appears to conflate it with the Constitutional Treaty (ibid 35)). For a discussion and rejection of the dual constituent power, based on a reading of the Treaty, see Dieter Grimm, 'Sovereignty in the European Union' in J Ellsworth and J van der Walt (eds), *Constitutional Sovereignty and Social Solidarity in Europe* (Nomos/Bloomsbury 2015).

[13] The influence of von Bogdandy here, cited by Habermas, is unmistakable: see, eg Armin von Bogdandy, 'The European Lesson for International Democracy: The Significance of Articles 9 to 12 EU Treaty for International Organizations' (2012) 23 European Journal of International Law 315.

[14] Habermas, 'Crisis' (n 10) 35.

[15] ibid 36. Habermas supports this claim on the basis that the Lisbon Treaty gives some limited power to the European Parliament in the simplified revision procedure under Article 48, an argument given short shrift by Grimm (n 12); cf Markus Patberg, 'The Levelling Up of Constituent Power in the European Union' (2017) 55:2 Journal of Common Market Studies 203.

[16] Habermas, 'Crisis' (n 10) 36 (citing Armin von Bogdandy, 'Grundprinzipien' in Bogdandy and Bast (eds), *Europäisches Verfassungsrecht: Theoretische and Dogmatische Grundzüge* (Springer 2010) 64).

Even though Habermas started from the presumption that it was states that were responsible for the origins of the project, the approach to European integration, thus, becomes entirely free-standing. If we take seriously Habermas's own co-originality thesis with regard to the EU, one might think that, whereas the juridical protection of (some aspects of) private autonomy is very real, the democratic expression of public autonomy must be entirely imagined or projected into the future. This, for Habermas, is no obstacle to proceeding 'as if' a European Constitution had been brought into existence by a double sovereign,[17] despite everything we know about the democratic deficit and the lack of a European public sphere.[18] In other words, the constituent power is relegated to the status of a counterfactual; as an individual (European) constitution-founding subject. A constitution-making power that exists only in the mind of intellectuals can finally substitute the unruly masses of modern democracy.

Law, Habermas had argued in *Between Facts and Norms*, was already the privileged mode of integration among strangers.[19] The process of *juridification*, instead of a corruption of the lifeworld, would now act as 'not only a rationalising but also a civilising force';[20] acting as a language which circulates throughout society and unifies all other subsystems including the political sphere. The priority of law over politics is firmly established: the constitution connects them through the 'legal medium', emphasizing the triumph of the juridical component and its style of practice and discourse. It is now, decisively, modern law that is supposed to perform the role of de-differentiation of the functional subsystems that had been so central to Max Weber's narrative of secularization. Law would be called upon to re-enchant the modern constitutional imagination.

Other constitutional theorists went further than Habermas in the depoliticization of the constitutional idea, discarding even the simulacra of constituent power. Disconnected from any particular polity or history, constitutionalism could then acquire a cosmopolitan character, 'according to which a set of universal principles' central to liberal democracy 'undergird the authority of public law'.[21] According to one of the leading exponents of this view, 'Constitutionalism' (with a capital 'C') was a 'distinct *cosmopolitan* framework for the construction of a coherently principled, yet pluralist world of public law'.[22] Although these free-standing principles were constructed

[17] The notion of popular sovereignty or constituent power split at the root is introduced here, a duality which is structural and built in from the beginning: 'the foundation of the European Union can be conceived retrospectively as though the citizens involved (or their representatives) were split into two personae from the very beginning; in that case every person as a European citizen in the constitution-founding process encounters herself, as it were, as a citizen of an already constituted national people' (ibid 38). See, further, Jürgen Habermas, *The Lure of Technocracy* (Polity Press 2015) 40.

[18] Even if we take *only* the Franco-German space, the absence of a 'real public sphere' has been well documented (see, eg Ulrich Krotz and Joachim Schild, *Shaping Europe: France, Germany, and Embedded Bilateralism from the Elysée Treaty to Twenty-First Century Politics* (OUP 2013) 112).

[19] Jürgen Habermas, *Between Facts and Norms: Contributions to a Discourse Theory of Law and Democracy* (MIT Press 1996).

[20] Habermas, 'Crisis' (n 10) 8.

[21] Mattias Kumm, 'How Does European Union Law Fit into the World of Public Law? *Costa*, *Kadi*, and Three Conceptions of Public Law' in Jürgen Neyer and Antje Wiener (eds), *Political Theory of the European Union* (OUP 2010) 125. cf Alexander Somek, 'Europe: Political, Not Cosmopolitan' (2014) 20 European Law Journal 142.

[22] Kumm (n 21) 135 (The debt to Dworkin was evident; if, for 'law's empire', we can now read 'constitutionalism's empire', it was largely built from the same materials as its legal ancestor. This strand of thinking would even lead to the introduction of a journal named 'Global Constitutionalism', declaring, in its inaugural issue, the new 'holy trinity' of human rights, democracy, and the rule of law).

by way of interpretation of the modern constitutionalist tradition that began in Paris and Philadelphia at the turn of the eighteenth century, their foundations in popular sovereignty would be gradually, but radically, loosened. In place of democracy, cosmopolitan constitutionalism offered abstract notions—such as respect for human rights, subsidiarity, and the rule of law—as defining concepts of constitutional interpretation, whether national or supra-national.[23]

Common to such accounts would be a rejection of any sense in which a constitution's authority must be tied to the exercise of a popular constituent power.[24] Public reason would be invoked in place of popular sovereignty as a standard for assessing institutional arrangements and outcomes in the multilevel systems, not only in Europe, but beyond.[25] Sovereignty would be 'neutralized', the discipline of *Staatslehre* abandoned.[26]

A new hook for this constitutional optimism would be the much-feted *Kadi* case, concerning the validity of EU regulations implementing a post-9/11 UN 'targeted sanctions' regime, in light of its alleged incompatibility with fundamental human rights.[27] In *Kadi*, Advocate General Maduro strongly reaffirmed the autonomy of the European Community (now European Union) legal order, contrasting it with the intergovernmental nature of the European Convention on Human Rights, and obliging the Court of Justice 'to act as the *constitutional court* of the *municipal legal order* that is the Community'.[28] He concluded that general principles of law must prevail over the comparatively weakly legitimated norms of the international order. Many European constitutionalists interpreted *Kadi* as an aggressive affirmation of a particular European 'constitutional identity', superior to, and distinct from, that ascribed to international law. Some even characterized it as a mature statement of judicial 'civil disobedience' towards the relatively immature and anarchic international order; a potential *Solange* moment for the European level.[29] Although other commentators

[23] ibid; cf Mattias Kumm, 'Constituent Power, Cosmopolitan Constitutionalism, and Post-positivist Law' (2016) 14 International Journal of Constitutional Law 697.

[24] For discussion, see Neil Walker, 'Post-constituent Constitutionalism? The Case of the European Union' in Martin Loughlin and Neil Walker (eds), *The Paradox of Constitutionalism: Constituent Power and Constitutional Form* (OUP 2008); Neil Walker, 'The Return of Constituent Power: A Reply to Mattias Kumm' (2016) 4 International Journal of Constitutional Law 906. Dyzenhaus would argue against constituent power more generally: see David Dyzenhaus, 'Constitutionalism in an Old Key: Legality and Constituent Power' (2012) 1 Global Constitutionalism 229.

[25] Mattias Kumm, 'The Cosmopolitan Turn in Constitutionalism: on the Relationship between Constitutionalism in and Beyond the State' in Jeffrey Dunoff and Joel Trachtman (eds), *Ruling the World: Constitutionalism, International Law and Global Governance* (CUP 2012) 268–70. Following MacCormick, albeit less excusably, given the rise in sovereignty claims in the intervening years, he proposed that 'in the law of the European Union, *the language of subsidiarity has completely replaced the language of sovereignty*' (ibid 293 (italics added)). It is extraordinary that subsidiarity continued to exert hold of the constitutional pluralist imagination, despite the fact that its juristic career was an abject failure.

[26] András Jakab, *European Constitutional Language* (CUP 2016) 116.

[27] See Joined Cases C-402 and 415/05P *Kadi and Al Barakaat International Foundation v Council and Commission* [2008] ECR I-6351.

[28] The Treaty, in his words, was 'not merely an agreement between states but an agreement between the *peoples* of Europe', creating a 'municipal legal order of transnational dimensions, of which it forms the "basic constitutional charter"' (AG Maduro in *Kadi*, para 21). The Court itself, although differing from the Advocate General in certain respects, also reaffirmed 'the constitutional principles of the EC Treaty' (para 141). It proclaimed the EC to be an 'internal [and] autonomous legal system' (paras 142–143).

[29] See Turkuler Isiksel, 'Fundamental Rights in the EU after Kadi and Al Barakaat' (2010) 16 European Law Journal 551.

suggested that a better route would have been to identify the principles of fundamental rights within international law itself (through an application of *jus cogens*), academics generally celebrated the European Court of Justice for emphasizing the 'separateness, autonomy and constitutional priority of the [EU] legal order'.[30]

If *Kadi* ostensibly offered renewed impetus to the legal-constitutionalist project, it was a thin gruel on which to base any robust constitutional optimism; illustrative, rather, of the further disconnect between constitutional discourse and constitutional reality. The post-9/11 executive response in Europe was not to protect human rights, in contrast to a dehumanizing US agenda (as Derrida and Habermas, amongst others, had proclaimed), but to Europeanize a security state, increasing powers of control and surveillance, notably with the impact of the European arrest warrant framework decision (examined in Chapter 6).

The increase in executive powers in the framework of European integration would provoke a new round of domestic constitutional challenges, highlighting a further aspect of authoritarian liberalism, namely the empowerment of organs and police powers of the state in the field of criminal justice, and a concomitant weakening of the rights of defence and protection against extradition. On the issue of extradition under the European arrest warrant, national constitutional courts had to insist on domestic constitutional amendments to conform with EU law, and increasingly struggled to reconcile constitutional rights with their EU commitments, culminating with the German Constitutional Court's refusal to execute an arrest warrant, in 2015.[31] These challenges were a clear sign that the misleadingly named 'dialogue' between national constitutional courts and the ECJ, far from occurring in a contrapuntal harmony, was sounding a seriously discordant tone. In spite of the language of 'openness towards European law' (*Europarechtsfreundlichkeit*) precedents were being established for further challenges to come.[32]

The problems of national constitutional discord were, in reality, even wider and deeper than suggested by the arrest warrant challenges. On the specific question of juridical authority to rule on the validity of EU law, the truce between domestic courts and the ECJ had, in fact, already technically broken, with the Czech court ruling a decision of the European Court of Justice ultra vires in a dispute over pensions.[33] In the *Ajos* case, the Danish Supreme Court had refused to disapply a provision of national law in favour of unwritten, but directly effective, principle of EU law on age discrimination.[34]

[30] cf an important exception: Gráinne de Búrca, 'The European Court of Justice and the International Legal Order After *Kadi*' (2010) 51 Harvard International Law Journal 1.

[31] Order of 15 December 2015, 2 BvR 2735/14 (*EAW II*) (BVerfG).

[32] See judgment of 6 July 2010, BVerfGE 126, 286 (*Honeywell* decision) (BVerfG). For a thick normative defence of constitutional pluralism, see Miguel Maduro, 'Three Claims of Constitutional Pluralism' in Matej Avbelj and Jan Komarek, *Constitutional Pluralism in the European Union and Beyond* (Hart 2012) 67–85.

[33] Judgment of 31 January 2012, Pl ÚS 5/12 (*Slovak Pensions XVII*) (Constitutional Court of the Czech Republic). See Jan Komárek, 'Playing With Matches: The Czech Constitutional Court Declares a Judgment of the EU Ultra Vires' (2012) 8 European Constitutional Law Review 323–37.

[34] Case No 15/2014 *Dansk Industri (DI) acting for Ajos A/S v The Estate Left by A* (*Ajos* case) (Supreme Court of Denmark). See Mikael Rask Madsen, Henrik P Olsen, and Urška Šadl, 'Legal Disintegration? The Ruling of the Danish Supreme Court in AJOS' (*Verfassungsblog*, 30 January 2017) <https://verfassungsblog.de/legal-disintegration-the-ruling-of-the-danish-supreme-court-in-ajos/> accessed 25 September 2020.

Little of this deterred theorists of constitutional sovereignty, constitutional pluralism, or cosmopolitan and global constitutionalism.[35] This was not only due to the influence of figures such as Habermas, Kumm, and von Bogdandy. It was also because the more aggressive juridical disputes were frequently proxy battles, in practice amounting to little more than domestic tussles between courts (as in the Czech case), and often of relatively little material consequence for the EU's overall constitutional authority and political stability.[36] The same could not, however, be said of the OMT dispute, to which we now turn.

3. Who is the guardian of the European Constitution?

The constitutional resistance to European integration, and to the European Court of Justice, spearheaded by the German Constitutional Court, which began in earnest at Maastricht, and then grew apace at Lisbon, pitted one discourse of 'legal constitutionalism' or 'judicial supremacy' against another. If the German court was rhetorically protecting a democratic public sphere, it was one that, in reality, was already in steep decline. The court's move was paternalistic, attempting to empower a parliament that did not really want the power, much less know how to use it, just as in the *Miller* litigation that would later occupy centre stage in the UK after the Brexit vote.[37] What the Karlsruhe court was doing was mounting a defence of the *sovereignty of the court*, attempt to fill a void that had emerged with the disconnect between rulers and ruled, substituting for a democratic culture that had been 'hollowed out', in part by the ascendency of very same juridical power and authority it was asserting!

The OMT case differed from its earlier jurisprudence in two ways, however. First, unlike the previous skirmishes between Karlsruhe and Luxembourg, there was actual engagement on the battlefield. Second, the stakes were far higher. OMT involved a crucial 'federal' institution exercising contested powers in a critical situation: the European Central Bank (ECB) finally acting to 'save the euro' when Mario Draghi famously promised, in July 2012, that the ECB, within its mandate, would do 'whatever it takes to save the euro'.[38] Just over a month later, the OMT programme was announced

[35] See, eg Jiri Priban, 'The Semantics of Constitutional Sovereignty in Post-sovereign "New" Europe: A Case Study of the Czech Constitutional Court's Jurisprudence' (2015) 13 International Journal of Constitutional Law 180, arguing that the Czech court actually 'addresses profound questions of constitutional sovereignty in global society, typical of legal and political systems evolving beyond the organizational framework of the sovereign constitutional state', and perceives sovereignty as 'an instrument for achieving the post-national rule of law and constitutional accountability beyond classical notions of power politics and state organization', legally confirming 'what legal theorists have been describing as a state of constitutional, legal, and political pluralism and the end of the EU law's absolute primacy doctrine'.

[36] There were, to be sure, more constructive encounters, such as the *Tarricco* saga, when the Italian Constitutional Court and the ECJ had been able to proceed through a more dialogical approach, negotiating the boundary rather than aggressively defending red lines (Case C-42/17 *Criminal proceedings against MAS and MB* [2017] OJ C52/12).

[37] See Michael A Wilkinson, 'A Constitutionally Momentous Judgment That Changes Practically Nothing? The UK Supreme Court's Decision on the Prorogation of Parliament' (*Verfassungsblog*, 25 September 2019) <https://verfassungsblog.de/a-constitutionally-momentous-judgment-that-changes-practically-nothing/> accessed 25 September 2020.

[38] 'Verbatim of the Remarks Made by Mario Draghi: Speech at the Global Investment Conference in London, 26 July 2012' (*European Central Bank*, 26 July 2012) <https://www.ecb.europa.eu/press/key/date/2012/html/sp120726.en.html> accessed 25 September 2020.

by way of press release, promising unlimited purchases of selected government bonds on the secondary markets.[39]

The stage was set for a showdown with the European Court of Justice, at a crucial juncture in the euro crisis. The question of 'who is the guardian of the constitution?', so significant in the crucible of late Weimar, had resurfaced, and at a critical moment for the future of the euro and the EU itself. The institution which represented the most prominent formal channel for the expression of Euroscepticism and resistance to the EU in the name of 'democratic discourse' (or 'militant democracy in one country') had the opportunity to send a clear signal. Would Karlsruhe finally 'bite'?

OMT constituted a second plank of the euro crisis response, alongside the European Stability Mechanism (ESM), but functioned in accordance with a different, functionalist, logic; one that could not be fully reconciled with intergovernmental interests and ordoliberal ideology. The unconventional monetary policy pursued by the ECB, albeit after considerable, and costly, delay, would be deployed ostensibly on the basis that the financial crisis had damaged the 'monetary transmission mechanism'. The explicit purpose was to make private credit more easily attainable; but reducing borrowing costs of member states was an expected side effect, helping to 'unblock the system' by encouraging banks burdened by toxic assets to lend into the real economy. Reducing the 'irrationally' high spreads on sovereign yields between the core and the periphery, and lowering borrowing costs (at least for member states that were, in theory, subject to an adjustment programme through the ESM), would reflect the 'irreversibility' of the currency.

Although the 'buying of time' by central banks was a 'worldwide field experiment' after the global financial crisis, the emergence of the ECB to the front of the stage was subject to very particular political, legal, and constitutional constraints.[40] These permitted restricted room for manoeuvre in comparison to the Federal Reserve or the Bank of England, as the ECB was charged exclusively with the goal of price stability (as we examined in Chapter 8). If the ECB informally obtained the backing of the German 'semi-hegemonic' government, a loosening of monetary policy sat uneasily with broader ordoliberal logic, as well the Maastricht rule-based orthodoxy, and some prominent members of the Bundesbank. Unlike the ESM, which, as Advocate General Kokott noted in *Pringle*, represented an expression of member state *sovereignty*, OMT was not designed, or even explicitly approved, by the collective 'Masters of the Treaties'.[41] OMT, in other words, was a threat to state sovereignty (and German semi-hegemony) in a manner that the ESM was not. Programmes such as OMT represented a fusion, less of inter-state power and liberal economic ideology, than of supranational technocratic power and the interests of transnational and domestic capital, amounting, as Blyth notes, to 'class-specific put options', benefiting the top end of the

[39] 'Introductory Statement to the Press Conference (with Q&A)' (*European Central Bank*, 6 September 2016) <https://www.ecb.europa.eu/press/pressconf/2012/html/is120906.en.html> accessed 25 September 2020. The ECB claimed the right to intervene, in order to guarantee the 'singleness of monetary policy'.

[40] See Wolfgang Streeck, *Buying Time: The Delayed Crisis of Democratic Capitalism* (Verso 2014) 165.

[41] Case C-370/12 *Thomas Pringle v Government of Ireland and Others* [2012] OJ C26/15 (Opinion of AG Kokott, para 138).

income distribution.[42] The self-empowerment of the ECB was a serious threat to the constitutional order as understood and defended by the German Constitutional Court.

Draghi's promise was widely praised by commentators as a crucial measure to protect the euro and avoid financial meltdown in its member states ('[n] ever has so much effect been gained by doing so little', was one endorsement). 'Words alone', noted the same commentator, 'calmed the markets'.[43] The OMT programme appeared as a 'watershed' in the eurozone crisis,[44] 'one of the most effective announcements any central bank has ever made', according to another commentary.[45] It was something for which, according to Habermas, all European citizens owed Draghi 'a debt of gratitude', his 'uttering a single sentence ... saved them from the disastrous consequences of the threat of an immediate collapse of their currency'.[46]

The reason for the apparent success of OMT was straightforward: financial investors would be encouraged to buy the bonds of distressed member states with the knowledge that they could later sell them on to the ECB. The prospect that the ECB would move into sovereign debt markets 'with the full weight of its balance sheet' was an offensive that 'no market participant could hold a short position against'. It was a promise to act as an indirect and conditional 'lender of last resort'. That is what Draghi meant when he said 'the euro is irreversible'.[47]

Aside from its distributional effects, there were, however, serious questions over the ECB's authority to pursue such a programme. The powers of the ECB had been drastically restricted by the rules set up at Maastricht; the ECB's primary objective was to ensure price stability and, in order to promote fiscal discipline, it was prohibited from monetary financing of national budgets (Articles 119 and 123 TFEU). A complaint was launched by Peter Gauweiler, a German Eurosceptic member of the Christian Social Union (CSU) party, with the support of the AfD and Die Linke parties. The German Constitutional Court ruled that OMT was ultra vires as a matter of European law, and, as a serious structural transgression of the delineation of competences, in violation of fundamental principles of the German constitution.[48]

The first ever preliminary reference from Karlsruhe to Luxembourg was not launched in the spirit of accommodation. In an area of tremendous political, economic, and even existential significance for the EU, the German court's conclusions finally seemed to match its argument, unlike its *Maastricht* and *Lisbon* rulings.

[42] See Mark Blyth, *Austerity: The History of a Dangerous Idea* (OUP 2013) 258–60, on the class-specific nature of programmes such as OMT and quantitative easing, benefitting those with assets. On the significance of the repo market and shadow banking in understanding shifts in state-financial market relations in Europe, see Daniela Gabor and Cornel Ban, 'Banking on Bonds: The New Links Between States and Markets' (2017) 54:3 JCMS 617.

[43] Blyth (n 42) 247.

[44] Nicolas Jabko, 'The Elusive Economic Governance and the Forgotten Fiscal Union' in Matthias Matthijs and Mark Blyth (eds), *The Future of the Euro* (OUP 2015) 82.

[45] See Carsten Gerner-Beuerle, Esin Küçük, and Edmund Schuster, 'Law Meets Economics in the German Federal Constitutional Court: Outright Monetary Transactions on Trial' (2014) 15 German Law Journal 281, 282.

[46] Jürgen Habermas, 'Why Angela Merkel is Wrong on Greece' (Social Europe, 25 June 2015) <https://www.socialeurope.eu/why-angela-merkels-is-wrong-on-greece> accessed 25 September 2020.

[47] Erik Jones, 'The Forgotten Financial Union: How You Can Have a Euro Crisis Without A Euro' in Matthias Matthijs and Mark Blyth (eds), *The Future of the Euro* (OUP 2015) 63.

[48] BVerfG, Order of 14 January 2014, 2 BvR 2728/13 ('*Gauweiler*' order) (BVerfG).

Accusations of methodological nationalism against Karlsruhe, hitherto of greater theoretical than practical import, were now pregnant with moment. Of particular significance was its potential to empower the German organs of state in any bailout negotiations by offering them the opportunity to play the 'Karlsruhe card', and reply, if asked to adopt a more flexible response, that 'our court won't let us'![49] Although technically limiting their room for manoeuvre, constitutional limitations, paradoxically, could strengthen Germany's hand in the intergovernmental arena of Eurogroup discussion, to the extent that they ruled out a broader mutualization of debt. And German refusal to take part (or the German court ordering the Bundesbank to desist) would be of considerable political-economic significance, likely to render any ECB or eurozone programme ineffective (or to provoke a constitutional crisis in Germany, if the Bundesbank refused).

Juridical conflict was, for once, direct and politically consequential. For the German court, the ECB must not subvert the conditionality ('austerity') imposed on debtor states under the ESM, or the various bilateral and multilateral loans, by a back-door programme of bond-buying.[50] On the other hand, from the perspective of the ECB, the OMT programme was essential to maintain the financial stability and 'singleness' of the currency, which had become a symbol of the success of the project of European integration itself. Although the German court offered a compromise solution, it was one which would have seriously limited, if not nullified, OMT, damaging the prospects of economic stability at a delicate moment.[51]

The German court compounded the difficulty for the ECJ by the manner of the referral and the particular intertwining of German constitutional law and EU legality. Karlsruhe indicated that, if unchanged, the OMT programme should be declared illegal, not only on the basis of EU law (OMT violating the division of competences between the EU and the member states, and, specifically, ultra vires the powers of the ECB), but of German constitutional identity (OMT violating the right of the German citizen to vote for the Bundestag, due to its potential impact on budgetary autonomy and the 'democratic discourse' of German society).[52] The German court construed constitutional identity idiosyncratically, divorcing its own doctrine from the more holistic perspective offered in Article 4(2) TEU.[53] Core German constitutional identity,

[49] According to Mayer, '[t]he reality of the Euro crisis is that constitutional law arguments replace political arguments ... [t]he Federal government is not entirely innocent in this development, as they do play the "Karlsruhe-card" domestically and in negotiations in Brussels ... [c]learly, some government bureaucrats have no sense of the potential damage to the community of law that comes with that kind of reasoning'. As the Constitutional Court increasingly 'over-reaches', 'politicians increasingly try to anticipate' its 'sensitivities'. (Franz Mayer, 'Rebels Without a Cause? A Critical Analysis of the German Constitutional Court's OMT Reference' (2014) 15 German Law Journal 111, 135–36).

[50] Wade Jacoby, 'Europe's New German Problem: The Timing of Politics and the Politics of Timing' in Matthias Matthijs and Mark Blyth (eds), *The Future of the Euro* (OUP 2015) 209.

[51] '*Gauweiler*' order (n 48), para 100: conditions of judicial guarantees of limited purchasing, no debt restructuring, and avoidance of market interference (which were anyway 'untestable', see Karsten Schneider, 'Questions and Answers: Karlsruhe's Request for a Preliminary Ruling to the Court of Justice of the European Union' (2014) 15 German Law Journal 217, 231).

[52] '*Gauweiler*' order (n 48) paras 26–30, 48.

[53] '*Gauweiler*' order (n 48) para 29.

it claimed, was exclusive and non-negotiable,[54] not only immune to balancing of any sort, but also solely for the German Constitutional Court to interpret.[55]

The double-pronged nature of its attack was significant, blurring the lines between the European and domestic legal orders, and putting the Luxembourg court in a difficult position. Even if declared by the ECJ to be within the powers of the ECB on a formal reading of EU law, the German court could declare it a violation of national constitutional identity. If so, OMT would be valid in the EU legal order with the exception of Germany (as a matter of German law). Germany would be in breach of EU law, and technically subject to the possibility of an infringement procedure by the Commission. But without Germany's participation, and without the support of the Bundesbank, the programme's credibility, which is what matters on the financial markets, could have been shattered. The implication was clear: Germany's economic power threatened to turn into a quasi-constitutional authority for the eurozone as a whole.

The ECJ stood firm, despite the weight of Karlsruhe's objections, and rejected the offer of a compromise. On the question of the authority to determine the legality of acts of EU institutions, including of the ECB, the Court of Justice was adamant about its exclusive authority: its ruling would be 'definitive'.[56] On the material question of ultra vires, the Court of Justice granted a wide margin of discretion to the ECB, amounting to what might be called a 'featherweight' review of its actions. In a 'controversial' area like monetary policy, the ECJ ruled, nothing could be required of the ECB except that it use its expertise 'with all care and accuracy'. Unsurprisingly, given this level of deference, the Court found no 'manifest error of judgment'.[57]

When the case returned to Karlsruhe, the German court essentially backed down, aside from noting that it would maintain a degree of surveillance, in case the OMT programme was actually triggered. It had achieved its goal of ensuring the spotlight remained on the imposition of conditionality (the significance of which we will return to in Chapter 11). The reality was that OMT had already done its work, and attention was turning towards the new quantitative easing policy (the public sector purchase programme), a multi-trillion euro asset purchase launched in 2015, through which the ECB eventually acquired bonds worth 20 per cent of the eurozone's GDP.[58] This would subsequently be challenged in the *Weiss* litigation, when the German court and the ECJ again clashed swords, with even more apparent fury than before. In *Weiss*, the German court found the ECJ's ruling ultra vires, specifically the ECJ's misuse of

[54] '[I]dentity review is not to be assessed according to Union law but exclusively according to German Constitutional Law', according to the German court ('*Gauweiler*' order (n 48) para 103).

[55] '*Gauweiler*' order (n 48) para 29. For analysis, see Monica Claes and Jan-Herman Reestman, 'The Protection of National Constitutional Identity and the Limits of Integration at the Occasion of the Gauweiler Case' (2015) 16 German Law Journal 917.

[56] Case C-62/14 *Peter Gauweiler and Others v Deutscher Bundestag* [2015] OJ C279/12, para 14. Unlike the Advocate General, the ECJ did not even make reference to Article 4(2) TEU, or to any process of balancing between the authority of EU law and national constitutional identity. The reference of the Advocate General to proportionality was, perhaps, significant, as the later *Weiss* case would demonstrate.

[57] ibid para 75.

[58] See 'Consolidated Financial Statement of the Eurosystem as at 2 October 2020' (*European Central Bank*, 7 October 2020) available at <https://www.ecb.europa.eu/press/pr/wfs/2020/html/ecb.fs201007.en.html> accessed 22 November 2020. By October 2020, the reported value of assets purchased under the PSPP was 2,295 billion euros. Inflation, however, had hardly shifted.

the principle of proportionality (which it deemed 'incomprehensible') to justify the ECB's programme, as well, it suggested, as the programme itself. It gave the ECB three months to do its homework, and demonstrate the programme's proportionality with regard to its adverse economic consequences.[59]

Weiss confirmed that the real winner of the euro crisis saga was not the ECJ, whose exercise of authority merely confirmed suspicions about its integrationist agenda, and its weakness as a guarantor of the 'rule of law': it was the ECB. Throughout the critical institutional tussles of the decade, the ECB had succeeded in expanding its mandate, as well as its institutional prestige. It had managed a transformation, from the Maastricht focus on maintaining low inflation, to the fight against deflation. It had turned the exception (unconventional monetary policy) into the norm. Even though it still lacked the possibility of direct government financing (prohibited by Article 123 TFEU), the ECB, it turned out, was the guardian of the 'European constitution'. Would money, rather than law, be capable of re-enchanting the constitutional imagination?

4. The new constitutionalists

This 'buying of time' with modern money would, in reality, only contribute to the evasion of serious reform of the euro, and of the EU, as we will examine in Chapter 11. But, for a new generation of European constitutionalists, the European Court's assertive rulings signified less the rubber-stamping of dubious emergency programmes, than the triumph of European law. The ECJ had finally stamped its authority over a recalcitrant domestic court on a decisive constitutional question.

For the 'new constitutionalists', the ECJ's ruling on OMT ended the constitutional compromise that had been formulated and embraced by scholars of European integration in the post-Maastricht era.[60] It signposted a new stage in the process of the constitutionalization of the European Union, towards a fully monist federal order, drawing the curtain on the play of constitutional pluralism. The end of the uncertainty between Karlsruhe and Luxembourg was essential for the EU to reach constitutional 'maturity', finally ending the conceptual 'fudge' that had prevailed since *Solange* in the 1970s. When compromise collapsed, as it necessarily would, equilibrium would need to be restored through affirming the ultimate authority of the European Court (or else

[59] C-493/17 *Weiss and Others* EU:C:2018:1000; German Constitutional Court Judgment of 05 May 2020 (2 BvR 859/15). See, for discussion, Marco Dani and others, 'At the End of the Law: A Moment of Truth for the Eurozone and the EU' (*Verfassungsblog*, 15 May 2015) <https://verfassungsblog.de/at-the-end-of-the-law/> accessed 25 September 2020.

[60] See Federico Fabbrini, 'After the OMT Case: The Supremacy of EU Law as the Guarantee of the Equality of the Member States' (2016) 16 German Law Journal 1003; R Daniel Kelemen, 'On the Unsustainability of Constitutional Pluralism: European Supremacy and the Survival of the Eurozone' (2016) 23 Maastricht Journal of European and Comparative Law 136. To buttress this point, Advocate General Cruz Villalón's Opinion in *Gauweiler* is relied on. According to the Advocate General, unilateral reservations of authority, such as that demanded by Karlsruhe, would soon lead to constitutional disintegration, and it would become 'an all but impossible task to preserve *this* Union, as we know it today, if it is to be made subject to an absolute reservation, ill-defined and virtually at the discretion of each of the Member States'; see *Gauweiler and Others* (n 56), Opinion of AG Cruz Villalón, para 59.

the constitutional construct of the EU would unravel).[61] It meant acknowledging that 'ultimately, in any constitutional order worthy of the name, some *judicial authority* must have the final say'.[62]

From the perspective of the new constitutionalists, the 'guardian of the European constitution' was decisively the ECJ. The EU would experience its federal 'constitutional moment' through the legal medium, against all the weight of evidence that suggested a de-federal and centrifugal dynamic.[63]

The insistence that a ruling on the supremacy of EU law by the ECJ would constitute a 'constitutional moment' represented the final disconnect of constituted and constituent power; a disconnect launched with post-war reconstruction, and central to the European constitutional construct. The new constitutionalists would exaggerate this dynamic, entirely disaggregating the legal constitutionalism from its political aspect, assuming a fully juridified version of constitutional federalism. Ironically, in so doing, they would mirror not only much of the constitutional pluralist literature they positioned themselves against, but the whole tradition of European 'free-standing constitutionalism', replicating its attempt to move beyond popular sovereignty and democratic constituent power.[64] In short, far from a representing a *rupture* from the status quo, the new constitutional moment would take legalistic constitutionalism to its limit.

Although the new constitutionalist claims appeared entirely to lack *credibility*, and looked increasingly like legal fetishism, removed from the realities of political power and democratic legitimacy, this was hardly a new phenomenon in the history of European integration. As we saw in Part II, the substitution of legal for political avenues towards integration had been spearheaded by the European Court of Justice from the outset, at the vanguard of a community of activist lawyers. This was how the European Union had ascended to 'constitutional' status in the Court and legal academy in the first instance, later bolstered by constitutional theories working to conceal the material weakness and brittleness of its political foundations and social supports, just when they were coming under scrutiny in the post-Maastricht era.[65] Although opposed to constitutional pluralism, the new constitutionalists would have got nowhere without it. But they would then turn fully *against* the constitutional pluralist turn, condemning pluralism as a means for domestic autocrats to justify violation of

[61] See Kelemen (n 60) 150. Kelemen's solution is, in fact, a declaration of incompatibility between the domestic constitution and continuing membership of the EU. Raising the constitutional stakes would, according to Kelemen, actually stabilize the EU legal order, by 'upping the stakes and increasing the costs of missteps, but at the same time reducing the chance of war'.

[62] ibid 139 (Italics added). cf Alexander Somek, 'Monism: A Tale of the Undead' in Matej Avbelj and Jan Komárek (eds), *Constitutional Pluralism in the European Union and Beyond* (Hart Publishing 2012).

[63] The idea of a constitutional moment is associated with the work of Bruce Ackerman; see Bruce Ackerman, *We, the People: Foundations* (HUP 1991). The centrifugal dynamic would be most obvious with the Brexit vote, but this was merely the tip of an iceberg (see Chris Bickerton, 'Beyond the Void: Reflections on Peter Mair's Legacy' (2018) 24:4–5 European Law Journal 268).

[64] Wilkinson (n 7). See also Joseph HH Weiler, 'The Political and Legal Culture of European Integration: An Exploratory Essay' (2011) 9 International Journal of Constitutional Law 678. Weiler notes that 'there has been a refusal to see the way in which the essential legal order of constitutional jurisprudence is part and parcel of the political democratic legitimacy crisis' (ibid 689).

[65] Neil Walker had actually warned precisely against such constitutional fetishism: see Neil Walker, 'The Idea of Constitutional Pluralism' (2002) 65 Modern Law Review 317.

the rule of law and European norms of liberal democracy, particularly in the cases of Hungary and Poland.[66]

The 'rule of law crisis' or crisis of 'constitutional degradation' appeared to give European constitutionalists a new vocation.[67] Authoritarian liberalism could now turn to the task of rhetorically defending politically liberal values against what would be labelled 'populism'.[68] The new constitutionalists not only became anti-pluralist, they accused constitutional pluralists of complicity in the populist turn, pointing out that authoritarians were now explicitly invoking constitutional pluralism in an attempt to justify departure from EU norms.[69]

A rarely noted irony in this move is that anti-pluralism is often taken to be one of the defining features of populism itself.[70] Was the juridical populism of the new European constitutionalists a mirror image of the political populism of the new authoritarians?

5. From Habermasian federalism to Schmittian federation

Central to the new constitutionalism emerging out of the various euro crisis conflicts was a claim that, although legal authority had been fully scaled up, the political foundations of the EU were ultimately determined at the domestic level, since membership of the EU was entirely voluntary. The basis for this claim was a formal version of an argument from state consent; one that could look to Article 50 TEU for textual support. This, in the view of the new constitutionalists, justified increasingly hierarchical juridical authority exercised by the ECJ.

This position revealed a significant inflection from the deliberative constitutionalism of Habermas and his followers, and a move towards a decisionistic constitutionalism reminiscent of Carl Schmitt. It led to a final irony. The new constitutionalists drew, in their support, on a state theory advanced by Martin Loughlin which was directed *against* the notion that constitutional authority was to be determined by judicial claims at all. Loughlin's statist theory had rejected constitutional pluralism, not because ultimate legal authority must be vested uniquely in the ECJ, but because political authority remained ultimately vested in the member states.[71] The new

[66] See Cormac Mac Amhlaigh, 'Symposium – Crisis and Constitutional Pluralism in the European Union' (2019) 21 Cambridge Journal of European Legal Studies 3 (on the uses and abuses of 'constitutional pluralism').

[67] For a survey of the literature, see Martin Loughlin, 'The Contemporary Crisis of Constitutional Democracy' (2019) 39 Oxford Journal of Legal Studies 1.

[68] See, eg R Daniel Kelemen and Laurent Pech, 'The Uses and Abuses of Constitutional Pluralism: Undermining the Rule of Law in the Name of Constitutional Identity in Hungary and Poland' (2019) 21 Cambridge Yearbook of European Legal Studies 59–74.

[69] ibid.

[70] See Jan-Werner Müller, *What is Populism?* (University of Pennsylvania Press 2016).

[71] Martin Loughlin, 'Constitutional Pluralism: An Oxymoron?' (2014) 3 Global Constitutionalism 9 (in Loughlin's reconstruction of the foundations of public law, constitutional development takes place through the dialectic of authority (*potestas*) and power (*potentia*); the generation of a belief in the authoritative '*right* to rule', in conjunction with the actual *capacity* to compel obedience or attract allegiance to the political community. In modernity, this dialect involves material and subjective elements associated with the apparatus of *statehood* and the set of beliefs on which it rests, central to which is the 'autonomy of the political domain'. Applied to the EU, the argument can be put in short form: the combination of political *incapacity* and *illegitimacy* is decisive in rejecting constitutional claims for the EU's governing authority. On the question of

constitutionalists seized on the argument from 'ultimate political authority', basing the legitimacy of integration on a formal notion of member state consent and the possibility of withdrawing it. Dissent *within* the Union, particularly from domestic courts, must be minimized; judicial supremacy at the supranational level must prevail. So, despite the scaling up of constitutional (qua juridical) authority, the new constitutionalists made no claim that political authority had fully (or even partially) shifted upwards in unison, nor that a new European *demos* had emerged on which to legitimate the increasing authority of the EU.

If the constitutional pluralist literature had *conflated* sovereignty and government, in the service of dissolving the former and enabling the move 'beyond the sovereign state', the new constitutionalists radically *divorced* them. The new constitutionalists' position could be bluntly put: if a member state objected to EU juridical supremacy (and, by extension, the supremacy of EU institutions such as the ECJ and the ECB), there was an obvious route: the exit door. Sovereignty, in other words, remained.

This disconnect between law and politics would be a less nuanced version of an older account of the dynamics of integration. Utilizing Hirschman's scheme of 'exit, voice and loyalty', Weiler had presented European integration along a two-track process; a fortuitous duality of normative supranationalism and political intergovernmentalism, achieving an equilibrium between legal authority, which had become strongly centralized through the ECJ's jurisprudence, and political power, which remained predominantly with the governments of the member states.[72] It was precisely because the member states remained in control of the basic political *contents* of the arrangement that they were willing to surrender control of its legal *enforcement*, which anyway depended not only on the ECJ, but also on national courts' acquiescence, as a feature of the decentralized judicial architecture. The framework, in other words, was meant to explain the maintenance of equilibrium without resorting to full 'exit', not to fall back on the possibility of exit as evidence of an imaginary current equilibrium. Equilibrium was maintained by preserving the domestic 'voice' of national political authority through formal and informal mechanisms internal to the EU's constitutional architecture; through its multidimensional institutional set-up and procedures of law-making and law-applying, including the continuing authority of domestic

power (*qua potentia*), the claim proceeds by contrasting the material elements of statehood at the domestic level with their absence in the EU, particularly with regard to its lack of resources for the essential tasks of providing for the *salus populi*: welfare and warfare (ibid 18). To this functional dimension, Loughlin adds a subjective element, which goes directly to the question of the governing relation between rulers and ruled. This demands a move beyond the legal text to consider by what 'political right' a governmental agency is able to act; to consider the set of arrangements 'through which rulers and subjects express their beliefs about the authority of government' and about that government's 'right to rule'. In short, there is the question of political loyalty and identity, which precedes any account of governmental powers and the way they are channelled through the constitution. In this foundational regard, the EU is similarly lacking, expressed by Loughlin through a version of the well-known 'no *demos* thesis').

[72] For the classic statement of this duality and its evolution in the early years of integration, see Joseph HH Weiler, 'The Transformation of Europe' (1992) 100 Yale Law Journal 2403; building on Joseph HH Weiler, 'The Community System: The Dual Character of Supranationalism' (1981) 1 Yearbook of European Law 267. See, further, Albert Hirschman, *Exit, Voice and Loyalty – Responses to Decline in Firms, Organizations and States* (Harvard University Press 1970).

(constitutional) courts.[73] This was why the German Constitutional Court's jurisprudence on fundamental rights, ultra vires, and constitutional identity was considered central to the constitutional and institutional balance, as it might help this equilibrium be preserved, over time.

These various features of the integration project were meant to protect the constitutional authority of the member states. They were designed to protect 'voice' in the EU, and even paid some attention to the material discrepancies in power *among the* member states, such as the rules on qualified majority voting in the Council, and the necessity of unanimity for Treaty change. These mechanisms, intended to facilitate equality, might permit the suspension of the question of exit, and even of the question of sovereignty itself. In short, the idea was that political voice (combined with a high degree of loyalty) prevented the need for exit, rather than the possibility of exit mitigating the absence of voice.[74]

The thrust of the argument offered by the new constitutionalists reversed this: with the possibility of exit available, the need for voice could now be discarded. This argument did not follow a theme of Kantian universalism, or Habermas's variation on that theme. It closely echoed the language of Schmitt; specifically, Schmitt's constitutional theory of the 'federation' (or '*Bund*'), an entity that was neither a loose alliance of sovereign states, on the one hand, nor a fully fledged federal state, on the other (in a different vernacular, neither a *Staatenbund* nor *Bundesstaat*).[75]

According to Schmitt, sovereignty does not disappear in this federated arrangement, neither is it pooled or divided: rather, it is *suspended*. For Schmitt, this could only be a provisional status, sovereignty inevitably reappearing in a time of crisis or in the moment of exception: the federation would be an inherently unstable phenomenon and eventually dissolve downwards or evolve upwards. Which way it is resolved would be determined, for Schmitt, by the political condition of homogeneity; this would determine whether political unity would be reasserted at the level of the federation, or by its member states.[76] In agreement with Schmitt, the new constitutionalists ultimately consigned any 'third alternative' to the graveyard, the 'chronicle of a death

[73] The Bundesverfassungsgericht (BVerfG) has been described as a missing channel for Germans to voice their Euroscepticism. See, eg Klaus Gärditz, 'Beyond Symbolism: Towards a Constitutional *Actio Popularis* in EU Affairs? A Commentary on the *OMT* Decision of the Federal Constitutional Court' (2014) 15 German Law Journal 189.

[74] Note that, as we examined earlier, a formal legal avenue of exit only came to exist, as a matter of EU law, with the Lisbon Treaty (Article 50 TEU).

[75] Carl Schmitt, *Constitutional Theory* (Jeffrey Seitzer tr, Duke University Press 2008). See also Olivier Beaud, *Théorie de la Fédération* (Léviathan, PUF 2007); Christoph Schönberger, 'Die Europäische Union als Bund: Zugleich ein Beitrag zur Verabschiedung des Staatenbund-Bundesstaat-Schemas' (2004) 129 Archiv des öffentlichen Rechts 81; Robert Schütze, 'Federalism as Constitutional Pluralism: "Letters from America"' in Matej Avbelj and Jan Komárek (eds), *Constitutional Pluralism in the European Union and Beyond* (Hart Publishing 2012); Matej Avbelj, 'Theory of European Union' (2011) 36 European Law Review 818; cf Signe Larsen, *The Constitutional Theory of the Federation and the European Union* (OUP 2021), especially 17–19.

[76] For discussion, see Signe Larsen, 'United in Diversity: Humanism, Homogeneity, and Hegemony' in Giorgio Baruchello, Jacob Dahl Rendtorff, and Asger Sørenson (eds), *Ethics, Democracy and Markets: Nordic Perspectives on World Problems* (Aarhus University Press 2016). 'Homogeneity' was the term picked up by the German court in its *Maastricht Urteil*, albeit, somewhat disingenuously, citing Heller rather than Schmitt.

foretold'.[77] Characteristic of the prevailing normativism in the legal academy, this momentous decision, however, is now entirely subsumed into the juridical question of *Kompetenz-Kompetenz*.[78] Judicial authority alone is scaled up; political authority is untouched. It is an odd echo of Schmitt, transfigured into a realm where norms and facts, law and politics, state and society, are uncoupled.[79]

The strength of the new constitutionalism—its simplicity—was also its weakness. A crude reduction of state theory, it obscured the transformational character of European integration; the transformation of political sovereignty in practice, effected by the changing state-society relations and growing void in democratic authority occurring through the post-war and post-Maastricht eras.

To justify a juridical federalism on the basis that the ultimate authority to leave (or renegotiate membership) remained with the member states would elide the material conditioning of political authority, and, indeed, the erosion of popular sovereignty *in the interim*.[80] It was not only that, prior to Lisbon, the formal option to leave the EU did not even exist in the Treaty; and, after Lisbon, few thought Article 50 would ever be triggered; nor even that, with regard to the euro area, there was no legal avenue of exit; indeed, one is yet to be juridically mapped out to this day. It is that it completely formalizes constitutional discourse by introducing a decisionism which is at odds with the fact that membership is an ineluctable part of the constitutional imagination for many, if not most, states of the European Union. Despite fluctuations in the popularity of the EU and its institutions, and the centrifugal forces pushing it apart, a more abstract loyalty to 'Europe' (and the project of 'European integration') is a crucial part of the process of state and constitutional transformation, in all the dimensions outlined in this book.

European integration as a process of state and constitutional transformation (outlined in Parts II and III of this book) revealed the precarity of the status quo, but also the apparent difficulty in transcending it. For all the various contestations, only an anticlimax would be reached in the euro crisis conjuncture.

In one sense, however, the new constitutionalists had stumbled upon a significant feature of the conjuncture. The capacity (or incapacity) for exit had *become* key to the project of integration in a way that it had not been during the first decades of the project. Soon, the related question of expulsion would also arise, with the rule of law crisis and the 'perfect storm' of populism giving a new impetus to the constitutionalist argument that supremacy of EU law must be respected at all costs.[81]

But there were two serious difficulties in raising exit to this level of constitutional significance. The political difficulty with basing the EU's enhanced authority on the possibility of withdrawal was that authoritarian populists in Hungary and Poland had

[77] Michael A Wilkinson, 'Constitutional Pluralism: Chronicle of a Death Foretold?' (2017) 23 European Law Journal 213.

[78] Recalling debates in early twentieth century German positivism; see Grimm (n 12).

[79] In basing its conclusions on *Kompetenz-Kompetenz*, the new constitutionalism is a mirror image of the approach taken by Grimm (n 12), but reaching the opposite conclusion.

[80] See Martin Loughlin, 'The Erosion of Sovereignty' (2016) 45 Netherlands Journal of Legal Philosophy 57(Loughlin, 'Erosion').

[81] For a broad overview of the 'perfect storm' of existential problems facing Europe by 2016, see, eg Conor Gearty, 'The State of Freedom in Europe' (2016) 21 European Law Journal 706.

no intention of using the exit clause, instead trying to reforge the EU in their own image. Conversely, expulsion was simply not catered for in the Treaty. And there was a second difficulty: exit assumed a voluntarism that was difficult to square with the material constitutional reality. Exit from the EU could not be presented as a simple formal option, reclaiming, at will, sovereignty that had been suspended. This would be amply demonstrated by the Greek crisis.

Sovereignty, in other words, had not only been suspended. It had been *eroded*. This should have been clear from the very same state theory the new constitutionalists purported to rely on:

> faced with extreme austerity conditions, the formal right of the Greek state to withdraw from these European arrangements was tested both in general elections and a referendum and has been shown, on capacity grounds, no longer to be a real right. The episode provides a stark case of a severe erosion of sovereignty, and one which highlights more general issues concerning the governing framework established for the Eurozone.[82]

As Loughlin explains, sovereignty is not merely a formal concept. 'Since sovereignty expresses a relation between right and capacity', he argues, 'there may come a point when developments at the level of governmental organization impose such strains on the right-capacity nexus that sovereignty is unable to carry its meaning as a representation of the autonomy of the political realm'.[83] This decline will not be counteracted by constitutional challenges of a juridical variety; on the contrary, if such rulings amount to 'all bark and no bite', then 'the existence of this supervisory jurisdiction is in danger of being transformed into the means by which a slow erosion of basic constitutional protections is in fact being legitimated'.[84]

The constitutional configuration of Europe would be tested, in January 2015, with the election of an anti-austerity government in Greece, beginning a contest that would symbolize the erosion not only of sovereignty, but of democracy, in its ancient birthplace. To see why, we need to examine the material constitution that had developed in the post-Maastricht period: neofunctionalist ideology based on the irreversibility of the euro; a hyper-financialized economy; a deepening and extension of neo-liberal hegemony; and the deteriorating condition of domestic democracy, specifically of the principle of popular sovereignty underlying it. This was highlighted by the Greek case, but, as we will see in Chapter 11, 'Greece' represented a much broader set of phenomena.

[82] Loughlin, 'Erosion' (n 80) 77.
[83] ibid 69.
[84] ibid 76.

11
The Material Constitution in Crisis: *Telos*, *Nomos*, and *Demos*

1. Introduction

The German Constitutional Court's resistance to the European Court of Justice (ECJ), ultimately unsuccessful in its bid to protect Germany's own 'democratic discourse', was only a (failed) attempt to preserve 'militant democracy in one country'.[1] It could do nothing for democracy in the rest of the eurozone. As with its *Lisbon* decision, as Fritz Scharpf put it, Karlsruhe failed a test of universalizability; it was 'fundamentally flawed' in failing 'to consider its generalized implications in the light of the Kantian categorical imperative'.[2] Indeed, by maintaining the pressure on the euro regime for conditionality and budgetary discipline, it served further to *repress* the range of domestic options for other member states (and for the EU as a whole).

The new constitutionalism that emerged in the euro crisis, insisting on supremacy of the ECJ, likewise did nothing to resolve the democratic deficits in the Union, but only exacerbated them. The notion that the EU's own constitutional future was definitively settled—that the EU had 'matured' into a federal unit—required a suspension of disbelief, impossible to reconcile with its increasingly fractious divisions and existential uncertainties.[3] The European Central Bank's programmes of outright monetary transactions (OMT) and quantitative easing (QE) were stopgap solutions to cover deeper structural design flaws of the euro. They bought time, but merely deferred the growing democratic legitimacy problems. The litigation was, in fact, a surface reflection of a *material* problem: a dispute not only over the symbolic unity of integration, or over juristic supremacy, but about the ideology of austerity and, ultimately, about the principle of popular sovereignty.

If both the 'old' and the 'new' constitutionalist responses could be characterized as an 'odd mix of Schmitt and Kelsen', combining Kelsen's legal normativism and Schmitt's political decisionism, Hermann Heller had been entirely abandoned. The social and democratic aspects of constitutional development had largely been discarded by courts— domestic and supranational—and commentators alike.

The French and Dutch 'no' votes on the Constitutional Treaty in 2005 should have sounded grave political alarms for the ruling political elites in Europe, following on the back of earlier failed referenda in the Republic of Ireland and Denmark, and the

[1] See, further, Michael A Wilkinson, 'Authoritarian Liberalism in the European Constitutional Imagination: Second Time as Farce?' (2015) 21 European Law Journal 313.

[2] See Fritz W Scharpf, 'The Asymmetry of European Integration, or Why the EU Cannot be a Social Market Economy' (2010) 8 Socio-Economic Review 211.

[3] For a dissection of the various different elements of the euro crisis, see Agustin Menéndez, 'The Existential Crisis of the European Union' (2013) 14 German Law Journal 453.

Authoritarian Liberalism and the Transformation of Modern Europe. Michael A Wilkinson, Oxford University Press.
 DOI: 10.1093/oso/9780198854753.003.0012

nearly failed French *petit oui* on Maastricht a decade previously.[4] The experiment of the Constitutional Treaty was not merely a failed 'public relations exercise', as some had speculated; it signalled the turn away from a democratic constitutional path. The democratic deficit, so prominent in debate between the Maastricht and Lisbon Treaties, would then, in Majone's words, become a democratic *default* through the euro crisis.[5]

When the euro crisis hit, the Maastricht constitution struggled to hold, and the crisis response became subject to multifaceted contestation, not only from powerful domestic institutions such as the German Constitutional Court, but also from social movements in the margins and, eventually, from positions of governmental authority (as in the Greek case). The various parts of the fragmented apparatus of the state and the European state system increasingly resorted to cajoling and coercing, undermining even the moderate checks and balances of constitutional accountability, and turning to emergency modes of governing, in an attempt to maintain the liberal economic order and the project of integration.

The ordoliberal rules of the game, established at Maastricht, had come into tension with the hyper-discretionary politics of neo-liberal structural adjustment, and particularly with the functional imperative to maintain the symbol of European integration, the single currency ('if the euro fails, Europe fails'). In turn, both ordo- and neo-liberalism came into conflict with the democratic and social movements against austerity, and in the case of Greece this was pushed (nearly) to the limit with the election of Syriza, an anti-austerity but pro-European government, in January 2015. After the circle was eventually squared by permitting 'rescue programmes', not as acts of democratic solidarity, but through a 'grey area' of Union law, and with strict conditionality attached, it would then require the pacification of an aroused and enraged populace.

In short, through the 'unfinished conjuncture' of the euro crisis phase, deep-seated instability in the regime emerged from contradictory imperatives, pertaining to distinct logics of the material constitution of Europe: *telos*, *nomos*, and *demos*.

The *telos* of European integration was premised on a neofunctionalist promise of unification or 'ever closer union' of the peoples of Europe, symbolized by the European Central Bank's (belated) technocratic intervention to secure the 'irreversibility' of the euro. The neofunctionalist *telos* of further and deeper integration, however, would come into conflict with the liberal economic framework that Maastricht was meant to constitutionalize and protect (section 2). The conflict between irreversibility and market logic would be deferred by tying the actions of the ECB to domestic neo-liberal structural reforms, in keeping with the ordoliberal spirit of the Maastricht rules. This deferral was materially underpinned by the growing financialization of the economy and the ideological and class dimensions of austerity politics, which conveys the *nomos* of the region in a new light, revealing not only the norms of ordoliberalism, but a geoeconomic and spatial strategy of production and capital accumulation (section 3). This new *nomos* would come up against the logic of the *demos*, amid growing local

[4] In the words of Hubert Védrine, rejection of the Constitutional Treaty by the French and the Dutch, 'marked the end of the enlightened despotism that had guided European integration since 1950' (Hubert Védrine, *History Strikes Back: How States, Nations and Conflicts are Shaping the 21st Century* (Brookings Institution Press 2008) 64).

[5] Giandomenico Majone, *Rethinking the Union of Europe Post-Crisis: Has Integration Gone Too Far?* (CUP 2014) 196–207.

demands for a reclaiming of sovereignty over the economy, illuminated briefly in the '*oxi*' referendum in Greece. This would be extinguished in Syriza's capitulation to the demands of the Eurogroup and Troika, representing the broader decay of democracy under the weight of an apparently resilient, but still essentially passive, authoritarian liberalism (section 4).

2. Economic liberalism and the *telos* of irreversibility

The constitution of monetary union, in accordance with the logic of the market, was part of a broader experiment of market-making, designed to remove obstacles to the four economic 'freedoms', and to pursue the goal of undistorted competition in a single juridical space. Certainly, the move from a 'microeconomic' to a 'macroeconomic' constitution would be a step change in terms of the constraints it would place on a member state's capacity to intervene in the economy (and its effect on budgetary issues normally subject to democratic contestation). But monetary union would be an acceleration of existing trends; a further depoliticization of the economy through externalized constraints. It was prefigured in the French move, under President Giscard d'Estaing, towards a stability-oriented policy in the late 1970s, in the run up to the European Monetary System, after the failure of the more federally inclined Werner Plan for economic and monetary union, presented in 1970.[6]

The Treaty of Lisbon did little, if anything, to change the terms of the debate; the last-minute removal of 'competition' from the objectives of the Treaty at the insistence of the French having little or no effect, either from a constitutional perspective or a practical political-economic one.[7] On the contrary, the attached protocol confirmed the significance of undistorted competition and its central place in relation to the completion of the internal market. The influence on the Commission, and on European scholars, of an efficiency-oriented, Chicago school-way of thinking about competition was also steadily growing.[8] Although Lisbon added a provision committing the Union to social dialogue, the reality was a downgrading of industrial relations, with social partners reduced to a set of interested parties, or 'one policy stake-holder among many'. Legislative initiatives in the social policy field were 'almost completely exhausted', with the Commission failing to adopt any social policy agenda at all in the crisis years between 2010 and 2015.[9]

[6] Ulrich Krotz and Joachim Schild, *Shaping Europe: France, Germany, and Embedded Bilateralism from the Elysée Treaty to Twenty-First Century Politics* (OUP 2013) 188–89 (after 1976, following the decline of the dollar, French president Giscard and prime minister Barre 'welcomed the EMS as an external constraint on French monetary and fiscal policies contributing to anchor low inflation expectations. In a way, France under Giscard accepted becoming more "German".' (ibid 189).

[7] The reference to the 'free and undistorted competition' objective contained in Article I-3.2 of the draft Constitutional Treaty was removed, apparently to placate the concerns of the French 'no' voters of 2005.

[8] José LB Sierra, 'Writing Straight with Crooked Lines: Competition Policy and Services of General Economic Interest in the Treaty of Lisbon' in Andrea Biondi, Piet Eeckhout, and Stefanie Ripley (eds), *EU Law After Lisbon* (OUP 2012).

[9] Ruth Dukes, *The Labour Constitution: The Enduring Idea of Labour Law* (OUP 2014) 151–52. The Commission would then suggest an improved system of 'monitoring' to tackle the negative consequences of austerity, which was having a devastating effect on the deficit economies.

Lisbon signalled a complete blockage of progress in the field of social policy. It did little to alter the dynamic of authoritarian liberalism, and, if anything, deepened it, leaving the EU unprepared to face the forthcoming crises. The 'many crises' of the period of euro-related turmoil that followed Lisbon would then exacerbate economic differences between nations, sharpen the divide between labour and capital, and increase divisions among labour organizations in the member states.

According to Maastricht orthodoxy, economic stability would be ensured by the financial markets setting bond yields at a level appropriate to the soundness of a state's finances, with the aid of credit rating agencies and information available to investors on the credit worthiness of the investment. Yet, in the decade prior to the outbreak of the financial crisis, there had been an extraordinary convergence of sovereign bond yields; interest rates for peripheral states plunged in the run-up to the introduction of the single currency, and through the first years of the new millennium. In combination with huge capital flows from French and German banks, this facilitated consumption-oriented growth in the periphery, and northern trade surpluses in the core, emanating, in particular, from Germany and the Netherlands. *Convergence* in interest rates, in other words, was contributing to *divergence* in economic performance.[10]

Competitiveness in exporter countries increased, not through productivity gains, but through wage repression, a characteristic of 'Modell Deutschland'.[11] The conditions for large export surpluses were relatively weak currencies and low wages in the surplus countries, partly as a result of the weakening of the working class and trade unions.[12] In other parts of the eurozone, particularly Spain and Greece, growth was experienced through domestic demand, the creation of asset bubbles, and, notably in Spain, a large housing bubble. What emerged was a form of hyper-privatized Keynesianism. The effect of this substitution of private debt for public demand-management was to lessen the pressure for domestic reforms, with clientelistic states 'buying time' through large flows of foreign capital and investment. Export-led and debt-led growth, thus, developed in uneven combination.[13] If spectacular convergence of yields seemed unlikely to have been due to similar economic fundamentals when, for example, Greece and

[10] For an overview of the critical political economy and post-Keynesianism on which this section draws, see Johannes Jäger and Elisabeth Springler, 'Critical Political Economy and Post-Keynesian Perspectives' in Jäger and Springler (eds), *Asymmetric Crisis in Europe and Possible Futures: Critical Political Economy and Post-Keynesian Perspectives* (Routledge 2015) 1–15. See also Costas Lapavitsas, 'With Time to Prepare: Planning an Exit from the EMU' in Eva Nanopoulos and Fotis Vergis (eds), *The Crisis behind the Eurocrisis: The Eurocrisis as a Multidimensional Systemic Crisis of the EU* (CUP 2019) 406–08.

[11] On the history and geoeconomics of 'Modell Deutschland', see Bob Jessop, 'Variegated Capitalism, *das Modell Deutschland*, and the Eurozone Crisis' (2014) 22 Journal of Contemporary European Studies 248(Jessop, 'Variegated Capitalism'). See, further, Abraham Newman, 'The Reluctant Leader: Germany's Euro Experiment and the Long Shadow of Reunification' in Matthias Matthijs and Mark Blyth (eds), *The Future of the Euro* (OUP 2015) 117–36; Costas Lapavitsas and others, *Crisis in the Eurozone* (Verso 2012).

[12] See Lapavitsas and others (n 11) 45; Andreas Bieler, Jamie Jordan, and Adam D Morton, 'EU Aggregate Demand as a Way out of Crisis? Engaging the Post-Keynesian Critique' (2019) 57 Journal of Common Market Studies 805.

[13] Lapavitsas and others (n 11). On the longer backstory of the Greek crisis, dispelling the myth of an over-inflated public sector, see Spyros Sakellaropoulos, *Greece's (Un)competitive Capitalism and the Economic Crisis: How the Memoranda Changed Society, Politics and the Economy* (Palgrave Macmillan 2019). On the broader long-term relations between core and periphery, stressing both interdependence and diverse productive capacities, see Andrea Ginzburg, Dario Guarascio, and Giuseppe Celi, *Crisis in the European Monetary Union: A Core-Periphery Perspective* (Routledge 2019).

Germany were compared, few seemed particularly concerned with the market signals at the time.[14]

Such development strategies, based on capital flows and divergent growth regimes, may well have been 'unsustainable' in the long run.[15] The global financial crisis, in any case, brought them to an abrupt halt, dramatically precipitating capital flight from Greece as bond yields widened, and Greek government debt was priced out of the market. When the banking bubble turned into a banking crisis, and then into a sovereign debt crisis, as liquidity dried up and banks demanded rescue, the situation started to become more politically problematic, a development that was hardly surprising.[16] Once it became clear that Greek fiscal fundamentals were not as healthy as previously thought,[17] the markets, still reeling from the global financial crisis that began with the collapse of Lehman Brothers in September 2008, took aim at Greece, and created panic in other weak links in the euro chain. In a short space of time, the yield spread on Greek, Spanish, and Italian bonds shot back up towards their pre-euro levels, and Greek bonds were eventually graded 'junk' in April 2010. The financial markets, which had facilitated the gush of liquidity, would now cause it to dry up, blocking the main avenue of growth, as well as causing more acute crises in the economic situations of the debtor nations, as the social effects of austerity hit home.

At the time of the first Greek bailout in 2010, Greek debt was mostly privately owned, held largely by French and German banks.[18] The Greek situation, although special in certain respects, was not unique, with more general concerns about the solvency of the co-called 'PIIGS' (Portugal, Ireland, Italy, Greece, and Spain) raising the fear of contagion. The financial problems in the Republic of Ireland and Spain were also bank-related, 'housing bubbles' having grown on the back of 'credit bubbles', and protecting these private banks from losses at such a delicate financial moment appeared vital. Banks were considered 'too big to fail' (at least outside Iceland, which conducted a rare field experiment in bankruptcy), but the banking system as a whole was also considered 'too big to bail', not only due to the financial costs, but the political costs of rescue at the conspicuous expense of the taxpayer. The subsequent bailouts of Greece, the Republic of Ireland, and Portugal 'were connected by European financial markets—both to each other and to the rest of Europe', which was how, as this process wore on, 'the European financial crisis evolved into a full-fledged sovereign debt crisis'.[19] Rather than debtor countries defaulting and northern European banks

[14] See Menéndez (n 3) 494–97.

[15] Bieler, Jordan, and Morton (n 12).

[16] See Mark Blyth, *Austerity: The History of a Dangerous Idea* (OUP 2015) 73 (noting that even Reinhart and Rogoff argue that, in 80 per cent of cases, a banking crisis is followed by a sovereign debt crisis. This is, supposedly, why a government should never let a bank go bust, a point Walter Bagehot emphasized more than 100 years ago).

[17] A 12 per cent instead of 6.5 per cent government deficit was announced shortly after the centre-left PASOK was elected in October 2009.

[18] European banks, not least those of the core in Germany and France, 'were attracted to the margin of interest that could be procured on peripheral euro-zone state bonds and concluded that the risk that the margin represented—massively under-priced as it was by the markets—would ultimately have to be borne by the European Central Bank (ECB) in the interests of the systemic stability of the currency union, not themselves' (Helen Thompson, 'Austerity as Ideology: The Bait and Switch of the Banking Crisis' Comparative European Politics 1 (2013) 729–36, 730).

[19] Erik Jones, 'The Forgotten Financial Union: How You Can Have a Euro Crisis without a Euro' in Matthias Matthijs and Mark Blyth (eds), *The Future of the Euro* (OUP 2015) 54.

being bailed out directly, the less politically problematic path, not least for France and Germany, would be for debtor countries to continue to borrow money to service their debt, there being little appetite for any kind of default, debt restructuring, or major reform of the fundamental political economic structure, a theme that would become recognizable.[20]

Despite numerous interventions, the general economic outlook in the periphery continued to worsen: debts continued to rise and unemployment to increase. Austerity was reducing the prospect of a return to growth in Greece, the Republic of Ireland, and Portugal, as well as destroying the hopes of many of their citizens, particularly the young: by June 2012, youth unemployment in Greece was running at over 50 per cent. The consequences of austerity would not only be socially devastating but also, according to increasing numbers of mainstream economists, essentially irrational. It did not impress the markets, with yields continuing to rise through 2012; despite historically low central bank interest rates, money was not being passed on through the general economy. Banks loaded with toxic assets were holding on to their resources, despite the huge injections of liquidity by the ECB.[21]

It was only with the heightened concern that the Greek crisis could spill over and create broader contagion, causing investors to target other, bigger, economies, that Draghi decided something had to be done, to ensure the 'irreversibility of the euro'. Action was justified, in the official view of the ECB, because the monetary transmission mechanism was not working. Variations in liquidity, and in bond yields, did not reflect the fact that the euro was a single currency. According to the ECB (with the ECJ deferring to their authority on this point), the spike in peripheral bond yields was based on unfounded fears of a break-up of the currency. After initial hesitation, the ECB finally acted, promising to buy unlimited government bonds on secondary markets for states in financial difficulty. Draghi loaded his bazooka and aimed, without needing to fire; the promise itself was enough to calm the financial markets.

The ECB's justification for intervention in September 2012 had, thus, been the 'irrationality' of sovereign spreads, given the singleness of the currency, a claim which would constitute a key disagreement between the 'expert opinions' of the Bundesbank and the ECB in the hearings in the German court.[22] The Bundesbank, with the German court concurring, rejected the notion that the market could have priced sovereign debt irrationally when the yield spread rose in the early stages of the euro crisis.[23] Markets

[20] See Liz Alderman and Jack Ewing, 'Most Aid to Athens Circles Back to Europe' *The New York Times* (New York, 29 May 2012) <https://www.nytimes.com/2012/05/30/business/global/athens-no-longer-sees-most-of-its-bailout-aid.html> accessed 25 September 2020. It has been calculated that total state support of the financial sector amounts to some 5 trillion euros (see Blyth (n 16) 249). Even the modest, voluntary, 'haircut' accepted by private creditors was accompanied by various sweeteners, and anyway dwarfed by the 1 trillion euros passed to the banks at nominal interest rates, beginning with the first act of Draghi as central bank president when he took over from Trichet in 2011.

[21] According to the ECJ in Case C-62/14 *Peter Gauweiler and Others v Deutscher Bundestag* [2015] OJ C279/12 (the '*OMT* case'): 'It is undisputed that interest rates for the government bonds of a given State play a decisive role in the setting of the interest rates applicable to the various economic actors in that State, in the value of the portfolios of financial institutions holding such bonds and in the ability of those institutions to obtain liquidity' (para 78).

[22] The German court, in the *OMT* case (Order of 14 January 2014, 2 BvR 2728/13 ('*Gauweiler*' order) (BVerfG)), had been keen to add that it found the expertise of the Bundesbank more 'convincing' than that of the ECB (para 71).

[23] ibid para 98 (describing as 'meaningless' the idea that a portion of the debt was irrationally priced).

were simply 'pricing in' the risk of default, based on peripheral profligacy and revelations of unsound finances. The ECJ, on the contrary, accepted the ECB's exercise of discretion, based on unjustified fears of break-up: the euro was indeed 'irreversible', as the French had insisted two decades earlier, and as the project of integration had been presented in the foundational period in Paris and Rome.[24] This was an indelible aspect of the *telos* of the Union.

But if conditions were allowed to be more lax under OMT than under the ESM (European Stability Mechanism), the ordoliberal principles on which European Monetary Union (EMU) was structured—sound finances and fiscal discipline—might be jeopardized. OMT risked moral hazard by encouraging financial investors to lend, and governments to borrow, in the knowledge that they could be rescued by the ECB in the future. This raised a more profound issue. Whereas the German government (in conjunction with other states) was able to influence ESM through its voting weight, this influence could potentially be circumvented by the ECB's unorthodox monetary policy. The concern was that ESM (an expression of member state sovereignty, even if using EU institutions), might be unilaterally outflanked by a technocratic agent acting with a broader 'European' remit.

If the ECB was becoming more flexible in the direction of monetary powers, moving away from an exclusive focus on fighting inflation, it was important to ensure more rigidity in the direction of fiscal authority, to prevent flexibility subverting the discipline of austerity (which had effectively been constitutionalized by the ECJ's ruling on the ESM in *Pringle*).[25] Karlsruhe's concern, in other words, was that ECB policy might permit profligate states to benefit *without* being disciplined; to have their cake (receive financial assistance) and eat it too (maintain fiscal autonomy). The ECJ did its best to assuage this concern, offering a clear message: connection to conditionality is required by the Treaty, thereby reconciling financial aid with fiscal discipline and the avoidance of moral hazard. The circumvention of the market that OMT undoubtedly represented would only be allowed on terms that would replicate liberal market ideology; conditionality would ensure that member states' finances were guided 'as if' under the dictates of market logic.[26]

But assuaging Karlsruhe's concern on this point raised an obvious constitutional difficulty. Insisting on a connection to conditionality made the ECB's programme look more like an economic policy measure, functionally equivalent to the ESM, which—according to the ECJ's decision in *Pringle*—was not something the ECB should be interfering with. This 'double life' of the ECB, acting both in monetary and economic matters, raised serious legitimacy concerns, highlighted by the Advocate General, although ignored by the ECJ.[27] The ECB would, thus, come to wield enormous power

[24] Making EMU irreversible was the 'great French success story of the Maastricht negotiations' (Kenneth Dyson and Kevin Featherstone, *The Road to Maastricht: Negotiating Economic and Monetary Union* (OUP 2003) 251).

[25] See Case C-370/12 *Thomas Pringle v Government of Ireland and Others* [2012] OJ C26/15.

[26] A situation referred to by the German court as 'parallelism'. This appears largely rhetorical because, in practice, OMT's effects on fiscal discipline were already very real, reducing yields in Spain and Italy without them ever entering into any formal adjustment programmes. See, further, Michael A Wilkinson, 'The Euro is Irreversible! . . . or is it? On OMT, Austerity and the Threat of Grexit' (2015) 16 German Law Journal 1049.

[27] *Gauweiler and Others* (n 21), Opinion of AG Cruz Villalón, paras 143–50. On this point, the ECJ is rather formalistic. The ECJ agrees with the ECB that OMT is about price stability and the 'singleness of monetary policy', but justifies it along the following lines: because the ECB only has competence to pursue

over a member state that found itself in a situation of requesting assistance. Not only would the ECB set monetary policy, it would also negotiate economic policy in its role in the troika, monitoring compliance with adjustment programmes to the level of detail where it could be dictating the opening hours of bakeries, and public spending on pharmaceuticals.

Maastricht's depoliticization of monetary policy had led to the politicization of the ECB, a process that would come to the fore in the 'Greek crisis' that played out over the first half of 2015. After the election of Syriza, in January 2015, on an anti-austerity platform, the ECB would also take on a new role, using the freezing of emergency liquidity assistance to Greek banks as a threat, potentially wrecking the entire payments system. In tandem with a flight of capital, and then a liquidity crisis, limits on cash withdrawals from Greek bank accounts (sixty euros per day) came as the ECB withdrew emergency liquidity, after Greek prime minister Alexis Tsipras promised a referendum on the memorandum of understanding at the end of June 2015.[28]

What was new in this moment was not the decision of the Eurogroup and Troika to manage Greece as if it were a protectorate, or an outpost of economic colonialism. That was well understood, long before Syriza obtained power.[29] What was new was the threat of 'Grexit': but not by Greece. Less than a month after the ECJ's ruling on OMT reinforced the 'irreversibility' of the euro, it became clear that, at least for one country, the euro may no longer be sacrosanct, but reversible: not Greece, but Germany. The so-called Schäuble plan, scribbled on the back of an envelope and presented at the Eurogroup meeting on 11 July 2015, signalled not only willingness, but preparation—however half-baked—for a 'temporary', managed Grexit.[30]

This was a truly political and constitutional *event*. It had previously been assumed, and on good authority, that European political elites—*especially* German ones—would never let the euro fail (Merkel had stated that, 'if the euro fails, Europe fails'). 'Defence of the Euro at any price' was a matter 'not only of economic expediency but also of German political and moral raison d'état.'[31] That still held, in a sense, but it did not mean that the 'weakest link' would be retained at any cost, rescued on conditions that might be acceptable to its people. On the contrary, the weakest link would be used in order to demonstrate to others that the principles upon which the euro must proceed, and the authority on whose control it rested, would be non-negotiable. It was openly noted by European political elites that a 'no vote' in the Greek referendum would be

price stability and the 'singleness of monetary policy', this is what the OMT programme must be intended to achieve. Unlike the Advocate General, the ECJ is unconcerned that the ECB is involved both as monetary broker in its role as Europe's central bank, and fiscal enforcer through its part in the Troika's adjustment programmes.

[28] See Ashoka Mody, *Eurotragedy: A Drama in Nine Acts* (OUP 2018) 418–19.

[29] Sakellaropoulos (n 13) describes Greece as a quasi-protectorate, 'where the burden of foreign intervention focuses on the economic functions of the state' (ibid 162–63).

[30] Stefan Wagstyl, 'Germany's Wolfgang Schaüble Puts Grexit Back on the Agenda' *Financial Times* (London, 16 July 2015) <https://www.ft.com/content/4bb34e4e-2bcf-11e5-8613-e7aedbb7bdb7>accessed 22 November 2020.

[31] Wolfgang Streeck, *Buying Time: The Delayed Crisis of Democratic Capitalism* (Verso 2014) 149.

punished,[32] as indeed it was. What was 'irreversible' was not formal membership of the eurozone, or the EU, but its ideological content.

3. Austerity: narrative and *nomos*

To expose the material constitution undergirding the rhetorical claims discussed in the previous section, we need to recall an aspect of moral hazard that is less conspicuous in the literature on the eurozone crisis. The set-up of the EMU should have deterred private creditors from investing too freely, and not only deterred states from 'over-borrowing'; the avoidance of moral hazard cuts both ways. In fact, the avoidance of moral hazard is targeted, in the first place, at private sector recklessness, maintaining the rational behavior of the creditor in the financial market, rather than at the avoidance of public debtor profligacy. The constitutional claim that the 'euro was irreversible' can, thus, be more accurately understood as having been made with the goal of encouraging private investors to keep lending, as much as being a statement of the unity of the single currency, so dependent had economic growth become on finance-led accumulation.[33]

There is another significant, but overlooked, feature of the ECB's programme, which highlighted asymmetries even among the 'debtor states' themselves. The effects of Draghi's announcement in 'shoring up' southern bond markets were vital,[34] putting to rest any fear of a 'doom loop' or 'death spiral' in Spain and Italy.[35] But although they did benefit from indirect bank recapitalization, neither Spain nor Italy was placed under a structural adjustment programme. If the effect of the ECB's programme on them was real, the notion of a link between financial support and austerity was revealed to be, at least partly, a fiction. The promise of financial support could, in reality, alleviate the market pressure for austerity by suppressing yields, irrespective of the legal argumentation that links them together.

The argument that conditionality mimics the pressure on states to retain fiscal discipline that would otherwise be enforced by the financial markets seems to be refuted by the evidence, which suggests that the fall in yields on government debt after 2012 had nothing to do with any promise of neo-liberal structural reforms, reductions in public expenditure, privatizations, regressive tax policies, and so on.[36] The fall in yields certainly did not correlate to any reduction of sovereign debt—always

[32] See Philip Altermann, 'Jürgen Habermas' Verdict on the EU/Greece Debt Deal—Full Transcript' *The Guardian* (London, 16 July 2015).

[33] Bob Jessop, 'Elective Affinity or Comprehensive Contradiction? Reflections on Capitalism and Democracy in the Time of Finance-dominated Accumulation and Austerity States' (2008) 28 Berliner Journal für Soziologie 9. See, further, Daniela Gabor and Cornel Ban, 'Banking on Bonds: The New Links Between States and Markets' (2017) 54:3 JCMS 617.

[34] See, eg Jonathan Hopkin, 'The Troubled South: The Euro Experience in Italy and Spain' in Matthias Matthijs and Mark Blyth (eds), *The Future of the Euro* (OUP 2015) 161.

[35] Jones (n 19) 63–64.

[36] To be sure, the financial markets' supposed preference for austerity is doubtful in terms of its overall rationality, given its contractionary effects, which became well documented after the 'expansionary contraction' thesis was 'disgraced' (see Massimo D'Antoni, 'From Monetary to Fiscal to Political Union: A Progression to Integration or a Recipe for Failure?' (2020) 23 Journal of International Economic Law 469).

touted as the ultimate reason for austerity—because debt continued to *rise* as austerity was pursued.[37] It was only when the ECB stepped in to promise bond-buying that the markets were calmed. According to Mark Blyth, it was 'central bank policy, not public sector cuts', which 'brought down yields and stabilised European sovereign debt markets'.[38]

But to understand 'austerity' in full, we have to look at it as a political and economic strategy, supported by a particular ideology, rather than as an economic theory or a rational plan for growth in the eurozone as a whole. Austerity is a strategy of capital accumulation, 'a hegemonic project based on ordoliberalism as a particular variant of neoliberalism'.[39] The crisis thus served 'as an occasion to move forward the boundaries of the possible' when it came to pushing through structural reforms. In other words, the euro crisis response was a manifestation of the 'shock doctrine'.[40]

On the surface, austerity works by 'reducing entrepreneurial cost', lowering the labour costs in the private sector, increasing 'profit per (labour) unit cost and boost[ing] the profit rate'. It is complemented by institutional changes, which 'on the one hand enhance capital mobility and competition' and, on the other hand, 'strengthen the power of managers in the enterprise and share and bondholders in society'.[41] On the fiscal side, austerity functions through 'consolidation', prioritizing budget cuts over public revenue, reducing taxes on capital and high incomes, and downsizing the welfare state. But it is also, and primarily, a *class* policy, constantly promoting 'the interests of capital against those of the workers, professionals, pensioners, unemployed and economically vulnerable groups.'[42]

The class dimension of austerity was obscured through the euro crisis, as it was accompanied by a moralization of the debt. German (and other) politicians pushed a misleading metaphor: that of the frugal Swabian household, which saves before it spends. This is misleading because there is little evidence that excessive public spending was causal, or that the metaphor is a sound one for government spending.[43] But it appeared to be an effective strategy. The *symptom* of the crisis—rapidly increasing public

[37] Blyth (n 16) demonstrates that post-OMT yields are *negatively correlated* with sovereign debt loads (ibid 251). According to Blyth, a central bank liquidity put 'designed to back-stop financial markets that are running out of funding (the purpose of OMT)' has little, if not nothing, to do 'with cutting the state's budget' (ibid 247).

[38] ibid 249.

[39] Magnus Ryner, 'Europe's Ordoliberal Iron Cage: Critical Political Economy, the Euro Area Crisis and its Management' (2015) 22 Journal of European Public Policy 275, 281 (arguing that ordoliberalism influenced 'the disciplinary conditionalities as codified by the Treaty on Stability, Co-ordination and Governance (TSCG), the attendant EuroPlus Pact, and the 'Six-Pack' of Regulations on macroeconomic surveillance').

[40] ibid. Ryner accounts for the pivotal role of German ordoliberalism as, in part, a response to US-induced externalities. The euro crisis response emulated the 'shock therapy' imposed on the new member states in the 1990s (see Chapter 6).

[41] John G Milios, Spyros Lapatsioras, and Dimitris P Sotiropoulos, 'The "Greek Crisis" and the Austerity Controversy in Europe' in John Marangos (ed), *The Internal Impact and External Influence of the Greek Financial Crisis* (Palgrave Macmillan 2017) 15.

[42] ibid.

[43] Sakellaropoulos (n 13). Such tropes as the frugal Swabian housewife 'played a crucial role in recasting the narrative of the financial crisis from one of dysfunctional financial markets to one of public finances and competitiveness' (Ryner (n 39) 282).

deficits—was henceforth treated as its *cause*, 'facilitating macroeconomic ex post rationalization and justification for fiscal and structural conditionality'.[44]

Once this moralistic tale took hold in the constitutional imagination, it conditioned the reaction: in order to avoid further fiscal indiscipline, states that requested assistance had to pursue the 'strict conditionality' that would be demanded were they still subject to the financial markets.[45] Ordoliberal concerns to mitigate moral hazard on the part of the public debtor are thereby assuaged: the state continues to act 'as if' subject to market rationality; the imposition of austerity enables the constitution of the EMU to be violated *as if* it were maintained. Crucially, this tale was also given a constitutional seal of approval, through the European Court's rulings.[46] Through official and unofficial narratives, a private debt crisis would, thus, be turned into a public one, in the course of the greatest 'bait-and-switch' in history.[47] Moral hazard and mutual suspicion are substituted for mutual trust and solidarity, or at least any residue of these that remained.

To explain the 'rationality' of this project, we need to turn away from its highly ideological narrative, and examine the way its particular configuration of law and politics served the spatial organization of power in society. We need to view austerity as a domestic and geoeconomic strategy of capital accumulation. This involved 'an institutionalized compromise between opposing social forces', and the construction of an imagined 'general economic interest': the interest of the EU or the eurozone as a whole.[48] But it was not based on such a construction; it was based on a class- and country-specific accumulation strategy.

The term *nomos* is helpful in reconstructing this. As we saw in Chapter 3, Carl Schmitt had presented the *nomos* of the earth in the ancient, spatial sense as a threefold 'concrete order', based on an original appropriation (*nehmen*), distribution, and production of land.[49] Together, this process would signify the origins and source of the material constitution, underwriting the positive law of each era. *Nomos*, in other words, literally grounded political authority. But the nature of this ground could change. As well as a spatial aspect, it had a temporal aspect, Schmitt sketching this diachronically across large-scale historical epochs.[50] The *jus publicum Europaeum* was specifically grounded on an epoch that coincided with the maritime 'discoveries' made

[44] Ryner (n 39). This was through 'the European Stability Mechanism (ESM), and the European Central Bank's (ECB's) Long Term Refinancing Operations (LTRO) and, above all, the Outright Monetary Transactions (OMT), which were necessary for saving the euro and which then could be construed as indicating successful European governance and even spillover' (ibid 276).

[45] Busting the myth of the inflated public sector in Greece, see Sakellaropoulos (n 13).

[46] See, eg *Pringle* (n 25).

[47] See Blyth (n 16).

[48] According to Jessop, 'economic hegemony exists where a given accumulation strategy is the basis for' such a compromise: see Bob Jessop, *The Future of the Capitalist State* (Polity Press 2002) 30.

[49] See Martin Loughlin, 'Nomos' in Thomas Poole and David Dyzenhaus (eds), *Law, Liberty and State: Oakeshott, Hayek and Schmitt on the Rule of Law* (CUP 2015) (Loughlin, 'Nomos'); and Martin Loughlin, 'Politonomy' in Jens Meierhenrich and Oliver Simons (eds), *The Oxford Handbook of Carl Schmitt* (OUP 2017). cf Oliver Simons, 'Carl Schmitt's Spatial Rhetoric' in Jens Meierhenrich and Oliver Simons (eds), *The Oxford Handbook of Carl Schmitt* (OUP 2017).

[50] It is interesting to note, as Schmitt does, commenting on its use in classical Greece, that *nomoi* and the Aristotelian notion of *politiea* could be created not only by land division, but also by the liquidation of *debt*; see Carl Schmitt, *The Nomos of the Earth in the International Law of the Jus Publicum Europaeum* (Telos Press 2003) 68.

by European peoples, and the overcoming of civil war, internally. This early modern *nomos*, based on land appropriation, accrual of the monopoly of legitimate violence, and a claim to radical title overseas, underwrote the foundations of the modern constitutional order. It provided nothing less than the social- historical conditions for the relative 'autonomy of the political', or 'an expression of the constituent power to establish order'.[51]

But, as scholars in the Marxist tradition have noted, appropriation, distribution, and production operate within a capitalist economy according to an internal logic of their own, and one that exists in an uneasy relation with the political—and geopolitical—space. This relation between political and economic logics, as a feature of *nomos*, is captured by an extension of Rosa Luxemburg's characterization of the process of imperialist *Landnahme* as signifying not only literal 'land-grabbing' ('simple robbery', as Arendt calls it), but also metaphorical market expansion. Spatial (or territorial) accumulation is integrated with increasingly intense processes of *commodification*. Luxemburg's insight suggests a political-economic reconstruction of the threefold order of *nomos*, as well as a related, but distinct, periodization in contrast to Schmitt's.[52] From this perspective, the changing character of *nomos* reflects the transformation of the state from a feudal to a capitalist, and then to an imperial organization of political and economic power.[53] In the post-war period of informal American empire and economic neo-liberalism, new types of late modern state power and spatial organization have then emerged, as the productive forces evolve.[54]

With this reordering of Schmitt's *nomos* in mind, the process of state and interstate development can be internally related (but not reduced) to the logic of capitalist social relations. Constitutional ordering is grounded not just on the initial—or subsequent—forceful accumulation, concentration, and protection of land (or property), but on a *continual transformation* of social relations. Constitutional ordering sets 'in train distinctive imperatives of competition, profit-maximisation, the compulsion to reinvest surpluses, and the need to improve labour productivity by developing the forces of production.'[55] It is not only original appropriation, or 'primitive' accumulation, that sets up the economic and social conditions for the market, as Smith, Marx, and Weber all noted,[56] but also the periodical reconstitution of these conditions

[51] See Loughlin, 'Nomos' (n 49).

[52] See Rosa Luxemburg, *The Accumulation of Capital* (Routledge 2013).

[53] Arendt's endorsement of Rosa Luxemburg's 'brilliant insight into the political structure of imperialism' (Hannah Arendt, *The Origins of Totalitarianism* (Harcourt 1966) 148) is interesting because Arendt, like Schmitt, tries to retrieve the Greek idea of *nomos*. Although Schmitt (n 50) omits discussion of Luxemburg's updating of Marxism for the imperial age, he does, briefly, address Marx's idea of original appropriation (ibid 333–34). He adds, 'if the essence of imperialism lies in the precedence of appropriation before distribution and production, then a doctrine such as expropriation of the expropriators is obviously the strongest imperialism, because it is the most modern' (ibid 334).

[54] See Leo Panitch and Sam Gindin, *The Making of Global Capitalism: The Political Economy of American Empire* (Verso 2012). For an exploration of the recent continuation of capitalist land-grabbing, see, eg Fredric Jameson, 'Aesthetics of Singularity' (2015) 92 New Left Review 101.

[55] Ellen M Wood, 'Logics of Power: A Conversation with David Harvey' (2006) 14 Historical Materialism 19.

[56] The identification of coercive forms of appropriation—whether through domestic corruption, war, or in forms of global imperialism ('political capitalism')—as central to the formation of the modern state is stressed by Max Weber. See, eg Richard Swedberg, *Max Weber and the Idea of Economic Sociology* (Princeton University Press 1998) 46–53.

through 'accumulation by dispossession' (through re-distribution and re-production of resources by political and coercive means).[57]

Social relations are, thus, transformed through direct and indirect interventions in society, which function to commodify and marketize, impose competitiveness, privatize, or shift private debt into public debt, and so on; in short, various aspects of what would become known as 'austerity'. The extent to which these processes can still usefully be categorized on the basis of a traditional class analysis is debated, but the class pedigree of *nomos* can hardly be doubted. As Hauke Brunkhorst bluntly puts it, 'no *nomos* without class rule'.[58] This is a feature of *nomos* also noted, right at its root, by Aristotle.[59]

In a geoeconomic sense, what had already been partly revealed after Maastricht's enlargement process—the renewal of traditional imperialist postures and predatory capitalism—would emerge in full view through the new key core-periphery relationships, captured in the unceremoniously titled 'PIIGS' (Portugal, Ireland, Italy, Greece, and Spain). If these relationships followed the combined and uneven development of earlier epochs, the acquisition or physical control of territory was now less central to economic domination. As we examined above, Germany's export-led regime (along with other countries such as the Netherlands) would increase the competitiveness of its productive capital after the introduction of the euro, not by increasing productivity, but by domestic wage restraint. This was a feature of its own authoritarian liberal policies, pursued by a 'third way' social democratic government under the auspices of Agenda 2010 and the Hartz IV reforms.[60] But it was also a feature of the extension of the European market to southern and eastern Europe.

The imposition of conditionality as a prerequisite for financial aid in the periphery was, thus, more than ordoliberal fetishism or punishment for countries such as Greece daring to oppose the status quo. It reflected Germany's intra- and extra-European export strategy, a strategy aimed not only inside, but also increasingly outside, the single market. In this arrangement, the European home market entered the equation 'not so much as a vital outlet' to absorb surpluses, but as a 'regional production platform for German exports'.[61] As Julian Germann outlines, 'spatial reorganisation of industrial activity is by no means limited to the Visegrád countries'. Germany now stands 'at the centre of supply chains that link the old EU to the current EU27', due, in large part, to 'the ability of German exporters to parcel out and optimise production' across a 'new industrial landscape in both East and West'.[62] The benefits would not only accrue to German capital, but to a 'neo-mercantilist German bloc'.[63]

[57] See David Harvey, *The New Imperialism* (OUP 2003) 36.

[58] Hauke Brunkhorst, 'Concrete Order Formation or Rational Will Formation? Constituent Power as the *Ratio* of *Voluntas*' in Michael A Wilkinson and Michael W Dowdle (eds), *Questioning the Foundations of Public Law* (Hart 2018) 88.

[59] For Aristotle, 'the rule of *nomos* means the rule of the middle classes as opposed to the rule of the very rich, on the one hand, and the rule of the masses or the poor, on the other', cited in Schmitt (n 50).

[60] See, eg Jessop, 'Variegated Capitalism' (n 11).

[61] Julian Germann, 'Beyond "Geo-Economics": Advanced Unevenness and the Anatomy of German Austerity' (2018) European Journal of International Relations 24(3) 590–613, 602.

[62] ibid ('According to an annual survey conducted by the Association of German Chambers of Commerce and Industry (DIHK) among its members, the 14 old EU countries are becoming an increasingly attractive host of foreign direct investment for German manufacturers seeking to cut cost.').

[63] Jessop, 'Variegated Capitalism' (n 11).

Once the implications of the spatial reorganization of Europe are drawn out, austerity appears to make *some* sense, at least from the standpoint of capital: 'structural reforms' offer avenues 'for German manufacturers to "nearshore" and optimise their production process'. This would significantly expand the spatial reach of the German model, and, in combination with domestic retrenchment, 'dramatically narrow the social circle of its beneficiaries'.[64]

The late modern turn from geopolitical to geoeconomic power, in terms of underwriting a new *nomos*, and the implications of this for the project of European integration, are captured in Claus Offe's stark assessment of the fallout from the global financial crisis:

> It used to be the case that, in order for one country or a group of countries to take full control of the economy and polity of another country, the former must occupy the latter by military means. This is no longer needed. Today one can have perfectly peaceful relations with a particular country and still literally own it—simply by appropriating its economy through a permanent trade surplus and by destroying its sovereignty by depriving the country (in an ad hoc fashion of rescue conditionality, if not through European law) of its budgetary and other legislative autonomy . . . Given this constellation of economic and political power, it does not come as a surprise that within those countries the situation is perceived as a new version of imperialism and dependency—a view the anti-European mobilisational potential of which yields very gloomy prospects for the future of European integration.[65]

In Offe's prognosis, the new *nomos* of the European area would generate significant countermovement, igniting a reaction against the perception of a neo-imperial formation. But how would this potential be realized? More pertinently perhaps, *who* would mobilize it?

4. The erosion of the *demos*

The euro crisis measures were frequently derided as the ultimate 'extend and pretend', 'kicking the can down the road' by denying the need for any serious discussion of debt restructuring, in an attempt to maintain the status quo by any means possible: 'there was no alternative'.[66] If they had the effect of 'buying time', they also reduced the willingness of political elites—national and European—to reform the structure of the euro governance regime by agreeing, for example, to Eurobonds, serious debt mutualization, or supranational economic governance. There was no 'falling forward', as had been assumed by the neofunctionalism of an earlier era: 'not even an attempt was made to create a democratically accountable fiscal union'.[67] And, not very

[64] Germann (n 61) 603.

[65] Claus Offe, 'Europe Entrapped: Does the EU Have the Political Capacity to Overcome its Current Crisis?' (2013) European Law Journal 595, 604.

[66] Yanis Varoufakis, *And the Weak Suffer What they Must? Europe, Austerity and the Threat to Global Stability* (Penguin Books 2016).

[67] Mody (n 28) 314.

surprisingly, 'the governments' willingness to adopt common institutional or economic measures declined once the pressure receded', in no small part thanks to the actions of the ECB.[68]

And yet, all this institutional fudging would not come without serious political and constitutional consequences. Although 'post-functionalism' had suggested that any renewed integrationist developments would be held back by a 'constraining dissensus', the reality was that institutions would continue to push forward in new ways, exemplified by the actions of the Eurogroup and the ECB. The combined effects of these actions would be to jeopardize 'the coherence and credibility of EU constitutionalism',[69] the rule-based order substituted for an order based on executive and technocratic discretion. The Polanyian countermovement would not occur through any re-politicization that would be recognizable in terms of a democratic plan of action, or public accountability at the supranational level. What would be the cost to an already deracinated democracy, and what would be the reaction of the *demos*?

By the time of the Lisbon Treaty negotiations, European integration was *already* described as having heralded 'the passing of majoritarian politics', discarding 'conventionally legitimated democracy'. This was not merely because it had introduced elements of technocratic rule within its governance structures, but because it had 'dispensed with the *demos*' itself, and, thus, had 'equally dispensed with the very foundation for legitimizing political representation'.[70] Democracy was already hollowed out, through decades of disconnect in state-society relations, as well as the legacy of ordoliberal and neo-liberal political and social philosophy (as laid out in Parts II and III).

EMU had taken this project a step further, allowing 'monetary policies to be freed from democratic deliberation' and 'masking the complex economic processes of re-distributing the costs and the advantages amongst the population'. If, from the perspective of the ruling class, the launch of the euro was a success, its depoliticization had 'provided conditions of possibility for the bureaucratic Caesarism to come'.[71] The increasing centrality of finance-led capitalism ('the most de-territorialised form of capital') in the post-Maastricht era favoured the emergence of an 'original form of authoritarianism', pursued by 'non-charismatic' institutions and coalitions.[72] As we have examined in this book, there was nothing particularly original about this authoritarianism, however, but for the fact that it was now partly organized across transnational lines.

The cumulative impact of the euro crisis on an already weakened domestic democracy was acute. Fault lines were evident from an early stage, when intimations of dissent would be dealt with swiftly, and in a politically brutal and often informal fashion. In late 2011, Greek premier Papandreou had been replaced by Lucas Papademos, an

[68] Nicolas Jabko, 'The Elusive Economic Government and the Forgotten Fiscal Union' in Matthias Matthijs and Mark Blyth (eds), *The Future of the Euro* 82–83.

[69] Nicole Scicluna, 'Integration through the Disintegration of Law? The ECB and EU Constitutionalism in the Crisis' (2018) 25 Journal of European Public Policy 187.

[70] Michelle Everson and Julia Eisner, *The Making of a European Constitution: Judges and Law Beyond Constitutive Power* (Routledge 2007) 27.

[71] Cedric Durand and Razmig Keucheyan, 'Bureaucratic Caesarism: A Gramscian Outlook on the Crisis of Europe' (2015) 23 Historical Materialism 23, 35.

[72] ibid 36.

American-trained technocrat and economist, and a former vice president of the ECB, after daring to propose a referendum on the second bailout package, to the horror of the Franco-German leadership (dubbed 'Merkozy' at the time).[73] It was not long before Italy's own premier, Silvio Berlusconi, had been replaced; again by an American-trained technocrat and economist, this time a former European commissioner, Mario Monti. But it also occurred more formally: once tied to the ESM, a country dependent upon aid would be stripped of any pretence of democratic government, losing fiscal sovereignty to the Troika. And even if it did not actually go to the ESM, it could be held under its threat.

This authoritarian configuration was established by a combination of means: inter-state geopolitics, cementing core-peripheral relationships of economic domination and dependency; institutional capacity, with the power and authority of the federal and democratically unaccountable ECB conditioning the credibility of member state resistance; and social-economic inequality, following a class logic of austerity, which was tied to ideological, as well as material, strategies of capital accumulation.

Various prognoses would predict that the *demos* would react to such a configuration. And, in a variety of ways, it did. Various social and political movements emerged to protest against what was perceived to be an austerity agenda imposed by the German-led Eurogroup and the Troika of institutions, as well as more generally against the inequalities of late capitalism and its authoritarian political structures, which had been laid bare after the financial crisis.[74] The slogan of the demonstrations in Madrid in 2011 was 'real democracy now!', with the movements adopting a 'radical reformist' strategy of change through the ballot box.[75] Anger in Greece about the conditionalities in return for credits erupted from the first bailout in May 2010; the second, agreed in March 2012, was accompanied by large-scale protests and rioting in Athens. This was, by then, part of a broader dynamic, connected to the global 'Occupy' movements and to the Indignados movement in Spain. The political party Podemos would emerge out of the latter movement with extraordinary speed, growing to become a major player in its own right, and bringing to an end the two-party system in Spain.[76]

In two elections in 2012, Syriza would overtake the traditional centre-left party PASOK, and establish itself as the main opposition group, with 27 per cent of the vote, a historic achievement for a radical left-wing challenger outside the mainstream centre. In January 2015, the Greek people elected Syriza to power. Syriza formed a coalition with the conservative Independent Greeks, with the promise to restore democratic self-government and, specifically, with a dual mandate to end austerity and, it seemed, to remain in the eurozone. Although the action subsequently centred in

[73] Together—with the support of Barroso, Lagarde, van Rompuy, and Juncker—they threatened to immediately stop financial support to Greece and, 'breaking a taboo, made clear that this vote would be about the future of Greece in the Eurozone' (Krotz and Schild (n 6) 205). Papandreou soon withdrew his plan.

[74] See Mary Kaldor and Sabine Selchow, 'The "Bubbling Up" of Subterranean Politics in Europe' (2013) 9 Journal of Civil Society 85; Donatella Della Porta, 'Mobilizing against the Crisis, Mobilizing for "Another Democracy": Comparing Two Global Waves of Protest' (2012) 4 Interface 274, 276.

[75] Paolo Gerbaudo, 'The Indignant Citizen: Anti-austerity Movements in Southern Europe and the Anti-oligarchic Reclaiming of Citizenship' (2017) 16 Social Movement Studies 36.

[76] Luigi Corrias, 'The Empty Place of European Power: Contested Democracy and the Technocratic Threat' (2017) 23 European Law Journal 482.

Greece, this was a microcosm of struggles being fought elsewhere across the continent, outside as well as inside the eurozone, and was indicative of broader trends.

The anti-systemic movements, thus, appeared to come to a head in 2015, with the potential of a radical rupture in the post-war constitutional settlement, not through a 'transformation from above', which had always threatened, but through a rupture *from below*. The project of rejecting austerity, but without offering a break from the liberal European order, would, however, turn out to be 'Mission: Impossible'. The Eurogroup leaders and the European institutions had clear advantages over Syriza. They were not only in a numerically and financially superior position to the Greek government, as they were also armed with the 'rules of the game': the constitutional structure of EMU. The Eurogroup itself had the advantage of institutional ambiguity, enabling them to play outside the rules: an 'informal group', according to Article 1 of Protocol 14 attached to the Treaty, existing almost entirely in a legal void, as caustically noted by its own president, Jeroen Dijsselbloem, when its convention of unanimity was swept aside in order to deal with a dissonant Greek finance minister.[77]

Although Syriza was elected expressly on a mandate to reject austerity, each representative of the Eurogroup could (expressly or implicitly) claim hypothetical resistance to any unconditional or non-austere bailout of Greece from their own constituencies—*as if* each had been explicitly mandated by its people to refuse the loosening of austerity not (merely) on themselves—but on *Greece*.[78] This was, of course, an easy and superficially compelling claim to make, but it had less weight when advanced by those with no national electoral 'constituency' to represent, such as the presidents of the various European institutions—Bank, Commission, Eurogroup, Council—and the global IMF.

The six-month long negotiations undertaken by the Syriza government, adopting a strategy of seeking an 'honest compromise' with the Eurogroup, appeared to explode the myth that intergovernmentalism was about rational inter-state bargaining, given that the effect of further austerity, particularly in the absence of debt restructuring, would likely be to increase Greek debt. This was bargaining in the shadow of a 'non-ideological ideology', according to Donald Tusk.[79] Syriza had the forlorn hope that 'justice', 'history', and 'European values' were on their side,[80] and that they were in possession of the 'better argument', convinced that rational consensus would prevail. This Habermasian belief was bolstered by a phalanx of Nobel Prize-winning economists

[77] See Jan-Werner Müller, 'Rule-Breaking' (2015) 36:16 *London Review of Books* (London, 27 August 2015).

[78] The point is not to deny that this might well be the reaction of other electorates; but it remains speculation. If their leaders had thought that loosening austerity was the right thing to do, if only they had a free hand to do so, they could have sought to persuade their electorate that it was right, or that it was in their own interests.

[79] See Peter Spiegel, 'The Donald Tusk Interview: Annotated Transcript' *Financial Times* (London, 16 July 2015) <https://www.ft.com/content/ff50e5a9-7b15-3998-a9f1-c11359dc01b8> accessed 24 September 2020. For a contextualization of the German lead on austerity, see Newman (n 11).

[80] See Helena Smith, 'Tsipras Favours Greek Jobless over Creditors in Defiant Policy Speech' *The Guardian* (London, 8 February 2015) <https://www.theguardian.com/world/2015/feb/08/greece-prime-minister-alexis-tsipras-unveil-anti-austerity-plan-parliament> accessed 25 September 2020

and noteworthy political scientists, supporting from their positions on the sidelines, but otherwise surely a sign of desperation in times of crisis.[81]

Greek prime minister Alexis Tsipras made clear that the project of reclaiming democracy and exercising collective autonomy over the economy would only take place within the European Union, apparently failing to understand that the very *raison d'être* of the EU was to constrain projects of that type.[82] This faith in Europe was so strong that hardly any serious preparations had been made to put Grexit on the table as a credible bargaining tool for the negotiations, even when armed with the result of a spectacular domestic referendum, and against all the odds. A serious Grexit strategy would have had less leverage than in 2010, when Greek default would potentially have had an enormous impact on a global economy still reeling from the collapse of 2008, but it would still have had some clout given the historical investment of the European political elites in the project of integration and its 'irreversibility'. Instead, Syriza believed that they could convince their European partners to ease the austerity programmes, restructure sovereign debt, and transition towards a pan-European social democracy. They, too, were hampered, but by a constituency (as well as a leadership) that was *not* willing or politically prepared to appear *un*-European by putting Grexit on the table.

Political mobilization in Greece, and elsewhere, was hamstrung as a result of the erosion of the *demos* in the specific sense of an abnegation of the practice and principle of popular sovereignty. This was not a small matter, as we can now see. It can be traced back through the decades of neo-liberalism to the founding of post-war Europe, as outlined in Parts II and III. Syriza's own 'indecision' had deeper roots, related to the Eurocommunist origins of its leadership team, and the 'perception that the EU could be transformed into a Europe of the peoples'.[83] There was no preparation for a break from EMU, let alone a rupture from the EU; 'the assumption was in essence that the articulation of rational discourse and invocation of the "European idea" could be catalysts for change'.[84] Neither the threat of exit, or of suspension of debt repayments, both potentially powerful weapons in the hands of the Greek government, would be brought to bear in the conjuncture.

A third weapon, the 'dynamism of the people', evident from the intense levels of social mobilization and solidarity movements over the course of the euro crisis, would effectively be 'neutralized' by the Syriza government, unwilling as it was to lead a radical alternative political programme. In excluding the strategy of rupture from the liberal order, and of exit from the EU, it seemed to confirm what it had rhetorically fought against: 'there is no alternative'.

[81] Habermas afterwards suggested that the treatment of Greece was 'an act of punishment against a left wing government' (Altermann (n 32)).

[82] A claim that would be taken up by DiEM25. See its manifesto: DiEM25, 'The EU will be democratised. Or it will disintegrate!' <https://diem25.org/manifesto-long/> accessed 25 September 2020.

[83] Sakellaropoulos (n 13) 232. Sakellaropoulos notes that, after the 1968 split in the KKE, a Eurocommunist minority emerged, with the Communist Party of the Interior adopting a favourable stance to the EEC and coming out in favour of Greek accession, judging that it could be transformed into a people's Europe, a stance that was maintained through the SEA and Maastricht Treaties, and became the majority position within Syriza (ibid 245–46).

[84] ibid 245.

The upshot of Syriza's capitulation would be the return of the New Democracy party to government in 2019, a centre-right formation, in the lowest electoral turnout since the end of dictatorial rule. By that stage, attention had long turned away from the euro crisis, and towards the 'rule of law crisis' that had been brewing in Hungary, and would then build in Poland. Authoritarian populism had emerged as an inflection of authoritarian liberalism. Unlike the Left's anti-systemic alternative, which only briefly flickered with the rise of Syriza, the right-wing nationalism offered by authoritarian populists did not require a rupture. It appeared to be materially (if not always rhetorically) compatible with a continuation of the post-war European settlement.

Conclusion

In a constitutional order based on popular sovereignty and parliamentary democracy, the extension of political consciousness and representation to the working class could destabilize the liberal state. As the 'social question'—the question of material inequality—became not just an economic, but a political, and even a constitutional issue in the interwar era, the liberal state struggled to maintain hegemony. The bourgeois *Rechtsstaat*, which protected private property and the separation of the economic and political spheres, was threatened. The response of the ruling class was to repress parliamentarism and turn to the courts or the executive branches in an attempt to maintain stability. Even those of its theorists, like Hans Kelsen, who retained an 'open' approach to democratic politics and the social question, turned away from the principle of popular sovereignty underpinning them.

Carl Schmitt, although often presented as an 'anti-liberal', shared this liberal fear. For Schmitt, democracy was the chief threat to the stability of the German state and its liberal constitution.[1] He did, to be sure, *deride* a certain type of liberalism associated with positivism and relativism, which was not strong enough to 'guarantee itself'; but he feared parliamentary democracy because of the likelihood, after integrating the working class into the franchise, that it could follow a path towards socialism. This path would signal the interpenetration of state and society, and the conflation of the political and economic spheres, in a manner that violated the essence of liberal thought of the 'long nineteenth century'.[2] The motivating fear for liberalism in late Weimar was Schmitt's fear; it is, thus, no surprise that he was closely associated with the political and constitutional machinations of its authoritarian turn.

The fear of a left-revolutionary, or even reformist, challenge to the liberal order of private rights, property, and formal equality travelled far beyond Weimar. As Karl Polanyi showed, the same dynamic played out in various settings across Europe (and across the globe). Governments responded in different ways to the social question, depending on local variations of political economy. But, where the state reasserted sovereignty over the economy and intervened in order to tackle the social question decisively, a breakdown could be averted. Where governmental response was to hollow out democracy, and pursue austerity, eroding social protections, subjugating unions, and subordinating political organization to the service of deflationary policies and

[1] See Renato Cristi, *Carl Schmitt and Authoritarian Liberalism: Strong State, Free Economy* (University of Wales Press 1998) 6: 'if liberalism were to restrict its apoliticism to the sphere of civil society, and acknowledge the necessity of a sovereign state that retained the monopoly of the political, Schmitt would not object to conservative or authoritarian liberalism'.

[2] As Kelly puts it, 'Schmitt suggested in his most famous work that the equation "state = politics" becomes void at the moment when state and society penetrate each other' (Duncan Kelly, *The State of the Political: Conceptions of Politics and the State in the Thought of Max Weber, Carl Schmitt, and Franz Neumann* (Cambridge University Press 2003) 275).

Authoritarian Liberalism and the Transformation of Modern Europe. Michael A Wilkinson, Oxford University Press.
 DOI: 10.1093/oso/9780198854753.003.0013

balanced budgets, it weakened society's ability to respond to fascism. It was, in other words, a politics of authoritarian liberalism that directly prepared the ground for the fascist takeover. And, in the German case, the ruling bloc eventually, if reluctantly, turned to fascist dictatorship.[3]

The collapse of liberal democracy was neither inevitable, nor was it reducible to simple economic calculations on the part of capital. The Weimar context mattered: heightened economic instability; the conditions for cultivating a resentment towards and, eventually, a violent reaction to the existing order of things; the balance of class forces; and a powerful threat from the radical Left. Nevertheless, despite local variations, a more general, transnational 'thought collective' would soon emerge to contemplate how to lay the foundations for a new economic liberalism, beginning with the meeting of the Walter Lippmann Colloquium in 1938 (as we saw in Chapter 2). This project only begins in earnest after the Second World War.

Post-war compromises

In the post-war era, liberalism in Europe would have to be constructed on a new basis if it were to regain ideological hegemony. Popular sovereignty, democracy, and parliamentarism could no longer be trusted to provide it with support, and would need to be constrained. This resettlement would, in part, be conditioned by external factors; not least the division of Germany, the position of European states sandwiched between the imperialist ambitions of two rival superpowers, and the choice of core European states to act as a bulwark to the US in the Cold War with the Soviet Union. But the foundations for a new order of economic liberalism would require domestic and regional supports. These would be based on permissive consent to elite-led projects of constitutionalism, with the political demobilization of the masses and the decline of parliamentarism reflecting a more passive form of authoritarian government than in the interwar period. This would be designed to function without dictatorship and the glorification of violent nationalist sentiment. It offered very different myths of redemption, constructed on the basis of legal, technocratic, and transnational forms of rule; bolstered by political networks—particularly Christian democratic ones—juristic initiatives, and the deradicalization of Left opposition.

The ordoliberalism and neo-liberalism that had begun to germinate on the cusp of the Second World War would offer new frameworks for reimagining the differentiation of the political and economic realms. Although they were far from straightforwardly implemented, either at the domestic or European level, the prescriptions of a new economic liberalism reconfigured the post-war constitutional landscape. The particular ideological linkage of market economics and liberal constitutionalism became a key conceptual plank in the process of Europeanization.[4] Its legacy could be

[3] David Abraham, *The Collapse of the Weimar Republic: Political Economy and Crisis* (Princeton University Press 1981) 205. See, further, Ian Kershaw, 'The Nazi State: an Exceptional State?' (1989) 1:176 New Left Review 47.

[4] Steph Dullien and Ulrike Guérot, 'The Long Shadow of Ordoliberalism: Germany's Approach to the Euro-Crisis' (2012) European Council of Foreign Relations Policy Brief 49.

seen, for example, in how the self-understandings of constitutional actors in Europe (domestic and supranational, including the European Court of Justice (ECJ) and the European Commission) were increasingly conditioned by the pressures of economic rationality and the logic of market competition.[5]

The post-war resettlement also reflected a class realignment. With the working class demobilized, unions turned to more cooperative forms of engagement with capital. The very notion of the bourgeoisie faded from view.[6] Trade unions and employers would increasingly negotiate wage-setting in cooperation with each other, and with the state, securing the 'social peace' through co-determination in conjunction with welfare corporatism.[7] In comparison with the objectives of interwar labour lawyers, the formal mechanisms for the involvement of labour in the administration of the EEC and the nascent European economy were 'markedly limited' from 'the first decades of their existence'.[8] By the time of the 'Dusseldorf programme', published by the DGB (National Federation of Trade Unions) in 1963, 'the policy aims of the unions were no longer directed towards the institution of economic democracy. Demands were made instead for the extension of codetermination within a Keynesian capitalist economy'.[9] The 'last remnants of Germany's Marxist tradition', already abandoned by the Social Democratic Party (SPD) at Bad Godesberg, were laid to rest.[10]

There were significant cultural aspects to this transformation. Ideas of the *public good*, understood on a political register, were elided, as economics turned to rational choice, and the 'optimization of market outcomes' became a dominant rationality.[11] The impact of depoliticization of the economy, which began as a feature of new academic specializations, was soon felt across the political and cultural spectrum. It extended far beyond the EU. Even the more expansive economic neo-liberalism that is often captured in the term 'globalization' has been understood as a direct descendent of ordoliberalism's differentiation of the political-economic relation, and the gradual reversal in their prioritization.[12]

This claim is not merely offered with the benefit of hindsight. It was also perceived *at the time*, as early as the 1950s, although largely unpursued in the academy. As constitutional theorist Carl Joachim Friedrich had already noted by 1955, and Foucault

[5] Even where social funds were available, such as in the reskilling of redundant Italian workers, and emigration to other parts of the Community, 'this was action always in the perspective of easing free movement within a common market, an economic, not a social policy' (Brian Bercusson, *European Labour Law* (2nd edn, CUP 2009) 107).

[6] Charles S Maier, *Recasting Bourgeois Europe: Stabilization in France, Germany, and Italy in the Decade after World War I* (Princeton University Press 2016).

[7] Wolfgang Streeck, 'Industrial Relations: From State Weakness as Strength to State Weakness as Weakness; Welfare Corporatism and the Private Use of Public Interest' in Simon Green and William E Paterson (eds), *Governance in Contemporary Germany: The Semi-Sovereign State Revisited* (CUP 2005) 139.

[8] Ruth Dukes, *The Labour Constitution: The Enduring Idea of Labour Law* (OUP 2014) 124.

[9] ibid 54.

[10] Peter Katzenstein, *Policy and Politics in West Germany: The Growth of a Semisovereign State* (Temple University Press 1987) 125. Katzenstein notes that, in the post-war era, a 'stable system of labour-management relations' helped to 'depoliticise questions of social policy', as the result of 'deliberate efforts by businessmen, union leaders, and labour judges' (ibid 131).

[11] Emilios Christodoulidis, 'The European Court of Justice and "Total Market" Thinking' (2013) 14 German Law Journal 2005.

[12] See Kanishka Jayasuriya, 'Globalisation, Sovereignty and the Rule of Law: From Political to Economic Constitutionalism' (2001) 8 Constellations 442.

would later explore in his lectures on neo-liberal governmentality in 1979, the decisive theoretical turn triggered by ordoliberalism had been to replace constituent power (or popular sovereignty) with individual economic freedom—a freedom to participate in the market—as the legitimating device for the whole constitutional order.[13] Freedom came to mean not only freedom from politics, but from any form of collective political identity, particularly an identity pertaining to class or economic relations. As German chancellor Ludwig Erhard put it, '[t]he revolution of our era is marked by the call for freedom rather than for class warfare', as if these must henceforth be considered strict alternatives.[14]

The class-conscious struggles of the interwar period were repressed, in order to secure political and economic *stability*. Democratic control over the economy to ensure that it was run to achieve social ends would no longer be a permissible goal. Self-determination by council systems, and the integration of revolutionary Workers' Councils as organs of collective political autonomy, would become distant memories. What had originally signified the extension of democracy to the economy, and even the socialization of the means of production, now meant the insulation of the economy from democracy. The reversal of the economic constitution which had begun in early Weimar would then be complete. The economic constitution became the 'anarchy of so-called economic freedom' in bourgeois society, so fiercely contested by the Weimar labour lawyers.

But this reversal signalled nothing like political anarchy. The bourgeois separation of the political and the economic was reinvented in the post-war era by a 'strong state' ensuring a 'sound economy'. This was based on formal equality and individual rights, bolstered by a new 'civil religion' of fiscal prudence, efficiency, and competition: the model of the German economic miracle. The economic constitution as the political form of the free-market economy was based on a political hierarchy buttressed by counter-majoritarian institutions.

In the ordoliberal imagination, democracy would be restrained, less for fear of it violating civil or political rights (as the theory of militant democracy maintains), than out of concern for its impact on economic stability. In adopting, and adapting, Schmitt's message of 'strong state, sound economy', the ordoliberals gave the sound economy a stronger legal-constitutional, administrative, and technical foundation; the exercise of governance functions would be subject to constitutional safeguards and expert guidance. The goal of the economic constitution was to avoid a politicization of the economy that would lead to a weakening of the state; that is, protecting the market economy by disarming any democratic or capitalist threat to it. If its main purpose was to protect the economy from political-democratic pressures, '*this could not be but authoritarian*', as Kanishka Jayasuriya puts it.[15]

[13] Carl J Friedrich, 'The Political Thought of Neo-Liberalism' (1955) 49 American Political Science Review 509; Michel Foucault, *The Birth of Biopolitics—Lectures at the College de France 1978–1979* (Palgrave MacMillan 2008). It has recently been suggested that Foucault's analysis on ordoliberalism drew on the 1961 thesis of Francois Bilger; see Arnaud Lechevalier, 'Why and How has German Ordoliberalism Become a French Issue? Some Aspects about Ordoliberal Thoughts we can Learn from the French Reception' in Joerges and Hien (eds), *Ordoliberalism, Law and the Rule of Economics* (Hart 2007) 23–48.

[14] Horst Friedrich Wunsche, *Standard Texts on the Social Market Economy: Two Centuries of Discussion*, vol IX (Derek Rutter tr, Gustav Fisher Verlag 1982) ix.

[15] Jayasuriya (n 12) 453 (italics added).

European integration did not play an exclusive role in this reversal, but it did play a crucial one, formalizing restrained inter-state sovereignty, and contributing to the depoliticization of state-society relations by offering an economic constitution 'writ large'. In compounding counter-majoritarianism and the suppression of democracy at home (later characterized as a democratic 'deficit'), European integration, crucially, eased the transition into what would be termed the 'neo-liberal state'; this was not a revolution, but the continuation of a counter-revolution that had begun several decades earlier. The EU was not contingently undemocratic, but 'inherently undemocratic' from the outset.[16]

Europe also offered an 'empty signifier', into which the political Left could channel its utopian energies, holding out for the emergence of a pan-European social democracy to come, if only given the time progressively to mature. Although plans for political union stalled, commitment to European integration became culturally entrenched across the political spectrum, to the extent that there remained little, if any, alternative to EU membership in the constitutional imagination (and, after Maastricht, to the single currency, as we saw in Parts III and IV).[17] A functionalist 'progressivism' is captured in the metaphor that the project can only move in one direction, and must continue forward if not to collapse, resembling a bicycle that falls over once the cyclist stops pedalling. In a play that resembles Walter Benjamin's automaton, seen and unseen forces will move the pieces into a winning position, and in a process that is presented as 'irreversible'.

The so-called post-war *Trente Glorieuses* must not be misunderstood. As a constitutional matter, there had been no victory of social democracy or democratic socialism, even at the peak of the post-war welfare state in the most socially minded of contexts.[18] On the contrary, the post-war settlement was politically passive: based on a fear of German sovereignty externally, political democracy internally, and a suppression of class consciousness in the social imaginary (as clearly attested by the protests against authoritarianism captured by the date '1968').[19] The symbolic liberal achievements of the period—the restraining of sovereignty, the elevation of fundamental rights, and relative economic prosperity—were facilitated by the material conditions of global Cold War superpower rivalry, the making of global capitalism, and an economistic frame of thinking. There was no capitulation of capitalism, or recognition, later

[16] See, recently, Eva Nanopoulos and Fotis Vergis, 'The Inherently Undemocratic EU Democracy' in Eva Nanopoulos and Fotis Vergis (eds), *The Crisis Behind the Eurocrisis: On the Multi-Systemic Failure of the EU* (CUP 2019).

[17] Even in the UK, membership of the Union exerts strong constitutional pressures; see, eg Neil Walker, 'Our Constitutional Unsettlement' (2014) Public Law 529; Martin Loughlin, 'The British Constitution: Thoughts on the Causes of the Present Discontents' (2018) 16 New Zealand Journal of Public and International Law 1. The 'constitutional' nature of EU membership for the UK would be clarified in the *Miller* judgments of the Supreme Court.

[18] See, eg Rudolph Meidner, 'Why did the Swedish Model Fail?' (1993) 29 Socialist Register 211.

[19] On the fragmentation between working class and bourgeoisie students, evidenced by the distrust between them, see, eg Sartre's interview with Cohn-Bendit in the *Nouvel Observateur* on 20 May 1968. 1968 was, in part, a revolt against socialist and even communist parties, whose achievements came to be seen as simply prolonging the capitalist system, and who represented the continuation of hierarchical (and patriarchal) structures. See 'Jean- Paul Sartre interviews Daniel Cohn-Bendit' (*Verso Books blog*, 16 May 2018) <https://www.versobooks.com/blogs/3819-jean-paul-sartre-interviews-daniel-cohn-bendit> accessed 22 November 2020.

forgotten, that the interwar breakdown was caused by a crisis of capitalism that needed to be structurally fixed. The equalizing of conditions was the upshot of a mix of ingredients, not least, and perhaps most of all, the destruction caused by the Second World War.[20] This is important to emphasize, in order to stress that the neo-liberal state of the 1970s to the 1990s—although materially different, in some respects, in its prevailing strategies of capital accumulation (in particular the increasing financialization of the economy, and declining economic power of organized labour)[21]—was not, from a constitutional perspective, fundamentally distinct to the post-war state and state system. As Leo Panitch puts it, 'the apt metaphor for the post-war regime is not a cage but rather a cradle, which capital had outgrown and found too constraining by the 1960s amidst the enormous expansion of foreign investment by multinational corporations and international investment banking (not least in the Eurodollar markets)'.[22]

The post-war order had successfully constrained capitalist excesses and any regional ambitions of leading states, but had not castrated them. They were constrained so that economic liberalism could be renewed and maintained. In other words, the excesses of the capitalist state would be limited for the sake of capitalism itself (akin to a Fordist growth model, in US terms), partly under the pressure of 'actually existing' socialism in the Soviet Union, and partly through compromise with social democratic and Christian democratic movements and trade unions, benefiting from global economic growth. When the constraints no longer served the interests of capital and its managers, these managers would revolt, in a process beginning in the 1970s and continuing through into the Maastricht era and the euro crisis, decades later.

Maastricht ambiguities

The liberal economic constitution would develop more fully in the context of momentous geopolitical, political, and ideological shifts taking place at the end of the 'short twentieth century'. This period would be marked by a number of events: the fall of the Berlin Wall, which restored the prospect of German hegemony; the failure of the European Constitutional project amidst heightened political discontent and juristic contestation by the German Constitutional Court, which ended the prospect (if not the hopes) of political union; Economic and Monetary Union (EMU), which entrenched the economic constitution by uncoupling monetary sovereignty from the political authority of the state; and European enlargement, which effected a radical deepening and widening of the EU's neo-liberal market rationality.

The two symbolic 'advances' of Maastricht—European citizenship and European money—were, nominally, on a par with regard to their quasi-constitutional status. But it would be money rather than citizenship that would come to symbolize the Europe of the twenty-first century. EMU had provided the new political symbol of integration, and created a new institutional apparatus, monetary governance now lying in the

[20] See Thomas Piketty, *Capital in the Twenty-First Century* (HUP 2014).

[21] See Ben Fine and Alfredo Saad-Filho, 'Thirteen Things You Need to Know about Neoliberalism' (2017) 43 Critical Sociology 685.

[22] Leo Panitch, 'Capital and Politics' (2015) 13 Perspectives on Politics 1075.

hands of a European Central Bank (ECB) that would soon take centre stage. If this created money without a state, it also represented a new phenomenon of states without money, as the eurozone members lost a key 'marker' of sovereignty; as Jean Bodin had expressed it, at the foundations of the modern age, the 'right of coinage' is part of an indivisible assemblage of sovereign powers.[23]

The liberal market ideology represented by EMU was becoming more generally pervasive and dominant throughout society. The single currency itself offered a symbol of the new 'economic messianism' that would lead the Union into the new millennium, based on 'the assumption of a sole and exclusive truth', curiously recalling Jacob Talmon's characterization of political totalitarianism.[24] This was reflected in the culture of 'total optimism' that dominated much thinking amongst political elites in general, and visions of European integration in particular.

Etienne Balibar described Maastricht as having put an end to the long European 'civil war' between economic liberalism and social democracy that took place across the short twentieth century. It signalled the decisive triumph of economic liberalism. The victory of capitalism was declared complete. Reflecting on the (re)birth of the EU at the Treaty of Maastricht, he noted how extraordinary was the setting of its liberal political-economic goals into explicit, detailed, and rigid constitutional guarantees:

> The EU in its constitutive moment (Maastricht) was endowed with a quasi-constitution ... where, for the first time in this part of the world ... a principle of political economy deriving from a specific ideological discourse (namely neo-liberal deregulation and unrestricted competition, believed to produce 'optimal allocation of resources' and spontaneously 'just' redistribution) was presented as the sovereign rule which all member states ought to implement in their national policies under close surveillance of the federal (or quasi-federal) organs of the Union.[25]

The first stage in this battle, however, was already long lost. Once *politics* had been reduced to a single political-economic logic, and the possibility of genuine renewal came down to the exercise of constituent power, the autonomy of the political was reduced to a bare formality or the prospect of a revolutionary rupture. This blockage of the constituent power, the 'undoing of the *demos*',[26] did not occur only after Maastricht. It was cemented at Maastricht, but its foundations were laid at the outset of the post-war project.

[23] See Étienne Balibar, *We, the Peoples of Europe: Reflections on Transnational Citizenship* (Princeton University Press 2004) 141–48.

[24] See Jacob L Talmon, *The Rise of Totalitarian Democracy* (Beacon Press 1952) 1–2. On economic messianism through the euro crisis, see Michael A Wilkinson, 'Economic Messianism and Constitutional Power in a German Europe: All Courts are Equal but Some Courts are More Equal Than Others' (2014) LSE Legal Studies Working Paper No 26/2014, <http://papers.ssrn.com/sol3/papers.cfm?abstract_id=2522919> accessed 7 September 2020.

[25] Étienne Balibar, 'The Rise and Fall of the European Union: Temporalities and Teleologies' (2014) 21 Constellations 202.

[26] As Wendy Brown would later describe it: see Wendy Brown, *The Undoing of the Demos: Neoliberalism's Stealth Revolution* (Zone Books 2015).

Constitutionalism, rather than 'ruling the world', came to rule only a 'void'.[27] With the space for the expression of democratic sovereignty largely vacated, and politics hollowed out, 'identity' would fill the gap, whether cultural, consumption-oriented, or juristic in form. The democratic constitutional struggles for material equality or 'effective autonomy', as Cornelius Castoriadis theorized, had reached an impasse.[28]

Yet, in a material sense, the 'void' was not empty. The political reconfigurations in the 'long decade' from Maastricht to Lisbon heralded less the ideological triumph of liberalism than the de facto domination of a 'disorganized' global capitalism that had begun in the aftermath of the Second World War, guided by informal American imperialism and a home-grown British variety.[29] In Europe, the effects of increasing flows of transnational capital had been managed by a variety of compromises between capital and labour, which were themselves starting to unravel by the 1970s and 1980s. After Maastricht, these compromises were placed under further pressure, by a combination of inter-state asymmetries, growing transnational corporate mobility, supranational market-making, the abandonment of class politics, and an ideological ascendency of market liberalization.

The judicialization of political authority, and increasing emphasis on 'negative' constitutionalism—on constraints of governmental power, particularly through economic constitutionalization (symbolized by the Court's cases from *Cassis de Dijon* through to *Viking* and *Laval*)—did not lead to the perfection of constitutionalism in Europe. Instead, it led to an increasing contestation: geopolitically, between core and peripheral EU states; politically, between different levels of government (eg national and supranational, subnational and supranational, and national and subnational); and ideologically, between different substantive visions of the good life (eg neo-liberal, republican, social-democratic). Far from replacing political issues, judicialization only displaced them, ultimately heightening and renewing tensions without giving them democratic channels to be voiced, either at the domestic or supranational level.

The 'empty place of power', a dominant rhetorical trope in so much modern democratic theorizing, appeared to be full: saturated by a mixture of ordoliberal ideology, technocratic managerialism, and asymmetric intergovernmental authority.[30] What was empty, drained of content, was the practice of democracy itself, unmoored from the principle of popular sovereignty, and disconnected from political representation. This was accentuated by a decline of class consciousness and a weakening of industrial organization. But it was starting to show increasing signs of social fracture, as reaction against soft authoritarian liberalism grew. If, as Perry Anderson had warned in 2007, the future political norm in Europe might be 'protestation after the event, not representation before it',[31] the protestation was about to get more dramatic, building

[27] A phrase made famous by Peter Mair, *Ruling the Void: The Hollowing Out of Western Democracy* (Verso 2013).

[28] See Cornelius Castoriadis, *Philosophy, Politics, Autonomy: Essays in Political Philosophy* (David Ames tr, OUP 1991).

[29] See Andrew Glyn, *Capitalism Unleashed: Finance Globalisation and Welfare* (OUP 2006); Sam Gindin and Leo Panitch, *The Making of Global Capitalism: The Political Economy of American Empire* (Verso 2012).

[30] On the significance of the empty place of power, theorized by French philosopher Claude Leforte, for constitutional theory, see, eg Panu Minkkinen, 'The Tragic Politics of Public Law' in Michael A Wilkinson and Michael W Dowdle (eds), *Questioning the Foundations of Public Law* (Hart 2018) 51–63.

[31] Perry Anderson, *The New Old World* (Verso 2009), 117.

through the euro crisis phase with the more direct political and constitutional challenges that arrived in its wake. Where would the material struggle for equality turn once democratic channels had been obstructed?

Europe entrapped

At the beginning of the new millennium, Balibar suggested that the 'impasse' in which the problem of sovereignty in Europe was stuck referred 'to the absolute blockage of the question of "the people" understood ... as *demos* or constituent political power'.[32] By the time of the Lisbon Treaty negotiations, another commentator had described European integration as heralding 'the passing of majoritarian politics', discarding 'conventionally legitimated democracy'.[33] This was not merely because it had introduced elements of technocratic rule within its governance structures, but because it had 'dispensed with the *demos*' itself, and, thus, had 'equally dispensed with the very foundation for legitimizing political representation'.[34]

To call this *sui generic* or, in Weiler's words, an entity pursuing its own *Sonderweg*,[35] now concealed the structural fault lines that were becoming ever more visible. The unresolved question of the nature of the polity, and of its constitutional consequences for its members, and its lack of centralized political-democratic authority, combined with weak public support, were exposing its fragility in critical political and economic moments.[36] Centrifugal and centripetal forces would begin to combine to make the project look increasingly precarious, not only on the periphery, but in the core of Europe. After the failed Constitutional Treaty, the Lisbon fudge did nothing to resolve the tensions, but only exacerbated them.

When the global financial crisis hit, it became clear that the Maastricht (and Lisbon) framework was not fit for purpose. With its commitment to a depoliticized monetary policy based exclusively on price stability, a radically independent ECB with restricted monetary tools, and the absence of flanking institutions capable of dealing with uneven development, socio-economic heterogeneity, or exogenous fiscal shocks, the Maastricht framework had attempted to supranationalize principles that had been designed for domestic constitutional consumption. It had also been designed in a particular constitutional context—that of a set of myths, including, first, the interwar hyperinflations, and then the 'economic miracle' of post-war reconstruction, and a

[32] Balibar (n 23) 157. The absence of 'the people' in Europe, he continued, was not only 'symbolic'; there was an absence of any 'real control' over the constitutional order that is imposed on their behalf. What we have witnessed, accordingly, is nothing less than 'the disappearance of the dialectic of constituent and constituted power ... [which] goes beyond the 'bureaucratization' and 'professionalisation' of politics, and the 'political apathy of the masses'. It 'implies the return to a technical, reglementary status of the law' (ibid 169).

[33] Michelle Everson and Julia Eisner, *The Making of a European Constitution: Judges and Law Beyond Constitutive Power* (Routledge 2007) 27.

[34] ibid.

[35] See Joseph HH Weiler, 'In Defence of the Status Quo: Europe's Constitutional Sonderweg' in Joseph HH Weiler and Marlene Wind (eds), *European Constitutionalism Beyond the State* (CUP 2003).

[36] cf Neil Walker, 'The European Union's Unresolved Constitution' in Michel Rosenfeld and András Sajó (eds), *The Oxford Handbook of Comparative Constitutional Law* (OUP 2012).

particular economic strategy of export-led growth—which was not suited to all the members of the eurozone.

The euro crisis revealed the specific contradictions of two structural edifices of EMU: fiscal discipline and the irreversibility of the euro. If fiscal discipline, sacrosanct to the German ruling class, pushed against a financial rescue that would disincentivize prudent economic management, irreversibility of the euro pulled in its favour, at least as far as assistance was necessary to avoid disintegration. The crisis also revealed the necessity of a different set of policy objectives and the institutions capable of delivering them, to deal with prolonged *deflation*, high levels of unemployment, and a lack of domestic demand.

The member states also lacked crucial tools to deal with the economic downturn. Unable to turn to monetary policy intervention, they were forced to pursue 'internal devaluation' as the only way to regain competitiveness. This would place further downward pressure on wages, working conditions, and public spending. It would occur after a more general decline in the bargaining power of trade unions, in the core as well as the periphery of Europe, and an increase in the relative power of transnational capital.[37] The result would be increasing *divergences* of political economy across the eurozone, despite—or rather due to—being locked into the institutional architecture of the single currency. Although, again, the resulting divergences 'reinforced and exacerbated forms of unevenness' that had characterized European political economy 'for much longer', traceable to the Single European Act, and even to the foundational period of the single market, they were now becoming more politically salient.[38]

The prospect of reclaiming national sovereignty, however, by exiting the EU was scarcely considered an option, either constitutionally, or (with the notable exception of the UK) politically. It was not until Lisbon that the legal route of exit from the EU was even written into the constitutional text and, when it was, it was not with the intention of it ever being used. The possibility of exit from the single currency *still* inhabits a constitutional grey zone; a significant omission, as we saw in Part IV. The German court's *Lisbon* decision reinforced the status quo domestically, preventing further integration towards full political union, short of a constituent change to Germany's Basic Law, and, probably, a referendum, if not a revolution.[39]

In Claus Offe's apposite characterization, Europe was 'entrapped', unable either to move forward or turn the clock backwards.[40] Yet, there was one institution that would

[37] See Andreas Bieler, Jamie Jordan, and Adam David Morton, 'EU Aggregate Demand as a Way out of Crisis? Engaging the Post-Keynesian Critique' (2019) 57 Journal of Common Market Studies 805 ('German trade unions were no longer able to match the power of capital. From the 1990s onwards, German production structures, too, had increasingly been transnationalized with Central and Eastern European states, especially, offering a skilled and yet comparatively cheap workforce' (ibid 811)).

[38] ibid 809 ('Free trade policies, as initially embedded within the EU Customs Union since 1968 and then especially the Internal Market from the mid-1980s onwards, when free trade was extended from trade in goods to trade in services and finance, have generally tended to reproduce long-standing developmental asymmetries and polarizing conditions between countries.').

[39] Dieter Grimm, 'Defending Sovereign Statehood against Transforming the Union into a State' (2009) 5 European Constitutional Law Review 353 (according to Grimm, an amendment to the Basic Law to provide for a referendum on a European state would suffice: 'a new constitution, as the Court thinks, would not be indispensable').

[40] Claus Offe, *Europe Entrapped* (Polity Press 2015).

appear to offer an escape. After the Commission and the Court had taken the lead in the foundational stages, it would now be the turn of the ECB.

The Commission, Court, and ECB had been grouped together, euphemistically, as 'the independents'. But, in reality, they were closely *dependent* on a combination (often uneasy) of asymmetrical geopolitical power and market liberal rationality. It was not, or not only, a vague 'idea of the European project' that held them together.[41] Although the ECB was formally constrained by the Maastricht rules, it had tools at its disposal that gave it a unique position to respond to a crisis of financialized capitalism. In eventually turning to unorthodox monetary policy, it would give the appearance that the principle of irreversibility and its duty of rescue prevailed, on the basis of a higher duty to protect the euro area as a whole. When this was challenged by the German court, the ECJ did its best to assuage fears of associated fiscal indiscipline. Rescue, in other words, would occur on terms—determined by the Eurogroup, led by Germany, and with the backing of the Troika—that maintained the ideology, and, to a large extent, the practice of 'austerity'. For all the accusations that Karlsruhe was a court that barked but never bit, the last laugh belonged to it.

In this unfinished conjuncture, so frequently compared to the 1930s, norms of democratic constitutionalism were bypassed, often swiftly and sometimes coercively, in processes led by domestic, as well as transnational, political elites.[42] The rule-based structure was softened and bent, justified on any basis of 'keeping the project going', or 'rescuing the euro at all costs',[43] an imperative reminiscent of the destructive, but ultimately failed, attempts to conserve gold in the interwar period.[44] The institutional beneficiaries of this emergency neofunctionalism were executive power-holders at national and supranational level, bypassing domestic and European parliaments and electorates.[45]

Democracy in Europe, which had already been skinned, now looked to be gutted. This was occurring with an abrupt transformation of mentality—from 'integration through law' to 'integration through fear'—using the threat of catastrophe precipitated by the potential collapse of the euro to push through institutional and political reforms. European and domestic elites, to the extent that they projected the need for a stronger political union, projected an authority that would be need to discipline and coerce, in order to ensure the conditions of a 'free and flourishing' transnational economy and, if necessary, to achieve this through means which conflicted with the

[41] cf Antoine Vauchez, *Democratising Europe* (Palgrave MacMillan 2015). Pierre Rosanvallon would also suggest that the supposed impartiality of independent technocratic institutions could be equated with new conceptions of democratic legitimacy (see Pierre Rosanvallon, *Democratic Legitimacy: Impartiality, Reflexivity, Proximity* (Princeton University Press 2011)). Anderson (n 31) 207, comparing Rosanvallon's work with Rawls and Habermas, notes that, although empirically richer, its apologetic character was more transparent; an attempt at ideological compensation for the deficit of actually existing democracy.

[42] See, eg Alexander Somek, 'Delegation and Authority: Authoritarian Liberalism Today' (2015) 21:3 European Law Journal 340–60; William Scheuerman, 'Hermann Heller and the European Crisis: Authoritarian Liberalism Redux?' (2015) 21:3 European Law Journal 302–12.

[43] Van Middelaar describes the breakdown of 'rules-based politics': Luuk van Middelaar, *Alarums and Excursions* (Agenda Publishing 2019).

[44] See Daniel Wilsher, 'Law and the Financial Crisis: Searching for Europe's New Gold Standard' (2014) 20:2 European Law Journal 241–83.

[45] See, eg Jurgen Habermas, *The Crisis of the European Union: A Response* (Polity 2012).

wishes of a democratic majority. Coercion and discipline would not appear as legitimate substitutes for solidarity, but they were effective ones, as long as exit from the EU was not seriously contemplated as a possibility.

Balibar now identified, in the euro crisis, a potential 'revolution from above', a transformation of Europe 'which the leaders of dominant nations and the Brussels and Frankfurt technostructure are attempting under the whip of necessity'.[46] Invented by Bismarck in the nineteenth century, this notion designated, according to Balibar, 'a change to the structure of the *material constitution*' on the part of the ruling classes, altering the 'balance of power between society and state, economics and politics'. Balibar speculated that this process was under way with 'the neutralisation of parliamentary democracy, the European Union's institutionalisation of budgetary and fiscal controls and the sacralisation of banking interests', all pushed forward 'in the name of neo-liberal orthodoxy'. Although these changes had been germinating for a while, they were now, for the first time, 'demanded as part of a new configuration of political power'.[47] In this new configuration, constraints on democratic self-determination were not predominantly 'constitutional', in the orthodox sense of the term, but were relayed by global capital markets and credit rating agencies, which, along with banks that were considered 'too big to fail', became constitutional actors 'for all material purposes'.[48] These material constraints would then be formally constitutionalized at the EU level through the provisions of the Fiscal Compact and the European Stability Mechanism, and reinforced by political actors, as well as interpretations of the European Court, notably in *Pringle* and *OMT*.

The effects of this mix of political decision (and indecision), ordoliberal constraints, and neo-liberal management (and legal rubber-stamping) were manifold: Germany was emerging as a 'reluctant semi-hegemon',[49] the flaws of EMU were being covered up rather than resolved, and the domestic electorates were becoming increasingly angry. But there were few political ways to channel this discontent other than in domestic spaces and through anti-systemic forums. There was a palpable sense that neo-liberalism was dying, but stubbornly resisting any plans for its own funeral.[50]

[46] Étienne Balibar, 'Europe's Revolution from Above' *The Guardian* (London, 23 November 2011) <https://www.theguardian.com/commentisfree/2011/nov/23/europe-revolution-from-above> accessed 25 September 2020.

[47] ibid. The notion of a 'revolution from above' is advanced by Sheldon Wolin, in a different context, but in analogous manner, as characteristic of the totalizing shifts in political and economic power generated by elites in postmodern democracy and its hybrid of the corporatist state (see Sheldon S Wolin, *Politics and Vision: Continuity and Innovation in Western Political Thought* (Princeton University Press 2004) 605).

[48] See Edoardo Chiti, Agustin Menéndez, and Pedro Teixeira (eds), *The European Rescue of the European Union: The Existential Crisis of the European Political Project* (ARENA 2012).

[49] 'Germany is Europe's paymaster. Even Franco-German summits are now really "German-German summits", Romano Prodi said recently'; see Jan-Werner Müller, 'What do Germans Think about when they Think about Europe?' *London Review of Books*, (London, 9 February 2012) <https://www.lrb.co.uk/the-paper/v34/n03/jan-werner-mueller/what-do-germans-think-about-when-they-think-about-europe> accessed 25 September 2020.

[50] Colin Crouch, *The Strange Non-Death of Neoliberalism* (Polity Press 2011).

Authoritarian populism

The harsher forms of authoritarian liberalism were bound to elicit strong social and political reactions, and even risk 'letting loose the kind of political passions that were so destructive during the inter-war years.'[51] Right across the eurozone, old animosities resurfaced. Despite the Treaty obligations protecting representative democracy, social justice, and solidarity, there was rarely direct reference to these in the response of political elites to the euro crisis. Although, in theory, there was potentially large redistribution among members, through the mutualization of risk in programmes such as the ESM, the quid pro quo for using these programmes was the total loss of fiscal sovereignty. Any prospective notion of transnational solidarity was stillbirthed by the language of austerity and moral hazard. The language of the tabloid press reflected this, resorting to clichés pitting nation against nation—'lazy Greeks' versus 'selfish' Germans—instead of identifying the *classes* within nations that had benefitted from decades of neo-liberalism, and those that had suffered its effects, accelerated by its measures of austerity for the poor and liquidity for the rich.[52]

The euro crisis proper, which had begun with a banking crisis, and become, over time, a sovereign debt crisis, and then a series of constitutional crises, would soon be supplemented by the 'migration crisis', and 'rule of law crisis', as governments of right-wing nationalism gained power in Hungary and Poland. The 'perfect storm' of multiple crises revealed the weaknesses of the rule-based structure of integration, as, first, the pillars of EMU crumbled, and then those of Schengen and Dublin weakened.[53] But it would be the emergence of what would be labelled 'political populism' in Hungary, and then in Poland, that occupied the attention of constitutional scholars. By the time of the '*oxi*' referendum in July 2015, when the Greek people rejected the memorandum negotiated with the Troika and Eurogroup, focus had, thus, pivoted from the crisis in the eurozone to the apparent dangers of populism, an accusation directed against Syriza itself.[54] This development was said to threaten the 'foundational values' of the EU, violating democracy *qua* the rule of law.[55]

The Maastricht re-foundation of the EU on the basis of democracy and the rule of law had been entirely rhetorical, however. While significant energy had gone into making the new members 'market-conform', little had been expended on ensuring they would be 'democracy enhanced'. On the contrary, the 'low-intensity form of democracy' that had become dominant in the West was assumed as the norm.[56] Democratic change was presented as a technical challenge, which 'de-politicised the meaning of democracy', detaching it from 'politics, from history, from society and

[51] Helen Thompson, 'Austerity as Ideology: The Bait and Switch of the Banking Crisis' (2013) 11 Comparative European Politics 729, 730.

[52] On the class politics of austerity, see, eg Wolfgang Streeck, *Buying Time: The Delayed Crisis of Democratic Capitalism* (Verso 2014); Mark Blyth, *Austerity: The History of a Dangerous Idea* (OUP 2015).

[53] Conor Gearty, 'The State of Freedom in Europe' (2016) 21 European Law Journal 706–21.

[54] Yannis Stavrakakis and Giorgos Katsambekis, 'Left-Wing Populism in the European Periphery: The Case of SYRIZA' (2014) 19:2 Journal of Political Ideologies 119.

[55] ibid.

[56] Susan Marks, *The Riddle of All Constitutions: International Law, Democracy and the Critique of Ideology* (OUP 2003) 70–73.

from economics'.[57] As David Kennedy noted at the time, the new members, unlike the old, had to 'undertake a long march not only through austerity but through formalism'.[58] The type of market liberalism imposed was a fantasy version of strict, deregulated laissez-faire economics that had been long discarded in the practice of most Western European states, in favour of soft technocratic versions.

The reality was that liberal democracy was in a fragile condition in the older members, as much as the new. Right-wing populism, itself, did not appear from nowhere in Central and Eastern Europe in the 2010s. As we saw in Part III, it was foreshadowed in the core of Europe in the early 1990s, particularly in France. Right and centrist populism would later grow elsewhere, notably in Germany and Italy, with the growth of Eurosceptic parties such as the Alternative für Deutschland, the Cinque Stella, and the rebranded Lega (formerly Lega Nord). It is ironic that the UK's home-grown domestic neo-liberal project of the 1980s, itself characterized as an 'authoritarian populism',[59] had such a significant impact on the course of European integration through the market liberalization agenda of the Single European Act.[60] And a further irony that Brexit would then be described, by Jürgen Habermas, as a victory of populism over capitalism.[61]

The failures of social democratic politics to remain embedded in working-class communities, and the domination of policymaking by liberal-technocratic elites, were critical for the rise of populist parties, in both East and West.[62] The traditional centre-left would be hit particularly hard in elections after the financial crisis, in a variety of locations across the EU, giving rise to a new phenomenon: 'Pasokification', named after the electoral collapse, in Greece, of the established socialist party, PASOK. But it also produced political beneficiaries. These would, predominantly, be those parties labelled populist, harnessing the discontent that had slowly emerged in the long decade after Maastricht, most successfully in Central and Eastern Europe, but across the whole European political space, and often with their own constitutionalist rhetoric and projects.[63]

In Hungary, Fidesz would be the major beneficiary of the 'disintegration of the culturally and ideologically integrated socialist working class'.[64] Hungary had been

[57] ibid 73.

[58] David Kennedy, 'Turning to Market Democracy: A Tale of Two Architectures' (1991) 32 Harvard International Law Journal 373.

[59] See Stuart Hall, 'Popular-Democratic versus Authoritarian Populism' in Alan Hunt (ed), *Marxism and Democracy* (Lawrence & Wishart 1980); Stuart Hall, 'Authoritarian Populism: A Reply' (1985) 151 New Left Review 115.

[60] According to Lord Cockfield, '[t]he gradual limitation of national sovereignty is part of a slow and painful forward march of humanity' *The Guardian* (London, 11 November 1988), cited by Alan Milward, *The European Rescue of the Nation State* (Routledge 1994) (Cockfield, 'Father of the Single Market', European Commissioner from 1985 to 1988, was the author of the White Paper on 'The Completion of the Internal Market').

[61] Thomas Assheuer, 'The Players Resign—Core Europe to the Rescue: A Conversation with Jürgen Habermas about Brexit and the EU crisis' *Die Zeit* (Hamburg, 12 July 2016) <https://www.zeit.de/kultur/2016-07/juergen-habermas-brexit-eu-crises-english> accessed 22 November 2020.)

[62] See Gabor Scheiring and Kristof Szombati, 'From Neoliberal Disembedding to Authoritarian Re-Embedding: The Making of Illiberal Hegemony in Hungary' (2020) International Sociology 1.

[63] Paul Blokker, 'Populist Constitutionalism' in C de la Torre (ed), *Routledge Handbook of Global Populism* (Routledge 2018) 113.

[64] Scheiring and Szombati (n 62).

subjected to harsh and imposed austerity after the onset of the global financial crisis, although led from outside the EU institutional framework notably by the International Monetary Fund.[65] The mandate that Fidesz received, in the 2010 elections, would be used 'to engineer a new class compromise between the political class, the national bourgeoisie and transnational corporations', the last-mentioned of which had become highly significant in terms of the dependency on foreign direct investment, and integration of production networks.[66] To protect itself against a possible political backlash from the losers of capital accumulation and transnational connectivity, Fidesz then 'occupied the democratic institutions, undermined the system of checks and balances and obstructed the channels of direct democracy'.[67]

It should have been little surprise that countries in Central and Eastern Europe, lacking a robust democratic political culture, but having undergone a brisk transition to market liberalism, would move sharply towards authoritarian 'illiberal' or 'populist' politics, in reaction. Fidesz's programme of illiberal and nationalist rhetoric, combined with defence of a 'Christian Europe', emulated aspects of both the political authoritarianism and the economic liberalism of the dominant post-war formation in Western Europe, mediated, on occasion, by conservative welfare packages. More generally, the right-wing beneficiaries of a failing political establishment would incorporate anti-elitist and populist rhetoric, pivoting away from a material focus on political economy, and turning to identity politics, cultural conservatism, and anti-immigration rhetoric.[68] But there was no rupture from the status quo. It was an inflection of the post-war settlement, and often labelled as such: a form of *authoritarian neo-liberalism*.[69]

The apparent electoral success of this formation also gave rise to a new phenomenon— Fideszification—as centrist parties co-opted the anti-immigration, anti-modernization, and cultural rhetoric of the far right, with some attempting to harness Eurosceptic opinion (notably Cinque Stella), but without any serious plan to leave the EU. Combinations of technocratic managerialism and political populism would also emerge, 'contradictory but mutually reinforcing tendencies', labelled 'techno-populism'; versions of authoritarian liberalism which incorporated an

[65] See Claire Kilpatrick, 'Constitutions, Social Rights and Sovereign Debt States in Europe: A Challenging New Area of Constitutional Inquiry' in Thomas Beukers, Bruno de Witte, and Claire Kilpatrick (eds), *Constitutional Change through Euro-Crisis Law* (CUP 2017) 279–326 (using the example of Hungary).

[66] Scheiring and Szombati (n 62).

[67] ibid. See, further, Gabor Halmai, 'Populism, Authoritarianism, Constitutionalism' (2019) 20:3 German Law Journal 296.

[68] On the relation between populism and constitutionalism, see Blokker (n 63); Jan-Werner Müller, 'Populism and Constitutionalism' in C Rovira Kaltwasser, P Taggart, P Espejo, and P Ostiguy (eds), *Oxford Handbook of Populism* (OUP 2017) 590(Kaltwasser and others, 'Oxford Handbook'); Luigi Corrias, 'Populism in a Constitutional Key: Constituent Power, Popular Sovereignty and Constitutional Identity' (2016) 12 European Constitutional Law Review 6; Zoran Oklopcic, 'Imagined Ideologies: Populist Figures, Liberalist Projections, and the Horizons of Constitutionalism' (2019) 20 German Law Journal 201. On the deeper historical connections between populism and popular sovereignty, reaching back into the nineteenth century, see Duncan Kelly, 'Populism and the History of Popular Sovereignty' in Kaltwasser and others, 'Oxford Handbook' (n 68) 511.

[69] Paul Stubbs and Noemi Lendvai-Bainon, 'Authoritarian Neoliberalism, Radical Conservatism and Social Policy within the European Union: Croatia, Hungary and Poland' (2020) 51(2) Development and Change 540; Adam Fabry, *From State Capitalism to Authoritarian Neoliberalism* (Palgrave 2019).

anti-establishment rhetoric, but retained most of the prevailing constitutional structures, depoliticizing strategies, and political economy of market liberalism.[70]

There was, thus, a marked sense of double standards in the EU and elite-led response to political populism. First and foremost, as Bojan Bugaric notes, the liberal moralist aversion to populism was suspect, since populism was a predictable response to the destructive forces of liberal market logic.[71] Reaction to, and dramatization of, the perceived departure from EU norms in Hungary and Poland also came in rather stark contrast to the relatively muted attention to the ascendance, in Austria, of a right- nationalist party, the Freedom Party (FPO), to government, as a junior partner, in October 2017 (itself in contrast to the earlier, but ineffectual, outcry in regard to Jörg Haider joining a coalition government in 2000).[72] This sense of hypocrisy would by heightened by the fact that Fidesz was accommodated within the dominant centre-right grouping, the European People's Party (EPP) group, in the European Parliament.

Brand new parties of the Left also emerged in the conjuncture, and others adopted a new, more strident style, with the notable electoral success of parties such as Podemos, in Spain, and Syriza, in Greece.[73] Although Left populism ultimately had little to show for its electoral achievements,[74] its successes were illuminating; particularly the election to government of Syriza, in January 2015. It revealed that the perceived danger to the EU, from the perspective of political elites, was less right-wing authoritarian populism than a left-wing democratic populism, one that would challenge the dominant paradigm of austerity and economic liberalism.[75] Syriza adopted a democratic, anti-austerity, yet pro-European platform, although it would just as casually be dismissed as populist, or even as 'extremist'.[76] And, being inside the eurozone, Greece was far more susceptible to coercive threats from the core.

As Ernesto Laclau had earlier noted:

[I]n the dismissal of populism far more is involved than the relegation of a peripheral set of phenomena to the margins of social explanation. What is involved in such a disdainful rejection is . . . the dismissal of politics tout court, and the assertion that the management of community is the concern of an administrative power whose source of legitimacy is a proper knowledge of what a 'good' community is.[77]

[70] Christopher Bickerton and Carlo Invernizzi Accetti, 'Populism and Technocracy: Opposites or Complements?', (2017) 20:2 Critical Review of International Social and Political Philosophy 186.

[71] See Bojan Bugaric, 'Could Populism be Good for Constitutional Democracy?' (2019) Annual Review Law and Social Science 41; see, further, Chantal Mouffe, *For a Left Populism* (Verso 2018).

[72] After the fall of the 2000 coalition government, the FPO rebranded itself as pro-EU, albeit maintaining the reactionary, conservative, and neo-liberal elements that characterized its development, and which had induced the earlier concern in 2000 around violation of the EU's core values.

[73] See, generally, Blokker (n 63). For discussion of Podemos, its connection to the populist theory of Laclau and Mouffe, and growth out of the Indignados movement and 15-M protests that emerged after the financial crisis, see Joaquin Valdivielso, 'The Outraged People: Laclau, Mouffe and the Podemos Hypothesis' (2017) 24 Constellations 296–309.

[74] See Anton Jäger, 'We Bet the House on Left Populism—and Lost' *Jacobin Magazine* (New York, 25 November 2019) <https://jacobinmag.com/2019/11/we-bet-the-house-on-left-populism-and-lost> accessed 22 November 2020.

[75] See Peter Spiegel, 'The Donald Tusk Interview: The Annotated Transcript' *Financial Times* (London, 16 July 2015) <https://www.ft.com/content/ff50e5a9-7b15-3998-a9f1-c11359dc01b8> accessed 22/11/20.

[76] See Stavrakakis and Katsambekis (n 54).

[77] Ernesto Laclau, *On Populist Reason* (Verso 2005) x.

The weakness of authoritarian liberalism

According to Jan-Werner Müller, by 2012 Europe had already reached a genuine conjuncture, breaching a democratic threshold by developing a *qualitatively* different relationship with its sovereign states.[78] For Müller, this transformation had a dual aspect: it was characterized both by the EU's increasingly intense (and often informal) intervention in the domestic life of its member states—most evident (and ominous) in the cases of Greece and Italy—and, equally disarmingly, by non-intervention or impotence to protect liberal democracy in others, most notably in the case of Hungary.[79]

There would, thus, be a notable asymmetry in the reaction of the EU, and its powerful member states, in dealing with reactionary, as opposed to self-styled radical forces. Anti-systemic parties of the Left, contesting austerity, but not the European Union as such—Syriza, Podemos, and the Left Bloc in Portugal— would be presented by the European political establishment, as well as by domestic elites, as a threat to necessary structural reforms, and even to the project of integration itself. Parties of the centre and Right were able to harness anti-establishment and Eurosceptic opinion more effectively, even as they were able to pursue their programmes from *within* the EU. In contrast to its 'success' in dealing with Greece—success in so far as the EU rebuked Syriza's threat to its economic liberal paradigm and micromanaged the process of imposing austerity—the EU would be relatively powerless in dealing with the apparent threats to democracy and the rule of law in Hungary and Poland. On the contrary, the EU started to shape itself in their own image, emulating populist strategies to define and defend a European 'way of life' based on Christian heritage.[80]

Müller's diagnosis of a qualitative transformation of the post-war project of constrained democracy was, however, revealing. The EU, from his perspective, was no longer able to maintain its *raison d'etre*: too authoritarian in one context (vis-à-vis Greece), not authoritarian enough in another (vis-à-vis Hungary). The inappositely named 'militant democracy', it turned out, and despite its initial interwar rationale, was far more capable of responding to the threat from the Left to liberal economic norms than to the threat from the Right to liberal democratic values.

Attention to the phenomenon of authoritarian liberalism suggests a different diagnosis of the conjuncture. The juridical and institutional conflicts were largely superstructural; underpinning them was, at each juncture of the euro crisis, an avoidance of serious debt restructuring, and of constitutional and political-economic reform. By conveying the impression that the crises were of liquidity rather than insolvency, the can would be continually 'kicked down the road'; the strategy of the ruling elites was

[78] Jan Werner-Müller, 'Beyond Militant Democracy' (2012) 73 New Left Review 39 ('Countries like Greece are now effectively forced to renegotiate their basic social contracts. Such interference, without any overarching supranational architecture to generate legitimacy, is both quantitatively and, I would argue, qualitatively new: it goes beyond what might have been covered under the old post-war European understanding of constrained democracies.' (ibid 44)).

[79] Infringement proceedings against Hungary were launched on the grounds of concerns over the independence of its central bank, judiciary, and data protection authority. For general discussion, see Carlos Closa and Dimitry Kochenov (eds), *Reinforcing Rule of Law Oversight in the European Union* (CUP 2016).

[80] As with Commission president Ursula von der Leyen's renaming of a Commission portfolio on security and immigration as a portfolio for 'protecting a European way of life'.

to 'extend, and pretend'. In order to face down domestic opposition to the EU, political elites had to adopt more direct avenues of de-democratization, bypassing parliament and juridical guarantees, in order to implement conditionality. But these measures would only defer and redirect, rather than address or redress, deep-seated deficits of legitimacy.

From this perspective, the post-war project had been all too successful. The conjuncture represented the final chapter of an ongoing transformative development: the deradicalization of politics, the hollowing out of democracy, and a decline of traditional class identities and organized labour, all in combination with an ideological faith in European integration. The containment of democracy, and distrust of any attempt to assert popular sovereignty over the economy, would be a continuation of post-war trends. What was new was the brief flicker of contestation, centred in Greece.

Contestation in Greece led to the hardening of the geopolitical, political, and material constitution of authoritarian liberalism, not only as a matter of political form, *but also of* economic policy and ideology. The first was frequently noted: 'the replacement of law by discretionary political fiat' was 'Schmittianism pure', according to Christian Joerges.[81] The second was less remarked upon, but the political logic of 'friend versus enemy' would increasingly come to form around those willing to support economic liberalism and austerity, and remain in the eurozone. A new enemy was identified, not an external or physical threat, but an internal and *ideological* enemy: those willing to advocate for a different kind of Europe.[82] This, too, signified not the strength of the prevailing configuration, but its weakness, the dominant structure apparently threatened by a political project in a country representing 1 per cent of the EU's GDP.

Undergirding the Schmittian rhetoric, was, to adapt the language of Gramsci, a *hegemonic project*, as well as an accumulation strategy and a 'state form'.[83] There was, as we saw in Chapter 11, a new *nomos* to accompany the *narrative* of austerity. But this amounted only to a *weak hegemonic project*. Germany was not able to exercise anything approaching a full geopolitical hegemony, not only due to its own lack of military and financial resources, but due to the absence of any consent (either domestically or outside of Germany) for its adoption of a leadership role. It could not assume the role of 'hegemonic stabilizer'; on the contrary, its insistence on rigid ordoliberal medicine was creating political instability. To the extent that it exercised a form of hegemony, it would be through the consent of other states, not to German leadership, but to the EU.[84]

The euro crisis exposed the lack of a coherent opposition to the status quo.[85] It highlighted both the absence of any centralized political-democratic authority to

[81] Christian Joerges, 'Europe's Economic Constitution in Crisis and the Emergence of a New Constitutional Constellation' (2014) 15 German Law Journal 985.

[82] See Spiegel (n 75).

[83] See Rune Møller Stahl, 'Ruling the Interregnum: Politics and Ideology in Nonhegemonic Times' (2019) 43 Politics and Society 333 ('To establish economic hegemony, whether by factions of capital or cross-class compromise, it is necessary to formulate a *Hegemonic Project*, not only to provide an accumulation strategy, but also a "State Form".')

[84] Costas Lapavitsas described this as a 'fetishisation of the EU': see Costas Lapavitsas, 'Marx at 201: The Legacy of Karl Marx of the Contemporary Study of Law, Politics and Society' (LSE, 27 March 2019) (recording can be accessed here: http://www.lse.ac.uk/Events/2019/03/20190327t1830vSZT/Marx-at-201 .

[85] See Stathis Kouvelakis, 'Borderlands' (2017) 110 New Left Review 5.

deal decisively with economic matters *and* the absence of a viable alternative to membership of the EU in the domestic constitutional imagination.[86] If, in other words, it revealed not a European Caesar, but a 'bureaucratic Caesarism', it also revealed the hollowness of domestic democracy, and lack of serious political resistance. In the final analysis, it was not Wolfgang Schaüble, but Yanis Varoufakis who confessed to wanting to act as the stabilizer, to 'save European capitalism from itself' and avoid a 'postmodern version of the 1930s'.[87] Due to the profound grip of the ideology of European integration on post-war cultural memory, as well as on dominant material interests and identity—not only of a transnational capitalist class, but of various professional, managerial, and intellectual classes—there was limited willingness to channel domestic dissent.[88] Europe remained the 'empty signifier' that will save all.[89]

The euro crisis signified, *pace* Balibar, less a 'revolution from above', than an 'erosion from below'; this explains why the crisis could not be capitalized on by political and social movements.[90] If the constraints of EU membership are properly characterized as external constraints, they are not, however, 'imposed from without'; they are the part of the apparatus of governing, through which the domestic political class rules over its own people. They are part cause and consequence of the disconnect between rulers and ruled.[91] What had occurred through the unfinished conjuncture was that the terrain had been exposed, economic liberalism revealing its authoritarian character. More than that, it also exposed that this character remained based on a fear of freedom, as much as on its repression from without.

[86] Even Krastev and Holmes, staunch defenders of liberalism, consider the absence of any alternative to the liberal order after 1989, and the order's increasing 'hegemony' and decreasing 'pluralism', to be a significant precursor to the populist turn (see Ivan Krastev and Stephen Holmes, *The Light That Failed: A Reckoning* (Allen Lane 2019)).

[87] Yanis Varoufakis, 'How I Became an Erratic Marxist' *The Guardian* (London, 18 February 2015) (based on a lecture delivered at the 6th Subversive Festival in Zagreb in 2013) <https://www.theguardian.com/news/2015/feb/18/yanis-varoufakis-how-i-became-an-erratic-marxist> accessed 22 November 2020.

[88] One of the extraordinary effects of the Brexit vote was that these classes were politically reawakened when they felt their interests and identity were threatened, even in a country traditionally more eurosceptic (see Daniel Cohen, 'Loud, Obsessive, Tribal: The Radicalisation of Remain' *The Guardian* (London, 13 August 2019) <https://www.theguardian.com/politics/2019/aug/13/brexit-remain-radicalisation-fbpe-peoples-vote> accessed 24 September 2020.

[89] Perry Anderson, 'Situationism a l'envers' (2019) 119 New Left Review 47 (a review of Adam Tooze's work).

[90] Panagiotios Sotiris, 'The Authoritarian and Disciplinary Mechanism of Reduced Sovereignty in the EU: The Case of Greece' in C Tansel (ed), *States of Discipline: Authoritarian Neoliberalism and the Contested Reproduction of Capitalist Order* (Rowman and Littlefield 2017) 171–89.

[91] Peter Mair, *Ruling the Void: The Hollowing Out of Western Democracy* (Verso 2013); Christopher Bickerton, 'Beyond the European Void? Reflections on Peter Mair's Legacy' (2018) 24 European Law Journal 268–80.

Bibliography

Abraham D, *The Collapse of the Weimar Republic: Political Economy and Crisis* (Princeton University Press 1981)

Accetti CI, *What is Christian Democracy? Politics, Religion and Ideology* (CUP 2019)

Accetti CI and Zuckerman I, 'What's Wrong with Militant Democracy?' (2013) 65 Political Studies 182

Ackerman B, *We, the People: Foundations* (HUP 1991)

Ackerman B, 'The Rise of World Constitutionalism' (1997) 83 Virginia Law Review 771

Ackerman B, 'Three Paths to Constitutionalism—and the Crisis of the European Union' (2015) 45 British Journal of Political Science 705

Ackerman B, *Revolutionary Constitutions: Charismatic Leadership and the Rule of Law* (Belknap Press 2019)

Adenauer K, *World Indivisible—With Liberty and Justice For All* (George Allen & Unwin 1956)

Adler-Nissen R, 'Opting Out of an Ever Closer Union: The Integration Doxa and the Management of Sovereignty' (2011) 34 West European Politics 1092

Aglietta M, 'The European Vortex' (2012) 75 New Left Review 15

Ali T, *The Extreme Centre: A Warning* (Verso 2015)

Alter KJ, *Establishing the Supremacy of European Law: The Making of an International Rule of Law in Europe* (OUP 2003)

Amable B, 'Dirigism and Modernism vs Ordoliberalism' in Hien J and Joerges C (eds), *Ordoliberalism: Law and the Rule of Economics* (Bloomsbury Publishing 2017)

Anderson GW, 'Constitutionalism as Critical Project' in Gill S and Cutler AC (eds), *New Constitutionalism and World Order* (CUP 2014)

Anderson P, 'Arms and Rights' (2005) New Left Review 5

Anderson P, *The New Old World* (Verso 2009)

Anderson P, *The H-Word: The Peripeteia of Hegemony* (Verso 2017)

Anderson P, *The Antinomies of Antonio Gramsci* (Verso 2017)

Anghie A, *Imperialism, Sovereignty and the Making of International Law* (CUP 2005)

Apeldoorn B van, 'Transnational Class Agency and European Governance: The Case of the European Round Table of Industrialists' (2000) 5 New Political Economy 157

Apeldoorn B van, *Transnational Capitalism and the Struggle over European Integration* (Routledge 2002)

Arato A, 'Dilemmas Arising from the Power to Create Constitutions in Eastern Europe' (1993) 14 Cardozo Law Review 661

Arendt H, 'Parties, Movements, and Classes' (1945) 12 Partisan Review 504

Arendt H, *On Violence* (Allen Lane 1970)

Arendt H, *On Revolution* (Penguin Books 1990)

Arendt H, 'The Aftermath of Nazi Rule: Report from Germany', *Essays in Understanding 1930–1954: Formation, Exile, and Totalitarianism* (Schocken Books 1994)

Arendt H, *The Origins of Totalitarianism* (Harcourt 1966)

Armstrong K and Kilpatrick C, 'Law, Governance, or New Governance? The Changing Open Method of Coordination' (2007) 13 The Columbia Journal of European Law 649

Arrighi G, *Adam Smith in Beijing: Lineages of the Twenty-First Century* (Verso 2007)

Asad T, 'Muslims and European Identity: Can Europe Represent Islam?' in Pagden A (ed), *The Idea of Europe: From Antiquity to the European Union* (CUP 2002)
Ashiagbor D, 'Unravelling the Embedded Liberal Bargain: Labour and Social Welfare Law in the Context of EU Market Integration' (2013) 19 European Law Journal 303
Assheuer T, 'The Players Resign—Core Europe to the Rescue: A Conversation with Jürgen Habermas about Brexit and the EU Crisis' *Die Zeit* (Hamburg, 12 July 2016) <https://www.zeit.de/kultur/2016-07/juergen-habermas-brexit-eu-crises-english> accessed 24 September 2020
Audier S, 'Neoliberalism Through Foucault's Eyes' (2015) 54 History and Theory 404
Augenstein D and Dawson M, 'Introduction: What Law for What Polity? "Integration through Law" in the European Union Revisited' in Augenstein D (ed), *'Integration through Law' Revisited: The Making of the European Polity* (Ashgate Publishing 2012)
Avbelj M, 'Theory of European Union' (2011) 36 European Law Review 818
Baccaro L and Pontusson J, 'Rethinking Comparative Political Economy: The Growth Model Perspective' (2016) 44 Politics & Society 175
Baccaro L and Howell C, *Trajectories of Neoliberal Transformation: European Industrial Relations Since the 1970s* (CUP 2017)
Baker E and Harding C, 'From Past Imperfect to Future Perfect? A Longitudinal Study of the Third Pillar' (2009) 34 European Law Review 25
Balakrishnan G (ed), *Debating Empire* (Verso 2003)
Balibar É, *We, the People of Europe? Reflections on Transnational Citizenship* (Princeton University Press 2004)
Balibar É, 'Europe: Final Crisis? Some Theses' (2010) 13 Theory & Event
Balibar É, 'Europe's Revolution from Above' *The Guardian* (London, 23 November 2011) <https://www.theguardian.com/commentisfree/2011/nov/23/europe-revolution-from-above> accessed 25 September 2020
Balibar É, 'The Rise and Fall of the European Union: Temporalities and Teleologies' (2014) 21 Constellations 202
Balibar É, *Equaliberty: Political Essays* (Duke University Press 2014)
Bartolini S, *Restructuring Europe: Centre Formation, System Building, and Political Structuring between the Nation-State and the European Union* (OUP 2005)
Bauer O, 'The Equilibrium of Class Strength' in Blum ME and Smaldone W (eds), *Austro-Marxism: The Ideology of Unity: Austro-Marxist Theory and Strategy*, vol 1 (Historical Materialism Book Series, Brill 2015)
Beatty D, *The Ultimate Rule of Law* (OUP 2005)
Beaud O, *La puissance de l'État* (Léviathan, Presses Universitaires de France 1994)
Beaud O, *Théorie de la Fédération* (Léviathan, PUF 2007)
Bebr G, 'The European Coal and Steel Community: A Political and Legal Innovation' (1953) 63 The Yale Law Journal 1
Beck U, *The Cosmopolitan Vision* (Polity Press 2006)
Beck U, *German Europe* (Polity Press 2013)
Becker P, *Die Deutsche Europapolitik und die Osterweiterung der Europäischen Union* (Nomos 2011)
Behrent MC, 'The Origins of the Anti-Liberal Left: The 1979 Vincennes Conference on Neoliberalism' (2017) 35 French Politics, Culture & Society 44
Bell D, *The End of Ideology: On the Exhaustion of Political Ideas in the Fifties* (HUP 2000)
Bellamy R, 'Gramsci, Croce, and the Italian Liberal Tradition' (1990) 11:2 History of Political Thought 313
Bellamy R, *Political Constitutionalism: A Republican Defence of the Constitutionality of Democracy* (CUP 2007)

Bellamy R, 'The Liberty of the Moderns: Market Freedom and Democracy in the EU' (2012) 1:1 Global Constitutionalism 141

Benjamin W, 'Theses on the Philosophy of History' in *Illuminations* ed Hannah Arendt (The Bodley Head 2015)

Bercusson B, *European Labour Law* (2nd edn, CUP 2012)

Berend IT, 'From Oil Crisis to Financial Crisis 1973–2009' in Stone D (ed), *The Oxford Handbook of Postwar European History* (OUP 2012)

Berlin I, 'Two Concepts of Liberty' in Hardy H (ed), *Liberty: Incorporating Four Essays on Liberty* (2nd edn, OUP 2002)

Berman P, 'From Laeken to Lisbon: The Origins and Negotiation of the Lisbon Treaty' in Biondi A, Eeckhout P, and Ripley S (eds), *EU Law After Lisbon* (OUP 2012)

Berman S, 'Institutions and the Consolidation of Democracy in Western Europe' in Fioretos O, Falleti TG, and Sheingate A (eds), *The Oxford Handbook of Historical Institutionalism* (OUP 2016)

Bernatavičius M, 'Independence of the ECB and the ECJ during the Sovereign Debt Crisis: From Active Leadership to Rubber-Stamping?' (2020) 35 Journal of Common Market Studies 1

Besselink LFM and Reestman J-H, 'The Fiscal Compact and the European Constitutions: "Europe Speaking German"' (2012) 1 European Constitutional Law Review 1

Bibow J, 'On the Origin and Rise of Central Bank Independence in West Germany' (2009) 16 The European Journal of the History of Economic Thought 155

Bickerton CJ, *European Integration: From Nation-States to Member States* (OUP 2012)

Bickerton CJ, 'The Collapse of Europe's Mainstream Centre Left' *New Statesman* (London, 1 May 2018)

Bickerton CJ and Accetti CI, 'Populism and Technocracy: Opposites or Complements?' (2015) 20 Critical Review of International Social and Political Philosophy 186

Bickerton CJ, Hodson D, and Puetter U, 'The New Intergovernmentalism: European Integration in the Post-Maastricht Era' (2015) 53 Journal of Common Market Studies 703

Bickerton CJ, Hodson D, and Puetter U, 'Something New: A Rejoinder to Frank Schimmelfennig on the New Intergovernmentalism' (2015) 53 Journal of Common Market Studies 731

Biebricher T, *The Political Theory of Neoliberalism* (Stanford University Press 2019)

Bieler A, Jordan J, and Morton AD, 'EU Aggregate Demand as a Way out of Crisis? Engaging the Post-Keynesian Critique' (2019) 57 Journal of Common Market Studies 805

Bilger F, *La pensée économique libérale dans l'Allemagne contemporaine* (Librairie générale de droit et de jurisprudence, R Pichon et R Durand-Auzias 1964)

Black J, 'Decentring Regulation: Understanding the Role of Regulation and Self-Regulation in a "Post-Regulatory" World' (2001) 54 Current Legal Problems 103

Blokker P, *New Democracies in Crisis? A Comparative Constitutional Study of the Czech Republic, Hungary, Poland, Romania and Slovakia* (Routledge 2014)

Blokker P, 'Populist Constitutionalism' in C de la Torre (ed), *Routledge Handbook of Global Populism* (Routledge 2018) 113

Blyth M, *Austerity: The History of a Dangerous Idea* (OUP 2015)

Bobbitt P, *The Shield of Achilles: War, Peace, and the Course of History* (Anchor Books 2003)

Bogdandy A von, 'Founding Principles of EU Law: A Theoretical and Doctrinal Sketch' (2010) 16 European Law Journal 95

Bogdandy A von, 'The European Lesson for International Democracy: The Significance of Articles 9 to 12 EU Treaty for International Organizations' (2012) 23 European Journal of International Law 315

Bogdandy A von and Bast J (eds), *Principles of European Constitutional Law* (Hart Publishing 2006)

Bohle D, 'Neoliberal Hegemony, Transnational Capital and the Terms of the EU's Eastward Expansion' (2016) 30 Capital & Class 57
Bohle D and Greskovits B, *Capitalist Diversity on Europe's Periphery* (Cornell University Press 2012)
Böhm F, Eucken W, and Grossmann-Doerth H, 'The Ordo Manifesto of 1936' in Peacock AT and Willgerodt H (eds), *Germany's Social Market Economy: Origins and Evolution* (MacMillan 1989)
Bomhoff J, *Balancing Constitutional Rights: The Origins and Meanings of Postwar Legal Discourse* (CUP 2013)
Bonefeld W, 'Authoritarian Liberalism: From Schmitt via Ordoliberalism to the Euro' (2017) 43 Critical Sociology 747
Bourne AK and Bértoa FC, 'Mapping Militant Democracy: Variation in Party Ban Practices in European Democracies (1945–2015)' (2017) 13 European Constitutional Law Review 221
Brennetot A, 'The Geographical and Ethical Origins of Neoliberalism: The Walter Lippmann Colloquium and the Foundations of a New Geopolitical Order' (2015) 49 Political Geography 30
Brown W, *The Undoing of the Demos: Neoliberalism's Stealth Revolution* (Zone Books 2015)
Brunkhorst H, 'Collective Bonapartism—Democracy in the European Crisis' (2014) 15 German Law Journal 1177
Brunkhorst H, 'Concrete Order Formation or Rational Will Formation? Constituent Power as the *Ratio* of *Voluntas*' in Wilkinson MA and Dowdle MW (eds), *Questioning the Foundations of Public Law* (Hart Publishing 2018)
Bryde B-O, 'The ECJ's Fundamental Rights Jurisprudence—A Milestone in Transnational Constitutionalism' in Azoulai L and Maduro MP (eds), *The Past and Future of EU Law* (Hart Publishing 2010)
Bugaric B, 'Could Populism be Good for Constitutional Democracy?' (2019) Annual Review Law and Social Science 41
Bulmer S and Paterson WE, *Germany and the European Union: Europe's Reluctant Hegemon?* (Red Globe Press 2018)
de Búrca G, 'The Quest for Legitimacy in the European Union' (1996) 59 Modern Law Review 349
de Búrca G, 'The European Court of Justice and the international legal order after Kadi' (2010) 51 Harvard International Law Journal 1
Cafruny AW and Ryner M, *Europe at Bay: In the Shadow of US Hegemony* (Lynne Rienner 2007)
Caldwell P, 'National Socialism and Constitutional Law: Carl Schmitt, Otto Koellreutter and the Debate over the Nature of the Nazi State, 1933–1937' (1994) 16 Cardozo Law Review 399
Caldwell P, *Popular Sovereignty and the Crisis of German Constitutional Law: The Theory & Practice of Weimar Constitutionalism* (Duke University Press 1997)
Callies G-P and Zumbansen P, *Rough Consensus and Running Code: A Theory of Transnational Private Law* (Hart Publishing 2010)
Callinicos A, 'Brexit and the Imperial Constitution of Europe' in Nanopoulos E and Vergis F (eds), *The Crisis Behind the Eurocrisis: The Eurocrisis as a Multidimensional Systemic Crisis of the EU* (CUP 2019)
Carr EH, *The Twenty Years' Crisis, 1919–1939* (Palgrave Macmillan 2016)
Cartabia M, 'The Legacy of Sovereignty in the Italian Constitutional Debate' in Walker N (ed), *Sovereignty in Transition* (Hart Publishing 2003)
Castoriadis C, *Philosophy, Politics, Autonomy: Essays in Political Philosophy* (OUP 1991)
Cederman L-E, 'Nationalism and Bounded Integration: What it Would Take to Construct a European Demos' (2001) 7 European Journal of International Relations 139

Chalmers D and Barroso L, 'What *Van Gend en Loos* Stands For' (2014) 12 International Journal of Constitutional Law 105

Chalmers D, Monti G, and Davies G, *European Union Law: Cases and Materials* (3rd edn, CUP 2010)

Chalmers D, Monti G, and Davies G, *European Union Law: Cases and Materials* (4th edn, CUP 2019)

Chambers S, 'Democracy, Popular Sovereignty, and Constitutional Legitimacy' (2004) 11 Constellations 153

Chapman H, 'The State' in Berenson E, Duclert V, and Prochasson C (eds), *The French Republic: History, Values, Debate* (Cornell University Press 2011)

Chapman H, *France's Long Reconstruction: In Search of the Modern Republic* (Harvard University Press 2018).

Chiti E, Menéndez AJ, and Teixeira PG (eds), *The European Rescue of the European Union: The Existential Crisis of the European Political Project* (ARENA 2012)

Christodoulidis E, 'The European Court of Justice and "Total Market" Thinking' (2013) 14 German Law Journal 2005

Christodoulidis E, 'Social Rights Constitutionalism: An Antagonistic Endorsement' (2017) 44 Journal of Law and Society 123

Claes M and Reestman J-H, 'The Protection of National Constitutional Identity and the Limits of European Integration at the Occasion of the Gauweiler Case' (2015) 16 German Law Journal 917

Clift B, 'The Political Economy of French Social Democratic Economic Policy Autonomy 1997–2002: Credibility, Dirigisme and Globalisation' in McIver M, Fishman N, Callaghan J and Jackson B (eds), *In Search of Social Democracy: Responses to Crisis and Modernisation* (Manchester University Press 2009)

Closa C and Kochenov D (eds), *Reinforcing Rule of Law Oversight in the European Union* (CUP 2016)

Cocks P, 'Towards a Marxist Theory of European integration' (1980) 34 International Organization 1

Cohen A, 'Constitutionalism Without Constitution: Transnational Elites Between Mobilization and Legal Expertise in the Making of a Constitution For Europe (1940s–1960s)' (2007) 32 Law & Social Inquiry 109

Cohen D, '"Loud, Obsessive, Tribal": the Radicalisation of Remain' *The Guardian* (London, 13 August 2019) <https://www.theguardian.com/politics/2019/aug/13/brexit-remain-radicalisation-fbpe-peoples-vote> accessed 24 September 2020

Cohen E, 'The Euro, Economic Federalism, and the Question of National Sovereignty' in Pagden A (ed), *The Idea of Europe: From Antiquity to the European Union* (CUP 2002)

Cohen J and Sabel C, 'Directly-Deliberative Polyarchy' (1997) 3 European Law Journal 313

Conway M, 'Democracy in Postwar Europe: The Triumph of a Political Model' (2002) 32 European History Quarterly 59

Conway M, 'The Rise and Fall of Western Europe's Democratic Age, 1945–1973' (2004) 13 Contemporary European History 67

Corrias L, 'The Empty Place of European Power: Contested Democracy and the Technocratic Threat' (2017) 23 European Law Journal 482

Corrias L, 'Populism in a Constitutional Key: Constituent Power, Popular Sovereignty and Constitutional Identity' (2016) 12 European Constitutional Law Review 6

Cowen D and Smith N, 'After Geopolitics? From the Geopolitical Social to Geo-economics' (2009) 41 Antipode 22

Craig P, 'Constitutions, Constitutionalism, and the European Union' (2001) 7 European Law Journal 125

Craig P, 'Subsidiarity: A Political and Legal Analysis' (2012) 50 Journal of Common Market Studies 72

Craig P, '*Pringle*: Legal Reasoning, Text, Purpose and Teleology' (2013) 20 Maastricht Journal of European and Comparative Law 3

Cremona M, 'Introduction' in Cremona M (ed), *The Enlargement of the European Union* (OUP 2003)

Cristi R, 'Carl Schmitt on Sovereignty and Constituent Power' (1997) 10 The Canadian Journal of Law and Jurisprudence 189

Cristi R, *Carl Schmitt and Authoritarian Liberalism: Strong State, Free Economy* (University of Wales Press 1998)

Crouch C, 'Breaking Open Black Boxes: The Implications for Sociological Theory of European Integration' in Menon A and Wright V (eds), *From the Nation State to Europe: Essays in Honour of Jack Hayward* (OUP 2003)

Crouch C, *Post-Democracy* (Polity Press 2004)

Crouch C, *The Strange Non-Death of Neoliberalism* (Polity Press 2011)

Cukierman A, *Central Bank Strategy, Credibility, and Independence: Theory and Evidence* (MIT Press 1992)

Curtin D, 'The Constitutional Structure of the Union: A Europe of Bits and Pieces' (1993) 30 Common Market Law Review 17

Dahl R, 'Epilogue' in Dahl R (ed), *Political Oppositions in Western Democracies* (YUP 1966)

Dahl R, *Democracy and its Critics* (YUP 1989)

Dale G, 'Karl Polanyi's The Great Transformation: Perverse Effects, Protectionism and Gemeinschaft' (2008) 37 Economy and Society 495

Dale G and Fabry A, 'Neoliberalism in Eastern Europe and the Former Soviet Union' in Cahill D and others (eds), *The SAGE Handbook of Neoliberalism* (SAGE Publications 2018)

Dani M, 'The Subjectification of the Citizen in European Public Law' in Azoulai L, Barbou des Places S, and Pataut E (eds), *Constructing the Person in EU Law* (Hart Publishing 2016)

Dani M and others, 'At the End of the Law: A Moment of Truth for the Eurozone and the EU' (*Verfassungsblog*, 15 May 2015) <https://verfassungsblog.de/at-the-end-of-the-law/> accessed 25 September 2020

D'Antoni M, 'From Monetary to Fiscal to Political Union: A Progression to Integration or a Recipe for Failure?' (2020) 23 *Journal of International Economic Law* 469

Davies B, *Resisting the European Court of Justice: 1949–1979: West Germany's Confrontation with European Law* (CUP 2012)

Dawson M and de Witte F, 'Constitutional Balance in the EU after the Euro-Crisis' (2013) 76 Modern Law Review 817

Deakin S, 'Social Policy, Economic Governance and EMU: Alternatives to Austerity' in Bruun N, Lörcher K, and Schömann I (eds), *The Economic and Financial Crisis and Collective Labour Law in Europe* (Hart Publishing 2014)

Deeg R, 'Change from Within: German and Italian Finance in the 1990s' in Streeck W and Thelen K (eds), *Beyond Continuity: Institutional Change in Advanced Political Economies* (OUP 2005)

Della Porta D, 'Mobilizing Against the Crisis, Mobilizing for "Another Democracy": Comparing Two Global Waves of Protest' (2012) 4 Interface 274

Della Sala V, 'Leaders and Followers: Leadership Amongst Member States in a Differentiated Europe' in Jones E, Menon A, and Weatherill S (eds), *Oxford Handbook of the European Union* (OUP 2012)

Delors J, 'Speech Delivered at the First Intergovernmental Conference (IGC) to be held in Luxembourg' (Luxembourg, 9 September 1985)

Demaret P, 'The Treaty Framework' in O'Keeffe D and Twomey PM (eds), *Legal Issues of the Maastricht Treaty* (Wiley Chancery 1994)
Denord F, 'French Neoliberalism and Its Divisions: From the Colloque Walter Lippmann to the Fifth Republic' in Mirowski P and Plehwe D (eds), *The Road from Mont Pelerin: The Making of the Neoliberal Thought Collective* (HUP 2009)
Dewey J, *German Philosophy and Politics* (revised edn, GP Putnam's Sons 1942)
Di Fabio U, 'A European Charter: Towards a Constitution for the Union' (2001) 7 Columbia Journal of European Law 159
Di Fabio U, 'Karlsruhe Makes a Referral' (2014) 15 German Law Journal 107
Drochon H, 'Robert Michels, The Iron Law of Oligarchy and Dynamic Democracy' (2020) 27 Constellations 185
Dukes R, *The Labour Constitution: The Enduring Idea of Labour Law* (OUP 2014)
Dullien S and Guérot U, *The Long Shadow of Ordoliberalism: Germany's Approach to the Euro Crisis* (European Council of Foreign Relations 2012)
Dunne N, 'Liberalisation and the Pursuit of the Internal Market' (2018) 43 European Law Review 803
Dunoff J and Trachtman J (eds), *Ruling the World: Constitutionalism, International Law and Global Governance* (CUP 2012)
Dunphy R, *Contesting Capitalism? Left Parties and European Integration* (Manchester University Press 2004)
Durand C and Keucheyan R, 'Bureaucratic Caesarism: A Gramscian Outlook on the Crisis of Europe' (2015) 23 Historical Materialism 23
Duranti M, *The Conservative Human Rights Revolution: European Identity, Transnational Politics and the Origins of the European Convention* (OUP 2017)
Dworkin R, *Taking Rights Seriously* (HUP 1978)
Dyson K, *States, Debt, and Power: 'Saints' and 'Sinners' in European History and Integration* (OUP 2014)
Dyson K, 'Ordoliberalism as Tradition and Ideology' in Hien J and Joerges C (eds), *Ordoliberalism: Law and the Rule of Economics* (Bloomsbury Publishing 2017)
Dyson K and Featherstone K, 'Italy and EMU as a "Vincolo Esterno": Empowering the Technocrats, Transforming the State' (1996) 1 South European Society & Politics 272
Dyson K and Featherstone K, *The Road to Maastricht: Negotiating Economic and Monetary Union* (OUP 2003)
Dyzenhaus D, *Legality and Legitimacy: Carl Schmitt, Hans Kelsen and Hermann Heller in Weimar* (OUP 1997)
Dyzenhaus D, 'The Politics of the Question of Constituent Power' in Loughlin M and Walker N (eds), *The Paradox of Constitutionalism: Constituent Power and Constitutional Form* (OUP 2007)
Dyzenhaus D, 'Constitutionalism in an Old Key: Legality and Constituent Power' (2012) 1 Global Constitutionalism 229
Eberhard K, *The Weimar Republic* (2nd edn, Routledge 2004)
Ehlermann CD, 'The Contribution of EC Competition Policy to the Single Market' (1992) 23 CMLR 257
Eichengreen B, *Golden Fetters: The Gold Standard and the Great Depression, 1919–1939* (OUP 1995)
Eichengreen B, *The European Economy Since 1945: Co-ordinated Capitalism and Beyond* (Princeton University Press 2007)
Eilstrup-Sangiovanni M and Verdier D, 'European Integration as a Solution to War' (2005) 11 European Journal of International Relations 99

Elden S, 'Reading Schmitt Geopolitically: Nomos, Territory and Grossraum' (2010) Radical Philosophy 18

Eley G, *Forging Democracy: The History of the Left in Europe 1850–2000* (OUP 2002)

Esping-Andersen G, *The Three Worlds of Welfare Capitalism* (Polity Press 1990)

Evans RJ, 'German Social Democracy and Women's Suffrage 1891–1918' (1980) 15 Journal of Contemporary History 533

Everson M, 'An Exercise in Legal Honesty: Rewriting the Court of Justice and the Bundesverfassungsgericht' (2015) 21 European Law Journal 474

Everson M and Eisner J, *The Making of a European Constitution: Judges and Law Beyond Constitutive Power* (Routledge 2007)

Fabbrini F, 'After the OMT Case: The Supremacy of EU Law as the Guarantee of the Equality of the Member States' (2016) 16 German Law Journal 1003

Fabry A, 'The Origins of Neoliberalism in Late "Socialist" Hungary: The Case of the Financial Research Institute and "Turnabout and Reform"' (2018) 42:1 Capital and Class 77

Fabry A, *From State Capitalism to Authoritarian Neoliberalism* (Palgrave 2019)

Fine B and Saad-Filho A, 'Thirteen Things You Need to Know about Neoliberalism' (2016) 43 Critical Sociology 685

Fioretos O, 'Coordinated Versus Liberal Market Economies' in Jones E, Menon A, and Weatherill S (eds), *Oxford Handbook of the European Union* (OUP 2012)

Fischer J, 'From Confederacy to Federation: Thoughts on the Finality of European Integration' in Joerges C, Meny Y, and Weiler JHH (eds), *What Kind of Constitution for What Kind of Polity? Responses to Joschka Fischer* (Jean Monnet Program Online Papers 2001)

Follesdal A and Hix S, 'Why There is a Democratic Deficit in the EU: A Response to Majone and Moravcsik' (2006) 44 Journal of Common Market Studies 533

Forst R, *The Right to Justification: Elements of a Constructivist Theory of Justice* (Columbia University Press 2012)

Fossum JE and Menéndez AJ, *The Constitution's Gift: A Constitutional Theory for a Democratic European Union* (Rowman & Littlefield 2011)

Foucault M, *The Birth of Biopolitics—Lectures at the College de France, 1978–1979* (Palgrave MacMillan 2008)

Fraenkel E, *The Dual State: A Contribution to the Theory of Dictatorship* (OUP 2017)

Frankenberg G, 'Authoritarian Constitutionalism—Coming to Terms with Modernity's Nightmares' in Alivar Garcia H and Frankenberg G (eds), *Authoritarian Constitutionalism: Comparative Analysis and Critique* (Elgar 2019)

Fraser N, 'From Redistribution to Recognition? Dilemmas of Justice in a Postsocialist Age' (1995) New Left Review 68

Fraser N, 'Behind Marx's Hidden Abode: For an Expanded Conception of Capitalism' (2014) 86 New Left Review 55

Friedrich CJ, 'The Political Thought of Neo-liberalism' (1955) 49 American Political Science Review 509

Fromm E, *The Fear of Freedom* (2nd edn, Routledge 2001)

Fukuyama F, *The End of History and the Last Man* (The Free Press 1992)

Fuller LL, 'Positivism and Fidelity to Law—A Reply to Professor Hart' (1958) 71 Harvard Law Review 630

Fuller LL, *The Law in Quest of Itself* (The Lawbook Exchange 2012)

Gabor D and Ban C, 'Banking on Bonds: The New Links Between States and Markets' (2017) 54:3 JCMS 617

Gamble A, 'Economic Recession and Disenchantment with Europe' in Hayward J (ed), *The Crisis of Representation in Europe* (Routledge 1996)

Garditz K, 'Beyond Symbolism: Towards a Constitutional Actio Popularis in EU Affairs? A Commentary on the OMT Decision of the Federal Constitutional Court' (2014) 15 German Law Journal 189
Gassert P, 'The Spectre of Americanization: Western Europe in the American Century' in Stone D (ed), *The Oxford Handbook of Postwar European History* (OUP 2012)
Gauchet M, *The Disenchantment of the World: A Political History of Religion* (New French Thought, Princeton University Press 1997)
Gay P, *The Dilemma of Democratic Socialism: Eduard Bernstein's Challenge to Marx* (2nd edn, Collier Books 1970)
Gearty C, 'The State of Freedom in Europe' (2015) 21 European Law Journal 706
Geary D, 'Employers, Workers, and the Collapse of the Weimar Republic' in Kershaw I (ed), *Weimar: Why Did German Democracy Fail?* (Weidenfeld and Nicholson 1990)
Genschel P, 'One Trap, Many Exits, but No Free Lunch: How the Joint-Decision Trap Shapes EU Tax Policy' in Falkner G (ed), *The EU's Decision Traps: Comparing Policies* (OUP 2011)
Georgious C, 'Unification from Above and Its Contradictions' in Nanopoulos E and Vergis F (eds), *The Crisis Behind the Eurocrisis: The Eurocrisis as a Multidimensional Systemic Crisis of the EU* (CUP 2019)
Gerbaudo P, 'The Indignant Citizen: Anti-austerity Movements in Southern Europe and the Anti-oligarchic Reclaiming of Citizenship' (2016) 16 Social Movement Studies 36
Gerber D, 'Constitutionalising the Economy: German Neoliberalism, Competition Law and the "New Europe"' (1994) 42 American Journal of Comparative Law 25
Germann J, 'Beyond "Geo-economics": Advanced Unevenness and the Anatomy of German Austerity' (2017) 24 European Journal of International Relations 590
Gerner-Beuerle C, Küçük E, and Schuster E, 'Law Meets Economics in the German Federal Constitutional Court: Outright Monetary Transactions on Trial' (2014) 15 German Law Journal 281
Gerstenberg O, 'Law's Polyarchy: A Comment on Cohen and Sabel' (1997) 3 European Law Journal 343
Gill S, *Power and Resistance in the New World Order* (2nd edn, Palgrave Macmillan 2008)
Gillingham J, *European Integration 1950–2003: Superstate or New Market Economy?* (CUP 2003)
Gindin S and Panitch L, *The Making of Global Capitalism: The Political Economy of American Empire* (Verso 2012)
Ginzburg A, Guarascio D, and Celi D, *Crisis in the European Monetary Union: A Core-Periphery Perspective* (Routledge 2019)
Giubboni S, *Social Rights and Market Freedom in the European Constitution: A Labour Law Perspective* (CUP 2006)
Glencross A and Trechsel AH (eds), *EU Federalism and Constitutionalism: The Legacy of Altiero Spinelli* (Lexington Books 2010)
Glenn HP, *The Cosmopolitan State* (OUP 2013)
Glyn A, *Capitalism Unleashed: Finance Globalisation and Welfare* (OUP 2012)
Glynn A, 'Social Democracy and Full Employment' (1995) New Left Review 33
Goldoni M, 'Reconstructing the Early Warning System on Subsidiarity: The Case for Political Judgment' (2014) 39 European Law Review 647
Goldoni M, 'Politicising EU Lawmaking? The *Spitzenkandidaten* Experiment as a Cautionary Tale' (2016) 22 European Law Journal 279
Goldoni M, 'Rousseau's Radical Constitutionalism and Its Legacy' in Dowdle MW and Wilkinson MA (eds), *Constitutionalism Beyond Liberalism* (CUP 2017)
Goldoni M and Wilkinson MA, 'The Material Constitution' (2018) 81 Modern Law Review 567

Goldthorpe JH, 'Problems of Political Economy After the Postwar Period' in Maier CS (ed), *Changing Boundaries of the Political: Essays on the Evolving Balance between the State and Society, Public and Private in Europe* (CUP 1987)

Gönenç R, Maher M, and Nicoletti G, 'The Implementation and the Effects of Regulatory Reform: Past Experience and Current Issues' (2003) OECD Economic Studies No 32, 2001/I

Grahl J and Teague P, 'The Cost of Neoliberal Europe' (1989) 174 New Left Review 33

Gramsci A, *Selections from the Prison Notebooks of Antonio Gramsci* (Lawrence & Wishart 2003)

Greenberg U, *The Weimar Century: German Émigrés and the Ideological Foundations of the Cold War* (Princeton University Press 2014)

Grémion P, 'State, Europe, and Republic' in Menon A and Wright V (eds), *From the Nation State to Europe? Essays in Honour of Jack Hayward* (OUP 2003)

Griffith J, 'The Political Constitution' (1979) 42 Modern Law Review 1

Grimm D, 'The Constitution in the Process of Denationalization' (2005) 12 Constellations 447

Grimm D, 'Defending Sovereign Statehood Against Transforming the Union into a State' (2009) 5 European Constitutional Law Review 353

Grimm D, 'The Achievements of Constitutionalism and its Prospects in a Changed World' in Loughlin M and Dobner P (eds), *The Twilight of Constitutionalism?* (OUP 2010)

Grimm D, 'Does Europe Need a Constitution?' (2010) 1 European Law Review 282

Grimm D, 'Sovereignty in the European Union' in Ellsworth J and Walt JWG van der (eds), *Constitutional Sovereignty and Social Solidarity in Europe* (Nomos/Bloomsbury 2015)

Guastaferro B, 'Beyond the Exceptionalism of Constitutional Conflicts: The Ordinary Functions of the Identity Clause' (2012) 31 Yearbook of European Law 263

Gunsteren H van, 'The Birth of the European Citizen out of the Dutch No Vote' (2005) European Constitutional Law Review 406

Haas EB, *The Uniting of Europe: Political, Social and Economic Forces, 1950–1957* (Stanford University Press 1958)

Habermas J, 'Remarks on Dieter Grimm's "Does Europe Need a Constitution?"' (1995) 1 European Law Journal 303

Habermas J, 'On the Internal Relation between the Rule of Law and Democracy' (1995) 3 European Journal of Philosophy 12

Habermas J, *The Lure of Technocracy* (Polity Press 2015)

Habermas J and Derrida J, 'February 15, or What Binds Europeans Together: A Plea for a Common Foreign Policy, Beginning in the Core of Europe' (2003) 10 Constellations 291

Habermas J, 'What Does Socialism Mean Today? Rectifying Revolution and the Need for New Thinking on the Left' (1990) 1 New Left Review 183

Habermas J, *Between Facts and Norms: Contributions to a Discourse Theory of Law and Democracy* (Polity Press 1996)

Habermas J, 'Three Normative Models of Democracy' in Benhabib S (ed), *Democracy and Difference: Contesting the Boundaries of the Political* (Princeton University Press 1996)

Habermas J, 'Why Europe Needs a Constitution' (2001) 11 New Left Review 5

Habermas J, *The Postnational Constellation: Political Essays* (1st edn, MIT Press 2001)

Habermas J, *The Crisis of the European Union: A Response* (Polity Press 2012)

Habermas J, 'Why Angela Merkel is Wrong on Greece' (Social Europe, 25 June 2015) <https://www.socialeurope.eu/why-angela-merkels-is-wrong-on-greece> accessed 25 September 2020

Hailbronner M, *Tradition and Transformations: The Rise of German Constitutionalism* (OUP 2015)

Halberstam D, 'Pluralism in *Marbury* and *Van Gend*' in Azoulai L and Maduro MP (eds), *The Past and Future of EU Law* (Hart Publishing 2010)

Hall PA and Soskice D, 'An Introduction to Varieties of Capitalism' in Hall PA and Soskice D (eds), *Varieties of Capitalism: The Institutional Foundations of Comparative Advantage* (OUP 2001)
Hall S, 'Gramsci and Us' in Hall S (ed), *The Hard Road to Renewal: Thatcherism and the Crisis of the Left* (Verso Books 1988)
Hall S, 'Popular-Democratic versus Authoritarian Populism', in Alan Hunt (ed), *Marxism and Democracy* (Lawrence and Wishart 1980)
Hall S, 'Authoritarian Populism: A Reply' (1985) New Left Review I/151
Hallstein W, *Die Europäische Gemeinschaft* (ECON 1979)
Halmai G, 'Populism, Authoritarianism, Constitutionalism' (2019) 20:3 German Law Journal 296
Haltern U, 'Pathos and Patina: The Failure and Promise of Constitutionalism in the European Imagination' (2003) 9 European Law Journal 14
Haltern U and Weiler JHH, 'Constitutional or International? The Foundation of the Community Legal Order and the Question of Judicial Kompetenz-Kompetenz' in Slaughter AM, Stone Sweet A, and Weiler JHH (eds), *The European Courts and National Courts—Doctrine and Jurisprudence: Legal Change in its Social Context* (Hart Publishing 1998)
Hamilton A, Madison J, and Jay J, *The Federalist* (HUP 2009)
Hampton JE, *Hobbes and the Social Contract Tradition* (CUP 1986)
Hansen P and Jonsson S, 'Building Eurafrica: Reviving Colonialism through European Integration, 1920–1960' in Nicolaïdis K, Sebe B, and Maas G (eds), *Echoes of Empire: Memory, Identity, and Colonial Legacies* (IB Tauris 2015)
Hardt M and Negri A, *Empire* (HUP 2000)
Harlow C, 'Citizen Access to Political Power in the European Union' (1999) EUI-RSCAS Working Papers 99/02
Harlow C, 'Voices of Difference in a Plural Community' (2002) 50 The American Journal of Comparative Law 339
Harvey D, *The New Imperialism* (OUP 2003)
Hayek FA, 'The Economic Conditions of Interstate Federalism' in *Individualism and Economic Order* (University of Chicago Press 1942)
Hayek FA, *Law, Legislation and Liberty: A New Statement of the Liberal Principles of Justice and Political Economy* (Taylor & Hudson 1982)
Heartfield J, 'European Union: A Process Without a Subject' in Bickerton CJ, Cunliffe P, and Gourevitch A (eds), *Politics Without Sovereignty: A Critique of Contemporary International Relations* (Routledge 2006)
Helgadóttir O, 'The Bocconi Boys go to Brussels: Italian Economic Ideas, Professional Networks and European Austerity' (2016) 23 Journal of European Public Policy 392
Heller H, 'Autoritärer Liberalismus' (1933) 44 Die Neue Rundschau 289
Heller H, '*Rechtsstaat* or Dictatorship?' (1987) 16 Economy and Society 127
Heller H, 'The Nature and Structure of the State' (1996) 18 Cardozo Law Review 1139
Heller H, 'Political Democracy and Social Homogeneity' in Jacobson AJ and Schlink B (eds), *Weimar: A Jurispurdence of Crisis* (University of California Press 2000)
Heller H, 'Authoritarian Liberalism?' (2015) 21 European Law Journal 295
Heller H, and Dyzenhaus D, *Sovereignty: A Contribution to the Theory of Public and International Law* (Cooper B tr, OUP 2019)
Heun W, *The Constitution of Germany: A Contextual Analysis* (Hart Publishing 2010)
Hinarejos A, *The Euro Area Crisis in Constitutional Perspective* (OUP 2015)
Hirschl R, *Towards Juristocracy: The Origins and Consequences of the New Constitutionalism* (HUP 2007)

Hodson D and Puetter U, 'The European Union in Disequilibrium: New Intergovernmentalism, Postfunctionalism and Integration Theory in the Post-Maastricht Period' (2019) 26 Journal of European Public Policy 1153

Hoffman S, 'Obstinate or Obsolete? The Fate of the Nation-state and the Case of Western Europe' (1966) 95 Daedalus 862

Holmes S, *Passions and Constraint: On the Theory of Liberal Democracy* (University of Chicago Press 1995)

Holtfrerich C-L, 'Economic Policy Options and the End of the Weimar Republic' in Kershaw I (ed), *Weimar: Why did German Democracy Fail?* (Wiedenfeld and Nicholson 1990)

Hooghe L and Marks G, 'A Postfunctionalist Theory of European Integration: From Permissive Consensus to Constraining Dissensus' (2009) 39 British Journal of Political Science 1

Hopkin J, 'The Troubled South: The Euro Experience in Italy and Spain' in Matthijs M and Blyth M (eds), *The Future of the Euro* (OUP 2015)

Höpner M, 'The German Undervaluation Regime under Bretton Woods: How Germany Became the Nightmare of the World Economy' (2019) MPIfG Discussion Paper 19/1

Huber K and Shackleton M, 'Codecision: A Practitioner's View from Inside the Parliament' (2013) 20 Journal of European Public Policy 1040

Ioannidis M, 'Europe's New Transformations: How the EU Economic Constitution Changed During the Eurozone Crisis' (2016) 53 Common Market Law Review 1237

Irving S, 'Limiting Democracy and Framing the Economy: Hayek, Schmitt and Ordoliberalism' (2018) 44 History of European Ideas 113

Isiksel T, 'Fundamental rights in the EU after Kadi and Al Barakaat' (2010) 16 European Law Journal 551

Isiksel T, *Europe's Functional Constitution: A Theory of Constitutionalism Beyond the State* (OUP 2016)

Isiksel T, 'European Exceptionalism and the EU's Accession to the ECHR' (2016) 27 European Journal of International Law 565

Islam S and Mandelbaum M (eds), *Making Markets: Economic Transformation in Eastern Europe and the Post-Soviet States* (Council on Foreign Relations Press 1993)

Issing O, 'Hayek, Currency Competition and European Monetary Union' (Annual Hayek Memorial Lecture hosted by the Institute of Economic Affairs, London, 27 May 1999)

Issing O, *Should we have Faith in Central Banks?* (Institute of Economic Affairs 2002)

Ivaldi G, 'Beyond France's 2005 Referendum on the European Constitutional Treaty: Second-order Model, Anti-establishment Attitudes and the end of the Alternative European Utopia' (2006) 29 West European Politics 47

Jabko N, *Playing the Market: A Political Strategy for Uniting Europe: 1985–2005* (Cornell University Press 2006)

Jabko N, 'The Elusive Economic Governance and the Forgotten Fiscal Union' in Matthijs M and Blyth M (eds), *The Future of the Euro* (OUP 2015)

Jachtenfuchs M, 'Theoretical Perspectives on European Governance' (1995) 1 European Law Journal 115

Jacobs F, *Sovereignty of Law: The European Way* (CUP 2007)

Jacoby W, 'Europe's New German Problem: The Timing of Politics and the Politics of Timing' in Matthijs M and Blyth M (eds), *The Future of the Euro* (OUP 2015)

Jäger A, 'We Bet the House on Left Populism—and Lost' *Jacobin Magazine* (New York, 25 November 2019)

Jäger J, and Springler E, 'Critical Political Economy and Post-Keynesian Perspectives' in Jäger and Springler (eds), *Asymmetric Crisis in Europe and Possible Futures: Critical Political Economy and Post-Keynesian Perspectives* (Routledge 2015)

Jakab A, *European Constitutional Language* (OUP 2016)
James H, 'Economic Reasons for the Collapse of Weimar' in Kershaw I (ed), *Weimar: Why did German Democracy Fail?* (Wiedenfeld and Nicholson 1990)
James H, *Making the European Monetary Union: The Role of the Committee of Central Bank Governors and the Origins of the European Central Bank* (Belknap 2012)
James M, *The Unfinished Revolution: Making Sense of the Communist Past in Central-Eastern Europe* (YUP 2011)
Jameson F, 'The Aesthetics of Singularity' (2015) 92 New Left Review 101
Jančić D, 'The Barroso Initiative: Window Dressing or Democracy Boost?' (2012) 8 Utrecht Law Review 78
Jaspers K, *Antwort—Zur Kritik meiner Schrift—Wohin treibt die Bundesrepublik?* (R Piper & Co 1967)
Jay M, 'The Weimar Left' in Gordon PE and McCormick JP (eds), *Weimar Thought: A Contested Legacy* (Princeton University Press 2013)
Jayasuriya K, 'Globalization, Sovereignty, and the Rule of Law: From Political to Economic Constitutionalism?' (2001) 8 Constellations 442
Jessop B, *The Future of the Capitalist State* (Polity Press 2002)
Jessop B, 'Variegated Capitalism, *das Modell Deutschland*, and the Eurozone Crisis' (2014) 22 Journal of Contemporary European Studies 248
Jessop B, 'Elective Affinity or Comprehensive Contradiction? Reflections on Capitalism and Democracy in the Time of Finance-dominated Accumulation and Austerity States' (2018) 28 Berliner Journal für Soziologie 9
Joerges C, 'Guest Editorial: The Commission's White Paper on Governance in the EU—A Symptom of Crisis?' (2002) 39 Common Market Law Review 441
Joerges C, 'Europe: A Grossraum: Shifting Legal Conceptualisations of the Integration Project' in Joerges C and Singh-Ghaleigh N (eds), *Darker Legacies of Law In Europe: The Shadow of National Socialism and Fascism over Europe and its Legal Traditions* (Hart Publishing 2003)
Joerges C, 'What is Left of the European Economic Constitution? A Melancholic Eulogy' (2005) 30 European Law Review 461
Joerges C, 'Europe's Economic Constitution in Crisis and the Emergence of a New Constitutional Constellation' (2014) 15 German Law Journal 985
Joerges C, 'What is Left of the European Economic Constitution II? From Pyrrhic Victory to Cannae Defeat' in Kjaer PF and Olsen N (eds), *Critical Theories of Crisis in Europe: From Weimar to the Euro* (Rowman & Littlefield 2016)
Joerges C, Meny Y, and Weiler JHH (eds), *Mountain or Molehill? A Critical Appraisal of the Commission White Paper on Governance* (2001) Jean Monnet Working Paper No 6/01, 2001
Joerges C and Neyer J, 'From Intergovernmental Bargaining to Deliberative Political Processes: The Constitutionalisation of Comitology' (1997) 3 European Law Journal 273
Joerges C and Rödl F, '"Social Market Economy" as Europe's Social Model?' (2004) EUI Working Paper Law No 2004/8
Joerges C and Rödl F, 'Informal Politics, Formalised Law and the 'Social Deficit' of European Integration: Reflections after the Judgments of the ECJ in *Viking* and *Laval*' (2009) 15 European Law Journal 1
Jones E, 'The Forgotten Financial Union: How You Can Have a Euro Crisis without a Euro' in Matthijs M and Blyth M (eds), *The Future of the Euro* (OUP 2015)
Judt T, *A Grand Illusion? An Essay on Europe* (New York Review of Books, Hill and Wand, 11 July 1996)
Judt T, *Postwar: A History of Europe since 1945* (Pimlico 2005)
Judt T, *Ill Fares the Land* (Penguin Books 2010)

Kahler M, 'The Survival of the State in European International Relations' in Maier CS (ed), *Changing Boundaries of the Political: Essays on the Evolving Balance between the State and Society, Public and Private in Europe* (CUP 1987)
Kahn PW, *Political Theology: Four New Chapters on the Concept of Sovereignty* (Columbia University Press 2011)
Kahn-Freund O, 'The Weimar Constitution' (1944) 15 The Political Quarterly 229
Kaiser W, *Christian Democracy and the Origins of the European Union* (CUP 2007)
Kaldor M and Selchow S, 'The "Bubbling Up" of Subterranean Politics in Europe' (2013) 9 Journal of Civil Society 85
Kaldor N, 'Escape from Socialism' *New Statesman* (London, 26 July 1963)
Kaldor N, 'The Dynamic Effects of the Common Market' *New Statesman* (London, 12 March 1971)
Kanishka J, 'The Strange Death of the International Liberal Order' (2010) 45 Economic and Political Weekly 75
Katz RS and Mair P, 'Changing Models of Party Organization and Party Democracy: The Emergence of the Cartel Party' (1995) 1 Party Politics 5
Katzenstein P, *Policy and Politics in West Germany: The Growth of a Semisovereign State* (Temple University Press 1987)
Kaupa C, *The Pluralist Character of the European Economic Constitution* (Hart Publishing 2016)
Kelemen RD, *Eurolegalism: The Transformation of Law and Regulation in the European Union* (HUP 2011)
Kelemen RD, 'On the Unsustainability of Constitutional Pluralism: European Supremacy and the Survival of the Eurozone' (2016) 23 Maastricht Journal of European and Comparative Law 136
Kelemen RD and Pech L, 'The Uses and Abuses of Constitutional Pluralism: Undermining the Rule of Law in the Name of Constitutional Identity in Hungary and Poland' (2019) 21 Cambridge Yearbook of European Legal Studies 59–74
Kelly D, *The State of the Political: Conceptions of Politics and the State in the Thought of Max Weber, Carl Schmitt and Franz Neumann* (OUP 2003)
Kelly D, 'Populism and the History of Popular Sovereignty' in Kaltwasser R, Taggart P, Espejo P, and Ostiguy P (eds), *Oxford Handbook of Populism* (OUP 2017) 511
Kelsen H, *Introduction to the Problems of Legal Theory: A Translation of the First Edition of the Reine Rechtslehre or Pure Theory of Law* (Clarendon Press 1996)
Kelsen H, *The Essence and Value of Democracy* (Rowman & Littlefield 2013)
Kennedy D, 'Turning to Market Democracy: A Tale of Two Architectures' (1991) 32 Harvard International Law Journal 373
Kennedy E, 'The Politics of Toleration in Late Weimar: Hermann Heller's Analysis of Fascism and Political Culture' (1984) 5 History of Political Thought 109
Kennedy E, 'Introduction' in Schmitt C and Kennedy E (eds), *The Crisis of Parliamentary Democracy* (MIT Press 1988)
Keohane RO and Hoffmann S, 'Institutional Change in Europe in the 1980s' in Keohane RO and Hoffmann S (eds), *The New European Community: Decision-making and Institutional Change* (Routledge 1991)
Kershaw I, 'The Nazi State: an Exceptional State?' (1989) 1:176 New Left Review 47
Kershaw I, 'Introduction: Perspectives of Weimar's Failure' in Kershaw I (ed), *Weimar: why did German Democracy Fail?* (Wiedenfeld and Nicholson 1990)
Kilpatrick C, 'Are the Bailouts Immune to EU Social Challenge because they are not EU Law?' (2014) 10 European Constitutional Law Review 393

Kilpatrick C, 'On the Rule of Law and Economic Emergency: The Degradation of Basic Legal Values in Europe's Bailouts' (2015) 35 Oxford Journal of Legal Studies 325
Kilpatrick C, 'Constitutions, Social Rights and Sovereign Debt States in Europe: A Challenging New Area of Constitutional Inquiry' in Beukers T, de Witte B, and Kilpatrick C (eds), *Constitutional Change Through Euro-crisis Law* (CUP 2017) 279
Kindleberger CP, *The World in Depression, 1929–1939* (University of California Press 1973)
Kirchheimer O, 'Notes on the Political Scene in Western Germany' in Burin FS and Shells KL (eds), *Politics, Law and Social Change: Selected Essays of Otto Kirchheimer* (Columbia University Press 1969)
Kirchheimer O, 'France From the Fourth to the Fifth Republic' in Burin FS and Shells KL (eds), *Politics, Law and Social Change: Selected Essays of Otto Kirchheimer* (Columbia University Press 1969)
Kirchheimer O, 'The Waning of Opposition in Parliamentary Regimes' in Dogan M and Rose R (eds), *European Politics: A Reader* (Little, Brown & Co 1971)
Kiss E, 'Foreign Direct Investment in Hungary: Industry and its Spatial Effects' (2007) 45 Eastern European Economics 6
Klimke M, '1968: Europe in Technicolour' in Stone D (ed), *The Oxford Handbook of Postwar European History* (OUP 2012)
Komárek J, 'Czech Constitutional Court Playing with Matches: the Czech Constitutional Court Declares a Judgment of the Court of Justice of the EU Ultra Vires' (2012) 8 European Constitutional Law Review 323
Komárek J, 'Waiting for the Existential Revolution in Europe' (2014) 12 International Journal of Constitutional Law 190
Komárek J, 'Playing with Matches: The Czech Court's Ultra Vires Revolution' in Steinbeis M, Kemmerer A, and Möllers C (eds), *Krise und Konstitutionalisierung in Europa* (Verfassungsblog I, Recht Im Kontext, Nomos 2015)
Komárek J and Avbelj M (eds), *Constitutional Pluralism in the European Union and Beyond* (Hart Publishing 2012)
Kommers DP and Miller RA, *The Constitutional Jurisprudence of the Federal Republic of Germany* (Duke University Press 2012)
Koskenniemi M, *The Gentle Civilizer of Nations: The Rise and Fall of International Law 1870–1960* (CUP 2001)
Koskenniemi M, 'International Law as Political Theology: How to Read *Nomos Der Erde*' (2004) 11:4 Constellations 492–511
Koskenniemi M, 'Conclusion: Vocabularies of Sovereignty—Powers of a Paradox' in Kalmo H and Skinner Q (eds), *Sovereignty in Fragments: The Past, Present and Future of a Contested Concept* (CUP 2009)
Kostal R, 'The Alchemy of Occupation: Karl Loewenstein and the Legal Reconstruction of Nazi Germany 1945–1946' (2011) 29 Law and History Review 1
Kostal R, *Laying Down the Law: The American Legal Revolutions in Germany and Japan* (Harvard University Press 2019)
Kouvelakis S, 'Borderlands' (2017) New Left Review 5
Krastev I and Holmes S, *The Light that Failed: A Reckoning* (Allen Lane, 2019)
Kreuder-Sonnen C, 'Beyond Integration Theory: The (Anti-)Constitutional Dimension of European Crisis Governance' (2016) 54 Journal of Common Market Studies 1350
Krishan K, 'On Civil Society: A Further Note on Civil Society' (2000) 41 European Journal of Sociology 167
Krotz U and Schild J, *Shaping Europe: France, Germany, and Embedded Bilateralism from the Elysée Treaty to Twenty-First Century Politics* (OUP 2013)

Krouwel A, 'Otto Kirchheimer and the Catch-all Party' (2003) 26 West European Politics 23

Krugman P, 'Europe's Austerity Madness' *The New York Times* (New York, 27 September 2012) <https://www.nytimes.com/2012/09/28/opinion/krugman-europes-austerity-madness.html> accessed 24 September 2020

Kumm M, 'How does European Union Law fit into the World of Public Law? *Costa, Kadi*, and Three Conceptions of Public Law' in Neyer J and Wiener A (eds), *Political Theory of the European Union* (OUP 2010)

Kumm M, 'The Cosmopolitan Turn in Constitutionalism: On the Relationship between Constitutionalism in and Beyond the State' in Dunoff J and Trachtman J (eds), *Ruling the World: Constitutionalism, International Law and Global Governance* (CUP 2012)

Kumm M, 'Constituent Power, Cosmopolitan Constitutionalism, and Post-Positivist Law' (2016) 14 International Journal of Constitutional Law 697

Kundnani H, *Utopia or Auschwitz: Germany's 1968 Generation and the Holocaust* (OUP 2009)

Kundnani H, *The Paradox of German Power* (C Hurst & Co 2014)

La Torre M, 'The German Impact on Fascist Public Law Doctrine: Constantino Mortati's Material Constitution' in Joerges C and Singh-Ghaleigh N (eds), *Darker Legacies of Law in Europe: The Shadow of National Socialism and Facism over Europe and its Legal Traditions* (Hart Publishing 2003)

Laak D van, 'From the Conservative Revolution to Technocratic Conservatism' in Müller J-W (ed), *German Ideologies Since 1945: Studies in the Political Thought and Culture of the Bonn Republic* (Palgrave MacMillan 2003)

Laclau E and Mouffe C, *Hegemony and Socialist Strategy: Towards a Radical Democratic Politics* (Verso 1985)

Laclau E, *On Populist Reason* (Verso 2005)

Lamers K and Schauble W, *Reflections on European Policy* (European Policy Documents No 189/96, 7 September 1994)

Landa I, *The Apprentice's Sorceror: Liberal Tradition and Fascism* (Brill 2010)

Lapavitsas C and others, *Crisis in the Eurozone* (Verso 2012)

Lapavitsas C, 'With Time to Prepare: Planning an Exit from the EMU' in Nanopoulos E and Vergis F (eds), *The Crisis behind the Eurocrisis: The Eurocrisis as a Multidimensional Systemic Crisis of the EU* (CUP 2019)

Lapavitsas C, *The Left Case Against the EU* (Polity Press 2019)

Lapavitsas C and Flassbeck H, *Against the Troika: Crisis and Austerity in the Eurozone* (Verso 2015)

Larsen S, 'United in Diversity: Humanism, Homogeneity and Hegemony' in Baruchello G, Rendtorff JD, and Sørenson A (eds), *Ethics, Democracy and Markets: Nordic Perspectives on World Problems* (Aarhus University Press 2016)

Larsen S, *The Constitutional Theory of the Federation and the European Union* (OUP 2021)

Lasser M, *Judicial Transformations: The Rights Revolution in the Courts of Europe* (OUP 2009)

Lasser M, 'Fundamentally Flawed: The CJEU's Jurisprudence on Fundamental Rights and Fundamental Freedoms' (2014) 15 Theoretical Inquiries in Law 229

Lechevalier A, 'Why and how has German Ordoliberalism Become a French Issue? Some Aspects about Ordoliberal Thoughts we can Learn from the French Reception' in Hien J and Joerges C (eds), *Ordoliberalism, Law and the Rule of Economics* (Hart Publishing 2017)

Lee BA, '*The Miscarriage of Necessity and Invention: Proto-Keynesianism and Democratic States in the 1930s*' in Hall P A (ed), *The Political Power of Economic Ideas: Keynesianism Across Nations* (Princeton University Press 1989)Le Gloannec A-M, 'Germany's Power and the Weakening of States in a Globalised World: Deconstructing a Paradox' (2001) 10 German Politics 117

Leonard M, *Why Europe Will Run the 21st Century* (Fourth Estate 2005)

Lerner D and Gorden M, *Euratlantica: Changing Perspectives of the European Elites* (MIT Press 1969)
Lindahl H, 'Democracy, Political Reflexivity and Bounded Dialogues: Reconsidering the Monism-Pluralism Debate' in Christodoulidis E and Tierney S (eds), *Public Law and Politics: The Scope and Limits of Constitutionalism* (Ashgate 2008)
Lindberg L and Scheingold S, *Europe's Would-be Polity: Patterns of Change in the European Community* (Prentice-Hall 1970)
Lindberg LN and Scheingold SA (eds), *Regional Integration: Theory and Research* (HUP 1970)
Lindseth P, *Power and Legitimacy: Reconciling Europe and the Nation-state* (OUP 2010)
Linz JJ, *Totalitarian and Authoritarian Regimes* (Lynne Rienner Publishers 2000)
Loewenstein K, 'Autocracy Versus Democracy in Contemporary Europe, I' (1935) 29 The American Political Science Review 571
Loewenstein K, 'Militant Democracy and Fundamental Rights, I' (1937) 31 The American Political Science Review 417
Loewenstein K, 'The Union of Western Europe: Illusion and Reality. I. An Appraisal of the Methods' (1952) 52 Columbia Law Review 55
Loewenstein K, 'The Union of Western Europe: Illusion and Reality. II. An Appraisal of the Motives' (1952) 52 Columbia Law Review 209
Loewenstein K, 'Sovereignty and International Cooperation' (1954) 48 The American Journal of International Law 222
Loewenstein K, 'The Bonn Constitution and the European Defense Community Treaties' (1955) 64 The Yale Law Journal 805
Loewenstein K, *Max Weber's Political Ideas in the Perspective of our Time* (University of Massachusetts Press 1966)
Lokdam HC, 'Banking on Sovereignty: A Genealogy of the European Central Bank's Independence' (LSE 2019)
Lord C, 'The Democratic Legitimacy of Codecision' (2013) 20 Journal of European Public Policy 1056
Lord C and Pollak J, 'Unequal but Democratic? Equality according to Karlsruhe' (2013) 20 Journal of European Public Policy 190
Losurdo D, *Liberalism: A Counter-History* (Verso 2011)
Loughlin M, *Sword and Scales: An Examination of the Relationship between Law and Politics* (Hart Publishing 2000)
Loughlin M, *The Idea of Public Law* (OUP 2003)
Loughlin M, 'In Defence of *Staatslehre*' (2009) 48 Der Staat 1
Loughlin M, 'What is Constitutionalisation?' in Dobner P and Loughlin M (eds), *The Twilight of Constitutionalism?* (OUP 2010)
Loughlin M, *Foundations of Public Law* (OUP 2010)
Loughlin M, 'The Concept of Constituent Power' (2013) 13 European Journal of Political Theory 218
Loughlin M, 'Why Sovereignty?' in Rawlings R, Leyland P, and Young A (eds), *Sovereignty and the Law: Domestic, European and International Perspectives* (OUP 2013)
Loughlin M, 'Constitutional Pluralism: An Oxymoron?' (2014) 3 Global Constitutionalism 9
Loughlin M, 'Nomos' in Poole T and Dyzenhaus D (eds), *Law, Liberty and State: Oakeshott, Hayek and Schmitt on the Rule of Law* (CUP 2015)
Loughlin M, 'The Constitutional Imagination' (2015) 78 Modern Law Review 1
Loughlin M, 'The Erosion of Sovereignty' (2016) 45 Netherlands Journal of Legal Philosophy 57
Loughlin M, 'Politonomy' in Meierhenrich J and Simons O (eds), *The Oxford Handbook of Carl Schmitt* (OUP 2017)

Loughlin M, 'The Concept of Constituent Power' in Dowdle MW and Wilkinson MA (eds), *Constitutionalism Beyond Liberalism* (CUP 2017)
Loughlin M, 'The British Constitution: Thoughts on the Cause of the Present Discontents' (2018) 16 New Zealand Journal of Public and International Law 1
Loughlin M, 'The Contemporary Crisis of Constitutional Democracy' (2019) 39 Oxford Journal of Legal Studies 435
Ludlow NP, 'Problematic Partners: De Gaulle, Thatcher, and their impact' in Jones E, Menon A, and Weatherill S (eds), *Oxford Handbook of the European Union* (OUP 2012)
Ludlow P, 'De-commissioning the Empty Chair Crisis: The Community Institutions and the Crisis of 1965–66' in Palayret J-M, Wallace H, and Winand P (eds), *Visions, Votes and Vetoes* (Peter Lang 2006)
Lutz FA, 'The Functioning of the Gold Standard' in Peacock AT and Willgerodt H (eds), *Germany's Social Market Economy: Origins and Evolution* (Palgrave MacMillan 1989)
Lütz S and Kranke M, 'The European Rescue of the Washington Consensus? EU and IMF Lending to Central and Eastern European Countries' (2013) 21 Review of International Political Economy 310
Luxemburg R, *The Accumulation of Capital* (Routledge 2003)
Mac Amhlaigh C, 'Symposium—Crisis and Constitutional Pluralism in the European Union' (2019) 21 The Cambridge Yearbook of European Legal Studies 3
MacCormick N, 'Beyond the Sovereign State' (1993) 56 Modern Law Review 1
MacCormick N, *Questioning Sovereignty: Law, State, and Nation in the European Commonwealth* (OUP 1999)
MacCormick N, 'Sovereignty and After' in Kalmo H and Skinner Q (eds), *Sovereignty in Fragments: The Past Present and Future of a Contested Concept* (CUP 2010)
Madsen MR, Olsen HP, and Šadl U, 'Legal Disintegration? The Ruling of the Danish Supreme Court in AJOS' (*Verfassungsblog*, 30 January 2017) <https://verfassungsblog.de/legal-disintegration-the-ruling-of-the-danish-supreme-court-in-ajos/> accessed 25 September 2020
Maduro MP, *We the Court: The European Court of Justice and the European Economic Constitution: A Critical Reading of Article 30 of the EC Treaty* (Bloomsbury Publishing 1998)
Maduro MP, 'Europe and the Constitution: What if this is as Good as it Gets?' in Weiler JHH and Wind M (eds), *European Constitutionalism Beyond the State* (CUP 2003)
Maier C, 'The Weimar Origins of the West German Rechtsstaat, 1919–1969' (2019) 62 The Historical Journal 1069
Maier CS, *Dissolution: The Crisis of Communism and the End of East Germany* (Princeton University Press 1997)
Maier CS, *Recasting Bourgeois Europe: Stabilization in France, Germany, and Italy in the Decade after World War I* (Princeton University Press 2016)
Mair P, 'Political Parties, Popular Legitimacy and Public Privilege' in Hayward J (ed), *The Crisis of Representation in Europe* (Routledge 1996)
Mair P, *Ruling the Void: The Hollowing of Western Democracy* (Verso 2013)
Majone G, *Dilemmas of European integration: The Ambiguities and Pitfalls of Integration by Stealth* (OUP 2005)
Majone G, *Rethinking the Union of Europe Post-crisis: Has Integration Gone Too Far?* (CUP 2014)
Majone G, 'From Regulatory State to a Democratic Default' (2014) 52 Journal of Common Market Studies 1216
Majone G, 'The Limits of Collective Action and Collective Leadership' in Chalmers D, Jachtenfuchs M, and Joerges C (eds), *The End of the Eurocrats Dream: Adjusting to Diversity* (CUP 2016)

Malkopoulou A and Norman L, 'Three Models of Democratic Self-Defence: Militant Democracy and its Alternatives' (2018) 66 Political Studies 442

Mancini FG, 'Europe: The Case for Statehood' (1998) 4 European Law Journal 29

Mandel E, *Europe versus America? Contradictions of Imperialism* (New Left Books 1970)

Mandel M, 'A Brief History of the New Constitutionalism, or "How we Changed Everything so that Everything Would Remain the Same"' (1998) 32 Israel Law Review 250

Manganelli S and Wolswijk G, 'Market Discipline, Financial Integration and Fiscal Rules: What Drives Spreads in the Euro Area Government Bond Market?' (2007) ECB Working Paper Series No 745

Manin B, *The Principles of Representative Government* (CUP 1997)

Mann M, 'Sources of Variation in Working Class Movements in Twentieth-Century Europe' (1995) New Left Review 14

Manow P, 'The Uneasy Compromise of Liberalism and Corporatism in Postwar Germany' (1999) University of California, Berkeley Center of German and European Studies Working Paper 5/88

Manow P, Schäfer A, and Zorn H, 'European Social Policy and Europe's Party-Political Center of Gravity, 1957–2003' (2008) 15 Journal of European Public Policy 20

Marcuse H, Habermas J, and Friends, 'A Discussion on Democracy and Critical Theory' (2008) 1 New Political Science 19

Marcuse H, *One-Dimensional Man: Studies in the Ideology of Advanced Industrial Society* (Taylor and Francis 2013)

Marks S, *The Riddle of all Constitutions: International Law, Democracy and the Critique of Ideology* (OUP 2003)

Marquand D, 'Reinventing Federalism: Europe and the Left' in Miliband D (ed), *Reinventing the Left* (Polity Press 1994)

Marquand D, *The End of the West: The Once and Future Europe* (Princeton University Press 2011)

Martin H and Armin S, 'Polanyi in Brussels? Embeddedness and the Three Dimensions of European Economic Integration' (2010) MPIfG Discussion Paper 10/8

Marx K, *Economic and Philosophical Manuscripts of 1844* (Dover Publications 2007)

Mathews J, *Extending Rights' Reach: Constitutions, Private Law, and Judicial Power* (OUP 2018)

Mayer F, 'Rebels without a Cause? A Critical Analysis of the German Constitutional Court's OMT Reference' (2014) 15 German Law Journal 111

McCormick JP, 'The Dilemmas of Dictatorship: Carl Schmitt and Constitutional Emergency Powers' (1997) 10 The Canadian Journal of Law and Jurisprudence 163

McCormick JP, *Carl Schmitt's Critique of Liberalism: Against Politics as Technology* (CUP 1999)

McCormick JP, 'Carl Schmitt's Europe: Cultural, Imperial and Spatial Proposals for European Integration, 1923–1955' in Joerges C and Singh-Ghaleigh N (eds), *Darker Legacies of Law in Europe: The Shadow of National Socialism and Facism over Europe and its Legal Traditions* (Hart Publishing 2003)

McCormick JP, *Weber, Habermas and Transformations of the European State: Constitutional, Social, and Supranational Democracy* (CUP 2007)

McCormick JP, 'Weimar Legal Thought' in Gordon PE and McCormick JP (eds), *Weimar Thought: A Contested Legacy* (Princeton University Press 2013)

Meidner R, 'Why did the Swedish Model Fail?' (1993) 29 Socialist Register 211

Meierhenrich J, 'Fearing the Disorder of Things: The Development of Carl Schmitt's Institutional Theory, 1919–1942' in Meierhenrich J and Simons O (eds), *The Oxford Handbook of Carl Schmitt* (OUP 2017)

Meierhenrich J, *The Remnants of the Rechtsstaat: An Ethnography of Nazi Law* (OUP 2018)

Menéndez AJ, 'European Citizenship after *Martinez Sala* and *Baumbast*: Has European Law Become More Human but Less Social?' in Maduro MP and Azoulai L (eds), *The Past and*

Future of EU Law: The Classics of EU Law Revisited on the 50th Anniversary of the Rome Treaty (1st edn, Hart Publishing 2010)
Menéndez AJ, 'The Existential Crisis of the European Union' (2013) 14 German Law Journal 453
Mestmäcker E-J, 'European Touchstones of Dominion and Law' (2007) 58 The Ordo Yearbook of Economic and Social Order 3
Michaels R and Jansen N, 'Private Law beyond the State? Europeanization, Globalization, Privatization' (2006) 54 The American Journal of Comparative Law 843
Middelaar L van, 'Spanning the River: The Constitutional Crisis of 1965–1966 as the Genesis of Europe's Political Order' (2008) 4 European Constitutional Law Review 98
Middelaar L van, *The Passage to Europe: How a Continent Became a Union* (YUP 2013)
Middelaar L van, *Alarums and Excursions* (Agenda Publishing 2019)
Miliband R, 'Constitutionalism and Revolution: Notes on Eurocommunism' (1978) 15 Socialist Register 158
Milios JG, Lapatsioras S, and Sotiropoulus DP, 'The "Greek Crisis" and the Austerity Controversy in Europe' in Marangos J (ed), *The Internal Impact and External Influence of the Greek Financial Crisis* (Palgrave Macmillan 2017)
Millet F-X, 'The Respect for National Constitutional Identity in the European Legal Space: An Approach to Federalism as Constitutionalism' in Azoulai L (ed), *The Question of Competence in the European Union* (OUP 2014)
Milward A, *The European Rescue of the Nation-state* (Routledge 2000)
Mirowski P and Plehwe D (eds), *The Road from Mont Pelerin: The Making of the Neoliberal Thought Collective* (HUP 2009)
Mody A, *EuroTragedy: A Drama in Nine Acts* (OUP 2018)
Möllers C, '"We are (afraid of) the People": Constituent Power in German Constitutional Discourse' in Loughlin M and Walker N (eds), *The Paradox of Constitutionalism: Constituent Power and Constitutional Form* (OUP 2007)
Mommsen H, *The Rise and Fall of Weimar Democracy* (University of North Carolina Press 2007)
Monnet J, *Mémoires. Nous ne Coalisons pas des Etats, Nous Unissons des Hommes* (Fayard 1976)
Moravcsik A, 'In Defence of the "Democratic Deficit": Reassessing Legitimacy in the European Union' (2002) 40 Journal of Common Market Studies 603
Moravcsik A, 'The European Constitutional Compromise and the Neo-functionalist Legacy' (2005) 2 Journal of European Public Policy 349
Moravcsik A, 'What can we Learn from the Collapse of the European Constitutional Project?' (2006) 47 Politische Vierteljahresschrift 219
Moravcsik A, 'The European Constitutional Settlement' (2008) 31 World Economy 158
Moschonas G, 'Reformism in a "Conservative" System: the European Union and Social Democratic Identity' in McIver M, Fishman N, Callaghan J, and Jackson B (eds), *In Search of Social Democracy: Responses to Crisis and Modernisation* (Manchester University Press 2009)
Moss BH (ed), *Monetary Union in Crisis: The European Union as a Neoliberal Construction* (Palgrave 2005)
Mouffe C, *The Democratic Paradox* (Verso 2000)
Mouffe C, *For a Left Populism* (Verso 2018)
Moyn S, *The Last Utopia: Human Rights in History* (HUP 2012)
Müller J-W, *Contesting Democracy: Political Ideas in Twentieth-Century Europe* (YUP 2011)
Müller J-W, 'Militant Democracy' in Rosenfeld M and Sajó A (eds), *The Oxford Handbook of Comparative Constitutional Law* (OUP 2012)
Müller J-W, 'Beyond Militant Democracy' (2012) 73 New Left Review 39
Müller J-W, 'What do Germans Think about when they Think about Europe?' *London Review of Books* (London, 9 February 2012) <https://www.lrb.co.uk/the-paper/v34/n03/

jan-werner-mueller/what-do-germans-think-about-when-they-think-about-europe> accessed 25 September 2020

Müller J-W, 'A "Practical Dilemma Which Philosophy Alone Cannot Resolve"? Rethinking Militant Democracy: An Introduction' (2013) 19 Constellations 536

Müller J-W, 'Rule-Breaking' *London Review of Books* (London, 27 August 2015) <https://www.lrb.co.uk/the-paper/v37/n16/jan-werner-mueller/rule-breaking>

Müller J-W, *What is Populism?* (University of Pennsylvania Press 2016)

Münchau W, 'The Wacky Economics of Germany's parallel universe' *Financial Times* (London, 16 November 2014) <https://www.ft.com/content/e257ed96-6b2c-11e4-be68-00144feabdc0> accessed 24 September 2020

Mundell RA, 'A Theory of Optimum Currency Areas' (1961) 51 The American Economic Review 657

Myrdal G, *Economic Theory and Underdeveloped Regions* (Gerald Duckworth & Co 1957)

Nachtwey O, *Germany's Hidden Crisis: Social Decline in the Heart of Europe* (Verso 2018)

Nanopoulos E and Vergis F, 'The Inherently Undemocratic EU Democracy' in Nanopoulos E and Vergis F (eds), *The Crisis behind the Eurocrisis: The Eurocrisis as a Multidimensional Systemic Crisis of the EU* (CUP 2019)

Negri A, *Insurgencies: Constituent Power and the Modern State* (University of Minnesota Press 1999)

Neumann FL, *The Democratic and the Authoritarian State: Essays in Political and Legal Theory* (The Free Press 1957)

Neumann FL, 'On the Preconditions and the Legal Concept of an Economic Constitution' in Kirchheimer O and Neumann FL (eds), *Social Democracy and the Rule of Law* (Allen & Unwin 1987)

Neumann FL, 'The Social Significance of the Basic Laws in the Weimar Constitution' in Tribe K (ed), *Social Democracy and the Rule of Law: Otto Kirchheimer and Franz Neumann* (Allen & Unwin 1987)

Neumann FL, 'On the Marxist Theory of the State' in Tribe K (ed), *Social Democracy and the Rule of Law: Otto Kirchheimer and Franz Neumann* (Allen & Unwin 1987)

Neumann FL, 'The Decay of German Democracy' in Scheuerman WE (ed), *The Rule of Law under Siege: Selected Essays of Franz L Neumann and Otto Kirchheimer* (University of California Press 1996)

Neumann FL, *Behemoth: The Structure and Practice of National Socialism, 1933–1944* (Ivan R Dee 2009)

Newman A, 'The Reluctant Leader: Germany's Euro Experience and the Long Shadow of Reunification' in Matthijs M and Blyth M (eds), *The Future of the Euro* (OUP 2015)

Neyer J, *The Justification of Europe: A Political Theory of Supranational Integration* (OUP 2012)

Nicol D, 'Europe's Lochner Moment' (2011) Public Law 308

Nicol D, 'Can Justice Dethrone Democracy in the European Union? A Reply to Jürgen Neyer' (2012) 50 Journal of Common Market Studies 508

Nic Shuibhne N, 'The Resilience of EU Market Citizenship' (2010) 47 Common Market Law Review 1597

Offe C, 'Challenging the Boundaries of Institutional Politics: Social Movements Since the 1960s' in Maier CS (ed), *Changing Boundaries of the Political: Essays on the Evolving Balance between the State and Society, Public and Private in Europe* (CUP 1987)

Offe C, 'The Problem of Social Power in Franz L Neumann's Thought' (2003) 10 Constellations 211

Offe C, *Europe Entrapped* (Polity Press 2015)

Oklopcic Z, 'Imagined Ideologies: Populist Figures, Liberalist Projections, and the Horizons of Constitutionalism' (2019) 20 German Law Journal 201–24

Olsen N, *The Sovereign Consumer: A New Intellectual History of Neoliberalism* (Palgrave Macmillan 2019)

Oltermann P, 'Jürgen Habermas's Verdict on the EU/Greece Debt Deal—Full Transcript' *The Guardian* (London, 16 July 2015) <https://www.theguardian.com/commentisfree/2015/jul/16/jurgen-habermas-eu-greece-debt-deal> accessed 3 November 2020

Oppenheimer A (ed), *The Relationship between European Community Law and National Law: The Cases* (CUP 1994)

Panitch L, 'Capital and Politics' (2015) 13 Perspectives on Politics 1075

Parker O, *Cosmopolitan Government in Europe: Citizens and Entrepreneurs in Postnational Politics* (Routledge 2013)

Pashukanis E, 'General Theory of Law and Marxism' in Beirne P and Sharlet R (eds), *Pashukanis: Selected Writings on Marxism and Law* (Academic Press 1980)

Patberg M, 'The Levelling Up of Constituent Power in the European Union' (2017) 55:2 Journal of Common Market Studies 203

Paterson WE, 'Beyond Semi-sovereignty: The New Germany in the New Europe' (1996) 5 German Politics 167

Peacock AT and Willgerodt H (eds), *Germany's Social Market Economy: Origins and Evolution* (Palgrave MacMillan 1989)

Peer Z, 'Transnational Private Regulatory Governance: Ambiguities of Public Authority and Private Power' (2013) 76 Law and Contemporary Problems 117

Peo H and Stefan J, *Eurafrica: The Untold History of European Integration and Colonialism* (Bloomsbury 2014)

Petersmann E-U, 'State Sovereignty, Popular Sovereignty and Individual Sovereignty: From Constitutional Nationalism to Multilevel Constitutionalism in International Economic Law' in Shan W, Simons P, and Singh D (eds), *Redefining Sovereignty in International Economic Law* (OUP 2008)

Phelan W, *In Place of Inter-State Retaliation: The European Union's Rejection of WTO-Style Trade Sanctions and Trade Remedies* (OUP 2015)

Piketty T, *Capital in the Twenty-First Century* (HUP 2014)

Plant R, *The Neo-Liberal State* (OUP 2009)

Plehwe D, 'Introduction' in Mirowski P and Plehwe D (eds), *The Road from Mont Pelerin: The Making of the Neoliberal Thought Collective* (HUP 2009)

Polanyi K, *The Great Transformation: The Political and Economic Origins of Our Time* (Beacon Press 2001)

Polonen K, 'The Search for a New Beginning' in Goldoni M and McCorkindale C (eds), *Hannah Arendt and the Law* (Hart Publishing 2012)

Poscher R, 'Heinrich Triepel: Introduction' in Jacobson AJ and Schlink B (eds), *Weimar: A Jurisprudence of Crisis* (University of California Press 2000)

Poulantzas N, *State, Power, Socialism* (Verso, 2000)

Poulantzas N, 'Internationalisation of Capitalist Relations and the Nation-state' (2006) 3 Economy and Society 145

Poulantzas N, *The Poulantzas Reader: Marxism, Law and the State* (Verso 2008)

Poulantzas N, *Political Power and Social Classes* (Verso, 2018)

Preuss H, 'The Significance of the Democratic Republic for the Idea of Social Justice' in Jacobson AJ and Schlink B (eds), *Weimar: A Jurisprudence of Crisis* (University of California Press 2000)

Preuss U, 'Constitutional Powermaking for the New Polity: Some Deliberations on the Relations between Constituent Power and the Constitution' (1993) 14 Cardozo Law eview 639

Preuss U, 'Political Order and Democracy: Carl Schmitt and his Influence' in Mouffe C (ed), *The Challenge of Carl Schmitt* (Verso 1999)

Preuss U, 'The Exercise of Constituent Power in Central and Eastern Europe' in Loughlin M and Walker N (eds), *The Paradox of Constitutionalism: Constituent Power and Constitutional Form* (OUP 2007)

Preuss U, 'Carl Schmitt and the Weimar Constitution' in Meierhenrich J and Simons O (eds), *The Oxford Handbook of Carl Schmitt* (1st edn, OUP 2017)

Přibáň J, 'The Semantics of Constitutional Sovereignty in Post-sovereign "new" Europe: A Case Study of the Czech Constitutional Court's jurisprudence' (2015) 13 International Journal of Constitutional Law 180

Přibáň J, *Legal Symbolism: On Law, Time and European Identity* (Ashgate 2007)

Ptak R, 'Neoliberalism in Germany: Revisiting the Ordoliberal Foundations of the Social Market Economy' in Mirowski P and Plehwe D (eds), *The Road from Mont Pelerin: The Making of the Neoliberal Thought Collective* (HUP 2009)

Puetter U, 'The Informal Eurogroup: A New Working Method and Institutional Compromise' (2001) ConWEB No 02/2001 <https://www.wiso.uni-hamburg.de/fachbereich-sowi/professuren/wiener/dokumente/conwebpaperspdfs/2001/conweb-2-2001.pdf>

Quint PE, 'Constitution-making by Treaty in German Unification: A Comment on Arato, Elster, Preuss, and Richards' (1993) 14 Cardozo Law Review 691

Rasmussen M, 'The Origins of a Legal Revolution: The Early History of the European Court of Justice' (2008) 14 Journal of European Integration History 77

Rawls J, *Political Liberalism* (Columbia University Press 2005)

Rech W and Grzybowski J, 'Between Regional Community and Global Society: Europe in the Shadow of Schmitt and Kojève' (2017) 13 Journal of International Political Theory 143

Reh C, 'The Lisbon Treaty: De-Constitutionalizing the European Union?' (2009) 47 Journal of Common Market Studies 625

Reh C and others, 'The Informal Politics of Legislation: Explaining Secluded Decision Making in the European Union' (2013) 46 Comparative Political Studies 1112

Rehmann J, 'The Unfullfilled Promise of the Late Foucault and Foucauldian "Governmentality Studies"' in Zamora D and Behrent M C (eds), *Foucault and Neoliberalism* (Polity Press 2016) 134

Reuter P, 'Techniciens et Politiques dans l'organisation Internationale' in *Politique et Technique* (Presses Universitaires de France 1958)

Risse T and Engelmann-Martin D, 'Identity Politics and European Integration: The Case of Germany' in Pagden A (ed), *The Idea of Europe: From Antiquity to the European Union* (CUP 2002)

Robbins L, *Economic Planning and International Order* (Macmillan 1937)

Rodrik D, 'How Far Will International Economic Integration Go?' (2000) 14 The Journal of Economic Perspectives 177

Röpke W, *Economic Order and International Law*, vol 86 (of Recueil de Course II, Collected Courses of the Hague Academy of International Law, Brill [1954])

Röpke W, *International Economic Disintegration* (William Hodge & Co 1942)

Röpke W, *International Order and Economic Integration* (Reidel Publishing Company 1959)

Rosanvallon P, 'The Development of Keynesianism in France' in Hall PA (ed), *The Political Power of Economic Ideas: Keynesianism Across Nations* (Princeton University Press 1989)

Rosanvallon P, *Counter-Democracy: Politics in an Age of Distrust* (Arthur Goldhammer tr, CUP 2006)

Rosanvallon P, *Democratic Legitimacy: Impartiality, Reflexivity, Proximity* (Princeton University Press 2011)

Roznai Y, *Unconstitutional Constitutional Amendments: The Limits of Amendment Powers* (OUP 2017)

Ruda F, *Hegel's Rabble: An Investigation into Hegel's Philosophy of Right* (Bloomsbury 2011)

Ruggie JG, 'International Regimes, Transactions and Change: Embedded Liberalism in the Postwar Economic Order' (1982) 36 International Organization 379
Ryner M, 'Europe's Ordoliberal Iron Cage: Critical Political Economy, the Euro Area Crisis and its Management' (2015) 22 Journal of European Public Policy 275
Ryner M, 'The Authoritarian Neoliberalism of the EU: Legal Form and International Politico-Economic Sources' in Nanopoulos E and Vergis F (eds), *The Crisis Behind the Eurocrisis: The Eurocrisis as a Multidimensional Systemic Crisis of the EU* (CUP 2019)
Sabel CF and Gerstenberg O, 'Constitutionalising an Overlapping Consensus: The ECJ and the Emergence of a Coordinate Constitutional Order' (2010) 16 European Law Journal 511
Sadurski W, *Constitutionalism and the Enlargement of Europe* (OUP 2012)
Sakellaropoulos S, *Greece's (Un)competitive Capitalism and the Economic Crisis: How the Memoranda Changed Society, Politics and the Economy* (Palgrave Macmillan 2019)
Sassoon D, 'The Italian Communist Party's European Strategy' (1976) 47 The Political Quarterly 253
Sassoon D, *One Hundred Years of Socialism: The West European Left in the Twentieth Century* (Bloomsbury Publishing 1996)
Sauter W, 'The Economic Constitution of the European Union' (1998) 4 Columbia Journal of European Law 27
Sauter W and Schepel H, *State and Market in European Union Law: The Public and Private Spheres of the Internal Market Before the EU Courts* (CUP 2009)
Scharpf FW, 'The Joint Decision Trap: Lessons from German Federalism and European Integration' (1988) 66 Public Administration 239
Scharpf FW, 'Negative and Positive Integration in the Political Economy of European Welfare States' in Marks G, Scharpf F, Schmitter P, and Streeck W (eds), *Governance in the European Union* (Sage Publications 1996)
Scharpf FW, *Governing in Europe: Effective and Democratic?* (OUP 1999)
Scharpf FW, 'Democratic Legitimacy under Conditions of Regulatory Competition: Why Europe Differs from the United States' in Nicolaïdis K and Howse R (eds), *The Federal Vision: Legitimacy and Levels of Governance in the United States and European Union* (OUP 2001)
Scharpf FW, 'The European Social Model: Coping with the Challenges of Diversity' (2002) *Journal of Common Market Studies* 645
Scharpf FW, 'The Asymmetry of European Integration, or Why the EU Cannot be a Social Market Economy' (2010) 8 Socio-Economic Review 211
Scharpf FW, 'Legitimacy in the Multi-Level European Polity' in Loughlin M and Dobner P (eds), *The Twilight of Constitutionalism?* (OUP 2010)
Scharpf FW, 'After the Crash: A Perspective on Multilevel European Democracy' (2015) 21 European Law Journal 384
Scharpf FW, 'De-constitutionalisation and Majority Rule: A Democratic Vision for Europe' (2017) 23 European Law Journal 315
Schattschneider EE, *The Semisovereign People: A Realist's View of Democracy in America* (Holt, Rinehart and Winston 1965)
Scheiring G and Szombati K, 'From Neoliberal Disembedding to Authoritarian Re-embedding: The Making of Illiberal Hegemony in Hungary' (2020) International Sociology 1–18
Schepel H, 'Constitutionalising the Market, Marketising the Constitution, and to Tell the Difference: On the Horizontal Application of the Free Movement Provisions in EU Law' (2012) 18 European Law Journal 177
Scheppele KL, 'Jack Balkin is an American' (2013) 25 Yale Journal of Law & the Humanities 23
Scheuerman WE (ed), *The Rule of Law Under Siege* (University of California Press 1996)

Scheuerman WE, 'The Unholy Alliance of Carl Schmitt and Friedrich A Hayek' (1997) 4 Constellations 172

Scheuerman WE, *The End of Law: Carl Schmitt in the Twenty-First Century* (Rowman & Littlefield 1999)

Scheuerman WE, 'Social Democracy and the Rule of Law: The Legacy of Ernst Fraenkel' in Caldwell P and Scheuerman WE (eds), *From Liberal Democracy to Fascism: Legal and Political Thought in the Weimar Republic* (Humanities Press 2000)

Scheuerman WE, 'Democratic Experimentalism or Capitalist Synchronization? Critical Reflections on Directly-deliberative Polyarchy' (2004) 17 The Canadian Journal of Law and Jurisprudence 101

Schiller K, *Konjuncturpolitik auf dem Wege zi einer Affluent Society*, vol 54 (Kieler Vorträge, Institut für Weltwirtschaft 1968)

Schilling T, Weiler JHH, and Haltern U, 'Who in Law is the Ultimate Judicial Umpire of European Community Competences?—The Schilling–Weiler/Haltern debate' (1996) Jean Monnet Working Paper 96/10

Schmidt MG, 'The Parties-do-matter Hypothesis and the Case of the Federal Republic of Germany' (1995) 4 German Politics 1

Schmidt VA, *Democracy in Europe: The EU and National Polities* (OUP 2006)

Schmidt VA, 'Trapped by their Ideas: French Elites' Discourses of European Integration and Globalization' (2007) 14 Journal of European Public Policy 992

Schmitt C, *Staat, Bewegung, Volk: Die Dreigliederung der Politischen Einheit* (Hanseatischer Verlaganstalt 1933)

Schmitt C, *On the Three Types of Juristic Thought* (Bendersky J tr, Praeger 2004)

Schmitt C, *The Nomos of the Earth in the International Law of the Jus Publicum Europaeum* (Telos Press 2003)

Schmitt C, *Legality and Legitimacy* (Duke University Press 2004)

Schmitt C, *Political Theology: Four Chapters on the Concept of Sovereignty* (University of Chicago Press 2006)

Schmitt C, *The Concept of the Political* (expanded edn, University of Chicago Press 2007)

Schmitt C, *Constitutional Theory* (Duke University Press 2008)

Schmitter PC and Lehmbruch G (eds), *Trends toward Corporatist Intermediation* (Sage Publications 1979)

Schneider K, 'Questions and Answers: Karlsruhe's Request for a Preliminary Ruling to the Court of Justice of the European Union' (2014) 15 German Law Journal 217

Schönberger C, 'Die Europäische Union als Bund: Zugleich ein Beitrag zur Verabschiedung des Staatenbund-Bundesstaat-Schemas' (2004) 129 Archiv des öffentlichen Rechts 81

Schönberger C, '*Lisbon* in Karlsruhe: *Maastricht*'s Epigones At Sea' (2009) 10 German Law Journal 1201

Schönberger C, 'Hegemonie Wider Willen: Zur Stellung Deutschlands in der Europaischen Union' (2012) 66 Merkur 1

Schulz-Forberg H, 'Crisis and Continuity: Robert Marjolin, Transnational Policy-Making and Neoliberalism, 1930s–70s' (2019) 26 European Review of History 679

Schupmann BA, *Carl Schmitt's State and Constitutional Theory: A Critical Analysis* (OUP 2017)

Schütze R, 'Federalism as Constitutional Pluralism: "Letters from America"' in Avbelj M and Komárek J (eds), *Constitutional Pluralism in the European Union and Beyond* (Hart Publishing 2012)

Scicluna N, 'Politicization without Democratization: How the Eurozone Crisis is Transforming EU Law and Politics' (2014) 12 International Journal of Constitutional Law 545

Scicluna N, 'Can the EU's Constitutional Framework Accommodate Democratic Politics?' (2017) 9 Perspectives on Federalism 98

Scicluna N, 'Integration through the Disintegration of Law? The ECB and EU Constitutionalism in the Crisis' (2018) 25 Journal of European Public Policy 1874

Scott C, 'Governing without Law or Governing without Government? New-ish Governance and the Legitimacy of the EU' (2009) 15 European Law Journal 160

Scott J and Trubek DM, 'Mind the Gap: Law and New Approaches to Governance in the European Union' (2002) 8 European Law Journal 1

Seidel K, 'Robert Marjolin: Securing the Common Market through EMU' in Dyson K and Maes I (eds), *Architects of the Euro: Intellectual in the Making of the European Monetary Union* (OUP 2016)

Seitzer J, 'Carl Schmitt's Internal Critique of Liberal Constitutionalism: *Verfassungslehre* as a Response to the Weimar State Crisis' (1997) 10 The Canadian Journal of Law and Jurisprudence 203

Selinger W, 'The Politics of Arendtian Historiography: European Federation and *The Origins of Totalitarianism*' (2016) 13 Modern Intellectual History 417

Selmayr M and Zilioli C, 'The European Central Bank: An Independent Specialized Organization of Community Law' (2000) 37 Common Market Law Review 591

Selmayr M and Zilioli C, *The Law of the European Central Bank* (Hart Publishing 2001)

Shapiro M, 'Comparative Law and Comparative Politics' (1980) 53 Southern California Law Review 537

Sierra JLB, 'Writing Straight with Crooked Lines: Competition Policy and Services of General Economic Interest in the Treaty of Lisbon' in Biondi A, Eeckhout P, and Ripley S (eds), *EU Law after Lisbon* (OUP 2012)

Simons O, 'Carl Schmitt's Spatial Rhetoric' in Meierhenrich J and Simons O (eds), *The Oxford Handbook of Carl Schmitt* (OUP 2017)

Simpson G, *Great Powers and Outlaw States: Unequal Sovereigns in the International Legal Order* (CUP 2004)

Slobodian Q, *Globalists: The End of Empire and the Birth of Neoliberalism* (HUP 2018)

Smith DM, 'Benedetto Croce: History and Politics' (1973) 8 Journal of Contemporary History 41

Smith H, 'Tsipras Favours Greek Jobless over Creditors in Defiant Policy Speech' *The Guardian* (London, 8 February 2015) <https://www.theguardian.com/world/2015/feb/08/greece-prime-minister-alexis-tsipras-unveil-anti-austerity-plan-parliament> accessed 25 September 2020

Snell J, 'The Trilemma of European Economic and Monetary Integration, and its Consequences' (2016) 22 European Law Journal 157

Snyder F, 'Globalisation and Europeanisation as Friends and Rivals: European Union Law in Global Economic Networks' (1999) EUI Working Paper Law No 99/8

Snyder F, 'EMU—Integration and Differentiation: Metaphor for European Union' in Craig P and de Búrca G (eds), *The Evolution of EU Law* (OUP 2011)

Snyder FG (ed), *The Europeanisation of Law: The Legal Effects of European Integration* (Hart Publishing 2000)

Somek A, 'Authoritarian Constitutionalism: Austrian Constitutional Doctrine 1933 to 1938 and its Legacy' in Joerges C and Ghaleigh NS (eds), *Darker Legacies of Law in Europe: The Shadow of National Socialism and Fascism over Europe and its Legal Traditions* (Hart Publishing 2003)

Somek A, 'Postconstitutional Treaty' (2007) 8 German Law Journal 1121

Somek A, *Engineering Equality: An Essay on European Anti-Discrimination Law* (OUP 2011)

Somek A, 'Constituent Power in National and Transnational Contexts' (2012) 3 Transnational Legal Theory 31

Somek A, 'From Workers to Migrants, from Distributive Justice to Inclusion: Exploring the Changing Social Democratic Imagination' (2012) 18 European Law Journal 711

Somek A, 'Monism: A Tale of the Undead' in Komárek J and Avbelj M (eds), *Constitutional Pluralism in the European Union and Beyond* (Hart Publishing 2012)
Somek A, 'The Darling Dogma of Bourgeois Europeanists' (2014) 20 European Law Journal 688
Somek A, 'Europe: Political, Not Cosmopolitan' (2014) 20 European Law Journal 142
Somek A, *The Cosmopolitan Constitution* (OUP 2014)
Somek A and Wilkinson MA, 'Unpopular Sovereignty?' (2020) 83 Modern Law Review 955
Soros G, *The Tragedy of the European Union: Disintegration or Revival* (Public Affairs 2014)
Sotiris P, 'The Authoritarian and Disciplinary Mechanism of Reduced Sovereignty in the EU: The Case of Greece' in *States of Discipline: Authoritarian Neoliberalism and the Contested Reproduction of Capitalist Order*, Cemal Tansel (ed) (Rowman and Littlefield 2017) 171–89
Spiegel P, 'The Donald Tusk Interview: Annotated Transcript' *Financial Times* (London, 16 July 2015) <https://www.ft.com/content/ff50e5a9-7b15-3998-a9f1-c11359dc01b8> accessed 3 November 2020
Stahl RM, 'Ruling the Interregnum: Politics and Ideology in Nonhegemonic Times' (2019) 47 Politics & Society 333
Stavrakakis Y and Katsambekis G, 'Left-wing Populism in the European Periphery: The case of SYRIZA' (2014) 19 Journal of Political Ideologies 119
Stein E, 'Towards the Supremacy of Treaty-Constitution by Judicial Fiat: On the Margin of the Costa Case' (1965) 63 Michigan Law Review 491
Stein E, 'Lawyers, Judges, and the Making of a Transnational Constitution' (1981) 75 The American Journal of International Law 1
Stie AE, *Democratic Decision-making in the EU: Technocracy in Disguise?* (Routledge 2013)
Stolleis M, 'Prologue' in Joerges C and Singh Ghaleigh N (eds), *Darker Legacies of Law in Europe: The Shadow of National Socialism and Fascism over Europe and its Legal Traditions* (Hart Publishing 2003)
Stolleis M, *A History of Public Law in Germany 1914–1945* (Oxford University Press 2004)
Stolleis M, *History of Social Law in Germany* (Springer-Verlag 2014)
Stolleis M, *Pubic Law in Germany: A Historical Introduction from the 16th to the 21st Century* (OUP 2017)
Stone Sweet A, *Governing with Judges: Constitutional Politics in Europe* (OUP 2000)
Stone Sweet A, 'Why Europe Rejected American Judicial Review and why it may not Matter' (2003) Yale Faculty Scholarship Series
Stone Sweet A, *The Judicial Construction of Europe* (OUP 2004)
Stone Sweet A, 'The Juridical Coup d'etat and the Problem of Authority' (2007) 8 German Law Journal 915
Strath B (ed), *After Full Employment: European Discourses on Work and Flexibility* (Peter Lang 2000)
Streeck W, 'Neo-Voluntarism: A New European Social Policy Regime?' in Marks G, Scharpf F, Schmitter P, and Streeck W (eds), *Governance in the European Union* (Sage Publications 1996)
Streeck W, 'The Internationalisation of Industrial Relations in Europe: Prospects and Problems' (1998) 26 Politics and Society 429
Streeck W, 'Industrial Relations: From State Weakness as Strength to State Weakness as Weakness; Welfare Corporatism and the Private Use of Public Interest' in Green S and Paterson WE (eds), *Governance in Contemporary Germany: The Semi-Sovereign State Revisited* (CUP 2005)
Streeck W, 'E Pluribus Unum? Varieties and Commonalities of Capitalism' (2010) MPIfG Discussion Papers 10/12
Streeck W, 'The Crises of Democratic Capitalism' (2011) 71 New Left Review 5
Streeck W, 'From Citizens to Consumers: Considerations on the New Politics of Consumption' (2012) 76 New Left Review 27

Streeck W, 'Markets and Peoples: Democratic Capitalism and European Integration' (2012) 73 New Left Review 63

Streeck W, *Buying Time: The Delayed Crisis of Democratic Capitalism* (Verso 2014)

Streeck W and Thelen K, 'Introduction: Institutional Change in Advanced Political Economies' in Streeck W and Thelen K (eds), *Beyond Continuity: Institutional Change in Advanced Political Economies* (OUP 2005)

Supiot A, 'Under Eastern Eyes' (2012) 73 New Left Review 29

Sutton M, *France and the Construction of Europe, 1944–2007: The Geopolitical Imperative* (Berghahn Books 2007)

Swedberg R, *Max Weber and the Idea of Economic Sociology* (Princeton University Press 1998)

Sweezy PM, 'Is the Marshall Plan an Instrument of Peace?' (1949) 1 Monthly Review 80

Talmon JL, *The Rise of Totalitarian Democracy* (Beacon Press 1952)

Tamanaha BZ, 'The Dark Side of the Relationship Between the Rule of Law and Liberalism' (2008) 3 NYU Journal of Law & Liberty 516

Tatham AF, '"Don't Mention Divorce at the Wedding, Darling!": EU Accession and Withdrawal after Lisbon' in Biondi A, Eeckhout P, and Ripley S (eds), *EU Law After Lisbon* (OUP 2012)

Teitel R, 'Post-communist Constitutionalism: A Transitional Perspective' (1994) 26 Columbia Human Rights Law Review 167

Teschke B, 'Decisions and Indecisions: Political and Intellectual Receptions of Carl Schmitt' (2011) 67 New Left Review 61

Teschke B, 'Fatal Attraction: A Critique of Carl Schmitt's International Political and Legal Theory' (2011) 3 International Theory 179

Teubner G, *Constitutional Fragments: Societal Constitutionalism and Globalization* (OUP 2013)

Teubner G, 'A Constitutional Moment? The Logic of "Hitting the Bottom"' in Poul F Kjaer, Gunther Teubner, and Alberto Febbrajo (eds) *The Financial Crisis in Constitutional Perspective: The Dark Side of Functional Differentation* (Hart Publishing 2011)

Therborn G, 'After Dialectics: Radical Social Theory in a Post-Communist World' (2007) 43 New Left Review 63

Thompson H, 'Austerity as Ideology: The Bait and Switch of the Banking Crisis' (2013) 11 Comparative European Politics 729

Thompson H, 'Returning to Democracy: The British Left and the Constitutional Temptation of the European Union' in Ekins R and Gee G (eds), *Judicial Power and the Left: Notes on a Sceptical Tradition* (Policy Exchange 2018)

Thornhill C, 'Carl Schmitt after the Deluge: A Review of the Recent Literature' (2000) 26 History of European Ideas 225

Thornhill C, *Political Theory in Modern Germany: An Introduction* (Blackwell 2000)

Thornhill C, *A Sociology of Transnational Constitutions: Social Foundations of the Postnational Legal Structure* (CUP 2016)

Thym D, 'In the Name of Sovereign Statehood: A Critical Introduction to the Lisbon Judgment of the German Constitutional Court' (2009) 46 Common Market Law Review 1795

Tietmeyer H, 'The Role of an Independent Central Bank in Europe' in Downes P and Vaez-Zadeh R (eds), *The Evolving Role of Central Banks: Papers Presented at the Fifth Seminar on Central Banking* (Central Banking Department, IMF 1999)

de Tocqueville A, *Democracy in America* (University of Chicago Press 2000)

Tomkin J, 'Contradiction, Circumvention and Conceptual Gymnastics: The Impact of the Adoption of the ESM Treaty on the State of European Democracy' (2013) 14 German Law Journal 169

Tomkins A, 'In Defence of the Political Constitution' (2002) 11 Oxford Journal of Legal Studies 157

Tooze A, *Wages of Destruction: The Making and Breaking of the Nazi Economy* (Penguin 2008)

Tooze A, *Crashed: How a Decade of Financial Crises Changed the World* (Allen Lane 2018)
Tóth GA, 'Hungary's Constitutional Transformation from a Central-European Comparative Perspective' in Glaser H (ed), *Norms, Interests, and Values: Conflict and Consent in the Basic Constitutional Order* (Nomos Verlagsgesellschaft 2015)
Tribe K, *Strategies of Economic Order: German Economic Discourse, 1750–1950* (CUP 1995)
Tully J, 'Modern Constitutional Democracy and Imperialism' (2008) 46 Osgoode Hall Law Journal 461
Tully J, 'The Unfreedom of the Moderns in Comparison to Their Ideals of Constitutional Democracy' (2008) 65 Modern Law Review 204
Tuori K and Tuori K, *The Eurozone Crisis: A Constitutional Analysis* (CUP 2014)
Tzouvala N, 'The Ordoliberal Origins of Modern International Investment Law: Constructing Competition on a Global Scale' in Haskell J and Rasulov A (eds), *New Voices and New Perspectives in International Economic Law* (Springer 2019)
Vail M, 'Europe's Middle Child: France's Statist Liberalism and the Conflicted Politics of the Euro' in Matthijs M and Blyth M (eds), *The Future of the Euro* (OUP 2015)
Varoufakis Y, *And the Weak Suffer what they Must? Europe, Austerity and the Threat to Global Stability* (Penguin Books 2016)
Vauchez A, 'The Transnational Politics of Judicialization: *Van Gend en Loos* and the Making of the EU Polity' (2010) 16 European Law Journal 1
Vauchez A, *Brokering Europe: Euro-Lawyers and the Making of a Transnational Polity* (CUP 2015)
Vauchez A, *Democratizing Europe* (Palgrave Macmillan 2016)
Védrine H, *History Strikes Back: How States, Nations and Conflicts are Shaping the 21st Century* (Brookings Institution Press 2008)
Verdun A, 'The Institutional Design of EMU: A Democratic Deficit?' (1998) 18 Journal of Public Policy 107
Vinx L, *The Guardian of the Constitution: Hans Kelsen and Carl Schmitt on the Limits of Constitutional Law* (CUP 2015)
Visser J, 'More Holes in the Bucket: Twenty Years of European Integration and Organized Labor' (2005) 26 Comparative Labor Law & Policy Journal 477
Voegelin E, *The Authoritarian State: An Essay on the Problem of the Austrian State* (University of Missouri Press 1999)
Waldron J, *Law and Disagreement* (OUP 1999)
Waldron J, 'Constitutionalism—A Skeptical View' in Christiano T and Christman J (eds), *Contemporary Debates in Political Philosophy* (Wiley-Blackwell 2009)
Walker N, 'The Idea of Constitutional Pluralism' (2002) 65 Modern Law Review 317
Walker N, 'Introduction' in Walker N (ed), *Questioning Sovereignty: Law, State, and Nation in the European Commonwealth* (Hart Publishing 2004)
Walker N, 'In Search of the Area of Freedom, Security and Justice: A Constitutional Odyssey' in Walker N (ed), *Europe's Area of Freedom, Security and Justice* (OUP 2004)
Walker N, 'Post-constituent Constitutionalism? The Case of the European Union' in Loughlin M and Walker N (eds), *The Paradox of Constitutionalism: Constituent Power and Constitutional Form* (OUP 2008)
Walker N, 'The European Union's Unresolved Constitution' in Rosenfeld M and Sajó A (eds), *The Oxford Handbook of Comparative Constitutional Law* (OUP 2012)
Walker N, 'Our Constitutional Unsettlement' (2014) Public Law 529
Walker N, 'The Return of Constituent Power: A Reply to Mattias Kumm' (2016) 14 International Journal of Constitutional Law 906
Walker N, 'Sovereignty and Beyond: The Double Edge of External Constitutionalism' (2018) 57 Virginia Journal of International Law 799

Wallace W and Smith J, 'Democracy or Technocracy? European Integration and the Problem of Popular Consent' in Hayward J (ed), *The Crisis of Representation in Europe* (Routledge 1996)

Weatherill S, 'After *Keck*: Some Thoughts on how to Clarify the Clarification' (1996) 33 Common Market Law Review 885

Weber M, *Economy and Society: An Outline of Interpretive Sociology* (University of Chicago Press 1978)

Weiler JHH, 'The Community System: The Dual Character of Supranationalism' (1981) 1 Yearbook of European Law 267

Weiler JHH, 'The Transformation of Europe' (1991) 100 Yale Law Journal 2403

Weiler JHH, 'Does Europe Need a Constitution? Demos, Telos and the German Maastricht Decision' (1995) 1 European Law Journal 219

Weiler JHH, 'Europe: The Case Against the Case for Statehood' (1998) 4 European Law Journal 43

Weiler JHH, *The Constitution of Europe: 'Do the New Clothes have an Emperor?' and other Essays on European Integration* (CUP 1999)

Weiler JHH, 'Federalism and Constitutionalism: Europe's Constitutional Sonderweg' in Nicolaïdis K and Howse R (eds), *The Federal Vision: Legitimacy and Levels of Governance in the US and the EU* (OUP 2001)

Weiler JHH, 'In Defence of the Status Quo: Europe's Constitutional Sonderweg' in Weiler JH and Wind M (eds), *European Constitutionalism Beyond the State* (CUP 2003)

Weiler JHH, 'On the Power of the Word: Europe's Constitutional Iconography' (2005) 3 International Journal of Constitutional Law 173

Weiler JHH, 'The "Lisbon Urteil" and the Fast Food Culture' (2009) 20 European Journal of International Law 505

Weiler JHH, 'The Political and Legal Culture of European Integration: An Exploratory Essay' (2011) 9 International Journal of Constitutional Law 678

Weiler JHH, 'Prologue: Global and Pluralist Constitutionalism—Some Doubts' in de Búrca G and Weiler JHH (eds), *The Worlds of European Constitutionalism* (CUP 2011)

Weiler JHH, '60 Years since the First European Community—Reflections on Political Messianism' (2011) 22 European Journal of International Law 303

Weiler JHH, 'In the Face of Crisis: Input Legitimacy, Output Legitimacy and the Political Messianism of European Integration' (2012) 34 Journal of European Integration 825

Weiler JHH, 'Van Gend en Loos: Individual as Subject and Object and the Dilemma of European Legitimacy' (2014) 12:1 International Journal of Constitutional Law 94

Weiler JHH, 'The European Circumstance and the Politics of Meaning: Not on Bread Alone Doth Man Liveth (Deut. 8:3; Mat 4:4)' (2020) 21 German Law Journal 96

Weiler JHH, Haltern U, and Mayer F, 'European Democracy and its Critique' in Hayward J (ed), *The Crisis of Representation in Europe* (Routledge 1996)

Weisbrod B, 'Violence and Sacrifice: Imagining the Nation in Weimar Germany' in Mommsen H (ed), *The Third Reich Between Vision and Reality: New Perspectives on German History 1918–1945* (Berg 2001)

White J, 'Emergency Europe' (2013) 63 Political Studies 300

White J, 'Policy between Rules and Discretion' in Hien J and Joerges C (eds), *Ordoliberalism, Law and the Rule of Economics* (Hart Publishing 2017)

Wilkinson MA, 'Political Constitutionalism and the European Union' (2013) 76 Modern Law Review 191

Wilkinson MA, 'The Spectre of Authoritarian Liberalism: Reflections on the Constitutional Crisis of the European Union' (2013) 14 German Law Journal 527

Wilkinson MA, 'Economic Messianism and Constitutional Power in a "German Europe": All Courts are Equal, but some Courts are more Equal than Others' (2014) LSE Legal Studies Working Paper 26/2014

Wilkinson MA, 'Authoritarian Liberalism in the European Constitutional Imagination: Second Time as Farce?' (2015) 21 European Law Journal 313

Wilkinson MA, 'The Euro Is Irreversible! ... or is it? On OMT, Austerity and the Threat of "Grexit"' (2015) 16 German Law Journal 1049

Wilkinson MA, 'The Brexit Referendum and the Crisis of "Extreme Centrism"' (2016) 17 German Law Journal 131

Wilkinson MA, 'Constitutional Pluralism: Chronicle of a Death Foretold?' (2017) 23 European Law Journal 213

Wilkinson MA, 'The Reconstitution of Postwar Europe: Liberal Excesses, Democratic Deficiencies' in Dowdle MW and Wilkinson MA (eds), *Constitutionalism Beyond Liberalism* (CUP 2017)

Wilkinson MA, 'Public Law and the Autonomy of the Political: A Material Critique' in Wilkinson MA and Dowdle MW (eds), *Questioning the Foundations of Public Law* (Hart Publishing 2018)

Wilkinson MA, 'Beyond the Post-Sovereign State? On the Past, Present and Future of Constitutional Pluralism' (2019) 12 Cambridge Yearbook of European Legal Studies 6

Wilkinson MA, 'Authoritarian Liberalism: The Conjuncture Behind the Crisis' in Nanopoulos E and Vergis F (eds), *The Crisis behind the Eurocrisis: The Eurocrisis as a Multidimensional Systemic Crisis of the EU* (CUP2019)

Wilkinson MA, 'A Constitutionally Momentous Judgment that Changes Practically Nothing? The UK Supreme Court's Decision on the Prorogation of Parliament' (*Verfassungsblog*, 25 September 2019) <https://verfassungsblog.de/a-constitutionally-momentous-judgment-that-changes-practically-nothing/> accessed 25 September 2020

Wilkinson MA, 'Flight, Fight or Fudge: First Reflections on the PSPP Judgment of the German Constitutional Court' (*Verfassungsblog*, 6 May 2020) <https://verfassungsblog.de/fight-flight-or-fudge/> accessed 24 September 2020

Wilsher D, 'Law and the Financial Crisis: Searching for Europe's New Gold Standard' (2014) 20 European Law Journal 241

de Witte B, 'The Closest Thing to a Constitutional Conversation in Europe: The Semi-Permanent Treaty Revision Process' in Beaumont P, Lyons C, and Walker N (eds), *Convergence and Divergence in European Public Law* (Hart Publishing 2002)

de Witte B, 'Do not Mention the Word: Sovereignty in Two Europhile Countries: Belgium and the Netherlands' in Walker N (ed), *Sovereignty in Transition* (Hart Publishing 2003)

de Witte B, 'The European Union as an International Legal Experiment' in de Búrca G and Weiler JHH (eds), *The Worlds of European Constitutionalism* (CUP 2012)

de Witte F, *Justice in the EU: The Emergence of Transnational Solidarity* (OUP 2015)

Wolin SS, *Politics and Vision: Continuity and Innovation in Western Political Thought* (Princeton University Press 2004)

Wood EM, *Democracy against Capitalism: Renewing Historical Materialism* (CUP 1995)

Wood EM, 'Logics of Power: A Conversation with David Harvey' (2006) 14 Historical Materialism 9

Wunsche HF, *Standard Texts on the Social Market Economy: Two Centuries of Discussion*, vol IX (Gustav Fisher Verlag 1982)

Zhang AH, 'The Faceless Court' (2016) 38 University of Pennsylvania Journal of International Law 71

Zielonka J, *Europe as Empire: The Nature of the Enlarged European Union* (OUP 2007)

Ziller J, 'Sovereignty in France: Getting Rid of the Mal de Bodin' in Walker N (ed), *Sovereignty in Transition* (Hart Publishing 2003)

Zweig S, *The World of Yesterday: Memoirs of a European* (Pushkin Press 2011)

Miscellaneous

DiEM25, 'The EU will be Democratised. Or it will Disintegrate!' (*DiEM25*, 2015) <https://diem25.org/manifesto-long/> accessed 25 September 2020

ECB, 'Verbatim of the Remarks made by Mario Draghi: Speech at the Global Investment Conference in London, 26 July 2012' (*European Central Bank*, 26 July 2012) <https://www.ecb.europa.eu/press/key/date/2012/html/sp120726.en.html> accessed 25 September 2020

ECB, 'Introductory Statement to the Press Conference (with Q&A)' (*European Central Bank*, 6 September 2016) <https://www.ecb.europa.eu/press/pressconf/2012/html/is120906.en.html> accessed 25 September 2020

ECB, 'Opening Remarks at the Session "Rethinking the Limitations of Monetary Policy": speech by Mario Draghi, President of the ECB, at the farewell conference honouring Governor Stanley Fischer, The Israel Museum, Jerusalem, 18 June 2013' (*European Central Bank*, 18 June 2013) <https://www.ecb.europa.eu/press/key/date/2013/html/sp130618.en.html> accessed 3 November 2020

Index

For the benefit of digital users, indexed terms that span two pages (e.g., 52–53) may, on occasion, appear on only one of those pages.